Marketing in Leisure and Tourism: Reaching New Heights

Marketing in Leisure and Tourism:
Reaching New Heights

by Patricia Click Janes

Venture Publishing, Inc.
State College, Pennsylvania

Venture Publishing, Inc.
1999 Cato Avenue
State College, PA 16801
Phone 814-234-4561; Fax 814-234-1651

Production Manager: Richard Yocum
Manuscript Editing: Valerie Fowler, Michele L. Barbin, Richard Yocum

Library of Congress Catalogue Card Number 2006931430
ISBN-10: 1-892132-65-6
ISBN-13: 978-1-892132-65-9

To the three who inspire me and enrich my life everyday in the way they live, laugh and love... Katharine, Lauren, and Gregory... Blessed am I.

Table of Contents

Acknowledgements..xiii
  *Textbook Development/Editing • Teaching
  and Student Resource Support*
Preface...xvii
  Chapter Elements • Teaching Resources
About the Author xix

Section 1
Understanding Marketing
in Leisure and Tourism

Chapter 1
Reaching New Heights—Integrating Marketing 3

What Is Marketing?.. 5
Historic Marketing... 6
  1960s • 1970s • 1980s • 1990s • 2000s
Marketing Defined Today 8
The Role of Marketing... 12
Why the Sudden Change?....................................... 15
Barriers To Applying Marketing 19
Why Is Marketing Important?................................... 19
Applying Marketing to For-Profit and Nonprofit
  Organizations... 20
Components of Effective Marketing............................ 20
Apply What You Know 21
Key Terms.. 21
Review Questions 22
Internet Resources: Marketing-Related Listservs..........22
References.. 22

Chapter 2
The Marketing of Leisure and Tourism Experiences...................................... 25

Leisure and Tourism Experiences: "Are We
  Having Fun Yet?"... 26
Flow 29
  Elements of Flow
From Products to Services to Experiences.................... 29
Why People Play: "It's About the Benefits"................. 33
Constraints to Experiencing Leisure 33

Phases of the Leisure and Tourism Experience 35
Designing Leisure Experiences.................................. 37
  Six Elements of a Leisure Experience
Economic, Social, and Environmental Impacts
  of Leisure.. 40
Unique Leisure and Tourism Marketing Issues........... 41
Considerations in Marketing Leisure Experiences 42
Philosophical Development 42
Apply What You Know 42
Key Terms.. 43
Review Questions 43
Internet Resources.. 43
References.. 43

Chapter 3
The Quality Service Foundation 45

Word-of-Mouth Marketing 46
Quality Culture... 48
What Is Quality Service?.. 48
  Expectations • Moment of Truth
Quality Service Systems 50
  *Step 1: Design • Step 2: Production • Step 3:
  Perception • Step 4: Outcomes*
Developing a Service Strategy................................... 62
Loyalty and Relationship Management 63
Loyalty Programs.. 64
  *Gaining Employee Loyalty • Gaining Nonuser/
  Stakeholder Loyalty*
Customer Relationship Management........................... 67
Apply What You Know 68
Key Terms.. 68
Review Questions 68
Internet Resources.. 68
References.. 69

Chapter 4
Enabling Marketing Action................. 73

What Is a Marketing Plan?....................................... 74
The Value of Marketing Planning............................... 75
How the Plan Should Be Created............................... 76
Systematic Process for Approaching Marketing........... 79
  *Annual Marketing Plan • New Organization
  Marketing Plan • New Offering Marketing Plan
  • Marketing and Communication Guidelines*

Elements of a Leisure and Tourism Organization
   Marketing Plan 80
   Overall Plan Summary • Organization Assess-
   ment • Global, Industry, and Competitive
   Assessments • Market Assessment • Brand
   Mapping • Target Marketing Objectives •
   Marketing Mix Matrix • Promotional Mix
   Matrix • Communication Mix Matrix • Leisure
   Experience Assessment • Communication Eval-
   uation • Market Research Plan • Marketing
   Plan Impact and Financing Considerations •
   Future Thoughts
Keys to Effective and Ineffective Marketing Plans 83
Funding Marketing Plans 85
Enhancing Marketing Budgets 85
   Trade • Bartering Firms • Partnerships
Evaluating Marketing Plans and Efforts 88
   Why Measure Marketing Efforts?
Apply What You Know 93
Key Terms 93
Review Questions 93
Internet Resources 93
References 94

Chapter 5
Understanding, Developing, and
Applying Market Research 95

Market Research 97
How Market Research Is Used 98
   Market Research Prior to Marketing Decision
   Making • Market Research During Marketing
   Decision Making • Market Research After
   Marketing Decision Making
Value of Market Research 99
Types of Market Research 100
   Secondary Research Sources
Challenges With Market Research 103
   Primary Market Research • Step 1: Problem
   Identification (Research Objectives) • Step
   2: Research Design • Step 3: Data Collec-
   tion Methods • Step 4: Analysis of Data •
   Step 5: Interpretation and Report
Ethical Issues in Research 122
Planning for Marketing Research 123
Satisfaction Measurement and Feedback 123
   Comment Cards • Importance-Performance
   Analysis • ServQual • Differences: IPA and
   ServQual
Apply What You Know 129
Key Terms 129

Review Questions 130
Internet Resources 130
References 130

Section 2
Developing a Leisure Services and
Tourism Marketing Strategy

Chapter 6
Developing the Strategy 135

Market Strategy Development 137
Organization Assessment 137
   History • Philosophy • Inventory • Organiza-
   tional Issues and Structure • Stakeholders •
   Strategic Objectives/Master Plans • Finan-
   cial Status and Goals • Historical Marketing
   Efforts • Image
Global Assessment 147
Industry Assessment 147
Market Assessment 148
   Current Consumers Served • Market Area
   Demographics
Competitive Assessment 149
   Identifying the Competition
Value of Assessments 152
Strengths, Weaknesses, Opportunities, and Threats
   (SWOT) Analysis 153
Apply What You Know 155
Key Terms 155
Review Questions 155
Internet Resources 155
References 156

Chapter 7
Target Market Approaches 157

Target Marketing 158
Market Segmentation 159
The Segmentation Process 160
   Variables Used in Segmentation
Various Approaches to Market Segmentation 162
   Understanding Consumer Segmentation:
   Post Ho • Cluster Analysis Technique •
   Understanding Market Segments: A Priori •
   Comparing Existing and Potential Market
   Segments

Types of Segmentation 167
   Benefit-Based Segmentation • Demographic
   Segmentation: Age and Ethnicity • Psycho-
   graphic Segmentation • Multidimensional
   Segmentation
Developing Segment Profiles......................... 169
Identifying Market Segment Potential 171
Popular Leisure and Tourism Organization Market
   Segments 173
   Seniors • Baby Boomers • Women • Gay,
   Lesbian, Transgender • Teens • Persons With
   Disabilities
Value of Target Marketing............................ 178
Importance of Strategy Assessment with Markets
   Identified... 179
Apply What You Know 179
Key Terms.. 179
Review Questions 180
Internet Resources....................................... 180
References.. 180

Chapter 8
Brand Positioning and Marketing
Outcomes 183

Brand Positioning... 185
Positioning Assessments: Brand Mapping.... 187
Brand Management and Identity................... 189
Protecting The Brand 190
Brand Identity 190
   Brand Name • Logo • Slogan • Collateral •
   Design
Brand Repositioning 192
   Examples of Leisure Organization Repositioning
Positioning Statement Approaches 193
Marketing Objectives................................... 197
   Specific • Measurable • Attainable or Mod-
   erately Risky • Reflective of the Organization
   Mission • Time Frame and Target Market
   Oriented
Demarketing... 201
Apply What You Know 202
Key Terms.. 202
Review Questions 203
Internet Resources....................................... 203
References.. 203

Section 3
Achieving Leisure and Tourism
Organization Objectives Through
Successful Promotional and
Communication Plans

Chapter 9
Processing Operational Decisions..... 207

Utilizing the Model: Three Steps................. 210
   Step 1: Marketing Mix • Step 2: Promotional
   Mix • Step 3: Communication Mix
Marketing Budgets and Scheduling Activities 216
Evaluating Operational Decisions................ 217
Market Research 219
Estimating the Impact: Revenue/Cost Summary 220
Apply What You Know 221
Key Terms.. 221
Review Questions 221
Internet Resources....................................... 221
References.. 221

Chapter 10
Organization Offerings, Distribution,
and Pricing 223

Organization Offerings 224
Product Life Cycle....................................... 225
Distribution 228
   Physical Sources • Physical Location •
   Physical Service Delivery
Pricing... 233
   Identifying the Pricing Objective • Assessing
   the Pricing Variables • Determining the
   Price • Evaluating the Pricing Decision
Yield Management.. 241
Apply What You Know 242
Key Terms.. 242
Review Questions 243
Internet Resources....................................... 243
References.. 243

Chapter 11
Promotional Brand, Collateral Design, and Events 245

Brand Image.. 247
Selecting a Medium 247
Promotional Collateral.................................. 250
Developing Promotional Collateral 251
   *AIDA • Style • Message • Guerrilla Marketing •
   Problem Messages • Design Elements • Editing
   and Proofreading • Professional Quality
   Production • Working With a Communications
   Professional*
The Internet as a Collateral Tool 261
Protecting the Brand Image and Identity 262
Promotional Pricing 263
Promotional Events or Events Marketing.................. 263
Apply What You Know 264
Key Terms.. 264
Review Questions 264
Internet Resources... 264
References.. 265

Chapter 12
Advertising, Public Relations, and Crisis Communication 267

Advertising... 269
Advertising Methods... 269
   *Newspapers • Magazines • Phone Book •
   Direct Mail • Billboards • Television • Radio •
   Internet • E-Mail • Listservs • Search Engines
   • Brand Spiraling*
Advertising Organizations 281
   *Public Relations • Media Relations • Public
   Relations in Any Type of Medium • Print
   Publication Public Relations • Audiovideo
   Media Public Relations*
Crisis Management 291
Crisis Communication Plan 296
Apply What You Know 297
Key Terms.. 297
Review Questions 297
Internet Resources... 297
   *Advertising • Public Relations • Crisis
   Communication*
References.. 299

Chapter 13
Relationships: Community, Sponsorships, and Stewardship 303

Partnerships... 305
Community Relations and Cause-Related Marketing 306
Sponsorships 311
   *Types of Sponsorships • Value of Sponsor-
   ships • Approaching Sponsorship Relation-
   ships • What Organizations Consider Before
   Agreeing to Sponsor • Sponsorship Packages
   • Measuring Sponsorship Investments •
   Strategies for Determining Which Organiza-
   tions to Sponsor*
Stewardship: Providing Quality Service Internally
   and Externally.. 318
   External Stewardship • Internal Stewardship
Apply What You Know 323
Key Terms.. 323
Review Questions 323
Internet Resources... 324
References.. 324

Chapter 14
Direct Marketing: Internal and External Sales 327

Direct Marketing.. 328
Direct Sales Process... 333
The Strategic Sales Process 333
   *Step 1: Prospecting • Step 2: Planning and
   Preparing • Step 3: Establishing Rapport •
   Step 4: Questioning • Step 5: Supporting •
   Step 6: Summarizing • Step 7: Closing*
Internal Marketing 338
Apply What You Know 341
Key Terms.. 341
Review Questions 342
Internet Resources... 342
References.. 342

Appendix A
Market Research Resources............. 345
   *Industry Associations with Research Informa-
   tion • International and National Data • Local
   Data • Databases for Secondary Market
   Research • General Secondary Sources*

Appendix B
Brainstorming Cards and Charts 349

List of Tables and Figures

Table 1.1 Organizations' Opinions of How Marketing Is Defined......... 5

Table 1.2 Organizations' Opinions of How Marketing Is Misunderstood 9

Figure 1.1 Organization Creation 10

Figure 1.2 Integrated Organizational Chart...................... 11

Figure 1.3 Traditional and Updated Organizational Charts 12

Table 1.3 Organizations' Opinions of Recent Marketing Changes 13

Figure 1.4 Duties of a Marketing Professional................ 15

Figure 1.5 Components of Effective Leisure and Tourism Organization Marketing.................... 20

Figure 2.1 A Paradigm of Leisure 28

Table 2.1 Economic Distinctions 31

Table 2.2 Differences in Products, Services, and Experiences 32

Table 2.3 Organization Features Versus Benefits 34

Table 2.4 Comparing Marketing Language Describing Organization Features Versus Benefits 35

Figure 2.2 Clawson and Knetsch's Five-Phase Model of a Leisure Experience 36

Table 2.5 Examples of Ways Leisure Organizations Can Address Each Phase 38–39

Table 2.6 Potential Impacts of a New Recreation Attraction on a Local Community.................. 41

Figure 3.1 Quality Service System Model........................ 51

Table 4.1 Effective and Ineffective Leisure Organization Marketing Objectives................ 84

Table 4.2 Effective and Ineffective Leisure Organization Marketing Communication Items 85

Table 4.3 Bartering Firms 87

Table 4.4 Evaluation Methods for Measuring the Impact of Communication Tactics.................. 91

Table 5.1 Comparison of Camper Satisfaction Scores....... 96

Table 5.2 Overall Camper Satisfaction 96

Table 5.3 Research Characterized by Source and Technique............ 101

Table 5.4 Advantages and Disadvantages of Types of Market Research 102

Table 5.5 Potential Bias and Error in Research 103

Table 5.6 Various Values of Each Method for Aspects of the Festival 106

Table 5.7 Henderson's Qualitative Methods................. 108

Table 5.8 Focus Group Examples 109

Table 5.9 Poorly Worded Questions From Leisure and Tourism Organization Questionnaires....... 114

Figure 5.1 Sample Questionnaire Without Open-Ended or Demographic Questions 117

Table 5.10 Advantages and Disadvantages of Common Data Collection Methods............... 121

Figure 5.2 Importance-Performance Analysis (IPA) Matrix..................... 126

Table 5.12 Feedback Methods 129

Figure 6.1 Marketing Strategy Development 138

Table 6.1 Leisure Organization Historical Time Frame of Events 140

Figure 6.2 A Camp's Offerings 142

Figure 6.3A Leisure and Tourism Organization's Operational Structure 143

Table 6.2 Historical Membership Revenue Data From a Campus Recreation Fitness Center 144

Table 6.3 Market Share Analysis 145

Table 6.4 Example of a Revenue/Sales Forecast for a Campus Recreation Fitness Center............. 146

Table 6.5 Global Assessment Topics and Issues........... 147

Table 6.6 Competitive Analysis of Three Athletic Clubs 150

Table 6.7 SWOT Analysis for a Rafting Organization 154

Table 7.1 Segmentation Variables Used to Identify Markets............ 161

Table 7.2 Cluster Analysis Profiles of Consumer Respondents From a Health Club 164

Figure 7.1 Determining Market Demand for Schaumburg, Illinois 165

Table 7.3 Age Segment Profiles..................... 168

Table 7.4 Determining Market Segment Size 172

Table 7.5 Competitive Market Focus Assessment........ 173

Table 7.6 Potential Market Segments 173

Table 7.7 Summary of Differences Between Traditional and New-Age Elders 175

Figure 8.1 Brand Development Continuum 186

Table 8.1 Positioning Strategies and Statements 195

Table 8.2 Actual Leisure and Tourism Organization Marketing Goals and Objectives................... 199

Figure 9.1 Marketing, Promotional, and Communication (MPC) Mix Model........................... 209

Figure 9.2 Step 1: Marketing Mix Brainstorm 211

Table 9.1 Lodging Industry Marketing Best Practices..... 213

Table 9.2 Promotional Statements for a Golf Course....... 214

Figure 9.3   Promotional Collateral Mix............................ 215

Figure 9.4   Communication Mix Brainstorm 217

Table 9.4   Sample Budget and Timeline from a Leisure and Tourism Organization................ 218

Table 9.5   Evaluation Methods for Communication Plan... 219

Table 10.1   Offering Examples 225

Figure 10.1   Product Life Cycle (PLC) Model.................. 228

Table 10.2   Marketing, Promotional, and Communication Mix Issues Related to the Product Life Cycle.. 229

Table 10.3   Distribution Sources and Leisure Industry Examples... 230

Table 10.4   Average Rates Offered to the Customer 232

Table 10.5   Reservation Cost by Distribution Channel....... 232

Table 10.6   Examples of Leisure Service Organizations Using Various Pricing Objectives 234

Table 10.7   Summary of Golf Rounds by Day of Week..... 236

Table 10.8   Approaches to Setting Prices 239

Table 11.1   Common Promotional Collateral 250

Figure 11.1   A youth camp 8½ x 11 brochure with compelling photos and simple messages....... 253

Figure 11.2   Features Only Example 254

Figure 11.3   Incomplete or Inaccurate Information Example... 254

Figure 11.4   Incomplete or Inaccurate Information Example... 255

Figure 11.5   Information Overload Example.................... 255

Figure 11.6   Anatomy of an Ad Flyer 256

Figure 11.7   Large Font Draws Readers In 257

Figure 11.8   Use of Lighting Draws Readers to the Basketball... 257

Figure 11.9   Levels of Information on a Resort Flyer........ 258

Table 11.2   Font Style and Size Considerations............. 258

Table 11.3   Sample Font Styles..................................... 259

Figure 11.10   An Evolution of an Academic Department's Image Through Promotional Design 260

Table 12.1   Print Medium Advantages, Disadvantages, and Costs...................................... 271

Table 12.2   List Broker Organizations and Contact Information................................... 274

Table 12.3   Multimedia Advantages, Disadvantages, and Costs...................................... 275

Figure 12.1   Sample Directional Billboard........................ 276

Table 12.4   Sample Media List 285

Figure 12.2   Proper Format and Content of a Press Release 287

Figure 12.3   Proper Format and Content of a Public Service Announcement 292

Table 13.1   Sample Community Relations List 310

Table 13.2   Examples of Sponsorship Partnerships 313

Table 13.3   Lodging Industry Human Resource Best-Practice Champions 320

Table 13.4   Internal and External Stewardship Activities 321

Acknowledgements

The concepts of this book have been formed throughout my career where I have been blessed by the influence of so many people. It is these people that have given me the ability to complete this book and to them I am forever grateful. Through great fortune, I learned from professionals that I consider the most passionate in the industry. They have created and worked for organizations that are quality driven with concern for employees and consumers alike, and who are focused, compassionate, and dedicated individuals with balance and priority placed on both their professional and personal lives. The book could not have been developed without the guidance, teaching, and vision of those who have been engaging industry professionals, teachers, leaders, students and friends. Thank you, as you have encouraged, allowed, and reminded me to have passion for what I do and believe (even when it may be unpopular), to learn from my mistakes, and to embrace my vision(s). The number of people who contributed to the development of the textbook is endless! Their critical thinking, dedication, and professionalism were significant contributions to this book and my hope is that I have not forgotten any of them below. I have chosen to highlight their involvement in specific sections although many made contributions in numerous areas. Each of those mentioned are people who embody a quote by Kathleen Norris... and it is this premise that captures my thought of what is in their hearts and what I have had the privilege of learning from them on this adventure as they have each made it special. Not only am I in awe of their abilities, I am inspired by their stories and am blessed by their friendships.

"Anything, everything, little or big becomes an adventure when the right person (or people) shares it."

My past employers and consultancies that I have had the privilege of growing under their culture and beliefs while contributing to their systems including Marriott International, The Embers, Lake Shore Bakery, McDonalds, Central Michigan University's Department of Recreation, Parks and Leisure Services Administration (RPL), Binder Park Zoo, Canton Leisure Services, LaBelle Management, and Michigan's Department of Natural Resources, Parks and Recreation Division. This list also includes the guest speakers who have willingly shared their expertise with my students and me, both on and off campus, many of whom have been videotaped for their thoughts to be shared with others beyond the scope of my institution.

My colleagues and mentors that have guided and believed in me, whom I confided in, learned from and gained support and encouragement, and whom I truly consider friends, including: Dr. Tom Jones, Dr. Roger Coles, Dean Wallin, Dr. Mary Wisnom, Tim Otteman, Suzanne Gareiss, Lori Stoudt, G. Patrick Doyle, Louise Stakle, Dr. Susan Wilson, Barbara McGuire, Jan Howell, John Beck, Dr. Joe Fridgen, Dr. Don Holecek; Chris Chamberlain, Andy Wardwell, Gwen Hart, Pam Lavora, Randy Webb, Ed Proenza; and teachers/coaches Bill Schmidt and Mike Tomsich who taught me at an influential age about passion and dealing with adversity and those who say "You can't." Additionally, my other colleagues at Central Michigan University (CMU) as well as the hundreds of professionals cited and referenced in this textbook.

My family and friends who provided unconditional love and support for my every activity; these people have been there just because... and I cannot imagine completing the book without their influence on my life. They provided continuous encouragement (even though they may not even understand what our industry is all about!). My ultimate teachers who were not in the leisure and tourism industry but themselves service professionals (a nurse and policeman) who instilled in me since birth the value of doing something you love, working when people need you (24 hours a day, 7 days a week) doing what you know if right and always being there for family and friends, my parents, John and Mary Ann Click. They are the two most influential people in my life as they embody high quality, hard working, and passionate people. They provided the foundation for me believing anything is possible and it is this vision that made me truly think I could complete a textbook. My sister Terry and brothers Tom and Bill share these beliefs and practices and are a source of constant inspiration and support. I would choose them as friends had I not been fortunate to get them in the deal. Lifelong friends Pam Staub, Mary O'Brien, Mary Grace Olson, Dianne Foran, Kristie Swan, Debb Leasher, Theresa Pollard, Sandy Osterman, Tammy Black, and Kim Bandlow. These people have become family, not by blood but by choice.

And, God's greatest gift to me is the chance to be a parent to my daily inspiration and to whom this book is dedicated to... my children, Katharine, Lauren and Gregory. They may never understand the contributions (or sacrifices) they made to me completing this book, but I do.

Textbook Development/Editing

Four graduate students and three undergraduate students were critical to the completion of this book and I could not have done so without them and their professional assistance and expertise. Natalia Buta, Amy Decker, Felicia Powers, Chelsie Martin, Chris Stovak, Andrea Pecoraro, and Darcie Schafer provided their unending willingness to assist where and when needed. They found all the "needles in the haystack" and detail required in this textbook's completion and still smiled when they knew the tasks were challenging and overwhelming. Most importantly, each would come to me and say "What else can I do?" "Tell me what you need and how I may help" and helped me maintain perspective and the vision. They are high-quality people who are or will be amazing professionals in our industry. Lucky am I and those they serve.

The students enrolled in Promoting Leisure Service Agencies and Programs (RPL 545) at Central Michigan University who edited chapters; provided input during focus group discussions; wrote review questions; provided insight on teaching support, such as audio chapter reviews; selected the final textbook cover; and challenged and critiqued concepts and practices from 2002–2005. I am amazed and continuously inspired by my students. They are the reason I pursued a higher education career after working in the leisure and tourism industry for several years. My decision to do so was the best professional decision I ever made. I learn from and am inspired by my students every day.

Geoff Godbey's encouragement and ability to say to me upon our first encounter (after I inquired about needing a specific textbook on leisure and tourism marketing)… "Why don't you write one?" and reminding me that although I had not done so before, I "had to start somewhere." Richard Yocum and the staff at Venture Publishing for preparing the manuscript and helping my words come alive while embracing my vision and ideas for the textbook. Never was I shot down for ideas from the cover vision to the inclusion of worksheets and cards to assist in student learning. They embody quality practices and the ability to see and develop a product even better than my vision. They made my concepts and thoughts more meaningful and concise, while challenging my ideas and helping create, as a result, a better textbook.

Dr. Al Ellard made a significant contribution to this textbook with his thorough chapter on a foundation concept in my approach to leisure and tourism marketing relating to the leisure "experience" itself. His ability to capture this concept and teach its relevance to the leisure and tourism industry was one of two critical issues I base all marketing practices on… the other being high-quality experiences. A. Scott Rood, Grand Valley State University, and Dr. Bob Pfister, East Carolina State University, both used the textbook with students and provided feedback to the strengths of the text and suggested improvements. Their insight and expertise was incredibly valued.

I had great interest in showing and highlighting leisure and tourism organizations that have taken theoretical concepts and successfully integrated them into their organizations' efforts. As a result, the book is an applied textbook that highlights how concepts can and should be used in over twenty *Real Life Stories*. I sought groups who do it well and asked to share their stories with others. Not only are these professionals' stories captivating, they highlight the right way leisure and tourism organizations should be operated—unfortunately, all are not managed in this way. My hope is that readers learn from those who "do it right," as I have had the great fortune of encountering. My thanks to all who allowed me to capture their high-quality professional practices:

- Don Schappacher and Fred Kindell, American Hospitality Management, Inc.

- Bernie and Carol Parks-Karl, Aurora Ice Museum, Chena Hot Springs Resort

- A. Scott and Cindy Rood, Big Apple Bagels

- Scott McKnight and Greg Geise, Binder Park Zoo

- Ann Conklin and Debbie Bilbrey-Honsowetz, Canton Leisure Services

- Craig Bonter, Cedarbrook Senior Living Resort Community

- Dan Sullivan and Peter Hopps, Collette Vacations

- Laurie Mier, Easter Seals of Tennessee

- Jeff Tuma, The Embers

- Paul Beachnau, Gaylord Convention and Tourism Bureau

- Tanya Donahue, Volunteer, Make-A-Wish Foundation

- Mary Carroll, Mt. Pleasant Convention and Visitors Bureau

- Hank Phillips and Doug Rentz, National Tour Association

- Jamie Furbush, Frankenmuth Convention and Visitors Bureau

- Jan Pung, Oakland County Parks and Recreation

- Jon Dierkes, The Palace of Auburn Hills

- Debbie Bilbrey-Honsowetz, Pheasant Run Golf Club
- Maureen Hollinrake, The University Club of Chicago
- Chris Shepler, Shepler's Mackinac Island Ferry
- Todd Leinberger, Spring Hill Camp
- Bruce Beckham, Lisa Schmiemann and Joseph Sobin, Tourism Cares; Tourism Caring for America
- Rich Fairman, Warwick Hills Country Club

In an effort to ensure I provided high-quality guidance to the all those who read this book, I employed the assistance of four guest editors who daily engage in using the marketing promotion and communication skills found in the final four chapters of the book. I sought those who, to me, embody the technical skills and daily practices of successfully implementing marketing promotion and communication practices. I am thankful for their expertise and friendship:

- Chapter 11: Karl Olmstead, Olmstead and Associates
- Chapter 12: Connie McCann, Marketing Communication Consultant
- Chapter 13: Bill Shepler, Shepler's Mackinac Island Ferry
- Chapter 14: Bill Underdown, Marriott International

Three Central Michigan University photographers significantly contributed to this book and have captured the essence of how leisure and tourism contributes to people's quality of life in visual form. Brian Roberts allowed me to tap into his professional expertise and took dozens of photos specifically for this textbook and the teaching resources and materials. He suggested ideas to support concepts throughout the book and used his expertise to capture the meaning in visual form… providing visual relief for students to teach marketing concepts visually. He taught me more about the power of visual communication than I knew existed, and his graceful way of doing so was inspirational. Peggy Brisbane's amazing photographs included in this book are those in leisure and tourism settings including CMU faculty, students and alumni. Robert Barclay recently captured the RPL students at CMU and provided his professional expertise as well. Alumni responded in force allowing their organization's images to be used in this textbook including Laurie Mier, Easter Seals of Tennessee; Janice Skoleces, Crystal Mountain Resort; Jennifer Hayes, The College of William and Mary; and Chris Bundy and Carol Moody, Mt. Pleasant Parks and Recreation.

Teaching and Student Resource Support

Dan Bracken provided his expertise to create resources for the textbook that I feel not only make it complete but add value to the readers' experience. Dan and his staff captured several professional guest presentations on video that complement material in the book for faculty to access and provide to students enrolled in courses. These presentations share how leisure and tourism organizations use marketing concepts, have learned from them, and found success when using them. Dan has also captured audio chapter reviews and readers will be able to listen to introductions and summaries of the material presented in each chapter. These audio reviews will be available in various formats for easy access, to allow all student learning styles to be more successfully addressed. His willingness to embrace my "out there" thoughts and find a way to make them reality is what I hope every reader understands from this book—that anything is possible and anyone or organization can "reach new heights." Please contact me at janes1pl@cmich.edu for further information to access support materials.

Finally, graphic designer Kelly Preece (and those at Venture) shared their skills in the textbook as well. Kelly developed the design concepts for the worksheets and corresponding cards that enable any person to contribute to the marketing process. She was able to make my vision easily understood while Venture made continued improvements. Her ability to make these resources professional and embody design concepts that enhance the message was a gift and I am thankful for her expertise and "yes, sure, absolutely" attitude.

Preface

Marketing in Leisure and Tourism: Reaching New Heights was designed with student learning and faculty effectiveness in mind. Students and colleagues have been involved in the entire text development process and provided critical feedback regarding everything from critiquing content, identifying supporting elements to aid in student learning, resources for faculty, and the design of the text's layout. The following provides an brief overview of text content and organization, student resources, and faculty support. Direct comments to the author are welcome by e-mail at janes1pl@cmich.edu.

Section One: Understanding Marketing in Leisure and Tourism

Chapters 1 through 5 provide a foundation for understanding leisure and tourism marketing. They include critical concepts about the experiences leisure and tourism organizations provide and how they provide them. Effective marketing is built from organization's development of high-quality leisure and tourism experiences. In this effort, organizations must utilize information to create the most effective system. In addition to chapters about leisure and tourism experiences, quality and research, this section introduces the concepts of marketing and the author's thoughts regarding a system for successful integration in any leisure and tourism organization.

Section Two: Developing a Leisure and Tourism Marketing Strategy

The concepts in chapters 6 through 8 are vital to successful marketing. They introduce the process for successful integration of marketing concepts by providing an applied system designed to uncover critical information for effective decision making. These chapters highlight concepts related to developing a marketing strategy for supporting an organization's mission and goals. They also provide a process for identifying beneficial information to create to a solid strategy because "anyone can spend a marketing budget but not everyone will be successful."

Section Three: Achieving Leisure and Tourism Organizational Objectives Through Successful Promotional and Operational Communication Plans

Chapters 9 through 14 address critical issues regarding leisure and tourism organizations' ability to successfully achieve marketing objectives. These chapters are placed within the tactical section of the book to address issues related to promotional and communication mix elements. Once an organization determines its strategy, an effective tactical plan to reach the marketing objectives must be determined. In these chapters, readers are introduced to a process for identifying all the potential tools available for reaching consumers with meaningful messages in effective ways.

Chapter Elements

Each chapter is designed to address unique learning objectives yet follow consistent pediological features that enhance student learning. The following components are provided in each chapter to support text material.

1. **Learning objectives** listed at the beginning of each chapter identify the key learning outcomes for the chapter. These highlight the elements of the chapter and prepare readers for information forthcoming.

2. **Important terms** are italicized for emphasis and provide a means for easily identifying the concept definition when first introduced.

3. **Photos, tables and figures** provide visual support for leisure and tourism marketing concepts. They visually enhance and expand on chapter components.

4. **Quotes** from leisure and tourism industry leaders regarding marketing concepts, their beliefs, and practices highlight key concepts in each chapter.

5. **Real Life Stories** highlight leisure and tourism industry high quality marketing practices and show applied theoretical concepts being used. These organization's stories share with readers how the marketing concepts have been used and how they have enabled them to be more successful.

6. **Key Terms** are a list of critical concepts/words throughout the chapter and readers should have a mastery of these concepts to fully engage in a better understanding of leisure and tourism marketing.

7. **Review Questions** are designed to engage readers in the critical thinking of important chapter components. Readers mastering these answers have grasped an understanding of chapter material.

8. **Apply What You Know** activities engage readers in integrating the concepts of the chapter and by completing activities at the end of each chapter. By completing the questions within each chapter, readers follow the process to develop an organization's marketing plan.

9. **Internet Resources** and addresses are provided that highlight sources for additional information and summarize the content found within each site.

10. **References** have been used throughout this textbook recognizing the hundreds (and thousands) of individuals who contribute to the body of knowledge about leisure and tourism marketing.

Teaching Resources

In an effort to provide a full range of resources for faculty adopting the textbook, the following materials are available to support the textbook concepts. The ability to engage students with a variety of teaching methodologies promote enhanced learning for various student learning styles. Blackboard access to these teaching resources is given to those adopting the book for a semester and the resources will continually be updated and further developed. The following are available:

Syllabi: Sample syllabi are provided as resources from faculty who have utilized the textbook. These samples provide ideas to faculty for additional teaching methodologies, assignments, and course organization.

Sample Marketing Plans: Completed student and professional organization marketing plans are provided as an aid to student learning. These plans can be shared with students and allow for a critique of strengths and weaknesses of content and format of plans.

Related Articles: Work completed by authors engaged in marketing understanding is shared in the resource section to complement textbook learning.

Sample Assignments: Various assignments are provided to stimulate ideas and/or provide resources to assist in course development.

Photographs: Additional photographs are provided that can be used for classroom presentations. These photographs assist in teaching marketing concepts visually. Many of the photographs have been used in the textbook as well.

PowerPoint Slides: Provided by chapter, PowerPoint slides have been designed to follow the chapter contents. These are designed to follow the chapter components

and faculty are encouraged to add materials to customize them to their individual teaching style.

Test Bank: At least twenty-five questions per chapter are provided in the chapter-by-chapter text bank. These questions are in true/false and multiple choice formats only. Additionally, an answer key is provided for each test bank.

Audio and Video Guest Speakers: Several leisure and tourism professionals have allowed their marketing related presentations to be shared with other students/faculty to aid in student learning. These video and audio materials are available to complement textbook materials and provide the "real life" context for leisure and tourism related marketing concepts.

External Links: Internet links are provided that complement textbook materials and provide additional resources to faculty to aid in student learning. These links are not inclusive of all resources available and will be continually developed and refined.

Discussion Board: All faculty engaged in using the *Marketing in Leisure and Tourism: Reaching New Heights* textbook are invited to join in discussion board conversations to identify the most effective teaching methods, discuss textbook concepts/components, and continually improve the outcome for students and teaching effectiveness for faculty.

In addition to the resources noted above, **audio chapter reviews** and **audio and video guest speakers** are being developed. Finally, all faculty using *Marketing in Leisure and Tourism: Reaching New Heights* are encouraged to visit the **Communication modules** which provide: announcements, discussion boards, group pages, e-mail addresses, etc. If you have adopted this book for your class and would like to use these resources, contact Dr. Patty Janes at janes1pl@cmich.edu

About the Author

Dr. Patty Janes is an associate professor at Central Michigan University in the Recreation, Parks and Leisure Services Administration Department. She joined CMU's faculty in 1991 after spending seven years with Marriott International in catering, sales, marketing, and training. Janes' teaching and consulting interests focus on leisure, tourism and hospitality businesses specializing in marketing, quality service, and human resource issues. Janes' research focuses on developing effective marketing strategies, enhancing industry training practices, and assessing quality of worklife issues in the hospitality, tourism and leisure industry. *Marketing in Leisure and Tourism: Reaching New Heights* is her first textbook. Janes has completed over 25 professional presentations, published 11 articles/book chapters, and provided consulting services to five leisure and tourism organizations since 2000.

Section 1

Understanding Marketing
in Leisure and Tourism

Chapter 1

Reaching New Heights— Integrating Marketing

Think about the last leisure experience you participated in. What influenced your decision to participate? Was it a friend who suggested you try it? Did a brochure tell you what it would cost? Were you excited after you read an article about how it was enjoyable? Did someone recommend the equipment? After being handed a free pass, were you unable to resist giving it a shot? Regardless of the factors that influenced your decision, marketing played a role in the process of the organization understanding what you wanted, ensuring you knew about it, and hopefully providing you with a quality experience.

As leisure and tourism organizations are faced with increased competition, greater economic challenges, and continued resource issues, it is vital now more than ever to provide tools to professionals that assist in overcoming these dilemmas and reaching the people they desire to serve with more efficient and effective operations. The need for integrating marketing practices has never been more important for the industry. The need for professionals to understand and embrace these practices is critical to long-term success in a changing environment. Even though the discipline is not new, the leisure and tourism industries have been slow to adopt marketing practices, whether a small business or a large governmental organization (Vogt & Andereck, 2002). So, here is your opportunity to reach new heights by learning about and eventually integrating successful marketing practices in the leisure and tourism organizations that employs you.

Rob Schumacker conquers difficult terrain; organizations find ways to use marketing to do the same.

At the end of this chapter, readers will be able to…

- Explain marketing and discuss its importance to leisure and tourism organizations.

- Describe marketing's evolution and what it has become today.

- List the barriers to effective marketing.

- Discuss the value of strategic marketing decision making.

- Understand the reasons why all organizations can benefit from marketing.

- Identify the components of leisure and tourism marketing.

You may question how a mountain climber represents a leisure and tourism organization's approach to marketing. Do we see marketing as an uphill climb? a long and difficult journey? an adventure filled with risk and danger?

Outdoor adventure recreators hope you are not thinking this way about their leisure pursuit. In the same context, this book is designed to ensure you don't think that way about marketing. Of course, marketing has an adventurous feeling and there are indeed challenges. But as with mountain climbing, the bottom line is, the more you do it, the more comfortable, prepared, and successful you will be. The more times you climb, and the more understanding you gain about how it works, the less fear there is to overcome. If you avoid high adventure recreation activities, you may never know how the thrill moves you. If you avoid integrating marketing in your leisure and tourism organization, you may never know the value of it to your organization. There are some people who will never climb a rock face, just like there are some who refuse to look at marketing differently then they have. So, the role of this textbook is to take a potentially fearful topic and make it

a less frightening and risky process. How can it become more thrilling and enjoyable? Let this book show you how to enjoy the journey.

Leisure and tourism organizations are not well-known for their ability to integrate marketing practices. Many organizations are known to use marketing as a reactionary tool. It has been used to find consumers to fill a program, to deal with the media following a crisis, or to share information about a special event. But in today's competitive, economically challenging, and ever-changing environment, marketing is more important than ever. Marketing is beginning to take a more central and critical role in effective leisure service decision making in a proactive manner.

Some leisure and tourism organization professionals feel they are applying marketing practices when they fax out 20 press releases regarding the grand opening of the health club, place posters on car windshields about Daddy-Daughter Date Night, do a restaurant promotion with the local radio station to host a Super Bowl party with their winning listeners, or call a reporter back about an interview regarding a hotel guest who was injured. While these are marketing-related practices, they are not all-inclusive of what marketing is. These actions alone do not integrate marketing into a leisure and tourism organization. These are operational decisions to communicate with audiences, but they may not be effective choices for your organization. Consider the following:

- Was there any press coverage or publicity from the press releases?

- Were the media choices appropriate for the intended audience?

- Did any attendees of the Daddy-Daughter date night find out about the program from the flyer?

- Were the people who attended the Super Bowl promotion part of the target audience?

- Are there defined targeted audiences that efforts are focused toward?

- Should there be other programs or services provided to targeted audiences?

- Was there any consideration for the organization's objectives?

- Were responses to the interviewer's tough questions appropriate?

If the organization is unable to answer these questions, then learning about marketing and the way in which to integrate it strategically and apply it successfully will be of extraordinary value.

These students learn to climb Colorado mountains like organizations learn to reach new heights in marketing.

Every organization applies marketing practices, whether they realize it or not. However, marketing is more than a single activity or a series of tasks. It is an integrated approach involved in every aspect of an organization.

What Is Marketing?

What comes to mind when you hear the word "marketing?" A group of undergraduate students studying leisure and tourism recently replied that marketing is "a tool to promote your product, a way to improve program attendance, advertising programs to the public, introduce programs to others, and sell what you offer." These responses are common. Marketing does indeed involve such descriptions, but they are only a small part of how marketing has evolved.

These professionals were also asked and responded similarly to this same question. What is surprising is the variation in the responses. Although many who were interviewed suggested marketing dealt with telling people about what an organization does, marketing appears to be interpreted in many different ways by the industry. Oftentimes there seems to be confusion regarding what exactly marketing is defined as. Table 1.1 offers opinions as to how organizations define marketing.

The term *marketing* is so misunderstood and debatable that Schultz (2001) suggested "marketing" not be used at all to reflect the purpose and importance of it. Rather he suggested "value creation" and "management" be used to more accurately reflect the function of marketing.

The concept of marketing is a complex and mysterious process. It is difficult to understand because society is used

Table 1.1
Organizations' Opinions of How Marketing Is Defined

Type of Organization	Marketing Defined
Country Clubs	Promoting the facility and overall philosophy.
	Getting the program or promotion out to the public or membership as fast as you can.
Parks and Recreation Departments	Getting the word or message out to the community.
	Selling your facility, services, and amenities.
	Identifying the group we are promoting to serve, and finding a way to bring that information to the public.
Indoor Athletic Complex	How we get information out to public.
Campus Recreation Program	Promotion. Everybody does marketing but half are unaware of its contributions.
Spa	The way you get the word out.
Arena	Opportunity to educate other people on our product.
Minor League Baseball	How we get the word out and get our name and message out to the masses.
Professional Basketball Team	Selling a product or service at a higher price to the most number of people, the most times possible.
Hotel	Using different mediums to try to raise our occupancy.
Camp	Marketing is such a broad thing. It's everything we say and portray, and that could be both externally and internally. It's just basically the image.
Golf Course	A way of drawing attention to your product.
Resorts	The heart, or engine, of a company: What's going to be driving the company forward to success?
	A way of getting information about a product out to people who are consumers and who might want to visit us.
	We have a product or service that we have to get out to the client.
Special Event Company	Presenting services or opportunities to a number of different constituencies, and providing information on the benefits of the services.
Marina	It all has to do with perception: The promotion and delivery of one's product.
Corporate Recreation	The ability to reach a target or your target audience in a creative or timely fashion.

to defining it simply with what they know. Every day, messages read in advertisements, heard in commercials, and seen on billboards make us think about marketing.

Marketing has evolved to be so much more than simply telling people about what an organization does through a two-by-two–inch ad placed in a well-circulated newspaper. Advertising is indeed a function within marketing; however, they are not synonymous. Advertising, promoting, and selling are all functions within marketing but they do not represent a complete view. Just like leisure and tourism programs and services are growing and changing, so is the term *marketing*.

Historic Marketing

Some would argue the concept of marketing has been around since the beginning of commerce. Others would debate that marketing began in the 1600s with the advent of newspaper advertising. Yet, others believe that marketing surfaced with television commercials in the 1950s. At that time Drucker (1958) suggested marketing had advanced further than other business concepts and was critical to economic development as it had become systemized. Regardless, the formal practice of marketing, through education, has existed for over 90 years (Cooke, Rayburn & Abercrombie, 1992).

The concept of marketing evolved considerably over the past five decades. How the role of marketing changed from the 1960s to the present follows.

1960s

In the 1960s, the concept of marketing was still being introduced to organizations. This idea was new, and businesses were cautious to adopt its principles. Those who believed in marketing focused primarily on getting tangible products into consumers' hands through the use of the 4 *P*s: product, place, price, and promotion. Matthews, Buzzell, Levitt, and Frank (1964) suggested "marketing is the performance of business activities that direct the flow of goods and services from producer to consumer" (p. 11). During this time, consumers were thought of as one mass market. Organizations had the product to sell and they used marketing techniques to find people to buy it. Further, nonprofit organizations did not even acknowledge its existence (Perreault & McCarthy, 1999; Weitz, Castleberry & Tanner, 1998). Marketing at this time focused on organizations that produced products. Little to no consideration was given to the service industry.

It isn't surprising that marketing evolved as society evolved. Changes identified through the last five decades oftentimes mirror societal changes as well. It wasn't until the late 1960s that society started to overtly and systematically question authority. Prior to this time people had greater trust in business and government, which created consumer confidence. By the late 1960s this trust had diminished and organizations could no longer expect people to blindly accept their products and services.

1970s

During the 1970s, organizations started breaking away from the strict product orientation to focus more on services and the consumer. Organizations who provided services (vs. products alone) could also apply the concept of marketing. Customers were no longer lumped together into one mass market— they were slowly being put into categories where their needs could be more easily addressed by organizations. Marketing was also more thought of as an entire process versus simply the 4 *P*s. Blake and Mouton (1972) described marketing as an entire cycle of activities, which starts with research and product decisions and continues through sales and servicing.

By the 1970s, a greater concern for safety, the environment, and people created a marketing function also concerned with these same issues. The focus on consumers— their needs, their wants, and their uniqueness—was apparent during this time and social marketing emerged. In the 1970s the city of San Diego created the Chicano Park located in Barrio Logan. Approximately 50 murals were painted depicting the Chicano civil rights movement and the struggles with ethnic empowerment of the time. It has become a popular tourist stopping point. Since its inception, the park has been a symbol of cultural issues and social marketing.

Oakland County residents at a park-sponsored Earth Day event in the 1970s.

1980s

The needs and wants of consumers were top priority by the 1980s. Organizations were using marketing as an innovative tool to identify, reach, and secure consumers. They also began using marketing as a competitive tool to develop strategies to devour the competition. Levitt (1986) suggested, "[Marketing] generates products, services and communications that target the specifically discovered needs and wants of specific, narrow, best-fit consumer segments" (p. 33). It was during this time organizations started to obtain feedback from customers to assure their product or service was meeting their needs. The relationship to consumer satisfaction and customer feedback was established.

In the 1980s the services marketing theme emerged with enhanced emphasis on customer satisfaction. The "salesman" of the past was no longer popular as increased interest in trust emerged, discretionary income expanded and increased competition for these monies allowed people to make choices and demand more. The quality movement flooded manufacturing industries and concern for consumer opinion expanded.

1990s

Feedback alone would not accomplish the mission of marketing by the 1990s. Customers would become integrated with the organization's operations whereby mutually beneficial relationships were established. Marketing evolved to become a way of doing business in the 1990s. McKenna (1991) suggested, "Marketing has shifted from tracking the customer, to blaming the customer, to satisfying the customer, and now to integrating the customer systematically" (p. 70). Marketing has become an integrated central focus of an organization.

A community recreation theater group from the 1980s.

Marketing is meant in the largest sense of the marketing mission—the business of centering the corporation's efforts around customers needs, so that customers bond to the company and continue to buy at a profit from the company in mutually satisfying long-term value exchanges. (Magrath, 1992, p. 1)

Connecting the organization to the consumer is the most essential component of organization operations. Trivers (1996) suggested, "This is a new mindset, grounded in the real wisdom of marketing—customers, customers, customers" (p. 3). Markets in the 1990s had become so specialized that they were called *fragments* of a market in which an organization was targeting. A target market once described as males between the ages of 18 and 25 has now become males, interested in competitive off-road biking, seeking a challenging and enriching experience, between the ages of 18 and 25.

This theme continued to develop in the 1990s and the concept of *services marketing* emerged recognizing that marketing within the service industry was different than that of the historic manufacturing industry. In 1991, McKenna stated, "Successful companies realize that marketing is like quality—integral to the organization. Like quality, marketing is an intangible that the customer must experience to appreciate" (p. 69). Quality became the foundation from which all marketing action was based. The technology explosion during this decade fueled the availability of consumer access and consumer information to aid in decision making. The theme centered on building valued relationships with guests.

2000s

In the 21st century the role of marketing continues to develop. Today, marketing is more holistic, involved with every aspect of the organization from customers and employees to programming and financing. Marketing has become integrated throughout the organization. McCarville (2002), a leisure author, found "marketing is a pervasive activity undertaken by virtually anyone interested in facilitating exchange with other individuals or parties" (p. 1). Marketing evolved to become everyone's role because marketing's function involves everyone. No longer does marketing reflect a simple list of 4 *Ps*, but rather a sophisticated list of involving itself in all aspects of an organization. Bialeschki and Henderson (2000) suggested, "In the past, marketing has been narrowly viewed with a focus on the participant. In the future, marketing will become a way of competing for funding dollars while remaining accountable to participants and communities" (p. 30). The focus on marketing in the 21st century has centered on a variety of relationships. Further, marketing's role is more complex within organizations because there are both strategic and operational elements used as marketing tools. Ballantyne, Christopher, and Payne (2003) suggested marketing activities must be viewed as systematic, holistic, and complex.

Today, with emerging interest in a balanced, holistic, and quality life, the concept of experiences has emerged. These experiences are based on not only consumers but also employees, volunteers and anyone involved with an organization. Marketing today is about integrating people into the organization and creating high-quality leisure service experiences.

Even though the concept of marketing existed for many years, this did not mean all types of organizations bought into integrating it. Over the past 40 years, marketing has been more aggressively written about, talked about, and practiced. Yet, the leisure industry has not followed these same beliefs about marketing during this time period. Jerry Bear (1981), during an educational session at the National Recreation and Park Association conference, stated

> Marketing is a technique that is a whole management and organizational philosophy that needs to be addressed by park and recreation organizations. Marketing is so much more than just selling and promoting and advertising. It is creating, building, and maintaining relationships… with the target markets in order to achieve our organizations objectives.

Marketing is the engine, or the heart, of a company.
Kelley Davidson, Wintergreen Resort

Yet, many in the leisure service industry were not quite ready for these thoughts, as it wasn't until years later the concept was more accepted by leisure industry professionals.

Havitz (2000) suggested marketing's tenure in the leisure service industry is only 20 years old and many still debate its use. Although more profit-oriented leisure organizations have used marketing as a tool, the level of integration has varied by organization size, interest, and marketing knowledge as well as the amount of competition for business that exists. There are many reasons the leisure industry has not readily accepted marketing as an organization function, including the following:

1. Literature failed to mention the leisure service industry until 20 years ago and primarily focused on manufacturing industries.

2. Not all nonprofit organizations felt the need to develop business skills and not all had the ability or background to integrate marketing successfully.

3. It has only been since the 1990s that marketing outcomes were required of accredited recreation academic programs, therefore professionals did not have the background needed.

4. Public organizations felt they could not adopt marketing practices—their mission was to serve everyone in a geographic area. They could not be perceived as an organization that focused on specific markets and employed marketing practices.

5. Many leisure and tourism organizations believe they are integrating marketing, yet few have approached it from a 21st century perspective.

Evidence suggests organizations are ready to integrate marketing now more than ever. Although, as McLeisch (1995) stated

> Traditionally, marketing has not been a popular subject in nonprofit circles… However, with flourishing competition in the nonprofit world, marketing and its attendant strategies must be taken into account to ensure the success—even the survival—of most nonprofit organizations. (p. 4)

Some leisure and tourism professionals indicated a variety of reasons why marketing is misunderstood in the industry in Table 1.2 .

Marketing Defined Today

People think of marketing as pure fluff. They think it is really easy and anyone can do it.
Lynne Ike, Van Andel Arena

Pick up ten books on marketing and you will discover few people agree on what marketing has evolved into today. In fact, few have ever agreed on the definition of marketing; however, what should be apparent is the existence of a similar theme in the message. Today, marketing has evolved to build on the relationship concepts of the 1990s and expanded to include people throughout every aspect of the organization. Those labeled "customers" are not the only ones within the marketing realm. Today, *marketing* is

> ...integrating effective strategic, operational and communication concepts and practices driven by various people that influence an organization and practiced by everyone within an organization (e.g., customers/guests, employees, volunteers, board members, donors, suppliers). These practices will ultimately deliver high-quality leisure experiences that reach and exceed the expectations of the people they serve while achieving organization objectives.

Marketing is a systematic process that controls an organization's activities in such a way that people's needs are efficiently identified and filled. Schultz (1999) suggested marketing is the way in which an organization is operated and managed: "It's not 'done' or 'carried out' by marketing people, but conducted by the entire organization" (p. 8). The distinctions between a business plan and a marketing plan are slowly eroding. Historically, a marketing plan would be a component of a business plan. More often now, marketing and business plans include similar if not the same elements. Marketing is more often viewed as a central activity within an organization. Further, strategic marketing plans combine the practices of strategic planning and marketing, which creates a unified approach or one system to identify the organization's needs and establish a plan for accomplishing organization objectives. The following provides an approach to marketing today that describes the strategic relationship:

Table 1.2
Organizations' Opinions of How Marketing Is Misunderstood

Type of Organization	Marketing Misunderstandings
Country Clubs	Everyone needs to be involved in the marketing program and make sure staff understands the plan, objective, and direction you are headed in with all the details.
	We think that we put things out and people read them.
Parks and Recreation Departments	People don't view it as necessary.
	In leisure services, we have traditionally just put things out on the street thinking people would just come, and we haven't taken a real business approach to it.
	The time and planning involved and how it all relates to each other on making the whole plan work—It's not just handing out flyers. You have to have a coordinated effort.
Indoor Athletic Complex	Limited by money.
Spa	Not enough money to spend, competition, and little time to capture audience.
Arena	People think marketing is pure fluff— Really easy and anybody can do it.
Professional Basketball Team	That it is fun-filled, slap people on the back, let's take somebody out to lunch, let's blow up some balloons and have a party type of a persuasion.
Hotel	People try to classify people into little niches and not everyone fits into those niches.
Camp	It's not incredibly important.
Golf Course	How to evaluate marketing decisions to prove the investment was worth it.
Special Event Company	Today we are marketing a lifestyle.
Resorts	That advertising goes directly into sales.
	The various components that are involved with Internet marketing and measuring the return.
	We have to realize that we're all part of a big picture and individual departments cannot just market themselves—They need to understand the broader view.
Marina	That an organization can just put up a sign and people will come, and that employees aren't important to marketing when actually quality employees are most important.
Corporate Recreation	Marketing to the wrong target audience and not using the best avenue to reach them.

- If the circus is coming to town and you paint a sign saying "Circus Coming to the Fairgrounds Saturday," that's *advertising*.

- If you put the sign on the back of an elephant and walk him through town, that's *promotion*.

- If the elephant walks through the mayor's flowerbed, that's *publicity*.

- If you can get the mayor to laugh about it, that's *public relations*.

- And, if you planned the elephant's walk, that's *marketing*.

The expanding nature of the people involved in organizations resulted in the need for marketing to play a central role to ensure a consistent brand message is communicated with various audiences. Gummesson (1999) suggested as many as 30 different relationships exist within an organization. Historically, the people of concern to marketing have been the customer or consumer. This has grown to include any people with which the organization intends to be involved or has been involved. Strategies must be in place to address all their unique needs and issues. Some have a direct role within the organization, including employees, customers or guests, and those who govern or provide economically to the organization. Others more indirectly influence an organization's actions (e.g., suppliers, environmental groups).

Quality has emerged as a foundation of the marketing concept. Leisure and tourism organizations recognize that poor delivery of the leisure experience will negate all efforts toward reaching people. One negative experience in a leisure and tourism organization will impact ten people directly because the person who has the negative experi-

ence will tell that many people directly. The impact is expanded, however, as those ten people will in turn tell ten others, who will tell ten others, and so on. Ultimately 250 people learn about the poor service experience. More money can be spent on ways to reach new consumers, but ultimately any amount of money spent will have little impact when so many others are personally telling people why they should not engage in the experience at XYZ leisure organization. On the other hand, organizations focused on exceeding the expectations of those they serve create a network of "salespeople" encouraging others to participate.

In today's leisure and tourism environment, marketing includes for-profit, nonprofit, and public perspectives. Because marketing is objective based, any type of leisure and tourism organization benefits from this approach. The organization's objectives can be people-related (e.g., serving the teen market in a community), funding-oriented (e.g., raising $75,000 to build a new playground), or profit-driven (e.g., netting 20% more profit than last year). Regardless of the profitability status, all organizations can apply strategic marketing principles to their organization.

Marketing has evolved to become a centralized function in organizations. Webster (1995) found integrating marketing efforts and developing a marketing culture in 173 service organizations produced greater marketing effectiveness. This concept is undertaken by first thinking about the way an organization is created. Organizations first develop products and services based on customer need. Once these are established, funding, through stockholders or other means, is acquired prior to providing the product or service to targeted audiences. Finally, employees are hired to provide these offerings. The role of marketing today is to integrate all these activities. This relationship is highlighted in Figure 1.1.

Over 250 people could be impacted by this alumni event at the College of William and Mary, if just one person has a poor experience.

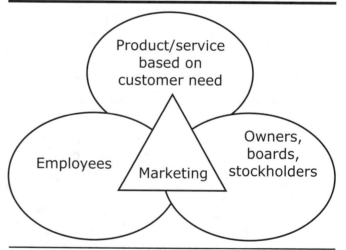

Figure 1.1
Organization Creation

Marketing has historically been concerned with consumer issues alone. This approach is viewed as limiting however and not the most effective for organizations. Viewing employees and volunteers as those subject to marketing processes is a recent phenomenon. Simms (2003) stated

> Marketers have started to realize that falling employee engagement [i.e., dissatisfied employees] is damaging external brand perceptions: the delivery is not matching up to the brand promise. So they are starting to lay claim to territory traditionally held by human resources—employee relations. The growing popularity of employee or employer branding is testimony to marketers' attempts to adapt the tools and techniques traditionally used to motivate and engage customers to secure the engagement and commitment of an internal audience. (p. 23)

Cony (2002) further suggested the importance of viewing staff as a target audience.

Other publics involved with the organization are those that influence the operation. These may be board members, shareholders, donors, nonusers, or anti-users (people who object to your organization operations, e.g., environmental group objecting to golf course development by wetlands). This holds true with other relationships within an organization, through ownership or leadership, and other vested parties such as volunteers and donors.

Marketing is used for a variety of functions in an organization, including the following:

- gathering information and data
- aiding in product, service, program, and facility development
- communicating with targeted and other markets
- developing relationships with people within and outside of the organization
- managing crises
- identifying and capitalizing on opportunities
- establishing the organization's image or brand
- assisting in funding
- creating consumer-based experiences
- exceeding the expectations of those served within an organization

Marketing provides resources to and supports all functions and departments within an organization. An organizational chart that integrates marketing, would resemble the organization creation in Figure 1.1 where marketing would influence and impact all aspects of an organization (Figure 1.2).

The more traditional organizational chart placed marketing's role as one additional function within an organization. Marketing's role was similar to the programming, fitness, or human resources department function. Historically, organizations have used marketing in a support role. Those within the programming department would solicit the assistance of the marketing department when they needed to develop a flyer to promote the new fall classes to be offered, the fitness department may ask for marketing to help with a brochure highlighting their offerings, and human resources may have asked marketing to write the classified advertisement for the new director position available. This use of marketing, however, is more reactionary. The programming and fitness departments made decisions about their offerings without the support of marketing. In this case marketing was simply viewed as a means to communicate with consumers, and it was not used in a strategic way. Marketing could have provided insight and data to each department to support their objectives.

Piece-meal marketing efforts in leisure and tourism organizations will not produce desired outcomes. Webster (1995) found those organizations with developed marketing cultures produced better results from their marketing

Figure 1.2
Integrated Organizational Chart

efforts. This culture suggests the entire organization places emphasis on the marketing function and the way in which employees adopt marketing practices. Figure 1.3 provides a more traditional organizational chart and shows marketing's historic role in leisure and tourism organizations and an integrated approach to marketing where the marketing function supports all areas strategically and operationally. Beirne (2004) suggested organizations are moving from decentralized marketing to integrating marketing within departments, such as operations, sales, and finance.

Leisure and tourism organizations have begun to more aggressively include marketing functions within their organizations. A variety of leisure organizations indicated they have recently changed the way they approach marketing. These comments are highlighted in Table 1.3.

Understand and recognize that this is the wave of the future. Dan Davis, Avondale Community Recreation

The Role of Marketing

Back in the early 1990s, McKenna (1991) suggested marketing had become "a way of doing business" (p. 69); it was no longer simply a function. Further, he noted the marketing was in everyone's job description. No longer was it limited to those with marketing titles. An organization's culture was one that embraced marketing practices.

This attitude, however, has not been prevalent in leisure and tourism organizations. Marketing has not become fully integrated in leisure and tourism organizations, and is often viewed as one of many functions within an organization. Even though marketing should be a function in everyone's job description, there is doubt that every employee's job description has this responsibility listed (if an organization has even provided job descriptions!).

It is common in leisure and tourism organizations to see one to three people assigned to the marketing function. Even though a person within the organization acts as the one responsible for "marketing," his or her role is to ultimately coordinate marketing efforts throughout an organization— It is everyone's role to understand they are ultimately responsible for the organization's success and all play a role in the marketing effort. Tew-Johnson, Havitz,

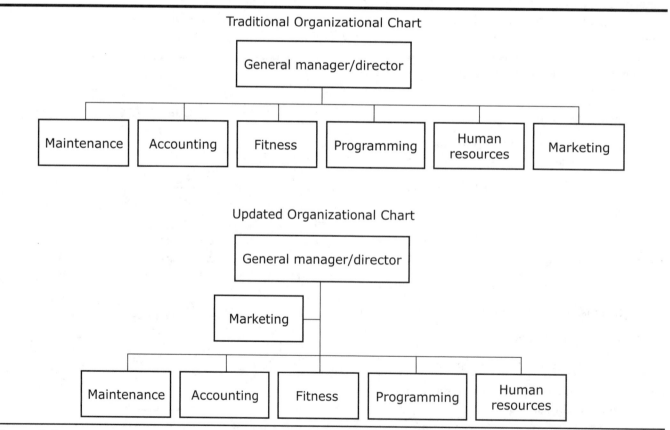

Figure 1.3
Traditional and Updated Organizational Charts

and McCarville (1999) stated all personnel must understand and embrace the complex process of marketing if an organization is to be successful in the long run.

Everybody should be a marketing person regardless of their job description. Don Schappacher, Owner and President, American Hospitality Management

The person or persons responsible for the marketing function within a leisure and tourism organization varies. The two distinct responsibilities of marketing—strategic and operational—may be completed by the same or different persons. Size and complexity of the organization are often determining factors on how many people are involved with these activities. Some duties may be shared by outside organizations as well (e.g., an advertising organization may design all the promotional materials).

The strategic elements of marketing center around understanding what is currently happening in the organization and within the environment. It is determining which markets to focus toward to achieve the organization's objectives. The strategic side of marketing sets goals and objectives to directly address the organization's needs and priorities. Conversely, the operational side of marketing makes these objectives a reality.

Marketing is geared toward not only customers but also other markets. Examples of additional markets of concern include employees, volunteers, boards of directors, nonusers, donors, and suppliers. The second difference is the expanding number of tools available to assist in marketing communications. These tools include event promotions, public and community relations, internal marketing, stewardship, advertising, sponsorship, and direct sales.

We focus marketing actions toward our 500-person volunteer force, as they are the key to us successfully serving youth. Daniel Varner, Think Detroit

Strategic responsibilities for marketing lie with someone who has access to all organization information. Esler and Sutton (2003) suggested the new marketing executive views marketing as "a science enabled by art"

Table 1.3
Organizations' Opinions of Recent Marketing Changes

Type of Organization	Recent Marketing Changes
Country Club	Assistance with internal marketing.
Parks and Recreation Departments	Added full-time marketing person. Three and a half years ago we did not have a marketing department, person or anyone.
Indoor Athletic Complex	Strategies
Campus Recreation Program	Suggestion from members of what they want to see; each works on marketing efforts in their area.
Spa	Competition
Arena	Communicate with all departments because previous marketing department was isolated.
Minor League Baseball	It is more of an image campaign.
Professional Basketball Team	Absolutely, we've gotten much more aggressive and strategic.
Hotel	Technologically. Marketing is the most important thing you can possibly do that nobody knows about. You are a secret until you're unlocked. Consumers have become a lot more educated.
Camp	There are more regional/geographic differences in people. More technological. More competition for kids' time.
Golf Course	Technology
Resorts	Organizations are no longer trying to be everything to everybody— They are more targeted. Marketing is more competitive.
Marina	A greater emphasis today on hiring and training employees.
Corporate Recreation	Information needs to be more concise today.

and has duties that are "broader than ever." The "science" part of marketing recommends the professional in this role must have business and financial knowledge. Further, Esler and Sutton stated for many companies this will be a new way of looking at the role of marketing and the time has come for a "dramatic turnaround and a marketing-led transformation…" (p. 5). Some of the new set of skills required include the following:

- networking between the various groups (e.g., employees, stockholders, customers)

- acting as voice of the customer

- representing image of organization

- analyzing data and converting this information into action, develops customer experiences

- integrating all in marketing efforts and develops the plan

First, the strategic role of marketing professionals is to believe philosophically in the importance of marketing, represent these beliefs through practice, and the engage others involved in the organization. Marketing professionals coordinate and integrate marketing information from all areas within an organization to develop effective strategies for each area to achieve their objectives. They further develop and assess all organization information, which leads to the creation of a future plan from which the organization operates. Williamson (1999) suggested even though organizations develop strategies, it does not mean they should not be prepared to identify and select strategic options for the future. Being prepared for the future and potential changes means an organization can reposition itself more quickly than others.

The second role within marketing involves the "art" of marketing—the operational decisions. These duties within marketing act as a support function that provide a level of expertise for consistent messages/communication with all publics. These duties include taking the future plan and creating marketing communications that allow an organization to achieve their objectives. This person must possess skills at developing, implementing, and evaluating operational ideas. Figure 1.4 highlights the role of a marketing professional within a leisure and tourism organization.

Examples of specific duties of a marketing professional include the following:

Strategic Duties

1. Coordinates meeting with all publics to develop organization objectives.

2. Shares information on current organization status and future trends.

3. Provides data on employee, customer, board member, supplier, and volunteer satisfaction.

4. Conducts a competitive analysis to determine organization's competitive edge.

Real Life Story: Crystal Mountain Resort Integrates Employees

Thirty-six holes of exceptional golf, splendid accommodations, superb downhill and cross-country skiing, excellent food, state-of-the-art conference facilities and entertainment for the entire family are just a few of the reasons Crystal Mountain Resort is voted, time and time again, a top resort in the Midwest. A secret behind their success is the approach they take with integrating employees in the marketing process.

Every staff member is involved in marketing by ensuring everyone is prepared every day to answer guest questions as well as provide exceptional guest service.

When employees arrive for work, they check-in at the time clock and pick up their nametag, a resort trail guide and a weekly activity guide. The trail guide highlights every area of the 1,500-acre resort; the activity guide highlights the resorts offerings for guests that week. Employees are better able to provide quality service and prepared to answer the most common questions. The organization's expectation is established, and every employee is equipped to handle questions. They have taken responsibility for marketing their resort.

With a marketing staff of 300 prepared on any given day and at any time to share information about guest activities and services, it is no wonder they are recognized for their efforts. They have found a simple yet very effective way to ensure employees are integrated in the marketing process.

Operational Duties

1. Creates brochures for staff recruitment.

2. Evaluates impact of attending trade shows.

3. Implements radio station promotions.

4. Supports staff training for preparing to serve a new market (e.g., seniors).

Leisure and tourism professionals view marketing as an important job responsibility. Analyzing over 75 professional job descriptions from various leisure and tourism industries revealed that each had mentioned, at least once, a marketing related responsibility. These ranged from sales, public relations, and promotional duties.

Marketing's role has become one that assists every area within an organization. Today, marketing may provide research about employee and guest satisfaction and may reach various audiences to communicate organization messages through brochures to stockholders, employees, and guests or customers. Marketing may provide strategies to areas to reach audiences of concern (e.g., environmental group does not like golf course development by wetlands).

Marketing is a very high priority. Without marketing our programs and services we don't have participants or customers, and then we don't have jobs. Jeremy Rycus, Corporate Recreation

Why the Sudden Change?

So, why has marketing changed so dramatically in such a short amount of time? The leisure and tourism market today is highly competitive and customers have a wide range of choices. They can choose between various activities, either passive or active, whether inside or outside the home. Leisure time and money are spent on both leisure and non-leisure activities including making choices between such things as taking a trip or buying new furniture, joining a bowling league or watching TV. The competitive world for leisure time and money is diverse and expanding. Organizations have become more sophisticated in their approach to marketing as a result of these and other influences, such as the following:

- increased competition
- challenging economy
- changing consumers
- funding challenges
- greater need for accountability
- advanced technology
- enhanced globalization

Competition for consumer discretionary spending and time has increased tremendously over the past decade. People have more leisure choices than ever before because

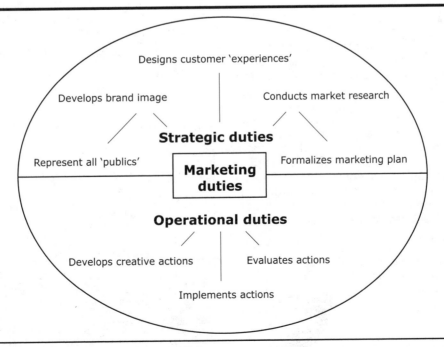

Figure 1.4
Duties of a Marketing Professional

there are more providers of leisure services than ever before. People are selecting from nonprofits, for-profits, and public organizations for their leisure experiences. Many public parks and recreation organizations offer fitness centers as do for-profit fitness centers. Through the increased

spending of discretionary income, the leisure and tourism industry has advanced its offerings to the consumer through the years. Competition grows with each new business in an attempt to gain those dollars. According to the U.S. Census Bureau (1963, 1983, 2003), $19.484 million was spent on

---

Real Life Story: Canton Leisure Services Integrates Marketing

Canton Leisure Services (CLS), an accredited community leisure and tourism organization, wanted to better utilize marketing in their overall organization operations. CLS had an $11 million annual budget to operate different divisions for a community size of 80,000, including a community center, five parks, two golf courses, a senior center, a banquet and conference center, and a performing arts center. CLS is located in a growing community where leisure is highly valued by residents and administrators alike. Challenged by the pressures of increased competition and providing more services with increasingly stretched resources (e.g., budget cuts), CLS realized integrating marketing practices would provide a resource to ensure they could sucessfully address these challenges. As their organization and community continued to grow, CLS had to operate differently than before to stay focused on their goals including

1. Create a sense of community and belonging.

2. Provide premiere facilities.

3. Develop and cultivate partnerships.

4. Utilize resources efficiently and demonstrate fiscal responsibility.

5. Create a healthy community.

6. Provide excellent customer service.

7. Empower staff.

In the past two years CLS added two staff members with "marketing-related" duties in their job descriptions. These positions, however, evolved and the job descriptions needed to reflect CLS's interest to integrate marketing better throughout the organization and to become more strategic in their marketing approach. As a result, CLS decided to form a marketing committee to determine how they would integrate marketing more successfully. This committee was comprised of the CLS director, area managers, one member from each division, the marketing and communication specialist, and several employees from various positions and divisions. The committee's objectives were as follows:

1. Promote CLS overall to Canton residents.

2. Develop the CLS brand as an organization strength showing uniformity, yet uniqueness, within all divisions.

3. Support all CLS divisions with marketing resources and activities.

4. Coordinate marketing-related activities between divisions to better utilize CLS resources.

5. Serve and satisfy more Canton residents.

As a result, the committee developed a list of actions to achieve their objectives and integrate marketing. These responsibilities were assigned to a committee member to coordinate and report back at their regular scheduled meetings. Their responsibilities were as follows:

1. Review and develop visual brand and ensure uniformity in brand communication.

2. Develop overall strategic marketing plan for CLS, leverage organization strengths, reduce overlap, and maximize resources.

3. Write communication standards/guidelines.

4. Integrate marketing throughout CLS:

    a. Evaluate and revise marketing specialist and communication specialist job descriptions.

    b. Clarify marketing roles and responsibilities of all staff.
        i. Train all staff on marketing concepts, tools, internal processes and support.
        ii. Develop an evaluation system and criteria for staff to measure marketing-related responsibilities.

5. Establish a process for developing, funding, implementing, and evaluating strategic marketing plans in each division.

6. Develop market research systems and support.

continued...

the leisure industry in 1960. By 1980 this number grew to $106.947 million and by 2000 this figure was $564.7 billion in the United States alone. Although one could debate the types of businesses included within the leisure groups measured, what cannot be debated is the overwhelming investment of consumers in recreation and the growth of leisure choices available to people.

Unfortunately, some organizations do not realize the importance of marketing until a new competitor enters the picture. Organizations that integrate marketing practices successfully are better prepared for the emergence of a competitor. Failure to develop strategies makes an organization ill-prepared to manage the challenges of competition and acheive organization objectives.

Real Life Story: Canton Leisure Services (continued)

As a result of these initial efforts, the job descriptions for the two staff were modified and their reporting relationship changed from the two staff reporting to different people, to both reporting to one centralized source who communicated with all departments. Job descriptions now focused on the actions to achieve organization objectives.

Revised Job Description: Marketing Specialist

1. Direct the development of annual organization and division strategic marketing plans, and development plans for new offerings.

2. Assist individual(s) responsible for preparing and implementating annual plans for approval by division directors and director.

3. Conduct various tactical communication activities as established in CLS Marketing Plan (e.g., act as sponsorship coordinator/liaison between organization and sponsors; conduct direct sales activities; handle all donations, community relations, and quality service efforts).

4. Support divisions with tactical communication plan activities as established in their respective annual marketing plans.

5. Conduct, evaluate, and communicate any organization/division market research activities.

6. Present regularly at organization and division staff meetings regarding "marketing" update and stay abreast of each divisions marketing activities.

7. Consult with divisions as needed or requested on marketing-related issues.

8. Develop, train staff about, and evaluate Communication Guidelines Manual.

9. Identify and establish opportunities for cross-marketing between/within divisions/organization.

10. Assist with the measurement of tactical marketing effort implementation.

11. Supervise Communication Specialist and ensure division of duties are completed.

Revised Job Description: Communication Specialist

1. Review and approve all communication materials developed within divisions (e.g., advertisements, press releases, flyers).

2. Maintain website and identify opportunities for enhanced communication.

3. Develop key promotional materials for CLS Annual Marketing Plan (e.g., seasonal activity guides, newsletter, brochures); write and review copy.

4. Conducts various tactical communication activities as established in CLS Marketing Plan (e.g., public and community relations, internal marketing, and advertising).

5. Assists with the development of organization and division marketing plans making specific communication plan suggestions.

6. Acts as media liaison establishing media relationships and public relations opportunities for CLS and all divisions. This includes identifying newsworthy events, writing press releases, producing CCTV cable shows, developing video projects, etc.

7. Maintains staff community relations assignments.

8. Places all CLS and division advertisements in media outlets to maximize resources, money/trade.

9. Consults with division directors/staff on promotional materials they develop that follows established guidelines.

10. Negotiates with organizations for publication of materials (identifies those organizations CLS will work with as "approved" vendor).

11. Consults with divisions as needed on suggesting tactical communication tools.

12. Purchases all promotional materials (e.g., clothing with logo, merchandise, giveaways, trinkets) and allocates to divisions as needed.

13. Supervises half time staff member to complete graphic design activities.

Even through CLS has just begun to make the changes necessary to integrate marketing success fully in their organization they have begun the process and are preparing for achieving their marketing committee objectives. Instead of reducing the role of marketing in their challenging times they realize the importance of further utilizing this function. They have employed the practices established in this chapter and represent how an organization can integrate marketing.

As the **economy** continues to pose challenges to leisure and tourism organizations, the roll of marketing must adapt accordingly. In troubled economic times, marketing is more important than ever as organizations must learn to be more efficient and effective. Marketing allows an organization to identify the most appropriate actions to take in an effort to achieve organizational objectives in troubled times. Yet, unfortunately, some organizations view this as a time for marketing to be cut or eliminated from leisure and tourism organizations, as they perceive marketing to be a luxury instead of a necessity. Only in economically prosperous times do some organizations support marketing. Marketing is, however, a system that must be in place during any economic time. Arnold (2001) interviewed Hugh Taylor, Vice President of Marketing for Hilton International. Taylor supported that organizations should not eliminate marketing budgets in difficult financial times, but rather invest more aggressively. Like any critical function within an organization, during economically difficult times, it must also learn to be more efficient.

Consumers have changed. Changing demographics, increase time demands, and greater sophistication of consumers have created the need for integrating marketing, strategically, more than ever. Today, increased population, longevity, potential workers, education, and persons with disabilities all affect how an organization caters to consumers. According to the U.S. Census Bureau (2000) between 1990 and 2000 the U.S. population increased by 33 million people, 1.7 million of which relocated from abroad. Two thirds of those relocating were noncitizens. In 2000, 25 million men and 31 million women were aged 55 and older. Sixty-one percent of women ages 16 and older were working or in search of a job. Workers with higher levels of education have higher earnings. Forty-four percent of Asians and Pacific Islander, 25 years or older, achieved at least a bachelor's degree, compared to 28% of White non-Hispanics, 17% of Blacks, and 11% of Hispanics. It has been determined that one in five adults live with a disability. It is imperative for organizations to acknowledge these types of diversities to streamline their marketing efforts.

Further, consumers are faced with increased demands on their time. More people work outside the home than ever before. They are busier with increased responsibilities of children and home and have longer commutes. The development and popularity of catalog shopping, drive-through services, technology simplifiers like cell phones, personal fitness, service companies, and reduced vacations trips are a result of changes in consumers.

Funding issues and greater need for *accountability* are prevalent in most organizations today. With increased pressure from the public to reduce taxes and exercise fiscal constraint, many communities have faced the challenge of reducing public services such as recreation (Glover, 1999; Hastad & Tymeson, 1997). Historically, local government has relied heavily on taxation to support programs, facility operations, and support services. While the cost of providing services has increased, local property taxation has not. It cannot increase proportionally, especially in the light of tax limitation initiatives in many states. Also, there is greater competition among local government departments for tax dollars and it is becoming increasingly harder to convince the public to support all these services with increased tax dollars (Artz & Bermont, 1970; Dubois, 1991; Hastad & Tymeson, 1997; Schmid, 1995). The demand for what are considered essential services (generally identified as police and fire protection as well as sanitation services) takes precedence over the funding of recreation services. As a result, public recreation departments have had to find new ways of maintaining programs and services while managing a decreasing budget. Hastad and Tymeson (1997) suggested these challenges have forced organizations to be more creative in the financing and delivery of recreation services.

However, funding challenges are not unique to public leisure and tourism organizations. Support for voluntary contributions such as those needed by the YMCA or other quasi-public leisure organizations are in high demand and competition for these contributions is greater than ever. Private and for-profit organizations also struggle with funding issues. Increased taxation, prohibiting tax laws, and greater competition have resulted in continued financial challenges to create a desired profit or develop enough interest to maintain services (e.g., private country club, corporate recreation programs).

Technological advancements are challenging organizations like never before. Increased access to the Internet created additional competitors for leisure time, money, and interest. Technology has advanced access between consumers and organizations. It has allowed gathering of consumer data at unprecedented levels (Ballantyne, Christopher & Payne, 2003). According to the U.S. Census Bureau (2000), 57% of students had access to computers at home and at school. Eighty-eight percent of families with a household income of $75,000 or more had at least one computer, 79% of which had one or more persons who used the Internet. Because of this

> Providers must think through how these technologies will impact not only the delivery of the products/service offering but how it will impact everything from customer interface points to actual product design. Marketing will need to be redefined and dynamic to adapt to the new technolo-

gies and be responsive to the customer. (Nykiel, 2001, p. 83)

Truax and Myron (1998) projected that marketing would take "the spotlight," as a discipline in the new millennium for various reasons, including "the speed of change in the market place requires greater responsibilities" (p. 11).

Enhanced **globalization** and access to a greater range of consumers has also impacted leisure organization interest in marketing. Ballantyne, Christopher and Payne (2003) suggested:

> In global and deregulated open markets, there are no certain prescriptions for marketing success that can be based on our past experience in relatively stable market systems. Open market conditions create higher levels of change and complexity within and between organizational boundaries. Establishing more open relationships with key customers, suppliers and other stakeholders can be seen as strategies for recreating stability, thus opening up value-creating opportunities in new ways. (p. 161)

These issues have been the most impactful to the desire of leisure and tourism organizations to invest in marketing. Hyland (2004) cited that during the past two years e-commerce increased by 53% where $44 billion was spent in 2002. However, there are still those who have yet to apply marketing practices that incorporate technology.

Barriers To Applying Marketing

Many leisure and tourism organizations believe they apply marketing practices. But not all integrate these activities throughout an organization. There are three basic premises as to why leisure and tourism organizations fail to integrate marketing. The first is *fear*: fear of not having the skills and not knowing how to apply and integrate marketing; fear of investing and producing minimal results; and fear of making an investment in time, money, and energy that doesn't provide results.

Another barrier is *disbelief* (or skepticism/doubt) in the impact of marketing. The belief that marketing will not help the organization improve; the belief that marketing only costs money and is too mysterious and risky to make an investment.

The final barrier is *no need*. When organizations feel there is no need to integrate marketing because they already have enough business, they are doing fine the way

they are. Why change what isn't broken? The safety of operating under the status quo is comforting to many organizations; yet, they are unprepared for the future.

Generally, these fears and disbeliefs are partially the fault of past marketing efforts. Those who have implemented marketing practices have not always done a good job proving its worth to an organization, and may not have always applied marketing practices correctly, hence creating fear. Not all marketing activities have produced results, hence creating disbelief. Finally, not all organizations have been shown the value of integrating and applying marketing within their organizations.

This text intends to remove fear and disbelief—to increase confidence and certainty when integrating marketing practices and techniques successfully. It will identify ways to maximize marketing opportunities, even with limited funding, and show ways to measure the return of the investment.

The most misunderstood concept in leisure marketing? People believe… if you build it, they will come… They don't view marketing as necessary. Ann Conklin, Canton Leisure Services

Why Is Marketing Important?

It wasn't all that long ago that marketing wasn't a priority of any organization. After all, marketing has only been around a short time. Leisure industries vary in their acceptance and utilization of the concept of marketing. Appiah-Adu, Fyall, and Singh (1999) found the value of the increased importance in the airline industry. They determined that a strong marketing culture produced better business performance.

Marketing provides organizations the opportunity to continue to look at their offerings from a *proactive* approach. Organizations value the integration of marketing for several reasons, including the following:

- it provides *focus* toward achievable outcomes
- it allows for *consistency* in messages shared
- it *improves* and is focused on all *relationships* (not just customers alone)
- it *integrates* the organization
- it is *cost-effective* (even though it costs money!)

Applying Marketing to For-Profit and Nonprofit Organizations

An abundance of books are available for leisure and tourism organizations to consult regarding marketing topics like social marketing, relational marketing, public sector marketing, nonprofit marketing, and services marketing. This book approaches the marketing concept in a practical, systematic way. It applies principles from each of these in one uniform fashion, suggesting that the concept of marketing itself is not unique, but the objectives of the organization are. Ultimately, all leisure and tourism organizations want to enhance the quality of life for people through the leisure experience. This is what makes the delivery of leisure and tourism experiences unique—what sets them apart from other service experiences. Marketing leisure and tourism experiences, whether from a for-profit, nonprofit, or public organization should be approached similarly. Hence, the need in the leisure industry is to have a book that deals with all the specific issues within the leisure experience. Each type of leisure and tourism organization will always have different objectives, but this will not impact the marketing process it will only ensure that each organization makes different decisions.

Further, the distinctions historically created between public and private, nonprofit and for-profit leisure and tourism organizations, is slowly blending. Past differences implied these organizations operated differently from one another and did not apply the same business practices. This is changing.

The differences in these types of organizations today lie largely in reporting relationships. The funding of these types of organizations is narrower than ever. Historically, private and public nonprofit leisure organizations relied on taxation, grants, and/or donations to secure operating and capital budgets. Today, more rely on user fees and charges, which is more similar to for-profit organizations. What they all have in common is the way in which they operate. Every organization, regardless of profit status has specific objectives from which to guide the decisions of the organization. There is no difference in applying marketing principles in these organizations.

Rosenstein (1995) found that nonprofit organizations did not apply marketing capabilities beyond the basic of levels. Comparing private and public nonprofits suggested the private organizations used marketing tools more often than the pubic nonprofits. Some have felt each discipline should apply related marketing techniques—that is, those who sell services should reflect on service marketing texts, those involved with providing social goods, social mar-

keting texts. However, it is suggested that the only differences between these type organizations is their differing objectives (Academy for Educational Development, 2001).

What is different between various leisure and tourism organizations are goals and objectives, the market(s) to attract, the message to communicate, and the way in which they are reached. The systems an organization creates to analyze, develop, implement, and evaluate will be unique. No two marketing plans are ever the same, regardless of profit status. What is also unique to marketing the leisure and tourism industry is just that, the fact that all marketing is related to leisure and tourism issues. Figure 1.5 highlights the marketing process for all types of leisure and tourism organizations.

Marketing is complex and ever-changing. A number of models and methods have been developed to help individuals and organizations apply marketing practices in an effort to simplify this process. These models have grown, changed, and expanded throughout the past decades to reflect a science that is in place today. This book is designed based on the components of this model.

Components of Effective Marketing

There are two foundational issues related to effective leisure and tourism marketing. The first is based on an organiza-

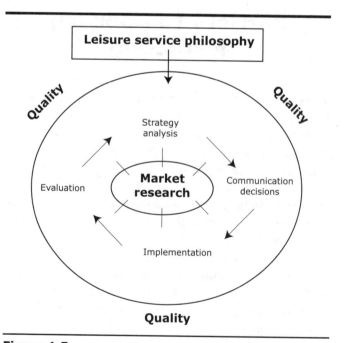

Figure 1.5
Components of Effective Leisure and Tourism Organization Marketing

tion's and an individual's leisure service philosophy. This model presumes professionals delivering leisure and tourism services have adopted a principal that suggests the delivery of these services is to create experiences that benefit the consumers served. This may be to enhance the quality of people's lives in some fashion. These issues are further clarified in Chapter 2, The Marketing of Leisure and Tourism Experiences.

The base consideration that overrides effective marketing decisions is the premise that all activities are driven by quality service standards. Each step in the marketing process must commit to and practice the belief that the role of the organization is to embody quality practices in everything it does. It is not just a consumer focus; it is a premise that applies to consumers, employees, boards of directors, vendors, facilities, policies, procedures, etc. It is not just limited to people. Quality service involves every aspect of an organization from the products, services, and experiences it provides to the standards (e.g., cleanliness, hiring) and processes it creates (e.g., policies/procedures). Chapter 3 further addresses this component of marketing.

Chapter 4 introduces a formal process for applying each of these components in a leisure and tourism organization. Enabling Marketing Action provides practical application of these principles through formal market planning. Further, it addresses issues of particular concern to leisure and tourism organizations, including funding marketing efforts and measuring the impacts of these marketing decisions.

If a solid leisure service philosophy and quality service commitment are the foundations of effective marketing, then market research is the heart of the marketing process. Research is needed throughout the marketing process and provides assistance to each phase within marketing. Research addresses issues related to understanding demographic and leisure trends, needs of targeted markets, satisfaction of employees, volunteers, and customers, and if the $10,000 per month billboard was worth the investment. Having staff with skills in analyzing and developing research to aid in marketing decision-making is a vital component within a leisure and tourism organization. Chapter 5 highlights basic research processes and issues.

Chapters 6 through 8 are dedicated to developing skills in strategic analysis. Anyone can spend a marketing budget, but not everyone can be successful at it. Therefore the key to effective decisions is analyzing and developing a strategy based on sound principles and evidence. During this phase, analysis of the current organization occurs, including understanding current systems, issues, and future plans. An assessment also occurs of the outside/external world, such as understanding leisure trends, legal issues, and technological developments. Based on these findings,

targeted markets are then developed. In Chapter 7 the process for target market creation is outlined identifying techniques for selecting appropriate markets. Once determined, organizations can develop a formal strategy for marketing. Chapter 8 highlights ways in which an organization can position themselves and develop or enhance the brand image. It is in this chapter that an organization learns to develop specific target market objectives. From these objectives, communication decisions are then based.

Once an organization identifies what they want to occur they then determine how they will accomplish it. Chapter 9 identifies the process in which an organization partakes to acknowledge and develop a strategic action plan, focusing on achieving the target market objectives. Chapters 10–14 provide insight into the marketing, promotional and communication mix decisions that need to be made in an effective marketing plan. The marketing mix is first addressed in this phase and related to the experience. Specifically, leisure and tourism organization offering decisions incorporate product, service, program, facility, distribution issues related to location and the Internet, and pricing considerations. Next, brand image and promotion decisions are made, followed by the various tools used to communicate with the targeted audiences in the communication mix. These tools include public and community relations, advertising, sponsorship, stewardship, selling, and internal marketing. These chapters highlight techniques for effective use of each decision and tool is shared helping organizations make successful decisions to achieve target market objectives.

Apply What You Know

1. Interview and investigate a leisure or tourism organization's approach to integrating marketing and compare it to the process discussed in this chapter.

2. Solicit marketing definition examples from textbooks or documents of previous decades and compare them to this chapter's discussion on the topic.

Key Terms

Integrated marketing	Organization culture
Marketing	Quality service
Marketing plan	Strategic marketing
Operational marketing	Target market

Review Questions

1. What is the definition of marketing today?

2. How has marketing changed over the last five decades?

3. What is the role of marketing and why can all leisure and tourism organizations benefit from it?

4. What are the six changes in emphasis toward marketing?

5. What are the three barriers of effective marketing?

6. What is the value of strategic marketing decision making?

Internet Resources: Marketing-Related Listservs

The *Association for Consumer Research* list (ACR-L) discusses consumer research. This list serves as a forum for researchers, practitioners, and graduate students working in the interdisciplinary field of consumer research.

http://www.acrwebsite.org

Adland is an e-mail discussion in digest format related to marketing online for those with small budgets looking for alternative solutions to their online business presence.

http://www.softfornet.com

Am-Political-Marketing is a forum for those engaged in political marketing to share and communicate ideas, information, and conference/event details. Political marketing as a topic includes lobbying, elections, referenda, and campaign communication.

http://www.jiscmail.ac.uk/lists/am-political-marketing.html

Elmar is a moderated list for the discussion of marketing and marketing research. Its focus is academic; it is sponsored by the American Marketing Association's Marketing Education Division. Note that you do not have to be a member of AMA to subscribe.

http://www.ama.org/elmar

I-Advertising offers a moderated discussion on all aspects of Internet advertising, including online media planning, media buying, campaign tracking, industry trends and forecasts, creative development, cost estimates, advertising sales, and other aspects related to the promotion of a business on the Internet through an ongoing new media campaign.

http://www.internetadvertising.org

References

Academy for Educational Development. (2001). *Social marketing lite*. Washington, DC: U.S. Department of Education.

Appiah-Adu, K., Fyall, A., and Singh, S. (1999). Marketing culture and business performance in the airline industry. *Journal of Travel & Tourism Marketing, 8*(3), 47–67.

Arnold, M. (2001). Suite success. *Marketing, 15*(3), 22.

Artz, R. and Bermont, H. (Eds.). (1970). *Guide to new approaches to financing parks & recreation*. Arlington, VA: National Recreation and Park Association.

Ballantyne, D., Christopher, M., and Payne, A. (2003). Relationship marketing: Looking back, looking forward. *Marketing Theory Special Issue: Conceptual development in relationship marketing, 3*(1), 159–166.

Bear, J. (1981). *Marketing the park and recreation product*. Presented at the National Recreation and Park Association Congress, Dayton, OH.

Beirne, M. (2004). Marketing: Circa 2025. *Brandweek, 45*(5), 26–31.

Bialeschki, D. and Henderson, K. (2000). Trends affecting non-profit camps: Issues and recommendations for the millennium. *Camping Magazine, 73*(2), 25–31.

Blake, R. and Mouton, J. (1972). *How to assess the strengths and weaknesses of marketing and sales*. Austin, TX: Scientific Methods.

Cony, S. (2002). Give your staff the marketing edge. *Camping Magazine, 75*(2), 42–43.

Cooke, E. F., Rayburn, J. M., and Abercrombie, C. L. (1992). The history of marketing thought as reflected in the definitions of marketing. *Journal of Marketing, 1*(1), 10–21.

Druker, P. (1958, January). Marketing and economic development. *Journal of Marketing, 22*, 256.

Dubois, L. (1991). Ribfest: A partnership of government and services. *Illinois Parks and Recreation, 22*(3), 32–33.

Esler, E. and Sutton, D. (2003). The new marketing executive. *Marketing Matters, 2*(13).

Glover, T. (1999). Funding the individual: An idea that spans the ideological spectrum. *Journal of Leisurability, 26*(4).

Gummesson, E. (1999). *Total relationship marketing: Rethinking marketing management. From 4 P's to 30 R's*. Oxford, England: Butterworth-Heinemann.

Havitz, M. E. (2000). Marketing public leisure services: Some (temporarily) pessimistic perspectives from an unrepentant optimist. *Journal of Leisure Research, 32*(1), 42–48.

Hastad, D. N. and Tymeson, G. (1997). Demonstrating visionary leadership through community partnerships. *Journal of Physical Education, Recreation & Dance, 68*(5), 47–51.

Hyland, T. (2004). The global outlook for internet advertising and access spending, 2003–2007. Retrieved June 6, 2004, from http://www.pwcglobal.com

Levitt, I. M. (1986). *The marketing imagination*. New York, NY: Free Press.

Magrath, A. J. (1992). *The six imperatives of marketing: Lessons from the world's best companies*. New York, NY: AMACOM.

Matthews, J. B., Buzzell, R. D., Levitt, T., and Frank, R. E. (1964). *Marketing: An introductory analysis* (4th ed.). New York, NY: McGraw-Hill.

McCarville, R. (2002). *Improving leisure services through marketing action*. Sagamore.

McKenna, R. (1991). Marketing is everything. *Harvard Business Review, 69*(1), 65–79.

McLeisch, B. L. (1995). *Successful marketing strategies for nonprofit organizations*. Etobicoke, Ontario, Canada: John Wiley & Sons Canada.

Nykiel, R. A. (2001). Technology, convenience and consumption. *Journal of Hospitality & Leisure Marketing, 7*(4), 79–84.

Perreault, Jr., W. and McCarthy, E. (1999). *Basic marketing: A global managerial approach* (13th ed.). Boston, MA: McGraw-Hill.

Rosenstein, D. M. (1995). *An empirical comparison of the role of marketing in private and public sector nonprofit service organization: An example from the heritage tourism industry*. Doctoral dissertation, Southern Illinois University at Carbondale.

Schmid, S. (1995). Partners in rec: Many cities are finding that in order to build recreation center, they must look at cooperation ventures with colleges and school districts. *Athletic Business, 19*(10), 31–38.

Schultz, D. E. (1999). We could be more efficient if we considered… *Marketing News, 33*(15), 8.

Schultz, D. E. (2001). It's now time to change marketing's name. *Marketing News, 35*(22), 8.

Simms, J. (2003). HR or marketing: Who gets staff on side? *Marketing London, 80*(9), 23.

Tew-Johnson, C. P. F., Havitz, M. E., and McCarville, R. E. (1999). The Role of marketing in municipal recreation programming decisions: A challenge to conventional wisdom. *Journal of Park and Recreation Administration, 17*(1), 1–20.

Traux, P. L. and Myron, M. R. (1998). Marketing: Meeting the changing needs of the people you serve. *Catalyst, 27*(1), 11–14.

Trivers, J. (1996). *One stop marketing: What every small business owner needs to know*. New York, NY: John Wiley & Sons.

U.S. Census Bureau. (1963). *Statistical abstract of the United States* (84th ed.). Washington, DC: U.S. Department of Commerce.

U.S. Census Bureau. (1983). *Statistical abstract of the United States* (103rd ed.). Washington, DC: U.S.Department of Commerce.

U.S. Census Bureau. (2000). *Statistical abstract of the United States* (120th ed.). Washington, DC: U.S. Department of Commerce.

U.S. Census Bureau. (2003). *Statistical abstract of the United States* (123rd ed.). Washington, DC: U.S. Department of Commerce.

Vogt, C. and Andereck, K. (2002). Introduction to special issue on park marketing. *Journal of Park and Recreation Administration, 20*(2) 1–10.

Webster, C. (1995). Marketing culture and marketing effectiveness in service firms. *Journal of Services Marketing, 9*(2), 6–21.

Weitz, B., Castleberry, S., and Tanner, Jr., J. (1998). *Selling: Building partnerships* (3rd ed.). Boston, MA: Irwin/McGraw-Hill.

Williamson, P. (1999). Strategy as options on the future. *Sloan Management Review, 40*(3), 117–126.

Chapter 2

The Marketing
of Leisure and Tourism Experiences

Authored by Al Ellard, ReD, with contributions by Patty Janes, PhD

Matt saw a poster advertisement in the local music store and discovered that his favorite group was coming to town for a live performance at the 12,000-seat outdoor amphitheater. He could not wait to attend his first concert, after all it was his favorite band, how could his parents say no? Unfortunately, his Dad, Trevor, was less than thrilled with the idea and did say no. He thought it was only two hours of loud music screeching through some speakers. As consolation, his Mom, Andrea, offered to buy him the group's new CD that was due to be released at the end of the month. Needless to say, Matt was devastated. He had already bought the new CD anyway.

"It's not just music," he pleaded, "There is so much more to it." This was more like an experience. The music was one thing but hanging out with fans before the concert in the parking lot, buying a T-shirt with the tour dates and cities listed, seeing all the fans get as excited as he was and hearing the music played live and learning the stories behind the writing of each song was the experience he was talking about. Trevor understood but shared that the "experience" was also about "paying $80 for a ticket, sitting in line for 30 minutes to park and exit the concert as well as

dealing with long rest room and food lines and disorderly people all night." Matt nodded excitely and agreed that this too was the experience he hoped to see for himself. He was even prepared to pay for his ticket with money he earned from mowing lawns and even had enough for a T-shirt and food during the concert.

His parents finally agreed to let Matt go if one of them went with him on the "experience." Matt's eyes lit up and he grinned from ear to ear. Trevor secretly looked forward to it. It had been 15 years since he had seen his last live band and it was long overdue, as he too remembered what an experience it could be.

• • • • •

Leisure and tourism experiences are so much more than just providing a core offering to the public. Matt's interest in the concert was not only about the music; it was so much more than that. The venue realized this, as they knew concertgoers enjoyed an opportunity to better appreciate the artist's talents. This was provided through high-quality sound production, an engaging show, and talented artists. These consumers also sought opportunities to socialize. The venue also addressed this through safety practices,

---

At the end of this chapter, readers will be able to...

- Define a leisure and tourism "experience."

- Understand why marketing leisure and tourism is different than marketing other services.

- Understand the motivations for leisure and tourism (the benefits-based movement).

- Describe constraints to leisure and tourism participation and experiences.

- State the components of the five phases of a leisure and tourism experience.

- Understand how leisure and tourism experiences are designed.

- Identify leisure and tourism impacts, including social, economic, and environmental influences.

- Describe unique leisure and tourism marketing issues.

- Develop a philosophical orientation to marketing leisure and tourism.

Posters help create anticipation for the experience.

by traditional service providers such as banks, insurance and financial companies, and healthcare organizations. This shift accompanied a fundamental economic change from a manufacturing economy to a service economy. Leisure and tourism services were generally lumped in with services and the leisure industry followed the lead toward services marketing. A new economic shift is again taking place that will replace the "service" economy with an "experience" economy. This new shift is fortuitous for the leisure industry, which has always been about marketing leisure experiences.

Experiences have always been the true product of the leisure industry, although leisure marketing efforts have been driven by the prevailing marketing winds of the time. Providing leisure services has always been about the experience. Even in for-profit leisure settings, the focus has been on creating high-quality leisure experiences that result in profitability. Nonprofit and public leisure providers have long employed leisure experiences to facilitate change in the lives of individuals, groups and communities. It is perhaps unfortunate that as a profession the leisure industry has allowed itself to be grouped with other service providers, as if leisure and tourism organizations exist merely as a convenience or to fulfill a useful service whenever called on. Were that the case, leisure providers would be no different than the power company, the Department of Motor Vehicles, or the Maytag repairman.

Leisure is more of an investment in your future or in your lifestyle, as it is something of an immediate and an intangible item. Jennifer Hayes, College of William & Mary

crowd control and open space for socialization opportunities before and after the event. They focused on the way in which their offerings benefited the consumers they wished to serve. In doing so, they created an experience for consumers to remember.

There is so much more to a concert than the music itself, and this venue concerned itself with the various needs of consumers. Unlike other types of consumer service purchases, quality-oriented leisure and tourism organizations provide enriching experiences for their consumers that enhance their quality of life. Matt talked about this first concert experience for years and compared other experiences to what he heard and how he felt as a result. The same wide grin came on his face each time he thought about the concert experience. Understanding the unique nature of providing leisure experiences is explained throughout this chapter.

Historically, marketing efforts focused on pushing products to people, creating a "need" and then providing a product to fill that need. By the 1970s and 1980s, the concept of a "product" grew to encompass services provided

Leisure and Tourism Experiences: "Are We Having Fun Yet?"

One of the key questions that must be answered to effectively plan and deliver leisure programs is: "What is the nature of the leisure experience?" The most simplistic approach to understanding leisure is to examine it as the use of discretionary time. *Discretionary time* is the time left after work, family, and other obligations have been fulfilled. Free time is a convenient way to quantify leisure and make comparisons between groups (Russell, 1996). The use of time budgets and diaries to monitor how individuals use their time is a common way to study leisure as a function of time. Unfortunately, merely having discre-

This Bingo consumer enjoys the complete experience.

tionary time cannot explain the experience of leisure. Defining leisure as time merely quantifies the time available for leisure and the kinds of uses we make of that time. One may choose to use leisure time sitting in the Lazy Boy with a remote in hand, engaging in a creative hobby, volunteering time to serve others, or going to the office to catch up on work. Based on the idea that leisure is discretionary time, each of these uses would technically be leisure because it is time to use at one's discretion. Defining leisure as discretionary time also fails to explain why many people attribute qualities normally associated with the leisure experience with nondiscretionary activities like work and domestic and family responsibilities.

The availability of discretionary time is frequently used to market products. Products designed for leisure consumption would naturally focus on a customer's discretionary time to pitch the product. Many products are designed to be used in leisure or to expand leisure time. Resorts market weekend getaway packages. At one time "the weekends were made for Michelob." Many newspapers include a "get a jump on your weekend" insert. Many products are touted for their power to "save time"—literally to create additional discretionary time for the user. Health clubs are incorporating day-care services for members while they workout. Airlines and movie theatres offer e-tickets to decrease the amount of time a consumer stands in line. Amusement parks are beginning to provide patrons with the opportunity to "cut" in line. For example, Disney's "fast pass" allows guests to avoid standing in line for many popular attractions. Of course, amusement park operators hope the time saved will be used spending money in the parks many shops and restaurants.

A second approach to examining the meaning of leisure and tourism is to try to explain it as *activities* people engage in. Many people, even parks and recreation practitioners, operationalize leisure as some form of activity. According to Clawson and Knetsch (1966), "Individuals choose their recreation activities within the range of opportunities physically and economically available to them" (p. 28). People are comfortable describing their leisure by describing what they do when they are not engaged in work or other obligatory activities. Activities themselves are neither work nor leisure. Many "do-it-yourselfers" find great satisfaction and enjoyment in doing their own home repair and improvements, woodworking, and other work-like activities.

Marketers use images of smiling people engaged in a wide variety of healthy, active, seemingly satisfying activities. Billboards, magazines, newspapers, television, and the Internet bombard society with images of activities we could be doing for leisure but stop short of guaranteeing their products will assure a leisure experience. Activities are merely vehicles that may lead to a leisure experience. Activities are insufficient to explain the leisure experience. No activity is always leisure to everyone under all circumstances.

A third approach to understanding the leisure experience has focused on identifying common themes participants attribute to a leisure experience (Mannell, 1999). Research methodology generally involves interviewing participants or having them record their thoughts and feelings while engaged in real or imagined leisure and work scenarios. From this information researchers have then extracted common elements. Lee (1999) summarized previous research into the characteristics of the leisure experience. Common characteristics cited included enjoyment/fun, relaxation, social bonding, a positive state of mind, companionship, intimacy, novelty, escape, communion with nature, aesthetic appreciation, timelessness, physical stimulation, intellectual cultivation, creative expression, introspection, freedom, peace, calm, and happiness. This approach may be useful from a marketing perspective because it provides images and outcomes that can be described to a prospective customer, however it still fails to tell what a leisure experience is. In a way this is like trying to explain the concept of a home by describing a house.

Neulinger (1974) approached it differently developing a framework for understanding how individuals experience leisure. Neulinger's leisure paradigm was concerned with factors that make a distinction between leisure and nonleisure. The leisure paradigm rests on a participant's *state of mind* rather than the time or activity engaged in. State of mind, however is more difficult to quantify because it is individually conceptualized by the participant and cannot be readily "observed" by an outsider.

The central factors of the leisure paradigm are perceived freedom and motivation. *Perceived freedom* relates to the freedom to choose, lack of compulsion or constraint, or the illusion that one is free to choose to engage in a behavior.

Motivation refers to the source of the satisfaction for engaging in a behavior. A person is intrinsically motivated when he or she participates in an activity merely for the sake of participating; the activity is self-rewarding. Figure 2.1 highlights this relationship.

Many athletes discover the paradigm of perceived freedom while participating in their chosen sport. Most people see sports participation as a matter of free choice—for love of the game. To the player, however, the freedom to choose is relative. Many people become involved in a sport because it is fun. Yet, others do so for various reasons. Some young athletes end up playing to please their parents rather than because they want to. People participate in sports to meet social expectations in the workplace, school, or peer group. College athletes and professionals play for scholarships and money respectively.

Extrinsic motivation results from participation motivated by anticipation of some payoff—the activity is not the reward, but leads to a reward. Work is often associated with the concept of external motivation. People work for a paycheck. When winning becomes more important than playing, then the motivation has shifted from internal to external. Playing golf to "schmooze" with the boss, volunteering to coach little league to make business contacts, or joining a gym to meet other singles are examples of external motivation for leisure participation.

Both perceived freedom and motivation exist on a continuum ranging between two extremes. Therefore one may feel relatively free at different times and may be motivated by some combination of external and internal sources of satisfaction at any given time. Few people may experience what Neulinger calls *pure leisure* (i.e., freedom and internal motivation), but leisure can exist to varying degrees in most aspects of our lives. Elements of leisure can even be found in work.

Neulinger's paradigm recognizes that leisure and work are not mutually exclusive. Although pure leisure and pure work do exist within the paradigm, so do the possibilities that work may be intrinsically rewarding or that things one chooses freely to engage in may provide a combination of external and internal satisfaction.

The business dinner and golfing with clients are long-held business practices that mix traditional work with leisure. Working vacations are more recent examples of the blurring of the line between work and leisure. Meeting planners regularly plan social and meal functions, recreational activities, entertainment, and even spouse and/or family activities to market professional meetings. Many retirees are among the vendors at crafts shows and flea markets; combining increased leisure and an existing hobby into a part-time income with opportunities for travel and socialization.

A PARADIGM OF LEISURE

Freedom					
Perceived Freedom			Perceived Constraint		
Motivation			Motivation		
Intrinsic	Intrinsic and Extrinsic	Extrinsic	Intrinsic	Intrinsic and Extrinsic	Extrinsic
(1) Pure Leisure	(2) Leisure-Work	(3) Leisure-Job	(4) Pure Work	(5) Work-Job	(6) Pure Job
Leisure			Nonleisure		

←——————————————— State of Mind ———————————————→

Adapted from Neulinger, 1976

Figure 2.1
A Paradigm of Leisure

Flow

Another approach to understanding the nature of the leisure experience has focused on gaining insight into the quality of the leisure experience. This approach generally requires that subjects be monitored while immersed in the leisure experience. Csikszentmihalyi (1975), in the development of the concept of *flow*, did extensive interviews with activity participants. Over nearly 30 years, Csikszentmihalyi and his associates have conducted thousands of interviews with individuals engaged in both leisure and work activities spanning dozens of countries, genders, age groups, ethnic, cultural, social, and economic backgrounds. Csikszentmihalyi describes flow as "the state in which people are so involved in an activity that nothing else seems to matter; the experience itself is so enjoyable that people will do it even at great cost, for the sheer sake of doing it" (p. 4).

According to Csikszentmihalyi the flow experience— or the "optimal experience"—shares some elements across all subject groups, activities, and cultures. The optimal experience is not exclusively a leisure experience, but the nature of leisure makes achieving an optimal experience highly probable.

Elements of Flow

A challenging activity that requires skill: The activity doesn't have to be a sport or physical activity. Social interactions and intellectual activities require their own kinds of skills for successful participation. The skill level should be challenging to the participant.

A merging of action and awareness: The activity requires complete concentration to the point of losing awareness of anything outside the activity itself. The participant has a sense of acting without conscious effort, automatically—being "in the zone."

Clear goals and feedback: Goals provide the participant with a way to assess progress and the activity provides feedback to reinforce participation.

Concentration on the task at hand: Because of the immersion of the participant in the activity, extraneous thoughts and concerns are temporarily suspended, permitting a separation from everyday problems and concerns.

Control: The participant has a sense that they have control over what will happen—or that they do not have worry about losing control. When skills match the level of challenge, the risk is minimal.

Loss of self-consciousness: The participant engrossed in an activity is not focused on self. In flow there is no room for self-scrutiny.

Transformation of time: Time may seem to move quickly: "Wow, where did the time go!" Or time may seem to move slowly: "It seemed like everything was moving in slow motion."

Not all of these elements are necessary for an optimum experience to occur, but descriptions of optimum experiences frequently include many of these elements.

We may have occasion to refer to our leisure in terms of time (e.g., "I can't want for the weekend!") or as an activity we enjoy (e.g., "I love going to the art museum!"). Both allow us to converse about our leisure in terms most people in our culture may well understand, but neither really expressed how we experience leisure.

Today, consumers increasingly desire neither goods nor services but sensation-filled experiences that engage them in a personal and memorable way. (Gilmore, 2003)

From Products to Services to Experiences

Chapter 1 presented an overview of the historical evolution of marketing. This evolution reflected a shift from manufacturing to services that occurred over the past 40 years. Just as there has been a shift from manufacturing to service, there is now a shift taking place from the provision of services to the creation of experiences. This shift will directly affect the way leisure is marketed. A glance at any dictionary will quickly affirm the differences between services and experiences (see box, p. 30).

In an effort to further explain these distinctions, consider the following illustration of the differences between service and experience:

I have my car serviced every 3,500 miles at the local fast lube, my community provides trash pick-up service, my physician provides me with health-care services, my financial planner advises me on financial and tax issues, and a kid down the street mows the lawn. All of these service providers are important because they all provide something I cannot or do not want to do for myself. They perform work, provide me with advice, offer convenience, make my life easier, or save me time and effort. For their service, I happily pay them for the service they provide.

Am I concerned about quality of the service I receive? Of course! I expect to be treated well as a customer and to get value for my dollar. I expect the service provider to stand behind the work—I even expect them to go a little beyond the call of duty on occasion. If a service provider did not deliver a level of service that met my quality expectations, I would find another provider.

But I have to ask myself, do these services rise to the level of an "experience?" I like it when the kid who mows the lawn also sweeps the sidewalk, I appreciate it when the person changing my oil wipes up a spill on the engine block (so it doesn't smoke all the way home), and I like it when my financial analyst finds a deduction I wasn't expecting. But do these occurrences transport me to a different level of being? Is my life path altered? Am I a different (hopefully better) person by these events? Not quite!

As the definitions imply, an experience has the power to change a person. Physically, emotionally,

sensually, spiritually—an experience has within it the power to transform. Because I have lived through an experience, I have learned, I have sensed, I have felt powerful emotions, I have responded at a deeper level than merely being the passive recipient of a service. I just can't say that about an oil change.

While services are done by someone else for my benefit, an experience requires that I be an active participant in its creation. I am both the recipient as well as an author of an experience. The outcome of an experience is not that I have saved some time or been convenienced, but that I am a different person because of my immersion in the experience. Leisure innately has the capacity to rise to the level of an experience whereas other service providers may attempt to create experiences to sell products but have difficulty rising to the same level.

In their book, *The Experience Economy: Work Is Theatre & Every Business a Stage*, authors Pine and Gilmore (1999) wrote about separating experiences from services, noting that experiences have always been around but they have been lumped in with the service sector. The new economy is characterized as one in which experience represents the new source of value. No longer satisfied with being the owners of products or being recipients of services, consumers are seeking experiences in which to be immersed that provide outcomes or meet needs far beyond mere product reliability and customer service. Dev and Olson (2000) quoted a major brand general manager who stated

> The customer's repurchase doesn't just depend on his or her experience at just my hotel, but on the total experience. So, to the extent that it depends on the total experience, I need to co-opt other partners in the process of managing the total experience. (p. 4)

Ser•vice (Noun)

- Employment in duties or work for another, as for the government
- The performance of work or duties for a supervisor or as a servant
- A facility providing the public with the use of something, such as water or transportation

Ser•vice (Verb)

- Assistance, help

Ex•pe•ri•ence (Noun)

- The apprehension of an object, thought, or emotion through the mind or senses
- Active participation in events or activities, leading to the accumulation of knowledge or skill
- An event or series of events participated in or lived through
- The totality of such events in the past of an individual or a group
- Personal knowledge derived from participation or observation

Ex•pe•ri•ence (Verb)

- To participate in personally; undergo
- To participate in or partake of personally
- To be physically aware of through the senses
- To undergo an emotional reaction

American Heritage Dictionary of the English Language (4th ed., 2000). Boston, MA: Houghton Mifflin.

A Crystal Mountain Resort skier enjoys the experience.

Customers are willing to pay a premium for memorable experiences. While recently attending a student banquet, a colleague bid several hundred dollars on a birthday catering package in the silent auction. She was not bidding for mere cake, cookies, and decorations, or merely because it would be more convenient than putting on the birthday party herself. What she was seeking was a packaged birthday "experience" that would provide lasting memories for the birthday girl as well as herself and the family. The success of Starbuck's coffee is an example of the economic value of an experience over a mere product or service. When a Starbuck's customer happily hands over up to $6.00 for a cup of coffee, what they are really buying is the experience that surrounds the ordering, creation, and consumption of the beverage (Pine & Gilmore, 1999).

Cabela's, Outdoor World, and REI retail stores also capitalize on the demand for experiences. REI's flagship store in Seattle, Washington, includes a 65-foot indoor climbing pinnacle and mountain biking testing trail and offers numerous instructional courses, programs, and events designed to immerse the outdoor enthusiast. Cabela's new store opening in Wheeling, West Virginia, will feature a soaring timber and fieldstone atrium and three walk-through freshwater aquariums totaling 55,000 gallons, stocked with fish native to the West Virginia, area accompanied by informative and educational kiosks detailing each species. Dual, sweeping grand staircases will lead to a mezzanine and a 250-seat restaurant in a park-like environment that overlooks the entire store. Patrons will be able to dine on such wild game as elk, caribou, ostrich, and buffalo. The mezzanine will also feature an art gallery featuring wildlife and outdoor-themed art. They are reaching new markets with the attitude, "This ain't your daddy's sporting good store!" Pine and Gilmore (1999) identify the key distinctions of the experience economy in Table 2.1.

It has been well established that there are several key differences between marketing of products and marketing

The smile on his face tells the story of his experience.

of services. Table 2.2 (p. 32) provides a summary of the key differences between marketing products and marketing services (Reisinger, 2001). In addition, marketing of leisure experiences has some key differences from marketing of traditional services. These differences are summarized in the final column of Table 2.2.

It is apparent that for most of the leisure industry the focus has changed from services to experiences. Le Bel (2005) found that researchers are starting to assess travel experiences from a broadened viewpoint. In Chaisson's (2002) interview, Pung stated that a new trend in county parks and recreation is users seeking "experiences rather than facilities" (p. 5). If we think of ourselves merely as

Table 2.1
Economic Distinctions

Economic Offering	Commodities	Goods	Services	Experiences
Economy	Agrarian	Industrial	Service	Experience
Economic function	Extract	Make	Deliver	Stage
Nature of offering	Fungible	Tangible	Intangible	Memorable
Key attribute	Natural	Standardized	Customized	Personal
Method of supply	Stored in bulk	Inventoried after production	Delivered on demand	Revealed over a duration
Seller	Trader	Manufacturer	Provider	Stager
Buyer	Market	User	Client	Guest
Factor of demand	Characteristics	Features	Benefits	Sensations

Table 2.2
Differences in Products, Services, and Experiences

Characteristic	Products	Services	Experiences
Focus	Manufacturer	Service Provider	Consumer
Product	Products generally consist of a physical object.	Work done for the customer, usually by a paid provider.	A personal experience.
Tangibility	Manufactured products can be examined before purchase.	A service cannot be touched, seen, tasted, felt, heard, or smelled before purchase.	An experience cannot be touched, seen, tasted, felt, heard, or smelled before purchase.
Production and Consumption	Products can be manufactured in one place, stored, shipped to another place for sale and consumption by the customer. Can be mass produced.	Service is produced as it is delivered by the service provider. The same service may be provided to many customers, but not simultaneously.	Experiences are created simultaneously by the provider and the customer. An experience is consumed by a customer as it is being created.
Heterogeneity	Products are homogenous from manufacturer to manufacturer and place to place due to standardization and manufacturing process.	Because services are delivered by people, each service experience is different. Service quality can decline under high demand. Standard procedures can reduce variance in quality.	No two people will have the same experiences because no two people are alike. People interpret things differently, come from different backgrounds, and have different motivations and expectations.
Consistency	Quality control can virtually eliminate any inconsistency in the product. The product performs consistently from one customer to another.	Because the performance of service personnel varies from day to day and from customer to customer it is difficult to assure consistency of the product.	Because the experience is an interactive product produced simultaneously by the provider and the customer, it is impossible to promise consistency of the product from customer to customer.
Perishability	Most products have some degree of imperishability. Even food products have some shelf life. Products can be produced and stored for some time before they are sold to the customer. Therefore, producers can produce product in surplus of demand taking advantage of business cycles.	Services cannot be produced and stored for later sale. Services are produced and delivered on demand of the customer. Service opportunities not used are lost. A hotel room or an airline seat that is empty today cannot be resold at a later date.	Experiences cannot be produced and stored for later sale. Unlike services, however, delivering an experience to the customer is not just a matter of selling the opportunity. For the experience to occur, both the provider and the customer come together as coparticipants in creating the product.
Ownership	Ownership of a product is transferred to the purchaser along with all rights of ownership.	The purchaser only owns a temporary right to have access to or benefit from a service. Purchase is based on a promise of performance.	Ownership of leisure products or rights to leisure services cannot promise a leisure experience.
Benefits Derived	Benefits of a product accrue to the purchaser as long as the product is in use. Benefits are tied to the use of the product.	Benefits are based on the ability of the service provider to deliver on the promise made.	The benefit is the experience. Products and services may contribute, but only the customer can evaluate the experience.
Quality Control	Mistakes in manufactured products can be discovered and corrected before the customer sees the product. The customer can examine a finished product that has undergone rigid quality control.	Mistakes in service are immediately evident. When mistakes occur it is too late to implement quality control. Standardized operating procedures and high-quality training of staff can reduce mistakes in service delivery, but cannot eliminate them. Customers can be compensated for poor service, but it cannot be undone.	Quality control applies only as far as the product and service providers can. Beyond that, the quality of the experience is subjectively evaluated by the customer based on personal experience, expectations, and performance.

service providers, then the focus is on how well we deliver the services. The purpose of this text is to look beyond merely providing quality services. The new challenge for leisure providers will be to orchestrate opportunities for consumers to become immersed in leisure experiences that meet their needs.

The industry is not like it used to be… People have changed regarding the experience they receive… People want to feel it, learn from it, and have an emotional connection to it. People choose experience not product. Susan Iris, Canadian Tourism Commission

Why People Play: "It's About the Benefits"

The larger question may be why people do anything. The answer is almost always because it meets a need for the individual. Theories of motivation generally agree motivation is an internal state or condition that activates behavior and directs goal-oriented behavior. Needs may fall into one of several domains. The *biological domain* includes needs generally associated with survival behavior, such as food, clothing, and shelter. Just as sleep is a behavioral response to the body's biological need for rest, other domains impact motivation. People are also motivated to act to satisfy needs in the social, cognitive, affective, and spiritual domains. People act to increase feeling good and to decrease feeling bad, to form social bonds and to build relationships, to be an accepted member of a group, to gain a sense of mastery, to effect change, to develop meaning or understanding, to solve problems, to reduce stress, to build self-esteem, and to understand one's purpose in life.

It is said that our lives are divided almost equally between work, maintenance, and leisure. Work is necessary to support modern lifestyles. Maintenance, including eating, sleeping, and personal/family care, is more or less necessary to insure survival. Taken together, work and maintenance account for two thirds of most people's time and consist of behaviors directed to satisfying requirements of living. Leisure, however, provides opportunity for individuals to meet the myriad psychic needs that remain unmet by daily living in the modern world.

How leisure can meet many psychic needs is reflected in the *Benefits Are Endless* movement. Begun in the United States in 1991 after its successful introduction in Canada, the Benefits Are Endless movement has marked a significant shift in how parks, recreation and leisure services are con-

ceptualized and communicated to communities. During the later decades of the 20th century parks and recreation organizations focused extensively on the inputs rather than the outcomes in their marketing efforts. The message being communicated consisted of acres of parkland managed, number of participants in programs, square footage of facilities, number of softball fields, qualifications of staff, expenditures, and revenues. Lost in this bureaucratic lingo was how individuals and the community benefited from the parks and recreation services that were being provided (O'Sullivan, 2004).

One of the outcomes of the Benefits are Endless movement was a clear delineation of the benefits of parks and recreation to people, families, groups, and communities. Identified benefits were grouped into four categories: individual benefits, social/community benefits, environmental benefits, and economic benefits. The benefits are endless movement challenges leisure service providers to undergo a paradigm shift away from marketing the features of programs and services to marketing the benefits of programs and services to people.

Leisure service providers must begin to think from the perspective of the customer's psychic needs rather than from the organization's static features. A water park, a beachfront condo or a seat in first class are merely features of a program or service. A leisure service provider must be able to link the feature to a need. Table 2.3 (p. 34) highlights these differences.

Marketing materials or collateral developed by an organization are used to communicate with prospective customers of the organization. Frequently, however, organizations fail to describe benefits for people and more typically communicate the features that they have. Table 2.4 (p. 35) illustrates the difference between organization collateral that describes features versus benefits (adapted from O'Sullivan, 2004).

Constraints to Experiencing Leisure

Just as it is important to understand what makes a leisure experience, it is equally important to understand the factors that prohibit individuals from experiencing leisure. Because leisure is an individual experience, each individual may approach a leisure experience under constraints that may inhibit their being able to fully experience leisure, or they may be faced with barriers that may prevent them from accessing the leisure opportunity. A constraint can be defined as any factor or factors perceived or experienced by individuals to limit the formation of leisure preferences and to inhibit or prohibit participation and enjoyment of leisure (Jackson, 1997). Constraints may either preclude or limit an individual's frequency, intensity, duration, or quality of participation in recreation activities. Constraints can be divided into two groups: participant-related constraints (i.e., interpersonal, intrapersonal) and structural constraints (i.e., external to the participant; Crawford, Jackson & Godbey, 1991).

Interpersonal constraints have been defined as barriers related to social interaction with friends, family members and others needed to facilitate leisure participation. Interpersonal constraints may be expressed as a lack of others to participate with, inability to coordinate times to participate with others, or differences in leisure preferences with other participants.

Intrapersonal constraints lead people to choose or to exclude selected leisure choices based on their beliefs, values, skills, self-concept, predispositions, or the expectations of others (e.g., peers and family members). Individuals may choose not to participate in selected leisure activities because they conflict with religious beliefs or personal values, for fear of embarrassment or failure, or due to perceived disapproval from friends or family.

While interpersonal and intrapersonal constraints tend have their greatest impact on the development of leisure preferences, *structural constraints* block the participant from engaging in the leisure activity. Structural barriers intervene between a person's preference for a leisure activity

and his or her actual participation in the activity. Commonly cited structural barriers include cost, time, equipment, facilities, and transportation. Overcrowding at leisure facilities, the cost to participate or to purchase equipment, over-extended personal schedules, and inaccessibility of areas or facilities needed to participate are other common structural constraints cited for not participating in a chosen leisure activity.

Constraints to leisure participation are not absolute, but relative. It was originally thought the presence of a constraint led to nonparticipation; that is, individuals chose not to participate or to cease participation when faced with a constraint. It has been more recently demonstrated that participation in leisure activities depends not on the absence of constraints but on the participant's ability to negotiate through the constraints (Jackson, Crawford & Godbey, 1993).

Participants negotiate constraints through either behavioral negotiation or cognitive negotiation (Jackson, Crawford & Godbey, 1993). *Behavioral negotiation* involves making an observable change in behavior that will enable participation. Observable behavioral changes can include changing the time, duration, or intensity of participation; learning new skills to be able to participate; finding partners with whom to participate; and reprioritizing the use of resources to be able to participate.

Cognitive negotiation involves the reduction of cognitive dissonance. Cognitive dissonance is described as a

Table 2.3
Organization Features Versus Benefits

Leisure Activity/Service	Features	Benefits
Bowling	Number of lanes Pro shop Bar/restaurant Leagues	Quality family time Fun
Valentine's Weekend Getaway	Seclusion Heart-shaped bed/tub Free flowers/champagne Free breakfast Romantic buggy ride	Rekindle a relationship Intimacy Communication Something unexpected Privacy
Fitness Center	Machine and free weights Cardiovascular equipment Certified staff Clean facility Personalized trainers Health and fitness products	Take control of one's life Improved health Sense of accomplishment Feel better about self
Religious youth camp	Wooded camp setting Games and activities Qualified facilitators Lessons Dining hall	Socialization Spiritual reflection Learn or advance skills

discomfort felt at a discrepancy between what you already know or believe, and new information or interpretation. Imagine standing at the door of a perfectly good airplane about to make you first parachute jump. Your mind tells you that you know what you are doing and you trust your equipment, but your heart tells you that you are going to die. That is cognitive dissonance. To reduce this dissonance you have to make a choice between the two dissonant perspectives. Agree with your mind and jump, or reason that you are not really interested in skydiving and land with the plane.

No two individuals experience constraints in the same way, therefore, negotiation strategies must be solved individually. In addition, participants may encounter different constraints at different phases of participation and must negotiate each separately. Negotiation of constraints is not a one-time proposition. Negotiation of constraints takes place at all stages of the leisure experience from the initial decision to participate and continuously throughout the participation phase. Finally, once negotiated, constraints are not eliminated, but may reemerge during other phases of participation.

Leisure providers must be cognizant of the barriers and constraints that limit or impede the individual's opportunity to experience leisure and be willing to generate strategies to help prospective participants negotiate those constraints. Recognizing that not all women are perfectly fit, outgoing, curvaceous, 5-foot 4-inch, 105-pound college cheerleaders who enjoy being on public display could broadly expand the market of women willing to join health and fitness clubs. Understanding the fear of broken bones, as well as the fear of appearing foolish, the ski operator may design instructional programs for beginners that do not require them to

mix with more highly skilled and daring skiers during peak hours, thus enhancing the retention rate of first-time skiers.

In a study of constraint negotiation by beginning women sea kayakers, Dominguez (2003) suggested a number of strategies that could be implemented to overcome common constraints women face in taking up and continuing to participate in sea kayaking. A constraint as basic as the inability of many women to physically lift and load a kayak without help was frequently cited by study subjects as a reason for not participating more. It was recommended that "the addition of a kayak loading section to the two-day basic course would serve to assist with this particular challenge of lifting and loading heavy kayaks, greatly increasing their ability to participate more frequently" (Dominguez, 2003, p. 180).

Phases of the Leisure and Tourism Experience

The optimal experience described by Csikszentmihalyi has powerful implications for planning leisure experiences. However, we would be wrong to think that the optimal (i.e., flow) experience only occurs like an instantaneous bright flash of light—a "eureka" moment. Because the optimal experience can occur under a variety of conditions, there are many opportunities to create and experience leisure before, during, and after the primary leisure situation. Think of a leisure activity or event as a sequence of experiences taking place over a period of time.

Clawson and Knetsch (1966, pp. 33–36) first identified five phases of the leisure experience: anticipation, travel to,

---

Table 2.4
Comparing Marketing Language Describing Organization Features Versus Benefits

Program	Focus on Organization Feature	Focus on Benefit
Parent and Child	*Mom and Me* A 45-minute session that meets twice a week and provides a chance for parent and child to play together and with others. Ages 2–3.	*Learning and Growing Together* Children (ages 2–3) play and grow while the parent learns play activities appropriate to the developmental needs of this age group. As an added bonus, both parent and child make new friends.
Youth Soccer	*Youth Soccer* Tryouts for youth soccer will be held on Monday and Wednesday from 4:00–5:30 p.m. at Turner Field. The fall league for children ages 5–7 and 8–10 will be scheduled for six weeks.	*Get in the Game* Kids ages 5–7 and 8–10 are invited to give soccer a try. Here's a chance to spend six weeks of the fall learning new skills, making new friends, discovering the feelings of being part of a team while staying physially active.

Adapted from O'Sullivan, 2004

on-site participation, travel from, and reflection. Crossley, Jamieson, and Brayley (2001) reiterated the five-stage model. O'Sullivan and Spangler (1998) streamlined the sequential process to three stages, including preexperience, experience and postexperience. Regardless, each model recognizes that the leisure experience is a culmination of a range of choices, actions, and events that take place over a period of time. Each phase of the leisure experience provides opportunities within which a participant may encounter a moment of flow—a peak or optimal experience. Figure 2.2 highlights the model.

During the *anticipation* phase of the leisure experience, the consumer is made aware of the opportunity and a sense of excitement for the experience is kindled. Organizations make a great deal of effort during this phase to communicate with the consumer both to make the customer aware of the opportunity as well as to motivate the customer to take action on the opportunity. The consumer must be made aware, informed, and persuaded. Expectations are established and a commitment is made by the consumer. Most marketing dollars are directed toward these activities. Their intent is to get people involved enough in the experience to commit to participation. Consider the following example:

> For some people planning a trip can be a great source of enjoyment and satisfaction. One can spend many hours searching online for attractions, alternate routes, scenic drives, the best local places to stay and to eat, and good deals on tickets. Learning about the destination can be a significant feature of the trip. Travel planning may begin in earnest over a year in advance. The search for the "perfect" trip can become a deeply engaging leisure experience by itself, while leading to a more enriching overall travel experience. Destinations are

quick to accommodate the travelers' information needs by providing high-quality, informative literature (e.g., brochures, newsletters, Internet sites) that further build anticipation for the planned trip.

The experience of *travel to* a destination can set a tone for the entire experience. Most families have at least one horror story about some family vacation trip. Cries of "He's touching me," "I'm bored," "How many more miles?" and "Are we there yet?" coming from the back seat followed by, "Don't make me stop this car!" bellowed from the front. Some organizations have found ways to enhance the anticipation of the experience during this phase. An amusement park may send a video highlighting all attractions for the family to watch on the DVD or VHS player in the car. Yet others may send a package of children's activities (e.g., coloring books, crayons, cards) to assist with the travel experience. Tour companies use videos, guides and en route activities to make the travel portion of the trip memorable. However, most leisure and tourism organizations fail to acknowledge this phase of the experience. Yet, regardless of the time it takes for consumers to reach a destination, organizations must remember that, whether it takes five minutes or five days to reach a destination, it *is* time spent on "the experience."

The *on-site experience* is the primary focus of the leisure and tourism organization, as the organization has great control over the quality of the on-site portion of the experience. Organizations that develop sound quality practices are more likely to engage consumers in meaningful ways to reach an optimal experience. Of course, this results in positive word-of-mouth advertising with consumers becoming the greatest source of reaching those in the anticipation phase. This concept will be further detailed in Chapter 3, The Quality Service Foundation.

Few leisure and tourism organizations have paid attention to the *travel from* phase of the leisure experience. The focus of marketing has historically been on getting the consumers to the organization and providing programs and services. Once the transaction is completed, the focus often shifts to bringing them back. The travel from stage is seldom addressed; however, this represents an opportunity for leisure service providers. What can be done to enhance the experience for a consumer who just completed a hard workout, attended an outdoor concert, or spent the day with the family at an amusement park? Leisure service providers have the chance to maximize the experience by offering a bottle of water with a logo to fitness consumers, a promotional CD with songs from various artists who will be performing during the season to concert goers, and a handheld game that ties in the parks activities as well as entertains to families.

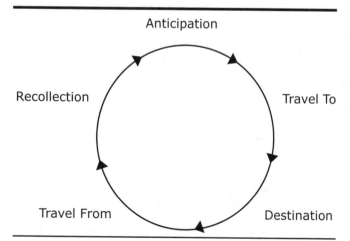

Figure 2.2
Clawson and Knetsch's Five-Phase Model of a Leisure Experience

Almost any leisure experience can be extended through *recollection*. When you drag out the slide projector, photo albums, CDs, or DVDs and subject your evening guests to your vacation, you are continuing and reinforcing a leisure experience through the process of reflection. Cruise lines, whitewater rafting companies, and theme parks contribute to the recollection phase of the experience by taking action photographs during the experience. Capturing the image of a raft full of terrorized urbanites as the raft plummets over a drop, or of a roller coaster as it enters the big drop, will provide participants with vivid reminders of the experience for years to come. These photographs help in reenergizing people in the experience, and it is not uncommon for consumers to sense the experience again. A whitewater rafter may, again, recall the experience, feel his or her heart racing and a sense of accomplishment for conquering the rapids. Leisure providers will enhance the experience by providing opportunities that will help consumers reflect on what they felt or experienced.

Recreation providers can meet the need for leisure experiences by taking advantage of opportunities at every phase of the experience process. Product development and marketing should be designed to enhance the leisure experience, beginning with building the anticipation and excitement about the experience and carrying through (not ending) with after-experience cues and reminders of the experience. Quality-oriented service providers will see each of these activities as contributing not only to the organization's objectives but also to the organization's

overall revenue. Table 2.5 (pp. 38–39) further describes examples of each of the five phases.

Designing Leisure Experiences

A recreation program is a "designed opportunity for a leisure experience to occur" (Rossman & Schlatter, 2000, p. 3). According to Rossman, to successfully design leisure experiences programmers must have an understanding of leisure behavior, the phenomenology of experiencing leisure, and how people interact within the leisure setting. Rossman's theoretical foundation for programming leisure experiences defines leisure activity as an interactional episode in which the participant is an active contributor to the creation of the experience, thus precluding the idea that a participant can be a passive recipient of leisure services.

The recreation programmer's role is to manipulate the elements of the activity situation to optimize the chances that participants will realize a leisure experience. Rossman and Schlatter (2000) identifies six elements the programmer can manipulate to give shape to the leisure situation. By careful manipulation of some elements of the situation, the programmer creates unique social situations for the participants. By understanding how social interaction occurs and how people are likely to act in a situation, the programmer can create situations in which the opportunity for participants to experience leisure is likely to occur.

CMU students receive a logo T-shirt when signing a major/minor with the department as a reminder about their educational experience.

Table 2.5
Examples of Ways Leisure Organizations Can Address Each Phase

Anticipation   Brochures, advertisements, billboards, flyers, websites, and telephone skills all impact the anticipation phase of a leisure experience.

Travel To   Signage, maps, CDs/DVDs/videos with music or promotional/entertaining information, children's activities (e.g., coloring books, crayons, books, games, puzzles) and discount coupons to supporting services along the way all address the time between leaving home or work and arriving at the leisure destination.

On-Site/Destination   The quality of the experience provided by staff is critical in creating an optimal experience for consumers.

Six Elements of a Leisure Experience

Interacting people: The programmer must either anticipate who the people will be and design the elements of the leisure experience for them, or design a leisure experience for a particular segment of people and market the program to them. The leisure experience changes when the participants change.

Physical setting: This includes the sensory characteristics of a setting that contribute to the success of the experience. Some elements of setting cannot be duplicated successfully. Some settings are inappropriate for the desired experience. In many cases, however, settings can be manipulated or altered to facilitate a desired experience.

Leisure objects: These include the key physical, social, and symbolic elements of an experience. Imagine starting

---

Table 2.5 (continued)
Examples of Ways Leisure Organizations Can Address Each Phase

Travel From	Water bottles with logo, music CDs, children's activities, popular sites to see along the way, trivia or other activities tied to attractions and areas, and videos are all ways in which a leisure and tourism organization can address the travel from phase.

Recollection	Merchandise, questionnaire/survey, photographs, thank you letters, telephone calls, promotional materials, and birthday/anniversary cards are all ways in which an organization can assist consumers in reflecting on their on-site experience (of course, this assumes the experience on-site was a positive one!).

a baseball game without raising the American flag and singing the Star Spangled Banner. The flag and anthem represent symbols strongly associated with playing of baseball games. Program planners must identify and make use of key objects essential to the leisure experience.

Rules: Rules guide the interactions during the leisure experience and include things like legal, civil, social, and relational guidelines as well as administrative and structural forms needed to carry out the experience. Rules give form and direction to the interactions and allow participants to experience freedom within the rules. At the same time, programmers can stifle a leisure experience by creating too many rules and too much structure.

Relationships: Programmers can enhance a leisure experience by building on existing relationships between participants or by creating opportunities for relationships to be developed within the experience. Many people desire to share their leisure experiences with friends, families, and social groups. Attempts should be made to foster these relationships. Mixers and ice-breakers may be planned to introduce individual participants.

Animation: Leisure experiences generally can be thought of as a series of events or actions that provide a sense of progression through the experience. Programmers create a sense of movement by sequentially unveiling the leisure experience to participants. Animation can be facilitated by providing a leader to direct the activity or by structuring the experience so participants are guided through the experience using signs, directions, or other cues that direct participation.

In their book *The Experience Economy: Work Is Theatre & Every Business a Stage*, Pine and Gilmore (1999) likened staging experiences to theatre. It is not enough to entertain customers; they must be engaged. Entertainment is merely passively absorbing an experience through the senses as in listening to music or watching a movie. Although there will certainly be many who may settle for entertainment, more consumers seek unusual experiences that offer opportunities for education, escapism, and esthetic experiences: to learn, to do, and to be part of something. The elements of an experience, according to Pine and Gilmore, include the following:

- Keep the theme consistent with the character and message of the enterprise staging the event.

- Alter the guests' sense of reality by altering how guests experience time, space, and matter.

- Harmonize impressions using positive cues to reinforce the theme. Inconsistent cues can leave the guest lost or confused.

- Eliminate negative cues that will detract from the experience.

- Mix in memorabilia. People frequently prize or cherish a tangible reminder of an experience.

- Engage all five senses. Services turn into engaging experiences when layered with sensory phenomena. The more sensory an experience, the more memorable it will be.

Pine and Gilmore (1999) further suggested that in the future, for experiences to truly have economic value, those who stage experiences will begin to charge for the experience rather than merely using experiences as a means to sell core products. Imagine being asked to pay an admission price to a business because the value of the experience they provide is sufficient to justify the cost regardless of whether you purchase products. Is it a leap to envision being charged admission to Cabela's? After all, consumers have many choices from which to purchase outdoor equipment—retail stores, catalogs, online. It is not necessary to drive to Dundee, Michigan, to visit the Cabela's store, which is advertised as the #1 tourist attraction in Michigan. Why are they coming? Is it the products?

Economic, Social, and Environmental Impacts of Leisure

Like all human activities, how we use leisure has the potential to make both positive and negative impacts on individuals, families, groups, communities, and society. The development of new recreation attractions brings with it a number of potential benefits. Likewise, the development of new recreation attractions carries a number of potential costs to the local community. Benefits and costs are frequently two edges of the same sword. One person may see a proposed tourist attraction as representing economic growth, jobs, and new tax revenues; another person may see the same proposed tourist attraction representing the loss of community character, an influx of traffic and undesirable visitors, and an increased tax burden on local residents. To some degree both may be correct. Table 2.6 illustrates this benefits-cost relationship, adapted from Crossley, Jamieson, and Brayley (2001, pp. 25–27).

Even local recreation developments may pose challenges for entrepreneurs who must wrangle with questions of how benefits and costs are distributed among individuals and groups in a community. In spring 1998, the DeKalb, Illinois, Park District Board of Commissioners voted to go forward with a project to construct an indoor sports and recreation center (Emanuelson, 2001). The project seemed like a slam-dunk. The $4.5 million facility was designed to house two indoor soccer fields, two gymnasiums, an aerobic dance facility, a wellness center, and offices. The center was slated to be built on a four-lane state highway, with 50 acres of buffer around the building. Yet it came as a surprise to many when the city of DeKalb objected to the sports and recreation center's construction on the grounds that it would negatively impact four homes on the other side of the four-lane highway.

In rural Maine entrepreneurs in three communities applying for permits to open paintball businesses were met with opposition by local property owners (Sherman, 2004). Questions were raised about the impact of paintball on a nearby salmon spawning stream, users of nearby public lands, parking, increased traffic and signage, noise, safety of adjacent property owners homes, cars, and persons and the "pot-smoking scum" paintball attracts. Skate parks are also frequently opposed because of the "type of kids" they attract.

Similarly, plans for a new Brooklyn Bridge Park in New York faced opposition from some Brooklyn Heights residents for "fear the park will attract hordes of people from outside the neighborhood to the narrow streets of well-preserved brownstones" (Robinson, 2001, p. 4). A lighted 11-field sports complex in Seattle, Washington, found opposition from homeowners two and a half miles away across a lake who argued the lighting would create an undesirable glow in the night sky (Perry, 2004).

The NIMBY (i.e., not in my back yard) mentality doesn't just raise its head when there is a debate about the location of a new prison or mental health facility. Any proposed development is likely to come under scrutiny. Recreation providers would do well to thoroughly explore the likely sources of resistance to proposed projects and work closely with potentially affected groups to minimize this kind of reaction.

Unique Leisure and Tourism Marketing Issues

Marketing professionals have begun to see a shift toward engaging customers on a personal level. McLuhan (2003) surveyed 140 senior-level marketing professionals who deemed this phenomena "experience counts." Their ability to engage customers was seen as a competitive advantage as they can stand out. "Brand experience is seen ideally as

---

Table 2.6
Potential Impacts of a New Recreation Attraction on a Local Community

Benefits	Costs
Increased nonresident visitation and spending on lodging, foodservice, leisure activities and local goods.	Loss of local culture and character, resident resistance to changes. Increase in crime, loss of security.
Increased opportunities for employment within community.	Mostly minimum wage, seasonal employment with the few career opportunities.
Increases in local economic activity through indirect and induced effects of leisure spending.	Out-of-town owners take profits out of the community.
Increased property values due to commercial development.	Local home buyers cannot afford to purchase property in their own community.
Increased tax receipts to local government from property tax, lodging, food and beverage taxes, and sales taxes.	Failure of increased tax revenues to keep up with increased local costs for pubic services and infrastructure costs.
Increased capital investment in the community.	Introduction of undesirable types of commercial development.
Improvements of local infrastructure, such as roads, highways, and utilities.	Increased traffic, congestion, construction. Inability to keep infrastructure up with the rate of growth.
Increased leisure opportunities for local residents.	Competition for leisure resources with nonresidents.
Diversity, greater appreciation of other groups and cultures.	Resentment of outsiders, them versus us mentality.
Attractions based on local people, culture, and history.	Exploiting local people/groups for profit.
Increased use of local natural resources.	Environmental damage from overuse.

permeating the whole of an organization, creating a variety of touch points to provide consumers with a direct personal encounter" (McLuhan, 2003, p. 27).

Considerations in Marketing Leisure Experiences

- Leisure and tourism organizations have the ability to create meaningful "experience" unlike other service industries, and they must think in terms of an experience.

- Experience is theatre. Unlike products and services, experiences are not just produced or delivered. Leisure and tourism experiences must be staged or created by organizations.

- Leisure and tourism experiences are not about entertaining customers; it is about engaging them.

- Experiences must have a theme that ties together the otherwise divergent parts for customers to be completely engaged.

- Leisure and toursim experiences are inherently personal. They cannot be mass-produced or delivered using a cookie-cutter approach.

- A consumer may not return because a part of the overall experience was not satisfactory; thus the necessity to collaborate with allied providers to provide a holistic approach to staging the consumer experience.

- It is not only the destination itself but also the experiences leading up to and following it that impact the leisure or tourism experience. Organizations must, therefore, address each of the five phases of leisure experience.

- The outcome of an experience is a memorable encounter that affects the consumer long after the primary event.

- Experiences have the capacity to change people.

Philosophical Development

The purpose of this chapter has been to establish a foundation for how we think about our role in designing and marketing leisure experiences. To do so, it is important to understand leisure, how it is experienced, and how to design and deliver leisure experiences. It is also necessary to understand what motivates people to seek leisure experiences as well as what constrains experiencing leisure.

Organizations that wish to enter the era of experience marketing must first undergo a significant shift in thinking. To embrace experience marketing, organizations must move from thinking of their product as a tangible good or a service. The true product of the experience economy is people. Experiences are created to meet the needs of people and not just to move more product or to rack up billable service hours. Companies are discovering that by wrapping their core products in successive layers of experience, they are establishing memories and building lasting relationships with people who also happen to purchase their products and services.

In the leisure and tourism industry, it is only about the experiences. Leisure and tourism experiences are even less about products and more about creating lasting, memorable, transforming experiences that meet the psychic needs of customers. It's about the customer.

Apply What You Know

1. Take a few minutes to think about the following questions. Think about the events, time, context, and circumstances within which the leisure experience occurred rather than on the particular activity itself:

   - What is the single most memorable leisure experience you have ever had?

   - What characteristics of the experience made it most memorable?

   - What was it about the time, place, others who shared the experience, things that may have preceded or followed the experience that contributed to its memorable character?

   - Describe what you were thinking, feeling, and sensing while engaged in that experience.

2. Think of one type of leisure and tourism organization (e.g., resort or community center) and develop a list of products, services, and experiences provided by that organization. Compare this list to the marketing materials provided by the organization and assess how they have described their organization and offerings.

Key Terms

Anticipation	Leisure paradigm
Behavioral negotiation	Marketing collateral
Benefits	Motivation
Cognitive negotiation	On-site experience
Discretionary time	Optimal experience
Economic distinctions	Perceived freedom
Extrinsically motivated	Psychic needs
Flow	Recollection
Intangibility	Service
Interpersonal constraints	Structural constraints
Intrapersonal constraints	Tangibility
Intrinsically motivated	Travel from
Leisure experience	Travel to

Review Questions

1. Name the common characteristics included in a leisure experience.

2. What are three approaches to understanding leisure?

3. What is the difference between the three approaches and Neulinger's leisure paradigm?

4. Explain the seven elements of flow.

5. Describe the constraints to leisure participation.

6. Explain the five phases of a leisure experience.

7. What are the differences between the elements of a leisure experience identified by Rossman and those noted by Pine and Gilmore?

8. What are the benefits and costs of integrating an attraction into the community?

Internet Resources

The *Association of Travel Marketing Executives* (ATME) is a professional association made up of travel industry marketers representing hotels and resorts, cruise lines, tour operators, online travel, and international tourist offices. ATME provides members with a forum for the exchange of creative ideas, effective marketing solutions, and valuable industry-related resources. On their webpage, an article by Dennis A. Marzella discusses outdoor adventure trends and how customers are looking for adventure and experiences during their travel time.

http://www.atme.org/pubs/archives

Adventure Travel provides news and information about adventures travel tours, interesting and exotic destinations, and fun activities. They provide an entire package of opportunities for leisure experiences from adventure cruise, adventure wedding to horseback riding, mountain climbing trips, and sailing vacations. The organization website makes an excellent job in promoting unique leisure experiences.

http://www.2adventure.com

The *Athletic Insight* is an online Journal of Sport Psychology. An article by Arthur J. Marr provides in-depth information about the theory of the flow experience. The article discusses the need for a synthetic theory of flow and the behavioral, cognitive and neuropsychological measures of flow.

http://www.athleticinsight.com

Information about Mihaly Csikszentmihalyi, the founder of the notion and theory of flow, can be found on the *Brain Channels* webpage. The website also provides a listing of the books written by Csikszentmihalyi and links to resources that discuss the theory of flow and the optimal experience.

http://www.brainchannels.com/thinker/mihaly.html

References

American Heritage Dictionary of the English Language (4th ed.). (2000). Boston, MA: Houghton Mifflin Company.

Chaisson, V. (2002). Marketing trends. *Michigan Parks and Recreation*, 14–22.

Clawson, M. and Knetsch, J. L. (1966). *Economics of outdoor recreation*. Baltimore, MD: Johns Hopkins Press.

Crawford, D. W., Jackson, E. L., and Godbey, G, (1991). A hierarchical model of leisure constraints. *Leisure Sciences, 13*, 309–320.

Crossley, J. C., Jamieson, L. M., and Brayley, R. E. (2001). *Introduction to commercial recreation and tourism: An entrepreneurial approach*. Champaign, IL: Sagamore.

Csikszentmihalyi, M. (1975). *Beyond boredom and anxiety*. San Francisco, CA: Jossey-Bass.

Dev, C. S. and Olsen, M. D. (2000). Marketing challenges for the next decade. *Cornell Hotel and Restaurant Administration Quarterly, 41*(1), 41–47.

Dominguez, L. A. (2003). *Constraints and constraint negotiation by women sea kayakers participating in a women-only course*. Unpublished doctoral dissertation, Michigan State University.

Emanuelson, D. N. (2001). Why some park districts and munici- palities don't get along: The NIMBY factor, politics and park district construction projects. *Illinois Periodicals Online (IPO), 32*(5). Retrieved June 21, 2004, from http:// www.lib.niu.edu/ipo/2001/ip010932.html

Gilmore, J. H. (2003, Autumn). *Frontiers of the experience economy: Batten briefings.* Charlottesvile, VA: Darden Graduate School of Business Administration.

Jackson, E. L. (1997). In the eye of the beholder: A comment on Samdahl and Jekubovich (1997), A critique of leisure constraints: Comparative analyses and understandings. *Journal of Leisure Research, 29*(4) 458–468.

Jackson, E. L., Crawford, D. W., and Godbey, G. (1993). Nego- tiation of leisure constraints. *Leisure Sciences, 15,* 1–11.

Le Bel, J. L. (2005). Beyond the friendly skies: An integrative framework for managing the air travel experience. *Managing Service Quality, 15*(5), 437–451.

Lee, Y. (1999, February). How do individuals experience leisure. *Parks and Recreation, 34*(2), 40, 42–46.

Mannell, R. C. (1999). *Leisure experience and satisfaction, in leisure studies: Prospects for the twenty-first century.* State College, PA: Venture Publishing, Inc.

McLuhan, R. (2003). Creating rapport with experiences. *Mar- keting,* June 19, 2003, 27–28.

Neulinger, J. (1974). *The psychology of leisure.* Springfield, IL: Charles C. Thomas.

Neulinger, J. (1976). The need for and the implications of a psychological conception of leisure, *Ontario Psychologist, 8*(2), 15.

O'Sullivan, E. L. (2004). *Benefits 101: The basics and beyond: A guide to the benefits movement in recreation programming.* Colchester, CT: S&S Worldwide.

O'Sullivan, E. L. and Spangler, K. J. (1998). *Experience mar- keting: Strategies for a new millennium.* State College, PA: Venture Publishing, Inc.

Perry, N. (2004, March 23). Magnuson Park ballfield plan finds objectors across the lake [electronic version]. *Seattle Times.* Retrieved June 21, 2004 from http://seattletimes.com

Pine, B. J. and Gilmore, J. H. (1999). *The experience economy: Work is theatre & every business a stage.* Boston, MA: Harvard Business School Press.

Reisinger, Y. (2001). Unique characteristics of tourism, hospi- tality, and leisure services. In J. Kandampuly, C. Mok, and B. Sparks (Eds.), *Service quality management in hospitality, tourism, and leisure* (pp. 15–49). Binghamton, NY: Haworth Hospitality Press.

Robinson, G. (2001, April 30). Not in my back yard. *Gotham Gazette.* Retrieved June 21, 2004 from http://www.go- thamgazette.com/iotw/nimby

Rossman, J. R. and Schlatter, B.E. (2000). *Designing leisure experiences* (3rd ed.). Champaign, IL: Sagamore.

Russell, R.V. (1996). *Pastimes: The context of contemporary leisure.* Dubuque, IA: Brown & Benchmark.

Sherman, J. (2004). *Nimby.* Retrieved from http://apg.cfw2.com

Chapter 3

The Quality Service Foundation

John and Mary Ann saved all month to enjoy a night out. They needed $150 to pay for the babysitter, dinner and a movie, complete with popcorn. After an enjoyable dinner, they arrived at the movie theater 20 minutes before show time. The line outside the theater was long, and unfortunately, it was raining. John waited in line while Mary Ann went to wait inside the theater.

Unfortunately, Mary Ann was told she could not enter the theater without a ticket and had to wait outside. After all, it was the premiere of the highly anticipated new drama. She elected to wait in the car instead.

John was pleased the line moved rather quickly. The ticket seller warmly greeted him as he gave her $20 for two tickets. He became enraged, however, when he was told he could not purchase the tickets unless everyone who was going to the movie was with him. John explained that his wife was in the car, but was told he would have to wait with her in line and he would need to go to the end of the line again. John asked for a manager. The manager greeted him and said he "didn't make the policy but had to abide by it" when confirming what the employee had said.

Needless to say, John and Mary Ann rented a movie and headed for home instead. It wasn't worth it.

• • • • •

As nice as the ticket seller was, it was not enough to create a quality experience for John and Mary Ann. In fact, John and Mary Ann proceeded to tell anyone who would listen about their movie experience. Hiring and training employees while providing good service to guests is important though not enough to create quality. In this case, the quality of the service came down to organization policies. Quality service involves every aspect of an organization.

Quality service… Everyone wants it yet not everyone is ready to commit to providing quality to guests, both internal and external. Organizations are known to show they are committed to quality by simply training employees on customer service. Some try to emulate quality service by teaching only front-line employees how to treat guests. The challenge is front-line employees are not the only ones who have guests to serve. Everyone in an organization does. Only training front-line employees does little to create a quality culture, which is essential to creating a quality driven organization. It all starts at the top. Owners, boards of directors and managers must accept their roles as practitioners and lead by example. Everyone in an organization must be trained and committed to the quality service standard if it is to become a reality. Those quality-driven employees may be faced with barriers to providing

---

At the end of this chapter, readers will be able to…

- Understand the impact of quality service on marketing.

- State the importance of quality experiences for word-of-mouth marketing.

- Define a quality service-oriented culture.

- Identify the critical components of the quality service system model.

- List the keys to providing quality service to internal and external guests.

- Describe empowerment practices and issues.

- Understand relationship management principles and loyalty programs.

- Develop and understand the importance of a service recovery system.

great service if everyone does not commit to being the best organization possible. *Quality is about doing the right things, the right ways, the first time.*

The foundation of effective marketing is quality service. A quality-oriented organization enables effective marketing to occur. Quality-driven organizations sell themselves to some extent. Providing quality service to employees, guests, suppliers, volunteers, and board members creates a sales force that sells the organization better than any newspaper advertisement could. This is the power of word-of-mouth advertising. The most efficient way for an organization to be effective at marketing is to integrate services throughout their organization that cater to stakeholders by investing excellence in every aspect of their experience.

In a competitive market, consumers can afford to be more selective with their choices. They can demand more, and today, individuals are seeking out services that meet their own unique personal needs (O'Neill, 2001). Service professionals need to recognize this transition and realize this trend is not likely to change. As a matter of fact, it is bound to get more difficult for service professionals to cater to the particular needs of the consumer.

These changes are apparent in the leisure industry as well, and there is increasing difficulty in managing a leisure and tourism organization now more than ever. Increased demands, placed by consumers, competition and shrinking management teams, have resulted in greater interest in quality service practices (Kandampully & Suhartanto, 2000). Competition increases customer choices, service expectations, and ultimately the value of the dollar spent. As the leisure industry becomes more competitive, professionals in the field are looking for better ways to gain a competitive advantage, attract and retain guests. Quality service is the way organizations differentiate themselves.

Word-of-Mouth Marketing

What type of harm do you think John and Mary Ann did to the movie theater? Consider this: John and Mary Ann told ten friends about their experience who in turn told ten others, who told ten others, who told ten others. Kenney (1999) suggested when an organization sells something to a consumer they are also selling it to family, friends, coworkers, and neighbors of that person. Ultimately, most estimates indicate that 250 people are impacted by every negative experience someone encounters at an organization through word-of-mouth. *Word-of-mouth marketing* is "oral, person-to-person communication between a receiver and a communicator whom the receiver perceives as noncommercial, regarding a brand, a prod-

uct or a service" (Arndt 1967, p. 5). Watkins (2002) suggested this number has expanded dramatically since the advent of the Internet. He stated, "the news of even the slightest bad experience a guest may have can be instantly spread around the world to thousands, maybe millions, of potential customers." (p. 4). How many potential consumers reconsidered their next entertainment option after hearing John and Mary Ann's story? Do you think any others thought twice about going to this theater? Do you think any chose another theater instead? Do you think anyone made a different entertainment choice? At a minimum, John and Mary Ann chose not to spend $20 there that evening.

When 250 people are confronted with a negative message about an organization, one could presume some will reconsider participating with that organization. No organization wants a negative message shared—especially an organization committed to quality.

What would have happened had John and Mary Ann had a quality experience at the movie theater? They may not have told as many people about this experience but with quality experiences people will, on average, tell three other people. Those three will tell three others, who will tell three others, who will tell three others, and so on. Ultimately, about 80 people would be positively impacted by the quality experience John and Mary Ann could have received. Do you think these people may consider going to a leisure establishment known for providing a quality experience? This positive word-of-mouth advertising can only occur if the organization delivers quality consistently. Organizations believe quality experiences result in repeat visitors, loyal customers, and a public that shares positive word-of-mouth communications with others. Tock (2002) suggests that 60% of private club business comes directly from referrals or word of mouth. Tian-Cole, Crompton, and Willson (2002) found service quality influenced wildlife refuge visitor's future participation intentions. The more satisfied visitors were, the more likely they would return and speak positively to others about the organization. This can be done by creating a quality culture.

Long-term relationships are critical in marketing today. You need to understand what consumers want and need, what resources are available, and communicate with those markets you are interested in serving.
Maureen McGonagle, DePaul University Campus Recreation

Real Life Story:
Oakland County Parks and Recreation—The Fridge

The Fridge is a marketer's marvel.

Michigan's first and only refrigerated toboggan run is among the nation's most unique winter recreation attractions. From a 55-foot-high tower, four riders on toboggans race at speeds of up to 30 mph along a 1,000-foot, ice-covered chute. The "winter water slide" is operated by Oakland County Parks and Recreation, an 11-park system located north of Detroit, Michigan.

The Fridge, nestled in 153-acre Waterford Oaks County Park, has all the elements of a great recreation marketing opportunity:

- a one-of-a-kind, exhilarating ride

- great appeal to kids and parents alike

- high potential for media coverage

- a perfect group outing/venue

- a snow—or no—outdoor winter activity

Yet, this visitor and media-friendly attraction presents the usual challenge for a county recreation department with limited promotional and advertising funds.

With that in mind, it's important to realize that no amount of marketing money can replace the importance of providing a fair value and excellent customer service. Satisfied guests who share their positive recreation experiences with families and friends are the best possible forms of advertising.

The Oakland County Parks and Recreation system strives to provide outstanding guest services including a video designed for groups outlining features of the ride and how to enjoy it safely. In addition, there are low-cost, one-time ride fees for those who want to "test drive" The Fridge and many other opportunities for reduced admission. Other marketing highlights include the following:

- A webpage (http://www.oaklandfridge.com) features a video clip depicting all the thrills and chills of The Fridge and offers a discount coupon that can be downloaded. Thousands of Internet coupons are redeemed each season.

- Large groups of 100 or more, such as youth clubs, church associations, scouts and business organizations, receive special attention with "exclusive" outings and significant discounts.

- Catchy, vinyl billboards posted on a major highway near the park are designed to create awareness and draw newcomers. The signs include the Web address so motorists can log on for details.

- Riders can "test drive" the Fridge for just $2 and apply the cost to the full admission price.

- Reduced-rate nights are offered for scout groups and youth teams. Groups are contacted via e-mail messages, personal visits, and promotional flyers.

- More than 100 four-second paid advertising spots run on a major Detroit area television station during The Fridge operating season. The spots create immediacy and reinforce The Fridge name.

- Advertisements with discount coupons have been placed in community recreation program booklets reaching hundreds of thousands of county residents. Ads were purchased or exchanged for mobile recreation units, such as skate mobiles and dunk tanks.

- The Fridge serves as a prime on-location site for live television weather reports. This free TV time results in extensive exposure throughout the entire metropolitan Detroit market.

- Partnerships with various media include ticket trades in exchange for advertising space in county-wide newspapers. Print ads provide another dimension to the marketing mix.

- Oakland County Parks has linked up with Kroger grocery stores to offer buy one, get one free Fridge admission offers with a Kroger Plus Card.

- As an extra convenience, advanced discount tickets are available at local parks and recreation departments

- News releases and "feature tips" about The Fridge are provided to a wide range of media outlets, resulting in extensive print and television coverage

- Family four-packs of Fridge tickets are provided to radio stations for giveaways in exchange for on-air mentions.

*Contributed by Janet Pung, Communications Officer
Oakland County Parks and Recreation*

Quality Culture

Total quality management, reengineering, continuous quality improvement, customer retention, quality circles, quality improvement teams, guest loyalty, consumer relations, relationship management, partnering, service marketing, guest service, hospitality—regardless of what you call it, each is a practice employed by organizations around the world in the attempt to strive for excellence. Yet, "service is one of the most overused words and under-delivered commodities in business" (Marconi, 2000, p. 42). Each incorporates specific practices but the philosophy is the same—find ways to improve and to be the most effective, efficient organization possible.

Improving quality service has been viewed as the way in which organizations can improve their position and remain competitive today. Quality service practices have emerged as the predominant strategy for organizations to reach their goals. In the country club setting Boughton and Fisher (1999) found quality was the driver of overall satisfaction. Service quality is one item that differentiates organizations, and it is a strategic process that involves every aspect of the organization (Kandampully, 1998). Organizations often blame service personnel for bad service, yet the real problem is the design of the service system.

Innately, it is hoped that a leisure provider's role in offering leisure service experiences is grounded in creating an experience that enhances the participants' quality of life. Unfortunately, leisure providers sometimes fail to provide this quality experience. It seems anyone can tell a recent story about a service establishment that did not deliver quality service.

Organizations that show their commitment to quality are not afraid to involve all their staff in the process. They are willing to learn information that may not be what they "want to hear" from employees or customers. They are willing to examine the organization from the top down. They are willing to make changes and make it a better place to be, visit, and work.

Being able to provide quality service requires every aspect of the organization to be analyzed. This includes hiring managers and employees that support the culture, allowing every policy to be evaluated, getting regular feedback from employees and customers, and turning over every stone. Those organizations willing and able to do such a task will be rewarded tenfold, *not* because they are jumping on the "customer service bandwagon," but because they are indeed concerned about employees and customers and have not lost sight of the reasons they are in business to begin with. Once the culture is developed, providing attention to detail and exceeding guest and employee expectations will be easier.

What Is Quality Service?

Quality service deals with the gap between consumer expectations of a leisure experience and their perceptions of that actual experience. Organizations are only as good as their ability to make that gap nonexistent.

Quality service is consistently exceeding expectations by anticipating guest and employee needs and going beyond to "delight" them, resulting in long-term lasting relationships that meet long-term goals.

Quality service is simply… Exceeding the expectations of those served in a leisure and tourism organization.
Craig Bonter, Entrepreneur

Why is quality important? In the leisure service industry, there are a variety of reasons why movement toward quality is critical. Godbey (1989) said it best over a decade ago when he suggested, based on economic constraints, participation in formally designed leisure services was diminishing, education levels were increasing, the amount of leisure time available was changing and the population was aging. As a result, consumers were more selective, sophisticated, and knowledgeable. This has translated to an increased need for leisure organizations to provide a higher level of quality to consumers for their leisure experiences.

If it is not a good experience then it doesn't matter.
Todd Leinberger, Spring Hill Camp

Expectations

If the key to quality service is the concept of perceptions and expectations, and "hard data" is not readily available, what is the first step you can take? Understand expectations.

Guest and employee expectations have changed with the increase in product and service choices, technology access, greater accessibility, and greater diversity. You cannot assume *anything*. Providing service to guests "my way" used to be acceptable, but the circle of influence has grown and expectations have changed because guests have changed. Guests are expecting greater interpersonal communication and greater attention to their situation. To be prepared for this change, organizations must first understand where guest expectations come from.

Service expectations are those beliefs consumers have before receiving a service experience that serves as the standards or references against which service performance is evaluated (Berry, Parasuraman & Zeithaml, 1988).

Ofir and Simonson (2001) found consumers were more negative about a service experience when their expectations were higher. They compared satisfaction ratings for an organization where one group of respondents were told favorable things about the organization and others were told negative issues (e.g., organization was under staffed). Those expecting more had greater disappointment to a negative service situation than those who expected less.

What would your expectations of quality service be if you were visiting Walt Disney World or going to work for the Los Angeles Parks and Recreation Department? Your answers to these questions would, more than likely, be based on at least one of the following categories:

Experience with the facility itself. You may have visited Disney previously or worked for the LA Parks and Recreation Department and had an expectation based on those past experiences.

Experience with other like facilities. You may have been to Six Flags or Universal Studios or worked for the Dallas Parks and Recreation Department. Therefore your expectation is based on those past "like" experiences.

Advertisements developed by the organization. Seeing pictures of staff and guests that are happy, diverse, and engaged on promotional literature and hearing a spokesperson describe what your experience will be like has left you with a specific expectation of these organizations.

Other people's perceptions. Others who have visited and/or worked at these organizations and have described their experiences. This word-of-mouth has created an expectation for you.

Seasonality issues also impact expectations. These change depending on the time of year you visit or work with an organization. Expectations will vary if you visit Disney in January when it is 60 degrees or in August when it is 90 degrees and humid, or during spring break and you expect it to be more crowded than if you visited when children were still in school. You may expect to work outside during the summer providing youth programming, but expect something different during other times of the year.

Personal needs also impact expectations. Whether you have particular needs because you are traveling with young children or want to experience a number of evening social activities, your expectations are impacted. In a work setting your needs also play a role in what you expect. Whether it may be special accommodations or mentorship for managing an upcoming project. Seth, Deshmukh, and Vrat (2005) suggest consumer expectations are impacted by time, number of visits to an establishment, and the competitive environment.

Since expectations play such a critical role in providing quality service, organizations must spend time to understand the expectations of those they serve. Some believe this task to be impossible, as everyone may expect something different. However, each of these expectations is manageable by an organization because all are influenced by how an organization operates. The following indicates what an organization should consider with each of these expectation areas.

Experience with my facility. Do you measure the service you provide? Are you consistent in your delivery?

Experience with other like facilities. Understanding competitors is very important. What type of service do they deliver? What do they charge? What do they offer? Being able to position your organization and better understand what consumers and employees may expect from you is valuable to anticipating what their expectations may be.

Advertising. What type of message are you communicating? Does it accurately portray your image and what you can do consistently? Or, are you conveying a message that is impossible to deliver (e.g., clean, new facility when you have not invested in the building in 25 years).

Word-of-mouth. What steps have you taken to understand what guests say about you? Have you developed a system for service recovery? Do you conduct exit interviews with employees, or are you available for guests to express their satisfaction or dissatisfaction?

Seasonal. Seasonality will also play a role; expectations may change based on the time of year. What can you anticipate the expectations of the people you serve to be based on the season? Have you asked people what they expect and compared those responses by season?

Personal needs. What steps do you take to understand the needs of each market segment you serve?

In essence, each one of the six expectation areas is manageable through quality-oriented leadership. Organizations can better understand or influence each expectation and better prepare for providing quality service to everyone they serve. Until you gain a more thorough understanding of your guests' expectations how can you manage these areas from which expectations are based?

As McCarville (2000) stated the challenge of dealing with expectations is "expectations tend to rise with performance levels. As the service improves, expectations become even more elevated. More elevated expectations make it more difficult to exceed those same expectations" (p. 28). Further, he suggested, "It is a goal well worth pursuing, however, because satisfaction has been linked directly to loyalty and repeat behavior."

It is important to understand the expectations of all guests. Delivering more than what is expected creates a quality service system. Building a quality service organization requires you to think about the gap that may exist between what is expected by guests and employees and what guests and employees perceive. Closing the gap between these two areas is the basis of quality service.

It's not what you say, but what is heard.
It's not what you show, but what is seen.
It's not what you mean, but what is understood.
Perception is reality. Author Unknown

In a quality service organization it is the leader's role to serve employees. After all, management invited employees to apply and selected them from the candidate pool, they are concerned with meeting their needs and expectations, and they create a positive work environment. As a result, employees then, in turn, serve either internal or external guests with the same high quality.

Everyone is serving someone. When organization members receive the same quality of service through courtesy, attention, responsiveness, and respect from managers then they in turn provide that same respect to the guests they serve. Simply look at an organizational chart within an organization to identify who serves whom.

A key concept in creating and implementing quality service practices is the notion of those interactions between leadership and the guests they serve, and the employees and the guests they serve. This concept is called a *moment of truth.*

Moment of Truth

Most research supports that we have thousands of moments of truth each day. Think of every time a service provider had the chance to leave a lasting impression with you. The advertisement on the radio, the quality of the toothpaste top, the telemarketer call, your call to the dentist, a stop at the bank drive-thru, lunch at a restaurant, an e-mail order for paper supplies, calling a store for directions, and on, and on, and on.

Every time you had the chance to leave a lasting impression with people you serve, you have had an opportunity to influence a moment of truth. A call to hire a candidate, passing an employee in the hall and using his or her name, delivering a paycheck correct and on-time, returning a telephone call within 24 hours, conducting a performance evaluation in person, and on, and on, and on, these are all moments of truth!

During *each* encounter one of three things happened:

1. The encounter was a positive one that may impact 80 potential visitors positively.

2. The encounter was neither positive nor negative, therefore a neutral experience.

3. The encounter was a negative one that may ultimately impact 250 people.

Think about how many positive, negative and neutral moments of truth you have had today. As service providers you have the choice to deliver quality service each day. You have the ability to influence whether a moment of truth is positive, negative, or neutral! Quality service providers give *all* they have, *every day*, in an effort to make a difference.

It is important to understand the needs of your guests to ensure that you deliver positive moments of truth. A key to quality-oriented leadership is understanding the needs of both employees and guests.

Quality Service Systems

The most important and fundamental key is creating and working in an organizational culture that understands, believes, conducts, and supports providing quality service to both internal (i.e., employees) and external (i.e., customers) guests. It is as simple as that. Organizations that are not committed to these practices will never reach the pinnacle they hope to achieve.

The foundation of an organization's system design is in the form of an organization's culture. Rousseau and Cooke (1984) defined culture as "the shared beliefs and values guiding the thinking and behavioral styles of members."

How people act, the environment in which they work, the experience the guest receives, the communication processes used, the mission of the organization and the man-

Attention to detail is valued in every service delivery.

agement style of leaders all play a role in forming an organization's culture. At times, subcultures may exist within an organization, which may complement or counter the overriding culture. Understanding these values and determining what the ideal quality service culture would look like is important in developing a quality service system.

Organizations that commit to providing quality realize it starts at the top. It begins with the owner, leader, manager, and directors who create and develop the operating system from which the organization is based. Williams (1998) concurred that without commitment by senior management to change the culture to be quality oriented, it is impossible for a customer-oriented organization to develop. In the United Kingdom, six leisure organizations were studied. Williams determined even though quality processes were introduced, commitment from senior leaders was missing and quality practices were "add-on" duties to existing positions.

Quality also involves all guests, internal (e.g., employees, volunteers, suppliers, board members) and external (e.g., visitors, consumers). Everyone serves someone in an organization. Managers serve employees, front-line employees serve customers, and some employees serve other employees. Quality also involves all policies, procedures, and processes. The cleanliness of the facility and the systems used to do everything from hiring and rewarding employees to providing a product or service for customers involves creating a quality system. Quality also involves interactions between employees and consumers, employees and employees, employees and board members, and board members and the community. As mentioned, the quality of this interaction impacts marketing significantly. Quality also involves reflecting on the quality of the interaction and gaining feedback from consumers, employees, volunteers, board members and suppliers on all aspects of the organization. This information is used to continuously improve and build a quality service system. The Quality Service Model shown in Figure 3.1 represents these components of quality service.

A quality service system is an integrated approach that occurs throughout an organization. It is not a pieced-together effort that allows for one department to "train

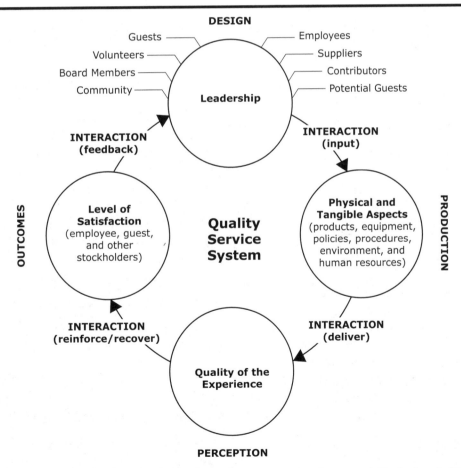

Adapted from Chang, 1998; Chang and Chelladurai, 1997; DiPrimio, 1987

Figure 3.1
Quality Service System Model

staff on service practices" and another to "address guest dissatisfaction through empowerment." It must be accepted, created, acknowledged and delivered by everyone in an organization.

Step 1: Design

Quality service is the result of the interactions between leadership, guests, employees, board members, and suppliers. The heart of the process starts at the top of the model.

Better relationships with all stakeholders results in a quality-focused organization. It is easier to keep guests happy than to keep finding new ones through marketing. Trotter (1995) suggested camps employ total quality management practices that follow H. Edward Deming's beliefs, which turned manufacturing environments into quality-oriented organizations. She suggests camps define quality through customer experiences and receive and respond to feedback from customers. The customers include both external (e.g., campers, parents, community) and internal (e.g., employees, board members, vendors) people involved in the organization. This base is the foundation of the Quality Service Model. Consider the following distinctions of internal and external guests:

Internal

- Consume services internally
- Cannot choose to go somewhere else
- Their needs are more apparent

External

- Consume product/service
- Can leave you to go somewhere else
- Needs may be more difficult to identify

Internal guests are not as often a focus for leisure and tourism organizations. Providing quality service to both internal and external consumers is critical however. J.W. Marriott said it best when he stressed the importance of putting employees first. If you treat employees well they in turn will treat customers well (Marriott, Brown & Marriott, 1997). Therefore, it is important for leisure and tourism organizations to remember to

1. Serve employees by meeting expectations as an employer.
2. Treat internal and external guests positively.
3. Remember, if an employee is no longer an internal guest they will hopefully be an external one,

and they will certainly be telling others about the organization they worked for.

Two examples of how organizations address the design stage include the survey and the focus group.

1. Survey: A camp conducts annual camper, parent, employee and volunteer surveys to understand needs, interests, and satisfaction (Leinberger, personal communication, 2004).
2. Focus Group: Annual focus groups are studied by a private country club with nonusers to learn about the organization image, perception, issues and reasons for no interest in participation (Ebert, 2002).

Great marketing starts with hiring, training, communicating, and involving staff. Rich Fairman, Warwick Hills Country Club

---

Step 2: Production

W. Edwards Deming (1986) suggested 94% of all quality service failures are caused by system designs (i.e., culture, leadership, and policies) and only 6% include carelessness, ignorance, bad temper, etc. Wakefield and Blodgett (1999) supported this in leisure service settings, finding the physical environment plays a significant role in consumers' intentions to return. In the sports industry, Hightower, Brady, and Baker (2002) agreed, suggesting the "servicescape" (or physical environment) relates to the quality of the sports experience. The importance of creating policies, procedures, and products that support quality issues is critical.

Organizations ask themselves the following questions:

- Are our systems quality oriented?
- Do we empower staff to take care of consumers and the organization?
- Do our policies support quality initiatives?
- Do we have practices that recruit, select and retain the best quality-oriented employees?
- Are we training employees to provide quality?
- Do we deliver our services, products and "experiences" in the best way possible?
- Have we established a system for recovery should something go wrong?

The leisure industry relies on people to make the employee and customer experience happen. Because many leisure experiences are consumed at the moment of production, the industry is more reliant on the effective leadership and management of employees and proper hiring and training to deliver high-quality experiences.

Brown (2003) profiled service organizations known for their service excellence. They know that "in order to make sure this quality experience happens again and again, these firms must give equal, if not even greater, attention to the quality of people they hire and the firm's ability to keep them trained and motivated" (p. 12).

Due to the unique nature of the leisure experience, no organization can anticipate all the potential various encounters between customers and employees. In an effort to manage this for employees, effective leaders pay particular attention to the norms of behavior influenced by the culture. Hiring appropriate personnel, training, and developing reward systems are found to be the foundation for this to occur (Brown, 2003).

Enz and Siguaw (2000) found in their analysis of lodging industry best practices that developing and training employees in quality service standards, empowering employees to do what is necessary to create satisfied guests, understanding guest wants and needs, and backing the quality experience through guarantees were ways in which these successful organizations developed and implemented quality service practices.

Leisure organizations are taking steps to address service quality. Janes, Wisnom, and Otteman (2004) found 42% of leisure organizations provide quality service training to employees. But is this training enough? Consider the following scenario:

A consultant receives a telephone call from a leisure business asking him or her to "train" employees on providing customer service. "The front-line staff" the consultant is told, "needs to treat customers better!" When asked if the entire organization is willing to go through training (not just the front-line) the organization states that they "didn't want to do that, they didn't need to." They simply wanted their front-line staff trained. In essence, the organization wanted to address organization concerns quickly and easily, or they may have just wanted to do the "popular" thing and be like other organizations that provide training on "customer service."

What is unclear is if they are ready or willing to truly build a quality service system. What makes them hesitant to be involved? "Oh," they say, "we are already customer oriented, we just need some training for our staff." The consultant knows that this type of service training may have no long-term impact, especially if employees return to the same old system where barriers to providing quality still exist, where employees are not served as guests, and where employees may not have the tools or empowerment to do their job successfully. Unless, of course, that system was indeed quality oriented.

If the system was quality oriented and leadership was committed to service, then there was no reason to hesitate. Those organizations willing to show they were committed and were willing to do it together will have a more successful experience in improving quality. They were willing to look at problems that may exist, they were willing to resolve issues. Yes, this took more work (and more money) but the payoff was not a short-term fix, it was a long-term service commitment.

There are organizations that send staff to customer service training, train staff internally on service, or hire consultants to train in-house. Are these organizations getting the return they hoped? Has training resulted in a change of behavior or attitude about customer service? Have customers and employees become more committed, more valued, and more successful at marketing? Let's say the front-line is trained on "customer service." What will happen when they return to work and management has not received the same training? Do you think their efforts will be rewarded or supported? How long will it take to mitigate any positive efforts training may have tried to develop? No matter how service oriented employees are, if the system from which they operate does not support quality service, then their efforts are wasted.

Consumer perceptions of exceptional service are often associated with employee interaction. The human elements are a critical piece, but they are not the only piece. It is the guests' collective view of an organization that determines their future intentions to return and to tell others.

A small example of a process issue is a growing concern in the "waiting experience." It is one of many considerations an organization must review. Dawes and Rowley (1996) studied the impact of wait time in the leisure industry. They concluded it may often be a consumer's first encounter with a service provider and it becomes a memorable part of the experience because guests may have had little else to occupy their mind while waiting. What is the wait time to buy a ticket to a game? Purchase snacks during the softball tournament? Ride the roller coaster? Check-in at the resort? Quality service organizations are trying to do two things: minimize the wait time and optimize the wait time (i.e., if it is necessary to wait, make it a pleasant experience for the guest).

To address these issues, leisure organizations have changed policies and procedures in organizations to improve the quality of the experience. Organizations now provide alternative means of purchasing tickets (e.g., online), they provide snacks in the stands, and they provide "quick tickets" to popular rides limit the need to wait for a long time. They also provide alternative means for checking-in through computer kiosks, extra staffing at peak times, and preregistration methods. Organizations have found one way to improve the production and quality of the organization experience—empower all employees.

Empowerment

Flexibility is what is delivered, not how it is delivered. That is consistency. Bill Shepler, Owner of Mackinaw Crossings and Shepler's Mackinaw Island Ferry

Empowerment is a frequently used word in recent times. Yet, not all organizations have been equally proficient at practicing and getting the full effect of this quality service technique. "Empowerment is the degree of freedom available to employees to make their own decisions and enable an organization to be as responsive as possible to guest needs" (Younis, 1997).

In essence, empowerment is doing whatever is necessary to ensure guests have an exceptional experience and their expectations are exceeded. Allowing employees to create their own solutions to guest issues and doing what it takes to satisfy the customer.

The degree of freedom is the quality issue, and all organizations handle the freedom differently. Quality service is limited because limits are placed on an individual to exercise that freedom. Most internal and external guests have a desire to do the right thing and to do the best they can.

Both internal and external guests have a basic need to be empowered. External guests want to be encouraged to express their needs and opinions. Internal guests want to do what is best for guests, themselves, and the organization.

Several scenarios exist to explain why employee empowerment has not been as effective in organizations as it can be:

1. An employee makes an empowered decision and is "punished" by his or her manager for making that decision.

2. Manager empowers staff but then "steps-in" and takes over offering something else to the guest.

3. An employee has the empowerment but is not comfortable using it so he or she lets a dissatisfied guest leave.

Organizations have learned that failure to develop an empowered staff is likely if the culture of the organization does not support quality measures. Some organizations are afraid to empower staff because they feel it will "give it all away." Organizations that employ empowerment practices have found this to not be the case. Employees are more likely to be protective of the resource (i.e., organization) and getting them to do something necessary for guest service is more difficult. Ritz Carlton allots each employee $2,000 per day to do what is necessary (Enz & Siguaw, 2000); however, on average less than 10% is utilized (Hoar, personal communication, 2005).

One of the reasons employees may not be ready to make decisions is that they have not developed self-efficacy. *Efficacy* is the power to produce an effect. In essence, those people who have the ability to make decisions believe they can make things happen in their life (versus having no control over things that happen in their life) and have greater efficacy. Fear exists because people feel they might lose something they already have, might not get something they want or are unsure of how people will react. The leader's role is to assist employees in developing self-efficiency. The best way to achieve this is to have employees (a) learn the basic skills, (b) identify and observe a role model, (c) seek out and utilize coaching, and (d) control anxiety (Steele, 1995).

Employers can empower their employees:

1. Give them information.

2. Provide employees with the tools to do the job. Establish boundaries for levels of empowerment, let them know what they can do!

3. Train employees on making decisions and gaining comfort in doing what is best for guests.

4. Coach and support employee decisions. Use experiences as opportunities to develop all the staff. Ask employees how the situation went? What would they do again? What would they do differently? BUT, support their decision and reward/recognize the effort.

Examples of how organizations address the production stage include the following:

100% guarantee. A health club developed a 100% guarantee on memberships. This health club looked outside of the health club industry to develop its membership policy. The policy states that for any reason a member may cancel the membership at anytime, extend the length of the membership for vacation or work out of town, or transfer the membership to any individual for any reason. This club found this policy alone accounted for an increase in revenue by 20% (Larson, 1999).

Training. The Ashley House Hotel developed service-quality training and orientation programs, which included employees becoming guests to understand the experience. Employees were also designated "captain quality" for a week and were required to be a guest in various departments. This resulted in decreased employee turnover (Enz & Siguaw, 2000).

Service program. Carlson Hospitality Worldwide implemented a total customer satisfaction program with employee empowerment and a chain-wide interactive, online database. The corporation conducts ongoing research with guests, employees and operators, it develops training programs and materials to support quality efforts, and employees are empowered to handle guest complaints. This corporation attributed the increase in average daily rate, occupancy, market share, and customer retention to this program (Enz & Siguaw, 2000).

Empowerment. A YMCA empowered employees to make any decision on behalf of the organization up to $100 (Sheridan, personal communication, February 13, 2001). Hoar (personal communication, 2005) believes empowering staff isn't just about solving guest problems, it's about providing an unforgetable experience. When consumers experience generosity through employees, it manifests itself into loyalty to the organization.

Step 3: Perception

It is important for the show to go on. Service providers must be ready when the curtain opens; delivery to guests, both internally and externally, is critical. The impact of a negative experience, as discussed, can be devastating.

There are two dimensions of providing quality service internally. First, getting leaders to treat employees as guests, and second, having each employee provide quality service to each other. Quality service to each other is not often researched. However, the way in which employees treat each other is another important element. Even if you do not supervise someone, providing quality service to the team is critical because they serve someone else.

Departments that serve other internal areas must understand the service requirements of their guests and ask those guests to evaluate them based on those requirements. For example, accounting may not serve an external guest but their job is to serve people internally in other departments. Internal guests should be asked to evaluate the performance of those areas that serve them. Quality organizations remember each person in an organization is always serving someone. Do you know the needs and expectations of those internal guests? Do you know how you are doing?

The benefits of providing quality service to the organization are often discussed; however, the value to an individual is not so readily addressed. There are several reasons employees benefit from providing quality experiences. Not only do they feel good about enhancing the life of someone else but also their paycheck reflects this commitment. Employees who follow quality practices are more likely to be promoted and recognized; have good relations with staff, reduced job stress, a more enjoyable job, and happier/positive guests; and can feel proud for their actions. Further, quality practices enable an organization to be more successful, resulting in not only having a job but also doing it fully staffed and receiving the number of hours desired.

Why would someone *not* want to provide excellent quality service? All too often it is due to organization barriers rather than personal issues. It is usually not because they don't want to… the system may not support them doing so.

Every person creates value for guests! Any one person can break the system, and the ability to provide quality effects both internal and external guests as well as the organization. Examples of how organizations address the perception stage include the following:

Training. Walt Disney World trains all employees (i.e., cast members) with thorough organization orientation (i.e., Traditions) training, job training, and quality service training prior to starting work.

Rewards. Employees are rewarded in a ferry boat company for providing great service internally and externally. The organization hosts monthly employee parties to celebrate their successes, recognizes efforts describing what employees did on behalf of quality service in weekly employee newsletters, and provides employees "company dollars" if superior service is provided or if organization objectives are met.

Johnston (2004) found in his investigation that consumers' perceptions of service excellence was based on four key factors: delivering the promise, providing a personal touch, going the extra mile, and resolving problems well.

Step 4: Outcomes

Measuring guest retention provides a benchmark to evaluate the impact of quality service initiatives. Measuring employee satisfaction is equally as important when all guests are of concern to an organization. Establishing a system for doing something with this information is critical. Organizations approach this quality service issue in many different ways. Some fail to address this area at all, some only measure guest satisfaction, and others gather information and use it to improve. Ideally, all leisure and tourism organizations would gather information from internal and external guests to better understand the quality of the experience, use this information to improve relationships with those they serve, and develop a system to enhance organization operations.

One type of system is designed to manage guest dissatisfaction. Creating a service recovery system to resolve guest issues before it impacts 250 other people is critical to an organization.

Service Recovery

Quality service today is all about guest relationships, retention, and loyalty. Involving guests on a long-term basis helps to identify needs and expectations, ensuring the organization creates a system that will be utilized by guests. A quality service system is not complete without a process for feedback from guests and a recovery system to insure all guests experience quality.

The impact a dissatisfied guest has on an organization is significant. Dresner and Xu (1995) found the greater the number of complaints in an organization, the lower the profitability ratio.

It's all been heard before… No one is perfect… We all make mistakes… Every organization has dissatisfied consumers… No one is exempt from service failures… This, however, does not imply that since everyone has dissatisfied consumers it is OK. Every dissatisfied consumer has a significant impact on a leisure and tourism organization. Just because organizations have these situations

occur does not make them less important and critical to minimize.

Working with people and addressing individual expectations is not an easy process. However, systematic steps can be taken to decrease the likelihood of service failure. Should it occur, specific techniques can be used to learn from the situation. Service recovery is a term used to describe the actions taken by an organization in response to a service failure or a dissatisfied consumer (Gronroos, 1988).

Regardless of the fact that "everyone deals with it," the goal is not diminished. All quality-oriented organizations should work to minimize the number of dissatisfied consumers and strive toward developing a system that reacts quickly and efficiently in response to potential situations. "In today's competitive environment, having a loyal base of satisfied customers increases revenues, reduces costs, builds market shares and improved bottom lines" (Babakus, Yavas, Karatepe & Avci, 2003, p. 272).

Boshoff (1997) stated "great service recovery cannot compensate for poor service delivery, but it can go a long way toward limiting its harmful impact" (p. 124). The leisure and tourism organization's reaction to a service failure can either build loyalty or turn a minor issue into a large dissatisfaction.

Smith, Bolton, and Wagner (1999) found consumers were less satisfied with process versus outcome failures. Process failures were the direct result of employee actions, whereas outcome failures were policy or predetermined activities. Consider the following research on the impact of service recovery:

- 27% to 96% of guests do not complain (45–96% referring to small product or service purchases and 27–37% referring to large-ticket products or services, such as cars or insurance).

- 45% to 63% of guests have not complained and will not return to buy a product or service in the future.

- 70% to 92% of people will return to an organization if their complaint is resolved.

Yet, even with research that supports the importance of service recovery, some organizations hesitate in managing dissatisfaction issues for the following reasons:

- Guests take advantage of organizations and just want free amenities. Some do. However, it is estimated that only 1% to 1.5% of guests may take advantage of an organization's commitment to quality service. Organizations that allow a small percentage of people to influence the poten-

Anticipating potential challenges at this park will reduce the need for service recovery.

tial success of pleasing the other 99% are at risk of never addressing quality.

- Organizations are not comfortable knowing how to handle the situation and do not know what to do to make the guest satisfied. No one suggests handling situations of guest dissatisfaction is easy. However, those situations that force individuals and organizations to develop new skills are often most rewarding. Developing systems and tools for addressing this issue is important for organizations and employees alike.

- Some guests are *wrong* and the organization does not feel they deserve to get something. As stated earlier, a guest's perception is his or her reality. You may not think the guest is right, but they are still the guest. Remember the premise "A guest may not be *right* but they are *never* wrong." Their perception is their reality. Let them disagree with dignity.

Why Are Guests Dissatisfied?

Guests are dissatisfied for a variety of reasons with an organization. Causes of dissatisfaction vary from a poor attitude by a service provider to competition. Pollard (2000) states 70% of consumers are dissatisfied because a service provider doesn't care. Not all dissatisfaction falls into this category, however, further findings indicate that 1% die, 4% leave due to a relocation, 10% for competitive reasons and 15% due to a product or service failure (Pollard, 2000). Hoffman, Kelley, and Rotalsky (1995) further found that in restaurant experiences, over 40% of all problems occurred because of service delivery issues, 21% occurred due to product defects, 18% due to slow service (e.g., procedures), 3% for facility problems and less than 2% for unclear policies.

Sources of guest dissatisfaction vary and include employees, the physical environment, other guests, and the organization's products/services, policies, procedures, operations, and marketing. Many of these areas have been studied, and organizations use this information to make operational changes. Levy (personal communication, November 5, 2005) suggests, however, that the impact consumers have on other consumers' experiences (e.g., loud consumers) has not often been studied and organizations need to better understand them.

Attitude of Service Providers

Service recovery systems vary from organization to organization and some are more quality oriented than others. Every person who has been a consumer can attest to those organizations that are effective at dealing with consumer dissatisfaction, but what specifically do they do? Organizations with effective recovery systems employ three basic principles: they identify, prepare, and learn from the dissatisfaction. But first, they must prepare the workforce for these difficult situations.

The attitude of the service provider handling these types of situations is key. Quality service providers believe learning of a guest's dissatisfaction is the best thing to happen to the organization because they are getting a chance to recover. In addition, service providers

1. See guest dissatisfaction as a service opportunity. A guest who tells you that you haven't created happy memories and exceeded their expectations is doing you a great favor. They are giving an organization a chance to recover versus telling 250 other people about a poor experience.

2. Know it is important to figure out ways to reach passive guests or guests that don't willingly share their dissatisfaction.

3. Understand handling these situations is not easy and know it is important to develop the skills to deal successfully with situations that are uncomfortable for people.

4. Make a commitment to use their quality service skills to handle the situation and to ensure the guest's expectations are exceeded. They say "I know I can handle this effectively and I will not subscribe to calling guests liars or complainers or placing blame/justification. A guest's perception is their reality, and my role is to serve them to the best of my ability."

5. Believe learning of guest dissatisfaction is only helping an organization to improve as a whole and effectively dealing with these situations allows the organization to grow as a service provider.

Steps to Effectively Managing Dissatisfaction

The individual attitude toward dissatisfaction and the choice of words used by a service provider greatly effects the service recovery environment. Guests are reluctant to complain because they expect nothing will be done and they will be "blamed," therefore, a basic need will not be met. It is important leisure and tourism organizations follow several steps in managing dissatisfaction issues.

Identify the dissatisfaction. Because all dissatisfied guests do not express emotional disappointment, it is important leisure service providers be trained in recognizing and understanding emotional cues. Nonverbal and verbal messages may be sent throughout an experience, and quality-oriented providers recognize and address the messages they are receiving. Service providers must encourage consumers to share their emotions and be ready and willing to handle the feedback presented (Smith & Bolton, 2002).

Be prepared to manage the dissatisfaction. Leisure service providers must also be trained in recovery efforts. They must feel comfortable and confident that assisting a consumer will directly have an impact on the organization. Quality service providers recognize aggressive, dissatisfied guests may not be easy to address, but any time a consumer brings their dissatisfaction to the organization's attention it is the best thing that could have happened to the organization. Boshoff (1997) and Swanson and Kelley (2001) found dissatisfied consumers are more positive about the service recovery if front-line employees resolve the situation. The role of these employees is to take care of consumers, hence it makes sense that they are equipped to deal with this type of interaction. When employees are prepared to successfully handle these situations they are more committed and loyal to the organization. Additionally, these employees know the needs of consumers better (Boshoff, 1997). Further, organizations should establish service recovery guidelines for employees and customers to understand. These guidelines should be consistently delivered by employees in case a service failure occurs.

Recover from the dissatisfaction. Hoffman, Kelley, and Rotalsky (1995) found recovery actions included a variety of remedies offered by organizations. Almost 24% offered free food, which was received most positively by dissatisfied consumers. Following in order of resolution satisfaction were discounts (4%), coupons (1%), management intervention (3%), food replacement (33%), correcting the existing order (6%), employee apology (8%). Twenty-one percent of organizations offered nothing to correct the service failure. Employee behavior and facility problems were found to be the most difficult to recover from. Not only are people the cause of most dissatisfaction but also they are the most difficult to manage.

Types of Dissatisfied Customers

Being able to solicit both negative and positive feedback is critical to ensure a quality service system exists and to make improvements based on guest expectations and needs.

Dissatisfied guests come in three basic forms. Each type should be understood to better prepare for learning about the dissatisfaction and recovery from the situation.

Passive. These types of guests walk out, don't say a word and possibly go tell 250 other people. They are the most dangerous for any leisure and tourism organization. They fail to inform the organization, not giving them a chance to recover, and therefore impact the organization the most.

Organizations must develop systems to gain information from passive guests. Ways to reach passive guest include questionnaire surveys, comments cards, mystery shopping experiences, proactive hospitality actions (i.e., see a situation and address it before consumers mention anything), talking to employees or board members who notice everything, or offer a toll-free phone number (or e-mail addresses) for guests to contact the organization. The most important point is to assure passive, dissatisfied guests feel welcome to share their dissatisfaction and are given a variety of means to do so.

Problem solver. Guests share their dissatisfaction positively, providing an indication on how you can help resolve the difficulty. "I am very disappointed that it rained today and I've been here 10 minutes. I would like my money back." They are in control of their emotions. This type of dissatisfied guest expects resolution to their concerns. They are rational and willing to work with an organization. If the organization does not recover from the situation, these guests may become aggressive.

Aggressive. Some guests get angry and lose control of their emotions. They share their dissatisfaction in expressive ways, like loud voice, angry face, and tense body. These guests are what most employees fear and think of when guest dissatisfaction comes to mind. Aggressive guests need to be quickly calmed and removed from the situation so other guests perceptions are not impacted. They are very difficult to assist until a service provider has allowed them to express themselves initially and have taken an obvious interest to hear their concern. Once they calm down and let anger subside they may experience a sense of guilt and embarrassment.

Smith and Bolton (2002) found that in a hotel setting those customers who respond emotionally to service failures significantly influence their recovery satisfaction, and these people will also more systematically evaluate the recovery effort. Ultimately, those customers who express more emotion (i.e., are more negative) may be less satisfied. It is important to consider the customer's emotional responses to ensure satisfaction or recovery is achieved.

Steps to Effective Service Recovery

Each dissatisfied consumer has different expectations of how the service recovery process should be handled. The more that is understood about individuals, the more likely organizations will be to respond in meaningful ways. Smith, Bolton, and Wagner (1999) found "customers prefer to receive recovery resources that 'match' the type of failure they experience in 'amounts' that are commensurate with the magnitude of the failure that occurs" (p. 356). Organizations should consider the type and amount of the service failure in establishing recovery processes. Further, "tailoring service recovery efforts will have the greatest positive impact on customer responses" (p. 369). The following highlights the seven-step process for recovering from a service situation: the LEAD (i.e., listen, empathy, ask questions, and discuss) and ACT (i.e., action, communicate, and theory of "*wow*") Service Recovery System.

Listen. Be receptive to receiving the dissatisfaction and *listen* without interrupting (and don't get defensive).

Empathy (i.e., sorry-glad-sure). Respond with sorry-glad-sure statements which expresses empathy. Let the guest know you are *sorry* this happened to him or her, that you are *glad* he or she brought it to your attention, and that you will be *sure* to do your best to resolve the situation for him or her.

Ask questions. Ask questions to understand the problem. This also allows the guest to know you are listening and truly interested in the situation as you are clarifying the story and making certain you understand exactly what transpired.

Discuss (i.e., they-can-alternatives). Find out what *the guest* wants and how you can resolve the situation for him or her. Discuss what you *can do* and provide *alternatives*, if necessary. Look for the guest to accept the resolution through positive body language (e.g., by nodding his or her head yes) and verbally ask him or her how they feel about that particular solution. Providing resolutions that are meaningless to guests will not allow an organization

---

Real Life Story: Collette Vacations' Keys to Service Recovery

Collette Vacations is a third-generation family-owned business. For 87 years, the company has taken millions of travelers around the globe on vacations that feature unique experiences, affordable prices, and inclusive dining and entertainment. Professional tour managers, who are full-time Collette employees, accompany travelers throughout their entire tour. Collette's trip cancellation waiver offers unique benefits, including the option to cancel at any time, for any reason, right up to the day of departure. Collette Vacations is committed to creating an extraordinary experience for all customers.

This type of quality service approach has allowed Collette to continue to thrive in an ever-growing and competitive marketplace. Their professional tour managers have the most important role in the satisfaction of their guests' experiences. Only one of 100 applicants make it through Collette's rigorous selection and training programs. Peter Hopps stated, "The first day of the tour is a critical moment to sell and deliver on the service Collette can provide. The tour guide is so important to quality service." His role at Collette is the guest relations manager. A title not so unique to leisure-related organizations, but his role and the way it is implemented is quite unique. Peter's job is to manage the service recovery process and to handle all guest dissatisfaction situations. Collette Vacations serves hundreds of thousands of customers each year, and Peter's role is to ensure each customer is as satisfied as possible to the unique tour experience.

Collette Vacations emphasizes the key to managing a service recovery process is to connect with them personally. Regardless of how Collette is notified of a dissatisfied customer, Peter contacts each person by telephone. Peter stated, "People are generally blown away that I call them and express concern about their situation." To begin each call, he thanks them for letting Collette learn of the dissatisfaction, because it is the only way they can learn to improve. As he learns more information, he does what he can to rectify the situation. Peter estimates he is able to satisfy over 95% of dissatisfied customers; the remaining 5%, no matter how hard he tries, are never satisfied. He does feel, however, that they leave the experience knowing Collette cares and tries their best to satisfy them. He believes Collette's commitment gives their organization a competitive advantage as they stand behind the unique tour experience they provide.

Salzburg 2005, 27th of May

to successfully recover from the situation. Ultimately, during this stage both service provider and guest should agree on the action that will be taken.

Action. Take action immediately. Do not wait to resolve this issue with the guest and respond as quickly as possible to the situation. The more time it takes to resolve an issue the less likely an organization will recover with a guest. Do not give the guest any additional time to discuss his or her dissatisfaction with others. Empowering staff to manage these situations is critical because staff are with guests most often.

Communicate (both internally and externally). Follow up internally in the organization and insure all processes, procedures and staff are informed to insure the situation does not happen again. For every one dissatisfaction an organization is made aware of, another 20 exist (i.e., passive guests). Therefore, learning from the experience is critical; establishing a system for documenting, discussing, and resolving internal issues is valuable.

Systematically categorizing consumer dissatisfaction issues is the first step to understanding if a larger problem exists. All too often organizations fail to track, monitor, and analyze the amount, type, and recovery steps taken to address consumer dissatisfaction situations. Hoffman, Kelley, and Rotalsky (1995) suggested analysis of how employees react to service failures and the response of consumers can be eye opening. These analyses allow organizations to

- Identify common service failures and address these issues internally.

- Use scenarios to improve on the management of service situations, and train employees in handling various encounters.

These staff members review golf outing details.

- Reward employees for improved efforts in tracking situations, reduce the number of incidents and/or handle the situations professionally.

Organizations must first track dissatisfaction. Employees must be encouraged and rewarded for addressing dissatisfaction situations and completing incident forms.

Using data to identify gaps in what is important and consumer satisfaction provides a way to better manage service recovery issues. Guests who are dissatisfied will become more loyal to an organization if their dissatisfaction is rectified; and, the sooner the better!

Theory of "wow." The final step in service recovery follows the definition of quality service. The action taken by the organization was one accepted by the guest. However, the guest's expectations may not be exceeded and further effort may need to be taken. Follow up with guest again to "wow" them. Do something they did not expect. Call them to ensure they are satisfied, write them a note thanking them again, send a free or discounted coupon, or mail a T-shirt with your logo. It does not have to be much. What it has to do is set you apart from your competition and do something special—something unexpected.

Further examples of ways in which organizations measure service experiences can be found in Chapter 5, Understanding, Developing, and Applying Market Research. The following highlights how organizations do this.

How to Practice the Theory of *Wow*

- *Research.* A community recreation organization conducts research on expectations and satisfaction of customers, and on hourly and management employees (Currie, 2000).

- *Service Recovery System.* A zoo develops a service recovery system that includes documenting and tracking each known dissatisfaction experience, responding to guests within 24 hours to resolve the issue, doing more than the guest expects and meeting with a quality committee that addresses internal issues as a result of the dissatisfaction.

- *Culture.* Babakus, Yavas, Karatepe, and Avci (2003) found culture plays a role in service recovery. Management's commitment to quality influences front-line employee service recovery performance.

Finally, a service recovery process must be in existence that allows staff to customize the recovery process, act quickly, and learn from the experience. Service providers must be able to individually address the needs of specific dissatisfied customers. They need to be able to adapt to each consumer based on their emotional state, needs and particular situation. Swanson and Kelley (2001) found dissatisfied consumers will be more positive about the recovery if it is handled quickly and in an efficient manner. In the airline industry, dissatisfied consumers were less pleased with the recovery process when it was more complex and took a longer time period to address. Additionally, the longer the recovery is delayed, the higher compensation the consumer will require (Boshoff, 1997). Hess, Ganesan, and Klein (2003) agreed, concluding in their research that the better the relationship between an organization and a consumer the more likely an organization will be shielded from the negative impacts of service failure. Loyal customers were more tolerant of dissatisfaction situations.

This model is not the only quality service system component to be addressed in leisure organizations. Clawson and Kneutch's model of the phases of leisure experience discussed in Chapter 2 also impacts quality efforts of a leisure organization. Each phase should be addressed with quality practices in mind. Both "systems" need to be addressed in a leisure organization to develop successfully a complete quality service system.

Malcolm Baldrige Award

Culture is part history, part leadership and part commitment. Ultimately, it is in the control of the people within an organization. Effective leaders enable an organization to be quality oriented. Malcom Baldrige, a former Secretary of Commerce, saw organizations could develop quality systems. Because of his efforts, Congress named the United States' highest quality award in his honor (National Institute of Standards and Technology, 2002).

This award is granted to businesses that employ quality service principles. Since 1988 the federal government has presented awards to small and large manufacturing and service organizations. In 1999 educational and healthcare organizations that adopt practices that embody quality became eligible. This was done to recognize organization achievements as well as to raise awareness of the value and importance of quality. The award is limited to two organizations in each category per year. From 1988–2002, 50 organizations received this noteworthy distinction. Of those 50, only one was a leisure-related organization, the Ritz Carlton Hotel Company. Although more awards could have been given, this award is only given to those that follow the guidelines established and truly model the practices of a quality service organization. Other quality awards exist; however, the Baldrige Award

1. focuses more on results and service.

2. relies upon the involvement of many different professional and trade groups.

3. provides special credits for innovative approaches to quality.

4. includes a strong customer and human resource focus.

5. stresses the importance of sharing information. (National Institute of Standards and Technology, 2002)

The Baldrige model epitomizes quality service principles. Seven categories must be addressed by organizations that apply for the award. Each category is considered by leading quality and management experts to be critical in developing a quality service system:

1. *Leadership.* Examines how senior executives guide the organization and how the organization addresses its responsibilities to the public and practices of good citizenship.

2. *Strategic planning.* Examines how the organization sets strategic directions and how it determines key action plans.

3. *Customer and market focus.* Examines how the organization determines requirements and expectations of customers and markets; builds relationships with customers; and acquires, satisfies, and retains customers.

4. *Measurement, analysis and knowledge management.* Examines the management, effective use, analysis, and improvement of data and information to support key organization processes and the organization's performance management system.

5. *Human resource focus.* Examines how the organization enables its workforce to develop its full potential and how the workforce is aligned with the organization's objectives.

6. *Process management.* Examines aspects of how key production/delivery and support processes are designed, managed, and improved.

7. *Business results.* Examines the organization's performance and improvement in its key business areas: customer satisfaction, financial and marketplace performance, human resources, supplier and partner performance, operational

performance, and governance and social responsibility. This category also examines how the organization performs relative to competitors. (National Institute of Standards and Technology, 2002)

A great deal of research has been conducted on the impact of quality service practices. Findings suggest those organizations with higher levels of guest satisfaction grow faster (as much as two times as fast) than those with lower levels of satisfaction *and* they charge more on average (9%; Blume, 1988). Moreover, quality efforts have been known to increase productivity, to create more satisfied employees and customers, and to improve profits.

Applying the Baldrige Award criteria has proved rewarding for many organizations. Those who have begun to apply the criteria indicate the process has helped to motivate employees, reduce turnover, achieve higher profits, create a better work environment, improve recruiting, increase productivity, collect and assess feedback, encourage sharing and relationships, stimulate change, and achieve organizational success. These organizations have had to rethink their basic organizational structures, employee (i.e., internal guest) development, job responsibilities, process involvement, and systems capabilities.

What has been learned from these successes and failures is there must be a balance between quality and organizational goals. All quality initiatives must be linked to the organization's mission and strategic goals. Many organizations have adopted quality principles successfully and the Malcom Baldrige Award has provided a basis to create a quality service system. The model in Figure 3.1 (p. 51) indicates how the components fit into an organization's system.

Studying six leisure organizations, Williams (1998) found six common elements emerge from those adopting quality practices:

1. culture

2. leadership (some have quality service managers)

3. feedback and monitoring

4. core service

5. specialist staff (making all areas feel the reason why they should be concerned with quality service)

6. training and human resources.

These same areas are addressed in the establishment of a quality award recognizing excellence.

The development and maintenance of a strong service culture is fundamental to quality service. Brown (2003) suggested:

managers of outstanding service organizations know that a truly guest-focused culture can help achieve three important goals. First, it helps guide the employee in making the intangible service product tangible. Second, it gives meaning and value to the work. Third, it helps to fill the gaps between what the organization can train the employee to do and what the employee must actually do to meet individual customer expectations across various situations. (p. 13)

Organizations often share their service culture through a mission statement. The existence of a mission statement alone, however, does not indicate the level of commitment by an organization. Organizations with service-oriented mission statements have also been known to deliver consistently poor service. What they need is a committed, well-defined, service strategy.

Developing a Service Strategy

Bonné (2003) suggested:

When companies offer sweeping, generic statements of goals and values, employees often shrug. Rather, workers really just care about how those goals impact them personally. A company might commit to customer satisfaction, but if workers don't see it reflected in their daily tasks—or feel they're being given pabulum from above—they sense a disconnect and can bristle… Companies simply don't understand their internal work structures and therefore are ill-prepared to reward and retain their best employees.

Therefore, it is important that organizations establish their expectations for service delivery. This can be done through the development of a service strategy. A documented service strategy provides an understanding of the organization's definition of service quality. It represents an organization's service values and establishes a goal/direction for quality efforts. Standards are created and a service culture emerges as a result of an organization first developing and then providing service based on this strategy to employees, guests, and all vested publics (e.g., donors, board members, volunteers).

This commitment, as Wirtz (2000) suggested, becomes "the guide for daily behavior, decision making and improvements. It focuses people's efforts in a common direction, builds customer relationships and distinguishes you from your competition" (p. 26). The development of a service strategy should involve leadership and employees. It is important both leaders and employees share expectations of service delivery and discuss their respective points of view to develop the vision together. If the leaders are not involved in the process, the commitment to an established strategy may not be evident. Conversely, should employees not be involved, the views of those closest to guest service may not be represented and buy-in to a top-down initiative may not be supported. Ultimately, Wirtz (2000) added the process "transforms vague concepts of quality and excellence into daily behavior and constant improvement" (p. 26).

Loyalty and Relationship Management

Athens (2003) reported that it costs six to ten times more to acquire new consumers rather than retain the ones currently served. She suggests a 5% increase in loyalty can produce a 95% increase in profitability. Historical marketing efforts have focused on identifying and securing new consumers for organizations. It is only within the past two decades that efforts have become more balanced between new and existing consumers. Insuring consumers are satisfied is the heart of a marketing effort because organizations realize the 80/20 rule holds true: 80% of revenue is generated from 20% of the consumers. Brannigan, Carey, and McCartney (2001) stated United Airlines suggested that 9% of its passengers accounted for 46% of its revenue in the booming late 1990s. Technology has played a role in helping organizations identify whom the 20% includes (Curley, 1999). This concept implies a group of loyal customers offer a majority of the organization's business. This is the power of word-of-mouth advertising. It does not, however, suggest other markets should be ignored.

It is a lot easier and less expensive to maintain an existing consumer than to go out and find a new one.
Rich Fairman, Warwick Hills Country Club

Coleman (1997) suggested organizations should concern themselves with both the returning and first-time customer. To even have a return customer, they must first be a new one. Therefore, it is critical that potential markets also be identified.

A level beyond having simply satisfied consumers is generating and developing customer loyalty. Organizations are finding ways to communicate with consumers in more personalized ways. As a result, they are building long-term relationships. The way in which organizations develop loyalty is through relationship management. Relationship management is developing techniques to engage consumers (e.g., visitors, employees, board members) for the long-term to produce desired outcomes.

Relationship management is a tactic used to provide quality service. It is the way organizations can exceed consumer expectations and add value to the exchange. These relationships are like partnerships, where neither party is dominant (Pressey & Mathews, 2000).

This concept has been in existence for the past decade, and as Tower (1997) noted, little agreement exists as to what it specifically means. However, the basic premise of the importance of developing a strategic approach to loyalty is that it is more expensive to find a new consumer than it is to maintain an existing relationship. Further, loyal consumers positively promote the organization's services more often than those who are not as loyal or who are dissatisfied.

In the leisure setting, developing loyalty means establishing a relationship that enables the customer to behave in ways meaningful to the organization. This is not necessarily just visiting/using leisure services, more often, it is also an emotional commitment to the organization/experience. In a leisure experience, some have described loyalty and relationship management as "the degree of attachment that a participant has to the leisure service in addition to the level of repeat participation" (Veldcamp & Backman, 1993, p. 8) and the ability to develop long-term, committed relationships between stakeholders (Terblanche & Malan, 2002).

O'Brien and Manross (2002) described loyalty in a recreation setting as one where users keep facilities safe and clean, they are willing to pay for services, they make financial commitments (e.g., bond) and they participate with the organization (e.g., volunteer). Solomon (2002) further defines loyal customers as partners. They may consume your services but they don't see themselves as customers, their perceived role is based on the benefits they offer to the organization. It is a state where consumer confidence is high and they are engaged in the organization at a level beyond a simple transaction. O'Brien and Manross (2002) highlighted the following issues for gaining customer loyalty:

1. Identify the behavior desired from various customers (e.g., more volunteerism, less vandalism).

2. Understand what influences loyalty (e.g., accountability, credibility and trust).

3. Stay in touch with organization stakeholders.

4. Develop policies guided by numbers 2 and 3.

5. Document and communicate the need for policy—Don't just say "trust me."

6. Don't exaggerate.

7. Clearly identify how you are investing organization resources.

8. Keep employees or leaders aware of their role in building loyalty.

9. Act on what is important to your customers.

10. Review organization practices annually including loyalty concerns.

Veldcamp and Backman (1993) indicated four levels of consumer loyalty exist. These range from low to high loyalty.

1. Those with high loyalty have a strong attachment and have high participation.

2. Those who participate often but do not have a strong attachment are "spurious."

3. Latent loyalty is based on consumers who have a strong attachment but do not participate in the leisure experience.

4. Low loyalty are those who have no attachment and do not participate in the leisure experience.

They found respondents with high versus low levels of loyalty indicated facilities, equipment, appearance of personnel, and presence of other participants were more important to their leisure service experience. No other pattern appeared comparing the level of loyalty and various satisfaction issues, including performance, responsiveness, assurance, and empathy. In the airline industry Long (1995) supported these findings, which indicated the more loyal consumers were (i.e., the more often they flew with one carrier vs. others), the more they valued their services.

Satisfaction is the base from which loyalty develops. It is a prerequisite of a long-lasting relationship, and consumers with developed relationships influence satisfaction evaluations (Bruning & Ledingham, 2000; Terblanche & Malan, 2002). O'Brien and Manross (2002) investigated the difference of customer satisfaction and loyalty in a park and recreation setting. Four measures provided the loyalty indicator, including credibility, trust, accountability, and voting support. They found that generally, loyal customers are inherently satisfied. However, they also found loyal customers were more likely to support a tax initiative than those who were simply satisfied and not considered loyal. Finally, they identified predictors of customer loyalty. The top seven, in priority order, included accountability, credibility, trust, always support district, public safety, customer service, and past experience.

It is not surprising that trust was identified as an issue in developing loyalty. Berry (1996) suggested trust was the "single most powerful relationship marketing tool available to a company" (p. 42). However, Sirdeshmukh, Singh, and Sabol (2002) found the consumer's evaluation of value was more influential on loyalty than trust was. Consumers prefer to have long-term relationships with organizations they trust. These findings suggest a combination of issues drive loyalty. Indicators suggest customer loyalty is a step beyond simple satisfaction. Finding ways to build loyalty will provide additional benefits to the organization. It is among this pretense that organizations have developed "loyalty" programs to bring extra value to those who are frequent consumers.

Loyalty Programs

Airline and hotel companies are well known for their consumer loyalty programs. These programs have existed since 1980 (Rogers, 2002). The more you fly a certain carrier the more points earned for free tickets or upgrades, stay so many nights in a hotel and earn free hotel nights. Even though the use of this technique has experienced highs and lows, more leisure and tourism organizations have developed and are continuing to develop loyalty programs. In the entertainment industry, frequent sporting event and concert consumers are provided rewards for the number of events they attend. They are provided tickets to sellout events in advance and are able to purchase merchandise at reduced prices. Athletic clubs offer punch cards, similar to those found in food and beverage establishments, where after purchasing ten days at the daily rate, consumers receive the next visit free.

Casinos monitor the amount of money gambled to provide incentives to gamblers to return to their organization versus other casinos. Kennedy (1998) found casino travelers were more likely to gamble and wager more when they were a valued member of the organization. Reda (2003) reported how Harrah's Entertainment provided free weekend reservations and valet parking to any reward card holder who produces $10,000 in casino worth a year. They do so to build loyalty as well as to obtain valuable consumer data. This data is used to understand consumer behaviors and preferences. Travel clubs and organizations offer incentives, such as spa and sauna days, depending on the amount of money spent on travel services. Although some have done this for over ten years, the majority have just begun to develop these types of systems.

A variety of leisure and tourism organizations are turning to relationship management practices, such as loyalty programs. Huang (1999) found four fundamental components were needed when baseball franchises established a fan loyalty program: (a) a consumer database, (b) a communication scheme, (c) a reward system, and (d) the acquisition of the resource for execution.

In addition to these types of benefits, loyalty programs also benefit the organization because they provide a means of tracking consumer use and maintaining databases on these users. As a result, organizations can target and customize their messages. Further, they encourage past consumers to develop the emotional attachment to their particular organization versus other competing organizations. Ultimately, they strive to have consumers who use their organization more often and sales or goals are accomplished as a result. Public, nonprofit and private/for-profit organizations use these types of programs even though the concept began in the for-profit/private industry. More nonprofit and public organizations recognize they compete for leisure time and discretionary income with for-profit organizations and must create programs and systems desired by the leisure user. Terblanche and Malan (2002) suggested nonprofit organizations are turning to relationship processes to manage decreased funding and participation that some leisure organizations have experienced. Even though the goals of each organization vary, loyalty programs are important to accomplishing a variety of goals (e.g., higher profit, increase usage, reduce crime, enhance the quality of life).

Kaczynski and Havitz (2001) suggested most literature has focused on organization versus consumer benefits. Loyalty programs provide benefits to consumers as they receive information that specifically meets their individual needs. Some suggest consumers identify three types of benefits as a result of developing long-term organization relationships: confidence benefits (e.g., comfort, safety, trust, consistency), social benefits (e.g., personal recognition, friendship) and special treatment benefits (e.g., time savings, discounts) were those identified prioritized values of the long-term relationship (Gwinner, Gremler & Bitner, 1998; Kaczynski and Havitz, 2001). In the leisure industry, Kaczynski and Havitz (2001) found differences existed in the benefits received from relationships between organizations and consumers. The private sector placed more importance on social and special treatment benefits than the public sector. They further suggested the importance of recognizing these benefits and allocating resources accordingly. Special treatment benefits were least valued by all leisure organizations where over 25% of the sample did not value them at all, whereas all groups valued confidence benefits the most. Leisure organizations that address the confidence and social benefits will distinguish themselves from other organizations and establish a competitive advantage (Kaczynski & Havitz, 2001).

Gaining Employee Loyalty

The loyalty concept is also one that relates to employees. The difference between a dissatisfied employee, a satisfied employee and a loyal employee can be described as follows:

- *Dissatisfied employee.* The employee comes to work late, does not hesitate calling in sick, does not come in for others who need time off, whispers to other employees, frowns.

- *Satisfied employee.* The employee comes to work on time, seldom calls in sick (or for a legitimate reason), will come in for others when asked, listens to negative talk but doesn't participate in it, smiles.

- *Loyal employee.* The employee comes to work early, helps out when needed (even before asked), promotes organization positively when not

Movie theaters have adopted loyalty programs as well.

working, encourages others to work and visit the organization, diffuses negative talk by walking away and encourages others to do the same, is positive and encourages others to serve others in this manner.

These processes apply to both internal and external consumers. Organizations are beginning to develop employee loyalty programs, too.

Gaining Nonuser/Stakeholder Loyalty

You may be thinking: How could a leisure organization develop loyalty in a person that is not a current user/customer? Nonusers can indeed be a market of concern in a leisure setting as many nonusers also influence and impact the organization's success.

A public recreation organization relies on nonusers to financially support its mission. Nonusers vote on tax or bond increases and a loyal nonuser would support these initiatives, even though they are not consumers. In a camp setting, nonusers would support the purchase of additional land for camp use. In a resort setting, nonusers would support the closing down of city streets to allow for an event to occur. Organizations need to develop loyalty programs practices for consumers, employees and nonusers. Pressey and Mathews (2000) provided seven indicators of this type of relationship:

1. high level of trust between both parties

2. high level of commitment between both parties

3. long-term focus on the relationship

4. open communication channels between both parties (information exchanged both ways)

Real Life Story: The University Club of Chicago

The University Club of Chicago, Illinois, is an established private club that developed a loyalty program two years ago, the "Membership Rewards Program." After 9/11, the market for hotel rooms in Chicago (and throughout the country) became very tight. Consumers suddenly were shopping for the best value their money could get them. Realizing the reciprocal members, traveling from out-of-state, had a tremendous amount of hotels to select from when they were coming into the Windy City, they knew they had to do something... quickly. Competition was fierce, not only with other hotels but also because they compete with four other private city clubs in Chicago, who also have hotel rooms within their facilities. They wanted to give those people traveling to Chicago another advantage to staying with them, something that they could not get with any other private club—that advantage being a loyalty program—something no other club had in the country.

There was an initial investment to have the frequent-stay punch cards made. Extensive traveling was done in marketing this program heavily to their biggest feeder markets, the Midwest and East coast. This was the first time in history that anyone from a private city club traveled to market their property. Clubs have always relied heavily on their own members to utilize the facility. Through the traveling, relationships were established and each club became more educated on their program. This was also a perfect opportunity to market other changes in the club (e.g., new athletic programming, renovated restaurant). Now, these trips are used to make sure each club has enough frequent

stay cards and informational brochures on file, as well as promote whatever else is going on in the club.

The club numbers fluctuate from month to month; however, during the first quarter of this past fiscal year, there was an increase of over 30% in room sales compared to reciprocal clubs. This increase in revenue more than covered the expenses of traveling and production of the cards. It not only brought in individual, transient guests but also it has helped in booking group trips from clubs from other cities, who want to stay with the Chicago Club and shop, dine, attend baseball games, and go to the theater.

Contributed by Maureen Hollinrake, Marketing Director, The University Club of Chicago

University Club of Chicago

STAY 5 NIGHTS:
*6th night free and Breakfast for two or
*6th night free and (1) one-hour massage

OR

STAY 10 NIGHTS:
*11th night free and Dinner for two or
*11th night free and (2) one-hour massages

Member Signature

Member Number

*Card must be presented at Front Desk to redeem.
Please call reservations at 312-726-2840
to reserve your room.

1 2 3 4 5 6 7 8 9 10

Membership Rewards
VIP

5. actions with the consumers best interest at heart

6. commitment to quality for both parties

7. interest in the service provider to retain the consumer

Some suggest these types of programs are losing ground. Consumers are tired of needing these cards at every organization they exchange with; they want to feel that same loyalty with or without a system to measure their purchases. Rogers (2002) suggested focus groups, brand experience, and the Internet have replaced these loyalty schemes. Regardless of the activity pursued, those organizations with more contact with more personally involved consumers create environments for relationship management to occur. The following highlights various ways to approach loyalty:

- **Donors.** Send a personal letter indicating specifically how the donation helped the organization. Regularly sending organization accomplishments/activities (e.g., newsletter) to donors. (The more commited a donor is to the cause, typically the larger the donation.)

- **Sponsors.** Volunteer to sponsor an organization's event/activity. Create a high-profile location or acknowledgement during an event (or on location) to profile a sponsor for a certain amount of time.

- **Employees.** Plan biannual or quarterly company family gatherings, parties, or events.

- **Consumers.** Offer an "Appreciation Day" on customers' birthdays by sending them a card and enclosing a special offer.

- **Volunteers.** Identify expectations of the volunteer, recognize efforts, and ask for input.

- **Local authorities** (e.g., police, city officials): Invite these individuals to worthwhile events and acknowledge their support in publications, and elsewhere.

- **Media.** Contact various media to understand "processes" for coverage, invite media representatives to the organization and provide "newsworthy" information to them.

- **Competitors/partners.** Design a culture where if a service isn't provided by your organization, you refer the consumer to other businesses. Chances are the consumer will be grateful for

the time you saved them in having to search for a place that had what they needed.

- **Suppliers.** Recognize special achievements and anniversaries of established partnerships.

- **Boards.** Send gifts to families to show how much you appreciate the extra time their loved one must spend away from home.

- **Nonusers.** Send communication updates to those who challenge and/or choose someone else. Invite these people to special activities and encourage an exchange of information.

The most important issue to consider when developing loyalty programs is to identify what would be of value to the intended audience and what these efforts will produce for the organization. If developing loyal employees is the objective, then what do these employees value? If developing more loyal consumers is the issue, then what do these different markets find valuable? Finally, would providing things of value to these groups produce intended results for the organization?

Customer Relationship Management

Common techniques for managing the relationship process are through customer relationship management (CRM). Rauchenberger (2004) suggested CRM as an overall organization culture in entertainment venues and staff is the center of this relationship. Others have suggested various techniques for supporting CRM culture, including software, data mining techniques, the Internet, research, and simple databases. Okula (2000) indicated that AMR Research of Boston predicts CRM software sales will increase from about $2 billion in 1998 to over $11 billion by 2002. CRM systems include information on customers, a means for analyzing this information and identifying patterns of behavior, identifying the appropriate plan for targeting consumers (e.g., which customers give you the most business), communicating this information to employees to build relationships, and finally, enabling a way for reaching the desired consumers in meaningful ways (e.g., e-mail a discount coupon for a program that the organization knows would interest the consumer; Curley, 1999; Zlotnich, 2003).

Organizations must also have an understanding of what others are doing to build loyalty, specifically with competitors. Research is used as a base for understanding loyalty issues and represents the foundation of marketing decision making. A few techniques are more frequently used in the leisure service industry.

Ephron (2001) suggested loyalty programs do little to build trust when consumers know why they are designed. How much effort you put into selecting a purchase may influence how much you will end up spending as consumers don't necessarily get the best price. Rebates, coupons, special offers, deals… they are all around. Now you have to check multiple airline sources to get the best price (e.g., Internet, Priceline, Orbitz, airline direct, travel organization). This same issue is emerging in several other leisure service industries as well.

Other ways organizations build loyalty are through relationship marketing techniques, stewardship and direct marketing which are discussed in subsequent chapters.

Apply What You Know

1. Profile a leisure and tourism organization loyalty program. Assess its value to the organization and consumer participants.

2. Conduct a mystery shopping assessment on a leisure and tourism organization to determine the quality service practices.

3. Review the Baldrige Winner Profile on the website http://www.quality.nist.gov. Identify the qualities of the winning organization.

4. Interview a leisure and tourism organization regarding their service recovery system and empowerment practices. Compare it to the discussion in the chapter.

Key Terms

Aggressive customers	Internal customers
Competitive advantage	Moment of truth
Customer dissatisfaction	Passive customers
Customer loyalty	Perceptions
Customer satisfaction	Problem solver
Empathy	Quality service
Empowerment	Relationship management
Expectations	Service strategy
External customers	Word-of-mouth marketing

Review Questions

1. List and describe the three types of dissatisfied consumers.

2. What are the seven steps used to successfully recover from a poor quality service experience (LEAD and ACT)?

3. How many people are potentially impacted by a positive experience? a negative experience?

4. Why is it important to develop a service strategy?

5. What is the theory of *"wow"*?

6. Define external and internal guests.

7. Define empowerment and explain how employers can empower employees.

Internet Resources

The *Quality Service Institute* is a company that provides assistance in developing customer service programs and strategies. On their website we can find valuable resources and training programs necessary to improve the quality and the customer service programs offered by an agency.

http://www.customer-service.com/

The *Wise Marketer* website aims to provide news, analysis, research and resources related to customer service and loyalty marketing. More than fifty articles can be found that talk about loyalty marketing and customer service programs. Links to other websites and resources are included.

http://www.thewisemarketer.com/features/index.asp

ICSA—The International Customer Service Association is dedicated to promoting awareness of the customer service profession by providing networking, education and research resources. Networking opportunities with customer service professionals are available by becoming a member of the association.

http://www.icsa.com/

On the *U.S. Small Business Administration* website one can find rules that should be used by the agency in order to provide quality service to their customers. Useful information about marketing for small businesses is also included.

http://www.sba.gov/managing/marketing/customer.html

The *Market Research* website brings together a comprehensive collection of published market research analysis. A separate link is dedicated to customer service analysis. About seventeen reports on customer loyalty are included. http://www.marketresearch.com/browse.asp?categoryid=941&g=1

References

Arndt, J. (1967, August). Role of product—Related conversations in the diffusion of a new product. *Journal of Marketing Research, 4,* 291–295.

Athens, D. (2003). *Using customer data to develop marketing programs.* Retrieved August 28, 2003, from http://www.marketingpower.com

Babakus, E., Yavas, U., Karatepe, O. M., and Avci, T. (2003) The effect of management commitment to service quality on employees' affective and performance outcomes. *Academy of Marketing Science Journal, 31*(3), 272.

Berry, L. (1996). Retailers with a future. *Marketing Management, 5,* 39–46.

Berry, L., Parasuraman, A., and Zeithaml, V. (1988). The service-quality puzzle. *Business Horizons, 31*(5), 35–43.

Blume, E. R. (1988). Customer service: Giving companies the competitive edge. *Training and Development Journal, 49*(2), 24–32.

Bonné, J. (2003). *Getting the best workers to stay: New thoughts on how firms should view employees.* http:/www.msnbc.com/news/977080.asp

Boshoff, C. (1997). An experimental study of service recovery options. *International Journal of Service Industry Management, 8*(2), 110–130.

Boughton, P. D. and Fisher, J. E. (1999). From measurement to action: How one club boosted business by listening to its members. *Cornell Hotel and Restaurant Administration Quarterly, 40*(1), 68–73.

Brannigan, M., Carey, S., and McCartney, S. (2001, August 28). Fed up with airlines, business travelers start to fight. *Wall Street Journal*, A1.

Brown, S. (2003). The employee experience. *Marketing Management, 12*(2), 12–13.

Bruning, S. D. and Ledingham, J. A. (2000). Perceptions of relationships and evaluations of satisfaction: An exploration of interaction. *Public Relations Review, 26*(1), 85–95.

Chang, K. (1998). *A systems view of quality in fitness services.* Columbus, OH: The Ohio State University.

Chang, K. and Chelladurai, P. (1997). *Determinants of quality in fitness/health services: A systems approach.* Presentation at the 5th Congress of the European Association for Sport Management (September 17–20, 1997).

Coleman, G. (1997). Marketing your day camp. *Camping Magazine, 70*(5), 31–33.

Curley, B. (1999). Profiting from the relationship. *Insurance & Technology, 24*(3), 34–38.

Currie, M. E. (2000). *A comparative study of the perceptions of quality service delivery in a community recreation setting.* Unpublished doctoral dissertation, Dalhousie University.

Dawes, J. and Rowley, J. (1996). The waiting experience: Towards service quality in the leisure industry. *International Journal of Contemporary Hospitality Management, 8*(1), 16–18.

Deming, W. E. (1986). *Out of the crisis.* Cambridge, MA: Massachusetts Institute of Technology, Center for Advanced Engineering.

DiPrimio, A. (1987). *Quality assurance in service organizations.* Radnor, PA: Chilton Book Co.

Dresner, M. and Xu, K. (1995). Customer service, customer satisfaction, and corporate performance. *Journal of Business Logistics, 16*(1), 23–41.

Ebert, M. (2002). The "Standing Tall" project: Using theater to address the effects of 9/11. *Stage of the Art, 15*(1), 10–16.

Enz, C. A. and Siguaw, J. A. (2000). Best practices in service quality. *Cornell Hotel and Restaurant Administration Quarterly, 41*(5), 20–28.

Ephron, E. (2001). Sheep to be shorn? *Mediaweek, 1*(13), 18.

Godbey, G. (1989). *The future of leisure services. Thriving on change.* State College, PA: Venture Publishing, Inc.

Gronroos, C. (1988). Service quality: The six criteria of good perceived service quality. *Review of Business*, 9, 10–13.

Gwinner, K. P., Gremler, D. D., and Bitner, M. J. (1998). Relational benefits in service industries: The customer's perspective. *Journal of the Academy of Marketing Science, 26,* 101–114.

Hess, Jr., R. L., Ganesan, S., and Klein, N. M. (2003). Service failure and recovery: The impact of relationship factors on customer satisfaction. *Academy of Marketing Science Journal, 31*(2), 127.

Hightower, R., Brady, M. K., and Baker, T. (2002). Investigating the role of the physical environment in hedonic service consumption: An exploratory study of sporting events. *Journal of Business Research, 55*(9), 697–707.

Hoffman, K. D., Kelley, S. W., and Rotalsky, H. M. (1995). Tracking service failures and employee recovery efforts. *The Journal of Services Marketing, 9*(2), 49–61.

Huang, Y. (1999). *An investigation of the current practice of relationship marketing programs within professional baseball clubs in Major league Baseball through a content analysis.*

Doctoral dissertation, University of Northern Colorado, Greeley.

Janes, P., Wisnom, M., and Otteman, T. (2004). *Quality of Work Life study* [Unpublished data] presented at the National Recreation and Park Association Congress.

Johnston, R. (2004). Towards a better understanding of service excellence. *Managing Service Quality, 14*(2/3), 129.

Kandampully, J. (1998). Service quality to service loyalty: A relationship which goes beyond customer services. *Total Quality Management*, 9(6), 431–443.

Kandampully, J. and Suhartanto, D. (2000). Customer loyalty in the hotel industry: The role of the customer satisfaction and image. *International Journal of Contemporary Hospitality Management, 12*(6), 346–351.

Kaczynski, A. T. and Havitz, M. E. (2001). Relational benefits in recreation services: Examining differences between operating sectors. *Journal of Park and Recreation Administration, 19*(2), 20–42.

Kennedy, E. N. (1998). An empirical analysis of the reasons why guests select and return to Las Vegas hotel/casino properties (Nevada). Quest Digital Dissertations Retrieved June 2, 2003, from http://0-wwwlib.umi.com.catalog.lib.cmich.edu/dissertations/preview_all/1390644

Kenney, B. (1999). The Kevin Bacon factor in marketing. *Brandweek, 40*(24), 26–28.

Larson, E. (1999, January). Fitness first! *Fitness management, 15*(1), 37–44.

Long, M. M. (1995). The ties that bind: An examination of consumption values at various stages of a relationship marketing program (consumer values). Retrieved November 11, 2003, from http://0-wwwlib.umi.com.catalog.lib.cmich.edu/dissertations/fullcit/9605624

Marconi, J. (2000, March 27). Total recall: How to build the value of a brand. *Adweek, 41*(13), 38–56.

Marriott, J. W., Brown, K. A., and Marriott, J. W., Jr. (1997). *The spirit to serve: Marriott's way.* New York, NY: HarperCollins.

McCarville, R. (2000, November). Satisfaction—The basis of client loyalty. *Parks & Recreation, 35*(11), 24–31.

National Institute of Standards and Technology. (2002). *Frequently asked questions about the Malcolm Baldrige National Quality Award.* Retrieved October 21, 2003, from http://www.nist.gov/public_affairs/factsheet/baldfaqs.htm

O'Brien, P. and Manross, G. G (2002). Building customer loyalty: Ten steps toward obtaining this valuable commodity. *Parks & Recreation*, 50–53.

Ofir, C. and Simonson, I. (2001). In search of negative customer feedback: The effect to evaluate on satisfaction evaluations. *Journal of Marketing Research, 38*(2), 170–182.

Okula, S. (2000). Trends in marketing: Customer relationship management. *Business Education Forum, 54*(4), 6–10. Retrieved September 30, 2003, from ERIC database.

O'Neill, M. (2001). *Service quality management in hospitality, tourism, and leisure: Measuring service quality and customer satisfaction.* New York, NY: Haworth Hospitality Press.

Pollard, G. (2000). Satisfying your existing members. *Australian Tennis Magazine, 25*(10), 19.

Pressey, A. D. and Mathews, B. P. (2000). Barriers to relationship marketing in consumer retailing. *Journal of Services Marketing, 14*(3), 272.

Rauchenberger, D. (2004, February/March). CRM: It's a culture, not a technology. *Facility Manager, 20*(1), 48.

Reda, S. (2003). Harrah's hits the jackpot with CRM. Total rewards program. *Stores, 85*(6), 64, 66, 68, 70.

Rogers, D. (2002, January). Loyalty's travel renaissance. *Marketing*, 20–21.

Rousseau, D. M. and Cooke, R. A. (1984). Technology and structure: The concrete, abstract, and activity systems of organizations. *Journal of Management, 10*, 345–361.

Seth, N., Deshmukh, S. G., and Vrat, P. (2005). Service quality models: A review. *The International Journal of Quality & Reliability Management, 22*(8/9), 913–949.

Sirdeshmukh, D., Singh, J., and Sabol, B. (2002). Consumer trust, value, and loyalty in relational exchanges. *Journal of Marketing, 66*(1), 15–37.

Smith, A. K. and Bolton, R. N. (2002). The effect of customers' emotional responses to service failures on their recovery effort evaluations and satisfaction judgments. *Academy of Marketing Science, 30*(1), 5–23.

Smith, A. K., Bolton, R. N., and Wagner, J. (1999). A model of customer satisfaction with service encounters involving failure and recovery. *Journal of Marketing Research, 36*(3), 356–372.

Solomon, J. (2002). Getting in touch with your customer. In an insider's guide to managing the sporting events. *Kinetics*, 91–115.

Steele, D. (1995). Unpublished manuscript. Change master series personal empowerment. Scottsdale, AZ: Steele Enterprises, Inc.

Swanson, S. R. and Kelley, S. (2001). Attributions and outcomes of the service recovery process. *Journal of Marketing Theory and Practice, 9(4)*, 50–65.

Terblanche, N. S. and Malan, J. H. (2002). Application of relationship marketing in non-profit organizations involved in the provision of sport and recreational services. *South African Journal for Research in Sport, Physical Education and Recreation, 24*(1), 113–129.

Tian-Cole, S., Crompton, J. L., and Willson, V. L. (2002). An empirical investigation of the relationship between service quality, satisfaction and behavioral intentions among visitors to a wildlife refuge. *Journal of Leisure Research, 34*(1), 1–24.

Tock, E. (2002). Eight great ways to create positive word of mouth. *Club Success, 8*(11), 4–5.

Tower, J. (1997). Using relationship marketing as a new approach for understanding the customer/leisure service provider relationship. In D. Rowe (Ed.), *Leisure, people, places, spaces. Proceedings of the 3rd Conference of the Australian and New Zealand Association for Leisure Studies* (pp. 204–210). Newcastle, NSW: University of Newcastle, Department of Leisure and Tourism Studies.

Trotter, K. M. (1995). Total quality management: Making camps successful. *Camping Magazine, 67*(5), 16–19.

Veldcamp, C. A. and Backman, S. J. (1993). Delivering high-quality recreation service: The role of loyalty. *Management Strategy, 17*(2), 1, 8.

Wakefield, K. L. and Blodgett, J. G. (1999). Consumer response to intangible and tangible service factors. *Psychology & Marketing, 16*(1), 51–68.

Watkins, E. (2002). Service in the age of the Internet. *Lodging Hospitality, 58*(2), 4.

Williams, C. (1998). The state of quality management in six leisure-related research sites. *The TQM Magazine, 10*(2), 95.

Wirtz, B. (2000). A service strategy: From cliché to action. *Marketing News, 34*(10), 26.

Younis, T. (1997). Customers' expectations of public sector services: Does quality have its limits? *Total Quality Management, 12*(3), 223–235.

Zlotnick, M. (2003). *Customer relationship management.* Retrieved October 10, 2003, from http://www.mplans.com/dpm/article.cfm/39

Chapter 4

Enabling Marketing Action

~~~~~~~~~~~~~~~~~~~~~~~~~~~~

Marketing without a strategy in place is the number one mistake made by companies. (*Top Five Marketing Mistakes Companies Make…*, 2005)

~~~~~~~~~~~~~~~~~~~~~~~~~~~~

In the past month, Tim, General Manager of the Oakland Ice Arena, has been presented with the following marketing communication decisions:

- Debb is selling Yellow Pages advertising and wants Tim to consider a half-page advertisement for $1,100/month.

- Craig, a Boy Scout, is selling $50 sponsorship opportunities for their annual banquet.

- Angie represents a company selling frequent shopper cards and wants to sell space for Tim to offer a free skate rental coupon (with a paid admission) at $250.

- Connie is from the local newspaper and wants Tim to buy an advertisement in the special section on Recreation and Entertainment for $30.

- Eric, the program director at Oakland Ice Arena, wants Tim to approve $125 he needs to copy and distribute flyers about the learn-to-skate program.

- Darcie wants Tim to donate four pairs of skates for the annual 4-H auction.

Leisure and tourism industry professionals are regularly approached with marketing-related opportunities. It is easy for Tim to say "yes" to everyone and spend over $1,800 this month alone. Even if Tim had this money to spend, would it be in the arena's best interest? If Tim's budget is limited, it is also easy for Tim to say "no" to the expensive things and "yes" to those he can afford. But should these decisions be driven by their cost? The dilemma for Tim is to determine which decisions will produce the greatest results and be the most effective choices. To make the best possible decisions, Tim needs to ask himself the following questions:

1. Do these ideas reach my targeted audience in a timely/efficient way?

2. Will these choices produce a return for the arena?

3. Are these the most appropriate choices to send my message?

4. Do we have the funds to do this, or can we "trade" services for this exposure?

5. What value is there for the arena to purchase these ideas?

6. What would happen if I did not purchase these suggestions?

At the end of this chapter, readers will be able to…

- Understand the value of marketing planning.

- Describe a systematic process for approaching marketing.

- List the elements of a leisure and tourism organization marketing plan.

- Explain the keys to ineffective and effective marketing plans.

- Understand funding options for marketing plans.

- Discuss techniques for evaluating marketing efforts and plans.

If Tim relied only on the opinion of the people selling these choices, he would buy everything. Of course, each person selling to Tim feels his or her communication vehicle is *the* best possible idea.

Anyone can spend a marketing budget, but not just anyone can spend it successfully. Patricia Janes

In an effort to effectively manage this situation, Tim should have a strategy and a plan for his annual marketing efforts so not to be confused, mislead or convinced that he should spend money that does not need to be spent. He should not plan day-to-day, but instead should have an annual plan for the organization's marketing activities. Not only does Tim need to be knowledgeable on the variety of communication ideas identified but also, most importantly, he needs a developed, strategic marketing plan to accomplishing his organization's objectives next year. In this marketing plan, Tim will identify the following:

1. where the arena is today, and where it is heading

2. external issues impacting the organization

3. knowledge about current consumers, nonusers, and the overall market conditions

4. who the targeted audience is, and why this is an appropriate choice for the arena

5. what he wants to accomplish this year

6. how he will make this a reality through communication decisions

7. how the success of decisions will be measured

8. when these decisions need to occur

9. how he will fund these decisions

This is how Tim can strategically integrate marketing into the arena to achieve his organizational objectives successfully and reduce the risk of making poor organization marketing decisions.

Instead of spending money randomly on marketing efforts where there is little guarantee of success, effective leisure and tourism organization marketing ensures any action taken is (a) directed toward an organization objective, (b) reflective of the organization's mission and values, (c) well-planned and thought-out (based on sound decision making), and (d) implemented properly. The results of these actions will produce intended outcomes in times when organizations are not successful. It will be evident why that occurred so the same mistake will not be made again.

In the leisure service industry, every organization implements marketing decisions, but these are not necessarily strategically determined. Few have established marketing plans that indicate and communicate the organization's strategy as well as their marketing approach (Forrester & Rubin, 1998). Nordin (2003) found only 16 of 55 (29%) campus recreation organizations had a marketing plan. Additionally, contact was made with 20 randomly selected leisure organizations to understand formal market plan development in other leisure industries. These leisure organizations, located in eight states, ranged in size, type (i.e., public, private, nonprofit, and for-profit), and location. Of the 20 contacted, seven had a written marketing plan, four had components of a marketing plan and nine had no documented marketing plan at all (Janes, 2003).

Those who did not complete a marketing plan indicated it was because of (a) a lack of knowledge on how to develop a plan, (b) limited time, (c) no perceived need because "we do it in our head," and (d) "everything changes so quickly" so there is fear that it would need to be rewritten every day. All nine organizations that had no marketing plan, however, indicated they knew plans were important. Bright's (2000) study supported these findings. He found that a lack of money, time and personnel (i.e., resources) were the reasons why marketing efforts were not adopted in leisure and tourism organizations.

The seven organizations that did complete a plan included various categories and information in their plans with no two looking the same. Most included the tactical marketing decisions regarding what they would do but few included any understanding/support on why these choices were made. Only one organization had an extensive, detailed plan. In all instances, the plan was not shared beyond the marketing department or executive office. It was used only by a select few. It was determined not everyone who was responsible for implementing activities viewed the entire plan—only their particular sections. Most of the plans were annual, a few were seasonal or quarterly. George (2003) stated, "most organizations leave the marketing plan sit on the shelf and seldom use it as the heart of their operation and the most important document they ever owned." The plan should be treated as a "living document, ever-changing and evolving" (p. 14).

What Is a Marketing Plan?

Toy, Rager, and Guadagnolo (1989) indicated that developing strategies in marketing has become an increased priority for public and private recreation providers. Formalizing marketing efforts through plans is a way to develop this process. Regardless of size, every leisure and tourism organization should have strategically implemented marketing activities and a documented marketing plan. Sevier (2000) suggested several reasons why marketing efforts do not work, including (a) a limited definition of marketing; (b) an unwillingness to address strategic issues; (c) no supporting data; (d) fuzzy goals or directions; and (e) unrealistic expectations, timelines, and budgets.

A *marketing plan* is a formal, written document that outlines the organization's current and future direction. It will "define, position, and lay out a strategy to build a brand" (Marconi, 2000). More specifically, it summarizes the organization's current status, the industry's current environment, the organization's marketing objectives, and the marketing actions that will be completed to achieve these objectives. The plan guides the organization into a predetermined future highlighting the decisions used to articulate the future direction. Instead of guessing why Tim had chosen the 4-H auction donation, Yellow Pages advertising, and Boy Scout sponsorship for the arena, a marketing plan would have not only clarified why these were effective choices but also indicated these ideas prior to being approached by all these people. Tim would have had this all planned out— no surprises, no guessing, less risk.

The Value of Marketing Planning

Leisure organizations may not understand the value of marketing planning for several reasons. Coakley (2003) suggested even in difficult times marketing is more important then ever.

"Why bother?" Maisner (2002) stated park and recreation organizations "striving to provide quality recreation and park facilities, programs and services without a comprehensive marketing plan, simply won't reach their full potential" (p. 7). Organizations that do formal marketing plans recognize the value and importance in doing so.

"We don't have time to plan!" No one has enough time. Spending time initially on marketing planning will save time and money afterward. Alan Lakein said, "Failing to plan is planning to fail"—and this couldn't be truer here.

"We serve (or market to) everyone." Leisure and tourism organizations must understand that every organization markets toward specific groups of people, even if their mission is to serve everyone. Even though all types of leisure and tourism organizations serve a large variety of people, no organization could afford to focus their marketing efforts in hopes to win over everyone. By investing valuable resources in the attempt to gain appeal by everyone, they fail to serve anyone. Most marketing plans focus on several targeted groups in an annual plan that warrants time, money, and energy from staff. The organization may be serving several other market segments, but choose to spend resources on only a select few.

"We have no competition." Every organization competes with another organization for consumer's discretionary time and money. In leisure settings there are two types of competition: direct and indirect. Suppose a parks and recreation department offers a youth softball/baseball program and no other area leisure service provider directly competes by offering a similar program. Although there is no direct competition, there is indirect competition, which includes organizations that appeal to a similar market segment in a similar way (e.g., an indoor hockey, basketball program). Competition may even be the movies, the arcade, or the beach. Finally, even if an organization still believes they do not have competition and demand is high, a new organization will be entering the market soon ready to compete with them. Complacency breeds disaster. Organizations need to be prepared for the emergence of a competitor at any time.

"Marketing costs money." Some marketing activities cost money. Often leisure and tourism organizations do not have large marketing budgets or a great deal of extra funding. However, marketing does not require a great deal of money. Any amount of funds or effort spent in the wrong way will fail to produce a desired result. Any leisure and tourism organization budget should be spent in the most effective way possible. If no money is available, efforts can be taken that do not cost the organization a penny. Some activities will cost an organization more money than they think they should spend. This belief often stems from a prior bad experience with a marketing activity that failed to produce a result, hesitancy based on fear of the unknown or the desire to spend money in other ways. The organization needs to ask itself the following questions:

1. What are our objectives? Do we need to do something to achieve these?

2. Are there other alternatives to reach our marketing objective?

3. Is this the most effective decision? Will it give us the greatest return?

At times, organizations must decide to take a risk but these choices will be less risky if sound planning was done prior to spending any money.

Shepler's found value in being strategic with their marketing efforts and spending resources to do so. Leisure and tourism organizations that have developed and applied formal, strategic marketing plans within their organization suggest there are several reasons to do so, including the following:

Act as a road map. They create a path for the organization to follow and shape the future of the organization. The plan identifies the organization's competitive advantages and selects the most effective route for achieving these objectives. They guide the organization to a destination (i.e., organization objective) and create new paths as change is needed. Marketing plans contribute to sustainable viability and growth for an organization. Marconi (2000) suggested a well-written plan should show how to get from one point to another.

Assist in management control and implementation. Marketing plans clarify an organization's focus. They explain who is responsible for which activities and when they are to occur. They create the action plan from which employees operate. They provide managers a tool to assign responsibilities and reward accomplishments. Ultimately, a marketing plan provides a tool/system to more effectively operate.

Inform new members of their role and the organization's focus. Marketing plans act as a training aid to communicate the organization's focus and direction. New employees understand their role in the process and are better able to contribute to the organization's outcomes. A plan instills confidence in stakeholders because they are more able to understand and appreciate the organization's plan for viability.

Help obtain resources for implementation. Marketing activities require organization resource investment. This investment may be in people, equipment/supplies, or money. A documented marketing plan allows everyone to buy into the marketing activities, in advance, and agree to expending the resources necessary to make the plan a reality. Because a plan provides rationale/evidence as to why these activities should be done, those making these types of decisions feel more informed and educated in sound decision making.

Stimulate "out of the box" thinking and the better use of resources. Formal plans allow members of the organization time to understand and digest the direction of the organization and the way in which it will get there. As a result of more feedback, the organization will approach these ideas more effectively than if one person alone decided and completed these activities. Instead of Tim spending $1,800 for the Yellow Pages advertising, others reading the marketing plan may suggest more effective ways to reach targeted groups. They may also suggest that the organization trade or barter their services for this advertisement. Documenting ideas provide others the means to understand, discuss, and commit to the more efficient way to achieve the organization's objectives. This results in more efficient use of resources. The old saying "two minds are better than one" certainly applies here.

Provide a reference to solicit when questions arise, staff changes or resources are needed. A formal, documented marketing plan provides a guide that can be accessed by any staff member at any time.

Developing a marketing plan takes time. This, of course, will vary based on the size and complexity of the leisure and tourism organization. Depending on the amount of time granted to working on the document, on average, anywhere from three weeks to four months will be needed to create a valued document. Typically, a formal plan is created prior to the annual budget to insure resources are allocated appropriately.

How the Plan Should Be Created

Wilson (2003) described an experience developing a marketing plan, which tells an interesting tale.

> The last thing I intended was to design a disaster. My boss wanted a marketing plan and I was going to do it right. With a copy of the company's objectives from the most recent memo, I closed my office door, started with a blank screen and created one of the most elaborate marketing plans you could imagine. I have no idea how many hours I invested into the marketing plan, but that binder was thick. It was just beautiful.
>
> I arranged the date for the presentation and the room was filled with all the key people. I began with confidence, but things could not have gone worse. The objectives were not in sync with recent changes, and the plan was far too complex. It didn't match available resources, people didn't feel a part of the plan, and I was the only one who felt accountable. All of my hard work was for nothing. I would never approach writing a marketing plan like this again.

Wilson further suggested most agree marketing plans are a good idea. However, many organizations have never produced a plan, and if they have, some express experiences like the one presented here. Ultimately, a plan must be created with the organization in mind. The process must be efficient and fit the organization's culture and style. The implementation must be attainable, and the plan must fit available resources.

Ideally, one person or department acts as the team leader to put the plan together. In the leisure and tourism

Real Life Story: Shepler's Mackinaw Island Ferry

Shepler's Mackinaw Island Ferry, a 225-employee, multifaceted transportation and marina facility, continuously strived to identify ways to remain competitive in a crowded marketplace. From market research findings they discovered some valuable information.

What they learned. From these findings they learned marketing research data provided them information, but the answers as to how and what they should do to improve the organization had to come from their analysis of the information. They concluded the following:

1. A large portion of their consumers made the decision to use Shepler's either before they left their home or once they arrived in Mackinaw City.

"When did you make your decision as to which ferry to take?"
SHEPLER'S CUSTOMERS

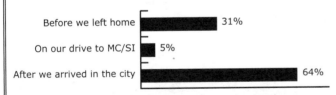

2. More of their largest competitor's consumers, however, made this decision on arrival to the city rather than prior to leaving home.

"When did you make your decision as to which ferry to take?"
COMPETITOR 1's CUSTOMERS

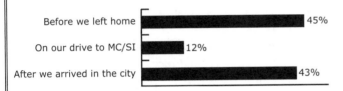

3. Compared with the two largest competitors, Shepler's consumers used the Internet to access information more often than either of the other two organization's consumers.

"Did you use the Internet to gather information on ferryboat services?"
YES

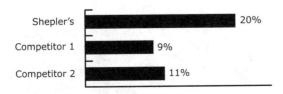

What they decided. Based on the data, they concluded they needed to capitalize on an opportunity to reach their consumers from home more often than trying to persuade them on their drive to the city. One of many tactical marketing activities they had always employed was the heavy use of billboards to communicate their message to consumers on the drive to northern Michigan. This, they decided, may no longer be in their best interest and by reducing the number of billboards, they would be able to invest more on their Internet site. They reduced their number of billboards from 67 to 52 this past year and made a significant investment in the Internet instead.

Making this change in tactics would not have been considered had it not been for market research data to provide a means for organization owners to understand the behaviors of their consumers as well as their competitor's consumers. The organization was concerned about spending the $50,000 needed to further develop their website to include options for consumers to purchase their tickets online—a plan neither competitor had implemented. This was one of their competitive advantages, however, and they went ahead.

The site was launched in June 2004 at 4:30 p.m. and by 4:39 p.m. the first purchase was made—a lighthouse cruise. Within the first month thousands of tickets had been purchased with few initial advertising and public relations activities to promote the new distribution system employed by Shepler's. Internet revenue the first season more than covered the cost of the redesign.

What they concluded. Shepler's concluded their investments in market research continue to provide a return to their organization. They believe the ability to strategically understand consumers, competitors, and their own organization in scientific ways enable their organization to remain a leader in their industry.

industry, this person may or may not have the word *marketing* in his or her title. As noted in Chapter 1, marketing is central to the organization but has two distinct roles; it is both strategically and operationally used in an organization. Some leisure and tourism organizations do not directly employ anyone in a specific market capacity. It may be a variety of employees who are responsible for these functions. Organizations that maintain a marketing staff have determined those individuals to be amenable for initiating and overseeing the two roles. However, the most successful organizations integrate marketing as part of everyone's job description. All organizations are designed differently; however, the individual responsible for the organization's strategy should be the team leader of this effort.

In the case of marketing plan development, the team leader would have the time and expertise to complete the strategic marketing activities. They would have access to all organization information. Once the plan is developed, a variety of people may have responsibility for implementing the plan.

The size of the organization will determine how many people will be involved in the creation of the plan. What is important to remember is that as many people should be involved as possible, without involving too many. Most teams consist of 4 to 15 people. At a minimum, all departments should be represented. This not only ensures each area has input into the plan but also assists in gaining buy-in for the direction of the organization, the way in which it will be achieved, and the resources needed to accomplish the activities. The involvement of others removes the mystery, hesitation, misconception, and confusion associated with the historical ways in which marketing was approached. Marketing unifies the organization. Everyone has a role and various views need to be communicated and considered.

Geehan and Sheldon (2005) suggested customers can also be involved, and doing so more successfully integrates marketing with various organization functions and aligns these actions more successfully with corporate objectives.

With all areas represented, each department claims a stake in the prosperity of the organization and how obtaining goals will occur. Dictating or mandating where the organization is heading and how it will get there deprives employees of a level of quality they need and deserve. Empowerment is necessary to create a system that ensures a sense of accomplishment or ownership. A quality leader is essential to facilitate the many functions in developing the initial plan. The leader is accountable for gathering information and presenting the findings to the team to begin discussions.

Those identified to participate in the marketing plan development provide insight into marketing plan sections. The team leader may prepare the document, but the decisions made represent the views of the group. The entire team analyzes the draft, makes suggestions, and agrees on the plan components.

Because a variety of employees are involved in the marketing process, regular meetings should be held with this team to monitor the plan's progress. Dedicated time to communicate internally regarding the operational activities and processes is critical to maintaining a central focus. Few organizations currently develop plans in this manner. Instead they presume an understanding of marketing is established with all employees. Those involved should have thorough knowledge and be trained on the concept of integrated marketing.

It is inevitable that outside issues, unforeseen circumstances, and internal changes may impact the completion

Involving more people in marketing decision making produces better results and gains employee committment.

of the exact plan; therefore, any decisions to make changes to the plan are discussed and decided by the team.

Regular meetings are important to truly integrate marketing. The marketing process today is constant—it doesn't just occur one time each year when an organization develops the plan. Leisure and tourism organizations need to learn to constantly gather and analyze information to develop a constantly shifting marketing plan that will change based on better information gathered. It will also enable the organization to more easily develop subsequent annual plans. As marketing discussions occur regularly these concepts and practices become ingrained in the organization's culture, ultimately integrating marketing so fluidly that an organization will question how they ever operated another way.

Systematic Process for Approaching Marketing

Marketing plans and guidelines come in various forms. Annual, new organization, and new offering marketing plans, as well as marketing and communication guidelines are all used in leisure marketing. Each of these plays a different role for an organization.

Annual Marketing Plan

The annual marketing plan directs organization communication activities for the year for all intended audiences. The plan includes various components all designed to address and to ensure the organization understands the past, present and future environments; the organization focus; the organization objectives; and the organization action steps.

Annual organization marketing plans are similar to plans designed for new or start-up operations. However, since there is no organization history or current organization data, a few noted changes are in this type of plan. Feasibility study information such as projections, comparisons, and forecasts are included. These types of plans are often designed to acquire funding as well as to achieve organization goals.

Marketing plans designed for new programs or services are smaller in scope. These plans are designed for organizations currently in existence that have added a new program to their current offerings. This type of plan determines whom the offering will target and how it will be communicated to the organization. This type of plan is focused on the specific objectives related to the new offering.

Often, leisure organizations have varied forms of marketing plans that represent their annual efforts. Some organizations believe they are completing annual plans but indeed are only conducting program marketing plans. In annual plans, programs and services are evaluated and may or may not be offered. The focus in annual plans is the markets of interest to serve, not a particular program. A bowling alley would develop a program-marketing plan when deciding how to communicate with adults to fill their seasonal bowling leagues. Annual marketing plans would think of the entire organization and focus on the markets that they are interested in. If a bowling alley wants to increase revenue from the adult market, then the annual plan would consist of strategies and actions that would make this occur. This may include the development of an adult league, but it may also include a singles' night and drop-in bowling. The difference is how the plan is approached. If an organization is driven by developing programs, then they will develop the program plans. If the organization issue is driven by marketing, then they will develop annual plans.

Few organizations integrate marketing as an organization plan, focusing marketing efforts toward the entire organization and not just on a program or service. Yet, this is the way in which organizations integrate marketing successfully.

New Organization Marketing Plan

This type of marketing plan is developed and implemented prior to the opening of a new organization. It may be as much as a year before the organization begins offering its products or servicess that marketing activities take place. The plan itself is directed toward opening day and is focused on accomplishing organization objectives prior to commencement of services. It can be any length of time, mainly because when an organization starts, this process varies greatly. The operational choices and objectives may vary from an annual plan due to the fact that the organization has not yet opened.

New Offering Marketing Plan

This type of marketing plan most closely resembles an annual marketing plan. It provides strategic and operational marketing viewpoints. Its length varies, but is typically shorter than an annual plan because it is based on one facet of an organization and its purpose is to introduce the new product, service, program, or facility.

This type of plan assists an organization in achieving specific product, service, facility or program objectives.

Operational marketing decisions are made and outlined based on each specific program. The program itself is often decided on in the annual plan, but specific detail can be outlined in a program/event marketing plan.

Marketing and Communication Guidelines

In a complex leisure and tourism organization, it is common to develop marketing and communication standards or guidelines that everyone in the organization must follow. Leisure and tourism organizations are faced with small marketing budgets and few dedicated staff. It is, therefore, important to train everyone on the concepts of marketing so everyone will have a responsibility, feel confident making decisions and utilize marketing tools effectively.

These guidelines are critical to establish organization expectations regarding marketing behaviors. It is common to see guidelines established for media relations, public and community relations, research, and promotions. These standards are designed by the organization and outline appropriate use of these tools in the organization in an effort to protect the brand, to create consistency, and to establish expectations of staff.

Leisure service marketing plans are unique, and no two are the same. They can only be written by those involved with the organization, whether it be internally as employees or externally by hired consultants. It may be in the leisure and tourism organization's best interest to hire outside professional marketing assistance if (a) internal skills are not apparent, (b) there are time issues, and (c) external eyes may identify inconsistencies in organization brand marketing. As Tyler (2002) suggested

> Utilizing an external advertising organization can be of great benefit to marketing efforts. When selecting an organization, keep in mind specific department goals, look for a marketing partner that has an understanding of the organization and… establish budget and decision-making guidelines. (p. 50)

Many different aspects give every marketing plan its own life. Even if the organization is identical in terms of offerings, the market, competition, and situation is never the same between two organizations. Therefore a cookie-cutter approach selecting the same plans for every similar organization will not work. What is effective is learning about other organizations' operations and building a base of ideas to tap into when the situation is right. Similar elements with a leisure and tourism organization marketing plan exist, even though the content within varies.

Elements of a Leisure and Tourism Organization Marketing Plan

For large organizations, which usually consist of multiple departments, the plan would be divided into divisions of the operation. Each division would develop their own marketing plan with the organization plan coordinating the activities of the individual departments. An example of this would be a resort. With so many divisions within the operation, an overall plan would be developed to represent the individual division plans. These individual plans may be rooms, restaurants/lounges, banquets/catering, human resources, engineering, financing, golf, and recreation. Each area has specific markets they serve and need to communicate with. Some of these may be the same as other divisions, but all should reflect the overall organization goals and objectives. In this case, each division would write their respective sections of the plan. Each division would be responsible for their plan and would submit these back to the team leader responsible for coordinating all marketing action. Once all plans were created, a final document would guide the entire organization.

Smaller leisure organizations, with a single administrative office or only a few departments, would not encounter this type of situation. They could develop a plan that includes all staff for achieving overall organization objectives. It not only suggests what should be done to achieve these objectives but also provides rationale as to why these things are being requested. It is a global assessment of an organization instead of being geared toward the outcome of specific activities, such as a grand opening, a new product or service introduction, or a program plan. The following sections describe the elements in an annual organization marketing plan.

Overall Plan Summary

This section is completed once the entire plan is written. It summarizes critical sections and provides the reader a quick snapshot of the entire marketing plan. Common elements within this summary include the following:

1. overall organization objectives (e.g., increase revenue by $100,000 by next year)

2. key research findings (e.g., 8% increase in county population is projected)

3. organization strengths, weaknesses, opportunities and threat assessment

4. specific target market objectives for the annual plan

5. action summary sheets highlighting tactical plans for achieving organization objectives

6. cost/revenue projections

Organization Assessment

The organization assessment requires a thorough review of the current situation facing the organization. A variety of issues are important to document and understand prior to being able to effectively market an organization. Often organizations assume these issues are well understood; however, it is a common mistake made by organizations to not begin their planning process with an inventory of the organization situation. Elements include the following:

1. history of the organization

2. organization philosophy (e.g., values, mission, beliefs)

3. operational structure (e.g., organizational chart) and organization stakeholders

4. offerings: a description of *all* of the facilities, programs, products and services available

5. financial status of the organization

Leisure Organization Marketing Plan Outline

- I. Table of Contents
- II. Overall Plan Summary
- III. Organization Assessment
- IV. Global, Industry, and Competitive Assessments
- V. Market Assessment
- VI. Brand Mapping
- VII. Target Marketing Objectives
- VIII. Marketing Mix Matrix
- IX. Promotional Mix Matrix
- X. Communication Mix Matrix
- XI. Leisure Experience Assessment
- XII. Communication Evaluation
- XIII. Market Research Plan
- XIV. Marketing Plan Impact and Financing Considerations
- XV. Future Thoughts

---

6. organization image: quality issues, marketing materials used and an evaluation of past marketing efforts

7. overall strategic objectives and goals of the organization (e.g., Where they are heading?)

This process allowed us to communicate the importance of and teach us how to conduct the steps critical to effective marketing… the analysis allowed us to develop action plans and materials that resulted in increased exposure and enabled us to more successfully achieve our objectives. Debra Bilbrey-Honsowetz, Canton Leisure Services

---

Global, Industry, and Competitive Assessments

This section of the marketing plan relies on skills in market research. A variety of assessments must take place to provide an organization with a thorough overview of issues that will impact an organization's success and the development of their marketing initiatives. Market research (see Chapter 5) is the tool by which this information will be gathered and used. Four categories of information are desired by organizations, including an analysis of the organization's (a) financial history and forecast, (b) competitive environment, (c) global concerns and issues (e.g., political, technological, and legal), and (d) industry-wide trends.

Market Assessment

All too often organizations believe they understand current market conditions, but when pressed for detailed information very few can confidently state an understanding of (a) who they currently serve, (b) where potential markets are, and (c) who the stakeholders are in their organization. The market assessment seeks to understand as much as possible about the current and future consumers of an organization as well as stakeholders. It formulates information about the current customers' participation patterns, needs/wants/ interests, behavior, and satisfaction—all of which are important to future planning. In addition, this type of information is important to understand characteristics of markets that may not be currently served by an organization, but are of interest. Finally, a thorough understanding of stakeholders, as well as nonusers, provides a base of knowledge from which effective marketing decisions can be made. As a result of this assessment organizations can complete a market forecast as well as identify their targeted markets. How is an organization to determine strategically the best path for an organization to take unless they understand potential demand for their offerings? Further discussion on these issues are reviewed in Chapter 6. The organization also identifies target markets' potential through the estimation of the market size.

Brand Mapping

Once an organization selects the most effective markets to focus on, the completion of the positioning process provides an organization with a reflection on information gathered in earlier sections of the marketing plan. Brand mapping assessment takes data gathered from the organization, competitive and market assessment and analyzes if the markets of interest are effective choices. It further begins to identify the issues the organization will face to truly target a market. Following the completion of this visual and analytical reflection, the organization completes the final assessment—a strengths, weaknesses, opportunities, and threats (SWOT) assessment. This reflection provides the organization with the opportunity to identify key focus areas, communication messages and strategies for securing this market. Chapter 8 highlights how this is completed. During this stage organizations also evaluate their brand identity.

Target Marketing Objectives

As further discussed in Chapters 7 and 8, once an organization finalizes that the targeted markets are indeed effective choices for the organization, clearly defined marketing objectives are established. Specific outcomes for each targeted market are written in this section which provides the organization with focused direction for all operational marketing decisions. This section simply indicates what the organization wants to happen with this target market specifically.

Marketing Mix Matrix

Once an organization determines what it wants to happen in the next year, the operational decisions of how an organization will achieve these objectives can begin. The first of these decisions relate to product, place, and price issues. Here an organization identifies if the products, programs, facilities, and services it currently provides are what it will need to achieve the marketing objective. At times, organizations indeed have the right product mix for a market and

can proceed reflecting on other potential decisions. There are other organizations that (on this reflection) discover that they need to change what they are doing by adjusting their current offerings. For example, will an organization's current operations appeal to area third-shift employees?

Based on these first decisions, an organization can then determine if the way in which they provide services is the most effective route and through the most effective sources. These place or distribution decisions are next reviewed for each targeted market.

Finally, based on new or revised product and place decisions, permanent pricing decisions can be made. Will a newly targeted senior market need a senior discount or AARP price? These types of decisions will vary by organization but should always be based on the needs/interests of the targeted market and the ability of the organization to successfully meet these needs. Chapters 9 and 10 will explain these issues.

Promotional Mix Matrix

Organizations are now ready operationally to decide how best to reach the targeted market(s) with the existing, new or revised decisions made in the marketing mix section. The promotional mix is most commonly associated with the term *marketing* because it is where promotional decisions are made. There are a variety of tools that a leisure organization can select from when determining the most appropriate way to reach the targeted markets and achieve organization objectives. Historical marketing textbooks lump all these decisions into the "promotion" category, yet, each tool is unique so it is critical to make distinctions between them. Organizations understand how a large variety of choices can be made. *Promotional decisions* in this text are defined as those that support the message being sent to "publics"—not the way in which the message is sent.

For example, an organization wishing to reach a market of daycare centers may use promotional tools to develop their brand image of the organization, identify the collateral needed to support the organization message, and determine what temporary promotional events will help reach the audience. These elements will be highlighted in Chapter 10.

Communication Mix Matrix

Once the promotional decisions are made, the organization can then use the variety of direct communication channels to reach the targeted market with the message intended for them. Chapters 11 through 14 highlight the various communication channels available to make this occur, including public and community relations, sponsorship and stewardship (i.e., quality service), advertising, direct personal selling, internal marketing, and research.

Leisure Experience Assessment

As previously described, the leisure experience is like no other "service" situation. Leisure experiences are not just a simple exchange between a consumer and an organization, but rather an experience that ultimately enhances the quality of life for those that participate. As a result, in this section of the marketing plan, it is important leisure and tourism organizations reflect on this uniqueness and identify specific ways in which the leisure experience can be enhanced for those targeted markets. Here an organization identifies how it can address the five phases of a leisure experience found in Chapter 2.

Communication Evaluation

Every leisure and tourism organization must identify how they will evaluate the entire marketing plan. More specifically, the marketing plan will suggest ways in which an organization can identify if the organizational and specific marketing objectives were achieved as well as if the operational decisions were effective ways to reach the targeted markets. Did the organization see an increase of $100,000 in revenue from last year? Did the organization increase the number of teens participants from the area by 10% over last year? Were the press release and advertisement effective ways to reach the intended audience?

All too often organizations are too busy to spend the necessary time and energy reflecting if their efforts seemed worthwhile. This is a critical step to integrating marketing successfully because it provides the foundation from which all future marketing planning efforts are based. This data allows the organization to understand what effective choices they made and which will need to be reconsidered. This topic is further outlined at the end of this chapter.

Market Research Plan

To make decisions regarding the marketing plan process and subsequent plans, research activities should be identified. This allows an organization to reflect on issues like consumer behavior and consumer satisfaction. Information and figures gathered have the potential to be the most

effective tools in making a decision about which markets to target and plan accordingly.

Marketing Plan Impact and Financing Considerations

The remaining sections of this chapter, as well as Chapter 8, examine how an organization projects the impact of marketing plan efforts and expands marketing resources. Further, issues related to identifying the cost of the marketing plan and how leisure organizations can maximize limited marketing funds are explored. These vital issues of a marketing plan need to be provided in easy-to-understand formats to gain support in leisure organizations. Few leisure service professionals have the luxury of not needing to provide this type of overview and understanding.

Future Thoughts

The final section of a marketing plan is the catch-all section that allows the author(s) a space for comments, suggestions, and/or concerns not clearly outlined in any of the previous sections. Often, when completing a document, future organization or marketing ideas, potential issues, or thoughts worth remembering are placed within this section.

Keys to Effective and Ineffective Marketing Plans

Some organizations develop vague, difficult-to-understand plans. Some plans do not commit to specific marketing objectives or outcomes. Some use language that suggests action is being taken, but do not clarify why these steps will be completed. These types of plans suggest to others that marketing is not result-oriented. It is no wonder marketing is misunderstood and people are confused when those who develop plans communicate this type of inaction. Marketing is mysterious but it doesn't have to be. Table 4.1 (p. 84) shows actual examples of this situation. After reading a marketing plan, it should be clear why an organization would pursue the identified action plans.

Some plans have no data to support activities, and some plans have too much data that is unexplained or misunderstood by readers. The plans don't commit to specific activities and are sufficiently vague enough for others not to be sure what exactly marketing people do. Table 4.2 (p. 85) highlights actual leisure organization marketing plan items.

Even though no two marketing plans will ever look identical, certain characteristics of effective and ineffective plans outside of the specific content drive the operational decisions. The keys to effective plans fall into two categories: content and format issues.

Content issues range from vague descriptions of activities to a lack of support justifying focused efforts. Effective content in marketing plans include

- target market specific operational actions

- research-based information

- specific, measurable, moderately risky objectives with a time frame for completion

- clarified historic and current organization issues

- examples of operational communication pieces (e.g., advertisement copy)

- multiple ideas about how to accomplish objectives

- direct relationship to organization's focus

- easily understood, clear writing style

- details

- identification and understanding of current and potential consumer markets

- list of and information about competitive organizations

- clear, detailed, supported operational ideas

- support for why these ideas are valid

In addition to content issues with marketing plans, formatting concerns can impact the effectiveness of the best ideas. Some plans have all the right information but are too lengthy, not well laid out, and poorly formatted. Some plans are not well-organized, and therefore information is not easily accessible. These types of plans are not often used by organizations. This document, like any communication piece, needs to address the needs of the audience and present it in a usable, readable, and understandable design. A marketing plan should reflect proper design considerations (Chapter 11). Some keys to effective formatting in marketing plans include the following:

- page number.

- table of contents

- summary page of action items, timeline, budget and key findings

- well-organized, logical flow of material

- thorough, concise writing

- sections to divide core content areas

- visual relief (e.g., use of bullets, tables, summaries, headings)

- structure

- sample communication pieces with captions to explain them

- consolidated analysis of competition for easy critiquing

- use of photographs or other visual aids to convey and support messages intended for readers

Table 4.1
Effective and Ineffective Leisure Organization Marketing Objectives

Type of Leisure Organization	Ineffective Marketing Goals/Objectives*	Effective Marketing Objectives
Campus Recreation Center	Continue to expand new categories for membership	Increase the number of family memberships from 0 to 50 by the end of 2008
Golf Course	Increase the number of groups	Garner two new corporate outings per quarter in 2008
Professional Sport Team	Reduce the "no-show" factor for tickets/seat sold	Decrease the average "no-show" factor from 35% to 20% by the end of the season
Athletic Facility	Increase member satisfaction next year	Increase member satisfaction scores for local, single members ages 18–39 from 80% to 90% by December 31.
Parks and Recreation Department	Maintain mutually beneficial relationships and participation with key publics	Maintain area senior citizen participation in center at 5,000 seniors served annually in 2004
Special Event Company	Expand customer base by 10%	Increase local market social events from 5 in 2003 to 15 in 2008

* actual examples from leisure organization plans

Funding Marketing Plans

As the economy shifts, the need for efficient use of marketing dollars is more critical than ever. The amount of a leisure and tourism organization budget dedicated to marketing varies, as does the way in which marketing is integrated into organizations.

A general guideline for establishing a marketing budget is 8% to 10% of revenue. Five percent of that is earmarked for labor (either inside or outside the organization) and the remaining money is used for implementation of the marketing plan. Therefore, a leisure and tourism organization with annual revenue of $1,000,000 would spend up to $100,000 on marketing activities, including staff and implementation funding. This is not surprising, as franchisees spend anywhere from 1% to 10% of revenue for the franchisor marketing rights in the lodging industry (Rushmore, 1995). These monies do not include their own marketing efforts as this goes to national or international advertising and promotional efforts.

Generally, those in the leisure industry have not had large marketing budgets, have been thrifty in their marketing funding, and have operated on little marketing budgets even when the economy was more fruitful. Herrick (2004) suggested that regardless of the size of venue, those in the leisure industry operate on a shoestring marketing budget.

The process of establishing the marketing budget most commonly occurs in one of two ways:

1. The organization establishes the amount, and the plan is built around that amount.

2. The marketing plan is developed and costs are identified; the organization discusses the plan and proposed budget, and negotiates the ultimate marketing allowance.

The amount provided and way in which the plan is developed will vary across organizations. The second method is a more ideal approach in integrating marketing however. Tools to maximize resources needed in this approach include the concepts of trade and barter. They are growing in popularity to enhance the amount of money or resources available to leisure and tourism organizations.

Enhancing Marketing Budgets

The leisure service industry has multiple opportunities to expand marketing budgets. These include trade, bartering firms, partnerships and measuring the impact of these past marketing efforts, then using this data to improve the effectiveness of choices.

Table 4.2
Effective and Ineffective Leisure Organization Marketing Communication Items

Type of Leisure Organization	Ineffective Communication Action Items*	Effective Communication Action Items
Campus Recreation Center	Advertise	Campus recreation coordinator will purchase four weeks (one per quarter) of 30-second radio spots on WCFX in 2008
Golf Course	Solicit companies	Golf professional will contact 30 largest employers employers in local market by April
Professional Sport Team	Give ticket holders a reason to come	Develop a list of promotional incentives (e.g., free food, fill your seats for ten games in a row and get a free team sweatshirt), secure sponsorship for each ticket to be used at each home game Mon–Thurs throughout the 2008 season
Athletic Facility	Tell single members about the "Single Services" program	Social coordinator will develop a brochure to be mailed to all existing single members highlighting the "Single Services" program by May.
Parks and Recreation Department	Conduct research	Communication specialist will conduct quarterly focus groups with senior participants regarding satisfaction with programs and services throughout the fiscal year
Special Event Company	Recruit event planners for familiarization tours and visits	Owner will host a wedding planning event in partnership with area wedding planners by March

* actual examples from leisure organization plans

No budget, no problem... You just need to be more creative. Colleen Steinman, Department of Natural Resources

Trade

Creating an exchange between two parties is the basic premise behind trade or bartering practices. Trading services for media exposure is one way in which leisure and tourism organizations can expand their marketing budgets. In this instance a fitness facility would work in cooperation with a radio station. A $600, six-month workout membership could be used as a promotional giveaway by the station, in exchange for $600 worth of media exposure on the radio advertising the fitness facility. In some industries, trade represents half of all marketing spending. More media/advertising campaigns are being funded through trade, either partially or fully, as many have found value in trade arrangements (Carlson, 2002; Carroll, 2000). However, these trade arrangements continue to be wasted. Organizations cannot risk creating trade opportunities with inappropriate or ineffective partners.

A strategic versus a tactical approach to trade relations must be taken. Identifying potential partners with similar markets of interest, similar ethical practices and complementary motives, understanding each other's goals for the trade experience, and creating boundaries for win-win relationships, will create an environment in which trade can be beneficial to everyone. Bell and Drèze (2002) suggested trust is critical in trade arrangements. Each party must not try to get the upper hand. Measuring the trade investment is also important.

Some organizations hesitate to participate in barter arrangements as they may be unsure how to do it or were negatively impacted by a previous barter attempt. Lithen (2002) further suggested organizations do not evaluate the barter deal as closely as they should. Oftentimes missed problems are associated with bartering. As a result, there are several keys to successful trade/barter agreements to keep in mind when developing and managing these relationships:

Trade partner must be a good match for what you are looking for. Is the value you receive what you need and not just any marketing exposure? Are there other things you can trade for (e.g., landscaping)—saving money in other areas of the budget that would allow for other marketing spending?

Objectives of each party should be clearly outlined. Why are they interested in trading with you? What do they hope to achieve? What do you hope to achieve? Ensure the length of the barter agreement reflects the needs of the organization. Determine if the barter arrangement is the best "deal" and if paying for media exposure nets more effective results (as time/type of exposures may be different if you paid cash versus traded the deal).

Investigate the organization with whom you are trading. Know your trade partner's reputation, ethics, trust, and likelihood of fulfilling their end of the arrangement. Will they be in business next year when the trade has expired? Will they fulfill the agreement as outlined and air ten spots during primetime?

Establish a fair market value for the trade exchange. Leisure and tourism organizations are known to underestimate the value of what is being traded. Partners must agree on the value of the exchange. Fluctuations of value exist by day of week, season, and time of day. These conditions must be clearly spelled out.

Start small and build confidence with trade experiences. By all projections this will continue to be a way to enhance marketing budgets and resources.

Trade arrangements are also used to stimulate use and enhance loyalty. A sporting goods manufacturer could provide a leisure site the opportunity to sell sporting equipment at a lower price for a slower time. This type of trade provides the retailer a product at a temporary lower cost. This gives the distributor more exposure in the sport facility as well as an opportunity for the sport facility to sell more sports products. Trade opportunities are not always available for everyone and this has been a problem for some organizations; that is, until the development of barter firms (Tyler, 1999).

Bartering Firms

The concept of bartering firms is the same as trade identified previously. An exchange occurs between two parties, but in this instance, an intermediary facilitates the exchange. Bartering firms developed as a means of managing obsolete products and excessive inventory. The growing popularity of barter firms has shown to be not only a way to get rid of excess inventory but also a way to provide services and a means to fund marketing activities (Carroll, 2000).

Barter firms provide a resource for trade opportunities by linking organizations to one another. These organizations have identified an interest in bartering, and firms host a large range of organizations and interests. An organization may sell their goods or services to one company and then spend that credit earned with someone else in the barter firm. Firms provide a directory of listings, newsletters, faxes, catalogs, and product expos (Freeman, 1998). Firms suggest most anything can be swapped as greater access to websites has expanded the reach of traditional barter firms.

An Australian study of barter arrangements indicated that most organizations work with barter firms to either rid themselves of inventory or expand their marketing budget without spending more cash. Birch and Liesch (1998) found the values for joining a barter firm include finding new customers, increased sales, and increased networking opportunities. Difficulties experienced by organizations included limited functionality of the trade dollar, limited trading opportunities and practical trading difficulties.

Organizations pay fees to belong to barter firms. Often an initiation fee, a monthly maintenance fee, and a commission for each trade is standard. The image of bartering has improved, as it has historically been known to be problematic. Today, it is viewed as a strategic way of operating (Wasserman, 2002). The use of bartering firms is still quite new, however, and organizations must approach this exchange like other trade arrangements by following the same guidelines for trade relationships identified with one addition. If using a barter firm, know where bartered goods and services are going. Identify who will specifically receive them, how will they be used, during what time frame, and so forth. An organization does not want bartered items competing with those already bought (e.g., an organization you work with buys tickets to an event through the radio station you bartered with at a lower price and in a better section of the arena). Table 4.3 provides a list of bartering firms.

Partnerships

Leisure organization partnerships continue to be a popular activity in the industry today. Pybus and Janes (2005) found the number and type of partnerships between leisure and tourism organizations expanded in the past five years, and it is projected to continue to develop in the next five years. These partnerships were for everything from shared services to programming to marketing.

In the area of marketing, partnerships are also referred to as co-op advertising, where an organization shares the

Table 4.3
Bartering Firms

Company Name # of Members	Website Phone	Location	Cost
New York Commerce Group Inc. 2,000	www.barteradvantage.com 212-534-7500	New York, NY	Initial: $400 cash/$200 trade Yearly: $200 cash/$100 trade
Alliance Barter 1,600	www.alliancebarter.com 585-244-0600	Rochester, NY	Initial: $500 cash Yearly: $150 cash
American Commerce Exchange 600	www.acxbarter.com 323-259-2340	Los Angeles, CA	Initial: 0 Yearly: $10 cash/$10 trade
ITEX 14,000	www.itex.com 425-463-4000	Bellevue, WA	Initial: Varies Yearly: $260 cash/$130 trade
International Barter Alliance 15,000	www.americantradeexchange.com 866-205-8554	Homosassa, FL	Initial: $199 cash Yearly: $120 cash/$120 trade
Barter Consultants International 1,000	www.barterconsultants.com 770-394-6364	Atlanta, GA	Initial: $395 cash Yearly: $15 cash/$15 trade
Illinois Trade Association 6,000	www.illinoistrade.com 847-588-1818	Niles, IL	Initial: $1,300 cash Yearly: $240 cash
Trade Exchange of America 6,000	www.tradefirst.com 248-544-1350	Oak Park, MI	Initial: $475 cash Yearly: $180 cash/$180 trade

Notes

- All barter companies charge a 5% to 12% commission on transactions. This is how their profit is made. Yearly fees are utilized to cover administrative/account costs.
- Cost may vary depending on two things: Whether the organization is profit or nonprofit, and how much revenue the organization generates.
- Some waive fees for nonprofits.
- Relationships can be established where profit-oriented companies can donate trade dollars to nonprofit organizations.
- The barter company being used does not have to be local/regional. It is possible to utilize national or even international trade organization services.
- Never underestimate the possibilities of what can be used as trade.

cost of a marketing activity with another leisure or non-leisure organization to expand the marketing dollar. Further, these activities may also expand community relations and/or find and promote newsworthy activities. Donations, in-kind services, and other joint ventures are also types of organization-to-organization partnerships.

The leisure industry is full of trade, barter, and partnership opportunities. This unique industry appeals to a broad range of people and industries because everyone has leisure time and interests. Unlike other industries that have a more limiting appeal to the masses, everyone embraces leisure opportunities.

The final area outlined to enhance marketing budgets relates to measuring the impact of marketing decisions made. The final section of this chapter discusses evaluating marketing plans and efforts.

Evaluating Marketing Plans and Efforts

Just as capital is spent on equipment and personnel in a business, marketing expenditures are an investment in building and contributing to the overall organization. With each of these types of decisions, organizations must estimate the return on investment. Yet, little research exists regarding current marketing evaluation practices and so it is unclear as to how many actually do this (Clark & Ambler, 2001).

Measuring the impact of marketing efforts can be difficult. Some organizations are so pleased to be done with determining and implementing marketing plans that they

Real Life Story:
Involving Others in Marketing Michigan's Little Bavaria

Frankenmuth, Michigan, is a top tourist destination, welcoming three million people annually to the community. Much of the Frankenmuth Chamber of Commerce and Convention and Visitors Bureau's marketing plan involves a unique relationship between private businesses in town, other destinations and the state tourism authority. Working cooperatively has proven to be an effective way to increase impact and reduce costs. They work with other destinations, such as Mackinaw and Holland, to put together itineraries that can be sold to group tours. The partnership with Frankenmuth, Mackinaw, and Holland is called the Triangle Tour. It gives tour operators a prepackaged option to visit all three destinations. It is convenient for the guests and effective for the destination.

An example of this type of marketing effort is an insert recently completed in the *Ohio Long Weekends* publication. It began as a brainstorm in Mackinaw and they contracted directly with the publication to have

a special, 20-page insert called "The Best of Michigan Getaways" produced. In this instance, Mackinaw invited Frankenmuth and yet another destination, Traverse City, to partner with them on this insert. Each community sold advertising space to their businesses to offset some costs. The publishing company handled the layout, design, and offered to write copy if needed. It was decided Frankenmuth would write their own copy to explain their story in their own words. It was very affordable for businesses that would have normally advertised in the magazine itself and the impact was incredible. The three destinations were able to stand out greatly in a publication that covered eight states worth of information. It was a worthwhile project and they look forward to doing more cooperative advertising and marketing in the future.

Contributed by Jamie Furbush,
Frankenmuth Convention and Visitor's Bureau

are ready to move onto the next issue or idea. Clark and Ambler (2001) suggested

> At the dawn of a new century, the measurement of marketing performance has never been more important for firms. Driven by the desire for sales growth, increasing customer orientation, the need for long-term performance measurement and demands for better accountability, increasing attention has been focused on the relationship between marketing activities and business performance. (p. 232)

Reflecting on the impact of marketing decisions is critical. Measuring activities not only provides information to improve but also shows how marketing contributed to organization goals and objectives and what value marketing efforts had on the organization overall.

The failure to measure marketing efforts has impacted the attitude of leisure and tourism organizations toward marketing and has contributed to the idea that marketing only costs money. It is our own fault that marketing is not readily accepted. One way to change this view is to ensure every effort is evaluated based on the effectiveness of the choice, the impact to the marketing objective, and the contribution to the organization objectives. George (2003), a marketing director, stated to "measure everything, then measure it again" (p. 14).

Why Measure Marketing Efforts?

Marketing efforts often go unmeasured by leisure and tourism organizations. For various reasons, organizations may not value evaluation or may not write clear, measurable marketing objectives and therefore have no basis from which to measure. Evaluation can be difficult to do as well. These efforts take time, energy, and resources—often limited commodities for organizations. However, failure to measure marketing efforts results in organizations potentially making repeated poor choices of ways to spend their marketing resources. Reda (1998) reported a retail pioneer once stated that half of his stores advertising was ineffective, he just wasn't sure which half. The following suggests the values for organizations taking the time to measure marketing efforts:

1. Ensure money, time, and resources are spent in the most effective ways.

2. Determine the most effective operational decisions.

3. Provide an understanding of deficiencies and identifies ways to improve.

4. Identify if efforts impacted the organization overall.

Metzger (2002) suggested the following scenario:

> Club A and Club B; both clubs are identical: same demographics; similar cities; same marketing strategy; each has 500 students and $250,000 revenue; each intends to spend 3% per year on marketing; and (at the moment) each is using the same tactical marketing.
>
> Now, visualize this dissimilarity: one year ago, Club A began to diligently record and track how each and every one of its prospects and clients learned about it. From this data, Club A learned to its great surprise that it had been spending 80% of its marketing dollars on a marketing tactic that was generating only 20% of its prospects. Armed with this information, Club A shifted its marketing dollars to align proportionately to the number of prospects each tactic was generating. In other words, it allowed the results to determine the flow of its marketing dollars.
>
> The results over time: assuming Club A's new marketing tactics proved to be 50% more effective in generating prospects (plausible); and assuming a 30% yearly attrition rate at both clubs, how many years it would take for Club A to double Club B's enrollment? The rule of 72 tells us in five years, Club A will be twice the size of Club B. Imagine, doubling your competition at no cost—only the simple discipline of asking every caller, visitor, or registrant how they first learned about the club. (p. 8)

There are several methods for evaluating marketing efforts. Three basic areas need to be measured:

1. Did marketing contribute to the organization's overall objectives? Did marketing efforts support the goal of increased revenue, increased community support, or an expanding number of publics served?

2. Were the marketing objectives achieved? Did the organization increase the number of senior citizens served from 1,500 last year to 2,000 this year?

3. Operationally, did each specific communication channel used and marketing decision made provide a return on investment? What exactly allowed the organization to achieve marketing and organization objectives (or what failed)?

Measurements can occur in a variety of ways. Not all efforts will see immediate results—Finding ways to measure long-term impact is also an important step. The most common approach is understanding if there was a return on investment (ROI). This is measured by identifying the response rate or revenue earned less cost factors. Cost factors can include labor (i.e., salaries/benefits), production, and fulfillment or actual cost of the activity (e.g., cost to run a full-page retail advertisement in the Sunday edition of the *New York Times* ranges from $50,000 to $140,000 depending on the type of business placing the ad).

Financial indicators of marketing's effects are valued (e.g., revenue data) and that this data was more often compared to marketing plan projections than historical data. Yet, consumer measurements were compared to historical data (Clark & Ambler, 2001). Financial measures alone indicate past performance versus current or future contributions of these marketing investments. Many support multilevel evaluation practices to measure performance more comprehensively and determine the efficiency and effectiveness of marketing decisions (Clark & Ambler, 2001). Some methods used to evaluate marketing efforts include

- Count the number of coupons returned.

- Track 1-800 numbers with advertising methods used (one number per method; e.g., billboards, newspaper advertisements, Internet/e-mail).

- Count the number of people in attendance at a promotional event.

- Count the number of media exposures gained through pitched stories, press release development, and media relationships.

- Compare satisfaction scores over a specific time frame.

- Ask people how they heard about the organization or event?

- Track the number of complaints and compare data from the past.

- Identify the number of new consumers.

- Maintain employee and consumer retention/loyalty figures.

What is more difficult is identifying what impact these activities had on revenue or other organization objectives. Was the increase in revenue directly related to marketing efforts, or was the warm, dry summer day the reason this year's 4th of July picnic was a greater success? How many of the number of calls received actually consumed an experience with the organization? Did media coverage have any impact on sales or participation? Did people in attendance consume, purchase, or contribute on a long-term basis? Did an increase in "awareness" impact any organization objectives?

Of course some values of marketing are not easily measurable. Marketing also impacts an organization by word-of-mouth advertising. How many others did consumers or employees tell about their experience with an organization? How did the organization improve product or service offerings? Were there system improvements? Did integrating marketing efforts enhance communication within the organization and between various stakeholders? These ways in which marketing can positively contribute to an organization are not as easily measured, but steps must be taken to evaluate as much as possible.

There are a variety of ways in which organizations evaluate the impact of marketing, including the following:

Quantitative

- Historical (i.e., preactivity) and current data comparisons (e.g., revenue, profit, market share, number of activities, number of participants/volunteers, employee turnover percentages, mix of business activity).

- Presurvey and postsurvey of consumers and employees to understand satisfaction levels.

- Script all encounters with "How did you hear about us/this event?" Record and analyze data.

- Compare predata and postdata from tracking usage via computer/registration systems. Frequent visitor cards, membership applications and loyalty programs support access to evaluation data.

Qualitative

- Observe attitudes of consumers and employees before and after activity.

- Use written comments on satisfaction surveys, and testimonial letters from employees, consumers or volunteers.

Once all communication channels are established in the marketing plan, one of the final steps is identifying how to measure objectives. Failure to identify the system to use in advance indicates a lack of commitment to evaluate efforts and impact. It should be clearly outlined and defined as to how specific and general activities are to be measured. Table 4.4 provides sample ways in which this could occur.

Doyle (2003) suggested marketing measurements should ideally include (a) monitoring effectiveness of marketing activities, (b) monitoring efficiency of the marketing team, and (c) monitoring the impact of marketing activities on brand development.

Regardless of the tools used to measure the impact marketing has on the organization and which marketing decisions were most effective, there are a few reminders to consider when developing the system for measurement.

1. It is critical that objectives be measurable, data be collected and analyzed, and historical records kept.

2. Communicate all data and results within the organization Ethical practices are critical—just don't share the "good" data.

3. Show how these results are being used to improve effectiveness of marketing efforts.

Only after an organization develops a well-thought-out and written marketing plan should implementation be completed. Spending the time, energy, and effort needed before implementing any operational marketing decision will pay off tenfold. Marketing strategy and operational plans are vary in approach and execution even though they are fully integrated. Both aspects are critical to successful leisure service marketing, yet each requires use of different skills and abilities. An organization should not presume everyone has both sets of skills. An organization with a good strategy but little ability to identify and implement an operational communication plan will be ineffective. Conversely, an organization with the ability to develop and implement operational ideas will be ineffective if these ideas are not based on a good strategy.

The development of a marketing plan ensures a leisure and tourism organization is approaching both sides of the large marketing process as thoroughly as possible, that more effective decisions will result, and that more inclusive integration will occur.

Table 4.4
Evaluation Methods for Measuring the Impact of Communication Tactics

Communication Tactic Mix	Evaluation Method(s)
All Tactics	"How did you hear about us?" script used with incoming telephone calls, program evaluations, member applications, and consumer surveys (e.g., quality service/satisfaction surveys, research, needs assessments)
Promotional Collateral	Track the distribution of materials (e.g., coupons), ask consumers to "show the logo pin for a 20% discount"
Public Relations	Subscribe to print media solicited and listen to oral media solicited to identify if organization is mentioned; search Internet for organization being mentioned; purchase a "clipping service" to search media for your name mentioned or hire staff to do this for the organization.
Community Relations	Survey participants at community presentations, meetings, etc.
Advertising Newspaper Magazine Telephone Book Direct Mail Billboards Television Radio Internet	Use a promotional code (e.g., a specific number [P618] or a specific name ["tell them Dana sent you"] for a 10% off discount), offer a coupon or special toll-free number; use a separate number, name, code, or coupon with each advertising tactic for the same "promotion" to track effectiveness of individual advertising methods Track Internet users (e.g., hits), develop e-commerce onsite so people can can purchase online, promotional code, or special 800 number
Direct Sales	Log number of calls and maintain contact to identify those that paid off and those that did not
Sponsorships	Survey sponsors/partners regarding the impact of the relationship to the organization
Internal Marketing	Survey employees, observe employee behaviors, mystery shop employees to see who/what they recommend
Quality Service/Stewardship	Develop and track loyalty programs (e.g., frequent consumer cards), survey consumers and employees on satisfaction

Real Life Story:
Mount Pleasant Convention and Visitors Bureau Evaluates Marketing

The Mount Pleasant Convention and Visitors Bureau sought to evaluate their investment in marketing efforts. As a destination marketing organization (DMO) they had a fiduciary obligation to the board and supporter that invested in their service to indicate how successful they had been. Therefore, each year staff measured efforts overall. One challenge over the past couple of years, not unique to other DMOs, was a reduction in funds available as hotel room nights (where their funding is based) were down since September 11th), therefore, less marketing communication could be done. DMO's had to identify priorities and streamline efforts. If they had not measured specific plan actions it would have made this task even harder.

This CVB did measure several outcomes from their activities and in 2004 they learned the following:

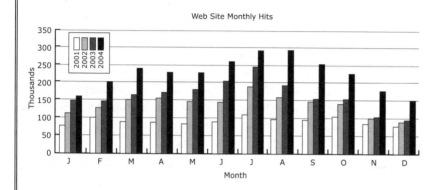

1. Their website secured more hits in 2004 than any year or month prior.

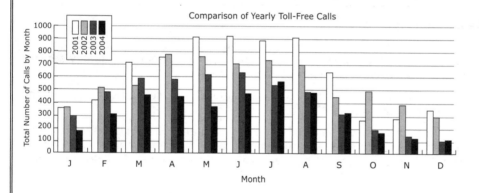

2. The number of telephone inquiries overall dropped steadily since 2001.

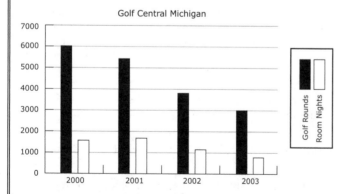

3. The number of golf rounds and room nights booked continued to drop since 2001.

As a result, this data suggested efforts directed toward investing more in website and communication promoting the website address had paid off. It also suggested that a challenge existed with reducing marketing efforts to the golf program as even though additional golf courses had been added to the state no other indicator (e.g., overall rounds of golf in other similar communities) could be blamed for this reduction.

Source: Mount Pleasant Convention and Visitor Bureau Annual Report. (2004)

Apply What You Know

1. Read an existing leisure and tourism organization marketing plan. Assess both the positive and negative aspects.

2. Use existing marketing plans to develop an outline of a marketing plan for a leisure service organization of your choice.

3. Complete the step-by-step process for writing a marketing plan for a leisure and tourism organization of your choice.

Key Terms

Assessment	Marketing plan
Bartering/trade	Partnerships
Brand mapping	Promotional mix
Communication mix	Return on investments
Marketing budgets	Target market objectives
Marketing mix	

Review Questions

1. Who should be involved in the development and incorporation of a successful marketing plan?

2. Why is it important to measure marketing efforts?

3. What are the different types of marketing plans?

4. Why don't most organizations complete a marketing plan?

5. What is one way an organization could trade to expand their marketing budget?

6. What is the definition of a marketing plan? Why is it important to leisure organizations?

Internet Resources

Bplans.com provides resources in order to help agencies to develop their business plans and strategies. A large collection of business plans and marketing plans samples are available on this website. A link to marketing plans software is included.

http://www.bplans.com/

Morebusiness.com is a website with a large collection of business related resources for entrepreneurs. Suggestions for developing business and marketing plans are included and useful samples of different plans developed by agencies are described.

http://www.morebusiness.com/templates_worksheets/bplans/

Action Plan Marketing is a business that provides marketing services for independent professionals in order to help them become better marketers. On their website marketing related tools, articles and suggestions are provided.

http://www.actionplan.com/

WebSiteMarketingPlan.com includes resources for developing and implementing marketing plans. Examples of marketing plans and marketing plan articles are part of the website.

http://www.websitemarketingplan.com/

Howstuffworks.com provides an article about How Marketing Plans Work written by Lee Ann Obringer. This article describes how an agency has to know the market, know its strengths and weaknesses and identify opportunities on the market to plan marketing decisions.

http://money.howstuffworks.com/marketing-plan.htm

The *SBA's Office of Women's Business Ownership* is a resource center for women entrepreneurs to address their need for business training and technical assistance. The link to marketing resources includes information about a wide variety of marketing, public relations and advertising topics.

http://www.onlinewbc.gov/docs/market/index.html

The *U.S. Small Business Administration* website includes valuable information about designing and implementing marketing plans. It includes a short description of the advantages and disadvantages of a marketing plan.

http://www.sba.gov/gopher/Business-Development/Business-Initiatives-Education-Training/Marketing-Plan/

Thewritemarket.com describes how to write a marketing plan and includes issues related to market research, target market, product and pricing strategies, as well as a link to related resources.

http://www.thewritemarket.com/marketing-plan.shtml

References

Bell, D. R. and Drèze, X. (2002). Changing the channel: A better way to do trade promotions. *MIT Sloan Management Review, 43*(2), 42–49.

Birch, D. and Liesch P. W. (1998). Moneyless business exchange: Practitioners' attitudes to business-to-business barter in Australia. *Industrial Marketing Management, 27*(4), 329–340.

Bright, A. (2000). The role of social marketing in leisure and recreation management. *Journal of Leisure Research, 32*(1), 12–17.

Carlson, J. (2002). Why trade dollars are wasted. *Brandweek, 43*(43), 18, 29.

Carroll, M. (2000, January). The benefits of barter. *Folio: The Magazine for Magazine Management, 1,* 141.

Clark, B. H. and Ambler, T. (2001). Marketing performance measurement: Evolution of research & practice. *International Journal of Business Performance Management, 3*(2/3/4), 231–244.

Coakley, D. (2003). More bang for your buck. *Agri Marketing, 41*(6), 32–34.

Doyle, S. (2003). Software review: Measuring the overall effectiveness of marketing (Part 1). *Journal of Database Marketing, 10*(3), 273–278.

Forrester, S. and Rubin A. (1998). A marketing panacea: Connecting to the four-year client. *National Intramural Recreation Sports Association Journal, 22*(3), 11–17.

Freeman, L. (1998). Getting direct results: Agencies drawing customers with measured marketing. *Advertising Agency's Business Marketing, 83*(10), 1–2.

Geehan, S. and Sheldon, S. (2005, November/December). Connecting to customers. *Marketing Management, 14*(6), 36–42.

George, G. (2003). Writing a marketing plan for tourism. Retrieved August 14, 2003, from http://www.tourismcenter.msu.edu

Herrick, J. (2004). Doing more with less: Stretching your marketing dollars in small facilities and small markets. *Facility Manager, 20*(1), 25–30.

Janes, P. (2003). [20 organization interviews]. Unpublished raw data.

Lithen, R. (2002). Pragmatic ideas for considering barter. *Brandweek, 43*(44), 20.

Maisner, J.M. (2002, Spring). On target. *Michigan Parks and Recreation,* 7–8.

Marconi, J. (2000, March 27). Total recall: How to build the value of a brand. *Adweek, 41*(13), 38–56.

Metzger, J. (2002). Are you tracking your tactical marketing? *Technique, 22*(1), 8.

Mount Pleasant Convention and Visitor Bureau Annual Report. (2004). Mount Pleasant, MI: Author.

Nordin, C. (2003). *The relationship between campus recreational funding models and marketing efforts.* Unpublished masters research report, Central Michigan University.

Pybus, D. and Janes, P. (2005, Spring). Recreation programming partnerships: What MRPA member organizations are doing. *Michigan Parks and Recreation,* 20–26.

Reda, S. (1998). Measuring marketing's ROI: Sophisticated new tools help retailers evaluate the payoff from advertising and marketing. *Stores, 80*(5), 22–26.

Rushmore, S. (1995). What a franchise costs over the long run. *Lodging Hospitality, 51*(6), 25.

Sevier, R. A. (2000). Preventing marketing efforts that bomb. *Trusteeship, 8*(6), 28–32.

Top five marketing mistakes companies make… and how to recover! (2005). Retrieved from http://www.gotomarketstrategies.com/tip_topfivemarketingmistakes.htm

Toy, D., Rager, R., and Guadagnolo, F. (1989). Strategic marketing for recreational facilities: A hybrid conjoint analysis approach. *Journal of Leisure Research, 21*(4), 276–296.

Tyler, G. (1999). Swap shop. *Supply Management, 4*(4), 38–39.

Tyler, E. (2002). NACMA corner: Effectively selecting and utilizing an external marketing organization. *Athletics Administration, 37*(3), 50.

Wasserman, T. (2002). The sultans of swap. *Brandweek, 43*(9), 30–34.

Wilson, D. (2003). Making marketing plans work. Retrieved October 10, 2003, from http://www.mplans.com/qam/article.cfm/4620

Chapter 5

Understanding, Developing, and Applying Market Research

Katharine, a camp director, presented camper satisfaction results to Camp Weedamoo's Board of Directors when the camp season ended. She indicated their efforts to improve had paid off and scores had improved from last year. Her presentation included the information shown in Tables 5.1 and 5.2 (p. 96).

The Board was pleased with her progress and gave all full-time employees a $100 bonus for their efforts. What Katharine did not indicate to the Board was important information that may have led the Board to another conclusion.

Katharine did not share that the results of the Year 1 data represented 525 camper responses from all camp

sessions held that year. Year 2 data included only 58 camper responses from the first week of camp, when the weather and staff were at their finest.

• • • • •

Statistics can be misleading. As in the camp example, Katharine presented data of something that was not entirely true. Some people misinterpret data and others misuse data. Marketing relies on this input and leisure professionals are consumers of data and information. It is important to understand the process by which data is gathered and disseminated. Data is a valuable source for effective marketing and it must be gathered professionally, ethically, and accurately.

The power of assessing, evaluating, understanding, and utilizing information in today's leisure environment is the catalyst for discovering the real value of organizations and establishing a competitive advantage. Wilson (2003) stated market research will benefit every organization: "If it does not provide new information, it will confirm what is known."

Data is critical to effective marketing. Organizations develop strategies, review progress, determine practices, and measure efforts with data gathered by or for the organization. Technology has enabled research and data to be instantly available and more easily accessible. There is so much information it can sometimes be overwhelming to

At the end of this chapter, readers will be able to...

- Define market research.

- Explain the value of research to effective marketing practices.

- Understand the problems with conducting and consuming research data.

- List various types of research tools and techniques.

- State the process for conducting primary research.

- Demonstrate how research is used throughout the marketing process.

- Demonstrate an understanding of measurement techniques for assessing quality (e.g., culture, IPA, ServQual).

leisure and tourism organizations. Clancy and Krieg (2002) suggested, "marketing today should be as much of a science as art, but we have a long way to go to make it a reality" (p. 42). Marketing research is the heart of the marketing effort. It is embedded throughout the marketing process as every marketing activity involves some type of market research. It is more accessible than ever before and, as a result, can more easily be used and misused.

Research relies on factual evidence to support marketing efforts. Using your "gut feeling" is not a proven method for decision making, and more times than not has shown to be a poor choice for leisure organizations. Uncovering information and facts about the organization, the environment, and its markets are vital to shaping the marketing process. From uncovering target markets to evaluating communication efforts (e.g., the use of billboards), research is a tool that will provide information that may confirm or contradict beliefs by those in the organization.

Although this chapter is not designed to make you a research expert, it is designed to introduce and to explain the research process as well as to make you a good consumer of research. Specifically, it will show how research can be (a) valuable to effective marketing practices, (b) accessed by leisure organizations, (c) conducted, and (d) misused or misunderstood because there are concerns with research that can be problematic for marketing efforts.

Many organizations understand the concept of marketing research but fail to utilize these tools to their advantage. Loomis (2000) suggested the absence of gathering

visitor's data in outdoor recreation has several significant consequences for organizations: "Recreation fares poorly in budget allocations for management, replacement of facilities, expansion of facilities, acquisition of lands for recreation and allocation of natural resources such as water flows" (p. 93). Stanton (2000) suggested, "Marketers should seek to make decisions with as much empirical data as possible and not look for excuses to avoid it" (p. 38). Organizations are often too busy and rushed to allow themselves the time needed to access, analyze, and integrate market research data. Some organizations may not be sure how to access data or may not understand why it may be valuable to their respective organization. Further, sometimes leisure organizations simply "don't know what they don't know." They don't understand market research or don't think they need it.

Masberg (1999) studied convention and visitors bureaus (CVB) use of market research as they represent the primary tourism marketing organization for communities. She found CVBs with average budgets of $10 million spent a range of $5,000 to $49,000 on market research activities. For the person primarily responsible for research, 10% or less time is spent on these activities which are largely managed in-house. Even though research was seen as "important and essential," CVBs generally did not provide enough resources to doing it completely and overall felt it was a low priority. Respondents further stated several reasons existed that kept them from conducting more research, including the following:

1. lack of research direction

2. standardization of research protocols, analysis, and reporting

3. lack of research training by those conducting the research internally

4. lack of confidence in the results therefore fear of comparison to past and future efforts

Marketing research is a valued, important tool used to improve an organization's bottom line and make well-informed marketing decisions. It is essential in every type of business because it is the eyes and ears that provide

Table 5.1
Comparison of Camper Satisfaction Scores

	Satisfaction Scores	
Camper Evaluation	Year 1 Mean	Year 2 Mean
Programs		
Challenging	4.0	4.1
Fun	4.2	4.3
Well-organized	3.8	4.1
Overall	3.9	4.0
Housing		
Safe	3.7	3.8
Comfortable	4.0	4.0
Accessible	3.8	3.9
Overall	3.8	3.9
Counselors		
Friendly	4.0	4.2
Organized	4.2	4.2
Fun	4.2	4.2
Overall	4.1	4.2

Higher scores indicate greater satisfaction
1 = Strongly Disagree, 5 = Strongly Agree

Table 5.2
Overall Camper Satisfaction

Camp Experience	Year 1	Year 2
Percent who would return to camp	68%	75%
Percent who indicated camp was a "great experience"	57%	62%

information to make informed decisions. It provides invaluable insight into consumers, and consumers define an organization's success (Deal, 1999). Market research provides information to develop a strategy based on data. This type of approach is considered *outside-inside marketing*—an organization relies on data gathered from consumers and other publics to develop the strategic marketing plan (Carroll & Carroll, 2001).

Market research is used in a variety of ways to benefit organizations. Marketing research has three characteristics within leisure and tourism organizations. First, it must be descriptive and gather facts. Second, it must be diagnostic and explain behaviors. Third, it must be predictive and use both descriptive and diagnostic data to assist in marketing decision making (Sutton, Irwin & Gladden, 1998). Such research may not identify the increased interest in indoor climbing walls, but it did identify that leisure consumers were interested in new, flexible, safe ways to participate in outdoor adventure activities.

~~~~~~~~~~~~~~~~~~~~~~~~~~~~~~~~~~~~~

Marketing research is so important to our organization. We need to find out what our customers want, need and desire as well as evaluate how we are doing. By knowing these things, we can improve as an organization and provide for everyone. Chris Shepler, Shepler's Mackinaw Island Ferry

~~~~~~~~~~~~~~~~~~~~~~~~~~~~~~~~~~~~~

Market Research

Market research is a systematic, objective process for generating information that will be used in decision making. It is the identification or creation of all possible data or information available to an organization, the assessment of this data, and the summary or interpretation of the data to be used for effective decision making. Without it, organizations would be left to intuition. With it, organizations indicate they make better decisions. Solomon (2002) suggested, "There are certainly bigger users of research than I have been over the course of my career. This has been a mistake, however. A little more research probably would have helped me to avoid a few mistakes" (p. 92).

Mahajan and Wind (1999) suggested market research today needs to do the following:

1. Provide an ongoing process for the diagnosis of organization, consumer, and "public" needs, opinions, or problems where treatments are tested until the best one is identified.

2. Integrate information technology to analyze the tremendous amount of information and data in a quick and efficient manner.

3. Apply both qualitative and quantitative research throughout the decision process, integrate marketing research continuously, and make it available throughout the organization. Include all forms of data gathering as a function of the marketing area.

4. Take a central role in shaping the organization's strategy.

Real Life Story: The Power of Data in a Private Club

A small, private country club needed assistance to increase the number of memberships and overall revenue at the club. In an effort to help them, first they needed to be asked about organization specifics to better understand their operation and needs. These first questions were about the number and type of memberships they currently had, the demographic characteristics of the members, current and historical financial reports, the pattern of golf play (e.g., number of rounds, days and times of tee time reservations), and historical information regarding memberships and golf play.

The club manager looked a bit shocked at the request and indicated that they had 230 memberships, but were unsure how that was broken down regarding types of memberships, the number of family members on the memberships and member gender, age, or other demographic characteristics. It was further determined by the golf professional that the tee time book (it was not computerized) had been thrown away at the end of the last season. Although the club manager and golf pro could answer these questions based on "gut feeling," their beliefs could not be confirmed.

They did not understand how this data could identify

1. need areas and potential markets for memberships

2. background of those currently served and potential for others "like" them

3. issues with patterns of play and potential opportunities for increasing revenue opportunities

Data, in this instance, could be used to develop the marketing plan, to sell the plan to board members, and to more effectively reach the goals of additional members and increased revenue.

As a professional in the leisure service industry, it is important one understands what market research is, where it can be located, how accurate or valuable the data is, and how it can be used to enhance marketing decision making.

The term *market research* creates an image in people's mind that involves computers, scientists, and reams of paper. Although the process does involve all three, it does not have to be difficult or time-consuming to be valuable. *Data mining* is the term coined in the marketing industry to represent the process that integrates a variety of data and information gathering techniques to identify and explain patterns and relationships in data that can be used to make projections about consumer behavior (Fitzpatrick, 2001). With data mining, organizations integrate research throughout the marketing process. James (2002) suggested market researchers must not only analyze data but also understand how this data impacts the organization's strategy and what the organization-wide issues are. Further, those involved with market research must share not only data but also make recommendations regarding the impact of this information on the organization overall.

We measure everything. If you don't measure it, you can't manage it. Kelley Davidson, Wintergreen Resort

How Market Research Is Used

Every facet of a leisure and tourism organization can benefit from the use of market research. Market research is used throughout the marketing effort: prior to marketing decision making, during marketing decision making, and after marketing decision making. It is used as a tool to uncover, analyze, and determine the future direction of leisure organizations.

Market research is used throughout the marketing process; hence it is the heart of the marketing effort. The following does not presume to be inclusive of all possible research ideas or efforts; a great number of opportunities to use data exists.

Market Research Prior to Marketing Decision Making

A *focus group* is often used to test out new ideas, such as whether a service will be used or purchased at a suggested price by a target market. *Secondary data* provides answers to questions relating to size, characteristics, needs and interests of target markets. A *survey* can be used to segment consumers into identifiable categories of like interests, behaviors, or demographic characteristics. A survey can

also be used to evaluate a current position or view held by participants by asking how they feel about the organization and how it compares to the competition. *Historical data* comparisons can be made from previous years to identify impact of efforts and opportunities for future initiatives.

Market Research During Marketing Decision Making

Telesurveys are used to support direct-mail efforts and increase response rates when targeted markets are contacted prior to receiving a direct-mail piece. For example, people with expired memberships may be contacted prior to mailing a membership renewal notice to discuss questions related to their membership. The organization learns specific information that can suggest how to reach/communicate with the members through the direct-mail piece. Those who have implemented this technique have experienced an increase in the effectiveness of their direct-mail efforts (Lowenstein, 1999). *Observation* can answer the question: What do the organization's consumers look and act like? *Focus groups* compare alternative communication strategies or plans to improve the implementation of a marketing plan. A *survey* can determine the view held by consumers on the value for price paid for the leisure experience.

Organizations conduct research, develop strategies, implement tactics, then do more research to see how they've done. Ray Artigue, The Phoenix Suns

Market Research After Marketing Decision Making

Secondary data can be used to evaluate how effective the marketing plan was at achieving objectives through analysis of sales, revenue, attendance, and profit data. A *survey* asks consumers how they found out about the organization to determine which marketing mix items were most valuable. Data can be used for recognizing accomplishments (or suggesting plans for improvement), planning similar or different choices in the future, and sharing it with other vested parties such as sponsors. With the *critical incident technique* respondents tell the story of the experience they received, and the organization can identify the important components of the service experience for consumers.

Market research is not a tool only available to large organizations. Small leisure organizations can benefit from and produce market research to become more effective organizations. Myers (n.d.) suggested, even in a small regional archery business, market research is just as valuable in his small organization as a large national organization. He stated, "His weapon of market knowledge is limited in power only by how diligently he builds his information base" (p. 22). Unlike other leisure industries, the archery business has little national data to select from, but a small business can gather regional market data themselves. Further, sources like U.S. Census, some archery companies, like Easton's, and other governmental sources tend to focus on frequent archery consumers. Although valuable data, this limits the type of information available to extensive users. McPherson (2002) supported research for small organizations like fitness firms as well because they too can benefit from what larger organizations have accessed for years. He found the International Health, Racquet and Sportsclub Association (IHRSA) provides general data on the fitness industry and specific information can be gathered locally by small organizations through surveys, focus groups or simple response cards consumers drop off after a workout.

At times, however, organizations are unsure what information could be helpful to their decision making. The old adage that sometimes "You don't know what you don't know" applies in marketing research. The following is a checklist of ideas where organizations have used primary market research to uncover information:

- What do you know about your consumers?
  – gender   – age
  – family status   – geographic residence
  – workplace   – income (if necessary)
  – individual/group status
  – consumption patterns
  – needs, wants and interests
  – benefits sought from an organization experience
  – satisfaction with the experience

- What attracts your consumers to the organization?

- How often they use competing organizations and why?

- How they heard about the organization?

- What do you know about potential target markets?

- What do you know about nonusers?

- What do you know about employees?

- What do you know about board members or owners?

- What do you know about volunteers?

- What do you know about suppliers?

- What do you know about your competition?

- What do you know about the industry?

- What do you know about the market?

- What do you know about your organization?

- What do you know about nonindustry events and trends?

Organizations conduct market research to understand consumers and forecast consumer trends (Bissell, 2000). Even though some organizations have not yet realized the value of it, Swaddling (2001) suggested there is no better information than that gathered direct from the marketplace. This process, however, is not limited to a research department but rather the entire organization. Research should be as much a cultural issue within an organization as an organizational one. "Keeping close to consumers is not relegated to the marketing department… it's fundamental to the way everybody thinks… from the top down" (Bissell, 2000, p. 14). McPherson (2002) interviewed a fitness center general manager who found a way to make gathering feedback a regular part of everyday business. Research must be conducted on a regular basis to understand changing consumer values and is the first step to exceeding guest expectations (Passikoff, 2002).

Research drives marketing decisions, as well as sells concepts/ideas to supervisors. Scott McKnight, Binder Park Zoo

Value of Market Research

Higgins (1999) suggested a recent increased interest in market research occurred for a variety of reasons, including the increased customer focus, greater demands for resource productivity, and increased competition. Organizations are finding greater value in utilizing market research as they search for each competitive advantage their organization holds. The variety of reasons why organizations should employ the use of marketing research include

- to improve marketing effectiveness

- to understand needs, wants, and interests of many "publics"

- to satisfy "publics" better

- to increase confidence in decision making

- to provide evidence to support initiatives (i.e., sells ideas to others)

The Association of Volleyball Professionals (AVP) used market research to better understand who their audience was. They conducted a study and learned it was not the young, hip, and disposable-income poor who watched them, but rather the "older, more settled (i.e., had families), [who] had more money than expected" (Solomon, 2002, p. 92). The integration of marketing research helped them to redefine their marketing strategies and better use their marketing dollars.

Key data about consumers that Sargeant (1997) found to be valuable include demographic data, lifestyle data (e.g., hobbies, interests, media exposure, competitive participation), behavioral data (e.g., likelihood of participating in this leisure experience), and attitudinal data (e.g., opinions about the leisure organization, their leisure participation, what influenced these behaviors). He used market research to help a charity better understand who their target markets should be.

Stanton (2000) stated that organizations (marketers) should seek to make decisions

with as much empirical data as possible and not look for excuses to avoid it. They should continually try to update their techniques and approaches… they should challenge themselves to find ways to incorporate real data into the way they make decisions. (p. 38)

Types of Market Research

Marketing research falls into two basic categories—primary and secondary research. *Primary market research* is data gathered by the organization for the intent of learning specific information. Often this type of data is based on a problem or area of need within the organization where the organization recognizes that if the data existed, their ability to make an effective decision would be greatly enhanced. The organization conducts this research or hires someone to conduct it for them based on their specific questions or issues. An organization's consumer and employee satisfaction data is an example of primary research because it is developed by the organization for the specific intent

Real Life Story: Data Improves Effectiveness at Spring Hill Camp

Spring Hill Camp, one of the largest summer youth camps in the nation which attracts over 10,000 campers each summer, spent an additional $150,000 in 2004 on an advertising campaign. The decision was based on poor registration numbers derived from historical comparisons on year-to-date enrollment figures. The data indicated enrollment was down by 2,500 campers from the same time last year, and they were worried about the impact this would have on their upcoming summer season. They began plans to develop strategies for communicating with past participants to try to capture more returning campers. Their satisfaction evaluations were excellent from the year prior so they did not understand why or how this could be occurring.

With the initial data they began to plan, then further analyzed the data to understand who was making the camper reservations. They soon learned their returning camper numbers were significantly higher than last year's numbers and it was not the returning market that was down, rather, they were down in new market exposure. The data, once thoroughly analyzed, revealed they would have spent money in areas that would have produced little return for the camp because the issue was not the returning campers. Therefore, they needed to develop strategies for reaching new markets instead.

The initial plan to reach these markets included television, radio and billboard campaigns geared toward their target markets in strategic geographic

locations. The camp director was startled at the $150,000 price tag to implement this campaign and initially thought they would need to compromise. However, in analyzing the plan and evaluating the potential impact of securing over 3,000 new campers, the cost to implement averaged only $50 per camper. Once analyzing the investment in these terms, they agreed it was worth identifying new campers and decided to spend the money strategically to find, communicate with, and secure this market for the upcoming season.

This organization could have spent marketing money in ways that would not have significantly benefited them (e.g., targeting returning campers) had they not analyzed their market research data. This has shown how the thorough analysis of marketing research data can assist in more effective decision making.

of understanding consumer and employee perceptions and experiences.

Secondary market research is information gathered by others and used by the organization to aid in decision making. In essence, it is someone else's primary market research data, that when used by others besides those conducting the initial research, becomes secondary. There are two basic forms of secondary research including internal and standardized market research. *Internal market research* is data gathered by the organization as part of their regular day-to-day operation. This may include guests registering at the membership desk of an athletic club, checking into a campground, completing a registration form for a basketball league/clinic, or reserving a tee-time at a golf course. It may also range from accounting figures

compared over time to head counts at an event. Every organization gathers data on a day-to-day basis but often does not recognize that they are gathering "data" beneficial to marketing efforts.

Standardized market research is data gathered by an outside organization or individual that is accessible to anyone who can find it. It is public information that is usable by all; however, the challenge is knowing that this type of data is available and identifying where and/or how to access it. Table 5.3 highlights various types of secondary and primary research as outlined by Kotler, Roberto, and Lee (2002).

There are advantages and disadvantages to using both types of research. Martin (1995) suggested no one method of research be used to make marketing decisions. A combination of experience, accounting data, consumer and

Table 5.3
Research Characterized by Source and Technique

Source	Technique	Description/Examples
SECONDARY	Analysis of existing data and statistics	Local, state, national, and international data in publications (e.g., Census Bureau) and reports on health and environmental indicators
	Literature search and review	Relevant articles in journals, periodicals, newspapers, and books
	Review of prior surveys and public	Custom surveys conducted by others in the past and syndicated studies (e.g., Gallup Poll)
	Databases and information systems	Commercial and online services (e.g., A.C. Nelson, Gallup, Arbitron, Medline) as well as internal databases
PRIMARY — *Qualitative in nature*	Personal interviews	Primarily face-to-face or telephone, sometimes referred to as "expert" or "key informant" interviews
	Focus groups	Moderator facilitates a focused discussion with 8–10 participants, typically for about two hours
	Casual observation	Data are gathered by observing relevant audiences in real situations (e.g., trying on life vests)
	Group meetings	Discussions with internal and external groups to identify issues, explore strategies, and build support
Quantitative in nature	Telephone surveys	Data are often gathered by research firms, most commonly using computer-assisted telephone interviewing
	Mail surveys	Often used when surveys are lengthy, detailed, require visual components, or need to be anonymous
	Intercept interviews	Respondents are approached for survey in locations such as malls, agency, or business facilities or at relevant sites (e.g., walking trails for physical activity surveys)
	Theater/Exposure testing	Respondents observe ads or other campaign components in a theater-like settings in which they "turn dials" to register responses, complete written surveys, or participate in follow-up interviews and discussions
	Controlled observation	Observation research is conducted on a large-scale basis using controlled procedures (e.g., recording use of bike helmets)
	Control group experiments	Program elements are implemented with one market, and key indicators are compared with similar markets without the exposure
	Internal records and tracking mechanisms	Using existing records to profile and measure relevant issues and monitor efforts (e.g., composition of litter on freeways)
	Knowledge, attitudes, practices, behavior (KAPB) study	Quantitative surveys of the target population to access levels of awareness/knowledge, attitudes, and behaviors related to the program focus
	Online surveys	Collecting data through electronic surveys

employee insight, and secondary research found via the library/Internet provides a well-rounded approach to data and information management. Often, organizations find it useful to access secondary information and then develop primary research for questions that are unanswered or cannot be accessed by secondary sources. Both types of research are beneficial in their own way and are highlighted in Table 5.4.

Secondary Research Sources

Secondary research comes from a variety of sources, including the organization, government, public record, or private data that is publicly shared or available.

Organization or *internal secondary data* is typically available to only those inside of the organization. This data is gathered on a regular basis and may or may not be used for marketing decision making. For example, a community center may have demographic information on the application for membership, but never analyze this data to understand the total number of members, ages, interests (e.g., How do they design programs for their seniors without this information?). Another example would be an entertainment venue that reserves seats but has never analyzed patterns of business (e.g., What shows have lower attendance than others and how can revenue be improved?). And an outdoor education center that conducts a program evaluation at the end of every interpretive class but has never analyzed the data (e.g., How could they learn from this to improve programming?).

Governmental sources are vast and seemingly endless providers of information. Government data is available for anyone who can find it. For example, the U.S. Census data provides general and specific demographic information about people in various geographic areas. This data is

valuable to leisure and tourism organizations because it provides an opportunity to understand the service area from which consumers are gathered. Governmental organizations also conduct specific research relating to a variety of topics. As an example, the U.S. General Accounting Office has completed research on gaming impacts. This may not be the first place one would look for gaming research, but it is available if one knows how to access it.

Other governmental sources include economic development offices (e.g., information on the number and size of businesses within a geographic area could provide insight for leisure organizations interested in this target market); city, county, and state organizations (e.g., youth crime statistics for the past five years in specific geographic areas could provide insight for public park and recreation professionals about the need for additional teen programming efforts); and federal organizations.

Public record sources for data are those organizations not affiliated with the government but provide access to research/data which can be useful to leisure and tourism organizations. Professional associations provide industry specific assistance and valuable data for decision making. Leisure associations such as the National Recreation and Park Association, International Association of Amusement Parks and Attractions, American Hotel and Motel Association, International Assembly Managers Association, Club Manager's Association, and the American Camping Association provide insight into industry specific research.

Other sources of information include chambers of commerce, convention and visitor bureaus and other nonprofit organizations (e.g., community foundations providing data on youth). Often these types of sources include a fee to access the information but may provide abstracts or executive summaries free of charge.

Publically shared private research data represents another source of secondary information for leisure organi-

---

Table 5.4
Advantages and Disadvantages of Types of Market Research

	Advantages	Disadvantages
Primary Market Research	• Applicable and usable for the organization (i.e., it addresses their particular issues and concerns) • Accurate and reliable (because the organization conducted the research) • Up-to-date	• Expensive • Not immediately available • Not as readily accessible (but moreso than ever)
Secondary Market Research	• Inexpensive • Easily accessible (you just need to know where/how) • Immediately available	• May be outdated • Potentially unreliable • May not be applicable to organization issue/question

zations. This data is gathered and funded by private sources (e.g., individuals, companies), yet shared with the public through professional journals, magazines, newspapers and other media sources. Not all privately generated data is accessible to the public, however. Only information individuals and organizations are willing to share is accessible. This data is often located utilizing search engines from library databases and Internet resources.

In each of these secondary sources, the greatest challenge to leisure organizations is finding and accessing the information. A wealth of information is available to leisure professionals but searching for useful information can be time consuming and exhausting. Secondary sources of information provided in Appendix A.

Challenges With Market Research

There has never been more information available to leisure service professionals as there is today. However, the over-whelming amount of information has provided evidence of conflicting reports, and professionals are more challenged than ever in understanding what all this means (Roggeveen, 2001). It is critical that research is free of error and bias. Anyone can make statistics work for or against them; however, ethical research provides the factual evidence and does not bias the findings. As leisure organizations rely on research it is important that potential problems in research be shared, making leisure professionals more aware of possible shortcomings. Then, professionals may take research for what it is worth.

When reading research conducted by others, careful consideration should be given to the methods used to conduct research. *Bad data is worse than no data.* Table 5.5 identifies potential bias and error that can result when others conduct research studies. These types of errors can be minimized through more effective questioning and research methods, including follow-up interviews to verify responses and pilot testing to ensure understanding.

Many problems and issues surround research, which makes utilizing it somewhat problematic. Data can be misused or misinterpreted—both of which result in utilizing

Table 5.5
Potential Bias and Error in Research

Sampling error	Associated with random sampling and likelihood that the sample and population mean are different.
Sampling bias	When sample fails to represent the population it was intended to.
Measurement error	A difference between information sought and information provided by the research/ measurement process.
Nonresponse error	Variation between the sample selected and the one that actually participated Respondents are either those who feel very positive or negative about the topic and are the ones motivated to respond.
Memory error	Respondents do not accurately recall events when asked about them from the past.
Ignorance	Either the question is unrealistic, or it is addressed to respondents who are not the people who can answer.
Misunderstanding	Respondents interpret the question in a way that it was not intended. Words may have dual or unclear meanings or questions may be worded in a vague way.
Dissimulation error	Exists when respondents lie about their responses so they do not appear ignorant or not intelligent.
Problem definition	Research concept may not accurately define the real problem or situation.
Surrogate information error	The information sought by the researcher is different than the information needed to solve the problem/answer the question.
Population specification error	The population required to gain the needed information and the one identified by the researcher is different.
Selection error	The sample selected was not obtained by a nonprobability sampling method.
Analysis errors	Potential improper use of statistical processes, data entry, calculation, interpretation, and missing or invalid information mistakes.

Sources: Semon, 2000; Stynes, personal communication, November 1997

information that is not accurate. This can lead to ineffective decision making. It is important that when using any data a clear explanation of the procedures used to gather the data is given. A "think tank" of 30 marketing hospitality and travel professionals indicated that a great deal of industry research is conducted with no systematic process and "companies that have a vested interest in the results" collect other data (Dev & Olsen, 2000, p. 44). Furthermore, consumer information needs to continue to be provided including who consumers are, why they buy, what they buy, and what motivates them to buy.

Trained market researchers can be valued assets to any organization. They provide expert advice and provide

insight into any potential irregularities that may exist in research. As a result the reliability and validity of the research is sound (Deal, 1999). They are not inexpensive, however. Researchers ensure data is reliable and valid and they will not cut corners at the expense of incorrect data (McPherson, 2002).

Primary Market Research

Primary market research is data discovered by the organization themselves. This data is gathered for the specific purpose of understanding issues that the organization believes to be important to future decision making. Learning about this information is viewed as so valuable that the organization is willing to invest time, money, and resources into answering the research question(s).

There are three basic forms of primary research:

- *Explanatory* research provides information on a new topic. The research is aimed to discover emerging issues/topics versus get good answers to problems (often qualitative).

- *Descriptive* research answers who, what, where, when and how much. It aims to describe a population and is the most often type of research conducted in the leisure industry (often quantitative).

- *Exploratory* research is where variations are explained and answers to the question "why" are obtained (often qualitative).

Several methodologies can be used to conduct primary market research. Determining which one to use is based on several issues including the budget and resources available for completing the research, timeliness of the research process, when information is needed and, most importantly, the information that is desired.

Prior to beginning the research process several considerations must be reviewed:

1. *Timeliness.* Can the research be done in a timely manner that will be available for decision making? What amount of time is needed from respondents to gain access to important information?

2. *Cost-effectiveness.* Can the research be done in a way so the benefits outweigh the costs?

3. *Usefulness.* If these questions are asked will the information be useful to decision making?

Once the methodology is selected, further considerations must include:

Real Life Story:
Misleading Market Research

A leisure organization located in a popular tourism destination welcomes over one million visitors a year. This organization hired an advertising firm to conduct a market research study to understand general views of their organization in comparison to the competition as well as reasons for using each of the organizations. The advertising organization conducted face-to-face interviews with randomly selected consumers in a downtown tourist area. The organization's report concluded:

There was little awareness of this business by local visitors, as 33% knew of the organization and 75% had never used this organization before, they were using the competition. The report stated that there was greater awareness of the competitors than this business and that strategies needed to be developed to increase this organization's awareness. Additionally, respondents who used competitors did so because of packages provided, discount coupons, and products available. It was also suggested the organization investigate these types of offerings and promotions.

If you were this organization, what type of organization decisions would you have made based on these data and findings?

In the fine print on the last page on the document, however, was the following discovery: "The data is based on 16 interviews conducted..." These statistics were based on few opinions yet it was suggested the organization should make changes immediately to develop more packages, offer discounts, and alter services. These researchers suggested this organization do similar activities as the competitors based on very few opinions. Based on the information provided, this organization could have made significant changes that were not representative of the large number of visitors using this organization and its competitors.

4. *Accuracy.* Will the information be accurate?

5. *Reliability.* Will the information be reliable?

Quantitative research tends to be a popular method to uncover information in the leisure industry and still represents the vast majority of the research conducted. Quantitative research answers questions that relate to understanding what, where, how much and who. It is "effective when studying large groups or samples and making generalizations about relationships among variables to a broader group or population" (Redmann, Stitt-Gohdes & Lambrecht, 2000, p. 135). Research done in this area seeks "explorations and predictions." The most popular type of quantitative research is the survey questionnaire. Quantitative research provides data on hypothesized versus actual experiences where participants are often asked to reflect back on their experiences. Common examples of quantitative research methods include survey, experiment, action and program evaluation. Common collection techniques include questionnaires, interviews, importance performance analysis, and ServQual instruments and tests. Some of these will be discussed in more detail later in this chapter.

This is not the only choice for gathering data. *Qualitative research* is gaining in popularity in the leisure industry. Qualitative research provides illustrative data and provides an in-depth understanding of opinions, attitudes, perceptions, and behaviors. It is "effective at examining in-depth understandings about a given phenomenon by a particular group of individuals at the expense of generalizability" (Redmann, Stitt-Gohdes & Lambrecht, 2000, p. 135). Research done in this area is naturalistic. Data collection is most often through participant observation and in-depth interviewing. This research method answers the question "Why?". Examples of qualitative research include historical, naturalistic, ethnography, and case study. Common examples of data collection techniques include interviews and focus groups, critical incident technique, observation (e.g., mystery shopping), and the Delphi technique.

Some of the more popular data collection methods used in the leisure industry include the following:

- *Focus groups* of consumers or nonusers gathered together to understand why they do or do not participate in the organization's offerings.

- *Mystery shopping* observation data where researchers provide a detailed explanation of their experiences as consumers in leisure service organizations.

- *Critical incident techniques* where consumers are asked to describe their experiences in detail

and researchers identify the specific issues that impacted the service experience.

Walsh (2000) suggested qualitative research can be valuable in the hospitality industry where understanding key information and relationships can be critical. This type of information can be helpful to support quantitative data as well as provide insight that is not expressed in this method. Onwuegbuzie (2000) suggested researchers that limit themselves to one form of research (quantitative or qualitative) are limiting the advancement of social science. Research through the use of both methods allows for researchers to select from the most appropriate tool to understand research questions and issues. Multiple advantages for valuing both forms of research include greater flexibility in investigation techniques, greater ability in understanding macro and micro issues, and use of one method to verify findings in the other method.

A blending of both quantitative and qualitative research methods is viewed as more favorable than either one alone (Redmann, Stitt-Gohdes & Lambrecht, 2000). Seaton (1997) found combining each method was valuable in a visitor survey at a festival. The investigator learned that the quantitative survey yielded a 99% overall satisfaction rating. Observational insights, however, uncovered information not measurable in quantitative methods. It further clarified conflicting survey responses. Table 5.6 (p. 106) provides an exhibit developed by Seaton to explain the various values of each method used in a study for aspects of a festival.

Sutton, Irwin, and Gladden (1998) used qualitative research methods to supplement quantitative survey research previously done. They gained insight into the motivations and emotions of respondents through video interviews that allowed participants to explain why they responded to specific survey questions in a particular way. They were able to observe nonverbal behaviors as well as listen to verbal responses to questions. Observation is another qualitative method employed to understand consumer behavior.

Regardless of the type of primary research selected, the same process exists for completing the research. Five steps are taken to conduct primary research:

1. problem identification (research objectives)

2. research design

3. data collection methods

4. analysis of data

5. interpretation and report

Step 1: Problem Identification (Research Objectives)

The base of all primary market research stems from the development of research objectives. Even though quantitative research tends to be hypothesis-based and qualitative research tends to be objective-based, each method uncovers information regarding a question that will provide data to address organization issues. These objectives state the specific purpose of the research and what is to be learned. One way to approach the development of research objectives is to consider the following:

At the end of the research project, I will learn about...

1. employee work life satisfaction
2. employee work needs and interests
3. employee demographic characteristics

At the end of the research project, I will learn about...

1. nonconsumer leisure interests
2. nonconsumer purchasing behaviors
3. competition strengths and weaknesses
4. nonconsumer demographic characteristics

At the end of the research project, I will learn about...

1. consumer importance and satisfaction with organization
2. consumer frequency and participation patterns
3. consumer loyalty behaviors
4. consumer demographic characteristics

The development of the objectives leads the researcher to write the inquiries based on the research methodology selected. Quantitative or qualitative research methods can be selected depending on the intent of the objectives outlined. Some objectives are more obviously quantitative as they answer questions that relate to what, where, how much, and who. Other objectives more closely relate to qualitative research because there is an interest in understanding why.

Step 2: Research Design

Qualitative Research

Some suggest qualitative research is so broad it is difficult to define. The methods used in this type of research are somewhat endless as the goal/role of this type of research is to collect unique data about a situation that is more

Table 5.6
Various Values of Each Method for Aspects of the Festival (Seaton, 1997)

Evaluative Dimensions	Questionnaire Survey Utility	Unobtrusive Observation Utility
Audience profiles	*Excellent.* Provided data on sociodemographics (i.e., place of residence, age, gender, occupational status and social grading), traveling distance, traveling time, and party size and composition.	*Modest but useful.* Provided some triangulated data on social grading, age, and gender to the main survey; provided additional descriptors of audience (stakeholders); facilitated accurate attendance counts.
Motivations	*Modest.* Limited to a few multiple-choice questions (i.e., "What is the main purpose of your visit to 'this area'?" and "What in particular attracted you to come to this event?").	*Modest but useful.* Extended insight into motivations excluded from questionnaire (e.g., motive of attendance at some events was parents wanting to occupy children who were on school vacation).
Satisfactions	*Poor/Modest.* Difficulty/impossibility of achieving responses during or at the end of many performances.	*Good.* Allowed judgments of reactions/satisfactions during all performances and some at end; provided triangulated data on some satisfaction responses to survey schedule.
Explanations of behavior	*Poor.* Limited to inferences drawn from behavioral responses inventoried in survey multiple-choice questions.	*Modest but useful.* Suggested reasons for liking or disliking some events excluded from the questionnaire survey.
Organization of event and scheduling issues	*Modest.* Limited to a few questions on pre-selected aspects (e.g., catering, parking facilities).	*Very good.* Facilitated judgments on unanticipated aspects; provided triangulated data on some responses to the survey schedule (e.g., on catering).
Performer reactions	*None.* No performer measures were included in survey (although this could have been monitored by a separate survey).	*Modest but useful.* Indicated some performer satisfactions and intentions to perform again at the festival.

real world and "rich" in detail (Jary & Jary, 1991, as cited in Cousins, 2002).

Qualitative techniques provide insight to a number of respondents' views, but are not as representative of the population as quantitative research can be. It utilizes a diverse set of approaches to complete the research. Qualitative research is not as popular as it should be in the leisure industry due to the perceived difficulty of conducting the research, greater researcher dependence, and no set of "rules" to follow. In addition, organizations are unsure of how to use the data. One fear of this research method is people use the data and fail to acknowledge the views are from a select small group of people and not necessarily the views of all consumers or enough that are representative of the consumer population. It does, however, provide valuable insight into consumer issues and has grown in popularity over the past fifteen years in the leisure industry. For example, the number of qualitative research dissertations more than doubled from 1990 to 2000 (Sevier, 2002).

Qualitative research seeks to understand the meaning and to explore and discover unknown information. The methods used provide an openness to the data gathering and an insider perspective not gained through quantitative methods. It is flexible and can help gain understanding of phenomena.

As suggested by Cousins (2002), the methods used in qualitative research are diverse and include the following:

- interviewing
- observation
- case studies
- personal experience
- introspection
- life story work
- historical, interactional, and visual texts
- psychoanalysis
- survey research
- cultural studies
- clinical research
- biographies
- ethnographies
- first-person accounts
- photographs

Cousins suggested these methods will continue to have ongoing debate, and the field of qualitative research is still plagued by questions of legitimacy. McWilliam (2000) suggested four criteria for reflecting on the quality of a qualitative data report: the information about (a) where the investigators are coming from, (b) what they did, (c) how they arrived at their findings, and (d) what the study means. Henderson (1991) provided a list of advantages and disadvantages of selected qualitative methods. Table 5.7 (p. 108) highlights this summary.

Qualitative Methods

In-depth Interviews

Individual one-on-one interviews are conducted when a researcher does not want any influence by others in a group setting. These are designed to solicit in-depth understanding of a topic(s).

Observational Research

A researcher studies a respondent engaging in an activity in a natural environment as it actually happens. This type of research is effective for understanding behaviors. A more recent term used to describe this research is *ethnographic*. It refers to cultural research done in "real-life environments and situations" (Daniels, 1999, p. 15). Although newer to the qualitative research field, this type of research is growing in popularity in market research environments as a valuable tool to understanding consumer behaviors.

Perceptual Mapping

Respondents determine where one organization is positioned against another. Instead of the organization answering this question, some use the technique with consumers and non-consumers to identify where organizations are positioned in terms of various criteria.

Focus Groups

A familiar, yet often misused, research method is the focus group (Stanton, 2000). A group of 8 to 15 people within a targeted audience (e.g., nonusers, female users, children between ages 12 and 16) are asked a series of questions by a trained mediator designed to understand an issue(s) of importance to the organization. Questions are developed from a set of research objectives. Multiple focus groups may need to be conducted depending on the information desired. Subjective information is gathered from respondents on their attitudes, feelings, reactions, beliefs, impressions and opinions. It is a flexible, two-way communication process between a mediator and the group of respondents. Groups larger than 15 can prohibit group discussion, therefore it is important to maintain an appropriate size group.

Focus group research has been primarily used in the private leisure industry until the last several years when other leisure organizationsdiscovered its value (Flood, 2002). Flood suggested focus groups provide insight in various leisure settings, such as wilderness settings. He stated focus groups compliment quantitative research by better understanding why visitors perceptions are the way they are regarding wilderness experiences.

A quality mediator is the "single most important determinant of the usefulness of focus groups" (Nelems, 2001, p. 1). It is particularly helpful for exploring specific topics.

Broad or sensitive topics are not well-suited for this type of research (Pearce, 1998). Often an outside mediator or facilitator is used to manage and guide this discussion. An individual trained in conducting focus groups will provide the necessary skills to gain the insight desired. A professional facilitator will first establish the format for discussion by explaining the purpose of the discussion. Then the facilitator will state there is no right and wrong answer because this is about the respondent's opinions. Facilitators establish ground rules so everyone has the opportunity to participate. Finally, they will reguide dominant participants, keep things positive, follow up on ideas generated by the group, and probe further to understand issues that quantitative data could not provide.

Facilitators of a focus group are skilled in several areas. They must understand (a) the purpose of the group meeting; (b) key topics/points that will be covered; (c) the topic; (d) the importance of listening, and that silence is an effective tool to solicit responses from the group; (e) they should not defend organizations, educate respondents in the process, or pretend to know it all; (f) their role is to gain information from respondents, and instead of answering questions they should turn it around to respondents to answer; and (g) flexibility is needed and they must be able to adapt questioning to flow with group responses, ultimately insuring all areas are covered by the end of the session (Nelems, 2001, p. 2). Facilitators must be able to adjust their questioning based on the way a group is proceeding.

Table 5.7
Henderson's Qualitative Methods (Henderson, 1991)

Method	Advantages	Disadvantages
Participant observation	• Face-to-face encounter in natural setting • Large amounts of data obtained • High interaction with respondents • Access to follow-up clarification • Wide range of data possible • Many possibilities for informants • Discovery of many possible relationships and interconnections • Data on nonverbal behavior and communication • Data on unconscious thoughts and behaviors • Useful in triangulation • Possibilities for validity checks • Allows for emerging designs and data • Provides contextual background	• Missed data • Misinterpretation possible • Relies on cooperation of subjects • Ethical dilemmas • Success depends on researcher • Difficult to replicate • Possible observer effects on observees • Discomfort in observer • Bias by researcher possible
In-depth interviews	• Face-to-face encounter • Facilitates cooperation in research • Access for probing and follow-up • Discovery of possible interconnections • Useful for validity checks, triangulation • Flexibility in formulation of hypotheses • Provides contextual background	• Misinterpretation possible • Requires training • Requires respondent cooperation • Difficult to replicate • Subject to researcher effects • Discomfort to researcher • Depends on interviewee honesty • Highly dependent on researchers abilities • Obtrusive and reactive
Unobtrusive measures	• Data easy to analyze • Wide range of types of data • Easy and efficient to administer • Easily quantifiable • Natural setting • Good for nonverbal behavior • Measuring devices may exist • Provides for flexibility	• Possible misinterpretations • Ethical dilemmas • May require expensive equipment • Depends on initial research question • Dependent on researcher's ability
Content analysis/ hermeneutics	• Data easy to categorize • Can use large amounts of data • Can be flexible with data • Wide range of types of data • Easy and efficient to use • Easy to generalize • Good for documenting major events • Validity checks can be done • Flexibility in hypotheses • Can get at subjective side	• Possible misinterpretation • Depends on initial research question • Minimal interaction with participants

Critical segments of focus groups include the following:

1. *Appropriate group member respondents*: Sampling techniques discussed earlier in this chapter can be employed to ensure the group is representative of the population from which an organization wishes to learn.

2. The *moderator* or *facilitator*

3. The *script* or *guide* from which a facilitator operates must include all questions of importance to the organization as well as any support material needed (e.g., photographs, brochures, samples).

4. *Analysis of the data/findings*: It is important that organizations not focus on one or two comments made by respondents but rather a summary of the data gathered. Both the words stated and nonverbal queues from respondents are important. Responses can also be analyzed based on the way group members responded to a participant's comments or what was not said but the organization thought would be discussed

Participants of a focus group are often encouraged to attend a session to share their information. Incentives range from free food/beverages to cash for attending. Often a session lasts no more than one hour and the information should be taped (with participant permission) for later analysis. The interaction that occurs between participants can be valuable because the ideas discussed might not arise from individual interviews (Yovovich, 1991).

Interpretation of focus group data is more difficult— The researcher's role is to hear *all* the information, not just what he or she wants to hear. This method, however, provides a unique way to understand specific information regarding consumer needs and motivations. The data gathered from a focus group is for projections and not quantitative—it cannot be quoted with percentages; it cannot be projectable as representative of all consumers' views (Yovovich, 1991). Some utilize focus groups to assist in developing a quantitative study to follow up with.

Knap and Propst (2001) used focus groups in parks and recreation settings and found them to be an "effective stand-alone procedure for conducting recreation needs assessments" (p. 62).

Sessions are held in a proper facility often with audio or video recording capability as well as one-way observation mirrors for observers to see the reactions of respondents. Examples of focus groups are shown in Table 5.8.

Three benefits of focus groups include the following:

1. Provide an opportunity to learn in-depth answers to questions.

2. Provide ideas to use in communicating messages to consumers because groups can simply talk, and organizations can learn valuable insights that often result in suggestions for better ways to share organization information.

3. Provide a two-way communication tool that solicits the support of those in the focus group.

New focus group techniques include online/Internet-based groups where respondents chat electronically with a remote facilitator. The facilitator types in questions and respondents type their answers where everyone can read each others' comments. Although this method is less expensive, nonverbal information is missing and there are limitations with real-time delays in type responses versus innate verbal responses. Webcasting and teleconferencing are other technologically driven tools used to conduct focus groups. This type of environment more closely resembles a typical focus group setting; however, participants are not limited to a geographic area (Nelems, 2001, p. 3).

Weber and Morgan (1998) found a way to evaluate and improve the effectiveness of direct mail through market research practices. They used a unique focus group technique to measure not the end result (e.g., how many people responded to the direct mail piece), but the components that went into the decision to respond. They developed a qualitative and quantitative method to identify how people respond to mail.

Table 5.8
Focus Group Examples

Type of Organization	Type of Focus Group Research
Country Club	Nonmembers to understand perception of club
University	Each priority audience (e.g., community leaders, corporate leaders, alumni, media, current students) hold a focus group to identify factors that impacted football attendance.
Human Service Organization	Employees identified complaints, challenges, and solutions to issues that stemmed from downsizing the organization

Once participants were selected, each received three envelopes to catalog their mail for ten days. During that time, the researchers mailed their test direct-mail piece as well. Participants were to place each piece of mail received over those ten days into one of three envelopes:

- mail that would have been thrown away without opening it

- mail that would have been opened, then thrown away

- mail that would have been opened, acted on, or kept to act on at a later date

Once the ten days passed, participants returned and met with a facilitator to discuss which items where placed in which envelope and why. As a result, researchers learned one direct-mail envelope was misleading— many never opened the envelope assuming it was a charitable donation request. In an effort to quantify these responses, a similar approach was taken on a larger scale.

Real Life Story: Athletic Club Uses Focus Groups

A member-driven athletic club uses focus groups to better understand member needs and nonmember issues with the club. Over the course of four evenings focus groups were conducted with 9 to 14 participants in each group. One group of nonmembers shared their responses to issues, including the nonmembers

1. perceptions of the club
2. interest in and barriers to membership
3. package desired to consider membership
4. improvements and long-term planning issues within club

Findings suggested nonmembers perceived the club to have outdated equipment in good condition/clean, good food/beverage services, a good location, possible financial difficulties because the parking lot was not often full and poor marketing materials did not represent the club in the most effective way. Costs to join for the services provided were barriers to membership. Nonmembers indicated several areas that would encourage them to consider a membership including hours, services (e.g., daycare/babysitting), updating equipment and offering flexible cost plans. Specific detail accounted for 12 pages of dialogue/ideas.

Three groups of members shared their responses to issues, including the following:

1. issues within the club as they related to their needs
2. club satisfaction with all areas
3. package desired that would include facilities and services that would meet member needs
4. improvements and long-term planning issues within club

Findings suggested participants averaged nine years of club membership. Overall, member comments suggested general satisfaction with club operations. However, service issues and concerns, updating and renovations of physical plant, and equipment were common themes that emerged as issues relating to their needs. Specific details regarding member issues and ideas were shared in over 20 pages of data. Members had interest in feeling comfortable and welcomed at the club at all times.

Overall, the final report was over 50 pages long. The club used this data to prioritize marketing/organization actions. They also followed up with a quantitative survey of all members regarding the concerns expressed by those in the focus group. This data proved critical for discovering specific, detailed information regarding the club.

A representative number of participants were sent the envelopes and researchers made telephone contact with them following the ten-day period to identify where the organization's direct-mail piece was placed. This research provided insight into "the actual percentage of their target market that opens the mail piece, the percentage that reads it and the percentage that plans to accept the offer." This method may generate quantifiable insight; however, it would be difficult to understand why participants behaved the way they did.

Even though many state the value of the focus group as a powerful research tool that can provide unique, valuable insight, it cannot be misused (Pearce, 1998). Some caution should be taken when using focus groups. Stanton (2000) stressed the significance of misusing this type of research. He fears organizations use the information suggested by the facilitator as the conclusion versus reading or listening to what respondents said. Another misuse is how organizations use the information gathered like quantitative data and try to put numbers to the results.

Young and Ross (2000) suggested research in the leisure industry is largely survey based, which can be costly, labor intensive, time intensive, and prone to data entry errors. They believe online research methods would address these limitations and should be considered as an alternative method for generating data for leisure and tourism organizations. They indicate though basic methods of online data collection has existed, this "method will not replace the traditional paper survey method" (p. 38). It can be an alternative with distinct advantages. They sited two leisure industry studies that used electronic research methods and found participants were favorable about the method over the traditional paper-and-pencil system.

Dillman (2000) suggested electronic methods "may have a more profound impact on research" (p. 352) than random sampling in the 1940s and telephone interviewing in the 1970s. Examples of electronic methods include disk by mail, where responses are placed on a disk and mailed back to the researcher; e-mail survey, where a questionnaire is attached or included in the message itself; and Web queries.

Young and Ross (2000) suggested several keys to developing online queries:

- Provide those responding with a password to gain exclusive access to the survey.

- E-mail respondents a message reminding them that their input is important.

- Create a questionnaire with those who have little or no computer skills in mind.

- Use an appropriate style of font.

These tools address many limitations of traditional research methods, such as data entry (e.g., these formats can be directly downloaded into analysis software), time constraints and poor environmental impact. However, some challenges also exist, including technological skill to respond; difficulty with Internet access, speed, or logging on to site; and problems navigating instruments.

Online focus group research does have unique challenges that traditional methods do not. Greenbaum (2000) suggested some organizations not substitute online focus groups for traditional methods based on the following differences:

1. Moderators have less presence and authority behind a screen.

2. Interaction between participants is different and limited with online application.

3. Nonverbal cues are nonexistent and moderators miss this communication from participants.

4. Lack of proof the participant is actually the person desired for the focus group; for example, organizations that want information from seniors have no proof a participant isn't 13 years old.

5. Organizations find data more convincing and real when viewed. Observations noted through reading, videotaping, or seen through a one-way mirror offer valuable insight.

6. Utilizing images or stimuli in the focus group is not impossible online, but it is more difficult.

Mystery Shopping

A popular qualitative research tool in the leisure industry, *mystery shopping*, is where trained observers (i.e., mystery shoppers) act as organization consumers to observe organization operations and service levels provided to other consumers and themselves. It assists with evaluating employee performance, monitoring the process and outcomes of service delivery, and benchmarking competitors' abilities (Janes & Rood, 2006). These observers then provide detailed feedback to organizations regarding their observations and at times make recommendations regarding service practices using a satisfaction rubric created by owners'/ managers' expectations of performance. This feedback can be in the form of narratives as well as quantitative rating scales. Wilson (1998a, 1998b) stated mystery shopping is a program implemented by focusing on whether or not the everyday service standards and procedures set by management are being met by employees in their absence.

Organizations report the information in a mystery shopping analysis provides keen insight into issues within the

Real Life Story: Mystery Shopping Tourist Attractions

Students enrolled in a leisure and tourism quality service course were required to evaluate the service practices of various leisure service providers through a mystery shopping research assessment. Through this experience, students observed and experienced the "service" as a consumer in an assigned establishment. They first indentified what they expected from the experience, then they evaluated the service they received directly (and/or the service they observed other consumers receiving). They observed many situations to see a variety of issues being handled by the staff/organization which made their conclusions more meaningful. Finally, they contacted the organization by telephone and e-mail and used their observations to produce a report.

Following the observations, students detailed as much of the experience as they were able in the final report. They cited specific interactions with staff members, detail on the interaction itself, observations and detail regarding the organization and its products, services, facilities, and programs. They detailed any insight into policies and procedures, the physical plant, and displays. Students then provided a summary of their experience as to what the organization may want to consider addressing as well as what the organization should continue to reinforce.

organization not revealed in traditional methods (e.g., comment cards). Staff often modifies their behavior when leisure management enters the organization. When leadership presence is not apparent, however, attitudes and interactions of staff may vary. Mystery shopping represents another way to utilize qualitative research to aid in decision-making. Cobb (1997) cited several reasons for organizations to utilize mystery shopping, including the following:

- Determine if needs of customers are being met.

- Identify problem areas and incorporate effective staff training techniques.

- Verify if actions, events and promotions were communicated correctly and carried out.

- Utilize information to develop a staff incentive program.

- Offer insight to help improve manager and staff performance.

- Evaluate whether standards set by corporate are consistently being met.

- Benchmark competitors' procedures.

This method has been used in large lodging properties as a tool to measure service quality. Little is yet known about other leisure and tourism organizations using the technique. Overall, Maret (2005) found that one billion is spent annually on mystery shopping, and its popularity is growing in leisure and tourism. Service quality was viewed as a competitive advantage not easily matched by competitors. Beck and Miao (2003) conducted a study to understand the perceptions of lodging senior management regarding mystery shopping. Most often it was conducted by outside organizations where employees were unaware of the evaluation. Largely, corporate offices initiated the evaluation and smaller, independent properties have not yet found the value in this type of research. Narvaez (2006) reminds organizations that normal cognitive limitations and biases must be accounted for when using this technique as reliable data is critical.

Critical Incident Technique

The process of collecting direct observations and experiences about human behavior, then categorizing it in a way that is useful to address and solve practical problems is called the *critical incident technique* (CIT). CIT studies tasks in terms of observable behaviors of those engaged in the task. Researchers ask respondents to provide detailed, factual descriptions of situations they wish to study in the form of written statements or incidents. Respondents are asked to answer open-ended statements to solicit detail

	IMPORTANCE			
PHYSICAL ENVIRONMENT	Low	Average		High
Safety	1	2	3	4	5
Cleanliness	1	2	3	4	5
Ample signage	1	2	3	4	5
Ambiance	1	2	3	4	5
Layout/accessibility	1	2	3	4	5
Overall exterior	1	2	3	4	5
Overall interior	1	2	3	4	5
OTHER: _____	1	2	3	4	5
OFFERINGS				
Product quality	1	2	3	4	5
Price/value	1	2	3	4	5
Product availability	1	2	3	4	5
Adequate equipment and supplies	1	2	3	4	5
Product display	1	2	3	4	5
Brochure/advertising	1	2	3	4	5
Staff identifiable	1	2	3	4	5
Staff appearance	1	2	3	4	5
OTHER: _____	1	2	3	4	5
INTERACTION				
Greeting	1	2	3	4	5
Friendliness	1	2	3	4	5
Aggressive hospitality	1	2	3	4	5
Appreciation	1	2	3	4	5
Honesty	1	2	3	4	5
Knowledge	1	2	3	4	5
Efficiency	1	2	3	4	5
Closing	1	2	3	4	5
OTHER: _____	1	2	3	4	5
LEADERSHIP				
Appropriate policies and procedures	1	2	3	4	5
Availability	1	2	3	4	5
OTHER: _____	1	2	3	4	5
SERVICE RECOVERY				
Positive response	1	2	3	4	5
Empathy	1	2	3	4	5
Listening	1	2	3	4	5
Offers for resolution	1	2	3	4	5
Satisfactory resolution	1	2	3	4	5
Response time	1	2	3	4	5
OTHER: _____	1	2	3	4	5

Mystery Shopper
E V A L U A T I O N

PRIOR TO EXPERIENCE

PART A

Please circle your response to the following quality service criteria based on your expectations prior to arriving at an establishment.

Agency: _____

Date/time: _____

Conducted by: _____

CHECK ALL THAT APPLY:
- ☐ I have been to this establishment before.
- ☐ I have heard from others about this establishment.
- ☐ I have viewed/heard about this establishment from marketing materials.
- ☐ I have not been to this establishment but have been to others like it.

describing incidents so the situation can further be understood. These incidents are considered data. For example, guests may be asked to provide a detailed, factual description of a service dissatisfaction they have experienced. Bitner, Booms, and Tetreault (1995, p. 136) used this technique in their research on dissatisfaction and provided a list of sample questions to which people could respond:

> Think of a time when, as a customer, you had a particularly dissatisfying interaction with an employee of a specific leisure industry or establishment.
>
> - When did it happen?
>
> - What specific circumstances led up to this situation?
>
> - Exactly what did the employee do or say?
>
> - What made you feel the interaction was satisfying or dissatisfying?

Responses to these questions are then placed into categories of themes or patterns are developed to learn issues (e.g., the sources of dissatisfaction, the factors that contribute to dissatisfaction, the successful recovery methods in dissatisfaction). In essence, any distinction related to service dissatisfaction (or other topics) can be understood from this type of research method.

This data can be collected in various ways, including responding to an open-ended questionnaire where customers write their own statements, through access to organization records (e.g., letters of dissatisfaction), and by individual or group interviews. It is considered a time-intensive process—many qualitative research efforts are. However, there are benefits to this approach because it can be the best choice for understanding distinctions of experiences. Incidents can be collected anywhere and can address very specific issues within an organization; however, it is not good for broad topics (e.g., "change"). The process provides greater detail than simple observation and insures that people's interpretations of an event are accurate even though potential memory bias exists when respondents are asked to recall a past situation. Potential issues in this research method includes a loss of intense "feeling" that direct observation would provide, concerns about vague word meaning, category labels, and coding of responses to the correct category.

Quantitative Research

As mentioned earlier in this chapter, a variety of quantitative research design choices are available to those interested in gathering data. The most common in the leisure service industry is the survey questionnaire.

Generally, data is collected in two ways in quantitative research. The respondents either complete the instrument (e.g., mail, web-based) themselves or another person asks them the questions and they respond. Self-administered responses are those in which the respondent completes the instrument; interviewer-administered are those when a trained research team member asks the questions and records respondent's responses.

There is no crystal ball to predict which data collection method is the "best" way to gather the information the organization needs to learn as no one right or wrong answer exists for all organizations. There are, however, advantages and disadvantages to each type of collection method that can be weighed to determine which would be the best for an organization.

Developing Instruments

After initially selecting a research design, the next step is the development of an effective instrument. The quality of questions is crucial to gathering information that will be valuable to an organization. Yet, this step is often given little consideration by leisure professionals and "garbage in equals garbage out". Table 5.9 (p. 114) shares actual questions from leisure and tourism organization survey questionnaires.

The questions in a research study are the means by which the information is gained. Improper questions, therefore, create potentially unusable information. Every question should be tested to ensure its usability prior to data collection. This process is called *pilot testing*.

Pilot testing ensures questions are indeed clear, accurate, and usable. Even researchers with refined instruments find beneficial suggestions made by pilot testing respondents. Ideally a researcher selects individuals to complete the instrument who match the sample intended (but are not part of the actual sample). As little as ten and as many as 50 people may be selected to provide feedback to the researcher regarding the wording of the questions, clarity of directions, format, and ease in responding. From this information, changes can be made to reduce the probability of error.

Every possible question an organization is interested in learning about should not be asked in one study. Organizations implement research for a variety of reasons. Questions should be limited to the primary purpose(s) of the study (e.g., understanding satisfaction). The objectives of the study drive or determine the questions asked in the instrument.

Questions

Questions must provide all possible responses and should not provide more than one possible response unless this is desired. The issue of ensuring that only one possible answer exists is called *mutual exclusivity*. A common example of this occurring is with an age question where someone who is 30 or 40 years old has two possible choices and those over 50 have no choice (Example 1a). A better way to ask an age question is to simply leave a blank for the respondent to fill it in (Example 1b). It takes as much time to write in the age as it does to place a checkmark.

Table 5.9
Poorly Worded Questions From Leisure and Tourism Organization Questionnaires

SERVICE AWARENESS
Are you aware of, and do you use the following?

	I am aware of	I have used	I am unaware of
1. Discounts and services offered through MESRA (Michigan Employee Services and Recreation Association)	☐	☐	☐
2. Discounts for travel and hotel accomodations	☐	☐	☐
3. Discount tickets for amusement parks	☐	☐	☐
4. Discount booklets for JAX car wash	☐	☐	☐
5. Quality Buying Power discount booklet	☐	☐	☐
6. Merchandise discounts (electronics, sportswear, and jewelry)	☐	☐	☐

Questions that are not necessary (e.g., unaware of).

Asking two questions in one.

V. Convention/Conference Service Planning	EXCELLENT	GOOD	FAIR	POOR	N/A
1. Convention/Conference Service Staff courteous & efficient?	☐	☐	☐	☐	☐
2. Were you contacted in a timely manner by the Convention/Conference Staff?	☐	☐	☐	☐	☐
3. Meeting rooms set up on time & to your	☐	☐	☐	☐	☐

How satisfied were you with the hotels/motels used on this tour?

GOOD   AVERAGE   POOR

Please list those hotels that did not meet your expectations.

_____   _____

_____   _____

Asking questions requiring respondents to remember information that is hard to recall and using a scale that does not indicate a beneficial range (e.g., no excellent).

Asking a question that does not allow for all possible responses. What about heavy metal, rap, or Christian music?

13) When you listen to the radio, what musical format do you listen to longest?

A. Easy Listening   B. Top 40   C. Country
D. Light Rock   E. Oldies   F. Alternative

19) Approval Rating   1 2 3 4 5 6 7 8 9 10

Question is unclear...approval of what? Scale is large and not defined. Is 1 a high or low approval rating?

Use of two different font types in one document, as well as two different scales.

My overall rating of this presentor(s) is: (circle one)	Outstanding	Very Good	Good	Fair	Poor

Overall:	Outstanding	Above Average	Average	Below Average	Poor
Rate this session in comparison to others at THIS conference.	1	2	3	4	5
Rate this session in comparison to other conferences.	1	2	3	4	5
Rate this session in comparison to other non-conferences.	1	2	3	4	5

Example 1a:
Age
__ Under 20
__ 20–30
__ 30–40
__ 40–50

Example 1b:
Age ____

Collectively exhaustive questions ensure every possible response exists. Questions that fail to provide this leave a respondent with the inability to complete the question accurately. A common example of this occurring is when asking respondents to indicate the highest level of education received. A respondent who has completed an associate's degree has no opportunity to indicate this (see Example 2a). A more appropriate way to handle this issue is to include an "other" listing if the possibility exists that more answers are likely (Example 2b).

Example 2a:
Highest degree held
__ high school diploma
__ bachelor's degree
__ master's degree
__ doctorate
__ technical certification

Example 2b:
Highest degree held
__ high school diploma
__ bachelor's degree
__ master's degree
__ doctorate
__ technical certification
__ other _____

Multiple questions asked simultaneously are another common issue in questionnaires that create challenges for the researcher. Often, the word "and" in a question denotes more than one question exists. The response will be unclear to researchers in the following example where staff may have been courteous but not efficient. Respondents may have scored the following example differently if the questions were separated.

Example 3:
Please circle a number for each statement using the scale provided:
Staff was courteous and efficient.

poor		average		excellent
1	2	3	4	5

Scales used in questionnaires also pose problems for researchers and respondents. Some scales include three or ten possible choices. A small number of choices does not provide enough distinction whereas a large number of choices provides too many distinctions. Example 4 portrays this issue. Most often, scales of 1 to 5, 1 to 6, or 1 to 7 are used in survey research because they provide a range of responses that are clearly identified. Selecting a scale with an odd number allows respondents to select a "middle" or

"average" score whereas even-numbered scales force respondents to select above or below an average score.

Example 4a:
Overall satisfaction:

low				average					high
1	2	3	4	5	6	7	8	9	10

Example 4b:
Overall satisfaction:

Poor	Average	Good
1	2	3

Likert scales provide a range of responses asking respondents to indicate their answer in a range from strongly agree to strongly disagree. This is often used to measure an attitude toward a leisure experience or facets within that experience. *Likert scale* questions provide an opportunity for respondents to answer based on their agreement with statements made on the instrument. For example

Strongly Agree	Somewhat Agree	No Opinion	Somewhat Disagree	Strongly Disagree
Essential	Significant	Moderate	Minimal	None

Semantic differentials list opposite responses to solicit an understanding of beliefs. For example, respondents are asked to indicate a registration speed where "1 = slow and 6 = fast."

Forced choice or *paired comparisons* are another way in which questions may be asked. These require respondents to select from limited options and can distinguish between priorities. For example, are indoor or outdoor offerings more important to you when deciding on a club membership? In looking at the list provided, which is the most important consideration you made when selecting this membership? (Spaulding, 2003).

Types of Questions

A variety of questions and formats exist in questionnaires. The basic four types of questions include fact, opinion/attitude, informational, and self-perception. *Fact* provides information about respondents (e.g., "What is your age?") *Opinion/attitude* provides information about feelings or beliefs (e.g., "In your opinion, should residents outside of the city limits be charged to attend city special events?") *Informational* provides information on what the respondent knows (e.g., "Indicate all the benefits of your membership.") *Self-perception* provides information about a respondent's own behavior in relation to other factors (e.g., "Has the information hotline addressed the issues regarding your questions?")

Questionnaire Format and Sequence

The flow of questions is yet another area that researchers concern themselves with because the goal is to get completed questionnaires. Research about this process suggests format can reduce this from occurring.

A typical format for mailed, Internet, and e-mail questionnaires includes an introduction (e.g., purpose of the study, how results will be used), warm-up questions (i.e., starting with these is as important as the introduction to prepare people to answer questions; these should relate to content but be easy to answer), core questions (i.e., those critical to the study; these take the most time and thought), and ending with demographic questions.

Demographic questions are at the end of this collection method so that when respondents begin to tire of the questionnaire, they see questions that require little thought left to answer. Conversely, with face-to-face and telephone collection methods, demographic questions should come first. These types of questions provide a means for developing rapport with respondents and ease them into responding to more difficult questions. Further, demographic questions may be used to identify the desired sample.

Failing to ask demographic questions about respondents limits the usability of the data gathered by organizations. A leisure organization questionnaire that fails to ask any demographic questions loses valuable information because the organization cannot distinguish between various market segments and their responses. As provided, this data is general in nature and little understanding of specific markets can be generated.

Instruments that provide choices for respondents to pick from are more likely to be completed. Open-ended questions take time to complete and are less likely to be answered. Use these sparingly when the information desired requires it. Close-ended questions may be easier to respond to, but at times can provide limiting information. Figure 5.1 provides a sample questionnaire without open-ended or demographic questions.

Finally, instruments should be professionally comprised with consideration given to the quality of the design. Visually appealing questionnaires are more likely to be completed than those with errors, poor design or visually limiting presence.

Overall, there are many distinctions that impact the effective development of survey questionnaires. Common questionnaire errors include the following:

- too long

- no explanation of the purpose of the research

- no instructions (e.g., circle one, check all that apply)

- no date (especially with continued research; e.g., programming evaluation)

- multiple questions in one question

- no "I don't know" or "no opinion" options when needed

- no ability to respond (i.e., collectively exhaustive)

- overlapping possible responses (i.e., mutually exclusive)

- unfamiliar technical terms, jargon, or words with unclear meanings

- unnecessary sensitive questions

- unprofessional document

- asking for information the organization already has

- asking questions unrelated to the purpose of the study

Validity and Reliability

It is important that all research efforts identify issues related to reliability and validity for consumers of research to understand the process by which the research was undertaken. This is done so potential bias and error can be understood.

Validity is the process used by researchers to ensure the instrument measures what it said it would measure. Face, criterion-related, construct and content validity can be addressed through a number of processes (Babbie, 1995). *Face validity* ensures the measurements made sense and the questions were not objectionable to potential respondents. Pilot testing assists in making certain face validity exists. *Criterion-related validity* ensures the research is correlated to something else that is already deemed valid. There are two types: (a) *concurrent validity*, where correlation occurs with something else that is measured at the same time; and (b) *predictive validity*, where after the immediate collection of data, criterion are verified with alternate sources. *Content validity* ensures the breadth of issues are covered in the instrument used in a study. Interviews, pilot studies and literature reviews can be instrumental in ensuring content validity was addressed in quantitative research. Each of these procedures provide additional insights that are helpful in confirming an instrument covers all related issues. *Construct validity* exists when a comparison of test scores is done with other tests that reflect the same theory or constructs.

Welcome and thank you for choosing our Hotel. Our Hospitality Promise assures that you will be satisfied with your stay and that we will meet the high standard you have come to expect. If, for any reason, you believe we have not met the standards we promise, or should you have a problem, please contact our front desk/Manager on Duty immediately.

The quickest way to resolve any difficulty, no matter how small, is to let the Manager on Duty know as soon as possible so we can correct it. In most cases we can solve your problem before you check-out. Please give us the opportunity to assist you.

If you still need assistance, after contacting our Manager on Duty, call 1-800-80 HI DEV (1-800-804-4338). Guest Assistance will need the names of our staff who attempted to resolve your problem.

Name: _____
Address: _____
City, State, Zip: _____
Country: _____
Tel #: _____

HOW WELL DID WE SERVE YOU?
Please let us know what you think about our service and accommodations so we can serve you better in the future.

Please check which best describes your satisfaction with your stay at this hotel.

Your Room Number _____

Date of your stay _____

During your stay, how satisfied were you with the:

	Very Satisfied 100%	Somewhat Satisfied 60%	Neither Satisfied or Dissatisfied 40%	Somewhat Dissatisfied 20%	Very Dissatisfied 0%
Outside appearance of hotel (curb appeal, grounds, building, etc.)	☐	☐	☐	☐	☐
Lobby conditions/attractiveness	☐	☐	☐	☐	☐
Service at check-in (friendly, efficient, etc.)	☐	☐	☐	☐	☐
Guest room/guest bath:					
• Overall cleanliness	☐	☐	☐	☐	☐
• Guest bath facilities (amenities, hot water)	☐	☐	☐	☐	☐
• Heating/air conditioning	☐	☐	☐	☐	☐
• Bed/pillow comfort	☐	☐	☐	☐	☐
• Television/remote/radio	☐	☐	☐	☐	☐
• Condition of furniture (dresser, chair, etc.)	☐	☐	☐	☐	☐
Service of hotel staff:					
• Responsiveness to needs	☐	☐	☐	☐	☐
• Friendliness of staff	☐	☐	☐	☐	☐
• Professional attitude and appearance	☐	☐	☐	☐	☐
Restaurant/deli/bar:					
• Quality of food/beverage	☐	☐	☐	☐	☐
• Restaurant cleanliness	☐	☐	☐	☐	☐
• Quality of service	☐	☐	☐	☐	☐
Telephone Services (wake-up call, messages, long distance, etc.)	☐	☐	☐	☐	☐
Lighting (brightness, good operating order, etc.)	☐	☐	☐	☐	☐
Hotel safety and security	☐	☐	☐	☐	☐
Accuracy of billing	☐	☐	☐	☐	☐
Service at check-out (friendly, efficient, etc.)	☐	☐	☐	☐	☐
Value received for price paid	☐	☐	☐	☐	☐
Regardless of what you paid: How satisfied were you with the:					
• Overall physical condition of this hotel	☐	☐	☐	☐	☐
• Overall service received at this hotel	☐	☐	☐	☐	☐
All things considered, please rate your OVERALL SATISFACTION with this hotel	☐	☐	☐	☐	☐
Would you recommend THIS hotel to a friend or business associate?	☐	☐	☐	☐	☐

Figure 5.1
Sample Questionnaire Without Open-Ended or Demographic Questions

Reliability of the research process indicates the degree to which the measure is repeatable. If this study is repeated will the same result occur? Several techniques can be used to ensure similar results with repeated measurements. *Test-retest reliability* is when a test is administered two or more times to the same group and reliability is checked through the positive association between scores. *Split-half reliability* is when test items are divided into two halves with each matched for content difficulty. Questions may be asked both positively and negatively to verify reliability. Finally, alternate forms can also be used to verify reliability. Two forms of a test are used and individuals take both to check the score and compare scores.

Babbie (1995) suggested researchers could cause measurement unreliability and if more than one researcher collected data, steps should be in place to ensure the research process is reliable. Training of persons collecting data and conducting data entry is critical to ensure reliability. Allowing people to conduct the research differently in a study causes possible reliability errors that can skew the data. Interrater reliability suggests one person conducting research would collect data similarly between two respondents where intrarater reliability suggests two different researchers would interview the same respondent similarly and get identical responses. These steps can be taken in survey research to ensure the process is reliable and that the findings are accurate.

Response Rates

Nothing is more frustrating in the research process than developing a good research instrument and having no one respond to it. The development of any research effort must consider that the people receiving the research may not have the time or interest in providing your organization information. Sudman and Blair (1999) stated:

> a disturbing trend in the past quarter century has been the slow, but steady, decline in sample cooperation. There is a broad range of causes, most of which are not under the control of the researcher. These include an increase in the percentage of working women, which reduces the likelihood of finding a respondent available for interviewing, reduces the pool of potential interviewers, and increases social isolation, which has led to less willingness to respond to strangers. Other factors include telemarketing activities that have created a noisy telephone environment and the increased use of screening devices to reject unwanted calls.

Increasing Response Rates. Dillman (1978) suggested an investigator should address four areas to encourage a

higher response in survey research. Respondents should (a) be provided a reward for completing the questionnaire, (b) be sent correspondence by first-class mail, (c) have a trusted relationship with the investigator, and (d) not incur any associated costs. Dillman (1978) indicated the total design method for mail survey research included first-class postage, postage-paid return envelopes, postcard reminders, and follow-up mailings to nonrespondents. Dillman recommended using certified mail for the third mailing to nonrespondents to increase the total response.

Others have supported Dillman's findings. Erdogan and Baker (2002) found that following up with an original replacement questionnaire yielded the highest response rate from other methods (e.g., postcard, photocopy of questionnaire, letter). This, they conclude, also costs the most to produce. Further, Janes (2000) found that personalizing the cover letter yielded a higher response than a generic introduction. One additional research team made additional suggestions regarding response rates. Sudman and Blair (1999) suggested contacting respondents more often and through mixed modes, including mail, fax, telephone, e-mail, Internet, and computer discs. Further, higher incentives for respondents may be necessary to gain the information. Conduct nonresponsive verification to determine if nonresponsive data indicates bias exists—report this in the final research accordingly.

Research efforts must be time sensitive. The longer it takes to provide information to the organization, the less likely people will participate. The research process must be specific to what information is to be learned. Mailed questionnaires should take no longer than 15 minutes to complete. Telephone and face-to-face can be longer; however, appointments should be made with respondents when longer time is needed. Generally, the shorter the time needed, the higher the response rate.

The research process should encourage participant response. It should be sent in a way that is most acceptable to participants (e.g., e-mail to computer users). Instruments could also be sent a variety of ways to give respondents choices (e.g., mail, e-mail, telephone, Internet). When mailing an instrument, it should have a postage-paid return envelope included. People are less likely to respond if they have to pay to mail a survey back. Hand delivering mail questionnaires enhances personalization and encourages responses. Respondents should be asked if this is a convenient time when asked via the telephone or face-to-face.

Incentives tied to survey research should be something of value to the participants. Leisure consumers may find value in complimentary leisure services, merchandise, or money. The reward must also be substantial enough that participants feel their time has been valued by the organization requesting the information. Sending 3,000 community members a questionnaire with a note indicating that one lucky respondent will receive a logoed sweatshirt may do little to encourage people to respond. Some research efforts provide respondents a summary of the research findings as an incentive. Everyone, however, does not value this type of incentive and careful consideration should be given to the incentive selected.

An often missed step in data gathering is acknowledging respondents efforts and sending a thank-you note following the completion of a study stating how the information was used and how it has been helpful to the organization. This may be done in a variety of ways. Some organizations provide results in organization newsletters, local newspapers, or personal letters. More times than not, respondents have no idea what has been done with the information they provided. This is particularly helpful when conducting research with organization consumers who have an interest in the outcome. Few organizations take this step, yet it will assist with building relationships with consumers and others as well as encourage future questionnaire responses as people feel their feedback was taken into consideration and acted on.

Nonresponse Concerns. Frankfort-Nachmias and Nachmias (1992) indicated that the most prevalent error in survey research is nonresponse error. This occurs when potential respondents fail to respond. If responses differ between respondents and nonrespondents on key variables potential bias exists. This may be due to something in the questionnaire or materials that influence people not to respond (Koff, 1992). To determine whether bias exists, data must be collected from a sample of nonrespondents. Comparisons are then made between respondents and nonrespondents (Frankfort-Nachmias & Nachmias, 1992).

Sampling Issues

Ideally, everyone in a population would be sampled, however, it is not realistic in all situations. Therefore, a sampling technique can be applied to provide meaningful information. Sample size is often a balance between accuracy and cost.

A *sample* is a specific number of people selected to represent a population the researcher will ask to respond. The *population* includes anyone who fulfills a set of parameters established by the researcher. An example of a population would be people who have visited the organization within the past year. In this case, 5,000 people are recorded on the organization's database as having visited. If the organization is unable to gain feedback from all 5,000 due to time or cost issues, they can determine the percent they anticipate responding as well as the number needed to be scientifically representative of the population.

If an organization wishes to compare data by subgroups, then the sample size must be larger. For example, a bowling center wants to compare data from league bowlers and non-league bowlers. In this instance each subgroup would need to have a probable sample size to complete the research with accuracy.

Science suggests that not all 5,000 people would need to respond to the organization to determine answers to questions from past visitors. *Sampling* is the process by which the researcher selects a random, nonbiased number from the population. If enough of the sample responds, a researcher can infer the results resemble the larger population, even though only a portion of the population was asked to respond to the survey. A *sample size* of 357 would need to be gathered from a population of 5,000 to be 95% confident with an error of ±5%. Should a researcher not get this many responses, the research would not be comparable to the population but rather to the number who responded.

Selecting the sample from within the population must occur without judgment and without bias. The sampling process is a scientific approach used to limit potential bias. Three common methods for identifying the sample include simple random, systematic, and stratified random. With *simple random sampling*, the desired sample is selected from the overall population randomly with every person having equal chance of being selected. For example, a golf course wishes to sample half of the 500 people with

---

> ## Real Life Story:
> ## State Park Understands Visitation
>
> Kerstetter, Zinn, Graefe, and Chen (2002) studied state park visitation. Of the over 1,000 people that responded, 78% had used the state parks and 22% had never visited a state park. When asked what constrained their state park use, respondents indicated a variety of issues including a lack of time (60%), lack of state park knowledge (34%), lack of family or friends to visit the park with (24%), and distance (22%).
>
> These issues, however, were not in isolation— Respondents indicated several constraints existed. Further, nonuser and former-user constraints differed. Therefore, researchers suggested a single approach to marketing is not likely to be effective for all publics.
>
> One problem with this research, however, was that some respondents indicated the parks and rides were too expensive even though no fee is charged for admission and no rides are available. This may indicate some misconceptions exist regarding the state park system. They conclude suggesting state park leaders must reach specific target markets to determine if reducing or eliminating constraints will be of value.

seasonal memberships. Conveniently, computers today complete this process easily, whereby 250 are randomly selected, with each of the 500 having an equal opportunity to be selected.

Systematic sampling provides a more precise way of selecting the sample. With the same example and an alphabetized list, researchers would select every other name to get the 250 names desired. To ensure that every person has the opportunity to be selected, a random beginning would be chosen. This is so the first person listed alphabetically has a chance of being included in the sample.

A variation of the systematic sampling method exists when groups of people are first separated into like areas. *Stratified random sampling* groups people by likes, desired characteristics and then randomly selects the desired number within each group. In the previous example, the golf course may want to separate first-year and returning members to ensure representation from each group. Therefore, the member list would first be separated, and from the respective groups a random number would be selected.

Other sampling methods exist to manage areas of a population. These types of sampling are more common when respondents are within specific geographic areas. *Cluster sampling* occurs when the population is divided into subgroups and the entire list of members in a cluster are sampled. An example of this would occur in a city where residents within a certain geographic area (e.g., low-income housing projects) are the desired cluster. *Area sampling* occurs when a list of residents may not exist within a cluster and particular city blocks are used to sample an area of the population.

Improper sampling can result in bias throughout the research process. Sampling bias is commonly perceived as negative when associated with using mail as a collection method.

Step 3: Data Collection Methods

A variety of data collection methods are available for quantitative research. Leisure organizations must decide which method more effectively collects the information based on study objectives, funding available, time limits and resources. Sometimes the decision will be quite obvious as one factor will force a selection (e.g., need the information immediately). However, at other times the decision will be more difficult to make and understanding each choice is critical. Technologically supported methods (e.g., e-mail, Internet) have increased in popularity as systems become available and other efforts have become more common (e.g., telephone, mail); however, this does not influence the selection of the method as each has unique advantages. The

advantages and disadvantages of the more common collection methods are reviewed in Table 5.10.

These collection method advantages and disadvantages presume the sample is specifically selected versus an open invitation for anyone to respond. If these collection methods are used with the general population (e.g., inviting anyone to complete the questionnaire), the results can be misleading, as the "population" would be the entire country versus specific groups of people. Respondents with strong views on the topics being researched are more likely to share feedback with researchers causing further issue with this process (Sudman & Blair, 1999). Coverage bias exists when the sample is not choosing to access or not having access to the Internet or other means (e.g., cellular phones, e-mail).

Solomon (2001) suggested combining an e-mail letter with an HTML or web-based questionnaire "provides an especially effective and efficient approach to Internet surveying." (p. 1)

White (2000) suggested even though some organizations have found value in online research efforts, others show concern. Proponents suggest speed and cost are positive trade-offs. Critics suggest these are not necessarily trade-offs for quality information. The Internet savvy markets are not representative of all populations. They tend to be rich, White, male, and technology oriented.

Stevens (2000) found ways to overcome this, however, by providing options for consumers to respond to surveys in various ways, such as online, by telephone, or at a central location. Further, as technology continues to develop the obstacles or limitations will be reduced (Heckman, 2000).

In an effort to conduct *ethnographic research*—studying people in their natural habitat and observing actual behaviors—researchers use technology to assist. Whether an organization desires information on participation patterns, satisfaction or advertising effectiveness, consumers are able to respond as the service is provided. Therefore, capturing a more reliable view of actual behaviors and beliefs, which are not impacted by time.

One example of an electronic marketing survey is inquiries being sent to people on wireless telephones, using both text-based and voice-based formats. Respondents answer questions and responses are sent back to researchers instantly. The benefits include the speed at which the data is collected, convenience of response (i.e., consumers control when they want to respond) and allows consumers to reply instantly at the point of consumption, and/or in a more natural environment. This form of research does have limitations though, including length of questions and limited graphic capability (Long, Whinston & Tomak, 2002).

Challenges in Quantitative Research

In summary, a variety of issues impact the accuracy of the quantitative research process. Some of these have been discussed in the previous section and others will be shared in the sections that follow. Possible errors in quantitative research include the following:

- sampling procedure
- number of respondents
- nonresponse bias

- poor questions
- reliability
- data entry errors
- misinterpretation of the findings
- ethical issues in reporting

Most research has potential errors embedded in the process and researchers have an ethical obligation to share these challenges.

Table 5.10
Advantages and Disadvantages of Common Data Collection Methods

	Advantages	Disadvantages
Mail	• Inexpensive • Same local/national cost • Limited bias • Able to sample large numbers • Can be anonymous for sensitive issues • Convenient to answer • No time pressure to respond	• Impersonal • Typically a low response rate • Longer time needed to obtain results
E-Mail	• Least expensive • Data obtained quickly • Convenient to answer • Same national/international cost • Able to sample large numbers • No time pressure to respond • Can combine e-mail and HTML methods easily	• Fear of anonymity/confidentiality • Limited to people with e-mail access • People changing e-mail addresses • Finding/Accessing e-mail addresses • Technical difficulties • Less personalized • More mistakes when responding • Spamming (i.e., junk e-mail from unknown source)
Hypertext Markup Language (HTML)/ Web-Based	• Least expensive • Data entry can be automatic, quicker results • Convenient to answer • Same national/international cost • Able to sample large numbers • Data obtained quickly • No time pressure to respond • Computer prompts to related questions only	• Respondent must find website to respond • Technical difficulties • Multiple responses possible from same person • Limited to people with Internet access • Sample may not want to access • Limiting the access to others not in sample • Lower response rate than mail • Respondent fear lack of anonymity/confidentiality • System speed varies in computers • More mistakes when responding
Face-to-Face	• High response rate • High flexibility • Timely • Open-ended questions are completed • Controlled clarification • Longest time to conduct research with prearranged meeting/appointments	• Expensive • Reluctance to respond • Inconvenient • Large number of staff needed • Intrarater reliability issues; same researcher asking questions differently with respondents • Interrater reliability issues; various researchers asking respondents questions • Time pressure to respond
Telephone	*Same as face-to-face plus:* • Lower cost than face-to-face • Easier to find hard to reach people • Sample more people in less time • Centralized data collection, quality control • Calling centers with trained personnel	*Same as face-to-face plus:* • Greater invasion of privacy • Higher refusal rate than face-to-face; less personal • Limited length of time to conduct • Unlisted telephone numbers • Call-screening devices (i.e., Caller ID) • Competition with "sales type" calls • No examination of visual materials

Step 4: Analysis of Data

Data must first be put into systems to professionally analyze the information gained from the research process. The coding, labeling, and storing of data provides easy access for those within the leisure organization and does not limit the access to the person who reads the information.

Data analysis varies for the type of research method selected. Quantitative research is often analyzed on statistical software programs (e.g., SPSS, SAS, Minitab). These programs provide a means for analyzing data by individual questions (e.g., 80% of the respondents were female), comparing responses to questions by demographic characteristics (e.g., children ages 6–10 prefer group activities to individual activities), and identifying statistically significant differences (e.g., males are significantly more interested than females in team sports). Qualitative research is often analyzed with computer assistance as well. Software programs, such as NUD*IST, provide a means to conduct content analyses and find common themes or patterns within the open-ended data.

Once data is put into some type of software, careful consideration should be given to potential data entry errors. An entry of 55 versus 5 will have an impact on findings. One method for checking for possible errors is to print range scores for every response insuring no response is beyond the range provided (e.g., a range of 1–5 is given yet the analysis shows that 0–55 exists. Therefore, a data entry error exists with the "0" and from "6–55"). Also, a random check should be conducted of various responses to verify that specific responses were accurately entered.

Once the data is "clean" (i.e., free of errors) it can be statistically analyzed. Training should be provided to researchers regarding the information to be learned and the statistical tests desired.

Following the completion of the tests, interpretation of the results are made. Then the findings and conclusions are shared with those within the leisure organization. It is important that any conclusions be documented and shared with those involved with the research (even respondents if researchers indicated they would do so) or those who would find the information beneficial within the leisure organization.

Step 5: Interpretation and Report

Neither qualitative nor quantitative research is not complete until data has been interpreted and shared in a formal process. In quantitative research, understanding statistical tests and accurately reflecting the meaning of the results is critical because these data will be utilized to make organization decisions. Any error in interpretation could result in ineffective decisions and potentially disastrous results. The processes used to interpret qualitative research vary; however, the importance of accurate interpretation is the same.

Ethical Issues in Research

It is crucial that leisure organization professionals conduct research that is ethical and accurate. With the access to information, many leisure organizations are relying on research to assist with decision making. This, however, can be problematic when the research being relied on is not done accurately, without bias and error. Although this chapter does not profess to provide enough support to establish research skills, it does provide a basic understanding of the research process from which decisions on the professionalism of research studies can be analyzed. Further, more leisure organizations are conducting their own research, and this chapter hopes to highlight and suggest proper processes and challenges with the research effort.

Any primary research conducted by a leisure and tourism organization should consider the following ethical issues:

- Are participants voluntarily contributing their data and are they informed of this consent?

- Are participants being deceived and do they have a right to unobtrusiveness?

- Is the data confidential?

- Has the data been shared for its value/worth and what is represented as both open and honest reporting?

It is important for those conducting market research to remember that research with consumers or employees must be relationship oriented. Pruden and Vavra (2000) even suggested market research and customer research are different activities and should be viewed as such. They view customer research as a process that not only collects valued information but also strengthens an organization's relationship with their consumers. It does not treat consumers as a number (as they suggest market research does) but rather a valued resource within the organization. Customer research uses the research process to build a relationship with their consumers. Research focused on relationships ensures any contact is of high-quality (e.g., professional questionnaires), personalized, protected (e.g., confidential, personal information is not shared beyond the organization), cognizant of consumers limited time (e.g., shorter in length but more frequently than once per year) and thankful for their response (e.g., a postcard that shows appreciation for consumers responding). Further, any consumer research that warrants additional follow-up would be completed immediately. Consumers sharing their dissatisfaction would be contacted immediately to resolve the problem.

Planning for Marketing Research

A leisure organization conducting one research study a year may think they are doing the "market research" necessary for decision making, but the bottom line is market research should be conducted every day in an organization that values feedback. When employees ask consumers and management asks employees about their experiences, valuable information is provided from which the organization can react. Organizations sincere in wanting feedback and acting on the information will be one step ahead of all others. Developing a culture that supports continuous feedback and

places the research function in the heart of the marketing process is the key.

Understanding consumer satisfaction is a common and important objective in leisure and tourism organizations. The remaining section provides insight into this area of market research.

Annual marketing plans include a research plan to identify projects that should be completed within the next year to aid in organization decision making. Table 5.11 highlights a marketing research plan being developed by a community organization.

Satisfaction Measurement and Feedback

The interest in measurement of service quality is high, and measuring the quality of the service encounter is an integral part of most managers' responsibilities (O'Neal, 2001). A common form of marketing research used in the leisure industry is measuring consumer satisfaction.

Table 5.11
Actual Market Research Plan in an Annual Marketing Plan

2005 Market Research Plan														
Actions	**Timeline**												**Budget**	**Responsibility**
	Jan	Feb	Mar	Apr	May	Jun	Jul	Aug	Sep	Oct	Nov	Dec		
Add question to all existing satisfaction surveys within each division regarding consumer characteristics and marketing evaluation (e.g., "How did you hear about _____?" "Who are you?" — e.g., gender, age, frequency of visits)														
Community use/needs assessment (users and nonusers) that includes questions on consumer characteristics/behaviors														
Satisfaction research (users) — Importance Performance Analysis that includes questions on consumer characteristics/behaviors														
Track data and maintain spreadsheet on tactical marketing activities (e.g., coupons, passes)														
Analyze users within each division to better understand markets served, potential target markets, and an evaluation of existing tactical marketing efforts (e.g., Did the promotional event to attract seniors work? Are there more seniors served?)														

Cline (1997) suggested it is necessary to learn about customer satisfaction in the industry. The best way to measure customer satisfaction is to identify if you are meeting customer needs. Asking customers is an important way to identify expectations, to determine if customers are satisfied, and to determine if the organization put their resources in the right areas (Evenson, 1999).

Keeping in touch with guests is critical in today's competitive environment. Losing sight of what is important to the people you serve can be disastrous. Quality service providers must be constantly focused on what is valued by guests. Understanding what guests need, expect, and experience is fundamental to quality practices.

W. Edward Deming said, "You can't manage what you can't measure," and this has been the case according to research. What organizations have learned is that feedback is vital. They realize there are a variety of reasons why an organization would want solicit opinions, including the following:

- Feedback is important to learn, change, and grow. Communication with internal and external guests is critical because it sets the organizational priorities.

- Good service keeps people coming back. Poor service loses external guests, and internal guests lose interest and hours.

- The organization gets a chance to make itself more efficient/effective.

- A dissatisfied guest tells ten people about the service they received (who in turn tell ten, and so on, becoming the 250 rule).

- Guests who were once dissatisfied and were recovered will be more loyal than someone who never had a problem to begin with.

- If given the opportunity to recover and you do nothing, the impact is far worse than never having been given the opportunity.

- A typical organization hears from only 4% of unhappy guests; therefore, for every one instance of negative feedback *a lot* more comments are being expressed to potential guests.

- Even if an employee no longer works for an organization, they will always be a potential external guest.

- Satisfied employees make recruiting efforts easier as the "choice" employer gets the calls.

Measuring consumer satisfaction is estimated to be the most common form of market research used by organizations today (Ofir & Simonson, 2001). Because this feedback is becoming more common, consumers expect to provide feedback to organizations in some way. They anticipate being asked to evaluate the organization's performance at some point and are often provided the means to give feedback prior to the experience (e.g., a comment card at the membership desk, feedback form on the back of a ticket), or they know, based on past involvement, that they will be asked to complete a questionnaire following the experience (e.g., recreation department craft class).

Ofir and Simonson (2001) studied this phenomenon and learned that satisfaction scores were lower when consumers expected to provide feedback to the organization. They suggest this could occur because consumers pay closer attention to service issues when they know they will be asked to provide feedback. Organizations should be careful to implement a system that provides the most accurate feedback possible. Comparing data from survey research collected in two different ways (e.g., with consumers who are provided advanced warning vs. those who have no idea you will ask them for feedback) can skew results. Organizations that gain feedback from the same consumers over time may have biased results. After the first evaluation those consumers will expect to complete others and may view the organization differently (Ofir & Simonson, 2001). Comment cards and other systems are problematic if not managed in the most appropriate way.

Comment Cards

A variety of tools are used to uncover information in the leisure industry. One of the more popular tools includes understanding current customers' views and opinions through comment cards (O'Neal, 2001). Although commonly used, some suggest problems with this form of evaluating customer service. O'Neal (2001) indicated a time lag in analysis, it relies on voluntary responses, and it is common to have a low response rate. Further, comment cards have been used to make fundamental organization decisions yet they are (a) not representative of the organization's customers as they represent extreme views of those very satisfied or dissatisfied guests, (b) not secured data as possible tampering by employees is possible since collection of the data is done at the front line level, and (c) asking questions that may not be proper to analyze customer satisfaction (Barsky & Huxley, 1999; Barsky & Nash, 2001).

Cline (1997) indicated although most leisure-related organizations use comment cards as a method of evaluating customer satisfaction, the trend is changing to more elaborate forms of evaluation. An approach growing in popularity in the leisure industry is guest satisfaction surveys since these provide a broad, cross-section of feedback (Baumann, 1998). Organizations are beginning to ask customers to complete a questionnaire measuring how well the organization performs in certain areas. For example, is the customer satisfied with staff service, cleanliness, and amenity selection? These questionnaires do provide some valuable information about the organization's performance that eliminates some problems associated with comment cards. However, critical information is missing.

Most evaluation instruments developed to assess services assume the organization can prescribe in advance what features of a service are important to the customer (Guadagnolo, 1985). Typically, satisfaction research ignores the level of importance these services provide to customers. Organizations may be spending resources on areas of little concern to customers. A thorough customer understanding and focus is missing in that type of research.

Today, customer needs vary over time. An evaluation that relies on organization predictions and is based on past observations is unlikely to be as accurate and useful as one based on current customer disclosures. Customer satisfaction is, therefore, a holistic function of both an evaluation by a customer of certain attributes and the customer's expectations of these attributes. Since each customer has different desires, the evaluation of a customer's satisfaction must include both an assessment of the attributes the customer feels are important and an assessment of each attribute's performance.

Since comment cards should not be the only method employed by organizations to measure satisfaction, Martin (1996) identified five common gaps organizations should be concerned with measuring the following:

1. *Consumer expectations and perceptions.* The use of ServQual or Importance Performance Analysis for employees or consumers can be used to do this and will be discussed in the next section.

2. *The organization's idea of consumer expectations and actual consumer expectations.* Use of focus groups or survey of consumer or employee needs is a method for identifying this. McColl-Kennedy and White (1997) found employees of five star hotels rated quality service attributes differently than their guests. Employees also rated hotel performance higher in each attribute than their guests. For example, guests rated personalized service as their number one determinant of quality service, whereas employees felt courtesy was the most important determinant.

3. *The organization's idea of consumer expectations and the creation of service standards.* Organizations develop procedures and policies with employee and consumer needs and expectations in mind all the time.

4. *Delivery of the service and the service standard.* Organizations train employees and managers to deliver the designed service standards to their respective consumers internally and externally.

5. *Service delivery and the commitment or promise made to consumers.* The way organizations deliver service and the communication and marketing processes used to create expectations should be evaluated.

Importance-Performance Analysis

More than 20 years ago a tool called the importance-performance analysis (IPA) was developed by Martilla and James (1977) to learn about both customer satisfaction and customer expectations. This technique accesses importance and performance information related to a customer's experience and translates this information into "easy to understand" management suggestions. In the hospitality industry, IPA has been a popular method used to understand the importance placed on attributes as well as how the organization performed on these same attributes. The attributes were analyzed not only by how satisfied consumers were with staff service, cleanliness, and amenity selection but also by how important these areas were to consumers.

Ultimately, the IPA attributes are evaluated and placed on a matrix (or *action grid*), basing their placement on their relative importance and performance to customers. Where the attribute is placed suggests to the organization the recommended focus of their efforts. The four grid quadrants are identified and interpreted as follows (Martilla & James, 1977):

Concentrate here. The upper-left quadrant includes attributes that are important to the customer, but for which performance is below average. These attributes require the most attention.

Keep up the good work. The upper-right quadrant includes attributes which customers view as important and for which your organization receives high performance marks. The organization is doing well with respect to these attributes. It is important that these attributes remain in this quadrant.

Low priority. The lower-left quadrant includes attributes which receive low marks on both importance and performance scales. Attributes in this quadrant require little attention because the customer views these areas as being lower in importance.

Possible overkill. The lower-right quadrant contains attributes, which received low importance ratings and high performance ratings. It is suggested that some attention could be diverted from these attributes to those in the "concentrate here" quadrant.

Therefore, an attribute placed into the "low priority" category need not be addressed by the organization. An attribute placed into the "possible overkill" category suggests the organization may be expending resources in an area customers are not concerned about. An attribute placed into the "keep up the good work" category reinforces organization efforts because customers state these items are both important and the organization is doing well providing them. Finally, attributes that are placed in the "concentrate here" category suggest these items are important, yet the organization is not doing well, and therefore should be a priority for the organization. Figure 5.2 highlights the IPA matrix. The IPA is customized to the particular needs of the organization; therefore, any issue the organization sees as appropriate can be evaluated. Having flexibility in the questions allows all facets of the organization to be understood

and identifies where the organization specifically needs to focus. Results on the IPA are visually plotted to make the data easy to understand. This visual plot identifies and categorizes organization attributes into four management suggestion areas as previously noted. IPA prioritizes what issues the organization should address first. Those items with a high rated importance would receive precedence. Further, the IPA identifies which attributes are considered overkill, those that are low importance and high performance by an organization; and low priority, those attributes that are of little importance and the organization is not performing well. These categories identify attributes of an organization to which they may be expending resources that are not seen as important by the customer.

The IPA axes serve as benchmarks for acceptable service quality standards and the category the attribute is placed in can change depending on the placement of the axes. Although the importance and performance mean or median scores are traditionally used to identify the benchmark, organizations can elect to move the performance grid line to a location that represents what they consider quality performance. An evaluation technique that can be adjusted to provide that information could help enhance quality service of the organization that uses it.

Janes and Wisnom (2003) found 42 leisure-related studies which employed IPA since its development in 1977. Eleven have been completed in the area of hospi-

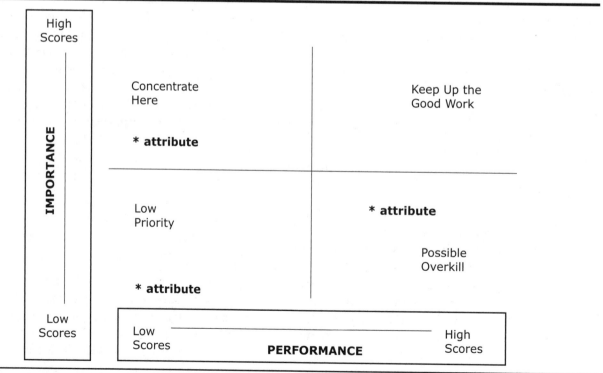

Figure 5.2
Importance-Performance Analysis (IPA) Matrix

tality, 21 in recreation and 10 in tourism. A majority (52%) of the studies were published in the 1990s, with five published since 2000. IPA was most frequently used to understand consumer opinions. However, in a few instances it was used to gain feedback from organization employees, organization management, and the general population.

They concluded the IPA has been used throughout the last three decades by hospitality related researchers as a tool to evaluate the views of staff, facilities, areas, or programs. Most often, self-administered survey instruments have been distributed after an experience transpired. Respondents evaluate the importance of specific attributes as well as the performance of the organization related to these attributes. On average, 30 attributes were evaluated and all were placed on an action grid to present the findings. The overall mean was used most often to determine which of the four categories an attribute was placed.

Vaske, Beaman, Stanley, and Grenier (1996) suggested IPA should also include segmentation variables to better understand the views held by various market segments. They found IPA could be limiting if these variables were not considered because various market segments may hold differing viewpoints.

These 42 studies provided insight into several issues related to the use of the IPA. Several researchers explored unique uses of the IPA, including when (a) organization employees were the intended sample, (b) data was collected by interview and survey, (c) attitudes toward operational policies were evaluated, (d) as many as 117 attributes were evaluated, (e) a variation of the action grid was used including a change of grid line placement, and (f) additional analysis of the data included quantitative methods such as the use of ANOVA (analysis of variance) and regression analysis.

ServQual

IPA is not the only popular leisure industry tool for evaluating satisfaction. Another popular method for measuring the difference between consumer expectations and experiences is through the ServQual model. Parasuraman, Zeithaml, and Berry (1985) developed one of the more popular measurement models in service organizations. Their ServQual model explores the gaps that exist between perceptions and expectations.

Over the past several years, few studying service quality have used IPA. ServQual became the most popular tool and most widely used instrument to measure service quality (Brown, Churchill & Peter, 1993). ServQual, adopted in the late 1980s, shared the same premise as the IPA, asking customers to share their expectations (i.e., importance)

and measurement of the experience (i.e., performance). It has even been adapted and used as a tool to measure employee internal service relationships or service quality—the service provided between employer and employee at an organization. It suggests a variety of service factors fit into five service categories,. These categories represent service quality: assurance, tangibles, empathy, responsiveness, and reliability (Zeithaml, Parsauraman & Leonard, 1990):

- *Assurance* is what the frontline staff offers customers—courteousness, respect, and cooperation.

- *Tangibles* are considered amenities like employees, facilities, equipment, and events or promotions.

- *Empathy* involves knowing the wants of a consumer and understanding their motivations.

- *Responsiveness* incorporates a readiness to assist customers and offer them service in a timely manner.

- *Reliability* is the capability of performing services promised with constancy and precision.

ServQual asks a total of 22 expectations inquiries and 22 perception inquiries. The questions are asked in each of the categories to understand the service quality of organizations. A seven-point Likert scale is used for each question. For example, an organization could learn that the expected responsiveness score from customer opinions was a 3.2 and the measurement of the experience was a 2.8 (i.e., the higher score meaning greater expectation and better performance). This result suggests customers expected more than they received, and this area should be of concern to management. Learning of the quality concern, managers would then look at each question and determine what specifically regarding responsiveness was an issue. If the performance score exceeded the expectation score, the organization would not need to be concerned with this area. The score can offer insight into issues facing the organization.

Currie (2000) stated scores can be derived that allow an organization to determine the overall quality of service, as viewed by the consumer. The ServQual equation to obtain a score is as simple as the perception score (P) minus the expectation score (E). These scores are also referred to as *gap scores*. There are five gaps outlined by Currie (2000) which can prevent an organization from being effective in offering quality services to consumers.

The first gap occurs because management's perception of customer expectations varies from actual customer desires. Those making the decisions are not necessarily experiencing firsthand what customers expect. Therefore, poor decisions are made when it is time for allocation of resources. This often stems from improper use of marketing research data. It is one thing to be able to gain the information; it is another to be able to have a system to analyze and use the data collected in a meaningful way. Other times the gap transpires because management does not interact with the customer firsthand.

The second gap arises because management does not have the ability to convert customer requests into service quality specifications for the company and employees. Often times the front-line staff performance is influenced by these standards created and the compensation accompanying them. The specifications emphasize the organization's priorities and the desired behaviors from the staff.

The third gap exists between the standards that were created and the quality of services rendered. Too often it is because the front-line staff fails to meet the criteria designed by management. To be effective the standards must be reinforced and proper resources need to be available.

The fourth gap arises when an organization offers services that it cannot complete. There is a breakdown between the external communications and what is actually available for consumers. Often the situation occurs when the organization has the best intentions, but because of inadequate financing or similar issues the staff is unable to follow through on what was promised.

The fifth gap occurs when there is a discrepancy between the levels of service the consumer received and the quality of service the consumer expected. Looking at the first four gaps and determining their effect on them is the best way to reduce the discrepancies within the consumer's overall quality experience.

Currie (2000) used ServQual to evaluate consumer satisfaction from various stakeholders in a recreation department. She found managers and front-line employees had similar opinions regarding what they believed consumer expectations to be and their views were similar to, but higher than, actual consumer opinions. Further, there were significant differences in what managers' views of consumer expectations were and the standards they implemented to reach these expectations. Managers indicated they did not provide consumers what they expected due to cost constraints. Yet managers estimated expectations higher than actual consumers did.

Although the ServQual instrument has been widely used in leisure related industries, there has been some criticism concerning its use (Babakus & Boller, 1992; Brown, Churchill & Peter, 1993; Grapentine, 1999; Mei, Dean & White, 1999; O'Neal, 2001; VanDyke, Kappelman & Prybutok, 1997). The most common criticisms include the following:

1. concerns with the ServQual dimensions—whether they are complete, accurate, and consistent across industries. McCarville (2000) agreed there is debate over the categories' applicability to leisure organizations, however, they do represent consumer concerns.

2. concerns with using two instruments—one for each of the two constructs (i.e., perceptions and expectations), to operationalize a third distinct construct (i.e., quality service).

3. concerns with the statistical properties of difference (i.e., gap) scores. The IPA cannot eliminate all the problems with this type of research, but does work to lessen some concerns associated with ServQual dimensions.

As noted, ServQual's framework is similar to IPA. Both assess customer expectations and organization performance.

Differences: IPA and ServQual

The way in which the information is obtained. IPA is customized to the particular needs of the organization, therefore, any issue the organization sees as appropriate. ServQual was designed to provide a generic measure that would be applied to any organization (Brown, Churchill & Peter, 1993; VanDyke, Kappelman & Prybutok, 1997). Baldrige criteria (as discussed in Chapter 3, p. 61) suggests quality practices involve every facet of an organization. Having flexibility in the questions asked allows all facets of the organization to be understood and where the organization specifically needs to focus.

Results on the IPA are visually plotted to make the data easy to understand. This visual plot identifies and categorizes organization attributes into four management suggestion areas.

ServQual is based on the size of the gap between expectations and performance. This prioritization, however, does not take into consideration the level of importance. If the gap between a low-rated importance item and a high-rated importance item is the same, they would receive the same priority. Based on importance, IPA prioritizes what issues the organization should address first. Those items with a high rated importance would receive precedence.

IPA identifies which attributes are considered overkill, those that are low importance and high performance by an organization, and low priority, those attributes that are of little importance and the organization is not performing well. These categories identify attributes of an organization that may be expending resources to an area not seen as important by the customer.

The IPA benchmarks for acceptable service quality standards can change. Although the importance and performance mean or median scores are traditionally used to identify the benchmark, organizations can elect to move the "performance" grid line to a location that represents what they expect or consider "quality" performance. For example, an organization that determines a score of 4 on a 5-point scale should represent the quality benchmark could develop their own line in the grid and set expectations of organization performance above or below the mean/median score.

Although these two methods are popular in leisure service settings, they do not represent all the ways in which data can be gathered. Many other forms of feedback have been used in the leisure industry. Table 5.12 highlights other ways to gain feedback from various consumers.

To accurately assess the feedback provided from the measurement techniques it is recommended that several different feedback mechanisms be used. The key to deciding and selecting which method(s) to use is to consider what you want to learn, the timeline, and the resources available. Once data is collected, use it to analyze, reward, identify root causes to problems, set goals, develop action plans, track trends, and implement and communicate findings. Let consumers know how their insight and efforts are being used.

Quality must be defined in the same way by you and by your guests since quality is their perception. Unknown

Apply What You Know

1. Assess primary and secondary research data from the organization selected in Chapter 4 to identify patterns and trends that would be helpful to understand.

2. Analyze a quantitative research-based journal article. Identify purpose, research methodology, sample, data collection methods, analysis techniques, findings, and potential limitations. How can the elements not discussed be problematic for the research?

3. Access websites listed in the text and analyze the data provided by these sources. Indicate how this information would be helpful to the leisure service organization your plan is for.

Key Terms

Area random sample
Cluster random sample
Critical incident technique
Data mining
Descriptive research
Explanatory research
Exploratory research
Focus groups
Importance performance technique
Internal market research
Market research
Mystery shopping
Perceptual mapping
Pilot testing

Population
Primary market research
Qualitative research
Quantitative research
Reliability
Sample
Secondary market research
ServQual
Simple random sample
Specialized market research
Standardized market research
Stratified random sample
Systematic random sample
Validity

Table 5.12
Feedback Methods

Internal Consumers (Employees)	External Consumers	All Types Of Consumers
• Exit interviews • Performance evaluations • Meetings • Quality circles	• Board members • Employees • Received correspondence • Tracking the number of and the reasons for giveaways • Toll-free telephone numbers • Empowerment/dissatisfaction forms • Guest advisory panels • Sales data • Guest complaints • Incidents/guest problems • Returns	• Mail, telephone, or face-to-face questionnaire • Interviews • Focus groups • Comment cards • Telephone calls • Mystery shopping • Management observation

Review Questions

1. Name five things that create confusion on questionnaires.

2. What are the two types of market research? Give two advantages and disadvantages of each.

3. Define data mining.

4. What are the possible errors in quantitative research?

5. What ethical issues need to be considered by leisure organizations in primary research?

6. Explain pilot testing.

7. What are the four categories of the IPA matrix?

8. Describe the difference between reliability and validity.

Internet Resources

Knowthis.com is a source of materials for those involved in marketing, market research, selling, promotion, and other marketing-related areas. This website includes articles, magazines, tutorials and links to other web pages that discuss market research issues.

http://www.knowthis.com

Marketing Today is an online marketing guide that provides articles with insights on strategies and tactics, and results of studies relevant to marketers. A special link is dedicated to the latest research, analysis, and trends.

http://www.marketingtoday.com

MarketResearch.com provides a comprehensive collection of published market research analysis that is available on demand.

http://www.marketresearch.com/

Market Research Society (MRS) is the world's largest professional association representing providers and users of market research. MRS provides publications and information services, conferences and seminars, meeting and networking opportunities for researchers.

http://www.mrs.org.uk/

Marketing Research Association is a source for information, assistance and training in marketing research. This association is also an important forum where marketing researchers discuss common problems, share ideas, and develop collective projects.

http://www.mra-net.org/

References

Babakus, E. and Boller, G.W. (1992). An empirical assessment of the SERVQUAL scale. *Journal of Business Research, 24*(3), 253–268.

Babbie, E. (1995). *The practice of social research.* Belmont, CA: Wadsworth.

Barsky, J. and Huxley, S. (1999). A customer-survey tool: Using quality sample. *Cornell Hotel & Restaurant Administration, 33*, 18–25.

Barsky, J. and Nash, L. (2001). One can't base management decisions on comment cards. *Hotel and Motel Management, 216*(12), 19.

Baumann, M. A. (1998). Surveys allow properties opportunity to improve guest retention. *Hotel & Motel Management, 213*, 40–41.

Beck, J. and Miao, I. (2003). Mystery shopping in lodging properties as a measurement of service quality. *Journal of Assurance in Hospitality & Tourism, 4*(1/2), 1–21.

Bissell, J. (2000). Market research needs a category focus. *Brandweek, 41*(1), 14.

Bitner, M. J., Booms, B., and Tetreault, M. S. (1995). The service encounter. In J. Batson (Ed.), *Managing services marketing* (3rd ed.). Fort Worth, TX: Dryden Press.

Brown, T. J., Churchill, G. A., and Peter, J. P. (1993). Improving the measurement of service quality. *Journal of Retailing, 69*(1), 127–139.

Carroll, S. R. and Carroll, D. (2001, August). Outside-inside marketing. *School Administrator, 58*(7), 32–34.

Clancy, K. J. and Krieg, P. C. (2002). Marketing science hasn't failed. *Brandweek, 43*(19), 42.

Cline, R. (1997). The value of human capital. *Lodging Hospitality, 53*, 20–22.

Cobb, R. (1997, July 31). Isn't it just common sense? *Marketing London*, 16–17.

Cousins, C. (2002). Getting to the "truth:" Issues in contemporary qualitative research. *Australian Journal of Adult Learning, 42*(2), 192–204.

Currie, M. E. (2000). *A comparative study of the perceptions of quality service delivery in a community recreation setting.* Unpublished doctoral dissertation, Dalhousie University.

Daniels, C. (1999). Real-life research. Observing what consumers actually do. *Marketing Magazine, 104*(19), 15–16.

Deal, K. (1999). The eyes and ears of business. *Marketing 104*(19), 18.

Dev, C. S. and Olsen, M. D. (2000). Marketing challenges for the next decade. *Cornell Hotel and Restaurant Administration Quarterly, 41*(1), 41–47.

Dillman, D. (1978). *Mail and telephone surveys: The total design method.* New York, NY: John Wiley & Sons.

Dillman, D. A. (2000). *Mail and Internet surveys: The tailored design method* (2nd ed). New York, NY: John Wiley & Sons.

Erdogan, B. Z. and Baker, M. J. (2002). Increasing mail survey response rates from an industrial population: A cost-effectiveness analysis of four follow-up techniques. *Industrial Marketing Management, 31*(1), 65–73.

Evenson, R. (1999). Soft skills, hard sell. *Techniques: Making Education and Career Connections, 74*(3), 29–31.

Fitzpatrick, M. (2001). Statistical analysis for direct marketers—In plain English. *Direct Marketing, 64*(4) 54–56.

Flood, J. (2002, May). Focus groups improve wilderness management efforts. *The Benefits of Parks & Recreation,* 24–31.

Frankfort-Nachmias, C. and Nachmias, D. (1992). *Research methods in the social sciences.* New York, NY: St. Martins Press.

Grapentine, T. (1999). The history and future of service quality assessment: Connecting customer needs and expectations to business processes. *Marketing Research, 10*(4), 4–20.

Greenbaum, T. L. (2000). Focus groups vs. online. *Advertising Age, 71*(7), 34.

Guadagnolo, F. (1985). The importance-performance analysis: An evaluation and marketing tool. *Journal of Park and Recreation Administration, 3(2),* 13–22.

Heckman, J. (2000). Qualitative research: Special report. *Marketing News, 34*(5), 15–20.

Henderson, K. A. (1991). Megatrends and organized camping in 2000 A.D. *Camping Magazine, 63*(6), 22–26.

Higgins, L. F. (1999). Applying principles of creativity management to marketing research efforts in high-technology markets. *Industrial Marketing Management, 28*(3), 305–317.

James, D. (2002). A seat at the table. *Marketing News, 36*(19) 19–20.

Janes, P. (2000). *The analysis of the human capital and segmented labor market theories as an explanation for the use, influences, and value placed on training in Michigan lodging organizations.* Doctoral dissertation, Michigan State University.

Janes, P. L. and Rood, S. (2006). [Using importance performance analysis in mystery shopping]. Raw data.

Janes, P. L. and Wisnom, M. S. (2003). The use of importance-performance analysis in the hospitality industry: A comparison of practices. *Journal of Quality Assurance in Hospitality & Tourism, 4*(1/2), 23.

Kerstetter, D. L., Zinn, H. C., Graefe, A. R., and Chen, P. (2002). Perceived constraints to state park visitation: A comparison of former-users and nonusers. *Journal of Park and Recreation Administration, 20*(1) 61–75.

Knap, N. E. and Propst, D. B. (2001). Focus group interviews as an alternative to traditional survey methods for recreation needs assessments. *Journal of Park and Recreation Administration, 19*(2), 62–82.

Koff, B. (1992). How to assess primary data collection techniques—Mail vs. telephone. *Medical and Marketing Media, 27*(1), 56–60.

Kotler, P., Roberto, N., and Lee, N. (2002). *Social marketing: Improving the quality of life.* Thousand Oaks, CA: Sage.

Long, J., Whinston, A. B., and Tomak, K. (2002). Calling all customers. *Marketing Research, 14*(3), 28–33.

Loomis, J. B. (2000). Counting on recreation use data: A call for long-term monitoring. *Journal of Leisure Research, 32*(1), 93–96.

Lowenstein, J. (1999) Telesurveys: A direct mail tune-up technique. *Folio, 28*(4), 45–48.

Mahajan, V. and Wind, J. (1999). Rx for marketing research. *Marketing Research, 11*(3), 6–13.

Maret, S. E. (December 20, 2005). Shoppers evaluate customer service on the sly. *Richmond Times Dispatch.* Richmond, VA.

Martilla, J. A. and James, J. C. (1977). Importance-performance analysis. *Journal of Marketing, 41*(1), 77–99.

Martin, C. L. (1996). The gap syndrome: The latest marketing tool is "gap analysis." *Bowlers Journal International, 83*(11), 117–119.

Masberg, B. A. (1999). What is the priority of research in the marketing and promotional efforts of convention and visitors bureaus in the United States? *Journal of Travel & Tourism Marketing, 8*(2), 29–40.

McCarville, R. (2000, November). Satisfaction: The basis of client loyalty. *Parks and Recreation, 28.*

McColl-Kennedy, J. and White, T. (1997). Service provider training programs at odds with customer requirements in five-star hotels. *Journal of Services Marketing, 11*(4), 249–264.

McPherson, D. (2002). Knowing your members' mind is key to a healthy bottom line: Inexpensive ways do exist for gathering information from current and prospective members to better serve their needs. *Fitness Management, 18*(4), 52–53, 55.

McWilliam, R. A. (2000). Reporting qualitative studies. *Journal of Early Intervention, 23*(2), 77–80.

Mei, A. W. O., Dean A. M., and White, C. J. (1999). Analyzing service quality in the hospitality industry. *Managing Service Quality, 9*(2), 136.

Myers, D. R. (n.d.). Analyze your local market: As a small retailer, you have the edge in the market-research game. *Archery Business*, 23–29.

Narvaez, L. (2006). Experimental mystery shopping: Are businesses spending their research dollars wisely? Retrieved from http://www.perceptivesciences.com/insights/white_papers/Experimental%20Mystery%20Shopping.pdf

Nelems, J. H. (2001). *Qualitative research overview.* Retrieved December 1, 2003, from http://www.marketingpower.com/content1060.php

Ofir, C. and Simonson, I. (2001). In search of negative customer feedback: The effect to evaluate on satisfaction evaluations. *Journal of Marketing Research, 38*(2), 170–182.

O'Neal, M. (2001). *Service quality management in hospitality, tourism, and leisure: Measuring service quality and customer satisfaction.* New York, NY: Haworth Hospitality Press.

Onwuegbuzie, A. (2000, November 19). *On becoming a bi-researcher: The importance of combining quantitative and qualitative research methodologies.* Paper presented at the Annual Meeting of the Association for the Advancement of Educational Research.

Parasuraman, A., Zeithaml, V. A., and Berry, L. L. (1985). A conceptual model of service quality and its implications for future research. *Journal of Marketing, 49*(Fall), 41–50.

Passikoff, R. (2002). You choose: Windshield or rearview mirror. *Marketing News, 36*(19), 23–24.

Pearce, M. (1998). Getting full value from focus-group research. *Ivy Business Quarterly, 63*(2), 72–76.

Pruden, D. R. and Vavra, T. G. (2000). Customer research, not marketing research. *Marketing Research, 12*(2), 14–19.

Redmann, D., Stitt-Gohdes, W., and Lambrecht, J. (2000). The critical incident technique: A tool for qualitative research. *Delta Pi Epsilon Journal, 42*(3), 132–153.

Roggeveen, A. L. (2001) *Integrating market research projections: The bias toward lower numbers.* Doctoral dissertation, Columbia University.

Sargeant, A. (1997). Don't be afraid of the numbers: Supplementing database records with marketing research. *Fund Raising Management, 28*(9), 22–27.

Seaton, A. V. (1997). Unobtrusive observational measures as a qualitative extension of visitor surveys at festivals and events: Mass observation revisited. *Journal of Travel Research, 35*(4), 25–30.

Semon, T. T. (2000). Better questions means more honesty. *Marketing News, 34*(17), 10.

Sevier, L. A. (2002, November). *A reflective strategy for learning the methods of qualitative research.* Paper presented at the Annual Meeting of the Mid-South Educational Research Association, Chattanooga, TN.

Solomon, D. J. (2001). *Conducting web-based surveys.* Retrieved from http://www.ericdigests.org/2002-2/surveys.htm

Solomon, J. (2002). *An insider's guide to managing sporting events.* Champaign, IL: Human Kinetics.

Spaulding, S. (2003). *Principles of questionnaire design.* Retrieved December 1, 2003 from, http://www.marketingpower.com/live/content1144.php

Stanton, J. L. (2000). The world of percentages: Focusing in on qualitative vs. quantitative data. *Food Processing, 61*(3), 36–38.

Stevens, B. (2000). Save money with online analysis. *Marketing News, 34*(23), 22–28.

Sudman, S. and Blair, E. (1999). Sampling in the twenty-first century. *Journal of Academy of Marketing Science, 27*(2), 269–277.

Sutton, W. A., Irwin, R. L., and Gladden, J. M. (1998). Tools of the trade: Practical research methods for events, teams and venues. *Sport Marketing Quarterly, 7*(2), 45–49.

Swaddling, D. (2001). Good data still worth the investment. *Marketing News, 35*(2), 20–21.

VanDyke, T. P., Kappelman, L. A. and Prybutok, V. R. (1997). Measuring information systems service quality: Concerns on the use of the ServQual questionnaire. *MIS Quarterly V, 21*, 195–208.

Vaske, J. J., Beaman, J., Stanley, R., and Grenier, M. (1996). Importance-performance and segmentation: Where do we go from here? *Journal of Travel and Tourism Marketing, 5*(3), 225–240.

Walsh, K. (2000). A service conundrum: Can outstanding service be too good? *Cornell Hotel and Restaurant Administration Quarterly, 41*(5), 40–50.

Weber, J. and Morgan, M. A. (1998). "Why" also important in direct mail effectiveness. *Marketing News, 32*(9), 11.

White, E. (2000, March 2). Market research on the Internet has its drawbacks. *The Wall Street Journal*, B3.

Wilson, A. (1998a). The role of mystery shopping in the measurement of service performance. *Managing Service Quality, 8*(6), 414–420.

Wilson, A. (1998b). The use of mystery shopping in the measurement of service delivery. *The Service Industries Journal, 18*(3), 148–163.

Wilson, D. (2003). *Market research.* Retrieved October 10, 2003, from http://www.mplans.com/dpm/article.cfm/46

Young, S. and Ross, C. (2000, June). Web questionnaires: A glimpse of survey research in the future. *Parks and Recreation*, 30–40.

Yovovich, B. G. (1991). Focusing on customers' needs and motivations. *Business Marketing, 76*(3), 41–43.

Zeithaml, V., Parsauraman, A., and Leonard, L. B. (1990). *Delivering quality service: Balancing customer perceptions and expectation.* New York, NY: Free Press.

Section 2

Developing a Leisure Services and Tourism Marketing Strategy

Chapter 6

Developing the Strategy

Bay Lanes Bowling Center recently hired their first marketing director, Lauren. She came from another bowling center giving her a great deal of experience in marketing these types of establishments. Anxious to get going, and to show the owner he made a good choice in hiring her, Lauren planned to place her first advertisement in the sports section of the local paper. Her goal was to focus on singles between the ages of 18 and 25.

Thank goodness she had enough sense to show the advertisement draft to the owner before it ran because the owner was not satisfied. The owner had little interest in targeting the young, single market. He felt they were already serving a large number from this group, and his interest was in serving families, youth (ages 8–13) and senior (ages 55+) markets. Lauren failed to understand where the organization was headed. Although this type of advertisement worked well in her last establishment, it was not a direction this center was interested in heading. The owner now wondered if he had made the right decision in hiring Lauren.

Had Lauren understood the owner's interest in these markets and developed a marketing strategy that took this into consideration as well as information on current business, trends, market demographics, and competitive information, she may have had evidence to sell the owner on the importance of the single market. She may have learned that no area competitor was pursuing that market; or vice

At the end of this chapter, readers will be able to...

- Define marketing strategy and situational assessments.

- Describe the marketing strategy development components.

- State the components of various types of assessments used to develop strategies.

- List elements within organization, global, industry, market, and competitive assessments.

- Understand the value of completing assessments.

- Describe why strategy is useful to effective leisure marketing.

- Understand how a strength, weakness, opportunity, and threat (SWOT) analysis is conducted.

versa, that all were attempting to target that age group. She also could have determined there were a large number of college-age people in the local area, and the organization had only served 10% of this group in the past year. She could have argued that here was a trend toward bowling centers attracting the 18 to 25 age market by utilizing programming. Lauren assumed that the organization would be satisfied seeing any marketing effort that produced a result—but she was mistaken. Developing a sound strategy was key in integrating marketing for this organization, as it is for other leisure service organizations.

• • • • •

The development of a marketing strategy creates the path an organization will take to ultimately identify consumer groups that will allow the achievement of organization objectives. An effective marketing strategy ensures the marketing budget will produce results for leisure service organizations.

Marketing strategy is an investigated, educated, well-thought-out plan used to determine organization marketing objectives and the most effective path for leisure service organizations to achieve their overall organization objectives. This involves gathering evidence from a wide variety of sources to making the most informed decisions possible.

Strategy development is an often misused, misunderstood step in effective marketing planning. Go-to-Market Strategies, Inc., said it best when they indicated organizations that have failed to develop a strategy should get one fast. They further suggested these organizations should "stop all marketing activities immediately and take the next three to six weeks to plan your approach" (http://www.gotomarketstrategies.com). Trapp (1991) suggested marketing strategy is an important determinant in the success of any business effort, including small business efforts. A strategy establishes and maintains a connection from an organization to its consumers. A marketing strategy's role is to determine two issues for an organization: (a) Who should the organization target as consumers? and (b) What is the best way to achieve this? A marketing strategy defines the process from which an organization will make these decisions.

Organizations that believe they "don't have the time" or "don't have the need" or "don't have the expertise" to develop a marketing strategy do not really understand the marketing function. Strategy is a critical step in marketing, Those organizations that believe marketing is simply placing an advertisement in the newspaper are mistaken. Marketing is only completed if thoughtful planning and analysis are done to make the best decisions on behalf of the organization. Otherwise, organizations are simply advertising. Marketing is an all-encompassing term that represents a variety of activities, and each activity needs to

be explored before determining how to spend marketing resources (e.g., time, people, money). Every tactical or communication aspect of marketing is more easily determined once the organization strategically determines the target markets and the organization's position. Strategy development is the most helpful but also the most difficult component of marketing.

In the initial stage of marketing plan development, strategy development will allow organizations to answer the following questions:

1. What is the historical development of my organization?

2. Where is my organization currently regarding financial status, organizational structure, and general practices?

3. Where is my organization headed in the future?

4. What is occurring in the industry and global environment that may impact my organization?

5. Who are my competitors, what do they provide, and how does my organization compare to them?

6. Who comprises my desired market?

7. What potential targeted markets are available to me?

8. What target markets make the best sense to pursue?

9. What are our organization's strengths and weaknesses?

10. How are we going to differentiate ourselves from the competition?

11. What outcomes do we strive to achieve with the target markets?

The strategic marketing process involves several steps, including assessment completion, target market development and analysis, organization assessment, and positioning. These steps ultimately lead to the development of marketing objectives from which all marketing, promotional, and communication mix plans will be based. The following three chapters will further explain the steps taken for organizations to be able to answer these questions.

Market Strategy Development

Marketing strategy is developed in a variety of ways. Various steps are taken by an organization to determine the best path to follow. Failure to do this may result in poor decisions being made. Therefore, a clear understanding of each of the necessary steps is important to any leisure and tourism organization.

The first steps in the process can also be referred to as a situational assessment. A *situational assessment* allows an organization to determine formally what is occurring inside and outside an organization at any given point in time. On a simple level, this is identified as the critical *three Cs* of marketing strategy development. Understanding the *company*, the *consumers*, and the *competition* of an organization are the three most important factors an organization must know prior to developing a marketing plan. The three Cs are further expanded to represent the variety of elements that need to be assessed. Organizations that delegate resources to conduct a situational assessment prepare themselves for managing issues ranging from changes in minimum wage on the amusement industry to the impact of September 11, 2001, on the travel industry. Figure 6.1 (p. 138) highlights the steps to develop a marketing strategy—the first of which are various assessments.

After the assessments are completed, a thorough analysis of the information gathered provides an opportunity for a leisure and tourism organization to identify and determine the markets to focus on better. Organizations then develop an in-depth understanding of potential target markets. All this information is again analyzed to identify the organization's strengths, weaknesses, opportunities, threats, and competitive position relative to each potential target market. Once the target market is solidified, a market objective is written for each target market the organization will focus on during the marketing plan time frame. Each of these topics will be further covered in Chapters 7, Target Market Approaches, and Chapter 8, Brand Positioning and Marketing Outcomes. Regardless if a marketing professional is internal or external to an organization, the following five assessments—organization, global, industry, market, and competitive—must be completed to effectively develop a marketing strategy.

Organization Assessment

The backbone of any effective marketing plan must include a knowledge base of the organizational environment. An *organization assessment* is a formal approach of documenting and understanding various components of an organization; it will provide insight into historical, current, and future directions. Several areas are evaluated, including an organization's:

- history
- philosophy (i.e., mission, values, and beliefs)
- product, service, program, and facility inventory/offerings
- organizational issues and structure
- various stakeholders
- strategic objectives/master plans
- financial status and financial goals
- historical marketing efforts
- image as viewed by those both inside and outside of the organization

Some authors have referred to this as an *internal audit* because what occurs during an organization assessment simply occurs "internally" (McCarville, 2002; O'Sullivan, 1991). Not all leisure service organizations have this information readily available. Information varies significantly across types of leisure service organizations and on how leadership desires to approach the organization's strategy efforts. Some organizations do not have defined mission statements, organizational charts, or strategic objectives. Others have never formally analyzed their financial results or projected into the future. Still others have never assessed the image they portray to others. Regardless of the number of leisure service organizations that approach it this way, the belief is that these components are important to understand the current and future direction of any organization. This process is important for any size organization. When an analysis is not completed missed opportunities, due to a lack of communication, occur. This process allows for a clearer understanding of the overall organization.

In a marketing plan, the information gathered from each of these areas is documented for all stakeholders to understand. Each year the various components are evaluated to ensure they are current. The up-to-date information should reflect the organization's situation and goals in the upcoming year. Many existing leisure organization plans fail to provide this data and insight. However, there are many reasons why an organization would find value in this assessment, including the following:

1. Ensures all those in the organization agree to the historical, current, and future direction of the organization.

stage one
Marketing, Promotional, and Communication (MPC) Strategy Development

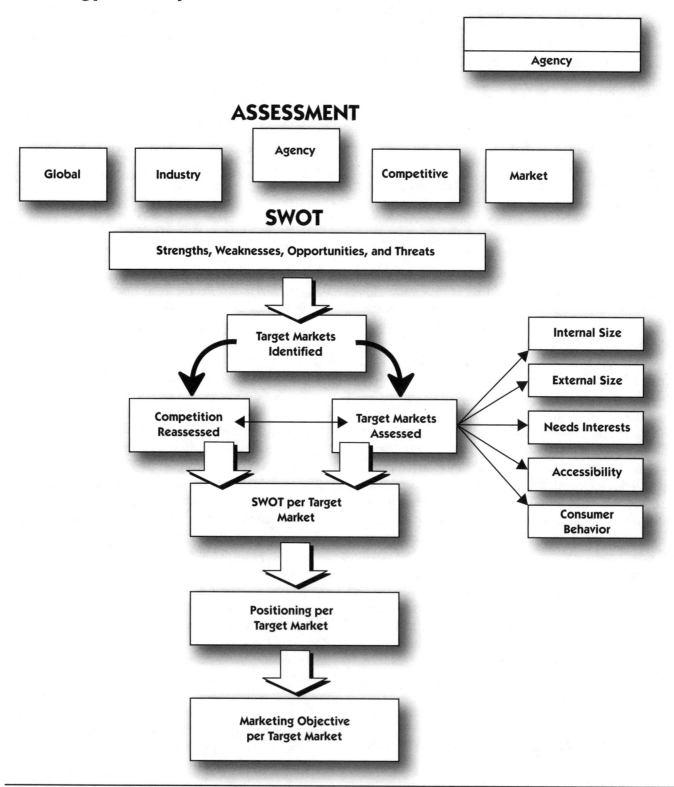

Figure 6.1
Marketing Strategy Development

2. Provides a means to communicate with staff, board members/owners and other stakeholders.

3. Provides various internal information in one source, which can be used for various functions, including training and funding opportunities.

4. Assists in determining organization strengths and weaknesses.

5. Identifies potential communication messages to be used in a communication plan.

History

The history of any organization is an interesting story that everyone associated with the organization should understand. This story provides a view of the company and allows those involved to gain a better perspective on how and why particular actions may occur. An organization's history impacts the current system and has the historical perspective, which allows others to understand and appreciate "why we do things the way we do." Further, this perspective provides potential competitive advantages from which the organization's "message" can be developed. The organization may use this historical perspective to communicate with various stakeholders.

Real Life Story: History Is the Story at Shepler's Mackinac Island Ferry

The Shepler family has owned and operated Shepler's Mackinac Island Ferry, Inc., since it began in 1945. Captain William H. Shepler created the organization by recognizing the need for transportation to and from Mackinaw City and Mackinac Island, which was an emerging tourist destination. He started the business by taking people by small watercraft and soon his son Bill was working along side him. The organization continued to grow throughout the years, adding larger vessels and more services for visitors and diversifying their offerings to include marina boat repair, long-term parking, and retail shopping. Bill's family continued the tradition and all his children have worked along side their father as soon as they were able. Today, the Shepler family operates their organization with the same family-oriented style. Even though over 200

employees are a part of the Shepler tradition, each is considered one of the family. This has become part of the Shepler culture experienced by both employees and guests.

Shepler's had never used this history in communicating with their consumers until 2000 when they decided that their family involvement and history were indeed a large part of what they did, how they operated, and what they valued. This was a competitive advantage for their organization as well. Other ferryboat organizations did not have the tradition or value placed in the same manner. They decided to use this message in communicating with various stakeholders in all publications and collateral. The photos here highlight Shepler's brochures from before and after the historical message was used.

1980 brochure:
One-color (blue) schedule

2000 brochure:
Full-color fold out includes schedule and family involvement highlights

Each organization should have a documented timeline of significant occurrences that have impacted the organization. This timeline should be maintained and start the formal marketing plan to give anyone reading it the opportunity to understand the "big picture" and value the rich traditions and history embedded in any organization. Table 6.1 highlights one leisure organization's historical timeline.

Philosophy

An organization's philosophy is represented in the mission, value statements, beliefs, and practices within an organization. Understanding the foundation of an organization is important prior to developing a strategy for the organization. Any strategy should be based on the same foundation from which the organization has been built and is currently practicing under. The organization's culture is developed through this philosophy because stakeholders belong or are involved with the organization based on how these beliefs impact them. Values, beliefs, and practices within the organization should be represented in an organization mission statement. A *mission statement* should embody both the values and the vision of an organization. It provides an understanding of what the organization is based on as well as what it strives to become—what every action should be based on. This information is valued for marketing strategy development as these are the priorities of the organization.

An effective mission statement should be communicated in 30 seconds or less and tell the organization's story, including what the organization is, does, stands for, and strives to be (Writing a Mission Statement, 2004). It is a process that staff should be involved in developing. If employees are unable to identify with an organization's

---

Table 6.1
Leisure Organization Historical Time Frame of Events

The National Intramural Association (NIA), founded in 1950, was the predecessor to what is now the National Intramural Recreational Sports Association (NIRSA). Dr. William Wasson arranged the first Intramural Conference at Dillard University in New Orleans where the NIA was initiated. Twenty African American men and women intramural directors from eleven historically Black colleges assembled and formed the NIA. Dr. Wasson was its president for the next five years.

Some of the noteworthy historical moments of the NIRSA include the following:

1952   NIA became interracial, inviting White intramural directors to the third annual conference.

1959   Female attendance at the annual conference was abated voluntarily.

1963   Exhibitors were allowed to show their products at the annual conference.

1971   The constitution was revised to accept women as members of the NIA.

1975   The NIA membership voted to change the name to the National Intramural-Recreational Sports Association (NIRSA).

1975   The first Executive Committee Student Representative was named.

1977   *NIRSA Journal* was first published.

1986   The National Office became a full-time operation.

1987   Mary Daniels, of The Ohio State University, was elected the first female NIRSA President.

1993   The NIRSA Foundation is established focusing on scholarship, membership development, and research.

1998   The NIRSA National Center officially opened its 16,089-square-foot, $2.2 million facility in Corvallis, Oregon.

1999   50th Annual NIRSA Conference and celebration held.

1999   Started the "for-profit" NIRSA Services Corporation.

1999   Initiated the celebration of National Recreational Sports and Fitness Day each February 22.

NIRSA memberships have evolved to form a network of highly trained professionals in the recreational sports field throughout the United States, Canada, and other countries around the world. The Association's rapidly growing membership is comprised of more than 4,000 professional, student, and associate members. Universities hold the majority of memberships, but they also exist in the military, correctional institutions, corporations, community parks and recreation departments, elementary/middle/secondary schools, not-for-profit organizations, and private enterprise. The Associate Member group consists of businesses that cater to the recreational sports world.

College athletics started from intramural activities, and even today many varsity teams start with intramural status. Intramural sports allow competition for all students; 80% of over 15 million students at the collegiate level are participating in various recreational sports programs compared to 2% in varsity sports. The field of recreational sports and participation in sports and fitness activities has grown tremendously. Consider the following:

• Nearly 11 million college students use recreational facilities operated by NIRSA's members.

• More than 1.1 million intramural contests are scheduled each year.

• More than 2 million individuals participate in collegiate sport clubs.

• More than $1.5 billion has recently been expended (or is approved to be spent) to renovate or build new "state-of-the-art" collegiate recreational sports facilities.

The major professional responsibilities of the NIRSA membership include the administration of informal sports, fitness programming, recreational facility operations, fiscal and personnel management, sport clubs, intramurals, outdoor recreation, and wellness programs.

mission, they are less likely to carry it out. Bialeschki and Henderson (2000) found mission statements were a priority for camps as determined by a study funded by the American Camping Association. The increased importance placed on mission statements centered on ensuring camps were mission driven and using it "as a roadmap for addressing today's societal needs" (p. 26). As an example, consider the mission and values statement for Mackinac State Historic Parks (see Box: Mackinac State Historic Parks).

Organizations that have not yet defined or developed their philosophical statements should ask these questions:

1. What does your organization stand for/believe?

2. What does your organization hope to achieve?

3. What are the fundamental ideas that guide your organization's decisions?

4. How does your organization put what is important into practice?

Inventory

To strategically plan for an organization, all offerings provided to stakeholders must be thoroughly understood. Identifying what the overall organization currently provides to consumers allows those developing the strategy within any area of the organization to understand what is currently available to work with, what may need to be developed, and what may not be necessary. Leisure service environments are complex and need to be analyzed on several different levels. The list is not as simple as "products and services." Various offerings need to be understood and analyzed, including the following:

- products

- programs

- facilities

- services

- policies and procedures

Each leisure and tourism organization has a variety of items that would be placed under each offering category. *Products* include the physical, tangible offering provided to the public. In a golf course, this may include 18 holes of golf, merchandise in the pro shop, or grilled hamburgers on the turn. *Programs* at a golf course may include company tournaments, youth leagues, and golf how-to clinics. *Facilities* at a course may include a pro shop, cart storage barn, clubhouse with restaurant/lounge, and a banquet facility. *Services* at a golf course may include private lessons, caddies available, club cleaning/repair services, hours of operation, and beverage cart offerings. Finally, *policies and procedures* are the aspects of an organization's offerings that impact consumers, from 100% guarantees to a nonsmoking facility, which are all a part of what an organization provides and how they provide it

Listing each of the organization's offerings under these categories provides easily accessible information that acknowledges all resources of the company for every department. For example, a community center that has a banquet/meeting facility as well as a fitness and aquatic center should review all organization offerings available to them, even if they do not currently utilize the services. If the banquet facility is writing a marketing plan, it would still be valuable to understand all organization offerings because these are resources available to them (whether they

---

Mackinac State Historic Parks

Mission Statement

At Mackinac State Historic Parks, we protect, preserve, and present Mackinac's rich historic and natural resources to provide outstanding educational and recreational experiences for the public.

Institutional Values

Institutional Values Statement

- Mackinac State Historic Parks holds the following values, which we group into the interdependent areas of Public Service, Resource and Program, and Staff. We understand that the success of MSHP depends on the conscientious practice of all these values.

- Faithful adherence by all staff and volunteers to these values enables MSHP to succeed in our mission and financial responsibilities. These values guide our decision making at all levels and areas of the organization, from executive budget decisions to daily individual decisions about personal conduct.

- The Institutional Values are organic, designed to change when necessary to meet the changing needs of MSHP.

Public Service Values

- We exist to serve the public. We listen to our audiences and invite their suggestions. We conduct visitor research and program evaluation to ensure that our products and services are meaningful and effective.

- We encourage broad and inclusive participation in MSHP parks and programs, making resources and activities accessible and welcoming for all people. We seek to engage volunteers in a meaningful way in our programs. We foster a sense of ownership of MSHP among the public.

use them or not) and may represent a competitive advantage. Formalizing a list may provide an advantage for an organization that is competing against a similar organization. For example, a golf course owned by a resort would also list all resort products, programs, facilities, and services in their organization assessment. They have more offerings

Facilities

Center Lake Bible Camp is located in Tustin, Michigan, on 120 acres of land nestled along the edge of Center Lake. Facilities include:

Dining Hall
- Seats 188 campers with an overflow space for up to 255
- Massive stone fireplace
- Piano
- PA system
- Beverage bar
- Scenic deck overlooking Center Lake

Lounge
- Stone fireplace
- Available for small group meetings

Recreation Room
- Located in lower level of dining room
- Billiards, foosball, table tennis, and air hockey
- Sunken fireplace
- Includes one meeting room and two housing rooms
- Restrooms with showers

Cabins
- Five guest cabins with private restroom/shower facilities
- Ten individual heated cabins

Bathhouse
- For use by RV area and camper cabins

Chapel
- Seating capacity of 285
- Piano
- Communication booth with mixing board, sound system, and multimedia set up
- Restrooms in foyer

Nature Center

RV Sites
- Ten sites available
- Includes water, electric and sewer hookup

Camp Store
- Carries various items (e.g., clothing, souvenirs, candy and various personal items
- Pop machines
- Ice cream/Snack shop

Sports Areas
- Soccer/football field
- Kickball/softball field
- Basketball court
- Volleyball court
- Skate park

Waterfront Campfire Amphitheater
- Seating capacity of 100

White Heart Ranch
- Includes barn that houses 15 horses
- Outdoor shelter
- Four platform tents
- Bathhouse
- Fire pit

High Adventure Activities
- 40-foot climbing wall
- 20- and 40-foot high ropes course
- Indoor climbing wall

Programs, Products, and Services

Camps

Base camp
Week-long camp jam-packed with a variety of activities, speakers, and music

Ranch Camp
A camp focused on horsemanship skills with horse care and grooming, riding instruction, trail rides, games and other fun activities

Canadian Adventure
A trip to Canada featuring towering cliffs, vast forests, rock climbing, canoeing, and hiking in the wilderness

Trail Camp
A horse-riding camp along the Michigan Shore to Shore Riding and Hiking Trail including sleeping out, cooking over an open fire, and tubing

France 2004
CLBC is partnering with Youth for Christ to help remodel a Christian camping ministry in France

Specialty Camps
A series of six different camps focused on discipleship, nature, adventure, extreme sports, and soccer.

Summer Activities
- Swimming
- Canoeing
- Waterslide
- Blobbing
- Fishing
- Paddleboats
- Basketball
- Soccer
- Football
- Volleyball
- Frisbee/disc golf
- Noah's Ark playground
- Minigolf
- Tetherball
- Nature center
- Paintball
- Giant's ladder
- Archery
- Riflery
- Bouldering wall
- Indoor/Outdoor climbing walls
- Two-level ropes course
- Crafts
- Flying squirrel
- Initiatives course
- Recreation room
- Horseshoes
- BMX bikes
- Hiking trails
- Shuffleboard
- Horse trail rides
- Hay rides
- Skate park

Figure 6.2
A Camp's Offerings (*Center Lake Bible Camp & Retreat Center Marketing Plan*, 2004)

available to them than a course not affiliated with a resort, and they could market this for a competitive advantage. Figure 6.2 highlights a camp's offerings.

Organizational Issues and Structure

Anyone involved in developing an organization marketing plan must also understand the overall organizational structure to best develop an effective strategy. This may include thoroughly understanding the departments, job duties, and capacity of an organization. This overview can be outlined in an organizational chart, job descriptions, and summaries that identify the number and type of employees.

Having this information allows an organization to identify all potential human capital and resources within an organization that can assist in developing the marketing strategy and implementing the actual marketing plan. Figure 6.3 highlights a leisure and tourism organization's operational structure.

Stakeholders

What would a leisure and tourism organization say if you asked, "Whom do you serve?" Often leisure service organizations view those they serve as "customers" who pay for the use of or participate in the services they provide. This list is more extensive than simple customers, however. With strategic marketing planning it is important the organization fully identify all the stakeholders that influence the organization and those they serve.

Most organizations, on closer analysis, understand there are a variety of "publics" they serve or are invested in. The stakeholders often include employees, volunteers, board members or investors, suppliers, community members, and nonusers or concerned publics (e.g., environmental groups). Organizations should identify all the publics they wish to serve and formally document this in their marketing plan. By detailing these individuals and how they relate to the organizational objectives, an organization can determine the most effective strategy to achieve desirable outcomes.

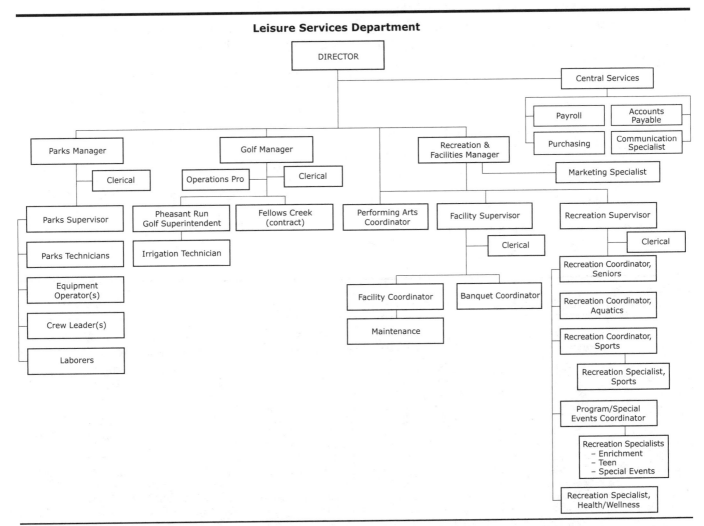

Figure 6.3
A Leisure and Tourism Organization's Operational Structure

Strategic Objectives/Master Plans

Someone in the organization knows where it is headed, but do all stakeholders understand what is important to the organization, where they would like to head, and what the priorities are? Most readers have probably been involved with an organization or company where he or she did not understand the strategic plans for the organization. In the community setting, master plans often formalize this understanding and provide an overview of the future direction. However, even in these settings, not all leisure service organizations communicate this well to those involved in the organization.

The marketing plan cannot be strategically developed without this type of information. This is critical to understanding in what direction the plan should head to achieve specific overall goal(s). Historic marketing efforts did not take into account the desired direction of the overall organization; this has caused leisure marketers great problems. All marketing efforts should be tied to organization objectives and should support the overall efforts of the organization. If this is not well-understood within the organization, it is risky to conduct marketing efforts that may not parallel the organization's desired path. Often times these relate to an organization's financial, operational, capital, and promotional plans. They may or may not include each of these areas depending on the direction of the organization for the near future. For example, the Binder Park Zoo's strategic objectives have both a financial and promotional focus:

- Increase awareness among key target audiences.

- Redefine the zoo image.

- Increase overall attendance by at least 40%.

Financial Status and Goals

Prior to developing a marketing strategy for a leisure and tourism organization, an understanding of the financial results and projections are critical to identifying and developing an effective direction to pursue. Current financial results include market share analysis, actual revenue, expenses, and profit throughout an organization. It is also valuable to understand specific projections and future goals of the organization. There are various reasons why these components are valued, including (a) understanding the strengths and weaknesses of the organization, (b) identifying areas on which to focus marketing efforts, and (c) highlighting potential resources for marketing implementation. Historical financial results are also valuable for understanding cause-effect relationships of past marketing related efforts, markets, demands, and other conditions (e.g., weather) that impact organization results. Table 6.2 shares historical revenue data for a membership in a campus recreation fitness center.

What can you conclude from this data? What other inferences can be generated as a result of this analysis? Consider the following questions:

1. Are there any revenue patterns in membership or guest revenue across time? Why are these patterns apparent (e.g., slower in the summer months)?

2. In what months is revenue the highest? Is that consistent over time?

3. When are the slowest revenue months? Could marketing efforts be more critical here?

Table 6.2
Historical Membership Revenue Data From a Campus Recreation Fitness Center

Month	2001		2002		2003		2004		2005	
	Members	Passes	Members	Passes	Members	Passes	Members	Passes	Members	Passes
January	42,456	85	47,275	1,155	53,387	1,829	55,010	1,996	40,540	2,010
February	17,630	110	27,376	1,895	27,572	1,423	27,200	1,525	24,110	1,170
March	16,263	118	51,050	2,056	18,478	2,292	21,097	2,465	23,645	1,535
April	17,477	645	17,578	3,980	13,126	3,424	18,962	4,108	12,711	12,050
May	12,478	996	17,898	2,555	14,249	3,007	15,874	3,001	16,014	4,110
June	16,003	1,208	17,394	5,862	44,205	3,215	44,255	3,150	45,672	3,760
July	9,731	1,164	9,412	4,413	13,156	4,607	10,123	4,988	10,840	5,103
August	24,199	2,225	13,375	4,079	14,858	5,438	15,305	5,623	19,473	5,111
September	27,855	1,309	37,185	3,756	21,636	4,315	24,556	1,654	23,333	1,480
October	21,692	1,899	31,008	4,005	25,302	3,969	26,032	4,566	24,009	3,673
November	21,952	1,633	19,732	2,100	16,530	1,185	16,999	1,527	15,550	984
December	10,205	1,420	11,680	1,506	18,435	1,784	19,246	1,815	14,710	970
Revenue	237,941	12,812	300,963	37,362	280,934	36,488	294,659	36,418	270,607	30,956
Total Revenue	**$250,753**		**$338,325**		**$317,422**		**$331,077**		**$301,563**	

4. What occurred in June that caused a member revenue increase between 2002 and 2003? Did any of it have to do with marketing (e.g., coupons, special promotion)?

5. What happened to overall revenue in 2003 and 2005?

6. What do we know about revenue in terms of various market segments?

7. Why was there an increase in passes revenue in April 2005?

If you had just started with this organization it would be difficult to answer many of the questions. In fact, unless you were directly involved in analyzing and discussing revenue cause-effect over each of the years determining a response to these questions would be near impossible. Ideally, revenue data from an organization will also include a critique of the year highlighting any changes in patterns and impacts on revenue (e.g., weather, competition, pricing changes, promotional efforts). This analysis would have stated the month for membership renewals was changed and were now sent in June rather than March as done in 2002; hence, the revenue shift occurred. Further, this analysis would have reported that late in 2001 a marketing director was hired and the first marketing plan was developed. The increase in revenue is a direct reflection on the organization's more strategic focus on marketing activities and outside memberships.

Further, this data can be broken into market segments to truly understand who the organization is serving, what impact they have on the organization overall, and what direction the organization should pursue as a result of these findings. Revenue data is valuable to identify the best possible path for leisure organizations to follow and

documenting fluctuations is critical. In the next two chapters it will become more apparent as to why this breakdown of data is critical by various market segments.

Other helpful financial data in marketing includes understanding the financial efforts of our leisure organization compared to others. A *market share analysis* compares data from competing leisure service organizations and provides an understanding of how each organization performed compared to the overall competitive market. Table 6.3 is a canoe livery's market share analysis.

In the market share analysis report WR Livery had a 116% market share, indicating they served more than their fair share of the market. Organizations under 100% lost rentals to competing liveries. These figures do not include data regarding revenue made from each rental; however, it provides an understanding of total livery demand in a market and who received the higher rental demand.

Other helpful financial results include revenue and sales forecasts. These forecasts are developed by the organization to project the anticipated revenue increases across various elements of the organization. This forecast indicates what areas the organization anticipates growth, maintenance, or decrease in revenue. Careful planning and research have gone into the development of this type of analysis tool, and it is valuable to the marketing efforts because it identifies specific measurable financial goals that must be supported through marketing efforts. Table 6.4 (p. 146) highlights a sample leisure and tourism organization revenue/sales forecast.

The sales forecast in Table 6.4 describes the projected revenue anticipated for the organization in 2006. In analyzing the data it appears the organization is projecting to increase revenue of guest passes more considerable starting in April 2006 and membership revenue in several months despite a poor revenue the prior year. The projected increase

---

Table 6.3
Market Share Analysis

Canoe Livery	# of Rental Canoes/Kayaks	Rental Capacity[1]	2005 Actual Rentals	Organization Rental %[2]	Market Share %[3]
WR	65	23,725	18,744	79%	116%
TT	23	8,395	5,954	71%	104%
RGR	70	25,550	15,916	62%	92%
LGR	30	10,950	5,726	52%	77%
BSA	25	9,125	6,549	72%	106%
Market Totals	**213**	**77,745**	**52,889**	**68%**	

[1] Rental days multiplied by number of rentals (e.g., 365 days x 65 available canoes/kayaks)
[2] Percent of rental capacity of canoe/kayak rental
[3] Percent market share is determined through the formula:

$$\frac{\text{Market Total Rental Capacity}/\text{Organization Rental Capacity}}{\text{Market Total Rentals}/\text{Organization Total Rentals}} \times 100 = \% \text{ Market Share}$$

must be supported by marketing activities. As such, the fitness center has decided to develop an aggressive campaign targeting local area hotel guests. In addition, revenue is projected to increase throughout the next years at a more moderate level; however, the significant membership increase that occurred between June 2002 and June 2003 must be maintained. Therefore, membership renewals must be sent to community members during this time again. Overall, the organization has projected an increase in membership revenue for the next year as well as an increase in guest pass revenue of over $20,000. Marketing activities must support this increase and determine how the organization will achieve these financial objectives.

Marketing history and forecasts provide organizations with a visual view of various market segments served and revenue garnished from each source as well as revenue projected from each source. This data was what was "missing" from this revenue history because total revenue did not reflect various market segments. This projection is done throughout the marketing process and will not be finalized until the marketing plan is developed. Hence, the value and reason why the market influences organization objectives.

Historical Marketing Efforts

Whether one is new to an organization or a returning employee, when preparing to develop the marketing strategy it is valuable to reflect on the previous year's marketing efforts (and further back if necessary). Ideally, organizations will have documented marketing efforts and evaluated their respective impact on the organization. Unfortunately, oftentimes this is not the case and little documented histori-

cal marketing data is available. At times, however, available staff can provide some insight into the past year's efforts and the impact they had on the organization.

Analyzing the past year's marketing plan is a good place to begin. Assessing where the organization was headed over the year and what the results were helps to identify potential growth areas, unforeseen challenges or successes, and effective communication efforts. Analyzing a critique of last year's marketing budget and determining what impact the efforts had on the overall marketing objectives will provide a breadth of data that will be valuable for the next year's plan.

Reviewing all promotional materials, including flyers, brochures, newsletters, websites, advertisements, promotional items, and displays provides an understanding of the brand identity, message sent to stakeholders, the markets desired or focused toward as well as the image portrayed. This analysis assists not only in comparing competitor marketing material but also in identifying if a unified brand system has been developed, including the use of a logo, slogan, and colors, and if it is representative of the future direction of the organization.

Image

At some point, to best prepare a marketing strategy, an organization must understand its image according to various stakeholder groups. Ideally, market research data will be available for organizations to access information regarding their image by employees, consumers in various markets, volunteers, and board members. Quality issues should be apparent in this analysis to understand how vari-

Table 6.4
Example of a Revenue/Sales Forecast for a Campus Recreation Fitness Center

| | Historic Revenue Results | | | | | | | | Forecast | |
| | 2002 | | 2003 | | 2004 | | 2005 | | 2006 | |
Month	Members	Passes	Members	Passes	Members	Passes	Members	Passes	Members	Passes
January	47,275	1,155	53,387	1,829	55,010	1,996	40,540	2,010	57,000	3,000
February	27,376	1,895	27,572	1,423	27,200	1,525	24,110	1,170	30,000	3,000
March	51,050	2,056	18,478	2,292	21,097	2,465	23,645	1,535	30,000	3,000
April	17,578	3,980	13,126	3,424	18,962	4,108	12,711	12,050	20,000	5,000
May	17,898	2,555	14,249	3,007	15,874	3,001	16,014	4,110	18,000	4,000
June	17,394	5,862	44,205	3,215	44,255	3,150	45,672	3,760	48,000	5,000
July	9,412	4,413	13,156	4,607	10,123	4,988	10,840	5,103	11,000	6,000
August	13,375	4,079	14,858	5,438	15,305	5,623	19,473	5,111	16,000	6,000
September	37,185	3,756	21,636	4,315	24,556	1,654	23,333	1,480	24,000	3,000
October	31,008	4,005	25,302	3,969	26,032	4,566	24,009	3,673	30,000	6,000
November	19,732	2,100	16,530	1,185	16,999	1,527	15,550	984	25,000	3,000
December	11,680	1,506	18,435	1,784	19,246	1,815	14,710	970	25,000	3,000
Revenue	300,963	37,362	280,934	36,488	294,659	36,418	270,607	30,956	334,000	50,000
Total Revenue	**$338,325**		**$317,422**		**$331,077**		**$301,563**		**$384,000**	

ous stakeholders perceive the organization. This data will provide insight about the organization's strengths and weaknesses as well as the future direction.

An organization's image is based on perceptions. These perceptions or expectations, as outlined in Chapter 3, The Quality Service Foundation, are based on several areas that an organization can better understand and prepare for. An organization can access satisfaction data, conduct a competitive analysis, evaluate promotional materials, and encourage quality experiences to gain a better understanding of what these expectations or perceptions may be.

An organization needs to reflect on these perceptions and ask themselves the following questions:

1. What do our stakeholders think and say about our organization?

2. What is our organization's reputation with each stakeholder group?

3. Are we proud of our organization's image?

4. Do we want to change any of the perceptions of these stakeholders?

Global Assessment

A *global assessment* is designed to formally analyze what is occurring in the world that may impact specific leisure service organizations. This includes the broader global view as well as the local view. The depth of the view is based on the reach of the organization's market (e.g., international markets would want to view a larger area assessment than a leisure organization that serves domestic consumers). These areas of interest impact the organization but the orga-

nization has little control over them. A look outside the direct leisure environment can provide a more complete assessment for marketing. Some of these issues may currently be impacting the leisure industry, but others may not. Those that are not may at any time become problems. An organization that is knowledgable about issues is better prepared to manage them once confronted with the situation. Table 6.5 highlights some topics of interest to a global assessment as well as the types of issues that may be relative to leisure service organizations.

Industry Assessment

Although leisure service professionals keep well acquainted with industry information, it is critical this insight be used during the strategy phase of the marketing plan process. An *industry assessment* is a thorough evaluation of industry-specific happenings that may impact a leisure and tourism organization. Professionals can access data regarding the leisure industry from trade associations, trade journals, other periodicals, and the popular press. As suggested in Chapter 5, Understanding, Developing, and Applying Market Research, several avenues for accessing data regarding the leisure industry exist. Leisure professionals must understand how to access this data as more sources of information become available. This type of information is valuable to market strategy development because it provides a base of resources that can help to identify the following:

1. *future product, service, program or facility development* (e.g., someone thought of spinning classes, rock climbing, skate parks). The popularity of the trends catapulted during the past five years—greater equity in sport participation

---

Table 6.5
Global Assessment Topics and Issues

Political issues	Minimum wage increase, rise in the cost of healthcare, taxation issues, special interest groups
Technological advancements	Computers, timesaving devices, improved safety, transportation advancements
Legal issues	Drunk driving laws, term limits
Economic issues	Employment levels, interest rates, inflation, change in work (e.g., flextime, telecommute), changes in organization structure
Societal trends	Lifestyle issues, diversity, changes in family composition, aging population
Health issues	Wellness interest, decline in youth fitness, rising healthcare costs, increased stress
Environmental concerns	User conflicts, energy concerns, ecotourism interest, environmental responsibility
Educational issues	Decreased support of extracurricular issues, increased emphasis on higher education, movement to lifelong learning, greater competition, choice at all education levels

and the blurring of public versus private involvement in leisure. Travel industry leaders suggested their interest in learning more about trends and many studies that currently exist are "either ad hoc (with no systematic process) or they are done by companies that have a vested interest in the result" (Dev & Olsen, 2000, p. 44)

2. *potential markets* (e.g., integrating persons with disabilities in all types of programming, seniors engaged in adventure recreation activities and partnerships between for-profit and nonprofit leisure organizations)

3. *answers to current or future challenges* (e.g., at-risk youth, competition between nonprofits and for-profits and alternative funding amidst budget cuts)

4. *new suppliers and technological advancements/ equipment* (e.g., electronic admittance cards to automatically analyze data, a speciality flooring manufacturer, online registration and payment)

Market Assessment

A *market assessment* provides a complete understanding of internal and external market segments, including use, satisfaction, interest, and behavioral information. This assessment is completed on those currently served in an organization as well as those desired by an organization. Caro (2001) stated a market analysis was a "critical building block in the club's success now and in the future" (p. 53). He further stated that today there is indeed a science to studying a market. Dev and Olson (2000) suggested the industry needs to better understand these topics.

Current Consumers Served

Having a thorough understanding of the consumers currently served in an organization is one of the most critical *C*s an organization must understand. When working with an organization on developing a strategy, the first questions asked include the following:

- What can you tell me about your current consumers?

- What do they look like?

- Where are they from?

- What do they do?

- What do they do when they are here?

- How satisfied are they with you?

- What are their needs, wants and desires?

Unfortunately, more times than not, small leisure service organizations are not able to share a great deal about their consumers beyond individual perceptions of what the markets look and act like, or general figures on internal data collected (e.g., amount of revenue/profit, number of visitors overall). In today's competitive, strategic environment it is more important than ever to have specific, detailed data about who is currently being served and whether they are currently being targeted or not. This data can assist an organization in a variety of ways, including the following:

- to understand various markets currently served which allows the application of target market practices

- to measure results of marketing efforts on specific marketing objectives

Real Life Story: Data to Understand Market Segments

A community parks and recreation department needed consulting help with their marketing efforts. The first several questions were asked to gain an understanding of the *company* itself (i.e., organization assessment), *competition*, and *consumers* (i.e., the critical "three *C*s"). Financial results and consumer information provided highlighted the overall revenue/profit earned for the year by months of the year and the overall number of consumers served throughout the year. Although this was helpful data, ideally it would have been separated into market segments. It would have been valuable to understand what percent of revenue was from the senior, family, or youth market. It would have been helpful to understand the exact number of consumers in each of these market segments as well. This data would have been easy to gather and analyze, but the organization had not seen value in doing so.

The following year, a part of the marketing plan identified how they would analyze revenue, profit, and consumer numbers. A simple additional registration line item, then coded to community "cards," provided the needed analysis.

Now, on a monthly basis, the revenue is subdivided by market segment, and the monthly consumer numbers are broken down into these segments. Over time, this data will be more valuable because comparisons can now be made regarding specific marketing efforts geared toward certain market segments.

- to more effectively address consumer needs, interests, and desires

- to better understand cause-effect revenue streams and sources that have negatively or positively impacted the organization

- to identify potential future markets to pursue by understanding who (and how many) are currently served and who is potentially available to serve (i.e., market demand)

Market Area Demographics

Another area important to understand is the *market demographics* for the geographic areas of interest to the organization. This information can assist in identifying the potential markets to be served by an organization. For example, if an organization knows their current consumer demographic analysis and compares this to the same geographic area to identify the potential demand, it becomes clearer to an organization if this is a market segment that should be pursued. The organization can ask themselves, "Are there enough people within this area that we have not yet served?" or "Should we pursue this market group?"

It is only through having data on both who the organization currently serves and the potential demand available in a market area that an organization can strategically determine the most effective path to follow. An organization may determine that, even though they are serving a current market (e.g., preschoolers), there are more to be served in the market area; or they may decide that they are not currently serving another market segment but may be interested in targeting another group (e.g., large companies).

In addition to general demographic characteristics, other social and economic trends need to be understood about market segments. An organization needs to understand the growth or decline of various age groups, changes in disposable income spending, concerns for "green" issues (e.g., conservation, pollution), personal health, organic products, and natural remedies (http://www.freedemographics.com) of the market in which they are interested. Several components of a market area can and should be analyzed, including the following:

- population and sociodemographic characteristics (e.g., census data)

- cultural characteristics

- various types and sizes of organizations (e.g., largest employers from Economic Development or Chambers of Commerce offices)

- needs and wants in specific leisure offerings

- socioeconomic background of the population

- consumer behaviors

The more that is known about the entire market, the more accurately an organization can select the effective strategy for them.

Competitive Assessment

Competition is the third C that must be thoroughly understood to be able to properly develop a leisure and tourism organization marketing strategy. When asked, some leisure organizations suggest they have no competition, yet most can verbally name who their "competition" is. However, not all leisure service organizations formalize their approach to analyzing their competitors and cannot tell specific details regarding their competition. Yet, Panico (2005) states, "Competition drives improvement. [It] creates the challenges and threats to motivate us to become healthier, excel in our professions, and generally accelerate our performance and progress toward any goal" (p. 69). Therefore, finding out about them is critical. Any leisure and tourism organization should be able to answer the following questions about their competition:

- What do they charge?

- What products, services, programs, or facilities do they offer?

- When are they open?

- Whom do they serve?

A successful strategy cannot be developed without this information. Leisure service organizations formalize their understanding of competitors in a competitive analysis. A *competitive analysis* documents competing organization capabilities, resources, and strategies. This helps to pinpoint the competitor's vulnerabilities and competitive advantages. An organization does not assess the competition to eliminate them. Today, an organization needs to understand the competition to differentiate themselves, to identify their own competitive niche, and to establish their own place in the leisure service marketplace.

Competition is anything, or one thing, that tries to get people's recreation and entertainment dollars.
Rich Fairman, Warwick Hills Country Club

Organizations summarize their findings of competitors in a table so they are better able to quickly assess and compare their organization to competitors. This information is updated as the respective leisure organizations change. For example, in the lodging industry, prices, services and offerings often change quarterly. Therefore, the competitive analysis is also completed quarterly to assess these changes. In some leisure industries the changes may be annually, biannually, quarterly, or even monthly. No one formula exists; organizations need to understand the fluctuations in organization offerings, prices, and so forth that necessitate the analysis of the competition.

It is important to understand as much about competitors as possible. This can be difficult, however, as organizations do not provide their list of activities, prices, and marketing strategies to competitors. You must gather this information on your own. Staff within organizations gathers this information in a variety of ways. Ideally, organization staff would personally visit all competitors and participate in their leisure "experience." A benefit within the leisure industry is being able to participate in other leisure experiences to assess competitive organizations' offerings. Organizations visiting another leisure establishment to conduct a competitive assessment would act like any other consumer. Unlike other consumers, however, they would absorb all they could about the organization. The organization staff could also drive by competitors, telephone and e-mail competitors, review websites and marketing/promotional materials, and read local newspapers and trade journals to gain a thorough understanding of the organization and their practices. Further, publicly held organizations have resources available that privately held organizations do not. A competitive analysis for an athletic club is shown in Table 6.6. The organization in this instance, the Wellness Athletic Club, would fill in their own organization infor-

Table 6.6
Competitive Analysis of Three Athletic Clubs

	Wellness Athletic Club	**Resort Sports**	**University Recreation**
Size (e.g., facility's sq ft, number of employees, number of holes)		20,000 square feet Staff of 20 Hours: 7 a.m.–11 p.m., 7 days	180,000 square feet Staff of 300 Hours: 8 a.m.–12 a.m., 7 days
Offerings (detailed) Products, Services, Programs and Facilities		Outdoor and indoor pool; 2 hot tubs; sauna; locker rooms; towels; aerobics; massage therapy; raquetball, wallyball, and basketball courts; fitness trainers; fitness center (i.e., Stairmasters, body treks, treadmills, bikes, weight machines); 2 tanning beds; outdoor tennis courts; pool tables; arcade/game room; golf simulator; incentive programs; free orientation; free 3-day passes; 1 free aerobics class; seasonal events; bar/restaurant connected to hotel and adjacent to golf course	Aerobics; aquatic center (i.e., hot tub tub; 2 pools; 2 saunas); 6 basketball/volleyball and 6 racquetball/wallyball courts; tennis and badminton courts; table tennis; big-screen TV seating area; indoor cycling center; fitness center (i.e., bikes, climbers, cross trainers, rowers, steppers, tread mills, free weights); weight training center; locker room; golf hitting nets; concession stand; bowling center; massage therapy; fitness trainers; injury care; health assessments; indoor track; billiards intramural programs
Fees (e.g., individual; group; AAA, AARP member; promotional discounts; other)		Single: $335 annual; Couple: $620; Corporate: $299 each; Aerobics: $1 (members), $3 (nonmembers); Tanning $3/10 min; Massage $25/30 min, $40/hr; Day pass with member $7.99, Day pass without member $14.50; One-, three- and six-month and pool-only bers); memberships	U student: $100/6 mo, $150/yr; Any student $150/6 mo, $300/yr; U staff/faculty $200/6 mo, $400/yr; U Alumni $250/6 mo, $500/yr; Limited $250/6 mo, $500/yr; Corporate $250/6 mo, $500/yr; Aerobics $1 (members), $3 (nonmembers); Massage: $25/30 min, $40/hr, $1/min; Day Pass with member $7 weekdays, $14 weekends; pass without member $10 weekdays, $20 weekends; Three- and six-month memberships available
Market segments served		Hotel guests; staff; adult community members; corporate memberships	U and other students; faculty/staff; alumni; community members
Quality rating (1=poor; 5=superior)		3	4

mation in the first column for easy comparison data. From the information provided various questions arise:

- What types of conclusions can be generated from this competitive assessment?

- What are the competitive advantages for each organization?

- What market segments does each pursue?

- How does the pricing compare?

- How should University Recreation position itself against Resort Sports?

What the Wellness Athletic Club must understand is that Resort Sports is a fitness center open to the public, but in a resort complex. The must also know that until recently community memberships not allowed. Wellness had heard "complaints" from current and potential members regarding hours of operation because 7:00 a.m. was the earliest any organization was open.

Wellness Athletic Club learned, after completing the competitive analysis, that consumers who expressed disappointment regarding opening at 7:00 a.m. had little other choice in the market. Professional adults were either forced to use the facility during lunch or after work if they were to be at work by 8:00 a.m. The 7 a.m. start did not allow enough time to exercise, shower, and get to work on time.

As a result, Wellness Athletic Club began opening its doors at 6:00 a.m. to more effectively target this market. This began to develop this organization's competitive edge—they were open for operation in time for 8 a.m. to 5 p.m. workers to exercise before work. This worked well. They secured over 100 memberships within one month of changing the time they opened. The value of understanding competitors is endless.

Both Wellness Athletic Club and Zane's Cycles found value in completing an assessment. There were several reasons why organizations would want to develop a formal analysis, including the following:

- allows an organization to strategically plan

- provides insight for target market selection

- provides a means for establishing a competitive advantage and differentiates your organization from the competition

- provides *critical* information for pricing

- helps to sell your ideas to others

Identifying the Competition

Organizations often answer who their competitors are without regard to the guests they serve. Identifying competitors to analyze can be more difficult for some types of leisure service organizations. To do this, an organization must ask themselves, "Who else do consumers consider (besides our organization) when they are making this type of leisure choice?" or "Why would a potential consumer buy from my organization rather than a competitor?"

Another approach is to ask consumers with which other organizations does yours compete: "Who would

---

Real Life Story: Zane's Cycles

Chris Zane, owner of Zane's Cycles, found his competitive advantage through the development of a lifetime service and price guarantee. Assessing other bicycle stores, Zane found that none had guaranteed their products or services and he felt this could be his niche.

If any item sold by Zane's ever needed maintenance or repair done, they do what it takes to get people bicycling again free of charge. In addition, if a bike sold is found for a lower price the difference plus 10% is refunded. These guarantees helped establish the edge for Zane's Cycles to achieve tremendous success. They have increased revenue continuously in an industry that does not see all achieve this success.

Other efforts completed by Zane's to differentiate themselves includes giving away any item that costs $1 or less to "bond" with customers and build valued relationships and providing a gourmet coffee/beverage bar with stools, magazines and a place to relax (some just stop for the free beverage but Zane's knows that they may be back, at least say good things about

their shop, or hang around long enough to find something else they may need). He has found unique ways to look at the bicycle shop business and set his organization apart from others (Lessons for All, 1998)

you have used if not our organization? Why?" and ultimately "Why did you select us?" A bowling center may find this answer easy because even in many smaller towns there are multiple bowling centers and each may view their competition as other bowling centers. A golf course may feel the same way; their competitor is another golf course in the area or in another community. Other leisure service organizations do not have a direct competitor. The senior center is the only one in the community, so who is their competitor? In this instance, it would be the possible other choices a senior may make if not going to the senior center, such as programs offered by the Commission on Aging or at a local assisted living center, the local bingo hall, or fitness center. These are considered indirect competitors. *Direct competitors* have a similar leisure activity they provide, whereas *indirect competitors* are other leisure organizations whose offerings are not identical to those provided by one organization but are those the market considers when determining how to use their discretionary time and money.

Other leisure choices are also competitors. Jim Jerecki (personal communication, October, 2004), the general manager of the West Michigan White Caps, a minor league baseball team, stated, "All entertainment choices were competitors." To some degree this is true. An organization must always think about competitors based on who else these consumers would specifically be visiting. A potential customer for a gambling racetrack would most likely not be considering a minor league baseball game because the desired outcome of the activities is different. Competition is more directly related to similar outcomes and offerings expected by the specific target markets.

Competitive analyses are most beneficial if they are conducted based on specific target markets. In the case of the minor league baseball team, breaking the overall organization into specific market segments helps to identify true competitors. If one of the markets of interest to the ball team were *local area families with children ages 5 to 14 looking for wholesome outdoor family entertainment* then competitors may be a local zoo; a water, amusement, or theme park; or a outdoor concert in the park. Conversely, if the same ball team identified *companies within a 45-mile radius with interest in group outings for clients, employees, or suppliers* as a market segment of interest then competitors may be a minor league hockey team that plays during another season; a sport/fitness center; a banquet hall with themed events; or an adult leisure center that has games, activities, food, and beverages. In these instances, competitors vary based on the market segment of interest. These competitors would also vary if the market segments were senior citizens, persons with developmental disabilities, or teenagers!

All leisure service organizations have indirect or direct competition that varies based on the specific target market of interest to the organization. Competitors may or may not be the same for each market of interest. What is most critical is that detailed information be gathered regarding competitors to make informed, strategic decisions that will be beneficial to one's own organization. Competitors of an organization will need to be reevaluated once the selection of a target market has been made. This topic will be further reviewed in Chapter 7.

Value of Assessments

A variety of values have been identified throughout this chapter as reasons why an organization would want to conduct various assessments. Each type of assessment has different value to the leisure and tourism organization, and in an ideal world each would be conducted. However, based on time, resources and expertise, not all may be completed in a formal manner. This, of course, lessens the value of conducting the assessment but any effort will improve the organizations effectiveness. Overall, the critical 3 *C*s must be analyzed and as much data gathered as possible before any decision is made. The efforts taken in these

Potential leisure and tourism indirect competitors

areas will dramatically increase the effectiveness of organization decision making.

Trapp (1991) found in his analysis of small businesses that those who developed marketing strategy practices had a positive impact on financial performance and that certain types of organizations engaged in marketing strategy practices more than others. At a minimum, when first implementing these steps, an organization can identify areas of weakness and develop steps to improve on these areas in the years to come.

Strengths, Weaknesses, Opportunities, and Threats (SWOT) Analysis

The purpose of a *SWOT analysis* is to review the organization's current potential as well as to evaluate its future potential. In essence it is designed to formally understand the organization's competitive advantages and develop a strategy for achieving organizational objectives. To complete this activity an organization must assess all information gathered to date, including data from the organization, global, industry, market, and competitive assessments. Based on these findings, an organization answers the question "What are our strengths?" They document the results, then answer the following questions:

What are our…	Questions to then ask…
Strengths?	How are we going to maintain these?
Weaknesses?	What are we going to do to improve on these?
Opportunities?	What are we going to do to capitalize on these?
Threats?	What are we going to do to minimize these?

All too often organizations utilize the tool and produce "shallow, misleading results" (Valentin, 2001). There are several modifications to the SWOT instrument designed to enhance the effect of shallow assessments; however, all are based on first understanding this technique and using it effectively. The first step in completing a SWOT is for organizations to be thinking in terms of what stakeholders would say about their organization, not necessarily what the organization would say about themselves.

Strengths of an organization are those that a specific market would describe as the positive attributes of an organization when compared to its competitors. They are the competitive advantages of this organization over others.

Wilson (2004) suggested an organization should consider not only the organization's offerings or tangible assets but also the people. Further, organizations need to identify how they will continue to maintain strengths. Questions that can be asked to stimulate this discussion include how stakeholders view your organization over the competition regarding

- products, programs, facilities, and services that the organization provides

- how we provide these (e.g., quality service)

- why consumers select us over others

- how we differ from our competitors

- how we are performing financially compared to others

Weaknesses of an organization are those elements that keep an organization from achieving a competitive advantage. These are factors that limit an organization from securing an edge over other organizations for specific market segments. They are the things an organization does not do well, but if they did, they would become a competitive strength for the organization. Organizations must identify these weaknesses and determine which are most important to improve. Questions that can be asked to stimulate this discussion include

1. What would stakeholders change about us if they could?

2. Why and how do competitors operate more successfully?

3. What have we identified as areas to improve on internally?

4. Do competitors have specific market segments conquered?

Opportunities are events that occur outside an organization that could provide potential for the organization. These could determine potential growth areas for the organization. Wilson (2004) suggested these can exist in the market or the environment, and an organization hopes to benefit from it in some way. Organizations need to identify how they will select and capitalize on opportunities that will benefit the organization. Questions that can be asked to stimulate this discussion include the following:

1. What market opportunities exist (e.g., those not focused on by others)?

2. What are the trends not yet captured in the market?

3. Internally, how will the organization be changing in the future, and what can be done to capitalize on these changes?

Issues identified as *threats* include "factors beyond your control that could place your marketing strategy, or the business itself, at risk" (Wilson, 2004, p. 2). Even though they occur outside or are external to an organization, organizations should have plans to address these issues if they occur. This plan addresses the answer to the question, "How can these be minimized?" Some threats may be competition, higher gas prices, or a decrease in discretionary spending. Some questions that can be asked to stimulate discussion include:

1. What is the competition doing that could impact our organization's development?

2. Are there changes in demand that will require our organization to act differently?

3. Are there changes in technology, the economy, politics, or regulations that will impact our organization?

Once these lists are generated, organizations again return to the questions about our strengths, weaknesses, opportunities, and threats to best utilize the information generated. For example, if an organization's strengths are service location and cleanliness, then an organization asks, "How are we going to maintain these?" These responses

identify priority actions for the organization. Table 6.7 shares a SWOT analysis from a leisure and tourism organization.

The global SWOT analysis provides an opportunity for the organization to reflect on itself as a whole. Its strengths provide evidence of tools to use in establishing the organization's brand image, which will be further discussed in Chapter 7.

There are several reasons why an organization would want to develop a SWOT assessment. A SWOT assessment provides

1. a tool to analyze the variety of data collected from the various assessments

2. an opportunity to identify the organization's competitive advantages

3. a focus for the organization—an idea of the steps to take to improve

4. justification for the marketing plan's activities and efforts.

All too often leisure organizations do not provide themselves the time to have staff analyze the data gathered and answer these questions. Often creative ideas to focus an organization are developed if this practice includes all those involved in each outlet of an organization.

As with a competitive analysis, these strengths, weaknesses, opportunities, and threats may change depending on the market segment being analyzed. Reflecting back

---

Table 6.7
SWOT Analysis for a Rafting Organization

Strengths	Weaknesses	Opportunities	Threats
• Low prices for raft trips, rentals, and gift shop	• Lack of additional recreational activities for the customer	• Offer more family-oriented benefits	• Area companies lowering their prices
• Specialize in whitewater rafting guiding and whitewater raft rentals	• Not within walking distance of the majority of local hotels	• Advertise customized trips	• Competition offering more recreational activities
• Customized trips	• Rely primarily on word-of-mouth advertising	• Due to the facility location, can target a large amount of people	• Complacency
• Customer service/customer-oriented business		• Rafting photography	• Unmonitored environmental issues
• River access—less shuttling necessary		• Rafting trips for company outings	
• Facilities—showers, restrooms, changing areas, storage areas, employee locker rooms		• Provide top quality experience for customers	
• Plenty of free parking			
• No cancellation fees or other hidden fees			
• Longer trips than the competition			

on the minor league baseball team, the strengths of this organization with the family market will be different than to the singles market. The competitors are different and the needs of each market are different; therefore, the SWOT analysis will be different. The family market may enjoy the variety of family-oriented activities offered during the game (e.g., promotional activities, between-inning contests, game stations around the stadium during the game), whereas the singles market may find the bar area located in the bleacher seats to be a strength. The SWOT analysis will need to be reevaluated once a specific target market has been identified as outlined in Chapter 7.

The development of a marketing strategy is the foundation of developing an effective marketing plan. Organizations that fail to take these steps may miss opportunities to better develop the organization and the ability to reach and serve desired markets. Various steps need to be taken to determine an organization's strategy, and organizations must allow the resources (e.g., time and money) to complete these activities.

Apply What You Know

1. Select a leisure and tourism organization to complete your marketing plan. With that organization in mind, conduct an organization assessment, a market assessment, a global assessment, and an industry assessment.

2. Access a toursim or leisure organization's website and identify all area direct competitors.

Key Terms

Competitive analysis
Direct competitors
Global assessment
Indirect competitors
Industry assessment
Market forecast
Marketing strategy
Market share analysis

Mission statement
Operational structure
Organization assessment
Organization inventory
Situational assessment
SWOT analysis
Three *C*s: company, consumers, competition

Review Questions

1. Define the five types of assessments and explain the value of each.

2. What three factors should an organization understand prior to developing a marketing plan?

3. What is a competitive analysis?

4. Explain why it is important to keep track of a company's history

5. What competitive advantage did Shepler's decide to use?

6. Define the two types of competitors. Why is it important to identify both?

7. What is a SWOT analysis? Describe each area and explain why it is important.

Internet Resources

MarketingProfs.com provides strategic and tactical marketing know-how for professionals, including marketing-related articles, opportunities for discussions with experts in the field and study seminars.

http://www.marketingprofs.com/

Online Marketing Today is a website designed to help agencies market their products and services online better. Marketing software, manuals and discussion forums are available.

http://www.onlinemarketingtoday.com/

On Point Marketing and Promotions provides marketing services for businesses, including marketing surveys, product sampling, and new product marketing services.

http://www.onpoint-marketing.com/

U.S. Census Bureau is a valuable source of information about the nation's people and economy. Offers relevant statistical data for different areas of interest, from agriculture and demographics to financial and market statistics.

http://www.census.gov/main/www/subjects.html

Freedemographics.com brings together information to analyze the demographic and market potential of any geographic area in United States. On this website you can create custom reports for any geography in seconds and perform accurate market analysis.

http://www.freedemographics.com/

Advanced Marketing Consultants is a firm that designs and implements management and marketing plans, and develops strategies for overcoming problems. Their website offers articles about marketing strategies and plans, target marketing, segmentation, marketing research and analysis.

http://www.marketingprinciples.com/

References

Bialeschki, D. and Henderson, K. (2000). Trends affecting non-profit camps: Issues and recommendations for the millennium. *Camping Magazine, 73*(2), 25–31.

Caro, R. (2001). On location: Certainty about the local marketplace can determine the success or failure of a health club before it even opens its doors. *Athletic Business, 25*(3), 47–53.

Center Lake Bible Camp & Retreat Center Marketing Plan. (2004). Tustin, MI: Author.

Dev, C. S. and Olsen, M. D. (2000). Marketing challenges for the next decade. *Cornell Hotel and Restaurant Administration Quarterly, 41*(1), 41–47.

Lessons for All from Bicycle Retailer Chris Zane. (1998, March). *Bottom Line/Business,* 13–14.

McCarville, R. (2002). *Improving leisure services through marketing action.* Champaign, IL: Sagamore.

O'Sullivan, E. (1991). *Marketing for parks, recreation and leisure.* State College, PA: Venture Publishing, Inc.

Panico, C. (2005) Competition: The ultimate energizer. *Global Cosmetic Industry, 173*(3), 69–70.

Trapp, P. (1991). *Marketing, strategy, and the small firm: A systematic inquiry.* Master's thesis, University of Illinois.

Valentin, E. (2001). SWOT analysis from a resource-based view. *Journal of Marketing Theory and Practice, 9*(2), 54–69.

Wilson, D. (2004, March). *How to perform SWOT analysis.* Retrieved from http://www.mplans.com/dpm/article.cfm/148

Writing a mission statement. (2004). Retrieved June 27, 2004, from http://www.bplans.com/dp/missionstatement.cfm

Chapter 7

Target Market Approaches

If you nail targeting and positioning, everything else will fall into place. Phil Kotler, Author of *Marketing Management*

Tom is the director of a large suburban recreation department. The community has doubled in size in the past ten years and the recreation department has grown in a similar fashion. The recreation department now has a community center with aquatics, sports and wellness areas, a senior center, a performing arts center, six large and two small parks, an ice arena, and an adventure center with a climbing wall and high/low ropes courses. Even with the community growth, funding challenges still exist for Tom.

As the city manager, Amy has encouraged him to find more ways to become less dependent on the general fund for his operation. As a result, several divisions of his department are now revenue producing. The department is now 40% self-funded, relying on 60% of his operating budget from the general fund. Today though Tom is facing greater challenges because Amy wants that ratio reversed to 60/40 in this next year.

Compared to other community recreation departments, Tom's recreation department is viewed as quite progressive. Tom and his staff have developed many innovative systems for a public recreation organization. Tom's approach to "marketing" is not unlike other public organizations. Marketing is viewed as a task to complete once the offerings were developed. Marketing is the way the department told the community about what they provided. Individual staff members develop their own marketing-related materials for programs and events. The city had a public relations staff member who would assist them as needed; however, as

---

At the end of this chapter, readers will be able to…

- Define market segmentation and target marketing

- Understand the value of target versus mass marketing approaches

- Explain the challenge of applying target market principles

- Describe the variables used to segment a mass market

- Explain the processes used to segment a market

- Identify and describe various market segments of interest to leisure and tourism organizations

- List the criteria used to determine an organization's target markets

- Understand why SWOT and competitive analyses should be completed once target markets are established

the department grew, more support was needed. Four years ago Tom hired his first "marketing" staff member who was responsibilities for developing all the promotional materials for the department. He soon realized there was more the organization could do to utilize marketing more effectively. He knew their marketing efforts were not well-thought-out and felt like they at times flew by the seat of their pants! Tom hired a second staff member that would focus on marketing. This staff member would concentrate on helping various outlets write marketing plans and become more strategic in how they approached marketing.

The mission of the department is to enhance the quality of life for all residents in the community by providing exceptional leisure service opportunities. Well-established values guide their organization and their marketing plans support their mission and values. For two years the department wrote and used marketing plans focused on serving the entire community. Their marketing objectives included

- to provide additional programs and events

- to prepare staff to deliver quality experiences

- to keep community members well-informed about offerings

- to develop community partnerships that expand the number of offerings

Although well-intended, the department was uncertain if their activities had any direct impact because they did not evaluate their plan. They could not attribute their success to date from the actions completed on behalf of these objectives. Community members used their facilities, attended their programs and events, and appeared satisfied. But, Tom knew that they would need to be "different" as they faced this difficult financial challenge.

Tom attended an educational session at a conference that changed the way he thought about marketing. He realized that if they quit focusing their efforts types of activities and started focusing their efforts on specific markets within the community, they would be able to more effectively serve community members' specific needs, utilize marketing resources, and achieve financial goals in revenue centers. They would begin by targeting specific markets, such as community conference groups in the adventure center; community corporations in the performing arts center; adult males with athletic interest in the ice arena; and families with children under age 13 in the wellness, sport, and aquatic facilities.

Tom changed the way the organization integrated marketing and found tremendous success targeting specific markets within the community. His one-time fear of taking a target market approach because he felt that would iso-

late some of the community residents was no longer a concern. The organization found that by really focusing their efforts on specific markets, they more easily identified marketing tactics that were more appropriate and effective to use and saved money as a result. They designed their offerings based on the needs of target markets, and these programs and facilities were better attended and utilized. This process enabled the department to serve community members more effectively as they zeroed in on what was important to these distinct groups.

They still served all segments of the population, but were more strategic in their use of marketing resources. Ultimately, the department also found they had greater financial success and they achieved more independence from the general fund. As a result, the operating budget was only 38% reliant on these funds the next year. Even though the department's mission was to serve the entire community, following target marketing concepts allowed them to do so much more effectively than before.

Target Marketing

At some point, all leisure and tourism organizations will discover the value of applying target marketing principles to their organization. Leisure and tourism organizations have approached this concept differently over the years. For-profit organizations began applying these practices long ago as they recognized that they needed to utilize "business" practices. They tended to focus on specific groups of people who were willing to pay for their offerings, whereas public leisure and tourism organizations approached marketing based on the mission of their organization—to serve everyone. They marketed to everyone and had little targeted focus. In both settings, however, some organizations were more apt to apply target marketing than others. There is great variance in the way leisure organizations have historically and currently approached target marketing.

Marketing is constantly changing as the market is changing; therefore, the way you analyze and speak to customers is also changing. Kelley Davidson, Wintergreen Resort

Leisure and tourism organizations are changing in so many areas, it is not surprising organizations' approaches to marketing are changing as well. Today, leisure and tourism organizations are approaching marketing based on zoning in on specific markets on which they choose to spend their marketing resources (e.g., time, people, expertise, money). Target marketing is seen as an effective, efficient way to approach marketing and to better serve both consumers and the organization.

So, how do organizations do this? How did Tom determine which markets to pursue? How did he know certain markets would produce a positive impact on the organization? The answers to these questions and the process organizations take to apply target market concepts are shared in this chapter.

The concept of *target marketing* appears to be understood by many people because it is a term conversationally used under the assumption that everyone understands what it means. The use of this term has joined the ranks of common language where it is shared in everyday life. We have heard about these *target markets* before. In the media they are described as college students; echo boomers; matures; baby boomers; generations X, Y, and Z; millenials; socializers; teens; and fitness activity avoiders. These descriptors all aim to suggest that target markets are specific groups of people with unique needs, values, interests, behaviors, and benefits sought from a leisure and tourism experience. But, do these markets relate to all leisure and tourism organizations? Individual market segments are defined based on the specific industry, organization, and market. Organizations have defined their markets in various ways. and individual leisure and tourism organizations must also determine the unique groups they serve and those they have interest in serving. Neal (2003) suggested either an organization mass markets or identifies distinctions of the market and segments it; however, there is no in between.

A target market is a group of people on which an organization would like to focus or "zero in." More specifically, though, a *market* is a group of consumers or potential consumers a leisure and tourism organization would serve. Therefore, a *target market* is the identification of groups of people with common characteristics toward which an organization's marketing efforts are geared. This is a group of people the organization concentrates on and uses resources to attract, satisfy, and build long-term relationships. They could be people currently served by an organization, or they may not be using the organization at the present time. Deciding to target a market is not based on if they are current consumers or not. The key to target marketing is "finding the most efficient, scientific way of segmenting the market and to choose a target group based on its potential profit contribution" (Clancy, 2003, p. 4). Four steps must be taken by an organization to establish its target markets:

1. Separate current consumer base into distinct market segments.

2. Separate the overall market into distinct market segments.

3. Select the market segments to target.

4. Identify if the potential target markets are worthy of becoming the organization's target markets.

Market Segmentation

Because we use the term *marketing* loosely, it implies this must be an easy thing to do. The process, however, is anything but simple. The first step of selecting the target markets for an organization is a process called *market segmentation*. This process is an analysis of the existing market. Identifying the various consumer types within that market is the first step in the development of consumer awareness. A market is made up of different types of consumers whose requirements are unique. Not all leisure experience consumers fall into the same "type." It is the process by which organizations separate a mass market of people into common characteristics. These characteristics are those distinct elements that make each group unique. In this process, their common needs, interests, beliefs, backgrounds, and behaviors for which a specific leisure service appeals separate people. Neal and Wurst (2001) suggested effective segmentation is determined when various segments respond differently to marketing, promotional, and communication mix variations. It is a balance between serving a mass market and serving one person and focusing in on his or her specific needs. It is finding the balance between "the ineffectiveness of treating all consumers alike and the inefficiency of treating each differently" (Carter, 1996, p. 287).

The concept of market segmentation has grown and changed since first being introduced in 1956. Smith (1956) suggested segmentation referred to developing products based on the various wants/needs of people. Today, this has developed into the search for groups of people with similar responses to market offerings. Segmentation has consistently focused on consumer behavior issues; however, the earlier definition addressed external influences—where people were already motivated to participate, demand was predetermined (Fennell & Allenby, 2002). Both identify and focus on the needs and wants of consumers. The current approach to segmentation relies on looking at both the population within a market and a profile of current consumers.

Fennell and Allenby (2002) suggested the key to identifying variables that should be used to describe a segment should "reflect the conditions that lead people to act and find brands worth pursuing" (p. 16).

Walk down a grocery store aisle and see how there has been a change in the way many organizations approach mass versus segmented marketing. Consumers are even segmented based on what they desire in a laundry detergent. They may have different interests, needs, backgrounds, behaviors, and beliefs about laundry detergent, and organizations have developed many different types of detergent in an effort to appeal to every distinct consumer. Some people prefer liquid over powder, bleach versus nonbleach, dye-free versus mountain air scent, with or without softener, in concentrate or regular strength… the list goes on and on.

It would be reasonable to assume if detergent manufacturers have identified distinctions in the laundry detergent market that people also have differences in their backgrounds, interests, needs, beliefs, and behaviors regarding leisure experiences. Even within a group of people who have common demographic characteristics, their needs, interests and behaviors may vary enough that a leisure and tourism organization would want to distinguish between them. For example, ask a group of peers this question: "What are you looking for in a fitness center experience?" You will have answers such as "I want to: lose weight, lower my cholesterol, relieve stress, reshape my body, socialize…." There are many different benefits people seek from a leisure experience, and what they need, want and desire will be different as well.

The Segmentation Process

It is important that an organization wait to identify market segments and select target markets until the assessment stage of the marketing strategy development is complete. Organizations use the data gathered in the organization, competitive, global, industry, market, and SWOT assessments to identify which markets should be pursued. Organizations who first determine the target markets without this consideration are potentially missing opportunities to learn about new markets, markets not being targeted, and markets being overmarketed. What organization would have thought about marketing toward single parents, gay couples, or persons with disabilities if it had not been for global, industry, and market data that suggested new, emerging markets to be served? What organization would have learned that the baby boomer market is being targeted by many leisure organizations, yet the senior and teen markets are more often ignored? The only organizations that would realize this would be ones that analyzed the competition. All of this information assists organizations in identifying target market approaches.

Variables Used in Segmentation

To identify market segments, several variables can be used to separate the mass market of people into smaller groups with common characteristics. Various authors approach this somewhat differently, yet each has shared important considerations in establishing a well thought out segmentation approach. Table 7.1 suggests variables that can be used to determine the distinctions between market segments. Clancy (2003) suggested organizations look not only at the segmentation variables highlighted in Table 7.1 but also at various market drivers when segmenting a market, including the following:

- category involvement (i.e., How important are leisure experiences to the consumer?)

- product preference motivators (i.e., What characteristics are most motivating?)

- product purchasing patterns (i.e., How frequently do they buy?)

- media habits (i.e., What do consumers watch, read, and listen to?)

Environmental variables include issues like geographic location and site locations where markets consume the leisure experience. The use of geographic techniques to segment a market is the oldest method and still most commonly used approach taken by organizations. This approach divides a market by the country, state, county or city a market lives or works in. Typically, a market is divided in this way based on the cultural differences within a geographic area. Organizations utilize this because of its logical simplicity and applicability. However, used alone, it does not consider other important considerations, such as buying motives and differences between consumers in a specific geographic area.

Neal and Wurst (2001) suggested the development of market segments by one type of variable is limiting because various people within an organization may want to look at market segments from various approaches. Some may want to look at markets in terms of geographic location whereas others may want to view a market in terms of needs or benefits sought. Therefore, segmenting a market based on multiple variables is more beneficial for marketing strategy development and tactical implementation.

Learning Resources Network (LERN; 2000) suggested in *The Marketing Manual for the 1990s* that geodemographic mapping can provide a visual means of comparing a segment based on their geographic status with the profile of those currently using an organization. For example, a computer map of the geographic area an organization is interested in is generated based on census data. Census data could provide a demographic understanding of each tract of interest to an organization. By overlapping current organization enrollment data on top of census tract maps, an organization can visualize and understand what census tracts they are currently serving. You can further determine if the census tract matches that of an organization's consumer profile. This provides an understanding of an organization's overall impact in a geographic area.

Person-specific variables include descriptors that characterize traits, including demographic and attitudinal variables (Fennell & Allenby, 2002). Demographic variables are those that describe what a market segment looks like. It assists in developing a consumer profile that specifies traits or characteristics of existing or potential consumers. Demographic techniques are also a commonly used approach when segmenting a market. Added to a geographic variable, they identify groups of people based on variables such as employment status, education, income, gender, family structure, age, religion, race, ethnicity, family status and education. These variables are often conveniently available to analyze, easy to interpret, and correlate with buying behavior. Fennell and Allenby (2002), however, suggested using these variables is problematic because it is difficult to differentiate consumers.

Some authors blend behavioral and psychographic variables together. A more recent trend is to further separate these because there are distinctions between them that are important to understand. Behavioral variables attempt to understand how people react and what they do whereas psychographic variables attempt to understand what people think. In particular, in the leisure industry the need to specifically identify leisure-related issues is important. Therefore, O'Sullivan (1991) separated leisure needs and interests because she found this was an important variable for leisure organizations to consider. It is important to isolate those variables of particular interest and value to leisure organizations specifically. All leisure organizations need to identify the leisure benefits sought from this type of experience.

It is important leisure organizations not only understand *who* people are and *where* they are from, but also *what*

Table 7.1
Segmentation Variables Used to Identify Markets

Consumer Distinction/Variable	Description	Market Segment Example (Health Club)
Consumer Location or Geographic Variables	*Where do they live and work?* Boundaries established by the location of where people live or work and the size of the area	Lives in Schaumburg, Illinois, or within the 60173 zip code
Consumer Profile or Demographic Variables	*Who are they?* Describes people by personal characteristics including gender, age, marital status, income, family status, race, ethnicity, religion, family composition, education level, occupation, and employment status	Single females, ages 28–45, with children under age 18, some college education, and income of $50,000 or more
Consumer Thoughts or Psychographics Variables	*What do they think and want?* Lifestyle, values, attitudes, personality, and loyalty status characteristics	Values family time and feels they have limited discretionary time and this is their single greatest resource
Consumer Leisure Needs and Interests or Benefit Variables	*What do they want in a leisure experience?* Benefits sought	Searches for both individual and family leisure opportunities, structured, with set times, to spend time together and "recreate" as well as burn stress and stay or get fit.
Consumer Behaviors or Behavioral Variables	*What do they do? How do we reach them?* Information sources used, what they need to be informed or knowledgeable, usage patterns, skill and specialization levels (e.g., competive vs. noncompetitive), meida preferences, and purchasing behaviors (e.g., how money is spent, readiness to buy)	Currently infrequent users (average 1x/mo), they will look to the Internet for information before deciding who to select, they will not want to be "sold" on a sales pitch but will want to have all the facts before making a decision on behalf of the family, reach them through children (e.g., schools, activities, worksite, and various support systems (e.g., churches)
Consumer Availability or Syncographic Variables	*When are they available?* Time elements such as season, time of year, month, day.	Available evenings and weekends

people want to buy and *when* and *why* they want to buy it. Behavioral and psychographic data helps organizations to understand this. Today's consumer has been influenced by the belief that there is less time available to them to participate in leisure activities yet they indicate in time diaries that they have more time (Godbey, 1998). The impact of some working longer (Steinberg, 1999) and others thinking they have less time will change how people conduct their activities. People today will shop around for better service, they will pay for services to help simplify their lives and provide more opportunities to do what they feel is important once work is done.

Syncographics, as a variable to segment a market, is a more recent consideration by a leisure and tourism organization as suggested by O'Sullivan (1991). She suggested, "The designation of this factor is fueled by the increasing importance of time-related factors within our society." Further, since discretionary time is a foundation for providing leisure experiences, identifying time available, use of time and time itself can prove to be a valuable method for segmentation. Time of day, time of year, day of week, length of time, and seasonal considerations are all ways in which the syncographic variable can be utilized.

These variables are used by leisure and tourism organizations to identify the various distinctions between leisure service consumers. An organization can segment a market by using any combination of variables. Each choice to add a variable reduces the size of the market. The process by which an organization identifies variables to use is a complex one.

Various Approaches to Market Segmentation

There are several steps involved in target marketing. The first two involve identifying the market segments of existing consumers, and a specific market or potential demand. The approaches an organization can take to segment a market are endless. Any variable may be used to distinguish one group of people from another group of people. There are "literally hundreds of thousands of different ways to divide customers into… segments" (Clancy, 2003, p. 3). As such, we have experienced a massive change in the way organizations approach the segmentation process.

Larger organizations would first identify the various components (e.g., wellness, senior center, golf course, community gym) within one leisure and tourism organization. Each of these will approach segmentation based on their own individual division versus an overall organization. Neal (2003) indicated an organization should next identify

its current and proposed positions within each of these divisions and select target markets based on opportunities that may exist.

Clancy and Krieg (2002) suggested the way in which organizations segment their overall market is oftentimes primitive. Some think a quick analysis of the market based on three or four variables is sufficient. This can lead to ineffective decisions regarding the market segments of an organization. They suggest effective segmentation can take months to complete and cost an organization a great deal of money. Many organizations look for the low-cost, quick ways to identify market segments; careful consideration should be given whether this is an effective process or not. Organizations must determine what and how far to break down an overall market to identify the "right size" of a market segment.

Understanding Consumer Segmentation: Post Hoc

Post hoc or *taxonomies methods* of segmentation refer to empirically based segmentation where an organization relies on primary research undertaken for the specific purpose of identifying target markets. An example of this would be data derived from a consumer satisfaction survey. Many variables can be also used to identify segments, including brand loyalty, values, use patterns, benefits sought, and lifestyles. One general concern for this type of segmentation process is the number and size of the segments are unknown until after data analysis is complete (Dolnicar, 2002; Neal, 2003).

With greater interest in understanding the unique issues of consumers, post hoc or taxonomies are growing in popularity within leisure and tourism organizations. Having ready access to data in organizations has provided an opportunity to apply market segmentation practices. In addition to understanding the answers to the segmentation variables in Table 7.1 (p. 161) there are several questions that should be answered to help identify markets within an organization (Veverka, 2001):

- Where are consumers coming from?

- What are their age groups and other socioeconomic attributes?

- How long do consumers stay? How often do they come? During what seasons do they visit?

- What is the consumers view on value for price paid?

- What did consumers spend money on? How much did they spend?

- What aspects of the consumers visit had the most impact? least impact?

- Why did the consumer decide to come to this organization?

- What experiences or benefits were these consumers seeking?

- How satisfied were consumers? Were their expectations met?

- How did consumers learn about the organization?

- How successfully were the five phases of the leisure experience addressed for consumers?

Organizations deciding to target a market do so with the intent that categorizing people based on expectations or preferences mirror the organization's strengths and lead to a competitive advantage (Dolnicar, 2002). Once an organization determines its target markets, then tactical plans are specialized specifically to attract these groups of people.

Cluster Analysis Technique

Cluster analysis allows organizations to conduct post hoc segmentation by utilizing multivariate data analysis techniques. This process divides people into subgroups according to specific criteria that highlight the group's similarities. The process is complex because it first requires deciding which algorithm to use to analyze the data, identifying which measure of association to use, and determining the number of groups that should be developed. Once determined, the data is then divided into corresponding subgroups to provide organizations with segments of consumers (Dolnicar, 2002).

Dolnicar (2002) analyzed tourism studies that used this approach to determine market segments. Tourism organizations find that grouping people by vacation activity preferences, benefits sought, and usage patterns (including spending) allows organizations to develop specialized products and opportunities to provide high-quality service. Dolnicar found that of the 47 studies analyzed that used post hoc cluster analysis techniques, some conclusions could be drawn regarding the process taken. Sample size of tourism studies ranged from 46 to 7,996 cases with 40% using between 200 and 500 cases. Sixty-three percent of studies used between 10 and 22 variables to group the respondents into categories. Two thirds of the studies used ordinal data in their formatting of data. Dolnicar found 45%

used factor analysis even though this technique is somewhat controversial, and 38% did not conduct any analysis.

Various methods exist for dividing data into groups with similar characteristics. The two most popular techniques are the hierarchical agglomerative and iterative partitioning methods. In the hierarchical agglomerative technique, "the basic idea is to merge individuals together stepwise, starting with each respondent representing one group and ending with one single large group" (Dolnicar, 2002, p. 9). Iterative partitioning relies on "a random splitting of the observations and then reallocate them in order to optimize a predefined criterion. The number of clusters decisions has to be made in advance of the analysis" (Dolnicar, 2002, p. 9). The use of these techniques was similar in the studies analyzed: 40% used hierarchical and 47% used partitioning algorithms.

The selection of clusters is important to this process because the result influences the outcome of groups. Tourism studies have tended to identify a number of heuristics and indexes as the means for establishing the number of clusters. Fourteen used heuristic procedures, twelve combined heuristic and subjective views, and five solely on subjective means. Slightly more than half of the studies discussed some type of validity analysis of the clusters.

In an attempt to find a more user-friendly approach to tourism segmentation, Arimond, Achenreiner, and Elfessi (2003) used a two-part cluster analysis on a large-scale tourism survey in Wisconsin. They found that the "typical" traveler is from Wisconsin (49%), between the ages of 30 and 54 (66%), a high school graduate (32.8%) and earns between $30,000 and $75,000 (60.8%). They stay for one to three days (77.2%) and spend $300 or less (58.3%). Using this approach, they segmented travelers into four clusters. The Nature Sightseer was the largest segment with 49.5% of all travelers falling into this segment. Attraction Enthusiasts made up 16.6% of the market, just over 5% were Outdoor Recreationists and 15.3% of the market fell into the Special Event cluster.

The reason for sharing this section on cluster analysis was to indicate the complexity and difficulty in properly identifying market segments in an organization. This section is not designed to conduct a scientific segmentation process but rather to indicate the steps taken, concern and value of this type of technique and to allow the reader to understand the process and language used in segmentation.

An example of conducting the post hoc method of segmentation is when an organization analyzes data from a satisfaction survey. In the survey, several questions were asked regarding respondent demographic, residence, leisure needs/interests, benefits sought from a health club, use and satisfaction of the club in particular. The data was then analyzed by cluster analysis with all variables being considered.

The result was scientifically predicting several consumer profiles based on existing consumers. The profiles were developed based on 775 member respondents and highlighted in Table 7.2.

Formica and Uysal (2002) used factor-cluster analysis, multiple discriminate analysis, and one-way analysis of variance to identify segments of travelers based on the environmental attitudes. Three distinct groups emerged: the conservationist, the anthropocentric, and the optimist. Demographic data was not found to be the variables that identified greater variance in the markets. Trip behavior, destination attributes, and travelers' choice of destination served as the most beneficial variables to understand this market segment.

This type of segmentation can be used externally to understand segments within a market. This provides several benefits for an organization. It allows them to

- Rely on past behavior to predict future performance.

- Understand their current share of the market overall (a market share analysis would also provide this insight).

- Identify current markets served and those drawn to an organization's current offerings.

- Understand market potential.

Understanding Market Segments: A Priori

The second type of segmentation that occurs is called *a priori*. A priori or *typological methods* of segmentation allow an organization to distinguish between consumer groups based on consumer purchase or usage of offerings. They do not provide opportunities to establish a competitive advantage because gathered data is not from consumers themselves. An organization segments based on general findings. This type of segmentation presumes the variables are known in advance. These include standard industrial classification (SIC) groups, basic demographic or geographic groups, usage groups (e.g., heavy vs. light users) and the values and life styles (VALS) classification system. Organizations that choose this type of segmentation method should remember that segmentation from over two years ago may be outdated. These segments must be frequently verified as to their stability, size, and response to marketing mix decisions. Failure to identify qualified segments will result in poorer results for an organization than if it had mass marketed. Organizations should consider the stability of the market and remember to verify that two market segments are indeed distinct (Dolnicar, 2002; Neal, 2003).

There is no one right way to break a market down or cookie-cutter process that makes this simple. There are only more effective or less effective ways of doing it. The listing of variables to select from is simply the variety of choices an organization can make to find those common elements. Someone cannot suggest to any organization there is only one right way to approach it.

The initial process to understand overall market segments is to list the potential variables people can be segmented by and assess if these categories are important distinctions for the organization. First, an organization should consider if there is some geographic boundary considered unique for the organization. Many leisure organizations have some type of geographic boundary that separates the entire world as a mass market to a smaller mass market. For example, the health club example in Table 7.2 identified their market is from Schaumburg, Illinois. This market could be further broken down into a subsection of Scha-

Table 7.2
Cluster Analysis Profiles of Consumer Respondents From a Health Club

Variables	Segment 1 Hard Bodies	Segment 2 Muscle Men	Segment 3 Overworked Moms	Segment 4 Stress Relief Dads
# of respondents	245	222	208	123
Geographic	Lives/works in Schaumburg	Lives in Schaumburg, Palentine, and Hoffman Estates	Lives in Schaumburg	Lives/works in Schaumburg
Gender	Female	Male	Female	Male
Age	20–34	20–34	35–44	35–44
Marital status	Married	Single	Single	Married
Family status	No Children	No Children	Children	Children
Benefits sought	Fitness	Body composition	Socialization/fitness	Stress relief/fitness

umburg, such as the northeast side of the community. If this market was uniquely different from Schaumburg overall, then they would be separated; because they are not in this example, they are left whole. Another consideration is made regarding demographic variables. For example, are males and females different in their needs, interests, and behaviors, regarding this leisure experience (e.g., health club)? If they are uniquely different regarding their needs, then an organization would consider separating them into two market segments. If they are not uniquely different, then they could remain unchanged. In the health club example, the organization has gone from a mass market approach to having two market segments, males and females from Schaumburg, Illinois.

Figure 7.1 highlights a visual representation of these two markets. The pie represents overall demand, and in this example, the geographic area of Schaumburg, Illinois,

is represented. The shape of the pie is determined by the size of the market. In this example, U.S. census data indicated there are 75,386 people in the Schaumburg, Illinois, market—51.3% (38,692) females and 48.7% (36,694) males. This would be considered a scientific estimate and the organization could feel very confident about this estimate of size. The issue of market size will be further explained later.

Each variable is addressed with the organization, saying, "If we further separate this market by this variable we are suggesting these groups are distinct from each other as it relates to our organization (e.g., health club)." They may decide that some variables do suggest unique differences whereas other variables do not suggest any difference. In this example, they further conclude this market could be further broken into age segments, marital status, family status, and behaviors. Note that in each instance, the

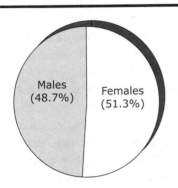

Figure 1: Market demand for females in Schaumburg, Illinois (est. 38,692)

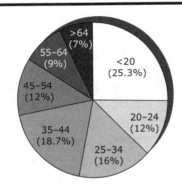

Figure 2: Market demand for females ages 35–44 in Schaumburg, Illinois (est. 7,235)

* widowed, divorced or never married

Figure 3: Market demand for single females ages 35–44 from Schaumburg, Illinois (est. 3,545)

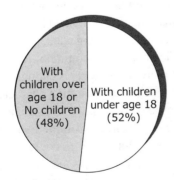

Figure 4: Market demand for single females ages 35–44 from Schaumburg, Illinois with children under age 18 (est. 1,844)

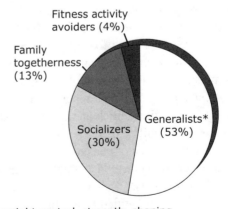

* weight control, strength, shaping

Figure 5: Market demand for single females ages 35–44 with children under age 18 from Schaumburg, Illinois with "generalist" interests (est. 977)

Figure 7.1
Determining Market Demand for Schaumburg, Illinois (pop. 75,386)

market demand description changes for each variable accepted until the full market description exists.

The pie again represents the U.S. census estimation percentage of females in Schaumburg, Illinois, in various age categories. U.S. census information provides this data so the organization can feel confident regarding the size of these market segments. It does not indicate the number of females in each age group; however, an estimation is made based on the ratio of females to males and applied to the age category. This is only an estimation because no scientific data is available that better identifies this figure.

In this instance, the percentage, of married versus single females between the ages of 28 to 45 from Schaumburg, Illinois, is an estimation. The U.S. census data does not separate this group in particular. It does suggest that within the overall market slightly over half (51%) of the households are married. This figure is therefore used as an estimation for this specific age category. Forty-nine percent of 7,235 people estimated are single females between the ages of 35 to 44 from Schaumburg, Illinois.

Data is available regarding the percent of married versus single households with children over and under age 18. This estimate takes these same percentages and applies them to this market segment. There are 52% of Schaumburg, Illinois single households with children under age 18. Therefore, the same percent estimation was applied to women ages 35 to 44. It should be noted that this estimation is low for this group because they would be more likely to have children under 18 than say the senior market over age 50. This should be considered a conservative estimate and approximately 1,844 single females in Schaumburg, Illinois between the ages of 35 to 44 have children under 18 at home.

A study of Canadian students over age 23, based on the segmentation by benefits sought, revealed that 30% of the sample were considered Socializers, 4% Fitness Activity Avoiders, 13% Family Togetherness Seekers and 53% Generalists. Generalists seek benefits related to weight control, strength, and shaping. Although this study was not completed on this market in particular, this is the best available data. Until research on this organization can be done, this data will be used to estimate the market segment size. Therefore, an organization that wishes to focus on fitness generalists would estimate the market as 977 people (53% of 1,844).

One of the markets identified from this exercise can now be described as *single females, between the ages of 35 and 44, with children under age 18, who are interested in socialization opportunities and weight control from Schaumburg, Illinois.*

In an organization, it is important there is agreement in the breakdown of the overall market. The organization should always question if the market should be broken down further. Each time a variable is considered, an organization must ask

(a) Will this, indeed, separate the market further? (i.e., The variable *leisure interests* is used, but the market's needs are the same.)

(b) If it does separate the market, does it matter? (e.g., The variable gender is used, but are females and males really unique in their needs of the organization's offerings?)

In this example, do you believe the needs of a single versus married parent are different? Do you believe that the needs of someone ages 18 and 40 are different? Do you believe that those interested in weight control and socialization are different than those who are looking for health improvement or stress relief? If there are no difference in their needs, then these market segments should be collapsed.

One additional consideration should be made: to break down a market when an organization would reach it differently. For example, the needs of females ages 35 to 44 with children under 18 may not be that different for those in Tucson, Arizona; Westford, Massachusetts; or Schaumburg, Illinois. However, if an organization requires different methods to reach them, the geographic variable is necessary. Therefore, "Are these groups unique in the way the organization would reach/communicate with them?" needs to be answered. If so, the market could again be segmented/separated.

Some who are reading this may believe there are other market segments that should be targeted by this health club—others possibly better suited for the organization. Ultimately, an organization will want to explore all potential markets. They first look at broad segments of the mass market, as is often done with age in a community leisure service setting. The mass market is divided into baby, toddler, preschool, elementary, teens, young adult, adult, and seniors in some geographic area. Some communities feel this breakdown of the market segments is enough; however, others further separate this by common characteristics that involves the process they make to participate in community leisure experiences. Common variables used are gender and leisure interests (e.g., competition vs. socialization, ability level, passive vs. active recreation/leisure, structured vs. unstructured opportunities).

Comparing Existing and Potential Market Segments

An analysis of existing and potential market segments should occur to understand what markets are available and what percentage the organization is already serving. To make this comparison, however, both types of segmentation, a priori and post hoc, would tend to use similar variables to segment the market. In the health club case outlined in this chapter, the existing consumer market and the overall market would need to be segmented by geographic home, gender, age, marital and family status, and benefits sought from health club experience.

An organization benefits from this comparison by learning if they are (a) already serving a great number of a specific market segment, (b) serving few of a specific market segment, and (c) unsure what is occurring with a specific market segment. For example, the ad hoc segmentation process with the existing consumers in the health club revealed that approximately 40 memberships matched the segmentation profile for single women, ages 35 to 44, with children under 18, with socialization and fitness interest, from Schaumburg, Illinois. The market, a priori segmentation process, identified approximately three fall into this same segmentation profile. Through gathering data on current organization consumers, an organization can determine if a market segment is appropriate to pursue. If they are serving 40 of a potential 240 people who fit this profile, this suggests there are more people who may be available to reach and serve.

Types of Segmentation

As suggested, there are numerous ways to segment a market. Some of the more popular segmentation approaches in the leisure industry are benefits-based, demographic, psychographic, and multidimensional.

Benefit-Based Segmentation

Leisure authors feel strongly about the importance of these variables in segmentation, and this author could not agree more. Benefits-based segmentation is where an organization combines the state of mind (e.g., opinions, interests, preferences, lifestyles), being (e.g., geographic, demographic characteristics) and product usage to identify segments based on the benefit people seek from the experience.

Ipson, Ellis, and Singleton (1995) suggested benefit-based market segmentation could be utilized in the leisure industry to identify specific groups of people with similar needs, interests, and patterns for consuming leisure experiences. Bichis-Lupas and Moisey (2001) found that rail-trail users could also be segmented according to benefits sought from the leisure experience. Four market segments emerged from their findings, including fitness seekers, typical outdoorsmen, group naturalists, and enthusiasts. These segments differed according to demographic and geographic variables. Two were identified as target markets based on their profitability, accessibility, and reachability.

Demographic Segmentation: Age and Ethnicity

Age is a common method used to segment a market. Rice (1995) suggested markets tend to be defined by age brackets rather than by defining experiences. Generational marketing defines market segments by birth years where significant external events have impacted them during important, formative years. A great deal has been written about groups of people defined by age. Baby boomers; Generations X, Y, and Z; teens; millenials; and seniors are all defined based on their age. Table 7.3 (p. 168) highlights the various age segment profiles Table 7.3 uses age as the predominate variable to segment a market.

Other variables may be used in the same manner. For example, race has helped to identify and classify a group of emerging markets. Various ethnic markets are known to have differentiated marketing strategies, promotional messages, tailored advertising, and product lines created just for them. Ethnic minorities represent approximately 30% of the U.S. population (U.S. Census Bureau, 2001). This market is projected to increase and is estimated to be 35% of total U.S. population in 2010 and as much as 50% by 2050 (U.S. Census Bureau, 2004).

There are various reasons why ethnicity can be a logical way to segment a market. Cui and Choudhury (2002) suggested in their review of relevant literature that there is various support for this market segregation process; however, many variables can be used to further segment ethic groups. This is because (a) there is diversity even among an ethnic group whereas typical segmentation variables can be used to segment a market (e.g., demographics, psychographics, behavioral patterns); (b) unique cultural differences among ethnic minorities suggest consumer motivations and responses to marketing activities will be different; and (c) consumers in ethnic subcultures often exhibit unique patterns in many lifestyle activities and consumption-related behaviors.

Today, ethnic minorities are more reachable than in the past. Nicodemus (2000) suggested camps should consider marketing to diverse ethnic populations. With the increase

Table 7.3
Age Segment Profiles

The Depression Cohort
(aka, the G.I. generation)
Born: 1912–1921
Age in 2005: 84 to 93
% of Adult Population: 7% (13 million)
Money Motto: Save for a rainy day.
Sex Mindset: Intolerant
Favorite Music: Big band

People who were starting out in the Depression era were scarred in ways that remain with them today— especially when it comes to financial matters like spending, saving, and debt. The Depression cohort was also the first to be truly influenced by contemporary media: radio and especially motion pictures.

The World War II Cohort
(aka, the Depression generation)
Born: 1922–1927
Age in 2005: 78 to 83
% of Adult Population: 6% (11 million)
Money Motto: Save a lot, spend a little.
Sex Mindset: Ambivalent
Favorite Music: Swing

People who came of age in the Forties were unified by the shared experience of a common enemy and a common goal. Consequently, this group became intensely romantic. A sense of self-denial that long outlived the War is especially strong among the 16 million veterans and their families.

The Postwar Cohort
(aka, the Silent generation)
Born: 1928–1945
Age in 2005: 60 to 77
% of Adult Population: 21% (41 million)
Money Motto: Save some, spend some.
Sex Mindset: Repressive
Favorite Music: Frank Sinatra

Members of this 18-year cohort, the War babies, benefited from a long period of economic growth and relative social tranquility. But global unrest and the threat of nuclear attack sparked a need to alleviate uncertainty in everyday life. The youngest subset, called the *cool generation*, were the first to dig folk rock.

The Boomers I Cohort
(aka, the Woodstock generation)
Born: 1946–1954
Age in 2005: 51 to 59
% of Adult Population: 17% (33 million)
Money Motto: Spend, borrow, spend.
Sex Mindset: Permissive
Favorite Music: Rock & Roll

Vietnam is the demarcation point between leading-edge and trailing-edge boomers. The Kennedy and King assassinations signaled an end to the status quo and galvanized this vast cohort. Still, early boomers continued to experience economic good times and want a lifestyle at least as good as their predecessors.

The Boomers II Cohort
(aka, Zoomers)
Born: 1955–1965
Age in 2005: 40 to 50
% of Adult Population: 25% (49 million)
Money Motto: Spend, borrow, spend.
Sex Mindset: Permissive
Favorite Music: Rock & Roll

It all changed after Watergate. The idealistic fervor of youth disappeared. Instead, the late boomers exhibited a narcissistic preoccupation that manifested itself in things like the self-help movement. In this dawning age of downward mobility, debt as a means of maintaining a lifestyle made sense.

The Generation X Cohort
(aka, Baby-busters)
Born: 1966–1976
Age in 2005: 29 to 39
% of Adult Population: 21% (41 million)
Money Motto: Spend? Save? What?
Sex Mindset: Confused
Favorite Music: Grunge, rap, retro

The slacker set has nothing to hang on to. The latchkey kids of divorce and day care are searching for anchors with their seemingly contradictory "retro" behavior: the resurgence of proms, coming-out parties, and fraternities. Their political conservatism is motivated by a "What's in it for me?" cynicism.

Generation Y
(aka, Generation Millennial)
Born: 1977–1993
Age in 2005: 12 to 28
% of Adult Population: 25.9% (69 million)
Money Motto: Money doesn't buy happiness.
Sex Mindset: Living in the moment
Favorite Music: Boy bands, rap, pop music, rock

Most parents of the members of Generation Y are from the Baby Boomers generation and fewer parents are from Generation X. They were the first to grow up with the Internet in a developed, prolific form, including music downloads, instant messaging and cellular phones. Characteristically, they are generally very tolerant towards multiculturalism and internationalism. They also tend to be very competent with technology and in people skills.

Generation Z
(aka, Homelander generation)
Born: 1994–2007
Age in 2005: unborn to 11
% of Adult Population:
Money Motto:
Sex Mindset:
Favorite Music: Pop music, hip hop, electronic music

Their parents are divided between Generation X and Generation Y. Generation Zers are often primarily raised by the television and technology, with few controls or guidances given to them by their largely fairly unsuccessful parents. However, they will often be hard-working and successful, if never as influential as other generations as a whole, and more confused and less assertive about their roles.

Source: http://en.wikipedia.org

in ethnic media (e.g., publications, television, radio), specialized markets are more accessible than ever before. It has become a recent trend to no longer ignore these markets. The focus has switched to differentiating the ethnic groups and integrating them as transcultural or crosscultural markets (Cui & Choudhury, 2002).

Psychographic Segmentation

Many organizations have identified and developed "categories" to describe various market segments. In this process organizations use lifestyles, values, attitudes, personalities, and loyalty issues to determine market segments. Chaker (1999) suggested how psychographic variables were used in an organization to create segmentation profiles:

- *fulfilleds*—practical consumers who care about durability and might like reading about finance

- *achievers*—make purchases that show off their status

- *experiencers*—young, rebellious, excitement seekers

- *makers*—people who have constructive skills, travel a lot, and value "image"

- *believers*—conservative, moral, often practical consumers, characterized by concrete beliefs with an affinity for hobbies like needlework

- *strivers*—try to emulate people who own more impressive possessions, but are weighted down by limited resources.

Hallab, Yoon, and Uysal (2003) found value in segmenting on the healthy living attitude. The study showed there was a greater benefit to the organization by grouping the overall market into clusters, for example, around their attitude toward healthy living.

Multidimensional Segmentation

The use of multiple variables to distinguish a market segment is called *multidimensional segmentation*. This is where an organization utilizes more than one category or variable to reflect a consumer's response to leisure offerings. Segmentation based on only one set of variables may be limiting to an organization, as additional distinctions within these markets may still exist. Multidimensional methods are cited as being more flexible for planning strategy and tactical

decisions, as well as being more effective overall (Neal & Wurst, 2001).

Moscardo, Pearce, and Morrison (2001) used this approach when they compared geographic origin to activity participation to identify market segments. This type of analysis was also used with downhill skiers to more effectively segment the market (Carmichael, 1996).

Developing Segment Profiles

Each target market established should be profiled to describe the "look" of the market. Each target market should become a "real" thing and should resemble those currently served or those wanting to be served. It is important that organizations know, understand, and relate to the needs of each market. One way to do so is to "become" them. Organizations who become the target market are better able to think like them and to approach organization decisions with the market's needs, interests, and desires in mind. The more an organization thinks like a single female with children under 18, living in Schaumburg, with interest in individual and family leisure opportunities to be fit and provide socialization, the better an organization is able to serve this group. The organization will make decisions with this market in mind. It is therefore important for an organization to thoroughly understand the market they wish to pursue.

Various leisure industries have developed consumer profiles to identify a typical consumer within various industries. Consider the following typical consumer profiles of leisure industries in 2004:

Lodging guests. In 2004, 50% of lodging customers travelled for business and 50% for leisure. The typical leisure room night is generated by two adults (51%) ages 35 to 54 (45%) and earning an average household incomes of $72,600. They travel by auto (74%), make reservations (90%), and pay $89 per room night (Shifflet & Associates, 2004)

Boaters. Barbagallo (2002) stated boaters listed on the national boat-owners mailing list are 95% male. They possess a great deal of discretionary income and devote extensive time on their boat for pleasure or for business.

Skiers. The National Ski Areas Association indicated that the average skier spent $1,000 annually on the sport. It is enjoyed by only a small percent of the population—the highly affluent (Maher, 2001).

Outdoor enthusiast. Mostly male market (more women are joining in, however), ages 30 to 49, owns his own house (valued at $126,000+), makes at least $40,000/year, is married, travels domestically, and holds a professional/managerial level job (Mummert, 1998).

Movie theaters. Seiler and Snider (2003) reported the Motion Picture Association of America suggests the core movie going audience is ages 12 to 29 (50% of admissions) whereas those 50 and over represent 17% of attendance. Adults ages 30 to 49 represent one third of all attendees.

Nude recreation. Razzouk and Seitz (2003) studied nude recreation areas to determine if participants could be segmented. They found individuals who participate in nude recreation are mostly educated, middle- to upper-income Caucasians who are fun-loving, family-oriented, sport-oriented, and enjoy socializing with others.

As each leisure industry can profile their respective markets, organizations can also develop their own profile. There are hundreds of different markets not shared in the health club example. As noted, an organization typically seeks more than one market segment they wish to target in an annual marketing plan. There are several approaches an organization can take to determine the number and type of markets it will pursue. Organizations that decide to target one main market tend to put themselves in a high-risk situation even though there are several potential benefits of this approach. Organizations that focus on one market tend to specialize and develop a strong market position within that segment. When an organization has "put all their eggs in one basket," however, they are more vulnerable to some impact to that market (e.g., negative economic situation) and more susceptible to an impact due to additional competitors. Also, when the potential that there may not be enough demand in a market segment to maintain an organization or concern the organization did not segment correctly, one target market may produce little results.

Some organizations identify several target markets so they are not vulnerable to market changes and competition. These target markets may or may not be similar to one another. Each, however, must have passed the test of selecting effective target market choices. Typically, in this situation, an organization may identify two to seven market segments to target.

Organizations who choose more than seven target markets may feel like they are further reducing the potential risk to an organization, but are really increasing the risk once again. Organizations who focus on too many markets may find that this is difficult to keep track of, serve, or maintain. They begin to apply mass marketing approaches to their organization and start to again serve no one. This approach lends itself to the challenges associated with mass marketing.

Some of the potential markets not selected in the health club example, but potentially viable include the following:

- senior males (over age 60) from Schaumburg, Illinois, interested in improving their health

- single seniors (over 60) from Schaumburg, Illinois, interested in socialization opportunities

- adult males (ages 20–34) from Schaumburg, Illinois, interested in increasing body mass and body sculpting

- females (ages 20–34) from Schaumburg, Illinois, interested in body composition and fitness opportunities

- married couples (ages 46–60) with grown or no children at home from Schaumburg, Illinois, interested in health and socialization

These five examples are all considered market segment profiles. They highlight the variables used to determine a unique group of people an organization is considering targeting. Again, an organization would ask, "Are the needs of these markets different? Would I reach or communicate with these markets in different ways?" As long as the answer to these questions is yes, then the organization has *potentially* identified a target market(s).

Understanding the needs of these Gen X snowshoers is valuable for the ski industry.

Identifying Market Segment Potential

The term *potentially* is added for several reasons at this step in the target market process. The organization may not be certain that these markets are indeed the ones that should be pursued. As noted, it is difficult to analyze the market clearly and every step to ensure the target market is appropriate should be taken. Typically, when organizations identify the two to seven target markets for an annual marketing plan, they determine which markets to target by answering the following questions:

- Which target markets are sustainable? Are they fragmented?

- Which target markets have the highest probability of success and the least competition?

- Which target markets have the greatest need for our expertise? Which target markets can we most effectively serve based on existing resources?

- Which target markets are reachable?

- To which target markets can we allocate resources?

- Which target markets most effectively assist in reaching our overall organization goals?

- Which target markets support our mission?

Based on these results, organizations should establish primary, secondary, and even tertiary markets to pursue. Yet, one additional analysis will confirm if these markets are indeed worthy of pursuing. The following concerns should be addressed to solidify if these target markets should be pursued by a leisure and tourism organization:

(1) Is the size of the market sustainable? Is this market fragmented?

Market fragmentation occurs when a market is divided so many times that, not only would it be difficult to find the group of people that fit the description, there may only be a few that actually fit the description. Further, the following must also be considered:

- Is the size of this potential target market known?

- Can the organization feel confident in the estimate?

- Is the size large enough to produce a significant enough effect on the organization?

- Is the size large enough to warrant these efforts (of developing a marketing plan)?

- Is the size large enough to be sustainable?

An organization can take several steps to determine the size of a market segment. An example of this was used in the health club scenario (see Figure 7.1, p. 165) where an estimation of the size was made as the overall and consumer markets were divided into segments. Oftentimes, as suggested, this estimate is developed from using both a scientific method as well as an educated guess. Ultimately, an organization needs to feel confident that the number they have estimated is accurate, and they will be comfortable sharing their rationale to others regarding this market segment.

U.S. census data was used to determine the number of single versus married people, with and without children, in various age segments. At times this was an exact number and other times an estimation based on percentages. However, the U.S. Census does not ask households to indicate the benefits sought in leisure experience. As a result, other methods must be used to develop the best "educated estimate" available. In this instance, there may be national, regional, or statewide data that was done by the health club industry regarding benefits sought from a health club experience. There may be data gathered by the Surgeon General's office that suggests why people go to health clubs, which may also be useful.

In this example, although the research did not study Schaumburg females specifically, the organization could reasonably estimate the national research suggests some pattern. In this instance, approximately 30% utilize fitness for socialization opportunities, 53% do so for general reasons, 13% for family togetherness, and 4% avoid fitness activities. The organization could get a reasonable idea on the size of the market knowing some of the data is based on scientific data directly related to their market and situation, and some data suggests this type of relationship would exist in a market other than the organization's.

If data was not available to help support the organization's understanding the benefits sought in a fitness experience (or any other variable for that matter), then the organization is left to present what it can and to make some conclusions based on their best educated guess. If while presenting the marketing plan to the county commission or club ownership/management, someone asks why the organization would ever want to market toward local teenagers, who are not engaged in school activities and have socialization interest, the evidence of market size is critical. An organization confident in stating what they know about the market, and then what they can best "guess," will assist in selling plan ideas, gaining support for marketing efforts and ultimately making better marketing decisions about which target markets to pursue. Table 7.4 highlights the size of the market in a different format to explain the process the health club example suggested.

Determining the size of the market is also a condition of selecting the best markets to pursue. There are, however, other considerations to address.

(2) Which target markets have the highest probability of success and the least competition?

If an organization has not yet completed a competitive assessment, this is yet another reason why it is important to do so. To determine where existing demand may be going as well as who is focusing on and meeting the needs of various markets, it is valuable to assess the competition. One tool that can assist in this analysis is completing a graph that depicts which competitors are focusing on which markets. Table 7.5 describes this type of analysis tool.

Table 7.5 provides an example of segmentation using several variables; however, any segmentation process could be used in this type of analysis. Several conclusions can be drawn from this assessment. It is evident that young adults (ages 18–27) and youth (ages 6–12) have several organizations focusing on their needs. Few organizations are targeting the very young youth (ages 0–5) and teen

(ages 13–17) markets. No organization is targeting the senior (ages 65 and over) and only one organization is targeting the 50–64 year old senior. This assessment suggests the senior market's needs are not being specifically addressed by organizations and this may be a potential market to pursue.

(3) Which target markets have the greatest need for our expertise? Which target markets can we most effectively serve based on existing resources?

Organizations would ask themselves, "Based on our current organization structure and offerings, what markets may benefit most from what we do? What are our organization's strengths, and which markets are we designed naturally to serve (versus making changes)?" Answering these questions often relies on a thorough understanding of all an organization can do and on assessing the organizations strengths, weaknesses, opportunities, and threats. Once again, if an organization is unclear as to the value of conducting an organization assessment or a SWOT analysis, being able to answer these questions is one of the main values of doing so.

(4) Which target markets are reachable?

Just because an organization has answered "yes" to all of the previous questions does not mean the market is reachable. If you cannot find the market to communicate with them directly, then the values of target marketing will not

---

Table 7.4
Determining Market Segment Size

Variable Used	Data Source to Determine Size	Estimated Market Size
Schaumburg, IL: Total population	U.S. Census data: City population (total)	75,386
Males vs. females	U.S. Census data: Percent female (51.3%)	75,386 * 51.3% = 38,692
Females by age segment	U.S. Census data: Estimation of percent of population in each age group	*(see breakdown below)*

Age	Est. %		% Female
<20	25.3	*38,692 =	9,789
20–24	12.0	*38,692 =	4,643
25–34	16.0	*38,692 =	6,190
35–44	**18.7**	***38,692 =**	**7,235**
45–54	12.0	*38,692 =	4,643
55–64	9.0	*38,692 =	3,482
>64	7.0	*38,692 =	2,708

Variable Used	Data Source to Determine Size	Estimated Market Size
Married versus single females in 35–44 age bracket	Estimation of 49% of households are single	7,235 * 49% = 3,545
Single, 35–44, family status	Estimation of 52% of households have children under age 18	3,545 * 52% = 1,844
Benefits sought	National study used to estimate the size of generalist market based on the national study's findings on benefits.	Socialization (1,844* 30%) = 553 **General (1,844* 53%) = 977*** Family Togetherness (1,844* 13%) = 240 Avoid Activity (1,844* 4%) = 74

* Single females with children under 18, between the ages of 35 and 44, from Schaumburg, Illinois, who are looking for general opportunities (i.e., weight control, strength, shaping).

be proven. You may have the best-designed leisure experience for consumers, but if they do not know about it then it really does not matter. Organizations need to reach markets and tell them what they have to offer as well as how these offerings can meet a market's needs.

(5) Which target markets can we allocate resources to?

An organization needs to determine what type of support it can provide to each potential target market. They need to determine if they have enough resources to set themselves apart from the competition and distinguish themselves as the best organization to fulfil needs and exceed expectations of this market. An organization would ask themselves, "Do we have the resources to establish a competitive edge in the marketplace?"

(6) Which target markets most effectively assist in reaching our overall organization goals? Which target markets support our mission?

An organization must always operate under the foundation of their mission, objectives, and goals. Because other competitors do not pursue a market does not mean the organization should target it. An organization may be able to reach soccer groups to fill slow weekends in a hotel; however,

the focus on corporate clients may not be a good match for active, enthusiastic, up-until-late-hours soccer groups.

If an organization positively answers each of these questions, then this market segment may indeed be worthy of pursuing. Before the final selection occurs however, markets are further evaluated in a positioning exercise explained in Chapter 8.

Popular Leisure and Tourism Organization Market Segments

So many potential market segments exist that it is valuable for organizations to stay current on materials that may introduce potential segments to an organization. Access to market research data is critical in market segmentation. A variety of sources can be used to identify potential markets (see Table 7.6).

Yet, within each of these market segments, there are greater distinctions to be made. Are all runners the same? Do they look and act alike? Are they searching for the

Table 7.5
Competitive Market Focus Assessment

Agency/Competitors	Market Segments						
	Senior 65+	Senior 50–64	Adult 28–49	Adult 18–27	Teen 13–17	Youth 6–12	Youth 0–5
Wellness center			▓			▓	
Community health and fitness				▓		▓	
University activity center		▓	▓				
Resort sports			▓				
T.E.A.M. sports					▓	▓	

Table 7.6
Potential Market Segments

Market Segment	Source
2.34 million U.S. weddings each year	http://afwpi.com/wedstats.html
601,209 same-sex households	http://www.gay.com
7.8 million single-parent homes	Monthly Labor Review (July 2002)
25% of men and 45% of women diet daily	http://womensissues.about.com
24 million runners (6+ times in 2002)	NSGA Sport Participation Study (2002) http://www.nsga.org/public/pages/index.cfm?pageod=150
7 million tai chi/yoga participants	NSGA Sport Participation Study (2002) http://www.nsga.org/public/pages/index.cfm?pageod=150
28.9 million people worked out in a club in 2002 vs. 26.5 in 2001	NSGA Sport Participation Study (2002) http://www.nsga.org/public/pages/index.cfm?pageod=150

same experiences? A competitive marathon runner from Florida certainly is different from a fitness-oriented, three-day-a-week, three-miles-a-day runner who lives in northern Canada. Their needs, expectations, and interests are different. Hence, it is important to further identify specific groups of runners (or any large group) into like characteristics.

Several market segments more recently addressed in leisure and nonleisure literature are worthy of consideration by leisure and tourism organizations. Table 7.3 (p. 168) highlighted several market segments defined by age. Some of these expand further, including seniors, baby boomers, women, gay/lesbian/transgender, teens, and persons with disabilities.

Seniors

Based on the large number of people that fall into the baby boomer generation, this quantity of people will always represent those with the most economic clout. Yet, much of this segment has not entered "senior" status.

Twenty years from now the over-50 market will have grown by over 70%, while the under-50 market by only 1%. Every leisure and tourism organization should consider this shift and respond to it accordingly. Historical methods for identifying this market have been based on age, where anyone over 50 was lumped into one category of "senior." After all, that is when one becomes eligible for an American Association of Retired People (AARP) card, and some organizations recognize this age for "senior discounts." This market reminds organizations that keeping the "blinders" on and not recognizing the various segments within this segment would be an opportunity missed (Rude, 1998).

Some suggest marketers have not focused on the senior market, yet seniors are spending an increasing amount on travel, recreation, and entertainment. This market is expanding as baby boomers reach senior status; they are healthier and living longer, have more money than seniors in the past, and are spending more. Brazil (1998) stated marketers would not suggest 30 to 50 year olds are one demographic group. Yet, many see no problem in lumping 50 to 70 year olds in the same group.

Szmigin and Carrigan (2001) suggested marketers have tended to shy away from targeting older consumers because it is perceived they are less likely to try new brands and are too set in their ways to change. Further, this market also felt younger and accepted the youthful messages viewed in marketing communication. They studied older consumer consumption habits in leisure and tourism services to understand if this indeed held true. Perceptions of 231 persons between the ages of 51 and 86 from higher than average socioeconomic status indicated they were indeed active consumers of tourism and leisure services. They felt very few organizations geared advertising messages to them because their age group was not well-represented in the media. They have interests in more than just the typical "older consumer" product or service (e.g., funeral plans).

This older generation has been viewed as a market to focus on by many in the leisure industry. Knutson (2001) found further segmenting the senior population at a private club proved valuable because "matures" (ages 50–64) were very different than "seniors" (over age 65). Significant differences exist between these segments and their dining patterns, importance placed on membership factors, overall opinion of the club as well as current and future directions of the club.

Many have found this market has several distinctions within it because all older consumers are not created equal. Mathur, Sherman, and Schiffman (2001) identified a new category of older consumers called the "new-age" elderly. They see themselves as younger in age and outlook. They are also more willing to accept change and be introduced to, and use, new products and services. They enjoy personal challenge and are open to new experiences (Mathur,

Senior working out at the Easter Seals Tennessee facility.

Seniors enjoy participating in "younger" activities.

Sherman & Schiffman, 2001). A study conducted by Mathur, Sherman and Schiffman analyzed the segmentation differences between traditional and new age elderly versus using only chronological age-based segmentation. The findings are summarized in Table 7.7.

New-age elders were slightly younger in chronological age and significantly younger in how old they felt in cognitive age. However, there was no differences in marital or employment status. This market of older consumers likes to travel and also will consider activities geared toward younger persons.

They found that by segmenting the elder consumer market by chronological age only did not provide the distinctions of the market like value-oriented variables did. Traditional methods of segmenting the older consumer market have relied on age as the primary variable to divide behaviors, needs, and interests. This research suggests profiling elders in a new-age category based on their value orientation is possible. They suggest it is important for marketers to target these groups using messages consistent with the new-age versus traditional appeals. "Marketers need to understand that it is not their perceptions of aging that are important, but that of their perspective market." (Mathur, Sherman & Schiffman, 2001, p. 271) Brazil (1998) supported this, suggesting the key to reaching a senior market is to recognize there are distinctions within the senior market and various subgroups exist. Even the baby boomers are divided into subcategories, where those in the top versus bottom have different values, needs, and spending behavior.

This data is not to suggest no leisure organizations have found value in pursuing this new-age senior. Many leisure-related organizations have found the value of the senior market. Recreational vehicles, motorcycles, snowmobiles, and personal watercraft have all experienced growth due largely in part to increasing perusal of the senior market (Dover, 1998; Fost, 1998a; McCune, 1999).

Baby Boomers

An American demographics study in 1999 suggested that of the 1,200 baby boomers (born between 1946 and 1965) surveyed, 73% felt recreation-focused businesses would be important when they reached age 65. "Computer-related services" was the only topic mentioned more often (at 80%). Third, at 33%, was "mental health services," and 64% suggested they plan on working in some capacity after they retire—36% of those expect to have a home-based business. These baby boomers have reached senior status as the oldest are now in their early sixties.

Table 7.7
Summary of Differences Between Traditional and New-Age Elders

Variable	Traditional Elder	New-Age Elder
Age	Chronological average age: 66.9 years Cognitive age: −7 years	Chronological average age: 63.3 years Cognitive age: −12 years
Marital and employment status	No differences	No differences
Values	Less decisive, individual decision makers, less control of their life, less satisfaction with health, social life and overall life, and less adventurous and willing to try new things.	More decisive, individual decision makers, greater control of their life, greater satisfaction with health, social life and overall life, and more adventurous and willing to try new things.
Travel and leisure behavior	40% exercise at least once each week, 3.73 days spend on air vacations and 1.14 days on international vacations.	70% exercise at least once each week, 8.71 days spent on air vacations and 4.91 days on international vacations.
Leisure activities	Significantly less interest in outdoor activities, foreign trips, financial markets and news, volunteer work/self-enrichment, learning new things, computers, and domestic travel.	Significantly greater interest in outdoor activities, foreign trips, financial markets and news, volunteer work/self-enrichment, learning new things, computers, and domestic travel.
Sources of information	Less use of travel agents, travel books, pamphlets and brochures, and travel videos. No differences existed with other mediums (e.g., newspaper and magazine ads, TV or radio commercials, magazine articles or use of travel clubs).	Greater use of travel agents, travel books, pamphlets and brochures, and travel videos. No differences existed with other mediums (e.g., newspaper and magazine ads, TV, or radio commercials, magazine articles, or use of travel clubs).

Real Life Story:
Cedarbrook Village Resort Targets the Senior Community

In an effort to successfully manage an oversaturated hotel market, challenging economy and escalating operating costs, owner Craig Bonter decided to convert his 150-room Ramada Inn into a senior living resort community. The hotel was among over 50 others in a primarily summer-only resort community. Of the 50+ hotels, only five stayed open year-round.

Recognizing the growing demand of the over 70 million American baby boomers who are beginning to turn 60 and the lack of adequate offerings for this market, Craig identified the potential to successfully meet the needs of this emerging market. As a result he could increase his potential for a year-round operation, minimizing seasonality issues. He could also better compete and manage challenging times.

He decided to convert his hotel into a place for various senior markets including traditional hotel segments, such as the transient and group senior market, and the more nontraditional hotel segments including local seniors and seniors in need of more permanent residences with assisted-living accommodations. Specifically focused on meeting the needs of the senior market, Craig set out to be the single destination for seniors whether they were already living in the area, vacationing, visiting family and friends, or needed more permanent accommodations.

In an effort to create a successful conversion, Craig evaluated his existing amenities. He knew he offered more services and amenities than any other senior living center with a pool, spa, restaurant facility with a liquor license, meeting space, walking distance to shopping, tourist attractions and other services, and a large variety of guest rooms. He partnered with the county's Commission on Aging to meet the needs of the local senior market by dedicating the restaurant facility and program areas for their offerings. These offerings would be extended to any of Craig's other senior visitors as well.

These changes, in addition to identifying other competitive advantages, provided the elements he needed to be successful in this venture. Instead of developing the facility for the type of senior most living center's did (i.e., a more high-end consumer), he instead focused on becoming an affordable senior living facility with more amenities than others that would better meet the needs of the baby boomer market. He recognized through his competitive analysis that there was a large gap in the midscale price range for senior living. This would provide him a unique position in the market.

Nationwide senior living chains are not traditionally serving that market segment. Craig recognized they have financial constraints that he did not. They could not build a new senior facility at a price that can warrant the more moderate extension of cost to the consumer. His facility already had hotel amenities; it provided him various offerings that would prove to be too costly for start-up operations to absorb.

Most senior living facilities need to charge high prices to recover the debt service from developing a facility and providing services. By converting the hotel, Craig was able to limit the burden of new development expenses. He did, however, need to make several changes to better meet the needs of these markets. Some of the changes that were necessary were

- Fire suppression/sprinkler system addition
- Change of zoning use (i.e., transient)
- Better lighting
- Larger parking spaces
- Bigger signage
- Softer colors
- Hard surface flooring to accommodate walkers and wheelchairs
- Increased heating/cooling systems
- Accessible restrooms
- Small kitchens/kitchenettes

In essence, he met the specific needs of the market segment he was now going to serve. As a result, he was better positioned for the future.

Women

Outdoor recreation manufacturers are broadening the market base by targeting women. This market segment is of interest to manufacturers because they control over half the U.S. wealth, make more than 80% of all purchases, and are becoming more active. Outdoor products are being designed for women from sleeping bags with a narrower top for shoulders and larger midsection for hips, to specially designed ski boots that more closely resemble the narrow heal and wider toe area that women have. Women are willing to pay more for gear specially designed to fit them (McCune, 1999).

Gay, Lesbian, Transgender

Many in the tourism industry are looking to nontraditional, markets such as gay and lesbians. As early as 1992, Wilson suggested this market is being courted by destinations and tour operators like never before. One of the reasons is because this market of people, predominantly, has a high discretionary income, no children and interest in travel. In 1992, the International Gay Travel Association (founded in 1983) boasted 600 members, yet today their presence has grown to 1,200 members with a new name of the International Gay and Lesbian Travel Association (http://www.traveliglta.com).

Teens

Teens are mature, independent, media savvy, and economically powerful. Often referred to as the baby boomlet based on their massive size relative to other age market segments (White-Sax, 1999), they have brand loyalty, like to shop, and have greater mobility options. Fifteen million teenage boys spend more than $50 billion annually on extreme sports. Boys ages 12 to 15 prefer alternative sports to baseball. Some are active in these sports while others within the market fantasize about participating (Horovitz, 1997).

Persons With Disabilities

Fost (1998b) predicted that a growing market for the leisure industries would be consumers with physical disabilities. He suggests there have been three external influences to

Both women and men enjoy outdoor activities.

All abilities can participate in leisure activities.

making this more of a viable market than before. First, the Americans With Disabilities Act (ADA) highlighted the needs of persons with disabilities and provided a means for accessing leisure experiences as both a consumer and employee. The ADA brought to light so many issues and concerns ignored by many organizations in the past. The second influence, improved and enhanced technology, provides additional opportunities for persons with disabilities. The third influence is that the baby boomer generation is aging while there are enhanced medical treatment options as well as continued growth in the disabled population.

Value of Target Marketing

The identification of target markets is not an easy one. Many organizations suggest there are countless benefits when applying target market processes, so there must be significant value in identifying these potential groups. One of the primary outcomes from target marketing is the ability to know why consumers behave the way they do and what meaning this behavior has on a specific leisure organization. The benefit of target market is simple—efficiency (Wilson, 2003). It allows organizations to more effectively reach consumers and use resources including time, money, and expertise better.

The more an organization knows about current or desired consumers the better able they are to make specific decisions to connect with and reach them. Many of the other values of target marketing have been identified in Tom's community recreation department situation highlighted at the beginning of this chapter. These and additional values include the following:

- more specific and effective use of marketing resources (e.g., budget, time, expertise)

- greater impact on overall organization effectiveness

- clearer understanding of markets needs, wants, and desires

- enhanced ability to identify competitive advantages and to establish positioning

- more strategic approach to organization development

Even though there are many values to conducting target market approaches, there must be a reason why every organization does not approach it this way. There are several potential failures and limits to market segmentation:

- It is difficult to segment markets correctly.

- It is difficult to identify the most appropriate variables to use to segment the group.

- Organizations can select a market segment that is not viable.

- It is difficult to define the size of the market.

- There is an expense to analyzing segments and a fear that an organization may not be doing it correctly.

- Organizations do not gain full leadership support for developing a segmented versus mass market approach.

- Organizations do not fully understand the concept.

Real Life Story: Understanding Target Markets in Fitness

Sova (1996) described her approach to marketing with her organization, Fitness Firm. She always thought everyone was her market and to grow her business she should try to expand the number of markets she served.

That was a mistake, she admits, as she really needed to expand her share of select target market(s). She now looks back and better understands why she was frustrated with the amount of money she spent on marketing and the return she received for that investment. First, she surveyed those already using the Fitness Firm. She found that over 85% were women, ages 25 to 35 with some college education and middle-class incomes. From this she realized that they really were her target market and began to approach marketing with this in mind.

As a result, her marketing investments provided greater returns. They continued to serve various market segments (e.g., seniors, children, persons with disabilities). Even though marketing dollars were not aimed at them, they continued to come.

"I learned that you will always draw some peripheral clients, but you don't need to spend marketing dollars on them." Finally, she recommends organizations decide whom they are targeting before they ever start up and identify specific geographic, demographic, socioeconomic and other variables specific to your organization. Once you do that, she suggests, you will provide better service, better products, and better marketing. As a result of these efforts, Sova grew her businesses to over 2,000 fitness centers located in 22 states.

Importance of Strategy Assessment with Markets Identified

To best manage these limitations, an organization does several things beyond learning about how to segment and apply target market approaches. Once target markets are identified by an organization, several final steps need to be completed before going after the market. The first of these is another assessment of the competitive and SWOT analyses.

Competitive and SWOT analyses, as outlined in Chapter 6, are important processes for developing a marketing strategy. At this point in strategy development, they play a particularly useful role as well. First, they assist in answering critical market questions as outlined in the previous section. Second, they provide a means to further understand if a market segment is viable.

Within each market segment identified it is valuable for an organization to identify specific changes to these analyses based on the specific needs of the target market itself. For example, the competitive analysis shared in Chapter 6 was for a health club. Would these health clubs still be a competitor if the target market was a senior over age 64? The answer to this question could be yes depending on the leisure service choices in an actual market. At a minimum, one could presume there are other choices a senior may make in a given market. Other competitors for this market type may be a senior center, community organization walking programs, or even a healthcare provider that offers classes on wellness, cholesterol, and weight management. This raises the concern that each potential target market may have unique competitors that have not been assessed in the initial competitive analysis stage. The same type of situation may occur with the teen market. Who would a community organization compete with regarding serving a teen? In this instance, the competitors may be school, a local arcade, or a "hang out" area in a park. Regardless, an organization should always reevaluate the competition once potential target market segments are identified. A second competitive analysis should be done with those organizations identified as another competitor for each potential market segment.

It is valuable for an organization to understand there are distinctions within each target market that make it unique. Those organizations that recognize these changes are better able to prepare, implement, and react to each specific market's needs. These same issues apply with conducting a SWOT analysis.

For example, with the SWOT analysis shared in Chapter 6, would the SWOT change if the potential target market segment was seniors? It is doubtful that teens would find a daycare center a strength of this organization, and they may find it a weakness that little children and parents would be there. Would they find the aquatic center a weakness? Most teens would consider it a great value. Therefore, a SWOT analysis must also be completed based on each target market so an organization can best determine what should be communicated to each market (e.g., strengths) and what should be addressed for each market (e.g., weaknesses). These helpful planning tools should always take into consideration each unique market an organization is serving or would like to serve.

Ideally, in a target market approach, a market will believe every aspect of the organization was designed with them in mind—every brochure written for them, every program with their needs in mind, every service with their expectations considered. Target marketing allows an organization to specialize its promotional message. A more specific message can be shared versus one that needs to represent the entire organization to all types of people. This type of message becomes generic and, therefore, the reason why so many organizations fail to even have some type of positioning statement. Chaet (1999) defined this as *concept marketing*.

Apply What You Know

1. Identify a segmentation approach (e.g., benefits-based, socioeconomic) for the leisure service organization you selected.

2. Determine and describe at least two target markets for your organization to pursue.

3. Conduct a SWOT analysis on these two markets.

4. Reassess the competitors for the two market segments you identified.

Key Terms

A priori segmentation
Benefits-based segmentation
Cluster analysis techniques
Demographic segmentation
Geographic segmentation
Post hoc segmentation

Market
Market fragmentation
Market segmentation
Market segments
Psychographic segmentation
Target market

Review Questions

1. Why is it important to select a target market before conducting or providing a service?

2. What is the difference between market segmentation and target market?

3. List the criteria used to determine an organization's target market.

4. Identify and explain the challenges of applying the target market principles.

5. What variables are used in market segmentation?

6. What is market fragmentation? What is its affect?

7. What is a priori? What purpose does it serve?

8. Explain why SWOT and competitive analyses should be completed once target markets are established.

Internet Resources

Target Marketing gives readers insights in subjects such as using databases and lists effectively, acquiring new customers, keeping the existing custumers, and developing strategies for specific target markets. Their website includes articles, know-how guides, and upcoming events.

http://www.targetonline.com

Target Market News provides corporate marketing news that targets minorities, including African Americans. Information related to consumer behaviors and expenditures, industry news, and the latest developments in African American marketing and media are included.

http://www.targetmarketnews.com

Free Bizsites.com links to useful sites to search target markets online. The statistical and demographic data available can be used as a baseline in identifying specific market segments.

http://www.freebizsites.com/target.htm

The *Virtual Advisor Interactive* website provides information for entrepreneurs related to company vision, company structure, target market, market and competitive analyses, and how to prepare a business plan.

http://www.va-interactive.com/inbusiness/starting_full.html

The *Plan Ware* website includes a complete guide to developing a business plan. The process of defining the target markets and additional resources are also described.

http://www.planware.org/gmarkets.htm

Entrepreneur.com is a valuable resource of articles and other materials related to marketing and sales. Useful materials about marketing plans and research, positioning, branding, niche marketing, and consumer loyalty can be found on this website.

http://www.entrepreneur.com/salesandmarketing

Business Forum Online addresses issues and questions of specific interest to the entrepreneurs. A special column is dedicated to target marketing as a tool in exploring market opportunities.

http://www.businessforum.com/target2.html

References

Arimond, G., Achenreiner, G., and Elfessi, A. (2003). An innovative approach to tourism market segmentation research: An applied study. *Journal of Hospitality and Leisure Marketing, 10*(3/4), 25–26.

Barbagallo, P. (2002). Boating enthusiasts. *Target Marketing, 25*(7), 56–57.

Bichis-Lupas, M. and Moisey, R. N. (2001). A benefit segmentation of rail-trail users: Implications for marketing by local communities. *Journal of Park and Recreation Administration, 19*(3), 78–92.

Brazil, J. (1998). You talkin' to me? *American Demographics, 20*(12), 54–59.

Carmichael, B. A. (1996). Conjoint analysis of downhill skiers used to improve data collection for market segmentation. *Journal of Travel and Tourism Marketing, 5*(3), 187–206.

Carter, D. M. (1996). *The sports marketing plan.* Grants Pass, OR: Oasis Press.

Chaet, M. (1999). Growing your club with concept marketing: A proven strategy for long-term success. *Canadian Fitness Magazine, 4*(3), 24–25.

Chaker, A. M. (1999, May 19). Lifestyles: No life of leisure. *Wall Street Journal,* S3.

Clancy, K. (2003). Marketing strategy overview. *American Marketing Association*. Retrieved December 1, 2003, from http://www.marketingpower.com/live/content1285.php

Clancy, K. J. and Krieg, P. C. (2002). Marketing science hasn't failed. *Brandweek, 43*(19), 42.

Cui, G. and Choudhury, P. (2002). Marketplace diversity and cost-effective marketing strategies. *Journal of Consumer Marketing, 19*(1), 54–73.

Dolnicar, S. (2002). A review of data-driven market segmentation in tourism. *Journal of Travel and Tourism Marketing, 12*(1), 1–22.

Dover, N. H. (1998). Where there's gray, there's green: Active seniors mean marketing opportunities. *Marketing News, 932*(13), 2.

Fennell, G. and Allenby, G. M. (2002). No brand level segmentation? Let's not rush to judgment. *Marketing Research, 14*(1), 14–18.

Formica, S. and Uysal, M. (2002). Segmentation of travelers based on environmental attitude. *Journal of Hospitality and Leisure Marketing, 9*(3/4) 35–49.

Fost, D. (1998a). Growing older but not up. *American Demographics, 20*(9), 58–65.

Fost, D. (1998b). The fun factor: Marketing recreation to the disabled. *American Demographics, 20*(2), 54–58.

Godbey, G. (1998). Toward another century of parks and recreation. *Parks and Recreation, 33*(7), 28–32.

Horovitz, B. (1997). Marketers get in line for extreme sports. *USA Today, 15*(182), 10B.

Hallab, Z. A. A., Yoon, Y., and Uysal, M. (2003). Segmentation based on the healthy-living attitude: A market's travel behavior. *Journal of Hospitality and Leisure Marketing, 10*(3/4), 185–198.

Ipson, N. M., Ellis, G., and Singleton, J. F. (1995). Benefit-based market segmentation: An approach to programming for adults by interest rather than age. *World Leisure and Recreation, 37*(1), 18–22

Knutson, B. J. (2001). Nature club members: Are they a homogeneous or heterogeneous market. *Journal of Hospitality and Leisure Marketing, 9*(1/2), 35–51.

Learning Resources Network (LERN). (2000). *The marketing manual* (Research Report No. 02-882) River Falls, WI: Author.

Maher, B. (2001). Hitting the slopes. *Target Marketing, 24*(1), 74–77.

Mathur, A., Sherman, E., and Schiffman, L. G. (2001). Opportunities for marketing travel services to new-age elderly. *The Journal of Services Marketing, 12*(4), 265–277.

McCune, J. C. (1999). Marketing the great outdoors. *Management Review,* 24–29.

Moscardo, G., Pearce, P., and Morrison, A. (2001). Evaluating different bases for marketing segmentation: A comparison of geographic origin versus activity participation for generating tourist market segments. *Journal of Travel and Tourism Marketing, 10*(1), 29–49.

Mummert, H. (1998). Outdoor enthusiasts. *Target Marketing, 21*(7), 64–66.

Neal, W. D. (2003). Principles of market segmentation. *American Marketing Association*. Retrieved December 1, 2003, from http://www.marketingpower.com/live/content1006.php

Neal, W. D. and Wurst, J. (2001). Advances in market segmentation. *Marketing Research, 13*(1), 14–18.

Nicodemus, T. (2000). Marketing your camp to diverse populations: Tips to reach ethnic markets. *Camping Magazine, 73*(4), 22–23.

O'Sullivan, E. (1991). *Marketing for parks, recreation, and leisure.* State College, PA: Venture Publishing, Inc.

Razzouk, N. and Seitz, V. (2003). Nude recreation in the United States: An empirical investigation. *Journal of Hospitality & Leisure Marketing, 10*(3/4), 145–157.

Rice, F. (1995). Making generational marketing come of age. *Fortune, 131*(12), 110–114.

Rude, J. (1998). Making the mature decision. *Athletic Business, 22*(1), 31–37.

Seiler, A. and Snider, M. (2003, May 6). The movie industry fights off the pirates. *USA Today.* Retrieved August 28, 2004, from http://www.usatoday.com

Shifflet, D.K. and Associates, Ltd. (2004). Cited by the American Hotel & Lodging Association, *2005 lodging indusrty profile.* New York, NY: AH&LA.

Smith, W. (1956). Product differentiation and market segmentation as alternative marketing strategies. *Journal of Marketing, 21*(7), 3–8.

Sova, R. (1996, July/August). Who is your target market? *RCRA Update.*

Steinberg, J. (1999, January). The millennial mind-set. *American Demographics,* 60–65.

Szmigin, I. and Carrigan, M. (2001). Leisure and tourism services and the older innovator. *The Service Industries Journal, 21*(3), 113–129.

U.S. Census Bureau. (2001). *The white population: 2000.* Retrieved from http://www.census.gov/prod/2001pubs/c2kbr01-4.pdf

U.S. Census Bureau. (2004). *Interim population projections by age, sex, race and Hispanic origin: United States, 2000 to 2050.* Retrieved June 27, 2004, from http://wnjpin.net/OneStopCareerCenter/LaborMarketInformation/lmi03/uspoproj.htm

Veverka, J. (2001). It's all about the visitors. *Legacy, 12*(2), 34–37.

White-Sax, B. (1999). Teens wield powerful financial influence. *Drug Store Use, 21*(9), 68–70.

Wilson, C. (1992, October 7). All-gay tours openly court big spenders. *USA Today,* 6.

Wilson, D. (2003). *Target marketing: Write a marketing plan and marketing plan examples.* Retrieved from http://www.mplans.com/dpm/article.cfm/44

Chapter 8

Brand Positioning and Marketing Outcomes

Bill has been the marketing director of the Brutus Resort and Spa for over ten years. He is good at what he does and has enjoyed a successful career at the resort as a result. Largely, his success has been from identifying specific target market segments the resort focused their attention and efforts toward. These included the corporate, association, and social group market as well as the transient family market. This has proved advantageous; the resort has averaged a 122% market share for the past five years.

Life has changed in the marketplace, however.

The Neekos Resort, less than three months from their grand opening, has added 400 additional guest rooms to the market. This new resort will be a direct competitor of Bill's resort because of similar amenities (e.g., large conference center, recreation complex, indoor/outdoor pools, fitness room, 18-hole championship golf course, indoor and outdoor tennis, children's activities, restaurants and lounge). They are 15 miles apart. It is anticipated they will have similar high levels of quality service.

Bill doesn't seem to be concerned. He knows the Brutus Resort and Spa has a commanding presence in the market. Therefore, he pays little attention to the new resort, because he knows guests have been satisfied with the services received. His plan is to continue to apply similar strategies that have proven successful for the resort. Bill develops the marketing plan for the upcoming year and submits it to the general manager, Tamara, and the resort owners for approval.

The marketing objectives identified in the plan for the Brutus Resort and Spa state the following:

- Increase the awareness of the resort.

- Use TV, radio, and direct mail for advertising.

- Further develop the customer loyalty program.

- Provide excellent customer service.

At the end of this chapter, readers will be able to…

- Define positioning and learn various positioning approaches—including competitive, offering, price, and strength—to identify an organization's niche or competitive advantages.

- Conduct and evaluate a positioning assessment.

- Define brand identity.

- Write a positioning statement for a target market.

- Write measurable marketing objectives.

- Estimate the impact and outcomes of marketing objectives.

In the past, Tamara approved these types of marketing objectives because the resort was doing well. However, this year is different. Unlike Bill, Tamara does not believe that The Neekos Resort opening will go unnoticed by their guests, and their past marketing efforts may not be as successful if they do not consider this new competitor in what they are doing. Tamara calls a meeting with Bill.

During the meeting, Tamara and Bill discuss the new competitor and review their own past marketing efforts to determine what has been most successful. What they realize is that they cannot identify which of their efforts were most successful. Did they increase awareness? Were television, radio, and direct mail effective in bringing in specific target markets? Were they simply successful in spite of themselves?

Bill and Tamara now realize although they believed they were applying target market strategies, they may not have been specifically focusing their marketing efforts in these directions. More importantly, they realized they could not determine if their marketing objectives were achieved, because they were not measurable. The marketing department did not prove their efforts had an impact. Further, they did not evaluate the impact of each tactical effort (e.g., direct-mail piece) and could not determine if these efforts truly provided a return to the resort.

Tamara asked Bill to rewrite his marketing plan so it would hold Bill and his staff more accountable for their efforts. She wanted to know what specific target market objectives he will have for the resort as well as the plan he has to achieve these objectives. She also wants to know how the resort needs to position themselves with the new competitor, and what their competitive niche may be.

Bill now realizes he must do several things before developing his "new" marketing plan for the upcoming year. First, he must learn about his new competitor and identify his competitive advantages over the new resort (as well as other competitors).

He must next identify how he is positioned with these target markets in the marketplacem which target markets he should continue to pursue, and identify new markets to consider. Based on his findings, he must write meaningful marketing objectives that will keep he and his staff focused, show the impact of his actions, and produce a measurable outcome that supports the resort's overall financial plan.

• • • • •

Thank goodness Bill and Tamara were able to see the potential problems they could have this upcoming year. Even though it took the emergence of a new competitor to make them realize the way they have approached marketing must change, the good news was they learned it before it was too late. Some leisure organizations fail to see this. They believe that doing things the way they have always

been done, if successful, is the way it should continue to be approached. They may say "Well, it worked in the past… why not now?"

What many organizations fail to realize is that every single day is different, and one change to the market will impact what an organization does and how they approach marketing. These changes could include the approach taken by a competitor (e.g., change in prices, services), the emergence of a new potential market, the shrinking of a market (e.g., a company going out of business), or the economy. Organizations must constantly evaluate what they do, how they do it and what is happening in the world, industry, and market. Each will influence these activities, hence another reason the steps in Chapter 6, Developing the Strategy, are so important.

Many organizations have a marketing plan that sets the direction for their marketing efforts. However, many also do what Bill had done—Establish a general guide for their efforts without committing to specific results. Although Bill felt he was target-market oriented, his objectives did not suggest this was the case. He did not specifically identify objectives for each target market. What outcome did he want this next year with the corporate, association or social groups? What did he want to happen with the transient family market? Was he ready to make a commitment as to what their efforts would produce? How could he measure if he achieved his marketing objectives? Was awareness increased? Did television, radio and direct mail advertising produce an effect? What market(s) were these efforts geared toward? These activities will be further clarified in the chapter ahead.

Leisure and tourism organizations today need tools that assist them in working smarter, not harder. With increased demands (e.g., funding, the economy, and competition) consumer expectations change. Any system that helps an organization, as opposed to adding one more thing to do, should be welcomed. Any organization can feel they are "marketing" as they complete activities that feel like marketing, such as placing an advertisement or developing a brochure. These steps allow them to check off task completed; however, just doing "things" will not solve larger organization issues and enable marketing to be a tool that assists leisure organizations. Properly executed marketing efforts allow organizations to better manage these issues.

At the center of a leisure and tourism organization's marketing efforts is the concept of their offerings as a developed brand. Brand, brand, and brand… Everyone is talking about the "brand." Organizations use this popular term to describe their marketing focus, yet not all understand what it means. The increased interest with branding is often associated with a competitive marketplace where organizations are battling for market share and establishing an identity (Cebrzynski, 1998; Stein, 1998). A brand is more than simply a logo, slogan, or organization name. Today it has evolved to become an asset within an organization just as capital, equipment, or people have been. Niemuth (2005) and Davis (2002) suggested it is a set of expectations a consumer experiences with an organization over time. Coughlin (2002) suggested it is the "perception of value" consumers believe they have received. It is an "accumulation of characteristics" that form an organization's identity and image (Kaplanidou & Vogt, 2003, p. 2). The goal of a brand identity is to have instant, favorable recall by stakeholders. It conveys expectations and lets stakeholders know what they can expect. Hopelain (2003) suggested

> Brand is defined as a set of expectations and associations evoked from experience with a company or product. It's about how customers think and feel about what the business or product actually delivers. If the experiences are positive, they likely result is a positive perception of the brand, increased likelihood of repeat purchase and positive word-of-mouth, and measurable bottom-line contributions in terms of increased market share and profitability. (p. 3)

It is, therefore, built on each consumer's entire set of experiences—from marketing activities focused on the anticipation stage of an experience, to the quality of the destination experience, to the recollection phase of an experience. A brand is all that an organization is; it is their culture. A brand represents how an organization structures and runs their business; it is their promise to consumers. It is what their name represents. Consumers buy a brand, not an organization.

Steiner is a spa company, yet few people would identify their organization name as one that provides quality spas. However, Mandara, Greenhouse, and C-Spas are brands with recognition. The spa market and other leisure providers are just beginning to build brand recognition, but organizations know a strong brand image sells itself. Traiman (2003) suggested "90% of all buy decisions are based on emotion and feeling" (p. 24). Branding consultant Karen Post (cited in Traiman, 2003) suggested brand is created on four foundations: what an organization (a) promises consumers emotionally, (b) states as their purpose or reason for being there, (c) describes as their experience and visually depicts this, and (d) determines as their position in the market.

McCarville (2003) suggested organizations have used communication channels to position their offerings versus other means. Today, positioning is about everything an organization does, from the quality of service and type of offerings it provides, to the price it charges and the way in which it is provided.

The development of a strong brand is explained in Figure 8.1 (p. 186). This continuum takes a look at an organization's process of little brand development to extensive brand development in relation to consumer and organization viewpoints.

The components introduced in this chapter are often not addressed by leisure and tourism organizations. The concepts of positioning, brand identity, and marketing objectives are critical transitionary elements that assist organizations in moving from the thought of pursuing a target market to successfully doing it. These steps are critical to effective marketing strategy development. Some suggest the most important component of developing a marketing strategy involves the concept of positioning.

Brand Positioning

The way in which a leisure and tourism organization solidifies its marketing strategy and transitions into making operational tactical marketing decisions is completed through positioning. *Positioning* is identifying the perception people have of a leisure and tourism organization as it relates to other leisure and tourism organizations. It is the reason people choose one experience over another. It is combining the process of target market identification and competitive analysis to assess an organization's current and desired position as it relates to a specific target market. *Brand positioning* more specifically relates to the way in which an organization manages the brand through marketing decisions that create and sustain a specific image of a brand (i.e., their organization's offerings) in consumers' minds. This is based on brand strengths as defined by a target market when considering the competition. This was first introduced by Ries and Trout (1986) as early as 1969. It was developed to improve the impact of marketing communication activities in a market flooded with advertising messages and brands.

Several positioning processes are conducted to create a perception in people's minds. Positioning itself has three distinct elements: (a) understanding an organization's current position called a *positioning assessment* or *brand mapping*, (b) understanding if this is where an organization wants to be positioned and if they want to serve this target market, and (c) developing a brand identity through a positioning or repositioning statement. Each step relies on the other.

Positioning assessments are used to determine what the current position is, whereas *positioning statements* are used to communicate the desired position of an organization.

There are many values to conducting these positioning exercises:

- Determine if a target market should indeed be targeted.

- Identify how the organization is viewed by the target market against its competitors.

- Understand if duplication of services exist.

- Establish a means for identifying what it will take to serve/secure that target market.

- Highlight the organization's competitive advantages.

- Establish a brand identity.

Positioning is a transitionary activity that occurs between identifying a target market and determining how an organization will communicate with and reach that target market. It secures that the target market is indeed one to focused on and establishes the way in which an organization should pursue the market.

The foundation of positioning is based on people's perceptions. As discussed in Chapter 3, The Quality Service Foundation, perceptions people have of an organization are formed in various ways. The better an organization understands what these perceptions are, the more effectively they can apply the positioning assessment because it often relies on subjective judgments regarding the organization, its competitors, and the needs of the target market. The more objective these judgments are, the more valuable the conclusions can be. Therefore, to conduct a positioning assessment, a thorough understanding of the organization, competitor, and target market assessments must be completed.

Understanding perceptions is important in any type of organization. If consumers do not understand what an organization wants them to know, then a misconception exists. How many times have you entered a store and said, "I didn't know they had this?" Leisure organizations want to minimize misconceptions about their offerings and be certain to communicate to their intended audiences.

Effective positioning assists organizations in focusing on the needs of target markets, identifying issues important to them, and identifying effective ways to communicate with them. Some authors suggest an organization should develop its position after first deciding what to offer consumers, then determine to whom the service will be directed. The approach to positioning that will be outlined in

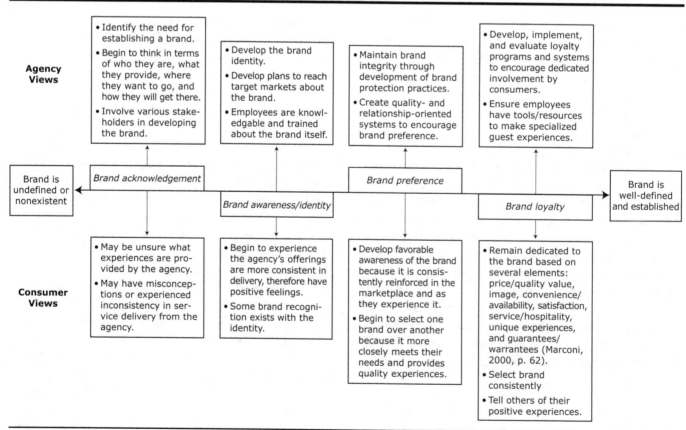

Figure 8.1
Brand Development Continuum

this chapter does just the opposite. It first identifies the target markets, then develops offerings based on the position desired by the organization.

In an effort to understand the most advantageous position for an organization, the positioning assessment must be completed, and an organization must evaluate how various target markets currently view it.

~~~~~~~~~~~~~~~~~

It was very enlightening to complete a competitive analysis and positioning assessment, as they forced us to candidly evaluate our services and provided a realistic view of our position as we had not seen it before.
Debra Bilbrey-Honsowetz, Canton Leisure Services

~~~~~~~~~~~~~~~~~

Positioning Assessments: Brand Mapping

In an effort to reap the benefits of conducting positioning, specific steps are followed. *Positioning assessments* or *brand mapping* provide a means to identify how target markets perceive an organization's brand. If their perception is not what an organization desires, then the organization can react with changing the marketing and communication mix to reach the desired state thus repositioning the organization. A positioning assessment provides a visual representation of an organization's status compared to any competitor in relation to a target market. This allows an organization to evaluate how it is viewed by the target market and how it compares to direct competitors. Central to this approach is understanding the needs of these various target markets (Green & Muller, 2002). Barnholt and Jackowski (2002) suggested leisure and tourism organizations must understand the people served to understand current positioning and to determine if repositioning the organization is necessary. Each target market identified by an organization should have their own positioning assessment because each market has unique needs and perceptions. A senior's perception of a skate park would be different than a teenager's. Therefore for each specific target market, an organization follows these six steps:

Step 1: Identify the two variables (e.g., needs, issues, priorities) most influential in the target market's decision to participate or consume an experience.

Step 2: Plot these two variables on a two-dimensional graph with each extreme placed on an end of the graph line.

Step 3: Plot the location of the target market on the graph.

Step 4: Plot the position of the organization on the graph.

Step 5: Plot the position of the competitor(s) on the graph.

Step 6: Interpret the positioning assessment graph.

In an effort to thoroughly explain this process each step will be outlined using the resort example introduced at the beginning of this chapter. The Brutus Resort and Spa is interested in targeting social wedding groups (e.g., engaged couples) from the local market who have interest in hosting their reception in the convention center as well as guest rooms for out-of-town visitors. They have budgeted for spending between $50 and $70 per person for the event. Although price and amenities are most important to this market, the quality of the facility is also a top priority. They want to host their reception and have their guest rooms at the highest quality facility they can afford. Step 1 is to identify two variables of most importance to local engaged couples in selecting a location for their wedding reception: price and amenities.

These variables could have been determined in a variety of ways. The most valuable way is to ask the specific target market, then an organization is not guessing and the analysis is more objective than subjective. Ask engaged couples who attend a local bridal show or who visit the organization as well as newly married couples who hosted their reception at the organization the following question: "What are the two most important issues for you when deciding on a location to host your wedding reception?" Be sure to ask demographic questions so you can further identify if within this market further segmentation should occur (e.g., Is there a difference between the needs of younger vs. older engaged couples?). For additional information, access a secondary research study that asked similar questions.

What is important to note is that failing to select the most important issues that face a target market could result an improper assessment of the organization's position. Applying target market principles is not a simple process.

Step 1
Two variables of most importance to local engaged couples in selecting a location for their wedding receeption:

PRICE and AMENITIES

The more objective the graph developed, the more effective the results will be.

In Step 2, an organization develops the graph to visually plot the issues most important to an engaged couple. The extreme of each variable is plotted at the end of each graph line.

In this instance, price and the number of amenities for engaged couples (e.g., decorations, linen, transportation, photography and floral services, guest rooms, resort amenities) were the most important issues for these couples when making the decision to select a facility. In Step 3, the target market's position is determined and plotted on the graph.

The target market is looking for a large number of amenities, realizing they may have to pay a slightly higher than average price. They are willing to pay a bit more for these added amenities, but do not have a "blank check" to get whatever they want. They are interested in amenities that make their event more unique. As a one-time event, they want to make their event as special and as perfect as possible. Step 4 plots the organization's position on the graph.

The Brutus Resort and Spa is more moderately priced for weddings, but has an average number of amenities to offer wedding groups. It is critical for an organization to understand all of their amenities at this step. A thorough organization assessment completed in Chapter 6, Developing the Strategy, ensures this occurs. Step 5 plots the competitors on the graph.

Because the organization conducted a thorough competitive analysis and understands not only what the competitors offer but also at what price for wedding groups, they are able to properly identify the position of the competitors. Once again, objective findings about these amenities and prices assists in properly positioning the other organizations compared to the Brutus Resort and Spa as well as the target market itself.

Step 6 involves assessing the positioning graph and making conclusions based on the findings. Conclusions need to be made regarding the organization's position, competitor's positions, and ways to improve an organization's position, should they decide to target this market. In this instance, these conclusions can be made:

1. The target market is looking for a large number of amenities and realize they may have to pay a slightly higher than average price.

2. The Neekos Resort is positioned more closely to the target market compared to the other organizations based on what they currently offer. Neekos is moderately priced and offers more amenities of interest to engaged couples than any other organization.

3. The Victory and La Premiere Hotels are furthest away from meeting the needs of this market. They both have limited amenities: La Premiere is priced the highest, and Victory Hotel the lowest.

4. Brutus Resort and Spa is priced appropriately for the target market, but does not provide the number of amenities they are seeking or as many as the Neekos Resort.

5. The Brutus Resort has the potential to improve its position by increasing the number/type of amenities offered to engaged couples.

The goal of any organization targeting a market should be to be so in tune with the needs of a target market that the organization is positioned right on top of the target market itself. If interested in serving this market, the organization should be better at serving and meeting the target market's needs than any other competitor. In this instance, should the amenities be exactly what interests engaged couples, the resort would also be able to charge slightly more for these services.

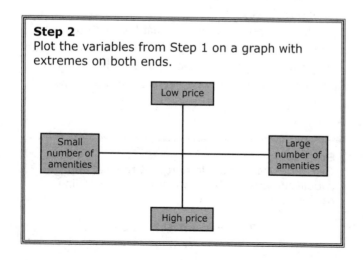

Step 2
Plot the variables from Step 1 on a graph with extremes on both ends.

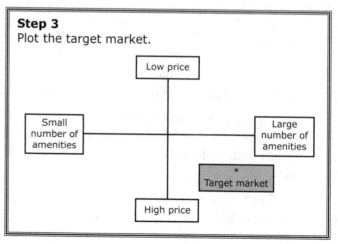

Step 3
Plot the target market.

Chapter 8: Brand Positioning and Marketing Outcomes   189

A limitation of this positioning assessment is that it can only address two variables at a time. However, in this instance, the organization had given each competitor a quality rating and could then evaluate this variable as well. In this case, the Neekos Resort is a new resort, similar in quality to the Brutus Resort and Spa. Therefore, it could pose additional challenges for the organization if it decided to pursue this market as this market is interested in high-quality facilities and services.

As a result of this assessment, the organization can determine one of two actions:

1. *Do not* target this market. The organization decides to pursue other markets because of the organization's current position, inability to improve its position, and/or amount of competitors pursuing the target market.

2. *Do* target this market. The organization decides this market is worthy of pursuing. It has identified specific actions that can be taken to improve the organization's position and more effectively meet the needs of the target market.

Positioning gives consumers a reason to participate in, consume, or buy a leisure experience. Leisure and tourism organizations must position themselves in the best way possible to targeted markets. Through the positioning assessment, organizations can identify ways in which it must move to establish and secure a position as the leisure service provider that addresses the markets needs better than any other. The assessment process keeps an organization focused on what is important to the market. It helps to establish the positioning statement based on these issues versus positioning based on an issue like price or other offerings that may or may not be important to a target market. Further, this type of assessment includes the competition and helps to identify an organization's competitive advantage in the marketplace.

Should the organization decide to target this and other specific markets the positioning assessment can also assist in determining a positioning statement for the organization. These positioning statements can be communicated to the target market and are used to establish a brand identity.

Brand Management and Identity

Brand management is the process by which an organization takes responsibility for the brand. The management of the brand requires that an organization make a long-term commitment to developing experiences based on a solid strategic approach to marketing as well as a willingness to invest in understanding consumer perceptions. Further, managing a brand requires consistency of all organization communications and activities that appropriately reflect an organization's image.

Some suggest management of the brand is a central focus within an organization—an element that one member is directly responsible for developing, analyzing, monitoring, communicating, and protecting. This needs to occur, in simple or complex leisure organizations, at the center of an organization with responsibilities delegated to divisions as needed (Nelson & Kersten, 2002). These duties must be central within an organization for several reasons:

1. Proactive brand management earns organizations money because there is internal versus external control of the brand. Other organizations will establish a brand identity for leisure and tourism organization if they do not do it for

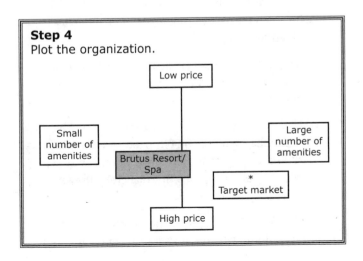

Step 4
Plot the organization.

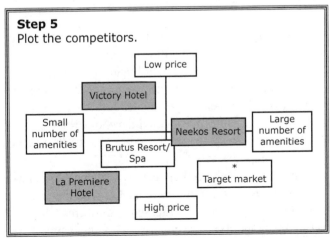

Step 5
Plot the competitors.

themselves. Competition can define other organizations through their own statements. For example, "VISA... Everywhere you want it to be:" Visa has established the American Express's brand as not being able to be used everywhere.

2. Strong brands lend credibility to other organization offerings. As new offerings are introduced by an organization, those with strong brand identities will have an easier time gaining consumer support.

3. Duplication of marketing and communication efforts is minimized with a centralized effort.

4. Control or protection of the brand is better managed with brand management at a high level within the organization. Organizations are able to react quickly to changes, challenges, and opportunities.

5. Brand measurements are more easily completed and consumer needs and perceptions monitored more closely with a centralized approach to brand management. (Nelson & Kersten, 2002)

Protecting The Brand

As organizations have further relied on a strong brand identity to represent their organizations they have also developed systems to protect the brand itself. The NFL Super Bowl brand was impacted with a less than wholesome halftime show in 2003. The National Hockey League was negatively impacted by a season-long lockout in 2004–2005 as was Major League Baseball in 1994–1995 with a 232-day strike (Standohar, 1997). Even concert venue brands are impacted (e.g., the Los Callejeros concert in Buenos Aires where 182 people were killed in 2004 ("News—Deaths Rise," n.d.).

Some aggressively protect the brand. Vermont is well-known as the only state that did not welcome a Wal-Mart store. They were protecting their brand as a wholesome state not subject to mass commercialization. Protecting the brand also includes employee guidelines. Are employees allowed to wear uniforms out after the end of their shift? Will any of their behaviors at the local pubs at 1:00 a.m. be less than complimentary to the brand?

There is a difference between wanting people to promote your business through merchandise with logos (e.g., hats, shirts) and employees dressed in uniforms not protecting the brand. Because employees *are* the brand, they

may be the only ones a consumer experiences at an organization. To that consumer they are the organization—all its values and all it is. Hence, the importance of quality leadership and developing a quality-oriented culture that not only concerns itself with external consumers but just as importantly, internal employees.

Of course, protection of the brand is not limited to nationally known organizations. Every leisure organization has the potential to develop or harm their brand identity. Organizations interested in protecting their brand identity focus on policing it by

- developing quality-oriented standards and practices to create a solid brand throughout the organization in everything they do

- establishing consistent communication messages

- regularly monitoring how the brand is communicated

- evaluating policies and procedures designed to maintain brand integrity

Brand Identity

The establishment of a brand identity allows an organization to communicate its position. It increases an organization's exposure and promotes name recognition (Woollen, 2002). It is how the organization communicates its message in written and verbal form. It is the way it looks. Consider the impact a first impression makes with people. Have you not formed an opinion of a date, professor, or presenter based on how they look. People tend to make first appearance judgments of people, the same way they do other things like the look of organization materials. Griffin (2002) suggested three types of brand identities exist:

1. *Monolithic*. The organization brand is the only brand and no other brands exist within the organization overall.

2. *Branded*. Individual products are given separate brand identities and the organization may or may not be known.

3. *Endorsed*. A symbolic relationship exists between the organization (e.g., the parent organization) and a brand within the organization (e.g., the child organization) whereby they promote each other.

As discussed, branding is an organization's values and established culture. All verbal and visual elements should support this brand (Kaplanidou & Vogt, 2003). They further cite Vermont's Department of Tourism and Marketing website, which indicates their belief about their brand to their partners. They stated, "Vermont brand is not a logo, set of official colors or a 'look and feel' on advertising website. The brand exists solely in the minds of the consumers and it encompasses heir overall perceptions and attitudes of Vermont" (*How to Use the Vermont Brand*, n.d.).

Elements to establishing the brand's identity include the brand name, logo, slogan, design, and collateral. Neisworth (n.d.) stated an organization should evaluate everything with their name on it and spread it out on a desktop. Do the materials have a distinctive look? Are the materials coordinated? Is the organization identifiable and easily remembered? If not, then they may not have established a consistent brand identity. The signage, corporate colors, stationery items, forms, contracts, dress code, vehicle identification, advertising, and myriad items that carry the organization name affect the image and brand identity.

Brand Name

What's in a name? Well, some organizations spend little time considering how their brand will be represented by their organization name (e.g., does the community recreation center provide an accurate identity for an ice arena?) Yet, this is often what people remember and associate with the experience created by leisure and tourism organizations.

Ask sports and entertainment venues across the United States the value of a name. In 2004, 20 new agreements were made with entertainment venues for exclusive naming rights. The terms of the agreements ranged from a few years to as many as 30 years; for example, Bank of America paid $140,000,000 to name the Carolina Panthers stadium (Miller, 2005). Throughout the last several years venues and other organizations have created their brand identity through giving naming rights to organizations that have paid for the opportunity. These organizations may or may not have any tie to the industry itself but do have interest in communicating with the same markets who attend professional games and entertainment events. They are using venue naming rights as an avenue for showcasing their brands to various markets (Menninger, 2000). By 2004, over 50% of MLB and NFL teams, 76% of NBA teams, and 87% of NHL teams had naming right agreements. This type of relationship is identified as *cobranding*, which will be further analyzed in Chapter 13, Relationships: Community, Sponsorships, and Stewardship.

Logo

The Nike swoosh and the Olympic rings create an image in people's minds about the organization, as well as the experience tied to that image. A strong, recognizable logo is a key marketing tool for any organization. It identifies an organization uniquely and ideally triggers positive associations among consumers. It can have an influence on attracting sponsorship deals, building loyalty, and consumer choice. Logos that are simple in nature and reflect the organization's core values are beneficial in creating a brand identity. It graphically represents the organization and what is unique about it. The image reinforces the name that builds a brand (Darlington, 2005).

Real Life Story: Naming a Leisure Facility

A community council and citizens on New Zealand's North Island looked to develop two needed leisure complexes together. One complex with aquatic facilities, initially named the "Upper Hutt Leisure Centre," was geared toward 10- to 14-year-olds. The name was not exactly what they hoped to establish a brand identity for a fun-filled, action-packed aquatic experience. It more closely resembled that of a typical community center with a wide range of services for a variety of markets.

Working with an advertising organization they first defined not only who they were but also who they wanted to be. They evaluated the markets they wanted to target, then developed an image that would appeal to those target markets. They viewed the facility not just as a building, but one with its own personality. One brand identity decision had to be developed— change the name of the facility.

Another advertising organization was hired to assist in this process. The steps included the following:

1. Hold focus group sessions with 10- to 14-year-olds to identify what they wanted in this facility.

2. Form a development team of council members, staff, and design students from the university to create a list of names and words that described the experience provided to consumers.

3. Survey hundreds of 10- to 14-year-olds with the list of names, and ask them to rank the list from 1 to 10 to produce a top-10 list of names

4. Establish a "Teen Board" consisting of ten teenagers whose first task was to pick the facility's name. They chose H2O Xtreme. (Bentley, 2002)

Slogan

Often, in leisure organizations, the brand slogan promotes the benefits of parks and recreation services and experiences. The core message shows how there are individual, community, environmental, and economic benefits to leisure experiences. Often these slogans are developed from an organization's positioning statement.

Collateral

The brand identity must be established and communicated throughout an organization consistently. This means the organization website, brochures, newsletters, uniforms, signage, newsletters, advertisements, and stationery must highlight and reinforce the same brand messages. Collateral decisions will be covered in Chapter 11.

Design

The design elements of a leisure brand are complex and several considerations must be made regarding the look of the brand identity itself. Chapter 11 will also examine design issues and considerations when establishing a brand identity within an organization.

Brand Repositioning

Organizations today need to continually look at their organization position and be prepared to reposition as needed. With changing consumer needs and the ability to quickly understand these changes, more organizations are viewing their brand position as an ever-changing entity. Those organizations that constantly look at their position and modify it as necessary are better able to sustain themselves in the long term. Other organizations forget to do this regularly and learn to reposition only after some type of issue emerges (e.g., new competition, changes within the organization).

Consumers' changing needs should drive positioning efforts. Tehrani (2002) suggested organizations need to assess, identify, and develop positioning processes every day. This may require repositioning that will require organizations to be flexible and adaptive to change so they may stay up-to-date with consumer needs. He further suggested, "It is better to be first than to be better," where those who lead are those who are remembered (p. 6). Positioning drives brand identity and repositioning must be considered continuously.

Organizations should consider rebranding under the following circumstances:

1. Sometimes there is no choice but to rebrand due to additions, consolidations, and acquisitions.

2. New competitors or those not viewed as a threat before.

3. An organization's new focus, vision, mission, or position.

4. The development of new target markets.

5. Changing economic conditions.

6. Changing consumer needs and tastes.

7. An outdate image. (Nelson, 2002)

Examples of Leisure Organization Repositioning

Kiley (1998) shared how *Colonial Williamsburg* repositioned the organization when attendance and revenue declined dramatically. They needed to address leisure trends in "extreme" recreation and "entertainment" to overcome an image of not appealing to the family market they wished to pursue. They were competing with Disney and Six Flags without their marketing budgets. To show families their historic appeal, they developed an ad campaign directly aimed at a non-Disney-type experience. Profiles noted historic figures such as Thomas Jefferson and George and Martha Washington.

A *Washington-based theater* reacted by developing a five-year plan to reposition the theater. Ticket sales and donations had decreased by the late 1990s. Research indicated people felt the theater experience was dull and predictable. From 1998 to 2002, the plan was implemented. It began with a new brand identity (i.e., logo), then included a biannual newsletter, direct-mail piece, cohesive seasonal brochures, print ads, posters, and an e-commerce website. The increased ticket sales of 28% and donations by 48% were evident of how consumers altered their perception of the theater. The result was a more accurate portrayal of what the establishment was capable of in consumers' minds (Jarvis, 2002).

In an effort to unify the various clubs owned by the same organization, Bally's Health and Fitness, Vic Tany, Jack LaLanne, and President's Health Clubs changed their individual brands and repositioned into one brand, *The Total Fitness* (Kirk, 1995).

National Express transportation group developed a brand identity for their new online ticket sales operation.

They changed everything from their logo, uniforms, signage, cabin interiors, cutlery, and in-flight entertainment. It was all assessed based on their new positioning statement of "speed with charm and style" (Travel and Leisure, 2002).

Winnebago lent its brand name/identity outside of the leisure market and suffered because of it. Their brand name appeared on nonleisure products and, before the organization realized that they had lost RV market share to Fleetwood Enterprises—their brand identity with the RV market had eroded. In an effort to reposition the brand they now focus on leisure-related offerings that add value to their direct brand. Their name now appears on tents, sleeping bags, and nonmotorized park homes. This made better sense for the organization because Winnebago as a brand was synonymous to the leisure and RV market, just as Kleenex is to the tissue market (Miller, 1998).

Binder Park Zoo (see p. 194) made changes to their brand prior to developing the brand's identity (e.g., logo, collateral). It is important to remember the organization's brand identity should not be finalized until after all decisions regarding changes in offerings/experiences, pricing, and distribution are made. If the brand identity decision is made prior to these decisions, then opportunities to more accurately reflect all that an organization includes may not be apparent. For example, had the zoo not considered the opening of the new exhibit in their brand identity decision, the positioning of the zoo would have been very different. Giraffes would not be included in the brand identity because giraffes were a part of a new exhibit. An organization must reflect on all that it is and all that it offers to targeted markets and compare these to the competition before establishing a new brand identity. This will further be dicussed in Chapters 9, 10 and 11, where specific decisions regarding organization offerings, prices, distribution, and brand will be made.

Positioning Statement Approaches

Based on the decision to pursue a target market, an organization then identifies a *positioning statement* to reflect the stance taken by an organization on behalf of the target market. Organizations specifically identify what value proposition consumers, employees, and shareholders can expect from an organization. They determine what competitive edge the organization will establish and be willing to share with others. Positioning statements should be developed based on the findings and conclusions from an assessment. It should reflect the strengths of an organization over its competitors for a specific target market. This positioning

statement can be anywhere from a few to as many as 100 words that identify one key brand promise to consumers. This statement includes the unique benefit a consumer will experience and describes who they are, what they offer, for what result and why someone would want this organization in particular ("Messaging," 2002). Clancy (2003) stated, "A powerful positioning [statement] leads to a powerful brand" (p. 2).

A positioning statement is a message so clearly communicated to a target market that it creates an imprint in the market's mind that sets it apart from others with whom an organization competes. It differentiates itself from the competitors in people's minds. Some leisure organization position statements include the following (Clancy, 2003):

- Walt Disney World as "family entertainment"

- Universal Studios Theme Park as "thrills and excitement for preteens and adults"

- Community recreation organizations used the National Recreation and Park Association's "Parks and recreation…The benefits are endless"

- Shanty Creek Resort as "We overlook nothing, except all of Northern Michigan"

- Pohl Cat Golf Club with "Stalk the Cat"

If an organization is focused on the needs of the target market not only the competitive advantages but also the issues of importance to a target market will emerge. Keller, Sternthal, and Tybout (2002) suggested differentiation alone is not enough to sustain a brand—it must also reflect on those aspects similar to other organizations. A positioning statement reflects the desired perception that an organization wants a target market to have. Mahajan and Wind (2002) suggested emotion can drive consumer decisions and organizations must use this to position its offerings. They must appeal to the heart as well as the head.

The leisure industry creates experiences that ultimately drive emotions. We can create our stories around these concepts, drive people's emotions and appeal to their heart. People are looking for something deeper in life, they are looking for meaning. Scott McKnight, Binder Park Zoo

There are a variety of ways an organization can approach the development of a positioning statement:

- Use market research to support organization positions.

Real Life Story: Binder Park Zoo

Binder Park Zoo (BPZ), a small zoo, was about to double in size with the development of a new exhibit called Wild Africa. They knew they had to do things differently. According to a recent market research study, the perception of the zoo was that:

1. You never hear much about it.
2. My children are too old to visit the zoo.

It was viewed by the market as a small children's zoo that did not do a lot—it was the same, old place. Their goal was to reposition the zoo as one that the entire family would enjoy, not just small children. They knew they had to look at the entire organization to not only communicate these changes but also tp insure these changes would occur within the zoo.

The zoo decided to make brand changes throughout the organization. First, employees were required to wear uniforms as shown in the photograph. In addition, all staff attended quality service training to place more emphasis and importance on the experience zoo guests received. Finally, the zoo's recruiting, hiring, and performance standards were improved.

With the addition of a large new exhibit, and in an effort to get rid of the children's zoo image that only appealed to the very young and old, BPZ modified their offerings to change the traditional zoo experience. Animals were integrated in a larger, more natural exhibit from cement cages. Every element of the exhibit matched the theme. Visitors were integrated into the experience as safari researchers and participated in interactive exhibits throughout the zoo. Elements, like animal carcasses, were placed in the exhibit not only to reflect a more native environment but also to appeal to 13-year-old boys. Finally, the experience changed to allow visitors to not only feed llamas but

also giraffes. An exhibit is situated 15 feet off the ground to allow people to feed the giraffes at different times of the day. Visitors are amazed at the giraffes' 18-inch tongue. This has supported the repositioning of the zoo's brand because it changed the experience.

Along with the change in practices, look, and experience, came a change in the way the organization communicated who and what they were. The repositioning of their brand identity was important in all that they did. Previously they had not established a consistent process for ensuring all materials identified their brand. Each collateral piece was changed to reflect their new sophistication that would be supported once visitors arrived, starting with a new logo.

The zoo knew the revised brand identity needed to be reflected in everything they did. In addition to being prominent on all uniforms, the logo and consistent look also needed to be present on all collateral. The images show the zoo's former collateral materials, as well as the redesigned materials. The new look has established a stronger presence in the market for the zoo, resulting in doubling attendance in the first year of the exhibit. A combination of redefining the brand with a new exhibit; new programs, services and facilities; addressing all internal brand issues (e.g., quality service training, uniforms, hiring practices); and communicating these changes in a strong brand identity, the zoo was able to capture a greater share of the market.

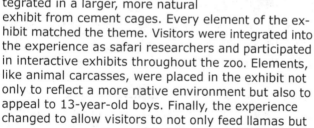

- Make sure all elements of the marketing promotional and communication mix reinforce your positioning.

- Make positioning statements as simple and succinct as possible.

- Position to individual markets—people want things to be customized. Gardyn (2001) supported this, and stated that research shows all types of consumers demand offerings and communication be directed to them personally.

- Be careful if positioning on price or against a competitor—that position is easily preempted.

- Use only one position statement for a target market.

- Don't position leisure offerings in such a manner that it cannot deliver on the positioning.

- Consider and review a number of alternative positioning statements before determining the most appropriate route.

- Don't expect positioning to occur immediately. Positioning might seem to be a simple concept but it is difficult to determine and apply. Effective positioning takes time and concentration.

Table 8.1 highlights various methods used to establish a positioning statement for an organization.

Each positioning strategy used to pursue a target may be entirely different from the strategy used for other targets of the organization or they may overlap. The Brutus Resort

Table 8.1
Positioning Strategies and Statements

Positioning Strategy	Definition	Positioning Statement Golf Course example	Positioning Statement Fitness Center example
Product	Identifying what is unique about the organization's feature offerings when compared to other offerings.	Watching TV or playing golf... there is NO comparison.	Work will always be there... You only have one body.
Benefits	Identifying what benefit the organization offers when valued by the target market.	You have never been so challenged.	You will never feel so energized with a half hour a day.
User	Creating offerings specifically for a market segment.	Built by and made for championship golfers.	Curves—for women only.
Usage	Seasonal issues and time elements are used to establish the position.	There is nothing like watching the sun rise on Hole #1.	Working out first thing in the morning sets your day off right!
Competitor	Organizations go directly after a specific competitor.	Nowhere else are tee times guaranteed.	There is not a club like it... access 24 hours a day.
Association	Used when there is no differentiation, whereby an organization partners with another to establish a position.	10,000 golfers can't be wrong... Make it 10,001.	Jack Lalane and Mari Winsor endorse us. Why not you?
Problem	When organizations have no competition, but need to position themselves against a specific problem.	No better form of stress relief than a two-inch ball.	A definite way to curb obesity problems.
Offering Class	Positioning one offering against another.	Choose your time of day and day of week, don't be controlled by league play.	Choose your time of day and day of week, don't be controlled by open gym night.
Price	Positioning based on price for offerings—services, programs, products, or facilities (i.e., experience).	Lowest price for golf in 60 miles.	More equipment, programs, and services at an affordable price.
Strength	Positioning based on an identified strength of the organization, specifically based on a target market's beliefs.	You've never seen a more perfect green!	You won't get better service anywhere.
Pleasant Alternative/ Self-Love	Positioning is based on the need to calm consumer frustrations, anxiety, and stress.	You deserve a chance to unwind.	You owe it to yourself to have a body you want and deserve.

and Spa may have completely different, or only somewhat different, positioning statement for the wedding market than the corporate group market because it is based on the needs of each market segment.

Although an organization may begin to develop a positioning statement at the conclusion of a positioning assessment, it is important that this decision not be taken lightly. All target market segments should be analyzed and identified, and decisions regarding offerings, pricing, and distribution should be made before this is finalized. The following describes several brand positioning recommendations:

1. Establish a brand position before building brand awareness. Organizations should understand what they are offering and to whom before establishing any communication patterns.

2. Develop a position on issues important to target markets. Understanding what consumers want and need is the foundation of effective positioning.

3. Write positioning statements that address not only competitive differences but also what is most important to target markets.

4. Lead positioning efforts; do not try to match competitor positions. Define your organization based on what you are, not what others do.

5. Know the ramifications of brand repositioning. A change in a positioning approach by an agency may turn off market segments the current positioning appeals to. Be prepared and certain that the repositioning is necessary and important. (Keller, Sternthal & Tybout, 2002; Tehrani, 2002)

As in Pheasant Run's experience (see Box), the positioning statement identified the uniqueness of their golf course over other championship courses. This statement allowed Pheasant Run to communicate their position to target markets easily and concisely in an area meaningful to the market. If the course fails to identify some type of statement, it runs the risk of their course being misconceived in consumers' minds or not being noticed by those markets they wish to gain.

Confidently determining the market segments to target is a significant step for an organization. This, however, is the first of many decisions an organization must make. Once an organization has identified the target markets it wants to pursue, it is important the focus, or goals of the organization, be reflected in a meaningful way. As earlier identified, the Brutus Resort and Spa failed to create meaningful measures to determine if marketing achieved any outcomes.

Leisure and tourism organizations must establish the goals for marketing efforts for each target market they pursue.

According to Cebrzynski (1998) and Martyka (2001) some authors state concern with too much attention on branding. They found some organizations focused so much on creating their identity that they began to forget about running their business. Other organizations were confused about their position and didn't convey a clear message about who they were (e.g., Boston Market couldn't decide and consumers went elsewhere). Holt (2002) further suggested branding based on copying styles of other organizations is also problematic. He stated that when organizations had success with mocking an advertising convention to develop their brand, it worked. However, dozens of other brands copied the technique and it failed. Further when organizations employ practices based on coercion (e.g., brand virus), they too will be thought of negatively. The Internet has grown as a source of truly understanding an organization's practices but if an organization creates a persona they can't live up to, they won't last very long.

Zambuni (2003) agreed that the concept of branding in organizations is "ubiquitous" because brands and brand experts are plentiful (p. 180). With the emergence of this concept, he suggests a "spectrum of quality and substance exist." He, like Holt, has concerns over this concept and he categorizes brand efforts by organizations into four types:

1. *Allegedly crooked:* The rise and fall of well-established brands based on unethical practices, such as Anderson, Enron, and WorldCom, has cautioned some regarding the truthfulness of a brand.

2. *Cynical window-dressers:* Organizations that create a respected brand image but use it to mask less than quality practices.

3. *Compensators:* A well-developed brand matched with equally good consumer experiences, yet these organizations cannot sustain the business because they have met consumers' needs at the expense of survival. They don't last long.

4. *Branding heroes:* Those who do it right.

Although more recent concern for the concept of branding exists, branding is still new to many leisure and tourism organizations. Zambuni (2003) agreed, stating, "In some industries branding and, indeed, marketing is still far from the center of power" (p. 183). As stated in Chapter 1, leisure organizations have been slower to apply marketing practices and in this sense can learn from those large, international organizations that have applied these steps already.

Potential issues with branding practices noted by these authors suggest leisure and tourism organizations learn two lessons including (a) ethical practices are of primary importance, and developing brands and brand identities that cannot be delivered fall into this category, and (b) copying others' creative ideas is not necessarily beneficial. Tait (2002) suggested a truly differentiating brand needs to have an original position and creativity is key.

Marketing Objectives

If the results of the positioning assessment confirm a target market is indeed worthy of pursuing, then an organization would write a *marketing objective* to solidify the importance of this market to the organization. A marketing objective represents the culmination of marketing strategy assessment, analysis, and decisions made by an organization to pursue a target market in an established measurable way. It reflects what the organization desires and needs to occur.

Real Life Story: Pheasant Run Golf Club

Pheasant Run Golf Club includes a 7,000-yard, 27-hole championship public course. They recognized the importance and value of establishing their identity within the market segments they wished to serve. It wasn't until they went through a positioning assessment exercise that they realized they had not identified or communicated their competitive edge to the market place. Not unlike other communities, golf courses were being built at a fast rate over the last few years. Now the market was not only oversupplied but also facing some economic hardship with large area employers announcing layoffs.

There were four other competing golf clubs in their area and Pheasant Run had not established what sets them apart, what makes them unique, and why their target markets would wish to golf there. One of their markets was described as *35–55 year old, white-collar males, within a 60-mile radius, who were frequent golfers (at least once a week)*. This market tends to golf with other men, have high-quality golf equipment and clothing, know golf etiquette, and do not appreciate others who do not know and do the same. They seek a challenging course which provides services they expect, including carts, caddies, beverage and food services both on and off the course, equipment cleaning and repair, upscale clothing, and merchandise.

From this assessment it became clear that every competitor was well-positioned to meet the two most important needs of this market segment. They all had similar difficult courses and a large number of services.

One conclusion that could have been drawn by Pheasant Run was to not pursue this market segment because every competitor was doing the same. They determined, however, this was the largest market segment, and there were still enough golfers to pursue. If the target market had been local females ages 25–60 who are inexperienced at golf, then the conclusion may have been to not pursue the market. If everyone was positioned to serve a small market segment, then it was not in the club's best interest to pursue it.

Therefore, in further assessing the services provided by each competitor, Pheasant Run learned that, with a few, minor differences, they all provided similar amenities regarding carts, caddies, beverage and food services on and off the course, equipment cleaning and repair, clothing, and merchandise. Pheasant Run had to identify what their niche would be in this very crowded market.

They knew other issues were important to these golfers. Having played each of the competitors' courses and having learned from golfers who had played each course through a market research study of competitors from both users and nonusers of Pheasant Run, the club identified a weakness of their competitors that was a strength of theirs—something very important to this golf market segment.

Golfers in this market segment were disappointed with "speed of play" at the other courses and became frustrated with setting a tee time then having to wait. Delays ranged from 15 minutes to 1 hour to get on other courses. Pheasant Run, however, prides itself by always starting golfers on time and ensuring speed of play is maintained. They do this by scheduling rounds at 10-minute intervals versus 7 to 9 as many clubs do. They realized this could be their competitive advantage. Their positioning statement became

Pheasant Run... a championship golf course where your tee time is guaranteed.

This established their competitive advantage and set them apart from the other courses. They had a distinct strength in an area important to this target market, and thus could establish a niche within this competitive market.

The priorities placed by an organization are the ends that need to be achieved. Smith (2002) stated that when marketing in the health club industry "nothing is more important than setting precise goals before spending your time, money, and effort" (p. 34).

It's harder than ever to justify a marketing budget when no one can figure out what they are getting for their money. Guy Jangi and Jordan Hochhalter, Partners, Mobium Creative Group

It is important to distinguish between a marketing goal and a marketing objective because many authors interchange these terms to mean similar things. A goal, in this instance, is an overall vision for an organization regarding marketing activities. *Goals* are broad statements that reflect where the organization is heading overall. They guide the thinking of an organization and establish what is important. For example, "Our goal is to increase our profitability, serve more community members, and enhance our quality of service."

Objectives have more specific outcomes. Based on these goals, an organization would write objectives to highlight what the organization specifically wants to happen. An organization at this point in marketing strategy development would write specific marketing objectives. Marketing objectives guide the entire operational (or tactical) marketing and communication plan. If it is unclear where the organization wants to head specifically, it is not only difficult to develop an appropriate action plan but also impossible to measure the impact or effectiveness of the plan (i.e., evaluation) to determine what worked well or not, and reward actions taken by staff. Marketing objectives enable an organization to plan the use of marketing resources (e.g., money/budget, people, time) more effectively, justify their activities, and highlight their contributions to the organization. Table 8.2 highlights some marketing objectives and goals taken from actual leisure and tourism organization marketing plans.

In assessing these objectives, what conclusions can you make? What objectives are more effectively written than others? Some organization goals are sometimes misinterpreted for marketing objectives. Those organizations that indicated they are creating a health community, raising brand awareness, and increasing statewide visibility have really written goals. Others have written more specific outcomes with measurable components. How would you know if the leisure organization created a healthy community? increased awareness? encouraged press coverage? How would an organization recognize outcomes if their efforts are not measurable? Specific and outcome-based objectives can be more easily understood by identifying the focus and tangible nature of what will occur as a result of marketing efforts.

Those objectives that suggest a measurable outcome are important, such as reducing the no-show factor by 50% or having 60,000 vehicles through an event. Further, one objective specifically includes the target market. They stated "The hotel will increase the social market by 5%." This is even clearer. Generally, many organizations have a tendency to write vague, meaningless marketing objectives. This may contribute to why marketing is misunderstood by organizations, why marketing budgets are cut in economic troubling times, and why it is difficult for organizations to prove the value of marketing. When objectives do not suggest a specific outcome and an organization does not hold staff accountable for producing results, the tasks are easy to let go because they are not important or valued by the organization.

There is an abundance of literature relating to the proper way to write an objective. Personal and professional objectives can be written using the same steps. There is no difference in the way someone would write their personal weight loss objective and how they would a marketing objective. Someone who states they "will lose weight" has written a vague and meaningless objective. Someone who writes a measurable, specific objective is more likely to determine if they accomplished what they set out to do. For example, someone who indicates a meaningful objective for weight loss may say he or she will "go from 175 to 160 pounds."

People who are more likely to accomplish personal and professional objectives write these statements in a similar way. They also communicate, act on, and monitor their progress. Marketing objectives should be approached in the same manner. Writing significant objectives benefits individuals and organization. Benefits include

- more likely to have and achieve results

- better able to identify the number and type of activities that will be needed to achieve an outcome (e.g., if the objective is 100 new groups versus 20, the tactical plan may change accordingly)

- remaining more focused on specific actions for a particular target market segment

- helps identify problems with marketing efforts

- helps track the value of marketing efforts

- provides a way to hold individuals and organizations accountable for actions

- can reward individual specific accomplishments

Marketing objectives are written internally, by the organization, and should reflect what they believe are the priorities of the organization. They should not be dictated because objectives developed by those responsible for implementation are more likely to be accomplished. There are six steps to writing an effective marketing objective that should be followed by any leisure and tourism organization.

SMART Marketing Objectives
Specific
Measurable
Attainable or moderately risky
Reflective of the organization mission
Time frame and **T**arget market oriented

Specific

Each meaningful marketing objective is written based on one specific outcome. They identify an area/issue that is concise and singular. Often times the word "and" may indicate the objective is focusing on more than one outcome—this should be avoided. In a personal example, "I want to lose weight and improve my cardiovascular health." In this instance, the way in which a person would pursue this objective would vary. The approach one would take to lose weight may be very different than one who wants to improve cardiovascular health. Therefore, these objectives would be separated and focused on individually. In Table 8.2, the country/athletic club wants to improve member retention and participation. Again, these outcomes could be approached differently. The way an organization would improve retention may be different than the way they would approach improving participation. In these examples, "and" was used in a way to include more than one outcome. Specific objectives focus on only one outcome.

Measurable

Some organizations suggest it is difficult to measure the impact of marketing; therefore, writing measurable objectives are not possible or important. Although it is agreed that it is sometimes difficult to measure, this cannot be the reason for failing to establish the specific outcome. It is no wonder marketing is an area often cut or reduced when times are tough when no proof exists about the impact marketing efforts have on a leisure and tourism organization. As suggested by the review of Table 8.2, marketing objectives that provide specific, measurable outcomes are easily understood. Those that indicate a 5% increase or 200,000 vehicles as an outcome provide a clear expectation of what they hope marketing will be able to help them accomplish. Without this focus, marketing actions would be difficult to determine. The amount, type, and frequency of such activities would be unclear. Should an organization host 2 or 12 promotional events? Should they place 3 or 6 advertisements? Should they solicit two or seven publications for positive media coverage? These answers would be extremely difficult to determine, as well as monitor, evaluate, and reward, if the overall objective was not measurable.

A measurable objective can be written in a variety of ways—Some are better than others. "Losing weight," versus "losing 5% of my current weight," versus "losing 7 pounds," versus "going from 175 to 160 pounds" are all ways to write a measurable objective. However, which is most specific? Which is truly measurable? Which could an organization evaluate and reward? Those objectives that include a before and after figure, such as "going from 175 to 160 pounds," are very specific and are the ones that are most effective. Those that use percentages (e.g., losing 5%) presume, however, that they also understand the current weight. Otherwise these figures are also meaningless because they are not measurable. Five percent of 100 pounds

---

Table 8.2
Actual Leisure and Tourism Organization Marketing Goals and Objectives

Type of Organization	Marketing Objective and Goals
Resort	Increase the revenue from the social market by 5%
Campus Recreation Program	Develop supportive programs using print ads, radio, and TV
Senior Olympics	Establish and increase statewide visibility
State Travel Bureau	Raise brand awareness and recognition of the state as a desirable travel destination
Hallmark Event (Winter Light Show)	60,000 vehicles with over 200,000 people
Conference Center	Increase the number of groups
Golf Course	Encourage press coverage for golf articles
Professional Sport Team	Reduce the "no show" factor by 50%
Country/Athletic Club	Develop member upgrades, retention, and participation
Municipal Recreation Department	Create a healthy community

and 5% of 200 pounds are very different. Unless the current numbers are known, it is difficult to evaluate if this person achieved his or her weight loss objective.

Ideally every organization must know the number of people they have served in a target market specifically over the course of some time frame (e.g., last month, last quarter, last year) to develop clearly measurable objective statements. If an organization does not know the number or type of consumers they have served it is difficult to apply these principles. Often, the first market research done with a leisure and tourism organization that has not approached marketing in this manner is to analyze data they may have. It can help an organization to better understand whom they are currently serving. Target marketing is more difficult if an organization does not understand everything about their existing consumers. If an organization does not have any data about their consumers, then a plan is established to gather this type of information within an organization over the next year. This is used to more effectively apply target marketing practices.

Organization marketing objectives, as identified here, should therefore include the same measurable components. Meaningful objectives include a specific, measurable outcome. Organizations objectives are written in a similar manner. Some suggest they will "increase revenue," versus "increase revenue by 5%," versus "increase revenue by $250,000," versus "increase revenue from $1,250,000 to $1,500,000." Of these four objective statements, the one that is most clear is the last one. It identifies where the organization currently is and specifically where they want to go.

Attainable or Moderately Risky

All objectives should have moderate risk—something attainable for an organization, but that will also push them to complete. Often times moderate risk is determined in two ways in a marketing objective. First, by the measurable figure as outlined in the previous section and, second, through a time frame that will be mentioned in a following section.

Marketing objectives, like personal objectives, can be written so they are impossible to achieve. For example, "I will go from 170 pounds to 100 pounds in 1 month" or "We will increase group revenue from $275,000 last year to $1,000,000 by the first quarter of next year." In these cases, the person or the organization have set themselves up for failure. What is the likelihood that they will be able to accomplish these objectives? In the first example, it certainly would not be prudent to do so (for the person's health) and in the second example, it seems near impossible unless

there were some significant organization developments occurring.

On the other hand, some objectives are written too simply. Objectives that fail to push an organization or individual to stay on focus with the objective, maintain actions, or activities to accomplish the objective or work at them for a short period of time are also ineffective. For example, "I will go from 170 pounds to 168 pounds in six months" or "We will increase group revenue from $275,000 last year to $275,001 this next year." (This presumes there are no market changes for the organization, and everything is expected to be the "same" this next year). Do these objectives push the individual or the organization? Do they keep them on focus and emphasize an outcome of value? These objectives are not risky enough to be valued. The person could wait to achieve his or her weight loss objective until a week or so before the ending date and the organization could do the same. They would feel like "they did it," but the outcome for the individual and the organization would not have been that beneficial.

Often it is only the individual or organization itself that can decide what the moderately risky figure should be. In the organization revenue example, increasing revenue by $1 may indeed be a moderately risky activity if market changes were occurring. Should there be a new competitor in the marketplace and troubled economic times by a large consumer, then this objective may indeed be appropriate. What is known is the organization or individual can determine this figure, what will make an impact on the organization, be worthy of focus in an annual marketing plan and require a variety of operational/tactical marketing and communication actions.

Several things can help an organization decide what is moderately risky. Understanding the specific target market size, as outlined in Chapter 7, is one issue. The second is considering the various assessments completed in Chapter 6 to understand the market industry and global and competitive impacts. Finally, the current number of those within the target market who are served in the leisure and tourism organization specifically should also be understood (ideally this will be understood in the market assessment as outlined in Chapter 6). Organizations who know how many people they are currently serving in a market segment can better identify what would be considered moderately risky. If a resort hosted 27 weddings from the local market area this past year, but knows that there were 750 wedding license applications at the county clerk office in the same year, they realize not only what they have but also what is the greatest possible potential. A moderately risky figure in a market with a large number of competitors may be increasing the number of weddings from 27 to 35. Yet in another market with less competition a moderately risky figure may be

65. There are many variables to weigh the common figures; however, to begin determining the figures rests in knowing how many were served and how many there are potentially to serve.

Reflective of the Organization Mission

All professional objectives should be reflective of an organization's mission. It is important that an organization step back and review this consideration because at times there may be specific, measurable, moderately risky objectives that do not match the organization's mission. These can contribute to the organization, but do not reflect the organization's vision or culture, what the organization is, or what it hopes to do. For example, just because an organization can increase group revenue from the soccer club market does not mean it is in the best interest of an organization that caters to a largely corporate client. The hotel or resort may not have the services to meet the needs of both groups well. Their largely corporate clientele may not appreciate a fun loving, sometimes rowdy group of youth and adults. Just because the objective can be achieved does not mean it is in the organization's best interest. Therefore, every objective should pass the "reflective" test that reconfirms this is an objective of value to the organization.

Time Frame and Target Market Oriented

A time frame is critical in any objective. If an objective does not clearly identify an ending date, how does an organization (or individual) determine what type and amount of actions to complete and when these actions will occur? An organization that states "We will increase group revenue from $250,000 to $300,000" does not indicate when it will evaluate if they accomplished their objective or not. An objective that states they will do it by "next year" also does not clearly show when the objective should be completed, as every time someone reads the statement it is always "next year." Ideally, a meaningful marketing objective includes a specific time frame or date for completion. This will guide the organization in establishing an appropriate plan based on an ending date that everyone commits to and understands. An example of an objective that includes a specific time frame is, "We will increase group revenue from $250,000 to $300,000 by December 31, 2005."

As noted previously, attainable, moderate risk can be defined through not only the measurable element within a marketing objective but also the timeline. Increasing or shortening the timeline can make an objective more or less

risky. Again, an organization is the one who needs to ultimately determine what the appropriate timeline is. This could be based on many issues, including moderate risk, fiscal year, target market patterns, or overall market demand. Unlike personal objectives, which reflect the focus of a particular person, marketing objectives must be written to reflect what a group of people (i.e., target market) relates to. This is the final, specific element of a meaningful marketing objective.

As noted in Table 8.2 (p. 199), many leisure organizations have not identified a specific market segment their objectives are focused toward. Most of these marketing objectives do not specifically acknowledge the market segment(s) the organization is wishing to pursue. Organizations may have broad objectives not specifically tied to a market. For example, the Winter Light Show marketing objective is to have 200,000 cars drive through the event. There was no identification of the type of people they would be interested in attending in those cars. Marketing objectives should be target market focused. In this instance, how will the organization specifically achieve this? Through what markets? With what actions? Keeping this objective as the marketing objective suggests a mass marketing approach. In this organization marketing plan, this is what the organization did. They placed advertisements in all area media (e.g., radio, cable, newspapers). Without a target market focus/presence these actions were in essence directed toward all people. Had they approached it with a target market focus their efforts would have been money well spent. For example, are college students a market of interest to this group or would families be a more likely group to be interested in this type of leisure experience? Reaching these target markets would vary and determining a specific orientation would be more effective than approaching it in a general way.

A marketing objective represents the outcome desired by the organization—what the organization wants to happen as a result of each marketing activities Leisure and tourism organizations must be willing to establish and commit to several elements of a meaningful marketing objective if organizations want to integrate marketing more successfully in their respective organizations.

Demarketing

The development of marketing objectives in this chapter has been viewed from a positive approach where organizations have interest in attracting market segments to their organizations. There is, however, another strategy that leisure and tourism organizations may decide to take related to discouraging the use of the organization or decreasing demand called *demarketing*. This practice employs marketing principles to reduce consumers' desires in an organization's offerings. Operational marketing tools are used, such as changing offerings, pricing, distribution, or promotional messages in an effort to protect recreation resources from overuse (McLean, Havitz & Adkins, 2002).

This concept can be extended to include using these techniques to disincent any marketing segment. In essence organizations demarket to many markets as the focus on serving specific target markets. For example, a community center that develops youth sport leagues, children activities, and playgrounds are demarketing to seniors because they are marketing toward youth.

Resorts that offer happy hours, singles dances, and adults-only activities are targeting adults and demarketing to families with young children. This natural approach, however, changes as it becomes purposeful and strategically planned. Whether interest in protecting a resource or simply not serving a market because of the impact it has on the organization or its consumers, the practice of demarketing is one that organizations should access as needed.

Price was found to be the preferred marketing tool used by municipal golf courses in an effort to demarket, whether for over use resource protection or conflicting user groups. McLean, Havitz, and Adkins (2002) indicated only one other study has evaluated demarketing in the leisure industry, noting that Sem and Vogt's (1997) work was theoretical, relatively, to federal park scenarios, whereas their empirical research focused on another leisure industry. Although they found price to be the preferred method for demarketing, they suggest all marketing tools were options to be considered. In comparison, Mclean, Havitz, and Adkins (2002) stated

It makes intuitive sense that an organization charged first with environmental stewardship overtly publicized situations wherein degradation of the resources has occurred. By contrast, managers' responses to the municipal golf scenarios clearly suggest that promotion of poor course conditions is not a desirable option. Likewise... limits to vehicular access are commonly used to curb access in outdoor recreation contexts, but parking was considered nearly sacred by respondents in this study, generating the lowest acceptability scores of any individual distribution-related item. (p. 105)

Apply What You Know

1. Conduct a brand mapping process for each of the organization's target markets . Determine the organization's position with each as compared to competitors and the market's needs.

2. Assess the brand identity of the existing plan, including logo, slogan, position strategy, and collateral.

3. Develop a position strategy for each target market using the various ways identified in the Table 8.1, Positioning Strategies and Statements.

4. Write SMART marketing objectives for each target group.

5. Estimate the expected revenue from each target market.

Key Terms

Brand	Demarketing
Brand identity	Logo
Brand management	Marketing objectives
Brand mapping	Positioning assessments/
Brand positioning	statements
Brand repositioning	Slogan
Cobranding	SMART objectives

Midland's light show.

Review Questions

1. What are the steps an organization should follow when doing a positioning assessment for a specific target market?

2. What are the three types of brand identities that Griffin (2002) suggested?

3. Why is it important to create brand identity?

4. After completing a target market assessment what are some reasons to not target a market?

5. What kind of role does an organization's mission play in selecting a target market?

6. What are marketing objectives?

7. Identify the steps to creating SMART marketing objectives.

8. Write a meaningful marketing objective using the SMART process.

Internet Resources

SMART: Strategic Marketing and Research Techniques is a consulting company which specializes in developing marketing research and analysis. Their market research expertise is focused on market segmentation, brand positioning, brand equity, image assessment, and customer satisfaction measurement.

http://www.s-m-a-r-t.com

OnPoint Marketing and Promotions provides marketing services, mostly related to promotion and advertising. Their website includes a glossary of marketing terms and marketing-related case studies.

http://www.onpoint-marketing.com/brand-experience.htm

Brandoctors.com brings together useful information for developing a brand. Materials about advertising planning, brand positioning and brand equity are included.

http://www.brandoctors.com/index_html.html

Sterling-Rice Group provides brand development consulting and creative advertising for businesses and entrepreneurs. Their website resources include materials on brand equity analysis, new product development, brand positioning, and relevant success stories.

http://www.srg.com/html/consulting.htm

The *Custom Fit Communication Group* is an organization oriented toward brand development for businesses and organizations. Their e-newsletter, *The Brand News*, includes a series of eight articles about the branding process.

http://www.customfitonline.com

The following link provides valuable information related to brand positioning strategies, positioning differences, and segmentation.

http://www.determan.net/Michele/mposition.htm

References

Barnholt, J. and Jackowski, M. (2002). First place: Before pursuing a partnership, analyze your ability to reposition your organization. *Athletic Business, 26*(6), 56–60.

Bentley, J. (2002). Keep it cool: How branding is integral to the success of council leisure facilities. *Australasian Leisure Management, 31,* 60–61.

Cebrzynski, G. (1998). Branding is a powerful tool—and the latest marketing "rage." *Nation's Restaurant News, 32*(48), 16.

Clancy, K. (2003). *Marketing strategy overview: American marketing association.* Retrieved December 1, 2003, from http://www.marketingpower.com

Coughlin, D. (2002, September/October). Find out what your customer wants and then deliver it. *NSGA Retail Focus, 22,* 16–22.

Darlington, H. (2005). Creating your brand. *Supply House Times, 48*(4), 166–168.

Davis, S. (2002). Implementing your BAM™ strategy: 11 steps to making your brand a more valuable business asset. *Journal of Consumer Marketing, 19*(6), 503–513.

Gardyn, R. (2001). Consumers are willing to exchange personal information for personalized products. *American Demographics, 23*(7), 50–55.

Green, B. C. and Muller, T. E. (2002). Positioning a youth sport camp: A brand-mapping exercise. *Sport Management Review, 5*(2), 179–200.

Griffin, C. P. (2002). Strategic planning for the internal marketing of communication of facilities management. *Journal of Facilities Management, 1*(3), 237–246.

Holt, D. (2002). Why do brands cause trouble? A dialectical theory of consumer culture and branding. *Journal of Consumer Research, 29*(1), 70–90.

Hopelain, J. (2003). Brand metrics strengthen business health. *Marketing News, 37*(7), 24.

How to use the Vermont brand. (n.d.). Retrieved from http://www.vermontpartners.org/htm/research_vtbrand.asp

Jarvis, S. (2002). Theater's rebranding efforts take a bow. *Marketing News, 36*(12), 6, 8.

Kaplanidou, K. and Vogt, C. (2003, August). *Destination branding: Concept and measurement.* Retrieved from http://www.travelmichignews.org/research.htm

Keller, K. L., Sternthal, B, and Tybout, A. (2002). Three questions you need to ask about your brand. *Harvard Business Review, 80*(9), 81–86.

Kiley, D. (1998). Shaking off the dust. *Brandweek, 39*(22), 20–21.

Kirk, J. (1995). Bally's brand workout. *AdWeek Midwest, 36*(23), 1.

Mahajan, V. and Wind, Y. (2002). Got emotional product positioning? *Marketing Management, 11*(3), 36–41.

Martyka, J. (2001). Regardless of branding, some failed: Emphasis on site identity took some start-ups' focus off good old-fashioned products and service. *Street and Smith's SportsBusiness Journal, 3*(48), 19–25.

McCarville, R. (2003). *Improving leisure services through marketing action.* Champaign, IL: Sagamore.

McLean, D. J., Havitz, M. E., and Adkins, K. D. (2002). Demarketing leisure services: The case of municipal golf courses. *Journal of Park and Recreation Administration, 20*(2), 90–110.

Menninger, B. (2000). Building a brand starts with a name: Prices going through the roof, but experts say venue naming rights still best branding device. *Street and Smith's SportsBusiness Journal, 3*(29), 6–12.

Messaging: How to tell the story of your business! (2002). *Go-To Market Strategies.* Retrieved October 2, 2003, from http://www.gotomarketstrategies.com/tip_07_02.htm

Miller, B. (2005). 2004 naming rights review. *Naming Rights Online.* Retrieved August 21, 2005, from http://www.namingrightsonline.com/2004final.htm

Miller, J. (1998). Winnebago climbs back into conversion vans; name licensed to Tenn. Company. *Automotive News, 5*(765), 24.

Neisworth, R. T. (n.d.). Corporate amnesia—Don't let it happen to you. *The Trendline.*

Nelson, S. (2002). To rebrand or not to rebrand? *Brandweek, 43(9),* 18.

Nelson, S. and Kersten, B. (2002). Positioning the brand within the organization. *Brandweek, 43*(44), 22, 24.

News—Deaths rise in Los Callejeros concert tragedy. (n.d.) *CSI Entertainment Insurance.* Retrieved August 21, 2005, from http://www.csicoverage.com/news-callejeros.html

Niemuth, B. (2005). A lesson in branding. *Target Marketing, 28*(11), 19–21.

Ries, A. and Trout, J. (1986). *Positioning: The battle for your mind.* New York, NY: Warner Books.

Sem, J. and Vogt, C. A. (1997). Demarketing as a new communication tool for managing public land use. *Trends, 43*(4), 21–25.

Smith, B. (2002). Target practice. *Athletic Business, 26*(3), 34–36.

Standohar, P. (1997). The baseball strike of 1994–1995. *Monthly Labor Review, 120*(3), 21.

Stein, R. W. (1998). "Branded" with success. *Best's Review, 99*(5), 67.

Tait, B. (2002). The failure of marketing "science." *Brandweek, 43*(14), 20, 22.

Tehrani, N. (2002). On differentiation and positioning: Every company wants to be a peacock in the land of the penguin. *Customer Interaction Solutions, 21*(3), 2–6.

Traiman, S. (2003, July). Exhibitionists show their brains: Convention leaders discuss sponsorship and branding in Tampa. *Venues Today, 2*(7), 24.

Travel and leisure. (2002, October 1). *Marketing,* 13.

Woolen, M. (2002, September/October). Design trends in sports venues: Branding your venue. *Facility Manager,* 24.

Zambuni, R. (2003). Branding in the USA—A triumph of technique over substance? *Journal of Brand Management, 10*(3), 180–183.

Section 3

Achieving Leisure and Tourism Organization Objectives Through Successful Promotional and Communication Plans

Chapter 9

Processing Operational Decisions

Stephanie heads up programs and special events for the leisure services department of the City of Guitpino, a growing suburban community. Her role is to develop and implement activities for 36,000 city residents. With her staff of six programmers, she is challenged every year to find new, innovative programs to add to the already impressive list of tried-and-true favorites. The program list had grown steadily since she was hired in 1997, and she is proud of her and her staff's accomplishments.

Each year Stephanie's staff holds a planning meeting where they discuss new ideas for programs and events. Each staff member is allowed to implement his or her favorite new idea and add it to the organization's offerings for the year. Each programmer decides how to price the program based on the organization's overall goal of breaking even. This planning meeting will be held in two weeks.

This year, a new director for the leisure services department, Theresa, has been hired. Theresa has been challenged by the city manager to develop a more efficient, yet effective recreation department. To this end, Theresa has asked Stephanie to analyze her participation patterns for the past three years. Although the data has been available, Stephanie had yet to review the figures for each of her programs in the past. Because her revenue had grown slightly each year, no one had ever asked for such an analysis.

Stephanie learned upon reviewing the figures that several of her programs had not broken even, overall partici-

pation numbers had remained steady, and they had made more money. It appeared a few events supported her department overall and subsidized those programs that did not break even. A slight increase in fees created the increase in revenue.

In her meeting with the new director, Stephanie discussed the way in which they had developed their offerings in the past. Theresa asked Stephanie to approach her department's offerings differently this year. This new approach would be based on first looking at the underserved market segments in the community, then identifying ways to best serve those markets with programs and events, then develop offerings to accomplish their organization goals. Stephanie agreed to try this approach and presented it to her staff at the scheduled meeting.

Her department staff readily accepted the new approach. Later they told her they appreciated a more practical, scientific approach to determine what they should offer. This method felt more comfortable and logical to them, and some of their ideas could still fit. The department approached program and event development in this manner over the next year, and saw substantial increases in numbers of historically underserved residents participating as well as increased revenue generated from more programs. This made Stephanie's department less reliant on the few, large, successful events and more able to spread the load evenly. The department had lacked a strategic process for

At the end of this chapter, readers will be able to...

- State the elements of the marketing mix and communication plan.
- Identify the three steps for making operational decisions.
- Explain factors to consider when finalizing the operational plan.
- Determine marketing budgets.
- Establish a process for scheduling tactical activities.
- Estimate the revenue/cost factors in strategic marketing planning.

identifying more effective ways to develop their organization's offerings, but now Stephanie implemented a new, more efficient strategy.

• • • • •

Leisure and tourism organizations have various methods for developing the experiences they provide consumers. The experiences are made up of various offerings packaged together with high-quality service to enhance a consumer's quality of life and leisure lifestyle. These offerings include various products, services, programs, and facilities in the leisure industry. Some organizations approach it as Stephanie had—staff would bring ideas and these would be implemented. Others forget to even look at new programs and simply rely on their old offerings and continuing to market them as Clark (2002) reported. Yet, others are more strategic—they revisit their offerings each year, understand the needs of the markets they target, and evaluate the past year's data and current trends to develop offerings for specific target markets.

Cruice (2002) suggested Australian community clubs are not as effective as they could be in applying marketing practices. In addition to becoming more strategic, clubs should operationally include a variety of activities in their marketing plan process. These include activities directed toward the clubs' strength—membership—which is often neglected. Communicating with members and potential members is valuable when building a club and maintaining strength through positive word-of-mouth communications. In addition, clubs tend to place little emphasis in areas that need attention, such as sponsorship, portraying a consistent brand image, events and fundraising activities.

Efficient, effective leisure organizations promote strategic identifcation an organization's offerings. These organizations are more in tune with the current environment and practices, and adapt ways to be flexible for the market and the organization. How organizations develop offerings and begin to communicate with targeted markets will be pursued in this chapter.

Sections 1 and 2 of this textbook introduced the processes designed to assist leisure and tourism organizations with determining *where they are currently and where they would like to be*. This third section of this textbook, Chapters 9 to 14, addresses *how organizations get there*. Section 3 is designed to introduce readers to how an organization achieves marketing objectives. Specifically, it will identify what an organization does once they have determined the most appropriate target markets to pursue. All of these decisions are reflected in the marketing, promotional, and communication mix.

There are so many different types of marketing tools presented to people on a daily basis that one may think this is a simple step in the overall marketing process. After all, as mentioned in Chapter 1, people often think of these operational issues when presented with the word *marketing*. Advertising, promotion, and public relations are words with which people are familiar. Even so, the approach to making these operational marketing decisions within an organization is quite complex and can be overwhelming if not properly utilized and thoroughly understood.

Because there are so many different choices available for organizations to choose from, it is important to follow a systematic process to identify all the possible tools available. Organizations should consider each available choice, then select the most effective tools to achieve the target market objective.

The marketing, promotional, and communication mix model establishes a framework for organizations to strategically apply these steps. As evident in Figure 9.1, the model begins with a specific target market objective. Each target market objective uses this model to determine the remaining decisions in a marketing plan. Each section in the model will be detailed in the following sections.

Once a specific target market objective is identified, an organization completes each category of the model in three phases. Step 1 addresses permanent organizational decisions related to offerings, distribution, and price. These elements are considered the *marketing mix*. Step 2 establishes the promotion and communication messages as well as temporary "shot in the arm" or promotional offerings. Specifically, this step transitions an organization between speaking directly with consumers and creating the right framework to attract these consumers. It establishes the brand identity, collateral, and promotional events for an organization to achieve its target market objective. These elements are referred to as the *promotional mix*. Step 3, the *communication mix*, helps identify the tools used to directly reach the target market.

Within the marketing, promotional, and communication mix model the process with which an organization makes decisions is an important one. The model and most marketing decisions have been historically based on the four *P*s of marketing principles developed in the early 1960s. He suggested that marketing decisions should evolve from *product*, *place* (i.e., distribution), *price*, and *promotion*. Many suggest this premise is still as valid now as it was back then (Motley, 2002). This premise, however, appears too limiting for today's marketing environment because the tools available to make organization decisions have grown since the four *P*s concept was introduced. This model further defines multiple distinctions within marketing decision making and creates a logical process for making such decisions.

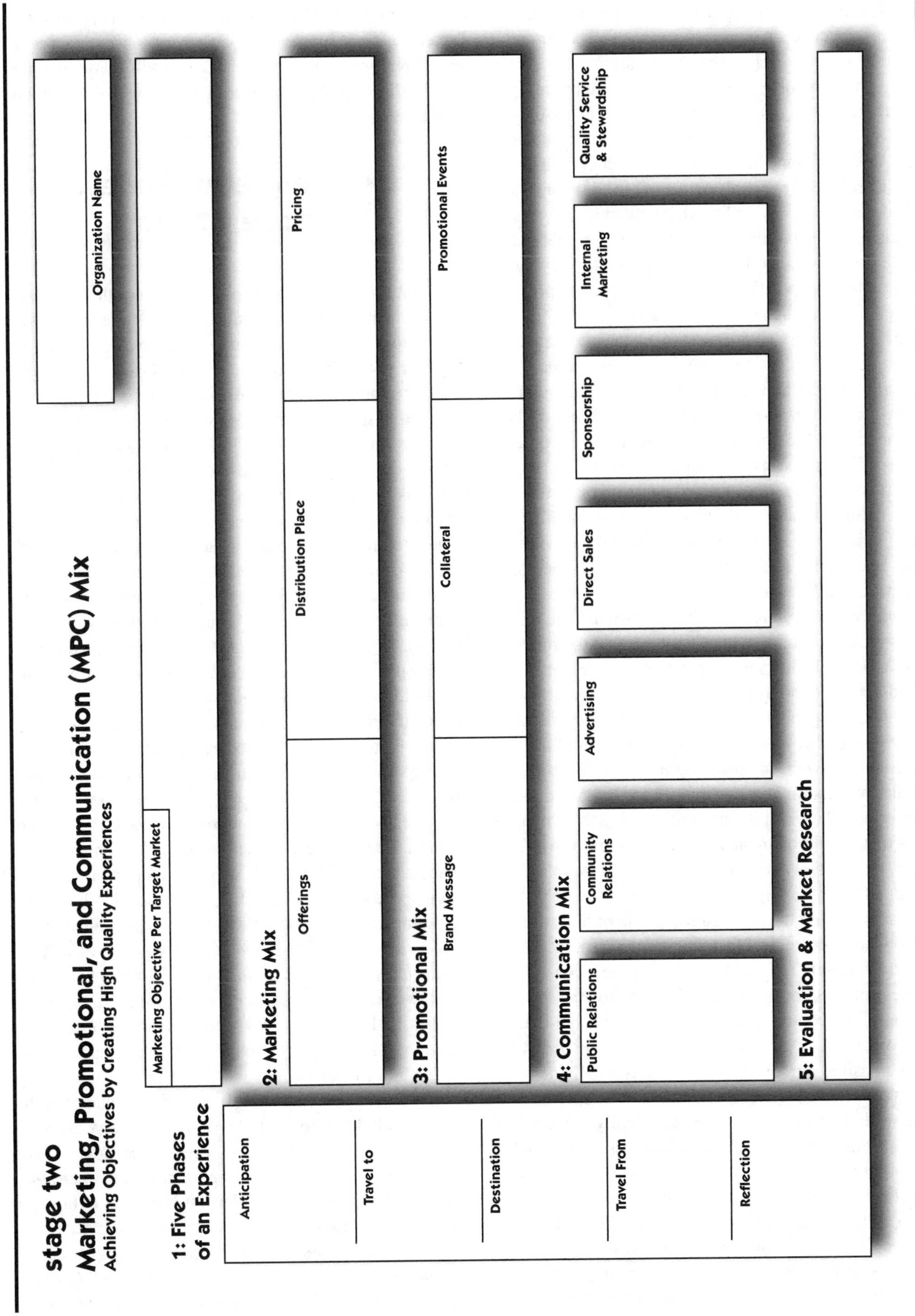

stage two
Marketing, Promotional, and Communication (MPC) Mix
Achieving Objectives by Creating High Quality Experiences

1: Five Phases of an Experience

Anticipation	Travel to	Destination	Travel From	Reflection

Organization Name

Marketing Objective Per Target Market

2: Marketing Mix

Offerings	Distribution Place	Pricing

3: Promotional Mix

Brand Message	Collateral	Promotional Events

4: Communication Mix

Public Relations	Community Relations	Advertising	Direct Sales	Sponsorship	Internal Marketing	Quality Service & Stewardship

5: Evaluation & Market Research

Figure 9.1
Marketing, Promotional, and Communication (MPC) Mix Model

Therefore, the MPC model suggests that based on the target market objective, an organization must first determine the marketing mix or what permanent changes it will need to make to organization offerings, distribution, and pricing. Based on these permanent decisions, an organization then determines or confirms the brand identity in the promotional mix stage. Once the brand is confirmed, an organization then decides what collateral materials are needed to communicate with intended audiences as well as what promotional events will be pursued. None of these decisions have yet reached the intended audience, but they are all designed to develop the most competitive position for an organization to provide for and reach an intended target market.

Once the temporary and permanent changes are made within the organization, they are then able to communicate directly with the intended target market in the communication mix. An organization may select from various tools to reach the market (i.e., public and community relations, advertising, direct sales, sponsorships, internal marketing, quality service/stewardship). An organization may select any combination of these tools to communicate with an audience in the most effective ways to reach the market. It is within these three sets of decisions that the essence of the marketing plan is established.

Four underlying premises exist in this model. First, the concept of quality, as outlined in Chapter 3, is also apparent in this model. Quality service practices, it is assumed, are embedded throughout these decisions. Second, it is important at this step in the marketing plan process to identify if Clawson and Knetsch's (1966) five phases of a leisure experience have been addressed in the marketing, promotional, and communication mix: Have the operational decisions reflected each of the five phases? Are there other decisions that should be made to address travel to/from? reflection? destination? anticipation? As suggested in Chapter 2, all too often organizations spend most of their operational efforts on the anticipation phase of a leisure experience and often neglect these other important facets. Organizations should reflect on their initial decisions and ensure these phases are addressed. Third, following the completion of the communication mix decisions, all marketing efforts must be evaluated to determine which have produced a desired outcome. Each action is ideally measured to evaluate its effectiveness. As outlined in Chapter 4, there are several ways for this to occur. Finally, market research is a component of this model, as it is throughout the marketing plan process. During the planning process, organizations become more aware of market research needed to make better, more informed decisions in future plans. Organizations discover, "If I had this information I could make more effective decisions regarding my organization." This type of constant reflection helps identify

what research would be most beneficial to an organization. Therefore, it is valuable for organizations to identify specific market research activities at the end of this marketing plan process to establish a means for gathering data throughout the next year.

Utilizing the Model: Three Steps

Organizations use the MPC model as a tool to apply the steps of the marketing plan process more strategically. This process forces an organization to focus on a specific target market in a systematic manner. It also allows an organization the opportunity to explore all possible tools available to them and ensures none are forgotten as potential choices.

Throughout each step a *brainstorming* or *modified ideation process* is used to develop the best possible set of decisions for an organization. Morais (2001) suggested the ideation process is a technique that "demonstrates the virtue of being inventive and systematic at the same time" (p. 22). A marketing plan development team, which includes staff identified in Chapter 1 (e.g., marketing staff, leaders, other employees), is brought together to complete the model. Morais (2001) suggested this group include people who not only are new to or fresh at the tasks but also possess the specific skills, knowledge, or abilities within the specific organization or marketing arena. Ideation begins with a specific, well-focused objective, similar to a target market objective. The team reflects on the various assessments, found in Chapter 6, completed to ensure the session stays focused on real world issues and facts. Then, starting with Step 1, the marketing plan development team conducts a "brain dump" or identifies all the ways each category could be used to achieve the specific objective. For example, if an objective was *to increase the number of youth ages 5 to 12 within a 30-mile radius at Click's Ski Hill from 257 lift tickets last year to 600 lift tickets this year*, the team would first decide what products, programs, facilities, and services would need to be added or changed to develop a high-quality experience for the targeted market. The brainstorm list may include offering youth group lessons, purchasing more youth equipment, changing the menu to include more youth favorite foods, and even building a warming hut nestled between the slopes. At this stage in the process, it is important to remember that these are only brainstormed ideas. It is critical to develop all the potential ideas and any attempt to eliminate ideas at this point would be detrimental to the process because the best potential ideas may never be considered. Groups identify more effective solutions to challenges because organizations are able to select from a larger list of potential ways to overcome these issues.

Step 1: Marketing Mix

Throughout the marketing, promotional, and communication mix decisions it is important an organization reflect on the needs, interests, and behaviors of the target market being addressed. The decisions made must reflect the unique elements for each target market. If the market was senior citizens versus teenagers, their needs, interests, and behaviors would vary greatly. This portion of the plan must reflect these unique differences. If it does not, the marketing plan process is no longer a targeted approach; it becomes a mass-marketing appeal.

Once all ideas are generated, each is placed in a matrix for evaluating and deciding which will be selected for the final plan. The matrix in Figure 9.2, which will be further outlined later in the chapter, highlights an actual leisure and tourism organization's global marketing plan process.

This list of ideas was generated for a municipal parks and recreation organization based on a plan for the organization overall versus one of their nine divisions (e.g., parks, theater, golf course, community center). This organization's overall target market objective was to increase the percentage of residents using their organization's services from 42% to 48% within the next fiscal year. Each individual division would be targeting specific market segments within the community, but this plan represented the overall organization objective.

The final list of decisions from the ideation process will be used in all collateral materials developed as permanent changes within the organization. The steps taken to determine which will be included must be completed prior to deciding the final plan decisions. The remaining components of the marketing, promotional, and communication mix model are based on these decisions. For example, if an organization decides not to develop a debit card system, then what they communicate with the market will be different than if they had decided to offer this service.

Marketing Mix Brainstorm

Actions	Timeline												Budget	Responsibility
	Jan	Feb	Mar	Apr	May	Jun	Jul	Aug	Sep	Oct	Nov	Dec		
Develop a global gift certificate/debit card for all divisions														
Implement a One-Stop Shopping service for residents														
Conduct a familiarization tour for new employee orientation of offerings														
Develop a "City Days" week that profiles all divisions														
Create reward cards (i.e., loyalty program) to support frequent users of divisions														
Develop a package that residents may purchase several events from various divisions at one price (reduced)														
Develop an outdoor aquatic facility														
Develop an employee services program that area employers can "purchase" based on division offerings														
Update department website														
Host a Chamber of Commerce business after hours event														

Figure 9.2
Step 1: Marketing Mix Brainstorm

Factors in Finalizing Operational Decisions

Once a list of potential ways to achieve a target market objective is established, the organization then must decide what decisions will make the final marketing plan. Factors to finalize operation decisions include the following:

- resources

- time frame established in objective

- organization culture, mission, and politics

- most effective method(s) for reaching the targeted market

- return on investment (ROI)

- evaluation of past marketing efforts

Resources. The reality for any organization is, unfortunately, there are limits to what they can actually do based on the resources available to them. These resources may drive organization decisions. In Figure 9.2, the organization may not be able to conduct a familiarization tour for employees because they do not have enough *staff* to complete this activity. They may need to eliminate this from the list or modify it so it can still be completed (e.g., develop a self-guided tour of all organization divisions for employees, which will include two free passes to each area so employees may bring a friend). Organizations need to remember, however, not to take "no" as the final answer until all possible avenues have been explored.

Expertise that is available or affordable may be another limitation to the brainstormed list that requires ideas to be eliminated. In the example in Figure 9.2, expertise may not be available or affordable to develop a debit card system for residents to prepurchase services.

In any of the instances in Figure 9.2, the *financial* resources may not be available to complete an activity. Each decision must weigh the financial issues that surround it. Money needed to conduct the "City Days" may not be accessible. However, sponsors could help reduce the financial burden. This will be further explored in Chapter 13.

Finally, the *tools* necessary to complete the activity may also not be obtainable. As in the illustration in Figure 9.2, these tools may include a service desk to conduct one-stop shopping or a scanner system for debit card purchases.

Time frame. The time frame established in the marketing objective may also limit certain ideas from being selected. In the example in Figure 9.2, if the marketing objective was to be completed within six months, developing an outdoor aquatic complex would not be feasible. This type of activity would take longer to complete and would be included in an organization's master plan. Even though a new offering may be completed within the time frame, an organization should begin communicating with consumers prior to introducing it.

Organization culture, mission, and politics. As much as we would like all ideas to be considered free and clear of internal organization issues, this unfortunately is not reality. Every *organization culture* is developed by boundaries established to indicate satisfactory and unsatisfactory activities. What would be acceptable in one organization may not be in another. Therefore, organizations must reflect on their culture to determine which decisions fit best into their operations. In addition to evaluating the ideas based on an organization's acceptable practices, the organization's mission and internal political systems should also be considered. Just because your area has the highest number of strip clubs in the state does not necessarily mean they would be good partners for providing community recreation opportunities to residents (a real story).

Effective methods. Of all the choices listed, an organization must evaluate which are the most effective methods for achieving the target market objective. Without considering cost, which would most successfully assist the organization in achieving its objective? What would impact the most people? What would be less taxing on the organization? Organizations must evaluate each idea based on this premise as well.

Return on investment (ROI). Each idea should be evaluated based on the return or value/benefit less cost (financial or otherwise) the organization would receive from the investment. Would investing $10,000 in a debit card system be worth it to this leisure and tourism organization? Would spending $50,000 on "City Days" be a good investment based on their objective? Would investing millions on an outdoor aquatic complex be worth the investment? To make this determination, the cost for each idea must be determined, and the return evaluated and measured. Estimation formulas for calculating an organization's return for their investment vary given multiple potential business drivers.

Evaluation of past marketing efforts. It is also valuable for an organization to reflect on their past marketing efforts to determine which worked well and which were not as effective as the organization had hoped. Insight into future ideas and practices can be learned from documented evaluation of past efforts.

No two organizations will have identical marketing plans because variables differ within markets. Market segments, competitors, economic, social, and legal issues all differ. Therefore, there is no one right answer for each of these factors. However, some suggest there are more preferred ways of reaching specific markets. Steinbach (2002) indicated there are methods in campus recreation settings that are more effective than others. These include literature on what the department provides overall (versus individual flyers), internal facility signage (e.g., scrolling message boards, kiosks, backlit signage), branding by establishing a logo/look for the department separate from the university, promotional events (e.g., special events during summer orientation), and face-to-face contact to establish relationships with consumers.

The lodging industry studied "best marketing practices" and identified 18 organizations' efforts and their methods of measuring success. Siguaw and Enz (1999) found few focused on the same operational decision that allowed it to be in the best-practices list. The best practices ranged from using research to making product and pricing decisions to utilizing a variety of promotional and communication tools. Table 9.1 highlights the market practice initiated/developed by an organization to receive this distinction.

YMCAs also combine a variety of tools to reach consumers. Clark (2002) shared the success of a YMCA in Ohio that started a promotion in January. They offered a reduced price on a membership and communicated this to the target market mostly through television. In February, they followed up with a direct-mail campaign reducing the price even further. He stressed the importance of sharing

---

Table 9.1
Lodging Industry Marketing Best Practices

- Relationship selling
- Offering group-price leisure stays to convention and meeting guests
- Alliances with national vendors
- Sales leads from all employees
- Consolidated sales offices
- Original books for promotional tools
- Vinyl-wrapped bus promotion
- Market research on guest satisfaction
- Targeted self-developed mailing lists
- Event booking centers, key account focus
- Development of new products and brands
- Memorable and effective advertising message
- Focusing on specific markets
- Sales training and strategy
- Global sales effort for key accounts
- Loyalty program
- Revised franchise agreements
- Creation of revenue manager position

---

a consistent message regardless of the medium selected to reach consumers. This YMCA also offered members an incentive to recruit other members because they found the majority of memberships came from referrals or word-of-mouth. Even though they used various other tools to communicate with consumers, these tended to be the ones that produced a large impact on their organizations.

Camp settings also indicate which communication tools are effective to reach new versus returning campers. Coleman (1997) suggested the following:

- Hold a camp fair.

- Offer the use of the facility to partnering organizations (e.g., United Way to local scouting organizations).

- Partner with another volunteer organization that seeks to serve the same target market and share the camp's philosophy.

- Host seasonal festivals or a sport's league.

- Volunteer staff expertise to assist in planning and presenting community fairs.

- Create a website that allows consumers to communicate with the camp directly from the site.

- Be visible in the community (e.g., decorate the camp house for Halloween and pass out treats with the camp logo on it).

- Write about the benefits of camp experience and make presentations to local elementary schools.

Overall, ensure the camp's name is positive and reaching children and families.

Janoff (2003) interviewed Reggie Williams, VP of Disney Sports and Recreation and learned that marketing Disney's Sports Complex included developing a strong brand positioning as well as finding ways to reach 30 different amateur sports markets targeted by the organization. The most popular tools used to reach these markets included developing advertisements that lead readers to the organization's website and placing these ads in various sport specific publications. They also sent close to 500,000 direct-mail pieces to sports-related people and groups (e.g., coaches, athletes, teams, organizations). Finally, sponsor partnerships were also regarded as positive relationships to support the organization. They have partnered with organizations, (with campaigns such as "Got Milk?") and Frito-Lay, to provide naming rights to facilities within the complex. The Milk House and Cracker Jack Stadium were developed within the partnership.

Attard (2003) suggested ways in which organizations could maximize communicating with markets on a shoe-string budget, including the following:

1. Network! Interaction is key to establishing relationships and creating partnerships. Working with groups creates an association that involves word-of-mouth opportunities and builds loyalties.

2. Develop a website and get it listed in the search engines. If you are not Internet savvy, contact a local web design company and negotiate a trade agreement.

3. Write a concise press release and send it to papers, radio stations, and TV stations. Because of federal laws, nonprofit organizations often can have free exposure through public service announcements (PSA).

4. Write an article about the benefits or unique features of your organization. Submit it to all the area newspapers. In some cases publications create a partnership that involve the organization writing a weekly/biweekly column in their area of expertise. This further exposes the public to your organization's name.

5. Develop the opportunity to exchange coupons or create joint mailings with noncompetitive companies that serve similar consumers. This expands the potential customer base and reduces the cost of mailing.

6. Purchase small ads in area newspapers (e.g., daily, weekly, alternative, buyers' guides, high school). If funds are limited, consider trading organization offerings for the space.

7. Place an ad for the organization in the Yellow Pages.

8. Try a give-away or sponsorship to gain exposure. Offer something free upon the referral of a friend or donate time, products or space for a charitable fundraiser.

Organizations must identify what will work for them under their circumstances. They must not rely on one technique they have always used, but rather combine multiple options based on a number of factors as suggested (Clark, 2002). Overall, an organization must ask themselves: What decisions could we make that would create a competitive difference for our organization to (a) serve this market, (b) meet its needs, and (c) achieve our objectives. They should also ask themselves: Are we being consistent? Do our messages have a similar theme, look, feel, and language? Are we communicating with our target markets frequently? Some suggest primary markets be reached at least twice a month and secondary markets once a month. This frequency, however, is not cut-and-dried as the marketplace is not either. Target market, target market objective, and considerations will impact the decision on how much is enough. Finally, the organization should ask: Do we have enough variety in our mix? Have we placed all our efforts in one market segment? Have we placed all our marketing dollars toward one or two communication vehicles? A combination of tools should be used to reach any target market (*Three Elements*, 2003).

Rule number one, you never want to put all your eggs in one basket. Lynne Ike, VanAndel Arena

Step 2: Promotional Mix

The promotional mix considers the decisions made in Step 1 to identify the permanent decisions for the organization regarding offerings, distribution, and pricing. In Step 2, the organization better formulates the brand identity and prepares to communicate with the target market by determining the collateral pieces needed to reach the market

Table 9.2
Promotional Statements for a Golf Course

Target Market	Positioning Statement
Local corporate outings	Memories "fore" the day
Local corporate transient golfers	Of "course" you can play
Experienced golfers from outside the local area	Private experience at a public club
Local area seniors	Golf at your leisure
Local area novice female golfers	A course for beginners and pros alike

as well as promotional events. All of the decisions made in Step 2 have not yet reached the intended audience, but are based on the marketing mix. Hence, the reason it is separated in the marketing plan process. These steps are critical tools to establish an effective message to target markets, and develop plans to reach them.

Brand identity. The brand identity of an organization must again be evaluated to determine if the message being sent to the target market is indeed the most appropriate. The organization should have already reflected on logos, general positioning statements, and other branding issues. However, when looking at specific target markets it is again important to reflect on positioning messages. Table 9.2 highlights a golf course's positioning statements based on the different target markets pursued. Communication to these markets would reflect different messages that are most meaningful to each.

Promotional collateral and events. The second facet of Step 2 includes making decisions regarding collateral the organization can use to communicate with the target market as well as develop temporary promotional events or activities designed to spur usage. These activities are often one-time, or "shot in the arm" events versus permanent

decisions made in the marketing mix (e.g., "City Days" in this instance would be considered a new but annual activity versus a one-time promotional event). Figure 9.3 highlights an organization's brainstorm list of all collateral and promotional events that could assist them in achieving their marketing objective.

The same factors described would be considered by an organization to determine which items to select from the promotional mix list. However, this list is developed in conjunction with the communication plan in Step 3, as there may be ideas generated in this list that determine which collateral items and promotional events to select. Therefore, the finalized list for Step 2 should not be determined until Step 3 is completed.

Step 3: Communication Mix

Once an organization determines the marketing mix (Step 1) and promotional mix (Step 2), they can then reach consumers directly. Organizations should view the communication mix as a "bag of tricks" where a combination of tools are used to achieve organization objectives. This maximizes

Promotional Collateral Mix

Actions	Timeline												Budget	Responsibility
	Jan	Feb	Mar	Apr	May	Jun	Jul	Aug	Sep	Oct	Nov	Dec		
Directions/map to all offerings														
Flyer to explain "packages"														
Discover guide (with accreditation on the next cover)														
Photographs of all offerings														
Overall division folder piece														
Leisure focus newsletter														
Daily event schedule for all divisions														
Promotional items (e.g., magnets) used for Blitz, "City Days," and other events														
Reward loyalty cards														
Familiarization tour passes														
Debit cards/gift certificates														
Calendar of events and frequently asked questions guides														
CD/DVD of offerings for consumers and employees (e.g., virtual tours, photographs, welcome by directors)														

Figure 9.3
Step 2: Promotional Collateral Mix

organization efficiency and effectiveness. Finally, the organization can now brainstorm to select the best tools for communicating with the target market. Step 3 includes all the ways in which the target market will be directly reached. All seven areas highlighted in Figure 9.1 (p. 209: public relations, community relations, advertising, direct sales, sponsorships, internal marketing, and quality service/ stewardship) should be considered to directly connect with the market. Again, it is important to consider the behaviors of the market: What do they read? Where do they shop? What do they do in their leisure time? Where do they work? Where do they live? That is what this was considered when a group brainstormed about ways to reach college students with outdoor gear rental and organized trip programs. Stuessy (2000) led a roundtable discussion regarding marketing outdoor programs and found several ideas for reaching students regarding information on trips and gear rentals. The group suggested the following (pp. 77–78):

1. Use flyers to advertise only one or two trips per flyer.

2. Assign a student group/organization to each trip for targeted advertising.

3. Contact residential advisors for dorm trips by floor.

4. Use special events to display available gear to rent.

5. Offer discounts and other trip registration specials.

6. Use computer databases to track consumer preferences by differentiating time of year, activity, length of activity, location, and cost of activity.

7. Send follow-up postcards thanking customer for their business and advertise another trip or registration discount.

8. Use collaborative efforts such as attaching flyers to a local pizza delivery business (e.g., "redeem this coupon for a 10% discount on any adventure trip").

9. Conduct raffles at social functions.

10. Utilize the university/college radio station.

Even though the group went into the discussion thinking of ways to reach the intended audience, several of the ideas generated did not directly communicate with an intended audience. Items 2, 3, 5, and 6 involved identifying target markets, promotional events or permanent pricing decisions, and market research activities. If the group had the

model to lead it through the range of choices it could make, the list would have undoubtedly developed a more strategic approach to identifying, selecting, and implementing the most effective ways.

An organization can use a variety of tools to communicate with a target market, including public and community relations, advertising, direct sales, sponsorships, internal market, and stewardship/quality service. Using the model in Figure 9.1 (p. 209), Figure 9.4 highlights the leisure and tourism organization's idea list of how they will reach residents regarding all their offerings.

Once this list is generated, organizations then select the actions of the final marketing plan by considering the issues in Figure 9.2 (p. 211).

Marketing Budgets and Scheduling Activities

As suggested, one way in which an organization determines which operational decisions to select is by identifying what each intended action will cost. These costs may be estimated during the initial step of the plan process, but will be finalized once the decisions have been made. Once the final set of mix decisions are determined, an organization must formally establish a budget to estimate all costs associated with the planned activities, establish a timeline for completing the activities, and assign who is responsible for the actions. Failure to complete any of these steps may result in failure to achieve the marketing objectives. Research suggests that when goals and objectives are documented and communicated with established time frames they are more likely to be achieved. Table 9.4 (p. 218) provides an actual organization example of a completed model. As shown, they have utilized the model format in different ways showing how the information can be shared using a similar tool, but adapted in a way that has more meaning for an organization. Highlighted sections are those that have been completed by the organization in Table 9.4.

Overall, the marketing, promotional, and communication mix model provides a means for concisely sharing the organization's operational plan in an easy-to-read, understand, and analyze format. Although the plan may be quite detailed, this section is an easy-to-pull-out component from which an organization can operate directly. Should someone in the organization desire additional support for why these actions are being taken, the marketing plan can be used to share this insight. However, the model becomes the reference for implementing the actions and monitoring progress and performance.

Evaluating Operational Decisions

Although previously discussed in Chapter 4, the issue of evaluating operational decisions is apparent at this step in the marketing plan process. A specific plan for identifying how each operational decision will be evaluated is a critical step to understanding and learning from these actions.

Organizations who fail to measure the impact of specific operational decisions may continue to make the same errors in subsequent years and may approach marketing in the same manner each year, unsure what worked and what did not. The goal of any marketing plan should be to measure all actions to be able to support next year's plan and establish a more effective plan in the future. Some actions may be more difficult to measure than others, but a plan should be established for the organization to agree

	Communication Mix													
	Timeline												**Budget**	**Responsibility**
Actions	Jan	Feb	Mar	Apr	May	Jun	Jul	Aug	Sep	Oct	Nov	Dec		
Employee Orientation/FAM Tour (i.e., orientation video, self-guided tour with free passes for two to all areas, and a contest for those who see all CLS areas)														
Quality service training—staff														
Sales and marketing training—staff														
Employee satisfaction/ performance evaluations														
Follow-up phone calls, e-mails, and letters to consumers														
Community and corporate sales blitz, follow-up on leads generated														
Present, distribute materials and magnets to homeowners' association														
Newsletter with Fun Facts shared with employees														
Incentive program for employees to sell services, facilities, etc.														
Employees receive Daily Calendar of Events and Frequently Asked Questions Guide to facilitate one-stop shop														
CCTV, cable TV show/advertising														
Billboard for all CLS offerings														
New homeowner direct mail														
Direct mail *Discover* (consider Web only and print small quantity for those who wish to receive by mail)														
Direct mail *Leisure Focus* newsletter														
Direct mail annual guide														
Website advertising to linked agencies (e.g., schools, builders)														
Global organization media stories of newsworthy events														

Figure 9.4
Step 3: Communication Mix Brainstorm

Table 9.4
Sample Budget and Timeline from a Leisure and Tourism Organization

Major Activities During Year: Jan — Membership; Apr — Annual Mtg; Jun — Golf Outing; Sep — Membership; Nov — Silent Auction
Jan–Mar — MSU/UM Sports sponsorship; Apr–May — Partner w/Youth; Jun–Aug — Day Camp; Sep–Oct — MSU/UM Sports sponsorship

Item Description	Jan	Feb	Mar	Apr	May	Jun	Jul	Aug	Sep	Oct	Nov	Dec	Totals	Budgeted	Deviation
Print Ad Production					$181								$181	$500	$319
Jackson Magazine 2/3		$750				$750			$750			$750	$3,000	$3,000	$0
Jackson Living 1/3						$675							$675	$675	$0
Jackson Cit pay 2x7 2x/mo@$16												$500	$500	$500	$0
Radio Spot Production		$330						$2,000					$2,330	$2,330	$0
MSU basketball											$200	$200	$400	$400	$0
UofM basketball											$200	$200	$400	$400	$0
MSU football								$100	$200	$200	$100		$600	$600	$0
UofM football								$100	$200	$200	$100		$600	$600	$0
WJKN spot schedule		$500							$500			$250	$1,250	$1,250	$0
WKHM spot schedule		$500							$500			$250	$1,250	$1,250	$0
K105.3 spot schedule	$750								$500			$250	$1,500	$1,500	$0
K1005.3 high school bball playoffs			$280										$0		$0
Television Spot Schedule															
WILX									$1,500				$1,500	$1,500	$0
WLNS	$1,670												$1,670	$1,670	$0
ABC 53	$1,700								$890				$2,590	$2,450	($140)
AT&T cable 2000	$1,016								$1,012				$2,028	$2,028	$0
Outdoor															
Adams (space)															
Production															
Projects															
Annual report				$8,000									$8,000	$8,000	$0
Website marketing			$275	$1,950									$2,225	$1,750	($475)
Ongoing Website development				$350	$233					$1,000			$1,583	$2,500	$918
Website searchable dbase				$2,300									$2,300	$2,500	$200
Annual Web hosting							$600			$129			$729	$729	$0
Account planning and media	$623	$398		$892	$345		$203	$300		$300		$300	$3,360	$2,100	($1,260)
Contingency					$345	$200	$200	$200	$200	$200	$200	$200	$1,745	$2,200	$455
Totals	$5,759	$2,478	$555	$13,492	$1,104	$1,625	$1,003	$2,700	$6,252	$2,029	$800	$2,900	$40,415	$40,432	$17

Media Trades

	Jan	Totals	Budgeted	Deviation
WKHM trade	$500	$500	$4,250	$4,250
WJKN	$500	$500	$3,000	$2,500
Adams trade		$0	$9,740	$9,740

Plan total with trades $57,422

Shaded areas = completed project at actual amount billed

on which actions they will evaluate. It should be noted any action not measured would be a continued risk to spend resources toward for the organization. Table 9.5 shares evaluation methods for the communication plan shared in Figure 9.4 (p. 217).

Market Research

At the base of the marketing, promotional and communication mix model, market research is a component that needs to be addressed by an organization. Throughout the marketing plan process, organizations may have identified times when data would have assisted them to understand issues and make decisions about the marketing plan, such as

- existing consumer sociodemographic characteristics

- consumer behaviors of targeted markets
- the number and type of consumers currently served
- market demand
- consumer satisfaction
- employee satisfaction
- impacts of past marketing efforts
- financial records by market segments served

In an effort to organize these thoughts and to ensure they are planned for in subsequent marketing plans, the model suggests an organization revisit this category at this point in the process. Doing so allows an organization to reflect on data that would be valuable to the organization and plan for it accordingly.

Table 9.5
Evaluation Methods for Communication Plan

Actions	Evaluation Method
Employee orientation/FAM Tour (i.e., orientation video, self-guided tour with free passes for two to all areas, and a contest for those who visit all CLS areas)	Record number of passes returned, number who entered contest, survey employees
Quality service training—staff	Survey employees, analyze survey data on resident satisfaction
Sales and marketing training—staff	Survey employees, mystery shopping of staff performance
Employee satisfaction/performance evaluations	Survey employees on satisfaction, analyze performance evaluations
Follow-up phone calls, e-mails and letters to consumers	Keep record of who was contacted
Community and corporate sales blitz, follow-up on leads generated	Track number of visits, track leads
Present, distribute materials, coupons, and magnets to homeowners' association	Track number of presentations, track number of returned coupons
Newsletter with Fun Facts shared with employees	Survey employees
Incentive program for employees to sell services, facilities, etc.	Track amount given to employees for revenue generated
Employees receive Daily Calendar of Events and Frequently Asked Questions Guide to facilitate one-stop shop	Survey employees, mystery shopping for staff performance/use
CCTV, cable TV show/advertising	Upon arrival, ask consumers how they heard about us
Billboard for all CLS offerings	Upon arrival, ask consumers how they heard about us
New homeowner direct mail	Send a coupon specifically for new homeowners, and track returning coupons
Direct mail *Discover* (consider Web only and print small quantitiy for those who wish to recieve by mail)	Upon arrival, ask consumers how they heard about us
Direct mail *Leisure Focus* newsletter	Upon arrival, ask consumers how they heard about us
Website advertising to linked agencies (e.g., schools)	Upon arrival, ask consumers how they heard about us
Global organization media stories of newsworthy events	Upon arrival, ask consumers how they heard about us

Estimating the Impact: Revenue/Cost Summary

The final analysis of the marketing plan, prior to implementation, rests in understanding how the results from established objectives compare to costs associated with completing the same objective. Any person responsible for creating a marketing plan should be able to defend the costs associated with it and be prepared to ensure the objectives are successfully achieved. Therefore, a simplified revenue/cost summary is prepared for each objective.

For example, for Click's Ski Hill the objective was to increase the number of lift tickets from 257 to 600 this next year. The incremental difference in revenue to Click's would be 343 lift tickets. Therefore, it is projected, if the organization did not pursue this target market they would not be selling more tickets than last year. The revenue generated from selling 343 more lift tickets is determined based on the average price for a lift ticket sold to this market. In this past year, youth lift ticket sales averaged $17 per session.

The incremental revenue is then 343 x $17 = $5,831. The cost of implementing the marketing plan is estimated at $3,500. Therefore, the revenue/cost summary projects pursuing this market and achieving the marketing objective will result in incremental revenue of $2,331. These figures are a simple estimate however and do not reflect the staff wages and fixed costs within the organization. In this instance, the organization may find it relatively easy to sell this plan to owners/board members when revenue exceeds costs. But, this is not always the situation presented.

If the cost for implementing the marketing plan was $7,500, how simple would it be to sell others on supporting this plan? In some instances, this may occur and be logical for an organization to sell others on supporting the objective. For newly targeted markets (e.g., if the ski hill had never pursued this market before) it may initially cost more to communicate with the market than the anticipated first year return. The concept of a product life cycle applies here and will be discussed in Chapter 10.

If the organization's objective was to increase attendance (without a revenue objective), then the comparison would also be explained in the same manner. The leisure services example throughout this chapter had an objective of increasing resident use of services from 42% to 48%. Therefore, the incremental difference is 6% of residents' population. A population of 36,000 indicates that the organization's objective is to serve an additional 2,160 residents. Would the board approve investing in $10,000 to reach and serve an additional 2,160 residents?

Once again, it is difficult to summarize revenue/cost impacts when data is not available to write measurable marketing objectives. How can an organization justify spending $5,000 when there is no understanding of the potential return? Certainly, this happens every day, and few marketing plans are written in measurable ways, however, this trend needs to continue to be addressed.

A revenue/cost summary can also be prepared by comparing the incremental difference in consumers by marketing costs to determine the marketing cost per new consumer. Using the same example, Click's Ski Hill will add 343 new consumers to the organization at a cost of $3,500. Dividing 343 into $3,500 suggests that $10.20 will be spent on securing each new consumer in this market segment. This is yet another way for an organization to justify its marketing efforts. This is what happened to Spring Hill Camp (see RLS box, p. 100).

With the reality of leisure and tourism organization marketing budgets being small by nature, every organization should be prepared to leverage the costs of marketing as effectively as possible. As mentioned in Chapter 4, a discussion on trade and barter should be explored to maximize plan elements while minimizing costs. As stated, every leisure and tourism organization has a commodity worth trading, and many other organizations find value in this type of trade relations.

What is most critical to understand at this point in the marketing plan process is the importance of estimating the costs and potential gains associated with the marketing plan. As previously discussed, all too often organizations do not establish marketing activities as measurable initiatives that contribute to overall organization objectives. If the return on investment in marketing is not measured, then organizations will continue to have challenges in gaining support for marketing-related activities, especially when financial issues are of concern within an organization. All marketing efforts should indicate how they support the organization's overall objectives and, more specifically, how they assist in achieving the specific marketing objectives.

The remaining chapters of this textbook provide additional insight into each component of the marketing, promotional, and communication mix model. This information will assist in clarifying the role of each tool and show how it can be used effectively. The final model should be completed once all chapters are read and a thorough understanding of each area is learned.

Apply What You Know

1. Estimate the costs for the items listed in Tables 9.4 and 9.5. Which activities would you recommend the organization complete and why?

2. Brainstorm components of the Marketing and Communication Mixes for your organization's marketing plan.

3. Take an existing brainstorm list and identify where each item would be placed in the marketing, promotional, and communication mix model.

4. Complete a marketing plan chart with final decisions, costs, reporting responsibilities, and an evaluation methods outline.

Key Terms

Brand identity	Operational decisions
Collateral materials	Organization culture
Communication mix	Promotional mix
Effective methods	Promotional statement
Evaluation	Resources
Marketing mix	ROI (return on investments)
Market research	Time frame

Review Questions

1. Identify and describe the three steps of the mix model.

2. What are the six factors in finalizing operation decisions?

3. What are the preferred methods of reaching the campus recreation market according to Steinbach (2002)?

4. Explain the second facet of the promotional mix.

5. Overall, what does the marketing, promotional, and communication mix model provide an organization?

6. Identify and explain the final analysis of the marketing plan prior to implementation.

Internet Resources

Cheap TV Spots provides media and advertising services for businesses. Their product offerings include TV commercials, billboards, posters, and bulletins.

http://www.cheap-tv-spots.com

Constant Contact develops e-mail marketing services for small businesses. Their goal is to improve the relationship between customers and the organization. E-mail campaign development, e-mail lists management and e-mail template design are some of the services they offer.

http://www.constantcontact.com

MyWorkTools focuses exclusively on digital business tools. One of their marketing tools, Zairmail Express Direct, allows businesses to launch effective direct mail campaigns quickly and reliable.

http://www.myworktools.com

Optimizer specializes in providing services that improve the organizations website traffic. Implementing search engine optimization, the organization will be ranked higher in search engine results pages.

http://www.optimiser.co.uk

AT&T Small and Medium Business Resource Center is a source of information and news for entrepreneurs. Website material describes how to establish a promotional mix. Useful links to Internet resources, professional associations, and publications are available.

http://www.att.sbresources.com/sbr_template.
cfm?docnumber=PL24_0000.htm

The *International Association of Business Communicators* provides a professional network for business communication professionals. The association offers opportunities for professional development, exchange of ideas and participation at conferences and seminars.

http://www.iabc.com

References

Attard, J. (2003). Local marketing ideas. *Marketing Plans Research*. Retrieved October 9, 2003, from http://www.mplans.com

Clark, T. (2002). Just imagine: When marketing for new members, there are many ways to get the message out. *Aquatics International—Los Angeles, 14*(3), 18–21.

Clawson, M. and Kneutsch, J. L. (1966). *Economics of outdoor recreation*. Baltimore, MD: Johns Hopkins University Press.

Coleman, G. (1997). Marketing your day camp. *Camping Magazine, 70*(5), 31–33.

Cruice, M. (2002). A sporting chance: How community sports clubs should approach their marketing. *Australasian Leisure Management, 31,* 58–59.

Janoff, B. (2003). Disney's quest to brand and market its sports division is a complex matter. *Brandweek, 44*(3), 10.

Morais, R. J. (2001). Analytical ideation: Power brainstorming. *Brandweek, 42*(3), 22.

Motley, L. B. (2002). Worth reviewing: The four Ps: Product, pricing, promotion, and place (distribution). *ABA Bank Marketing, 34*(3), 48.

Siguaw, J. A. and Enz, C. A. (1999). Best practices in marketing. *Cornell Hotel and Restaurant Administration Quarterly,* 31–43.

Steinbach, P. (2002). Participants wanted: Campus recreation marketing has evolved to include some new promotional ideas, and a few twists on old ones. *Athletic Business, 26*(4), 47–48, 50, 52, 54, 56, 58.

Stuessy, T. (2000). Marketing outdoor programs on the college campus. In M. Freidline, M. Phipps, T. Moore, and J. Verstee (Eds.), *14th International Conference on Outdoor Recreation and Education: ICORE 2000 Conference Proceedings* (pp. 61–68). Boulder, CO: Association of Outdoor Recreation and Education.

Three elements every marketing mix should have. (2003, July) Retrieved July 8, 2003, from http://www.gotomarketstrategies.com

Chapter 10

Organization Offerings, Distribution, and Pricing

Dana and Jack had wanted to travel to the Walt Disney World Resort for years. Their three children were now at an age that they were easier to travel with, and they would be intrigued by a high-quality Disney experience. They also knew that Disney would be an expensive trip, so they had been saving for over a year to have enough money to make the trip. They wanted to maximize their savings and create a memorable trip but did not want to spend it wastefully. Therefore, Dana set out to find the highest quality, least expensive transportation route she could for her family of five.

Dana started preparing for the trip as she had previous trips by contacting a travel organization. They needed airline, rental car, and lodging arrangements, and she knew this inexpensive service could save her time and money. In speaking with the travel agent she learned that a few years ago they added a fee to travelers' arrangements to offset the commission no longer paid for by the airlines. Dana learned that for using this service she would pay an additional $40 per airline ticket booked. No longer were the airlines paying travel organizations to be a distribution source for them. The travel agent was still a link to consumers for the airlines, but they no longer needed to financially support them because new distribution sources existed.

A new distribution source that had emerged in the travel industry and kept the airlines from having to pay commissions was the Internet. Dana knew this was also a source for travel arrangements but had shied away from using it because every time she had done so before she ended up spending hours and hours searching through a maze of services. In an effort to potentially save money however, she decided to spend the time finding out the most efficient, effective way to make her travel arrangements. With one quick entry titled "Disney World vacations," she was greeted with over 130,000 hits.

Various travel sources were located through these sites including individual home pages for lodging, car rentals and airlines, the Walt Disney World Resort itself, Internet-only travel organizations, tour operators, destination marketing organizations as well as sites where one can set their own price restrictions, such as Priceline, Travelocity, Expedia, StudentUniverse, Site 59, Orbitz, CheapTix, Hotwire, Worldres, and TravelWeb. All seemed to guarantee convenience and the lowest prices available. Needless to say, Dana was overwhelmed.

After four hours of searching, frustration increased. She realized each provider had different prices and offerings

---

At the end of this chapter, readers will be able to...

- Understand the elements within an organization's experiences or "offerings."

- Discuss the product life cycle and identify operational decisions based on the offerings phase.

- Explain the components of distribution and share examples of how organizations use distribution as a marketing tool.

- Discuss the Internet as a distribution tool.

- Understand the distinctions between identifying a pricing objective, assessing a pricing variable, and determining the price and evaluating these decisions.

- Explain the concept of yield management and the role it has in leisure and tourism organizations.

- Demonstrate the ability to make well-grounded pricing decisions that will achieve an organization's objectives.

for a trip that had an established date set. Some providers said that the hotel and airline seats were unavailable whereas others would offer them to her but at somewhat different prices. As a consumer in this maze of offerings she realized she may never know if she received the best price. All she knew was that she was tired of spending so much time on saving what would turn out to be only a few hundred dollars. However, that money would be the difference in buying her children Mickey Mouse ears, sweatshirts, and photographs to remember their trip or not, so she pressed on.

• • • • •

The advent of the most sophisticated technological advancement in recent history, the Internet, has created a wave of opportunity for all types of organizations. Undoubtedly, it has endless benefits for consumers and providers alike. It is not, however, without its challenges as well. As Dana discovered, the travel industry has become more complex than ever as a result of the advent of an additional distribution systems. How does an organization differentiate its offerings in a new world of competitors? How do consumers select a provider and how does an organization develop brand loyalty once they are found by a consumer? How does a consumer find the best value? Do they feel they received the best price?

What the travel industry is experiencing is not unlike what other areas of leisure and tourism are also faced with. The Internet as a distribution source for linking consumers and suppliers is growing in popularity. This linkage provides an organization's offerings at a specific price to consumers. Therefore, an organization must decide three marketing mix issues to best prepare for this opportunity. These include making decisions about the leisure and tourism experience/ offerings, distribution channels, and pricing.

As noted in Chapter 9, the first set of decisions following the development of marketing objectives are decisions related to offerings, distribution, and pricing. These sets of decisions represent those permanent choices an organization makes toward achieving its marketing objectives. Specific target markets must be considered when these decisions are made, and individual consumer practices and behaviors must be evaluated.

Organization Offerings

Leisure and tourism experiences are unique offerings in the world of consumption opportunities for people. As explored in Chapter 2, consumers desire experiences that immerse them in ways that provide outcomes far beyond traditional interactions. A leisure and tourism experience has the power to change a person physically, emotionally, sensually, and spiritually.

These experiences can be further broken into various categories of organization offerings. *Offerings* are the range of provisions provided to consumers by the organization. These offerings can be in the form of products, services, facilities, programs/events, delivery, policies/procedures and the physical environment. They are regular/permanent changes in an organization's offerings focused on the needs/wants of the target market. Donath (2005) noted that central to an organization's success is the ability to develop new offerings based on a solid knowledge base.

Product offerings are physical goods presented to the consumer. For example, a golf course provides a 9- or 18-hole course to consumers. *Services* are the way in which these products are offered to the consumer as well as the amenities that support the primary product offering. For example, various services support the golf course itself, including caddies, carts, and club cleaning. *Facilities* are yet another unique dimension to leisure and tourism service offerings where physical structures are available to consumers. In this example, golf courses have clubhouses, driving ranges, and putting greens. *Programs/events* are also part of a leisure and tourism organization's offerings that create an experience. Programs/events include scheduled activities that complement the products offered to consumers. In this example, leagues, tournaments, and golf clinics would be available at the golf course. The way in which an organization's offerings are *delivered* also impacts the experience received by consumers and other stakeholders as well as the way an organization determines its policies and procedures. The *policies/procedures* shape the experience by establishing boundaries for participation as does the *physical environment*. The physical environment also makes up the leisure and tourism experience as consumers' perceptions are formed on the physical attributes of the organization itself. An example of this is the cleanliness of the facilities. Table 10.1 provides examples of each type of offering.

The various components of a leisure and tourism experience fall into two distinct categories: tangible offerings and intangible offerings. The intangible components include those experiences consumers leave with because they have impacted them in some way. These include programs, services, delivery, and policies/procedures. Tangible offerings include those consumers can see, feel, or touch and take with them. Product, facility, and physical environment offerings fall into these categories. Wakefield and Blodgett (1999) found the physical environment played an important role in the leisure and tourism experience. They found in three leisure and tourism organization settings that these tangible elements played a significant role in consumer's intentions to return and their willingness to recommend the organization to others.

Even though many authors suggest a leisure and tourism experience is intangible, this author would suggest it can be made up of a combination of intangible and tangible offerings. Ultimately, the leisure and tourism experience is a multifaceted operation because it involves various types of offerings comprised of physical and human elements.

Our patrons and guests have come to expect a "newness" in our product on an annual basis. Whether this comes in the form of new rides or attractions or even in the way we promote our parks—new leads the way. Gary Stony, Chairman of the Board, International Association of Amusement Parks and Attractions

Within each of these offerings it is important to recognize that people do not buy these offerings, they buy how these offerings impact them whether tangible or intangible. People simply buy *benefits*. They buy how each of these offerings specifically benefits or impacts them directly.

Product Life Cycle

Theodore Levitt of Harvard University first introduced the concept of the product life cycle (PLC) model for the manufacturing sector (cited in Ivy, 2000). Its purpose was to identify and predict stages of growth that a product would pass through. Similar to a human life, products would pass from introduction (i.e., infancy), to growth (i.e., childhood) through maturity (i.e., adulthood) and to an eventual decline (i.e., death). Unlike with an actual life however, a product could indeed avoid decline or death. It is suggested that not all products will successfully pass through each phase of the PLC, rather only those that have the strength to live through adulthood. Figure 10.1 (p. 228) and Table 10.2 (p. 229) highlight a visual representation of the PLC as well as a condensed explanation of distinctions between the stages (Walle, 1994, as cited in Ivy, 2000).

At the introduction phase, a product is unknown and the organization must make the consumer aware of the product and inform them of its potential use. Sales/participation is low or nonexistent and over time this begins to emerge

Table 10.1
Offering Examples

	Examples			
Offering	*Golf Course*	*Athletic Club*	*Resort*	*Community Center*
Products	9/18 holes of golf, carts, golf merchandise, equipment	Multipurpose center, athletic clothing, equipment	Guest rooms with resort amenities	Community center with with various products
Services	Caddies, club cleaning	Certified trainers, body composition assessments, nutrition consultation	Concierge, bellstaff	Online registration
Facilities	Clubhouse, golf course, driving range, putting green	Basketball courts, fitness rooms, restaurant/lounge	Tennis courts, aerobic rooms, free weight room	Gymnasium, banquet/meeting rooms
Programs/events	Leagues, tournaments, clinics	Fitness classes, basketball leagues, swim classes	Children's activities, corporate events, theme classes	Craft classes, health screenings, blood drives
Delivery	Trained professional delivering high quality golf lesson to a consumer	Certified trainers coach members on proper weightlifting techniques	Recreation staff members encourage guest participation in a poolside trivia contest	Executive Director walks through activity areas to greet guests
Policies/procedures	Mandatory carts, collared shirts, tee time guarantee, reimbursed if less than half of round is not completed due to weather	Proper exercise clothing, one-year minimum membership, limited transferability of membership, guest fee at $30/visit	Pool closed at 11:00 p.m., no children under 14 in fitness rooms, $20 down payment for borrowed equipment	Community residents only, no children under 15 without an adult present, open recreation hours in gym 7–11:00 p.m., adults only swim 8–10:00 p.m.
Physical environment	Fresh flowers planted in flower beds, trash picked up, groomed lawns	Immaculate locker rooms with various toiletries/amenities provided, towels, sweat-free exercise equipment	Ample signage identifying recreation areas, clean children's area	Well-maintained older center with equipment in working order, well-lit parking lot

Real Life Story: A Unique Competitive Edge—The Embers Restaurant

The Embers restaurant began in 1958 in a rural community as a fine dining establishment, a rarity for the times. Clarence Tuma had a vision to create an elegant place for patrons to have a high-quality dining experience that centered on consistent great service and exceptional food... a vision they still deliver on today. The 700-seat restaurant has gone through 12 additions to now include 26,000 square feet of catering space, a more casual restaurant, and a bar. Almost 50 years later this established restaurant is a regional icon and attributes much of their success to one simple thing... a unique competitive advantage.

The Embers was featured in *The Farm Journal* in the late 1960s, which proved to be the turning point for their broader appeal. They subsequently received state, regional, and national recognition as a quality-oriented establishment where guests would be guaranteed an exceptional experience. There were several ways in which they made this occur. Their success can be attributed to established standards of service, efficient systems, extensive training, hands-on leadership, and unique product offerings. Servers worked in teams and everyone knew their role. Never would a water glass be empty, nor would one be interrupted by service staff. The systems were clearly outlined and staff was not allowed to work until they passed an exam showing they knew exactly what to do and how to deliver the experience at such a high level.

Finally, Mr. Tuma was there every day, garnishing every item as it left the kitchen to insure high quality and doing so in the dining room where he could observe and participate in high-quality service delivery. This strong leader did what it took to make the experience exceptional. If it meant washing dishes or shoveling the sidewalk, his style proved motivating to his staff, as everyone was willing to do whatever was necessary to ensure an exceptional guest experience.

This same culture is one that Tuma's son, Jeff, has maintained throughout time. The Tumas attribute their success to one additional item, and this, they say, sets them further apart from their competition— the "One Pound Pork Chop." This item was on the first menu and cost $2.95. The creation of this unique menu offering became what the restaurant has become known for. Today, the pork chop has the same appeal. The four-inch pork chop represents 25% of revenue and has been the number one selling item since day one. Jeff Tuma, owner since 1987, states that their success stems from the fact that this menu offering is still "unique" and offers them a competitive advantage in the complex restaurant industry. As a service to consumers, right from the start, Embers guests were given the recipe for the pork chop. The Tumas shared their secrets far before it was popular to do so.

Even the Hog's Breath Inn in St. Louis, Missouri, found the recipe of value and asked to feature it on their menu 1,000 miles from The Embers. The Tuma's welcomed them featuring the pork chop and would even occasionally have their guests mention that they had The Embers pork chop there.

CLARENCE TUMA'S
personal   RECIPE
The Embers Original One Pound Pork Chop

Recipe For Six 1-Pound Pork Chops

MARINATING SAUCE

2 Cups Soy Sauce
1 Cup Water
½ Cup Brown Sugar
1 Tbsp. Dark Molasses
1 Tsp. Salt

Take soy sauce, water, brown sugar, molasses and salt. Mix together and bring to a boil. Let cool. Put chops in a pan with bone-side up. Pour the sauce over the pork chops and let stand over night in refrigerator. Next day take pork chops out of sauce, place in baking pan and cover tightly with foil. Put in 375 degree oven and bake until tender. About 2 hours.

While chops are baking combine all red sauce ingredients in heavy sauce pan or double boiler.

RED SAUCE

1/3 Cup Water
1 14-oz. Bottle Heinz Ketchup
1 12-oz. Bottle Heinz Chili Sauce
1/2 Cup Brown Sugar
1 Tbsp. Dry Mustard

Dilute dry mustard, sugar and water together leaving no lumps. Bring all ingredients to a slight boil. The red sauce is finished. After chops are tender remove from oven and dip in the red sauce. Take chops after dipping and place in baking pan and bake for 30 minutes in 350 degree oven or until slightly glazed.

Marinating sauce and red sauce can be reused if brought to a boil and stored in refrigerator or frozen.

For an extra flavor keep at room temperature until you are ready to put on charcoal pit or grill, have grill as high as possible from coals, not a large bed of coals is needed. Place finished chops on grill, let cook slowly, a little blacking does not hurt chops, grilling should not take more than 15 minutes.

I sincerely hope you and your guests enjoy our Pork Chop as prepared and served by you.

Should you encounter difficulty in preparing our Pork Chop, please feel free, as one chef to another, to drop in and discuss these problems with me.

SINCERELY

CLARENCE TUMA
The Embers

and grow. Promotional statements are geared toward the needs of the targeted markets. Pricing may be high to capture top of market or to recover costs (e.g., technology, industry) or low to penetrate the market and spur consumption. Organizations utilize heavy advertising, promotion, and public relations tools during this phase to introduce the offerings and to induce trial and use. Quality issues become apparent as the offerings are being introduced for the first time. Leisure and tourism offerings on the cutting edge fall into this category. Every leisure and tourism service offering was at one point in time in the introduction phase. Think about the first time you heard about Pilates, parabolic skis, indoor climbing walls, or youth sports camps run by professional teams.

Real Life Story: New Suite Seating at The Palace of Auburn Hills

The Palace of Auburn Hills, a 22,000-seat arena owned by Bill Davidson, operates under the auspices of Palace Sports and Entertainment (PS&E). Entertainment action within The Palace includes the three-time NBA champions Detroit Pistons and the two-time WNBA champions Detroit Shock. The Palace also hosts concerts, family shows, and a variety of special events. PS&E owns both The Palace and DTE Energy Music Theatre, an outdoor amphitheatre. Together these venues average 300 events and 3.5 million guests annually.

The Palace has been voted "Arena of the Year" eight times by *Performance* magazine and twice by *Pollstar* magazine, and it is listed among North America's top-grossing arenas annually. Voted "Best Outdoor Concert Venue" in *Pollstar's* 2000 Readers' Poll, the DTE Energy Music Theatre has been listed as the most attended amphitheater by *Amusement Business* in each of its 14 years under PS&E ownership.

Built in 1988, the Palace was noted as a state-of-the-art facility. The Palace continues to find ways to be a leading provider to entertainment consumers by developing unique product offerings. The Palace of Auburn Hills undertook its largest enhancement project yet in 2005 with the development of a new concept in venue suite seating. This concept in arena seating labeled "bunker suites" by The Palace are designed not only to expand offerings different market segments but also to find ways to develop additional revenue opportunities.

This new premium seating at The Palace of Auburn Hills allows business associates, employees, family, and friends to be treated like VIPs while enjoying the exciting sports and entertainment action in a distinctive way. Instead of suite seating within the arena during an event, these suites were built to be used before and after events. These suite holders enjoy the entertainment experience in premium courtside seating versus away from the action as most other suite offerings do. This allows The Palace to expand their offerings to meet the needs of consumers they were historically unable to serve.

Bunker suites cost between $350,000 and $450,000 per year and are more like formal living rooms than the other suites. Using upscale custom materials and furnishings, each of the binker suites is individually designed to create a special experience.

Each 400–500 square foot suite holds 22 people and contains high-end amenities, including a 42-inch LCD television, espresso and cappuccino machine, wine chiller, ice maker, mini-kitchenette, and powder room. Each suite is assigned a suite Captain whose sole purpose is to cater to every need of the suite holder. An additional kitchen and pantry area is also under construction to serve only this suite area.

Each bunker suite comes with four front-row Pistons seats and eight prime Pistons and Shock seats within the first five rows of the lower level. Each suite holder receives an allowance of $50,000 for food and $20,000 for tickets to other Palace events, in addition to the 12 Pistons tickets that come with the suite. Bunker suite holders enter the arena through the loading dock (the same entrance the players use), travel past the visitor's locker room, and use the same tunnel to the court as the players.

During the growth stage sales/participation is growing, as are competitors. The product is becoming well-known and brand recognition is emerging. This brand identity needs to be communicated to markets where benefits of participation are evident. Pricing tends to rise as demand increases (unless its the technology field where the reverse occurs). Distribution systems are expanded to broaden reach to target markets. Quality issues are improved on and the offering should be very high quality. Organizations place continued emphasis on advertising, promotion, and public relations, and begin to utilize other tools more moderately, such as sponsorship, personal selling, stewardship and internal marketing, to build brand loyalty. Leisure and tourism examples at this stage of the PLC include developing skate parks, cities building stadiums for sporting events, and smaller performing arts venues bringing in major performers and Broadway shows.

In the mature stage or saturated stage, sales/participation has flattened or is slightly falling because a large number of competitors exist in a market that has balanced demand. Focusing on building brand loyalty is evident during this stage. Promotional statements tend to be reminder oriented, positioning against competitors while expanding on competitive advantages. Organizations must differentiate offerings and price according to what the market will allow. Less emphasis is placed on advertising and public relations, whereas increased focus is placed on personal selling, sponsorship, stewardship, community relations, and internal marketing to build and maintain loyalty. Leisure and tourism examples at this stage include climbing walls, golf courses, and movie theaters with stadium-style seating.

Many organizations keep from falling into the decline or death stage in the PLC by utilizing various strategies. At this point, revenue is extremely low and competitors reduced to only the strongest and most successful. Loyalty practices are the most successful tools to use as organizations prepare for reemergence into the introduction stage of the PLC. Three main strategies exist for reemergence. The first is product modification. The aerobic industry has done this as they have modified aerobics to include steps, slides/glides, bicycles, weights, balls, and even strip tease classes. Other modifications examples include when leisure equipment has become new and improved (e.g., inline skates with better ball bearings, golf balls with improved distance capabilities), or when offerings have small modifications to services (e.g., free golf carts, continental breakfast with hotel room, and a larger number and type of activities offered to campers). Thomas Cook Travel did this when they introduced a new brand called Cultura that modified typical prepackaged trips by allowing more flexibility and consumers could tailor design their trip (Rogers, 2003). Some suggest modifying or renewing a product line provides quicker returns to the organization by not requiring significant marketing investments as a new offering would need (Frater, 1991).

The second reemergence technique is expanding to new market segments. Organizations typically targeting one market decide to introduce their offerings to another potentially untapped market segment (e.g., golf industry pursuing seniors or novice female golfers).

Third, organizations also attempt to broaden and to maintain life through the development of new offerings. These may be either within an existing target market by expanding their current offerings or introducing new offerings to a completely different target market.

The PLC is a valuable concept to leisure and tourism organizations because products are no longer the only type of offering that passes through a life cycle. Every organization offering passes through a life cycle and the PLC. For example, a new no-smoking policy would be at an introduction stage as would a renovated communication center. The PLC is designed to provide a means for understanding current life stage and more importantly provide a tool to understand mix tools to use based on this stage. An analysis of an organization's offerings at the PLC stage helps an organization determine the communication mix to select.

Distribution

This section will attempt to provide a simplistic view of distribution issues as it relates to leisure and tourism organizations specifically. *Distribution* is the way in which a leisure and tourism and tourism organization connects to consumers to ultimately provide a leisure and tourism service experience. It is the physical source used to reach them, the physical location in which to offer the experience, and the physical delivery of the service itself. These are highlighted in Table 10.3 (p. 230).

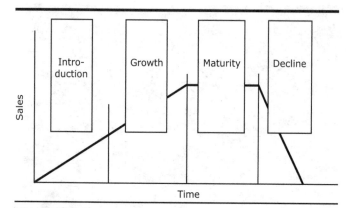

Figure 10.1
Product Life Cycle (PLC) Model

Table 10.2
Marketing, Promotional, and Communication Mix Issues Related to the Product Life Cycle

Issue	Introduction	Growth	Maturity	Decline
General organization belief	No one knows about this new and exciting offering, therefore, we need to get the word out and build our consumer base!	We have emerged and must continue to penetrate the market. We must focus on maintaining our strength/lead in a marketplace that has increased demand and a growing number of competitors.	We are one of many suppliers in a market with established demand and need to continue to differentiate our offerings, evaluate targeted markets and be extremely strategic in our approach.	If we have not modified our offerings, introduced what we offer to new target markets or developed new offerings, then we have perished and have hopefully diversified with other offerings.
Revenue/ participation	None	Growing and peaks as demand is at its top while supply is still relatively low	Maximized/flat and can be declining as the influx of competitors all split the flattened demand	Quickly eroding
Offerings	New, unique, competitive edge, unknown to most	More well-known	Well-known, yet some confusion about which competitor offers what	Reduced consideration to only those few that have sold well
Pricing	High to recover costs of launching or low to penetrate the market and spur consumption	Higher to take advantage of increased consumer demand	Priced at what the market will allow based on supply and demand	Low
Distribution	Selective (e.g., Internet, self)	Expanding to broaden reach to target markets	Extensive to maximize reach to target markets	Selective. Those not producing returns are phased out
Competition	None	Some and regularly increasing	Many. All competing for a small piece of the pie	Few. Weaker competitors have already disappeared
Promotional positioning statement	New, benefit-based, aimed at the needs of consumers	Leading. Brand benefits need to be evident	Position against competitor, and differentiate offerings	Position for a new market modification, or position on price
Promotional mix	High-quality collateral and publications to share message(s) regarding organization offerings; heavy use of promotional events and coupons to engage consumers to trial/use	Growth in the number and type of high-quality collateral with positioning messages changing throughout life cycle; moderate use of promotional events	Reduction in the number and type of high-quality collateral with positioning messages changing throughout life cycle to narrower target market; heavy use of coupons to encourage brand switching; limited promotional events	Use of collateral previously developed; limited use of coupons and promotional events; preparation for reentry to the introduction phase with modified or new offerings
Communication mix	Heavy advertising, public relations to expose offerings to as many as possible within target markets	Reduced, but still heavy advertising, public and community relations; moderate sponsorship, personal selling, stewardship, internal marketing to build loyalty.	Heavy personal selling, sponsorship, stewardship, internal marketing to ensure loyalty; continued use of community relations; modified advertising, public relations	Limited and focused on relationship-oriented activities to maintain loyalty
Quality issues	Attempt at high quality, however, issues emerge with delivery of offerings; steps taken to correct mistakes/imperfections	Quality should be very high and a strength for the organization with a growing numbers of competitors who have not advanced as well	Quality should remain very high and could be the differentiation among a large competitive market	Quality should remain high
Production costs	High	Decreasing	Stable	Increasing
Marketing costs	High	Decreasing	Stable	Declining
Brand loyalty	N/A	Developing	Strong	Limited and declining

Adapted from Ivy, 2000; Onkvisit and Shaw, 1989; Zikmund and D'Amico, 1989

Physical Sources

First, organizations connect with consumers through physical sources. These sources vary depending on the type of leisure and tourism organization and the divisions within a leisure and tourism organization. For example, a community center may connect with consumers directly by providing a direct telephone line to make all program reservations. An entertainment venue, however, may elect to allow an additional organization to connect to their consumers. For example, Ticketmaster is a common physical source for venues to connect to consumers. Ticketmaster outlets sell tickets to events held at the venue and, in turn, charge consumers a fee for the convenience. In other instances, the organization is the one who pays for the service of an additional distribution system. The travel organization example at the beginning of this chapter explains this relationship. Currently, hotel and car rental organizations pay a commission to travel agents if they sell their offerings to consumers. These organizations have elected to connect to consumers in a broader fashion in an effort to reach and serve more consumers. Even amusement parks sell discounted tickets through grocery stores and parks and recreation departments.

There are several reasons why an organization would pursue a physical distribution source:

- to reach more consumers

- to provide alternative ways to reach consumers

- to maximize organization resources

- to better meet the needs of consumers

As discussed, the Internet is the most recent physical source that connects an organization to a consumer. The example at the beginning of the chapter noted this change in the travel industry. This development changed the use of distribution sources for airlines and other travel partners. Watkins (2002) suggested that hotel companies should be forming new marketing strategies as a result of the airlines no longer paying commissions to travel agencies and the airlines decided to no longer use travel agencies as a distribution source.

Organizations have selected to develop their own website distribution system as well as distribute their offerings through other websites. More organizations have selected the Web as a primary distribution source because it is less expensive than utilizing other physical sources. Watkins (2002) suggested for the lodging industry that a website is less expensive to process a reservation than 800 numbers, travel organizations, airline systems, and other type sources.

In some instances the organization has a great deal of control over the physical source. The physical source may be owned by them directly or established in a formal contract. Reservation centers with 1-800 numbers are often in this type of arrangement. The organization often staffs the center or contracts with an outside organization to do this service for them. In this case, the organization has some control over how the distribution source manages to connect with consumers. With a contractual relationship the organization's control may be less; however, there are often provisions for termination of the arrangement. This of course is not a desired situation as the negative impact to consumers may already have been done.

Organizations may decide to control organization inventory directly and only allocate to other distribution sources. They decide what is prudent. For example, an airline may allocate a certain percentage of their seats to a travel agent and another percentage to various Internet

Table 10.3
Distribution Sources and Leisure Industry Examples

Distribution Element	Examples			
	Golf Course	*Athletic Club*	*Resort*	*Community Center*
Physical source	A community organization that books golf outings for all courses in the geographic area	A hospital rehabilitation program that refers all outpatient services to an area athletic club	A travel organization 1-800 call center	An organization website with online registration
Physical location	Providing golf lessons/clinics at a local organization for employees during their lunch hours	Providing aerobic classes at an off-site location	Providing recreation activities off site	Providing a mobile recreation unit that allows programs/equipment to be available anywhere
Physical service delivery	Training staff who work with senior citizen or novice female golfers	Ensuring all staff are CPR/First-Aid certified	Developing a service recovery system for consumers to share feedback and for the organization to learn from the experience	Assessing the organization's culture regarding quality service practices and implementing ideas for enhancing the organization culture

services. They may be the only ones, however, that have access to all available seats.

A leisure and tourism organization must decide on the distribution source(s) it will use to reach consumers. Whether an organization directly controls the distribution sources or not, several factors need to be evaluated and considered for each source selected. Pybus and Janes (2004) found when surveying public leisure and tourism organizations that successful partnerships included three elements: verbal and written communication, compatible (not necessarily comparable) goals, and knowledge of your partner. Further, a variety of factors can influence the success (or lack of success) of a partnership arrangement, including changes in leadership, forced partnerships, political atmosphere, funding, compatible versus comparable goals, and the dimensions of the partnership itself.

Technological influences. The aggressive development of technological advancements has impacted the leisure and tourism industry like all other industries. These advancements have also dramatically impacted marketing. Nykiel (2001) suggested technology has impacted everything from the prepurchase to postpurchase process.

Internet. The Internet is not only a recent phenomenon with great impact but also a system that influences marketing in several ways. First, the Internet is a distribution source for organizations. It is also a collateral tool used to communicate information about an organization as well as an advertising source to connect directly to consumers. It is a varied process organizations use in a variety of ways. These other topics will be further discussed in Chapters 11 and 12.

The U.S. Census Bureau (2000) projected 51% of all U.S. households had access to a computer and Internet access had more than doubled between 1997 and 2000. According to the Travel Industry Association of America (2004), 56% of U.S. adults used the Internet. More married couple households were likely to have a computer and Internet access than households with two or more people or people living alone. The Internet is influencing how society manages information as people use it to communicate to others via e-mail, access information on businesses, health practices, or government services and learn information about news, weather, or sports. Hyland (2003) stated that Outlook notes usage in homes and workplaces was still growing and in 2002 online commerce increased in spite of a challenged economy. He further suggested consumers are using websites for shopping, recreation, education, research, and communication, and online advertising would increase from 57.7 billion in 2002 to 93.1 billion in 2007 and compound at a rate of 10% annually. E-commerce and Internet advertisers will continue to grow as a result.

O'Connor (2003) studied the top 50 international hotel brands and supported the challenge of lodging properties' use of various Internet distribution systems. He found all used a variety of distribution systems simultaneously. "Price is key to selling successfully online" (p. 89) and even though one third of all pricing is consistent, generally lodging properties' use of multiple electronic business-to-consumer distribution systems is not.

O'Connor found a variety of online distribution systems beyond an organization's own website. These include

---

Real Life Story: Fitness First

Fitness First, a 60,000-square-foot publically funded enterprise in Illinois, focused on providing *the* best customer service for its 2,400 members. To determine what they could do, they looked both inside and outside the health club industry. As a result they developed a Total Customer Satisfaction Guarantee. The Guarantee included the following changes in the policies and services offered to members:

1. Members receive credit for illness or time away simply by completing a written request. As a result, members receive full use of their memberships.

2. Memberships can be transferred from one person to another.

3. Members who move from the area can receive a prorated refund of their membership fees.

4. Members can cancel their membership at any time.

As a result of this new approach, employees felt they were better able to serve members. The organization experienced a 17% increase in sales the first year. The elements of the guarantee were not typical of fitness centers and provided a unique opportunity to serve consumers and better meet their needs. It provided the competitive advantage they were looking for and developed trust between the organization and its members (Larson, 1999).

traditional travel agent oriented services online called global distribution systems (GDS) like Travelocity. Whereas others are database and reservation engine driven like travelweb.com, or strictly web-based with inventory and reservations all online like worldres.com. Finally, auction-type websites also exist (although not studied here) such as Priceline.

His research analyzed pricing provided for a double room on specific dates with each of the 50 brands, and the lowest general public rate available. In addition, O'Connor recorded each brand's central reservation service (CRS) verbally to identify the price available through this source. Table 10.4 highlights the average rates provided to consumers in his study, and although difficult to generalize, it appeared Expedia was the most consistent in providing the lowest price, which also has a higher transaction cost.

Further, he found that various lodging brands were significantly different when providing the lowest rates. The best value was not at the properties' own website all the time, although economy brands tended to have the lowest price three out of four times. Moderate and luxury brands offered lowest prices at their website 50% and 10% of the time, respectively.

In this instance, distribution channels that provided the lowest price had higher transaction costs because other distribution sources cost more than the organizations' own website (e.g., 10% commission is paid to travel organizations). Therefore, lodging properties should consider distribution sources with lower costs to them, thus providing more competitive prices. They should also evaluate the prices provided on their own website and at their CRS because these were often not the lowest price offered.

Many organizations use the Internet as a distribution source—a way to connect to consumers and other stakeholders in a more cost effective way. O'Connor (2003) cited Dresdner, Kleinwort, and Benson's breakdown of costs for lodging reservations via traditional and online distribution methods. As Table 10.5 depicts, the costs for online reservations is lower than a traditional travel agent. It has become the most effective form of reaching a large market of consumers. It is used as a process to communicate offerings, manage service issues and questions, make reservations and even registration arrangements. It does not, however, reach all market segments because not everyone has a computer or Internet access.

Physical Location

Organizations make distribution decisions based on their offerings. All too often an organization presumes its offerings must be provided in the same physical location where they have always offered them. At times organizations fail to identify alternative methods for distribution. For example, a leisure and tourism organization offers recreation programs, equipment, and services to community members in their own neighborhoods versus making consumers come to the community center. Oakland County Parks did this

Table 10.4
Average Rates Offered to the Customer

Channel	Mean	Standard Deviation
Hotel/company website	$159	112
Expedia	$152	116
Travelocity	$166	134
TravelWeb	$162	115
WorldRes	$181	168
Voice (CRS)	$163	117

Source: O'Connor (1993)

Table 10.5
Reservation Cost by Distribution Channel

Route		Transaction fee					Total cost
	Customer	Traditional travel agent	GDS	Switch	CRS	Hotel	
Traditional route		$5.90	$3.20	$0.20	$4.20		$13.50
	Customer	Online travel agent	GDS	Switch	CRS	Hotel	
Online intermediary route		$3.00	$3.20	$0.20	$4.20		$10.50
	Customer	Hotel-company website				Hotel	
Direct online route		$1.50					$1.50

Source: Dresdner Kleinwort Benson/Accor (2001)

This county park system brings the pool to consumers.

decades ago and still provides a mobile recreation unit to area residents. They offer community members their services at a location of the consumers' choosing versus only at the parks. An organization that distributes what it does in many locations expands its ability to reach consumers. Ultimately, Oakland County Parks will reach more consumers because it is able to reach more people through an expanded distribution system.

Physical Service Delivery

Service delivery is considered a part of the distribution system. The way in which an organization prepares for the connection between consumers and the organization plays a role. Organizations that implement quality service practices are concerned about how their offerings are distributed. As noted in Chapter 3, the delivery of leisure and tourism experiences by staff is oftentimes more valued than the product, facility, service, or program itself because it significantly contributes to the overall leisure and tourism experience.

Organizations that ensure consumers receive their tickets in a timely manner, are greeted immediately, and begin programs and classes on time are all contributing to the distribution system within an organization. Consumers need to feel their needs have been addressed through the physical service delivery sources. Ultimately, organizations that exceed consumers' expectations are the ones that will be the most successful.

Pricing

The final, permanent decision an organization must make regarding their offerings is the price to charge consumers. These prices are permanent decisions for the organization versus promotional or temporary discount prices to entice usage. This element of the marketing mix is an easy-to-do (but not necessarily easy to determine), highly visible, consumer-sensitive issue within a marketing plan. Every organization, regardless of profit status, evaluates their offerings and decides on a price for each aspect of their organization's offerings. Kyle, Graefe, and Absher (2002)

Real Life Story: The Value of Franchising—Big Apple Bagels

Cindy and Scott Rood were the operators of a regional water theme park and golf driving range for 15 years. When their tenure there ended, they looked for other opportunities. Cindy knew she very much enjoyed working with people and wanted to remain in the leisure/hospitality industry. Scott knew he wanted his own small business—and sought a concept with a proven track record.

They turned to a method of distribution called *franchising.* Franchising provides companies rapid growth and new operators with existing brand identity. Franchisees pay a lump-sum fee for a specified time period (typically 10 years) and ongoing royalties based on sales. After considerable research they chose to purchase a franchise from Big Apple Bagels. This was not an easy decision for them. This decision was going to commit ten years of their lives and a considerable financial commitment.

How did Scott and Cindy select Big Apple Bagels? They noticed a high product quality and a commitment to excellence in all aspects of the business. This allows stores to stand apart from the crowd and enjoy high consumer appeal. Every year *Entrepreneur Magazine* publishes a ranking of franchise companies—"the Franchise 500." Big Apple Bagels consistently earns a spot in that ranking and is the only bagel franchise on that list. They visited store locations and spoke with franchise operators. In 1998 they bought their first franchise and have been involved with six locations since.

The franchise arrangement is a tradeoff between being an independent business and joining a chain where control is held by the franchisor. Advantages

Cindy and Scott like include franchisor support in marketing, advertising and promotions; operational guidance and assistance; product development; chain-leveraged vendor pricing; and the network of franchise operators who support one another. Disadvantages in being a franchisee include potential lack of autonomy and being part of a collective group in the downturn of a product life cycle. Product redevelopment and franchisor support has kept their Big Apple Bagels stores successful in a competitive environment.

Key to a successful arrangement is the day-to-day relationship between the franchisee and franchisor. Cindy and Scott did their homework and found in Big Apple Bagels a corporate support team they liked and have enjoyed working with. For them, the franchise distribution option has worked well.

suggested public leisure and tourism organizations have placed little concern on pricing decisions, yet it is regarded the most important element of the marketing mix. Organizations tend to respond to competition through cutting prices to meet competition or do nothing. Neither are effective strategies. Cross and Dixit (2005) state organizations fail to place the time and effort needed to properly set prices and set a differential in the market. Developing a price strategy and determining the price to charge can be a frustrating process for some. Pricing decisions not only influence consumer usage but also predict organization success.

Staff at various levels within an organization may have input on pricing decisions. Some may decide the price to charge all on their own. For example, a municipal recreation organization programmer may determine the price to charge for a craft class. Others may only make recommendations about the price they believe should be charged to management or owners. The more prepared a leisure and tourism organization professional is for these types of decisions, the more successful their decisions will be.

Many organizations have wished for a crystal ball to predict the outcome of a specific pricing decision. Some have even flipped a coin to make a pricing decision. Unfortunately, the crystal ball does not exist and the coin is not the best answer. Shipley and Jobber (2001) suggested the lack of seriousness in pricing development stems from a narrow view of pricing based only on cost. They suggest organizations employ a multifaceted approach to pricing. An organization can use several tools to determine the most appropriate price for everything from a sleeve of golf balls to a craft class to a family special event to tickets for a concert to a membership at a club. There are four steps taken in any pricing decision:

1. Identify the pricing objective.
2. Assess the pricing variables.
3. Determine the price.
4. Evaluate the pricing decision.

Identifying the Pricing Objective

For each offering an organization is pricing, they must first ask themselves: What outcome do we want from this pricing decision? Traditionally, one of four responses emerge:

- We want to make money.
- We want to break even.
- We want to have as much participation as possible.
- We want to turn off certain market segments or demarket.

These responses are typical for all types of leisure and tourism organizations. Regardless of profit status, all leisure and tourism organizations will set all four types of objectives. A public leisure and tourism organization will set prices based on trying to make money, break even, host a large number of attendees, or even turn off a market as does any quasi-public, private, or profit-based leisure and tourism organization. Table 10.6 highlights how various leisure and tourism organizations may establish each type of pricing objective.

Certainly, the combination of offerings and pricing naturally turns specific market segments off and on as discussed in demarketing. By the simple nature of setting any price however, specific markets will be either attracted to consuming an organization's services or not. Charging $300 versus $800 per year for an annual fitness center membership is this type of example. There are markets of people willing to spend $300 and those willing to spend $800. Certainly, if the market that is willing to spend $800 can have their needs met for $300, then an organization can also serve this market segment. However, the reverse does not hold true. The market who is willing to spend $300 may not be willing to spend $800. Even if the price is $0, some market segments would be turned off by an activity that charges nothing. They may believe the offering will be substandard in quality as a result of price, or it will attract too many people and be too crowded.

Table 10.6
Examples of Leisure Service Organizations Using Various Pricing Objectives

Pricing Objective	Golf Course	Athletic Club	Examples Resort	Community Center
Make money	Golf rounds	Membership	Guest Room	Adult athletic programs
Break even	Bag service	Wellness classes	Recreation activities	Youth athletic programs
Participation	Clinic	Grand opening reception	Fireworks display	Special events
Turn off a market	Youth golfers	Families with young children	Soccer groups	Nonresidents

Assessing the Pricing Variables

Once an organization determines the pricing objective, they can establish a strategy for determining the price they will charge. To do this, an organization must assess mixed variables that influence the success of the pricing decision. These variables can represent a puzzle to a leisure and tourism organization. When all pieces are put in place, a pricing decision can be made. Generally, five variables need to be assessed to prepare to make a pricing decision. These variables include history, demand, competition, willingness to pay, cost, and margin.

History. History of an organization's prices and the impact of these prices on participation, revenue/sales, and profit tell an important story that must be understood by leisure and tourism organizations prior to establishing a price. Organizations that understand the relationship between prices charged and organization results and demand are better able to anticipate the future. This, however, is not the only assessment that needs to be understood by organizations. Organizations that limit their assessment to history alone are missing information that would help in making yet a better decision because the past is no guarantee of the future. It only tells part of the story.

Returning consumers also recall prices charged by an organization. Their previous exposure to a pricing level can become the expectation, and organizations should be aware of an increase beyond what would be considered reasonable. Cohen (2002) interviewed Anne Carpenter, who specializes in pricing strategies. Carpenter suggests consumers should be surveyed to determine their reaction to a potential price increase.

Demand. Demand for a specific leisure and tourism service offering is another variable that needs to be understood by organizations prior to developing pricing. Holecek (personal communiation, 2000) stated demand is when consumers will buy more at a lower price than at a higher price or, in essence, the relationship between the amount that can be sold at any given price. As price increases the number of people interested decreases. Ideally, an organization will have documented historical demand and forecasted future demand. Each leisure and tourism industry will vary on how they approach understanding this issue; however, it is important to know as much as possible. For example, Indianapolis, Indiana, hotels and resorts need to understand when the Indy 500 time trials and event will take place. Demand for their rooms will be very high and pricing can reflect their objective to make money. Conversely, demand for golfing in Florida in August will be lower than in March and changes in prices are reflected during these months. A course may wish to break even during the slow months and price themselves to make money during the peak season.

Documented demand is important to analyze and thoroughly understand. It is not just a gut feel for high, moderate, and low demand times—ideally, documented evidence exists.

Other leisure and tourism industries are developing pricing strategies based on demand. Ski hills have experienced rapid changes in their industry over the past ten years, including increased interest in snowboarding (now 30% of ski hill users), increased interest in Canadian skiing due to attractive exchange rate, trend of children pursuing indoor versus outdoor leisure and tourism activities, and leveling off of people participating overall in the industry. Organizations change offerings to be selected among the stiff competition; however, they see little returns based on these issues. To better manage, they have turned to customized ski passes for consumers. Consumers can now get half or full day, midweek/weekend, multipass, or package passes with resorts. Others have cut prices to appeal to new markets and/or diversified with tubing hills, Nordic trails, sleigh rides, paragliding, and ice skating (Palmeri, 2003).

Seasonality is an issue throughout the leisure and tourism industry. It is well-known some organizations experience fluctuations in revenue or participation based on time of year, day of week, or time of day. This is not limited to the leisure and tourism industry, and knowing these demand patterns is vital to setting appropriate prices. Organizations miss opportunities to achieve their pricing objective by failing to understand demand by time of day, day of week, and time of year. This type of market research becomes an important tool for leisure and tourism organizations to understand demand patterns in their own organization as well as others. Table 10.7 (p. 236) provides a golf round summary for Pheasant Run Golf Club by day of week. This evidence indicates that Monday and Tuesday are the slowest days for the club when adding 18- and 9-hole rounds together whereas Saturday and Sunday are have the highest demand. This type of data can be used to sell others on new concepts like the pricing decisions the club has made. This data can also be used to track demand over time and to identify if marketing strategies geared toward other markets are working (e.g., senior citizens, novice female golfers).

This type of data does not reflect all demand for golf in the area, however. The ideal information would provide data on the overall market demand and the organization's demand. Internal demand information should be gathered. Organizations who do not have this type of data often plan to analyze their offerings this way in subsequent marketing plans once they see the value of doing so. As suggested in Chapter 9, this type of suggestion would be added to the market research section of the marketing plan.

Data on market demand can be more difficult to obtain. Certain industries have systems in place for gathering this information and understanding market demand. A market share analysis described in Chapter 6 provides this type of information. Organizations learn how their demand compares to overall market demand. The lodging industry has a more sophisticated system that can analyze market share data by comparing competitors' data against the organization's data. This type of assessment lets an organization know if their demand is representative of overall market demand. Smith Travel Research (2004) developed the STAR report that tracks demand by month, weekday and weekend; now they can track lodging occupancy, average room rate and revenue per available room by individual day using daySTAR. They collect numbers daily from over 10,000 lodging properties and provide benchmark data for properties to understand demand as well as their success at obtaining their share of the market.

Other leisure and tourism industries also share this type of demand data in different ways. A retail distributor of snowmobiles can learn from the manufacturer the number of snowmobiles sold in their store versus other area stores. Entertainment venues learn of number of tickets sold to various venue events in their city for different events or other cities for the same event. Most any organization can learn this information if they have a relationship with competing organizations where they all share general demand information. This is how market share analyses started in the lodging industry, where directors of marketing would share monthly figures with each other and then complete a market share analysis. From this, Smith Travel Research's STAR report was developed.

Competition. Although the premise of conducting a competitive analysis was discussed in Chapter 6, it may not be until now that an organization can understand the value of completing one. An assessment of an organization's competition provides critical information for determining an organization's price. Understanding what each competitor charges for offerings provides a base for establishing the prices within a leisure and tourism organization. Organizations can use competitive information to determine if they will charge more, less, or the same amount as competi-

tors. They may decide to position their organization by price within the market place but cannot determine what the price should be without an analysis of the competition. This assessment is another piece to the pricing puzzle.

Willingness to pay. Determining what the market will bear is a consideration that must be made by leisure and tourism organizations. Leisure and tourism organizations must understand the specific target market(s) focused toward to answer this question successfully. Asking consumers about their willingness to pay is an approach taken by many organizations to understand consumer preferences and price sensitivity. Some have conducted primary research studies to ask a consumer or potential consumers the question about willingness to pay for an organization offering. This data is helpful in establishing a pricing decision, and any information that can be obtained (through secondary research or an organization's own primary research) should be used to assist an organization in determining a price.

Kyle, Graefe, and Absher (2002) did this in a public recreation area where they estimated consumers willingness to pay for an individual weeklong pass to a scenic area and what they felt was an appropriate price for this offering. They found consumers were not willing to pay for the proposed increase the organization was considering taking and a substantial drop in visitation would occur with the increase. But, smaller increases in fees would yield the desired revenue increase because less consumers would refuse participation. Establishing loyalty with consumers is critical because they will have greater willingness to support changes in the organization. Solomon (2002) stated, "If you price your event at a point greater than its perceived value, you risk losing all but the hardcore fans" (p. 97).

Cost. Cost needs to be assessed prior to making any pricing decision. An organization must understand the cost for providing the offering prior to establishing its price. All types of costs need to be included, such as fixed, variable, and administrative costs. An organization must understand the complete cost for providing any offering. For example, a craft class may cost $4 per person, which includes sup-

Table 10.7
Summary of Golf Rounds by Day of Week

	Mon 18	Mon 9	Tue 18	Tue 9	Wed 18	Wed 9	Thu 18	Thu 9	Fri 18	Fri 9	Sat 18	Sat 9	Sun 18	Sun 9	Total 18	Total 9
April	222	37	278	97	177	96	139	50	380	116	436	128	375	127	2,007	651
May	421	88	425	148	402	131	379	182	462	210	684	120	702	130	3,475	1,009
June	538	177	603	118	469	121	336	113	734	246	869	133	1,210	199	4,759	1,107
July	581	149	552	194	662	242	1,114	216	629	173	806	130	895	162	5,239	1,266
Aug	460	129	521	128	535	227	518	179	600	218	832	145	940	155	4,406	1,181
Sept	222	50	425	50	293	65	425	102	464	128	777	115	728	82	3,334	637
Oct	289	53	113	29	249	55	308	47	494	121	345	42	290	43	2,088	390
Total	2,878	686	3,008	867	2,899	948	3,436	922	4,108	1267	4,972	840	5,376	906	25,611	6,401

plies, facilities overhead, instructor fees, and marketing/registration. Each of these elements must be considered as well as any subsidy the organization is receiving. Any type of organization may be receiving a subsidy. Public organizations may receive tax dollars, quasi-public organization may get donations and even for-profit organiza-

tions, like a resort recreation department, may receive support from the room division of the resort.

Organizations should utilize a combination of all these elements to determine their pricing strategy. Failure to address one area may lead an organization to a decision that may not be as effective as it could be. Organizations

Real Life Story: Unique Pricing Structures at a Golf Course

Pheasant Run Golf Club established prices for their organization unlike other golf courses in the area. This par 72, 27-hole, championship course covers 320 acres. The course is intermingled between single-family homes, native areas, and wetlands. It has bent grass tees, greens, and fairways connected by 10.5 miles of paved cart paths. Supporting services include a 10,000 square foot practice green and 3,500 square foot clubhouse with a restaurant/bar, pro shop, and catering options. It is owned and managed by a municipality.

Thinking outside the box is a skill some managers fail to possess, but not at this course where demand played a large role in establishing prices for the golf course. Unlike other courses that may offer seasonal prices, such as reduced price golf in the shoulder season or at twilight, Pheasant Run took it a step further. They offered golfers different prices based on day of week, time of day, and time of year.

They identified the market demand in these same categories to establish opportunities for setting reduced prices and thereby inviting another market segment to the course. For example, this club offers the least expensive rate to someone willing to golf on Monday or Tuesday mornings. The club also offers its highest price during high demand times—weekend mornings. Therefore, men, ages 35–55, from within 30 miles, with middle upper class incomes, who are knowledgeable and experienced golfers, and are serious about the game, own nice quality equipment, and look for individual challenges with a mid/high handicap will be willing to pay the highest price for this type of course in the area. However, other markets may not be as willing but they may consider other times that are more affordable. For example, senior citizens may not

be willing to pay $63 for a round of golf but will pay $39. They are available during the day and would be a good market to consider now that prices are more in line with what this market would be willing to pay.

The following Golf Club Rate Card highlights the various pricing decisions made by the club. They have tracked the number and type of golfers and have found this to be very effective in helping them to maximize revenue at the club despite significant budget cuts. They continue to contribute positively to the organization so other public recreation offerings may be provided that do not make a profit.

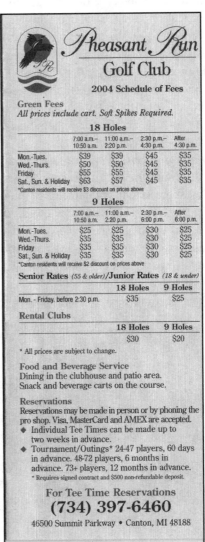

Pheasant Run Golf Club
2004 Schedule of Fees

Green Fees
All prices include cart. Soft Spikes Required.

18 Holes

	7:00 a.m.–10:50 a.m.	11:00 a.m.–2:20 p.m.	2:30 p.m.–4:30 p.m.	After 4:30 p.m.
Mon.-Tues.	$39	$39	$45	$35
Wed.-Thurs.	$50	$50	$45	$35
Friday	$55	$55	$45	$35
Sat., Sun. & Holiday	$63	$57	$45	$35

*Canton residents will receive $3 discount on prices above

9 Holes

	7:00 a.m.–10:50 a.m.	11:00 a.m.–2:20 p.m.	2:30 p.m.–6:00 p.m.	After 6:00 p.m.
Mon.-Tues.	$25	$25	$30	$25
Wed.-Thurs.	$35	$35	$30	$25
Friday	$35	$35	$30	$25
Sat., Sun. & Holiday	$35	$35	$30	$25

*Canton residents will receive $2 discount on prices above

Senior Rates *(55 & older)* / **Junior Rates** *(18 & under)*

	18 Holes	9 Holes
Mon. - Friday, before 2:30 p.m.	$35	$25

Rental Clubs

	18 Holes	9 Holes
	$30	$20

* All prices are subject to change.

Food and Beverage Service
Dining in the clubhouse and patio area.
Snack and beverage carts on the course.

Reservations
Reservations may be made in person or by phoning the pro shop. Visa, MasterCard and AMEX are accepted.
◆ Individual Tee Times can be made up to two weeks in advance.
◆ Tournament/Outings* 24-47 players, 60 days in advance. 48-72 players, 6 months in advance. 73+ players, 12 months in advance.
* Requires signed contract and $500 non-refundable deposit.

For Tee Time Reservations
(734) 397-6460
46500 Summit Parkway • Canton, MI 48188

that find all the pieces to the puzzle and master all four elements develop more strategic, well-thought-out, and effective pricing decisions.

Margin. Finally, margins need to be considered when establishing a price. Margins are the amounts an organization must consider to fulfill organization goals. These amounts vary depending on the organization's pricing objective. If a program cost $7 to deliver and an organization wants to make a profit, they could charge whatever the market would bear. Even though $10 may make them a small profit, consumers may be willing to pay $30 and therefore the profit margin could be much higher.

Determining the Price

Once an organization has identified the pricing objective and assessed the variables that influence the pricing decision, they are prepared to set the price for the offering. What the organization has learned in the assessment, however, may influence what type of approach they will take. What is of utmost importance is that organizations consider all known variables prior to determining the price. Setting price on demand and cost alone, while failing to address competition or margins, can be devastating. Table 10.8 discusses various approaches to establishing a price. Three of them—variable or differential pricing, market skimming or exclusivity pricing, and market penetration or discount pricing—are further explained next.

Variable or differential pricing is when an organization offers different prices to different market segments. This is a typical practice in many facets of the leisure and tourism industry, yet a foreign concept to others. Attractions typically offer groups of consumers lower prices than individual or transient consumers. Lodging properties typically offer discounts to partnered organization affiliates, such as

Craft costs include materials, facilities, marketing and instruction.

AAA or AARP, and offer lower prices to corporate consumers who provide the properties with a large number of guests each year. Entertainment venues and airlines offer different prices based on the type of seat a consumer prefers. First class or those closer to the "action" will generally pay a higher price than those willing to sit at the back of the plane or in the upper part of the arena or stadium. Even public leisure and tourism organizations often provide one set of prices for residents and higher prices for nonresidents. This too is a form of variable pricing called *scaling down*. This is when an organization knows that they may not sell all seats or tickets so they tier the price offerings. *Scaling up* is when there is one price for all seats or tickets because the orgnization knows they will sell out.

Another form of variable pricing is when offerings are priced in consideration of one another and given different prices. Examples of this are a one-year versus a six-, three- or one-month membership, or venue seats with different prices based on distance from the arena floor or stage.

Organizations may determine that setting a price very high is a strategy worth pursuing when they wish to capture the high-end users. The intent of *market skimming* or *exclusivity pricing* is to start high with the notion of lower it to attract additional market segments. The computer and high tech industry does this when introducing new offerings. The price will be highest when an offering is first introduced versus when something newer comes along that is faster, bigger, and fancier.

Market penetration pricing or *discount pricing* occurs in the opposite fashion of price skimming. This is where an organization decides to offer a low introductory price in an effort to attract a great deal of participants. New and emerging offerings may use this type of approach when the objective is to increase participation. The mindset at this pricing decision is the organization plans to increase the price at some point in an effort to achieve another pricing objective, such as making a profit or breaking even. Another belief is competitors will be slower to enter into the marketplace when they see there is little return because the price is so low.

One of the challenges of price penetration is increasing the price at some later point. Consumers used to one price point may not be pleased with an increase in price unless the value is established and brand loyalty exists. Inevitably as a price increases some markets may no longer be interested in the offering. This is to be expected because certain price points may have more appeal to certain markets. Even though Wal-Mart has been successful with its low price strategy, Murane (2002) suggests this is a difficult thing to do because it easily jeopardizes a brand's value perception.

However, this approach is worth considering if the increase does not impact the primary target markets the organization is interested in serving. One important consideration for easing consumers into a higher price is clearly notifying all consumers of an introductory price and available only for a predetermined time. Further, some organizations use coupons or other type of tangible tool to give consumers the feeling the price is only a "special."

Some pricing decisions are based on the psychological aspects of how people think about price, where "pricing is a marketing strategy intended to influence consumers' perceptions and decision-making" (Naipaul, 2002, p. 2). Organizations must evaluate if charging consumers $1.99 is different than $2.00. Some authors suggest it is and a higher demand results when prices are just below the nearest round figure (Coulter, 2001). People believe $1.99 is only a dollar and $2.00 is two dollars, not just a penny different. Individuals process and decode pricing from left to right whether price is in verbal or written form (Coulter, 2001). Organizations must also decide if they should charge for a program when the objective is participation. Oster (2000) stated charging a fee, even a nominal amount to cover at least some of the service costs, suggests to consumers that the service is of more value than something for free. Consumers in turn will take it more seriously. Some evidence suggests a nominal fee will increase commitment by attendees. Some organizations that experience initial interest by consumers who call to reserve a space then fail to show have implemented this type of fee and attendance has improved. Others suggest coupons can cheapen an offering because some consumers believe the quality/value is lower than initially perceived or the offering

---

Table 10.8
Approaches to Setting Prices

Types of Pricing	Definition	Examples
Variable/differential	Charge certain customers differently based on the capability to pay and incentive to use reward	Members pay one price; nonmembers pay another
Market skimming/Exclusivity	Customers pay for "exclusivity"	Premium prices for trendiness or what some people consider reflects high social esteem
Market penetration/Discount	Low prices	Customers buy because prices are low
Breakdown	Prices are broken down into palatable segments	A $1,000 membership sold in installments or explained as costing less than $2.75/day
Pay one price and Pay as you go	Pay one price and get unlimited use, or pay for each single use	Amusement Parks: pay one fee at the gate and ride all the rides all day or pay for each ride separately
Bundling and Unbundling	Sell services as a package deal, or broken up and sold separately	Selling programs as a whole, or splitting them up and selling them as separate units
Captive	"Locking" in customers by initially selling cheap, then charging a premium for necessary components	Signing membership contract then exposing hidden costs, or buying a cheap razor handle but blades that fit are expensive
Psychological	Prices do not approach what is perceived as too much	Charging $99 instead of $100. Listing members' prices next to what nonmembers pay.
Hidden costs	Not displaying extra costs needed to complete the service	Tipping, taxes, charging more for previously undisclosed parts or labor
Fixed to variable	One set price begins the process, the next costs are determined by use	Entrance fees followed by usage fees, such as paying to get into a bar, then for each drink
Creative variable	Setting prices according to certain time or length in an imaginative way	Selling sub sandwiches by the inch; selling boaters marina space by the meter
Price performance	Price determined by value perception	Museums ask guests to use their discretion when leaving a donation for entry
Differing segments	Same program sold differently (with different prices) to appeal to different customers	Athletics lessons priced for groups, children adults, and seniors
Product line	Prices arranged to get customers to focus on "deals"	Expensive goods/services are displayed next to more reasonable priced goods/services

may be overpriced in the first place. A potential problem exists when consumers who did not receive a discount feel neglected or offended.

Community organizations experience additional pricing challenges that other organizations do not. Sport and Recreation Victoria (1995) stated, "Pricing is an issue of perennial concern to recreation service providers because it is extremely difficult to develop a scale of fees which is readily accepted by the community" (p. 46). They further suggested this contention is for many reasons:

- different views of the role government should play in providing recreation opportunities

- varying opinions on the extent to which munici-pal assets should be managed on a commercial basis

- differing definitions of fairness and equity

- status quo based on past practices

- discrepancies in why fees are assessed, who should pay them, and the amount to charge

- the availability of different pricing strategies

- philosophical beliefs impact the way things are carried out

- resistance to change and the inability to deter-mine the basis of the existing pricing strategy

- sensitive political relationships and the need/desire for support affect management of issues

- ineffective data management of provision costs

Real Life Story: Ice Museum—A Distinctive Experience

Bernie and Carol Parks-Karl bought the Chena Hot Springs Resort from the Alaskan government in 1998. The resort was not a profitable venture for its past owners. Determined to make the operation a success-ful resort, the Karls' used their backgrounds as Alas-ka's largest recycler to create their own self-sufficient community over 60 miles from Fairbanks, Alaska. They sought to create Alaska's only year-round resort property. Today, winter is the busiest time of year despite record cold temperatures as low at -60°F. The Karls' formula is quite simple—meet the needs of their market using all available resources and leave visitors with memorable experiences.

Their property's master plan is a work in prog-ress. They create the Alaskan experience for visitors. They are not as concerned about high AAA and Mo-bile ratings as offering a remarkable, all-inclusive Alaskan experience. One of the ways the Karls' are acheiving this is by developing the first and only Ice Hotel Museum in the United States.

The Aurora Ice Museum at Chena Hot Springs Re-sort is now the largest year-round ice structure in the world. Created from over 14,000 tons of ice and snow, it is a constantly evolving structure. Twelve-time world champion ice carver Steve Brice and his staff created this work of art. All elements within the structure were carved by hand over many hundreds of hours, including chandeliers, beds, bar stools, and three-foot high chess pieces. Even the martini glass-es at the bar are carved from ice; popular drinks, such as apple martinis, are served in them.

The first structure in 2004 was an instant success, but was unable to withstand the 24-hour sunlight and 90°F temperatures of the Alaska summer. The Karl's used their knowledge and improved the pro-cesses so the structure could withstand both the winter and summer seasons by finding an alternative energy source to create and maintain the facility. The resort's unique ice structure is now able to be a year-round

facility because of the hot springs. A state-of-the-art absorption chiller uses hot water from geothermal wells to cool the building and an exoskeleton surrounds the ice hotel museum. This enabled year-round operation to be maintained at an internal temperature of 20°F. The Karls' knew their largely international customer base wanted this type of remarkable Alaskan experi-ence year-round and provide it.

This hotel/museum welcomed over 10,000 visitors in the summer of 2005 alone. It has four guest rooms, a wedding chapel which hosts over 50 weddings a year, five enclosed galleries including a 600-block igloo and castle bailey, and an Ice Bar with caribou-skin covered seats.

Today, the hotel/museum's occupancy permit does not allow typical overnight hotel accommodations; however, it does allow visitors to experience this unique facility in 12-hour increments. This is only the beginning for the Karls' unique way of creating expe-riences for the people they serve.

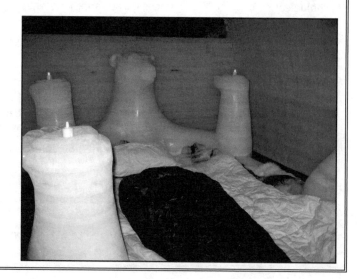

Evaluating the Pricing Decision

Monitoring participation and/or revenue or profit data is necessary to monitor the impact of the organization's pricing decisions. Detailed information regarding how revenue was earned is critical. For example, one organization may assume they were more successful if revenue increased from the previous year. This alone, however, may not be an indication of organization success because they also increased their prices at the beginning of that year. In assessing participation data, they may learn they had actually served less people than the year prior, but by charging more, offset the difference and made more money. It appears the increase in price either turned a particular market off their services, the service they provided did not support the pricing increase, or some people may have been unwilling to pay for the service provided.

Organizations should be concerned with using price as a tool for solving organization problems or issues. Some find price to be a "quick fix" for organization problems. Some assume if the price is lowered, then participation and revenue would increase. Price wars were a marketing strategy in the late 1980s and early 1990s and were found to be an easy-to-use but troublesome approach to solving these concerns. For example, two bowling centers are competing for league teams. In an effort to increase their participation numbers, one center decides to reduce the price for the league entry fee and the weekly cost to bowl. Once learning of this pricing strategy, the other center decides to match these prices. Once again, to establish its position as the most economical league in town, the first center reduces its prices again. The lowest price doesn't always do the best. Organizations that charge low prices need to sell more to makeup in total revenue. Ultimately, the consumer wins because they receive a very attractive price—but not for long. As the war continues, services begin to drop at the centers because they cannot afford to hire more staff or provide the services they had in the past. Eventually, neither center wins and they may even go out of business from using price as a positioning tool.

Price can also be impacted by other variables. For example, in an entertainment/event venue the popularity of the artist or success of the professional sports team will impact the price an organization is able to charge for tickets. In recreation settings, current trends or fads may be able to charge more because of heightened demand. Organizations that are able to anticipate and understand these issues will develop a more effective pricing strategy as a result. Zyman (1999) stated this is the largest form of marketing. Time of day the offering is provided, as well as day of week and season, also impacts the price that can be charged. Movie theaters often use this approach when they discount the midnight or daytime movie because demand is lightest during these hours.

Understanding the impacts of pricing decisions is needed to make subsequent pricing decisions. It is important an organization develop a system for evaluating this type of data to learn cause-effect relationships to prices and about price sensitivity.

Yield Management

Yield management is concerned with understanding the balance between the amount an organization sells of its offering at the best price possible. All too often leisure and tourism organizations measure their "success" in a linear fashion by examining the number of participants in a particular program, the number of tickets sold at an amusement park on a given day, or the percentage of seats filled at an event. These measurements are considered *perishable units* or *inventory*. The yield would be the comparison of an organization's perishable units or inventory by the number sold or consumed. An organization determines its yield by comparing potential inventory to actual inventory. For instance, the Pheasant Run Golf Club has the potential to serve over 6,000 rounds a day, yet serves, on average, a little over half of this between Monday and Wednesday. Therefore, there is an opportunity for the golf course to maximize its yield because it is only serving a 50% yield on those days (see Box).

$$\text{Yield} = \frac{\text{Actual Booking}}{\text{Inventory/Perishable Units}}$$

Determining the actual yield amount requires estimating revenue per unit or inventory. Therefore, when an organization offers variable pricing and different inventory is purchased at different prices, it must determine what the estimated revenue potential is for the given day. For example, in a 16,000 seat venue:

5,000 seats at $30/ticket = $150,000
4,000 seats at $45/ticket = $180,000
7,000 seats at $60/ticket = $420,000
Total Potential Revenue = $750,000
    Actual Revenue = $600,000 = 80% yield

Organization offerings not consumed that day are lost forever. Often in the leisure and tourism service industry, a yield left unsold can never be recaptured. Golf courses, lodging properties, entertainment venues, attractions, leagues, special events, programs, and sporting events all have offerings that if not sold on any given day, the opportunity is lost. This opportunity lost is a yield management issue. Yield management allows an organization to strategically organize an organization's inventory of offerings in a way to be sold as effectively as possible to achieve organization objectives. Organizations can open and close classes or change rates at any given point at any distribution source to achieve revenue or participation objectives. This strategy would seek to make money for the golf course and help the public organization serve more people. Regardless of the objective of an organization, yield management attempts to maximize the opportunities for organizations by combining the elements of pricing and distribution.

This concept is more common in for-profit leisure and tourism organizations, but can relate to public and non-profit organizations as well. Each leisure and tourism organization has a yield about which to be concerned. For example, a public organization trying to serve as many residents as possible by serving 20 in a crafts class with a potenital inventory of 20 (i.e., 100% yield). Lovelock (2004) suggests successful yield management requires knowing the various types of consumers served and the price they are willing to pay at any given time. Loyalty programs are designed to improve an organization's yield because returning consumers provide great benefits to organizations. An organization concerned about its yield tries to maximize an inventory and sell it as effectively as possible.

The airlines and the lodging industry are well-known for their yield management practices. They realize they have a certain number of seats or rooms to sell every day and use distribution and pricing to maximize their yield. In a 300-seat airplane or 300-room resort, the organization determines which physical distribution sources will be allowed to "sell" their offerings. They may decide to allow an Internet travel service to sell their rooms or seats within a specific price range, but allow another provider to sell their offerings at a different price range. They can turn their inventory of seats/rooms to various distribution sources on and off and change prices accordingly. They may find they are able to sell rooms and seats for more money when people call them directly versus allowing a discount travel provider to broker a certain number of seats/rooms (i.e., inventory). This can change by day of week, time of day, or time of year.

Organizations hire yield managers to do nothing else but manage the balance between identifying physical distribution sources and determining prices. This is why two people sitting next to each other on the same flight may have paid hundreds of dollars different for the same ticket. Four individual guests checking into a hotel may also be paying various prices for the same kind of guest room. Managing the balance between pricing and distribution is

not an easy task; however, it is a significant issue in all leisure and tourism organizations. The more flexible the organization is about adapting to opportunities, the better they are able to fulfill their organization objectives. The Internet has allowed many organizations to communicate with people quickly and provide opportunities to maximize yield for their organization.

The leisure and tourism industry will continue to build on this type of system for managing inventory that, if left unsold, can never be recaptured. Community programs, golf courses, entertainment venues, and even bowling alleys will begin to manage inventory on a day-to-day, week-to-week, and season-to-season approach to attempt to reach consumers and maximize inventory. Public recreation organizations will also address their yield issues and consider ways to fill those seats. Perhaps in the future, all leisure and tourism organizations will be able to connect to former craft class attendees to see if they would be interested in this class a week before the class is scheduled to begin... maybe even with a 25% discount since they were loyal consumers from the past.

Apply What You Know

1. Select a target market and generate a list of possible offerings a particular leisure and tourism service organization (e.g., a resort) could offer.

2. Select a target market and identify five distribution locations, sources, or service delivery options.

3. Evaluate the prices charged for offerings within the leisure and tourism organization marketing plan you are completing. Make recommendations based on determining a pricing objective, assessing variables of concern, and developing a strategy and price. Be able to sell these decisions to the organization by describing why you made the recommendations you did.

Key Terms

Competition	Market penetration
Cost	Market skimming
daySTAR	Organization offerings
Demand	Physical location
Distribution	Physical service delivery
Intangible offerings	Physical sources
Margin	Pricing

Product life cycle
Scaling down/scaling up
Tangible offerings

Variable pricing
Willingness to pay
Yield management

features, customer benefits, cost of production, competitors' prices and by getting feedback from consumers, salespersons, and consultants.

http://myps.sitesell.com/

Review Questions

1. Identify and describe the various forms of organization offerings.

2. Describe the elements of a product life cycle and one communication choice you would make for each.

3. What is regarded as the most important element of the marketing mix?

4. Identify the four steps in a pricing decision.

5. Describe the five variables that should be assessed to prepare for a pricing decision.

6. Name and give an example (not mentioned in the book) for five of the approaches to setting prices.

7. Explain how yield is determined and create an example to describe it.

Internet Resources

MatrixOne helps businesses to improve all the phases of the product life cycle from introduction and growth to maturity and decline. Matrix's services are directed toward developing, building and managing products.

http://www.matrixone.com

Adexa Product Life Cycle Management provides services for companies to plan, manage, and schedule product lifecycles by accelerating the introduction of new products and optimizing all product life cycle phases.

http://www.adexa.com/solutions/solutions.asp

Web Marketing Today provides information about Internet marketing with links to key articles, newsletters, books, and seminars. Valuable articles about product marketing, distribution, and pricing are included.

http://www.wilsonweb.com/wmt5/issue82.htm

Make Your Price Sell is an online service that gives insights for organizations on how to price their products. The technique used by the organization is based on the product

The *Association of International Product Marketing and Management* website includes articles about product marketing, management, and product pricing. AIPMM provides access to the latest information, training, and resources for product professionals.

http://www.aipmm.com/html/newsletter

References

Cohen, A. (2002). Pricing panic: Raise rates or stabilize? *Sales and Marketing Management, 154*(1), 13.

Coulter, K. S. (2001). Odd-ending price underestimation: An experimental examination of left-to-right processing effects. *The Journal of Product and Brand Management, 10*(4/5), 276–292.

Cross, R. and Dixit, A. (2005). Customer-centric pricing: The surprise secret for profitability. *Business Horizons, 48,* 483–491.

Donath, B. (2005, November 1). Marketers: Rethinking innovation approach. *Marketing News, 39*(18), 6–7.

Dresdner Kleinwort Benson/Accor. (2001). *Travel and tourism intelligence—The international hotel industry: Corporate strategies and global opportunities.* London, UK: Economic Intelligence Unit.

Frater, J. (1991, September). New profits from your current product lines. *Appliance Manufacturer, 39*(9), 29–30.

Hyland, T. (2003). *The global outlook for Internet advertising and access spending, 2003–2007.* Retrieved June 6, 2004, from http://www.pwcglobal.com

Kyle, G., Graefe, A., and Absher, J. (2002). Determining appropriate prices for recreation on public lands. *Journal of Parks and Recreation Administration, 20*(2), 69–89.

Larson, E. (1999, January). Fitness first! *Fitness Management, 15*(1), 37–44.

Lovelock, C. (2004). *Services marketing* (5th ed.). Upper Saddle River, NJ: Prentice Hall.

Murane, P. (2002). Low price no bargain as brand building tool. *Advertising Age, 73*(26), 34.

Naipaul, S. (2002). *Psychological pricing strategies and consumer response behavior: An empirical investigation in the restaurant industry.* Doctoral dissertation, The Ohio State University.

Nykiel, R. (2001). Technology, convenience, and consumption. *Journal of Hospitality & Leisure Marketing, 7*(4), 79–84.

O'Connor, P. (2003, February). Online pricing: An analysis of hotel-company practices. *Cornell Hotel and Restaurant Administration Quarterly*, 88.

Onkvisit, S. and Shaw, J. J. (1989). *Product life cycles and product management*. New York, NY: Quorum Books.

Oster, S. (2000, October 15). Pricing in the nonprofit sector. *The Nonprofit Times*. Retrieved August 29, 2005, from http://www.nationalcne.org/pubs/oster01.htm

Palmeri, C. (2003). An uphill battle on the slippery slopes. Can cheap tickets and snowboard "terrain" save the ski resorts? *Business Week, 44*, 1.

Pybus, D. and Janes, P. (2004). Expanding public recreation programs through partnership arrangements. *Current Municipal Problems, 30*(4), 408–422.

Rogers, D. (2003). Cultura to offer tailored holidays. *Marketing*, 2.

Shipley, D. and Jobber, D. (2001). Integrative pricing via the pricing wheel. *Industrial Marketing Management, 30*, 301–314.

Smith Travel Research. (2004). *Smith Travel Research announces major advancement in U.S. lodging industry performance tracking*. Retrieved June 8, 2004, from http://www.hospitalitynet.org/news

Solomon, J. (2002). *An insiders' guide to managing sporting events*. Champaign, IL: Human Kinetics.

Sport and Recreation Victoria. (1995). The pricing of leisure and recreation opportunities. Melbourne, Australia: *Leisure Industry Information Bulletins*, 4.6, 1–8.

Travel Industry Association of America. (2004). *New report shows use of Internet among travelers on the rise*. Retrieved July 17, 2006, from http://www.tia.org/research-pubs/topStories.html

U.S. Census Bureau. (2000). *Population profile of the United States: 2000*. Retrieved from http://www.census.gov/population/pop-profile/2000/chap10.pdf

Wakefield, K. and Blodgett, J. (1999). Customer response to intangible service factors. *Psychology & Marketing, 16*(1), 51–68.

Watkins, E. (2002). The travel agent: R.I.P. *Lodging Hospitality, 58*(5), 4.

Zikmund, W. and D'Amico, M. (1989). *Marketing* (3rd ed.). New York, NY: John Wiley & Sons.

Zyman, S. (1999, June 7). Marketing: Gurus. *Business Week, 3632*, 59.

Chapter 11

Promotional Brand, Collateral Design, and Events

Edited by Karl Olmsted, Chief Creative Thinker, Olmsted Associates Inc., Creative Thinking for Communications

Gregory and Jenna were a brother-sister team who volunteered to plan a family reunion for their mother's side of the family— a first in their family's history. Their mother had 11 siblings who in turn had 50 children, who in turn had over 120 children. As many as 300 people from 30 different states would be joining them for a weekend filled with activities for family members and their spouses. In an effort to develop a plan to accommodate all of these people for an entire weekend, they decided to host the reunion in a large tourism destination where they could access hotel accommodations, attractions, activities, food and beverage facilities, and at least one location for all 300 to be together for the actual reunion itself. They decided on two possible cities and contacted the area convention and visitors bureaus (CVBs) to gather general information on the area first. They e-mailed each organization and asked them to send travel guides and related brochures/information for their event. They informed each CVB what they were planning.

Within days they received both of the CVB's promotional materials. Community #1 provided a personalized letter to Gregory and Jenna and included a large meeting planner's guide with information on meeting space at all the area hotels and information about various attractions and food/beverage facilities. The letter acknowledged their event and explained how the information could be used to plan for their important weekend. The materials were professionally presented in four-color, glossy publications. Photographs enticed them right away as a town full of exciting opportunities for the families to participate. Community #2's materials came in a slightly different format. They included individual brochures from all 25 hotels and many area attractions, but did not have any type of meeting planning guide. Some of the brochures were four-color; others were one- and two-color with varying degrees of professionalism. the presentations certainly gave each community a different feel and presence.

Gregory and Jenna reviewed both communities' materials and websites to make their top selections in lodging properties and attractions. After reviewing the materials they leaned toward Community #1, but felt they just could not decide without visiting both, so they decided to make a weekend of it and drive to both locations. Even though they were fairly close each community, it had been years

---

At the end of this chapter, readers will be able to...

- Develop a brand image for an organization.

- Understand the distinctions in the promotional mix.

- List the various types of promotional collateral used by an organization to communicate with consumers.

- List the factors to consider medium and promotional collateral.

- Explain the purpose of an AIDA model.

- Show competence in collateral design.

- Understand promotional pricing practices.

- Identify event marketing practice.

since either had visited those areas' attractions and neither knew much about the lodging properties.

Are they glad they did! The decision was easy once they visited both communities. They even surprised themselves by jointly agreeing on Community #2 as the site for the family reunion. What surprised them the most when visiting Community #1 was the town's feel was much different than the publications suggested. The photographs were enticing, yet when they saw the sites they had selected from the materials and websites, they were very different than depicted. For example, what one hotel didn't tell you was their photographs must have been taken years before when the property was new. The facility must not have been updated in 20 years! In another they visited they were surprised to find single 20-somethings all over the resort; the photographs suggested a large family presence, yet no families were seen anywhere. The amenities and experiences provided reflected those for young singles, not a family market.

• • • • •

As much as an organization does not want to underrepresent their ability in promotional marketing materials, they certainly do not want to overrepresent it either. As discussed in Chapter 3, organizations create consumer expectations in many ways, one of which is their promotional marketing materials. Gregory and Jenna expected Community #1 to be very different than it was based on the high-quality, four-color, glossy, well-coordinated, photographed, and personalized materials sent to them.

As valuable as these materials were to create a professional, well-thought-out image of the community, the reality was the community was very different. The brand image portrayed was not what they experienced. Conversely, the community that undersold its image with less professional looking materials was selected. This could have been because Gregory and Jenna expected less from this community and their expectations were exceeded. However, Community #2 was fortunate to be considered. The lesson here is not that underselling an organization is beneficial because consumers' expectations will always be exceeded. Community #2 was lucky Gregory and Jenna were able to visit and see it firsthand before deciding; other consumers would have made the decision based on materials alone. What is important to understand is organizations and communities need to create a visual and auditory image that most closely resembles what consumers will experience. Failure to do so results in consumer dissatisfaction when organizations cannot deliver what it suggested or disinvolvement because consumers never make it to an organization due to the lower quality materials.

The premise of brand image, promotional materials, design, and events are the heart of the marketing, promo-

tional, and communication mix decisions. It is the transition activity between determining an organization's offerings and reaching consumers directly. Many authors suggest "promotion" is an all-encompassing term used to describe the communication plan process; however, it simply begins the communication process. This set of decisions creates the look and feel of the organization that reaches stakeholders and has a positive, neutral, or negative impact. An organization may have the best set of offerings to provide consumers, but they may never reach the people intended. A lot of great leisure and tourism ideas fail simply because no one ever knew about it. How organizations develop transitional activities and materials to reach consumers will be explored in this chapter.

Promotions are temporary changes in offerings and pricing used to create awareness and offer incentives. Promotion has been historically thought of as the fourth *P* in effective marketing and part of the communication plan, and has always lumped a variety of activities under this one umbrella. This is misleading, however, because elements within the promotional mix do not directly communicate with consumers or stakeholders. Just because an organization develops a brochure doesn't mean anyone reads it. Just because an organization decides to host a grand opening promotional event doesn't mean anyone knows about it or attends. Just because an organization decides to offer 2-for-1 memberships does not mean anyone knows about and acts on it. What it does mean is organizations are establishing the message(s) for stakeholders and the materials or temporary activities to achieve marketing objectives. These sets of decisions are so valuable and distinct to the overall marketing process they should be isolated and visited as independent, specific activities. Promotion is designed to establish the framework from which an organization communicates. Promotion is newly defined because it establishes the "communication" presence through the message (i.e., image), design of collateral, and promotional events.

The answers to these questions guide every promotional and communication mix decision:

- What do we want to happen with a specific target market?

- What is important to this market? Where do we find them?

- How will the market respond to messages we develop to achieve the organization's objectives?

An old adage states the entire promotional and communication mix to answer these simple questions:

Who…
says what…
in what way…
to whom…
with what effect?

Specifically, who (i.e., the organization) will say what (i.e., the message/brand identity that represents all marketing mix decisions) in what way (i.e., the communication mix decisions), to whom (i.e., the target market), with what effect (i.e., consumer feedback). These sets of decisions guide the promotional and communication mix decisions in the remaining chapters.

It's more of an image campaign than it was in the past.
Neil Neukam, Toledo Mud Hens

Brand Image

Brand image is the result of several activities, including brand identity and quality of service. The organization's image is probably the first aspect of marketing a consumer will encounter (Scott, 1996). The image of a community can change as well. In Gregory and Jenna's situation, one community did not present its image in a way that it could deliver. In Gregory's and Jenna's minds, they exaggerated what the community was about and what it could provide. Organizations are constantly changing offerings or experiences they provide to consumers within a community; being able to capture and communicate that image is difficult.

There are several ways in which an organization can understand what image to portray to depict their organization's (or in the case of a CVB, their communities) offerings or experiences most accurately:

1. Ask stakeholders (e.g., consumers, employees, volunteers, nonusers, board members) their opinion.

2. Evaluate differences in organization vision, mission, and perception of image.

3. Audit all marketing collateral and communication materials to assess uniformity, messages, and professionalism.

Marketing, promotional, and communication issues in the leisure and tourism industry are not well-studied (Johnson, Tew & Havitz, 2002). Johnson, Tew, and Havitz (2002) found people reacted differently to various promotional collateral materials sent to them to entice their inter-

est in attending a large homecoming event at a university. They used an experimental design to measure the impact of an informative brochure, an informative and persuasive brochure, a website, and a personal appeal. Measuring not only respondents attitude toward the materials but also their participation and intentions to participate, they found the personal appeal and the website were more effective than the brochures. In this instance, this market found these sources more appealing and valued. The leisure and tourism industry needs to continue to learn about consumer's reactions to communication mediums, messages, and materials. Is there a gap between what the organization image is and what they organization wants the image to be? Why is this occurring? How can the organization address this gap between their vision/mission and reality? Only if they understand reality can a true comprehension of image be obtained.

When establishing a brand image, remember an organization must be consistent and understand the most important message they need to communicate to consumers. What is most important to them? Chapter 8 further discussed brand issues and positioning statement development based on consumer needs. These statements are direct reflections of what is important to consumers. These statements convey to target markets what is important to them and what the organization wants them to understand.

It is easy to be a critic of all promotional materials and the image others portray of their organization or community, but it is very difficult to develop a comprehensive design plan that portrays an organization or a community in the best, most accurate way possible. Brand image is the result of many hours of design, analysis, and critique to develop the most accurate, positive approach to communicating to stakeholders about an organization, program, or in this instance, a community.

Selecting a Medium

A *medium* is any means used to disseminate information about an organization to consumers. Unlimited options are available to organizations to reach target markets. Understanding each potential tool and the pros and cons of each will assist in determining which are the best to select. A variety of tools will be explored in this and the remaining chapters. When organizations determine the tools they will use to reach a specific target market they must consider several issues. The factors used to finalize operational decisions (see Chapter 9) also relate here:

1. *Do we have the resources to do this well?* If an organization would like to do a commercial, do

Real Life Story: Design Changes at a Convention and Vistors Bureau

The Mt. Pleasant Area Convention and Visitors Bureau (CVB) is located in a small, rural community of about 30,000. The bureau markets to tourists and convention groups and represents the 1,500 hotel rooms in the market. In addition to a 20,000-student university, the community is also host to a large gaming venue. This multifaceted gaming venue is the community's number one attraction and is estimated at bringing over 15,000 people to the facility daily. Although gaming has been in the community since the mid-1980s, the large venue opened in the later 1990s.

The brand image the CVB has portrayed in its literature has varied over time. In the early 1990s, the CVB portrayed the community as depicted in the first brochure. This image was quite simplistic. It did not have a strong presence to showcase all the community's strengths but instead focused on one aspect. No real identity was established. To improve on this, they tried to create an image on their promotional materials highlighting a homey, folksy, and safe community... a nice place to live and a nice place to send sons and daughters to for their higher education. The community was largely known as the home of the univer-

sity. The school was the number one employer, and the community consisted mainly of students. The new look included positioning statements that described a location where a heart symbol was part of the logo and slogan of "in the Heart of Michigan." The CVB attempted to position the community in this manner. They realized the photograph from the previous brochure was limiting because a host of other leisure and tourism opportunities people could engage in were not well-represented in this collateral material. The next brochure highlights the CVB brand image in the mid-1990s.

The CVB revisited this image again and decided to depict the community in another way. The increased popularity of gaming in the community and the development of the large casino facility prompted the CVB to include this in the promotional materials. The university was no longer the number one attraction or number one employer. The gaming venue was now a popular reason for people to visit. The CVB knew it was time to establish a stronger image and show more appropriately how the community had evolved. The third brochure highlights a the "new and improved" image of the community as depicted by CVB promotional materials during the mid-1990s.

WOW!, Mt. Pleasant's new promotional positioning statement, described what the CVB hoped people would believe once they visited the community. This certainly wasn't the small town, folksy image portrayed in earlier years, but the community wasn't the same as it was before either. The use of fireworks, a couple dancing, and dramatic colors produced an image of the community as a fun, exciting place. Based on the photograph, it became evident the families depicted in earlier pictures were not the primary market of interest any

| Early 1990s | Mid 1990s | Late 1990s | 2000 |

they have the budget, expertise and facilities to produce a high-quality commercial?

2. *Does this medium match the time frame we have allocated?* Understanding each medium's time frame for production through publication may or may not match the organization's time frame for gaining exposure.

3. *What is the most effective medium for reaching the targeted market?* Organizations that understand their target markets inside and out select only those mediums that reach them directly.

Advertising in an AARP magazine to reach teenagers does not make sense. Not all mediums make sense for all markets.

4. *Will this choice produce a return on the organization's investment (ROI)?* Organizations must measure the return they anticipate based on the resources expended (e.g., financial, trade/barter, expertise, time) and ensure this is the best use of their resources. Just because a prime time television commercial could reach an organization's target market does not mean investing

---

Real Life Story: CVB—continued

longer. The 30-something crowd was what appealed to the community. Could the community deliver on this expectation? The university did not like the change in communication message because the parents of the students who attended the university would understandably be less than pleased to send their son or daughter to a place that was all about *WOW!* They disliked it so much that the university removed the cover from every guidebook before sending it to parents visiting for parent's weekend. This brand image obviously had challenges for the CVB as well— It did not communicate the community in the most accurate way possible. Fireworks and dancing opportunities were not readily available and stakeholders felt this was not an accurate depiction. The next group of brochures are from subsequent CVB materials.

This design continued to attempt to communicate the various activities visitors could participate in while in Mt. Pleasant. The range of activities included colle-

giate sports, gaming, and various outdoor activities. *WOW!* continued to be the positioning statement used because stakeholders did agree Mt. Pleasant had more than people expected. However, photographs used in some years were limiting because they were not all true. The photographs of a football player were not the university's team but rather one from another university. One photo depicted people dancing on a beach but the closest beach was over an hour away. Some photos were unclear and difficult to understand the meaning. The issue of creating an image that is more than what is offered was the challenge with these promotional pieces. The *WOW!* positioning statement remained; however, the look and feel of the publications had changed. These publications indicate how a community is challenged by creating an brand image that not only changes along with it but also accurately describes an experience that consumers will receive upon visiting.

2001

2002/2003

2004

2005

$500,000 makes sense to attract another 1,000 consumers.

5. *Have we used this type of medium before? What was the outcome?* An organization should evaluate past marketing efforts with this medium and reflect on the process, the outcome, and what was learned.

6. *Does this choice support our organization's culture?* There are unlimited options available to an organization, but it does not mean that each supports the mission, vision, and politics of an organization.

Overall, the more one knows about a target market, the better one can select the most appropriate ways to relate to and reach them. Always learn to think like the target market. Once an organization begins to identify the type of mediums it will use to communicate with audiences, it also identifies the promotional collateral it will need to reach these markets. These materials should be used to support chosen communication activities. Advertisements will need to be designed, flyers created, brochures developed, newsletters written, commercials produced, CDs burned, media kits made, photographs shot, and merchandise made. The variety of tools used to support the communication mix are called *promotional collateral*.

Promotional Collateral

Promotional collateral is defined as visual aids that support an organization's communication activities. Promotional collateral, special goods, and promotional items are considered attention-getting giveaways. They have a long shelf life that ideally provides a great deal of exposure. These are tangible objects consumers receive, and organizations can select from hundreds of items to use. There are, how-

ever, challenges with this form of promotion. They can be very expensive, it often takes time to personalize and order quantities, and organizations have to identify effective ways to distribute these materials to targeted consumers in meaningful ways. The scope of these materials is as broad as the imagination. Table 11.1 highlights common promotional collateral items.

Promotions can be used in two distinct ways within the leisure and tourism industry. First, promotions can act as appreciation or value-added items. These are sometimes referred to as *nonprice promotions* when they are designed to encourage repeat usage and loyalty. They also address the reflection stage (discussed in Chapter 2) for consumers because looking at a logo'd pen, photograph, or T-shirt can remind them of the positive leisure experience. Corporate sponsorship can defray the cost of the promotions, however, the sponsor maintains control of the message. Therefore, some organizations decide to purchase nonprice promotions themselves to maintain control.

Second, promotions can be used to entice participation with target markets. These are sometimes referred to as *sales promotions*. Price promotions can include discounts, free admissions, and value-added amenities to the experience (e.g., free lunch with a paid admission, first-class upgrade). Entertainment promotions can be nonprice or sales-related promotions where the consumer participates in the experience, such as fireworks, contests, special days, celebrity visits, or activities.

Leisure and tourism consumers may benefit from promotions geared to attract them to an organization or reinforce their decision once they arrive at the organization. The promotional Spider-Man hand given to consumers at a major league baseball game was a welcomed addition to the experience. However, this did not attract the consumers, it really showed that they were appreciated and was used as a value-added amenity. If the organization wanted to use promotions as tools for attracting new consumers then this would need to have been communicated by the organization prior to delivering the experience. Price-conscious

---

Table 11.1
Common Promotional Collateral

Postcards	Brochures	Letterhead	Business cards
CDs	Flyers	Posters	Annual reports
Catalogs	Point-of-sale displays	Exhibits	Coupons
Advertisements	Commercials	Contests	Giveaways
Sweepstakes	Photographs	Videos	DVDs
Mascots	Newsletters	Programs	Trading stamps
Novelty items	Merchandise	Sales incentives	Free samples
Banners	Websites	E-mail	Floats
Parades	Sandwich boards	Radio station events	Slogans
Themes	Donations	Gift certificates	Annual reports
Employee correspondence	Policy manuals	Want ads	Job announcements

consumers tend to search for sales promotions that further discount the cost of their experience.

In the leisure and tourism industry it was found consumers respond favorably to various promotions. Wakefield and Bush (1998) suggested promotions in the service industry are different than for products. They surveyed baseball patrons regarding their attitudes about sales promotions and found that nonprice promotions appealed to loyal consumers but did little to attract new ones, whereas sales promotions were popular with price-conscious consumers. Nonprice promotions appealed to highly involved consumers and sales promotions appealed to consumers who may not participate in the leisure and tourism experience if a price promotion did not exist. Therefore, organizations must thoroughly understand the market the promotion is intended for and the overall organization objective. If the baseball stadium is full on a regular basis (as the team is winning!) then nonprice promotions will be an objective worthy of pursuing. However, if the stadium has many seats to fill, then sales promotions may be the approach an organization should take (Wakefield & Bush, 1998).

The decision to develop a promotion based on an incentive or enticement needs to be determined prior to the actual design of the collateral piece. The style, message, and overall design may change based on the type of incentive provided. In addition, other factors may play a role in deciding which type of promotion to implement. The following list provides suggestions about what else should be considered to determine the promotional collateral for an organization:

- marketing objectives
- target market needs/interests
- product life cycle considerations (i.e., new offerings are promoted differently than mature ones!)

This group of Hurricane Katrina volunteers have T-shirts as reminders of their experience restoring tourism to the Mississippi Gulf Coast.

- organization's competitive strengths may be communicated more effectively with certain types of collateral
- quantity required to reach a market
- timing
- method of distribution
- message
- budget
- is it fun, unique, useful, and lasting?

In sum, organizations must analyze if their materials have a quality look; communicate a distinction; identify with a reflective symbol/logo, slogan, color, style, and look; and provide an appearance that is truly deliverable by an organization.

Developing Promotional Collateral

With thousands of messages confronting consumers each day, it is no wonder organizations strive to be the one seen, heard, and acted on. Part of the decision-making process is selecting the most appropriate medium to reach a target market and doing so with a meaningful message. Another decision, however, is reaching consumers visually in ways that provide meaning.

AIDA

The AIDA model has been around for over 70 years. This system is designed to help organizations develop collateral that produces results. Collateral should address the four elements of the AIDA model to ensure promotional tools are used in the most effective ways possible. Each letter of AIDA stands for an element—attention, interest, desire, action—that should be contained in each collateral piece.

Attention. Collateral should stimulate a target market to want to look at, read, and continue to pursue the material. It is designed to reach markets in meaningful ways and inform them of the organization's experience or offerings. A distinct, innovative identity helps organizations stand out from the abundance of messages trying to attract attention. Organizations do this in both the design and messages developed to communicate with target markets. These issues will be explored throughout this chapter.

Interest. The second phase is building interest where attention without interest serves no purpose. Collateral should introduce or remind target markets of the benefits of participation. Markets should understand how the organization benefits them directly and addresses their specific needs. The features outlined should be tied to these benefits directly. These benefits must be prominently displayed and easily understood. Are target markets excited or smiling when they see your materials? Cony (2002) suggested camp settings all too often fail to develop interest and instead provide "factual straight-and-narrow" materials because they are concerned they will not be trustworthy or taken seriously. Leisure and tourism organizations provide such unique experiences that this is the time to convey the benefits—it is not a time to be concerned with boring. Cony suggested camps use photographs of staff in outrageous costumes; campers laughing hysterically; quiet camper moments, such as reading in an Adirondack chair; and other visual realities. Before and after photographs used by health clubs and weight loss organizations are designed to do this in their promotional materials.

Desire. Collateral should persuade a target market to become motivated to participate in the organization. The design and copy should describe the pleasures of participating in the leisure and tourism organization's experience. Markets should understand the value of participation and feel they can enjoy it in advance.

Action. All collateral should provide a means for targeted markets to reach an organization where continued contact can be maintained. Organizations should identify a "call to action" request that will stimulate a consumer to respond. If an organization has appropriately developed attention, interest, and desire there is nothing worse than making it difficult for target markets to act.

This model is first considered by organizations when looking to develop collateral to support the communication mix. Once the overall premise of the piece is determined, then an organization can further develop the style of the piece keeping the intended outcome in mind (e.g., call to action vs. thank you).

Style

The look or feel of an organization's materials ideally have a predetermined style associated with them because the organization's brand and overall image should already be established. All materials have some sort of style, but those with well-thought-out, established styles make target markets want to read, see, or hear a message.

The style of a collateral piece must reflect the brand image and identity discussed in Chapter 8. Cohesion be-

tween all organization materials is critical if an organization places importance on developing a consistent, well-recognized brand identity. The style determined for the overall brand must be conveyed in all promotional collateral. Therefore, the logo should be reflected in the same manner (e.g., type, colors). However, this can be modified with consideration of the target market's specific needs to develop a collateral piece based on a specific style of importance or interest to a market. Organizations must always ask themselves if the style they have selected is appropriate for the target market. Does this style communicate a message? In the brochure sample in Figure 11.1, the style reflects the interests of a young person in a way that also appeals to a parent. The information is concise, detailed, and addresses issues a parent would be concerned with while engaging youth visually. There are many styles an organization can use to develop the look, theme or concept of promotional pieces.

Message

The specific message or words used to communicate with markets is also a part of the collateral piece that must reflect the style of the organization and the AIDA model. Although a style or theme helps to establish and communicate a message, elements within the words themselves should also be considered. The *message* itself is the information sent by an organization to an audience. The content is important but how the message is presented has been found to be especially important in gaining consumer participation.

Today, the trend in design is "less is more." Because people can be overwhelmed by too many messages or too much information, a simple, straightforward message is more likely to be acknowledged. Design today should reflect simplicity to engage readers and listeners enough that they commit to action. Perry (1999) stated saying everything about your organization will muddy the waters; developing one simple message will be more valued than several. This action may simply be visiting an organization's website for more information or even contacting the organization to participate in the experience. The key is to provide an adequate amount of information without overburdening consumers with nonessential information.

Zyman (1999) stated relevant marketing messages need to be sent. Organizations need to send reasons to consumers to buy, and promotional collateral can be used by organizations in a variety of ways to communicate with consumers. For example, brochures may be placed in travel welcome centers or brochure racks; newsletters can be distributed electronically, direct mailed, or simply placed on a desk within the organization; promotional merchandise may be provided at a direct sales presentation or offered to consumers as one of the first 100 in attendance; organization videos may be sent to the media, played during a community service presentation, or mailed to consumers; and coupons can be placed in newspaper advertisements or discount books, or passed out directly by employees to people they know could benefit. These various tools used to communicate with consumers and other stakeholders will be reviewed in Chapters 12 through 14. However, a specialized form of marketing communication has reemerged as another tool to share promotional materials—guerrilla marketing.

Guerrilla Marketing

How does an organization get a message out in a small business? The answer lies in a concept Jay Levinson first coined as guerrilla marketing. *Guerrilla marketing* practices have been evident for a number of years; yet, they have

taken on a new edge now being employed by all types of organizations both large and small. Also referred to as extreme marketing, grassroots marketing, and "feet on the street marketing," it has a surprise element in its approach (Hatch, 2005). The premise behind these practices is to reach consumers at the grassroots, sidestepping the traditional means of communicating with consumers. The large number of television, radio, print, and Internet ads has been the reason these practices have become more popular. These practices circumvent traditional means (Hays, 1999).

Hays (1999) suggested a way this occurs is through employee teams who promote organization products to younger consumers directly, face-to-face. Referred to as *foot promotion*, or creating your own word-of-mouth, organizations attempt to get more personal with consumers and develop instant two-way communication. Consumers may receive promotional items, such as free samples, coupons, or brochures from the teams who in turn are available for questions and encourage participation, purchase, or use.

Figure 11.1
A youth camp 8½ x 11 brochure with compelling photos and simple messages

A guerrilla marketing example is from the Big Apple Bagel store. Store co-owner/manager, Cindy Rood, likes working with people. She spends as much of her day at the customer counter interacting (i.e., marketing) with her customers. She gets to know them by name—not only what they order but also where they work. Every day she adds to her "informal database" the names of key individuals who make decisions regarding which sources to use for catering events and potential wholesale leads. Once she identifies a repeat customer she gives them a sales packet to take back to the organization's decision maker(s). This way of reaching the customer directly through one's daily routine is part of guerilla marketing.

The greatest opportunity for a sale is with your present customer. Therefore efforts are made at providing a quality product with excellent customer service and giving the customer a reason to remain loyal. Loyalty programs include daily specials, frequency punch cards, and bounce-back offers.

Cindy will devote an hour here and there to canvass the market area around her store personally. She will bring samples and leave literature. If possible she will try to speak directly to a decision maker. She makes it a point to get involved in the community. Product donations are given to area not-for-profits. Support is given to the local youth athletic teams. Fundraising programs are offered to area schools. Efforts are made to increase the word-of-mouth communication involving Big Apple Bagels. The goal is to add reach and frequency to a modest paid advertising budget that involves direct marketing, selected couponing, and newspaper inserts.

Mobile marketing is another term used to describe marketing efforts that are taken to consumers in large portable tractor-trailers where samples are provided to consumers. Mobility Resource Associates (n.d.) is a company which promotes organization offerings at large special events, such as the Indy 500. They suggest their organization is designed to provide experiential marketing where consumers see and feel an organization's offerings directly.

Viral marketing is another method that is growing in popularity as a tool used to communicate with target markets. In this instance the premise is to spread positive word-of-mouth advertising in a strategic way. The goal is for others to create a "buzz" and get people talking about the organization's products, services, facilities, or programs. It is essentially contagious just like a flu virus (Montgomery, 2001). In one instance, an internal person to the organization may start a chat room conversation about an organization's offerings in a positive way, pretending to be a consumer who simply enjoys the organization's offerings. Some use e-mail as the tool to infest a market with information on an organization (Bannan, 2000).

Yet, in another instance of guerrilla marketing, an internal staff member may throw a reception/party with the intention of getting guests' views of a new service they are offering. This type of approach is called *undercover marketing*—organizations deceive potential consumers by engaging them in product/service use without their knowing. In one instance, consumers were asked by two "tourists" to take their photograph. In this case, the tourists were actors and their intent was to get people to try the new cameras they were selling. When the Good Samaritan agreed to take the tourists' pictures the "tourists" talked to them afterward about the positive aspects of the camera. Bigge (2002) refers to this as *roach bait marketing* where unwitting consumers get a sales pitch by a seemingly ordinary consumer.

In all instances, these marketing tools are designed to connect directly with people in meaningful ways. How-

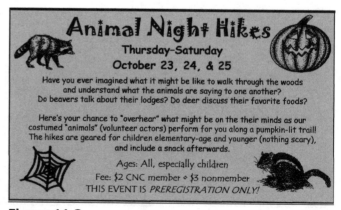

Figure 11.2
Features Only Example

Figure 11.3
Incomplete or Inaccurate Information Example

ever, the way these organizations are conducting their activities may be considered less than honest.

Messages should highlight an organization's strengths and competitive advantages as viewed by the target market. Information learned from the SWOT and competitive analysis will identify the elements to emphasize in promotional materials. Components of the message include four basic elements:

1. A headline that highlights a specific benefit (e.g., Have More Energy).

2. Simple, clearly organized body copy, with relevant information that answers who, what, when, where, why, and how.

3. Visuals for focal point and support.

4. A tag line or call to action.

Problem Messages

Features only. The newspaper advertisement in Figure 11.2 provides a list of offerings an organization provides. These offerings are actually features of the organization. The fact they offer leagues, lessons, and events highlights just what they provide. They do not, unfortunately, say how these things benefit individuals. They are not specific on why anyone would want to participate even though they use the NRPA's slogan of "Parks and Recreation… The Benefits Are Endless" they have not sold others on *how* they are endless. The concept of features and benefits will be explored in Chapter 14. Consumers need to understand how an organization's best features can benefit them directly.

Incomplete or inaccurate information. The flyer in Figure 11.3 does describe the experience in descriptive, benefits-based language. However, the organization fails to include all relevant information (e.g., Where does the event take place? What time on October 23–25? Who do you contact to register? How do you register?). Even though they did address who, what, and why, they failed to thoroughly answer when, where, and how.

The brochure in Figure 11.4 failed to mention the prices for the "sample" packages started at these prices and that all courses could not be purchased for the indicated amounts. The organization had hundreds of callers assume they could purchase a golf package at high-end golf courses for the

Figure 11.4
Incomplete or Inaccurate Information Example

Figure 11.5
Information Overload Example

price mentioned. The organization created an expectation based on the message conveyed in the brochure itself.

Information overload. Promotional collateral can be so filled with information that people fail to read it at all because it is too busy and too cluttered. The magazine advertisement in Figure 11.5 (p. 255) is so full of words, typestyles, and information that it hurts to look at it. It is unclear what they are offering or want consumers to purchase. People would really have to concentrate to understand what this is all about.

Once an organization determines the style and message for the collateral materials they then can determine the physical look of the piece by considering various design elements.

Design Elements

Various considerations are made in the design phase when developing collateral materials. As mentioned, the interests of the target market must be understood so the development of engaging designs becomes easier. Several elements within design decisions will be explored here.

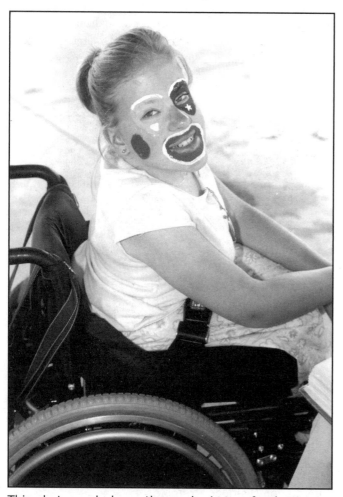

This photograph draws the reader in to a focal point.

Focal point. A focal point draws a reader's eye in and makes him or her want to continue to read. Look at any document and note where your eyes instantly go. Oftentimes it may be to a larger item, photograph or darker print. Regardless all promotional collateral material should have a strategically placed focal point on every page, and every item of a document should direct readers attention and entice them to continue. The eye generally travels upper left to lower right.

Photographs. Organizations use several methods to develop a focal point. Photographs of people are often used to make it easy for readers to relate to an organization because "a picture is worth a thousand words." The use of photographs are effective in publications because they personalize the piece, especially in the leisure and tourism industry when it is far easier to convey information and get people interested when they see what is possible. Photographs also make the collateral piece easier to design around. The people in the photograph must relate to the target market, however, or readers will have little interest. Photographs must be high quality regardless of whether black-and-white or color photographs are used. Captions also make photographs easier for readers to understand.

Anatomy of an ad/flyer. Almost all professional graphic designers and art directors use a formula of key elements in any print ad or flyer. If you look closely at print adver-

Figure 11.6
Anatomy of an Ad Flyer

tising in particular you'll start to recognize variations on a classic communications formula. Using the anatomy of an ad or flyer, illustrated in Figure 11.6, will help you to create more effective communications. The formula uses an attention-getting, message-defining kicker line (typically smaller); a large dramatic photo or illustration; a clever creative headline; descriptive body copy sharing more comprehensive details; a signature logo and branding slogan; and vital contact information, including a street address, telephone number, and web address. A "call to action" could be created by adding a term such as "Act NOW and Call," prompting the consumer to take an action.

Consistency is key. Lack of standardization is the number one mistake made when trying to manage an organization's communications identity by both professional and nonprofessional communicators. Consistent use of color, type, formatting, and application or presentation of the logo may sound like common sense, but you'd be surprised how difficult this can be. Large organizations spend extensive amounts of time and money developing standards and guideline manuals for managing their various applications consistently.

To apply basic standards to your communications you can begin by making sure your logo is presented consistently. Your logo should only appear in the organization's standard color(s) or white or black. Your logo should also be presented consistently because it is placed in various communications, without variation of size relative to any associated logotype or organization name. Other elements that will help you standardize your look are consistent use of a small family of typestyles.

Negative or white space. Negative or white space provides visual relief for readers. Less is more. One of the greatest design elements of all is the lack of design or white space. When creating print communications it is the one element you can use to make your piece as interesting, legible, and professional as possible. Keep in mind that audiences will always be turned off by busy crowded designs. A good rule of thumb is any ad or flyer should be composed of 40% or more of white space. KISS—keep is simple silly—even at the expense of editing unnecessary copy. Keeping your designs clean and simple is one of the best steps toward a professional look.

This allows readers eyes to easily flow through a piece. Professional designers tend to use this concept more often than those who have little experience. Often, leisure and tourism organizations producing their own materials feel the need to fill all the space provided, yet, allowing for this unused space not only helps develop a focal point it also creates interest. Figure 11.7 shows a simple advertisement with large size font draw readers to their simple message. The use of white space to compliment the focal point accents the message. In Figure 11.8, the basketball draws a reader's eyes into this advertisement for sport turf. Simple

Figure 11.7
Large Font Draws Readers In

Figure 11.8
Use of Lighting Draws Readers to the Basketball

wording and visual imagery make this message quick, easy, and attractive.

Levels of information. Consistent headlines and body copy patterns help the reader understand what they are reading and what materials are more important than others. To illustrate this concept, study the resort activity flyer in Figure 11.9.

Various levels of information are identified in this resort handout. For example, readers are initially drawn to the large headline describing what the publication is—a listing of what is happening at the resort this week. That is a level of information considered to be most important. Nothing else is similar to this and therefore, readers are drawn to the next most important level—the date. Even though each day of the week is listed first, the dates have more prominence and considered more important because of their size. The days of the week all have the same font size and style letting a reader know that they have equal importance. Finally, the body copy across days of the week all have equal importance. Readers would first be drawn to the bold heading at the beginning of each activity description and some would skim each of these body headings to identify those of interest and never read the copy below. In this instance, all activities have the same level of importance. The organization, however, could differentiate an activity they want to give more attention to, such as one that had low participation or one that is particularly noteworthy.

Fonts. Fonts must be used that support an image, theme or concept. They are used to help communicate a message to target markets. People use various style fonts and well as various size fonts to create a message to consumers. Even though hundreds of font choices are avail-

able to select from, most designed copy use a small variety that are easy to read, relate to a variety of audiences, and support the message. Those organizations that do not have a great deal of experience designing promotional materials tend to use a variety of font styles. There are, however, guidelines to using fonts that should be considered (see Table 11.2).

Popular font styles for copy design include Helvetica, Arial, Times, New Baskerville, Hedoni, Futura, and Optima. This is not to imply that all designs must include this style font. If a target market would be attracted to a look then that type of style should be used. For example, if marketing toward children, then the font may be more childlike because parents will understand simply by the use of the font style that the message is intended for children. The choice of font style supports the overall concept a designer is trying to develop. For example, a simple message regarding the features of a circus take on a different meaning when the font selected supports the message to an intended audience. In Table 11.3, which one would be most attractive to children and create a fun, exciting, childlike experience?

Example 2 communicates a message that the target market would look for. Example 1 appears matter of fact, simple, and straightforward, and Example 3 suggests a more formal experience.

Clip art. Different designers have beliefs about the use of clip art, however, most agree that clip art is often overused. It is a quick, easy and available tool that many

Figure 11.9
Levels of Information on a Resort Flyer

Table 11.2
Font Style and Size Considerations

---

1. Body copy should be 10 point to **12 point size font;** never less than 9 point (this is 7 point).

2. ALL CAPS ARE HARD TO READ AND SHOULD BE AVOIDED.

3. **This goes for all bold text, too.**

4. *The same can be said when using all italics.*

5. Limit the use of multiple font styles and *keep* to NO MORE than 3. Messages are difficult to read! Just because the tool is available does NOT mean it has to be used.

6. When using different font styles for headers and body copy, be sure to use those in the same "family." Helvetica and Arial are in the sans serif family; Times New Roman is in the serif family.

7. An effective technique used by professional graphic designers is mixing a sans serif font (for headlines and subheadings) with a serif font (for more readable, smaller level text and body copy).

think provide visual relief to materials and support a message. However, this is not always the case.

If an organization decides to use clip art, there are two general considerations:

1. Never use clip art that doesn't support the concept or message.

2. Never combine unrelated clip art styles.

If at all possible, organizations are better off using actual photographs to create a look or feel to communicate their message.

In the past several years, the availability of better quality, copyright free, stock illustration and photography has increased. It is now possible to download it directly off the Internet at sites like Gettyimages.com. This creates the benefit of being able to acquire just the right image, purchased nominally ($75 to $125) or even free, for your communications.

Color. Color is a powerful tool used to communicate messages in collateral materials. Certain colors can be used to support any concept or look. If the theme was mystery, the use of bright yellow and neon orange do not support that image whereas blacks, grays, and deep colors would. If the theme was a celebration, then bright colors would be effective choices versus beige and brown. Organizations should also use contrasting colors if using more than one. Yellow and white are not as effective choices as are black and brown. Common rules about colors include

1. Bold, bright colors attract attention and suggest lively and fun programming/activities.

2. Red is an action color that stimulates the brain's right hemisphere and helps people to recall something. It is difficult to read with a dark background and a lot of text however.

3. Yellow denotes happiness and is eye-catching. Reasoning is controlled by the brain's left hemisphere which is stimulated by this color.

4. Green is a stable, secure color.

5. Blue is soothing, quiet, cool, and orderly. It establishes credibility. It is not an effective color to help people concentrate.

6. Some colors, such as pastel yellow, bright orange, fuchsia, orchid, lime green or bronze, produce irritating or harsh effects.

Not all organization's budgets allow for four-color or full-color processing however, and many are limited in being able to use color financially. This does not mean, however, that organizations cannot use any color because black and white are colors too. One-color processing is common in leisure and tourism organizations who produce short-term, small-quantity collateral pieces. Even though black and white are considered colors, the options available to organizations is broader than that. An organization can maximize its use of color in several ways:

1. Select color paper to print on, thereby expanding the look to two-color processing.

2. Use a color other than black for ink, such as dark blue, to create a different concept.

3. Reverse colors so one color is the background (e.g., green) and the letters are white.

4. Produce a larger quantity. The price per piece decreases significantly when the quantity is increased.

Selecting colors to support a message is critical because the message may never be read simply due to color choices.

Table 11.3
Sample Font Styles

Example 1	Example 2	Example 3
Join us for...	Join us for...	Join us for...
Clowns	Clowns	Clowns
Cotton Candy	Cotton Candy	Cotton Candy
Games	Games	Games
Rides	Rides	Rides
Acrobats and more!	Acrobats and more!	Acrobats and more!
(Font: Verdana)	(Font: Comic Sans)	(Font: *Apple Chancery*)

In Figure 11.10 see how the evolution of brochures used in a leisure and tourism curriculum changed from 1982 to 1992 to 2002. The use of colors dramatically impacted the theme, look, and feel.

In 1982 the use of primary colors promoted the fun-loving, exciting type of academic major that would appeal to undergraduate students looking at a brochure rack filled with departmental brochures. The primary colors would appeal to those who wanted this type of career. (Remember, this discussion is about color—not the use of images in the brochure!). Plagued by image issues of only being a fun-loving and not a serious degree, the department chose to use simple colors (i.e., teal and gray) to communicate a more professional program in 1992. This type of look would not have appealed to those who grabbed the first brochure, but it did convey the "importance" and "seriousness" of this career and industry. The 2002 brochure combined effective elements from both the 1982 and 1992 brochures. The use of both bright and classic colors (i.e., maroon and gray) supported both the images of "fun and exciting" and a "professional program" in 2002. (The use of a full-color photograph helped too!). It is also important to note, the evolution of typography over the years—it is now cleaner, more credible, and offers greater readability.

Every organization changes and the brand identity must reflect these changes as well. Even in a leisure studies program, the image of the department must reflect the changes within the program, changes within the times, and changes within trends in design. Promotional collateral establishes a vehicle to communicate with stakeholders about an organization's image and must be revisited continuously.

The fascinating and challenging issue about collateral design is all of the design concepts reviewed will play a factor in the effectiveness of the message being absorbed by the intended audience. Each plays a role and cannot be underestimated. An organization may have selected appropriate colors, identified effective font style and size, and used high-quality photographs to convey a message, yet failure to develop a focal point and fill space may be the only reason the piece is not given any attention. As in Figure 11.10, each decade's brochure used a different style font to communicate the intended message as well as different imaging selections (i.e., clip art, nothing, and photograph). Each choice was supported by each individual design elements. Leisure and tourism organizations must pay particular attention to each of these areas.

  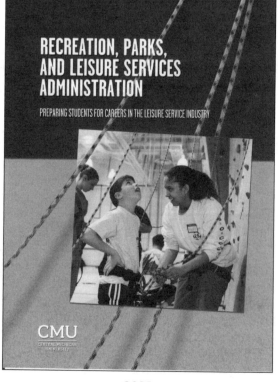

1982   1992   2002

Figure 11.10
An Evolution of an Academic Department's Image Through Promotional Design

Editing and Proofreading

I know, I know… What fool would produce promotional collateral and not check it for errors and omissions? Well, many professionals can share stories of the "piece that got away." As shown in Figures 11.3 (p. 254) and 11.4 (p. 255), this happens. In Figure 11.4, for example, the developers simply forgot to ad "starting at…" This resulted in hundreds of phone calls from hopeful golfers who wanted to play the area's championship golf courses at these low rates. To err is human; however, this type of error can cause significant impacts on the organization and the individual. Accuracy in communications cannot be stressed enough.

Techniques for editing promotional collateral include

1. Have multiple people who were not involved in the development process read it (i.e., fresh eyes and minds).

2. Read the message backward to identify misspellings and other errors (this way you are not caught up in reading what your wrote).

3. Develop relationships with proofreaders outside your organization for low-cost proofing (e.g., English teacher/professor, librarian).

Professional Quality Production

As stated, leisure and tourism organizations are faced with developing high-quality collateral with ever-shrinking funding. Aside from trade and barter options with printing service firms, leisure and tourism organizations can also develop high-quality materials internally. Several ways an organization can develop professional-looking materials, in-house include

1. Use paper weighted above 20 pound (i.e., common copier paper).

2. Use glossy paper to develop a polished look.

3. Print copies with high-quality printers (e.g., laser).

4. Take a desktop publishing class to improve design techniques and use software made for print design.

5. Use professionally designed preprinted templates customized for your organization.

6. Purchase noncustom, preprinted shells from your local stationery store.

Not all organizations can afford to hire design professionals to develop organization collateral. But then again, they can't afford not to if the organization does not possess the internal skills to do so.

Working With a Communications Professional

When fixed costs of communicating (e.g., any purchased media time, printing, staff resources, postage) are factored in, even when an organization is not working with a professional graphic designer or communications practitioner, it takes some resources.

Having a professional work with an organization offers many advantages. Professionals not only develop a communications strategy and improve the quality and professionalism of communications but also save money on larger projects. Targeting audiences more effectively and using printing specifications or production techniques that save money can achieve this. In many cases professionals can save an organization enough money to cover the fees for their involvement.

Even when organizations cannot afford design professionals they can apply the basic premises introduced in this chapter to develop more effective promotional collateral.

The Internet as a Collateral Tool

Internet technology affords communicators another important, relatively low-cost, and timely communications channel as part of an overall marketing mix. It is not only a source of information, but a vehicle to reach consumers with promotional materials. It is estimated that over 20% of all U.S. Internet users have redeemed a promotional coupon online (Nua Internet Surveys, 2002).

As discussed in Chapter 10, the Internet is used as both a distribution source and communications tool. Often the website itself is the source for both of these conditions to exist. The first step in integrating the Internet as a marketing and communication tool is to design an effective site. Once developed, an organization cannot rely on this alone and must strategically get consumers to the site through utilizing communication mix tools, including search engines, e-mail, Internet advertising, and publishing the organization's website on all collateral and promotional materials. Design of the site itself will be reviewed here; the communication elements will be discussed in Chapter 12.

Developing, improving on, or maintaining an organization website is a challenging, time-consuming task. There are so many issues to consider, such as layout, content, colors, photographs, links, and format. Simply having a website is not enough however—an organization's site must be effectively designed to meet the needs of visitors.

"Websites can be thought of as miniature information booths containing what an organization wants to make available to the public" (Poff, 1999, p. 2). Outdoor programs use the Web for a variety of functions, including (a) trip planning and facilitation, (b) communication between staff, (c) providing general contact and FAQ information, (d) sharing operational information (e.g., hours of operation, location, policies), and (e) sharing resource information through links to related sites.

Further, camps have been known to use Internet sites for reaching family members during a camper's experience with daily photos of activities and even Web cameras to watch them at camp. Information on staff members, weekly news, surveys for feedback, and direct e-mail access for questions, concerns or compliments (Salzman, 2000). More organizations are using virtual reality experiences and other multisensory systems as added features on their websites which are designed to engage consumers more regularly and keep them visiting their website.

Even aquatic facilities suggest what should be included in their sites. The basics include operating hours, facility features, programming schedule and details, and admission fees. Interaction with consumers is also critical. Sites include comments forms, online registration, chat time, and subscriber lists (Moore, 2001).

Friedman (2002) agreed. He found that a British food service company discovered a way to provide not only information on their website but also entertainment, hoping to appeal to consumer's needs. They added chat rooms and screensavers for website visitors to use. Organizations must design websites to be interactive with consumers because no other form of marketing communication allows this to occur so fluidly or thoroughly.

For an organization to develop and design a website that does what an organization would hope, they must consider the type of relationship they are seeking from consumers and other stakeholders and create a system to match these objectives (Rowley, 2001). Overall, sites should quickly communicate with visitors (a) who they are, (b) what they provide, and (c) how to navigate through the website. Further, websites must provide what visitors are looking for, or what customers want to accomplish by visiting the site. A homepage needs to do all this. If it does not, consumers will not access additional pages of information.

Leisure and tourism organizations should link organizations and resources that add value to their website and better serve their target market's needs. Further, these links should be supporting partners that match the organizations expectations regarding reliable, trustworthy organizations.

A multitude of sources suggest how to specifically design a website. A Google search on "Internet site design standards" produced 7,970,000 hits. Therefore, it is recommended readers consult various sources and design professionals when creating this important, valuable promotional collateral tool designed to reach consumers.

Direct consumers to websites with all promotional materials (e.g., billboards, brochures, stationary, signage). Organizations should also consider other aspects of their organization that reach consumers, such as automated voice mail answering systems. These should include information, such as whom to contact for further information and the website address. Stevens (2001) suggested organizations not only crosspromote their website but also the organization's telephone number or other ways to reach them.

Protecting the Brand Image and Identity

As discussed in Chapter 8, the protection of the brand must be maintained throughout the development and design of all promotional collateral. Guidelines are often established by organizations to facilitate this process. For example, a visual branding guidelines or a graphic standards booklet could be created for an organization that wants to ensure all staff protect the use of the brand. These guidelines establish allowable uses of the logo, slogan, and photographs as well as color, typology, and presence. These guidelines would be adhered to for all promotional materials including paychecks, advertisements, employee nametags, trophies, websites, and multimedia presentations.

This restaurant used a large promotional chicken to draw these bikers in on their 250-mile mountain biking trip.

Promotional Pricing

Temporary decisions to change an organization's prices (as opposed to a permanent change) is considered a *promotional pricing* activity. This type of pricing may come in the form of a discount coupon, special rate code, 2-for-1 deal, or some other type of affiliation. Many leisure and tourism organizations do it to entice participation, but sometimes at the expense of regular consumers.

Feinberg, Krishna, and Zhang (2002) found consumer preferences for organizations were negatively impacted by promotional pricing that provided reduced prices to new consumers over regular users. They suggested the deal percentage and the number of consumers made aware of the promotional price impacted the long-term influence. The more consumers aware of the deal and the better the new price, the more dissatisfied regular consumers will be. Further, they suggest organizations not overpromote to a market segment or an incorrect segment as a method for better managing the use of promotional pricing.

Promotional Events or Events Marketing

Promotional events are designed to stimulate interest in an organization's experiences and offerings. This is commonly referred to today as *events marketing*. Special events are temporary and not designed to be regular organization offerings like a league or annual special event would be. These are considered "shot in the arm" programs designed to increase awareness. They are developed for a variety of reasons and outcomes. Thse range from hosting a grand opening to increase awareness of a new organization or offering(s) to a celebrity demonstration to showcase and encourage participation.

Mead (2001) found automakers have developed leisure-and-tourism–oriented promotional events to capture consumer interest. They host outdoor recreation events and bring vehicles to these events, such as mountain biking, kayaking, canoeing, rock climbing, or hiking programs and competitions. Instead of focusing on mass media, automakers have turned to a more personalized approach that gains direct consumer feedback in the process. Events are considered the "ultimate face-to-face marketing medium" (Spethmann, 1999, p. 28). Often these events can be profitable endeavors for organizations in addition to achieving organization objectives.

Beer companies are partnering with campus recreation organizations to host special events, such as arm wrestling competitions (Steinbach, 2002). The nature and type of

events an organization can develop is unlimited. Examples of promotional mix items include the following:

- Host an open house to invite the target market to tour the new areas.

- Create coupons for the target market that provide a free meal for one.

- Establish a slogan for the department.

- Write and print brochures about each department and the overall organization.

- Work with a radio station on a joint promotion to educate people on the benefits of recreation.

- Have a department mascot that visits children in hospitals and schools.

Real Life Story:
Stars of the Moscow State Circus

The organizers of the Stars of the Moscow State Circus have developed a strategy to entice consumers to attend events by incorporating the use of hired professionals, designing tickets as promotional collateral, and creating a specific promotional pricing. Once the corporate office in Sarasota, Florida, has determined event locations local marketing organizations are hired to promote the circus in the town and surrounding communities. Through these professionals the areas are canvassed with a few posters in key locations and a plethora of tickets.

The tickets, which are much like coupons, are mailed or delivered to local businesses, schools, and organizations. They have been developed to utilize three design elements. Red, yellow, and white colors in the ticket draw attention; the art, placed on the front, is of interesting or well-known characters; and the word "free" in an enlarged font becomes the focal point.

The promotional pricing is achieved by offering one free child admission with the purchase of one adult admission. Parents take their children to see the two-hour event and save $7.50 per child. Adult tickets are $20 a piece. There are usually two shows per day. On average 2,000–2,500 people attend, often creating sold-out shows, all of which is done through strategic promotion.

- Buy a large number of trinkets to distribute with logo/name and slogan on them.

- Create a float to be used in all local parades.

- Create a point-of-sale display for school offices to promote your offerings.

The radio industry is well-known for its use of promotions to reach targeted markets. Mackin (personal communication, 2004) suggested the addition of community partnerships helped to leverage their listening audience from 3,000 to 8,000 average daily listeners. They added a resort giveaway contest, discount day featuring a local business, special event for working women, and a $5,000 shopping spree.

Apply What You Know

1. Identify one promotional collateral item the organization you are completing your marketing plan for could use. Design it using the guidelines provided throughout this chapter.

2. List at least three promotional events the organization you are completing your marketing plan for could provide to encourage participation and achievement of the marketing objectives.

Key Terms

AIDA	Promotional collateral
Brand image	Promotional pricing
Events marketing	Promotions
Guerrilla marketing	Sales promotions
Medium	Style
Message	Undercover marketing
Mobile marketing	Viral marketing
Nonprice promotions	

Review Questions

1. In the story at the beginning of the chapter, what was determined when Gregory and Jenna visited the two communities?

2. Name four actions that should be taken to understand an organization's image.

3. What considerations should be determined when deciding on a type of promotional collateral?

4. List six common promotional collateral items.

5. Identify and describe the elements of the AIDA model.

6. List three common message problems found in the design of advertisements, flyers, etc.

7. Describe the elements of design.

8. Create a guerrilla marketing tactic.

Internet Resources

GfK Gral-Iteo is a marketing research company for businesses that offers consumer research; market and competition research; brand, products, and services research; advertising; and public opinion research.

http://www.gfk.si/eng/2_3_brand_image.php

BrandingAsia.com provides resources for organizations who are interested in brand creation, development and management in Asian countries. Their website offers access to news, articles, case studies, and branding tips.

http://www.brandingasia.com/columns/temporal10.htm

Tutor2u.net brings together materials about a variety of topics mainly for teachers and students. The website includes materials related to marketing which discuss brand image and positioning, promotion, adverting, and relevant case studies.

http://www.tutor2u.net/revision_notes_marketing.asp

Ad Marketing Group specializes in advertising sales, custom publishing, and creative design. Their offerings range from logo design and letterhead to sale posters and banners.

http://www.admarketinggroup.com/pages/services_blueroom.html

Promo Magazine provides insights into using promotion marketing as a strategic component of the marketing mix. Trends, issues, articles, news, and stories on promotional topics are available on their website.

http://promomagazine.com/event

References

Bannan, K. (2000, June 5). It's catching. *Mediaweek, 10*(23), 20–26.

Bigge, R. (2002, July 29). Creative ads spark creative counterattacks. *Marketing Magazine, 107*(30), 8.

Cony, S. (2002, September/October). How creative! *Camping Magazine, 75*(5), 10–11.

Feinberg, F., Krishna, A., and Zhang, J. (2002). Do we care what others get? A behaviorist approach to targeted promotions. *Journal of Marketing Research, 39*(3), 277–291.

Friedman, A. (2002). British chain's Web methods click to boast guest loyalty. *Nation's Restaurant News, 36*(47), 58.

Hatch, C. (2005, March). When should you try guerilla marketing? *ABA Bank Marketing, 37*(2), 53.

Hays, C. (1999, October 7). Guerilla marketing is going mainstream. *New York Times*, p. C1.

Johnson, Tew, C. and Havitz, M. (2002). Improving our communication: A comparison of four promotion techniques. *Journal of Park and Recreation Administration, 20*(1), 76–96.

Mead, S. (2001, May 28). Marketers gain feedback, cost efficiency from events marketing. *Automotive News, 59*(32), 22.

Mobility Resource Associates. (n.d.). *About MRA*. Retrieved from http://www.gomra.com/about.asp

Montgomery, A. L. (2001). Applying quantitative marketing techniques to the Internet. *Interfaces, 31*(2), 90–108.

Moore, M. (2001). Water and the Web can work wonders: A good Web site can become an aquatics facility's most effective marketing tool. *Aquatics International* (Suppl.), S-4, S-6.

Nua Internet Surveys. (2002). *Online coupons are a hit with U.S. consumers*. Retrieved June 27, 2004, from http://www.clickz.com/stats

Perry, P. (1999, February). Creating effective display advertisements. *Funworld*, 81–84.

Poff, R. (1999). Outdoor programs online: Creating a link with participants, staff and community. *U.S. Indiana*, 2–7.

Rowley, J. (2001). Remodelling marketing communications in an Internet environment. *Internet Research: Electronic Networking Applications and Policy, 11*(3), 203–212.

Salzman, J. (2000). Blending technology with camp tradition: Technology can simplify camp operations, *Camp Magazine, 73*(2), 40–43.

Scott, J. (1996). Effective marketing. *RCRA Update*, 5–6.

Spethmann, B. (1999, May). In any event. *Promo XII*, 6, 28.

Steinbach, P. (2002, April). Participants wanted. *Athletic Business, 26*(4), 47–58.

Stevens, R. P. (2001). Time to decide: Integrate or disintegrate. *B to B, 86*(14), 20.

Wakefield, K. L. and Bush, V. D. (1998). Promoting leisure services: Economic and emotional aspects of consumer response. *The Journal of Services Marketing, 12*(3), 209.

Zyman, S. (1999, June 7). Marketing: Gurus. *Business Week, 3632*, 59.

Chapter 12

Advertising, Public Relations, and Crisis Communication

Edited by Connie McCann, Marketing Consultant

Dianne, Mary, Pam, and Kristie were college roommates who stayed in contact for over 25 years. They enjoyed a lifelong friendship that could be instantly renewed each time they conversed. They realized it was a special bond, even though they may not be in contact with one another as frequently as they would have liked because they lived in distant geographic locations throughout the United States. They were also working and raising families. Once every five years, however, they committed to a girls-only get-together in different locations to enjoy uninterrupted time together. They had already done the spa thing, cruise thing, theater thing, sun thing, and shopping thing, so they searched for their next adventure together. One leisure interest appealing to all four was a new passion for golf. They decided their next get-together would be to attend a golf school.

Mary and Pam did most of the planning because they were great organizers and the most avid golfers. They knew they needed a school that would address a variety of skill levels because Kristie had just joined her first league and Dianne started playing in grade school. They also knew

they needed a location that would include activities other than golf even though they would spend the majority of their time golfing. They needed a location that would provide opportunities to socialize and catch up, not just an intense school where they would play 36 holes a day and have time for little else. The school did not need to be for

---

At the end of this chapter, readers will be able to…

- List elements of the communication mix.

- Identify factors in selecting the communication mix in an organization marketing plan.

- Define and understand distinctions between advertising and public relations.

- Describe various advertising and public relations methods.

- Understand advantages, disadvantages, and costs of print media and multimedia sources.

- Write a properly formatted press release and public service announcement.

- Describe effective ways to work with the media.

- Identify strategies for crisis communication management.

women only. Even though price was a consideration it was not a primary issue because they did not make this trip often, and they had planned to pay for a very nice experience.

Pam's approach to finding the golf school for their trip was to search the Internet and canvas her *Golf Digest, Golf for Women,* and *Golf Illustrated* magazines. Even though her first choice for this trip was not to stay in her local area of Florida (a popular location for golf schools), she knew the owner of a local golf school who served on the local chamber of commerce board with her and thought she would visit his facility. Mary decided to talk to the pro at the club she belonged to and a few friends she knew who attended golf schools in the past. Based on their first steps, Pam identified three schools worthy of further investigating, and Mary found two that sounded like everyone would enjoy. Only one school was a duplicate, making both Pam's and Mary's lists. Therefore, in an effort to identify which of the four schools to select, they decided to contact each organization directly to ask questions and receive any promotional materials and pricing information they could.

From the list of four it was easy for Pam and Mary to decide the location for their trip. They chose the school both had put on their list of potential locations. This school seemed to reach them from all different angles while communicating the same, consistent message. Pam read about this golf school in an article on "Golf Schools" and visited their website, which not only addressed their needs but also provided up-to-date photographs to visualize the "experience." This same club was mentioned to Mary by her club pro and a friend of a friend who went to the school and was very pleased with it. She mentioned the school surprised her with a photo of her golfing (that she didn't even have to pay for) and the school still contacts her by sending golfing tips during the golf season even though she attended the school two years ago.

• • • • •

Organizations that use a variety of means to communicate with target markets and to create meaningful messages for consumers and potential consumers will have an advantage over those that do not. Organizations that put all tactical marketing resources into one basket may not achieve the objectives they want.

A variety of advertising, public, and community relations tools are used to communicate a message to consumers. In this example, Pam used Internet search engines to locate potential schools, spoke with someone who served in a community organization with her, and read articles and advertisements in golf-related publications. Mary used word-of-mouth to learn from people she respected and who were knowledgeable about golf schools. The people who spoke highly of the school not only experienced it but also received direct mail from the school, addressing Clawson

and Knetsch's (1966) reflection and anticipation phase. The types of tools an organization can identify and select from to reach consumers will be explored in this chapter.

To be successful in the recreation and leisure industry today, professionals must realize the value of using a variety of marketing and communication tools to share an organization's message, menu of services, or offerings. Organizations that do not do this will not grow or even maintain positive financial performance. Connie McCann, Marketing Consultant

Once an organization has decided what they want to occur in their organization (i.e., marketing objective) and what they will need to do in their organization for this to occur (i.e., marketing and promotional mix), they finally have an opportunity to share these decisions with the identified target markets through the communication mix. The communication mix incorporates a variety of tools and techniques designed to share an organization's message directly with their target markets. Organizations decide which of these will reach their targeted markets most successfully and develop action plans to achieve their marketing objectives based on these tools.

Even though all elements of the communication mix exist, not all organizations are equipped with the talent and expertise to utilize these tools effectively. Therefore, understanding each of these tools and the proper techniques for successfully utilizing them goes hand-in-hand. Chapters 12 through 14 will introduce tools and techniques to utilize and how to determine their value for achieving organization objectives.

The communication mix is the critical link between an organization and its target markets. Without marketing communication a terrible thing can happen… *nothing.* And, without properly implemented marketing communication a terrible thing can happen as well… *nothing.* Therefore, when to use and how to apply each of these tools is the final element to achieving organization objectives. Properly executed communication mix elements link targets markets to organizations and provide returns for both.

Organizations begin this process as they have the others—brainstorming all the ways they can reach and communicate with targeted markets. However, the challenge becomes identifying which tool or technique the organization should pursue and include in the final marketing plan. John Romero, a casino marketing executive, suggested in an article on direct marketing, "Market to your best customers first, your best prospects second, and the rest of the world last" (Raphel, 1999, p. 54). Walters stated they communicate all the efforts in their community-based recreation department three to five times in their marketing plans (Chaisson, 2002). The following list highlights additional considerations an organization should make. These will be discussed throughout the next three chapters:

- target market response/behaviors

- reach of choice

- impact on objective

- organization's brand image should be enhanced through this selection

- marketing objectives

- timing for the organization and deadline for the medium

- effectiveness of choice

- budget or trade opportunity— You may be able to make a large trade with one medium over another with a similar return. (*Note:* Cost may be influenced by size, color, location, and number of exposures.)

- return on investment (as average cost per exposure)

$$\text{Average Cost per Exposure} = \frac{\text{Cost}}{\text{Number of Prospects in Reach}}$$

Advertising

Advertising is probably *the* most common form of marketing, or at least what people think of first when they think of the term. Most people see, hear, and feel advertising every day, and most organizations have probably used advertising as a vehicle to communicate with consumers. Some suggest anywhere between 1,200 and 4,000 messages from advertisements are heard each day by consumers (Irwin, Sutton & McCarthy, 2002; Leger & Scholz, 2002; Mackin, personal communication, October 21, 2004). However, Tehrani (2002) suggested up to 90% of advertising dollars are wasted. This is due to developing ineffective advertising, including poorly designed, unimaginative, obscure, and dull materials. Based on this premise, some debate exists as to whether advertising is the most effective choice for organizations to reach consumers. Advertising is in essence paying for media-related attention; rhere are questions about whether a return for this expense is evident.

Reebok spends half of its marketing budget on advertising; sports, retail, and viral efforts make up the remain-

der. Cassidy (2002) quoted Povinelli from Reebok who stated they have had to change their mix in advertising, although advertising is still the tool they use for a broad reach. Various markets have specific communication needs. For example, to reach the growing youth market Reebok has added interactive displays in shoe stores and shoe displays in music stores. Several suggestions for improving the effectiveness of advertisements incllude the following:

Design and layout of ads. Poorly designed ads will not be read no matter where they are placed. Headlines and visuals are critical to gain attention. Body copy must capture readers, hold their interest, and reflect what appeals to each target market segment.

Positioning advertisements in publications. Some research supports that right-hand pages toward the beginning of a publication more effective than left-hand pages toward the back. Also, ads placed near related editorial information receive more effective coverage. (*Note:* Newspapers will not guarantee positioning unless it is a full-page ad; magazines will provide it for an additional fee.)

Size of advertisement. Larger ads receive more attention than smaller ones. Readers are more likely to remember full-page versus half-page ads.

Frequency of appearance. Ads need to appear at least 12 times to be considered in consumers' minds and encourage greater comfort in the organization's offerings (McCann, personal communication, January 5, 2006). Frequency may be increased by using daily versus weekly papers, putting three inserts in one issue, or having a "blitz" prior to a big event.

Color of ads. Color also impacts advertisement effectiveness. For example, red headlines are more effective. Yellow is a valuable background color shown to improve readability when acting as a backdrop for black or red colors. Further, four-color advertisements capture readers' attention better than black-and-white ads (Fisher, 2002; Tehrani, 2002).

These suggestions are not exclusive and do interrelate. For example, using the color red in an advertisement can be very effective, but not if you use a small font. Also, an advertisement may use the right colors, but a poor design loses the message.

Advertising Methods

Organizations can choose from many advertising methods:

- newspapers

- television (e.g., cable, local, national)

- radio

- magazines/periodicals/journals
- Internet/e-mail
- billboards/busboards/benchboards
- direct mail
- Yellow Pages
- electronic displays (e.g., LED strips, interactive computer kiosks)
- signage
- sponsorships
- Chambers of Commerce
- church bulletins
- cooperative or exchange advertising with organizations
- posters
- point-of-purchase displays
- grocery bags
- restaurant placemats
- bowling alley score sheets
- cash register receipts

Examples of advertising include

- a full-page advertisement in a magazine that targets the same market
- a listing in the Yellow Pages under "recreation," "athletics," "health" or related category
- a video of your department to play on a local cable channel
- a billboard to promote a department
- a website and/or e-mail distribution of letters/ activity reminders
- direct mail to past patrons
- a paycheck stuffer for large area employers to distribute to employees
- a bulletin board to post other leisure/recreation opportunities in the area

When making advertising decisions, organizations must consider what choice is best to reach the target markets, and the frequency and reach of each choice. *Frequency* relates to the number of times an organization will need to

use this type of medium to truly communicate a message to targeted markets. For example, placing one advertisement on the radio is not as effective as placing several advertisements on the radio. Frequency of a message impacts the effectiveness of the medium. *Reach* relates to the amount and type of consumers each medium can access. How many people pass by a billboard on an interstate versus a county road? What is the circulation of a local newspaper in Mt. Pleasant, South Carolina, versus San Francisco, California? How many people listen to one morning radio show over another and what type of market listens? In addition to these issues, related market segments that read, listen to, and watch these mediums must also be considered. Do families with children under age six watch shows after 9:00 p.m.? Do seniors listen to Top 40 radio stations? Do teenagers read the local paper?

Mackin (personal communication, 2004) shared that organizations need to hit target markets hard with an offer to act and hit them often—Let them see the organization brand all over the place in positive ways.

As highlighted throughout this text, careful consideration of the target market's behaviors by an organization will guide the organization's selection of the most effective communication mix items to use. Once again, understanding the needs and behaviors of the organization's target markets is *central* to effective target marketing.

The most common types of advertising mediums will be discussed in greater detail, including print media and multimedia sources. Print media includes newspapers, magazines, telephone books, and direct mail. Multimedia includes billboards, television, radio, and the Internet. Each of these has unique advantages and disadvantages to consider. For example, high-visibility posters are easy to produce; however, the message is often lost in settings where the organization's poster is one of many others. In addition, time is needed to deliver and post these messages to ensure exposure is gained versus simply mailing the posters to other organizations in the hopes they will display them.

In Table 12.1, each of the print choices is displayed. In addition, price ranges are provided according to various types of geographic areas. Rural, suburban, urban, and national classifications are used to estimate the costs associated with each of these four common print choices. For example, if an organization wanted to purchase a half-page advertisement in a rural paper they may spend between $400 and $1,000 per day, in a suburban market this price increases to $1,900 to $4,500, in an urban setting this half-page would run $36,000 to $73,000, and for a nationwide paper $47,000 to $162,000. Organizations must understand the costs associated with various advertising tools to determine what an organization can and cannot do.

Newspapers

Once considered to be the information vehicle where people access news, weather, and local, national, and international information, this communication vehicle is changing. Although many still read it, it has become less of a priority for many consumers because new sources of information have emerged, especially with younger consumers. The circulation of Sunday papers has dropped consistently over the last several years. This represents 40% of the newspaper industry's advertising revenue (Moses, 2003). Newspapers are no longer the timeliest source for information because it is now offered in electronic form as well which provides news every minute, every day. Pung stated in

Table 12.1
Print Medium Advantages, Disadvantages, and Costs

		Newspaper	Magazine	Phone Book	Direct Mail
Advantages		• Reach (quantity) • Immediacy • Time spent reading • Controlled circulation • Local emphasis • Free production/design	• Highly selective • Efficient • Long life • Display quality	• Easy to produce • High visibility • Free listings • Free distribution	• Selectivity • Broad reach • Controlled circulation
Disadvantages		• Reproduction quality • Messy • Reach (segmentation) • Short life	• Expensive • Ad variations • Production/design • Time placement sensitive	• Expensive • Deregulation • Multiple headings	• High costs • Timing • Junk mail image
Circulation, Ad Cost/Size (With Color), and Duration	*Rural (pop. 7,900)*	• Circulation 4,161 • $412–$1,074 • Half or full page • One-color, add $90; Four-color, add $240 • For specific location, add 10% • One paper, any day	Info not available	• Circulation 28,000 • $2,092–$3,800 • Quarter, half, or full page • Four-color included • Cover, inside cover, and back • One year	• $40–$150
	Suburban (pop. 38,000)	• Circulation 40,000 • $1,921–$4,428 • Half or full page • One-color, add $265; Four-color, add $585 • Any page except 1st • One paper, any day	• Circulation 16,500 • $600–$1,100 • Half page • Four-color, add $500 • One issue	• Circulation 30,650 • $5,600–$8,496 • Half or full page • Half page color, add $1,876 • Full page color, add $2,088 • Cover, inside cover, and back • 1 year	Info not available
	Urban (pop. 2,896,016)	• Circulation 679,327 • $36,540–$73,080 • Half or full page • Four-color, add $5,210 • For specific location, add $1,000 • One paper, any day	• Circulation 181,186 • $5,515–$8,380 • Half page • Four-color, add $2,856 • One issue	• Circulation 1,345,800 • $40,000–$300,000 • Half or full page • Half-page color, add $13,000; Full-page color, add $18,000 • Cover, inside cover, and back	• 4,000 names minimum • $100–$1,000
	National	• Circulation 2,136,068 • $47,500–$162,000 • Half or full page • Half-page color (M–Th) $75,400, (Fri) $92,000; Full-page color (M–Th) $115,800, (Fri) $141,300	• Circulation 21,289 • $76,935–$124,460 • Half page • Four-color, add $47,525 • One issue	• Dependent on business and advertising needs	• 1,000 names minimum • $160–$1,000

Chaisson's (2002) interview that newspapers have become less important in marketing for large county recreation department because there are so many more media choices and targeting smaller, more specific groups relies more heavily on other forms of advertising.

Friedman and Fine (2003) found the same trend in movie theater marketing. Historically 10% to 25% of a wide-release film's marketing budget was earmarked for newspaper advertising. Research suggests consumers have made up their minds about the movies they want to see before reading a newspaper. Newspaper advertising spending is slowing whereas "Internet outlays skyrocketed" by 70% in the same time frame (p. 17).

Newspapers end up complementing what organizations do in other forms of advertising. This medium has become more similar to television advertising as a supplement to a communication mix because it tends to be less personalized. National newspapers are published every day, while some local papers are offered daily, weekly, or monthly. Advertising is considered an integral part of a newspaper, and some look for the advertisements as much as the paper's stories. The advantages and disadvantages of traditional forms of newspapers were identified in Table 12.1; however, some of the problems with this form have been eliminated with electronic newspapers. The advantages of the electronic newspaper form of advertising are high reproduction quality, no ink mess on hands, a large reach, and a long life. Disadvantages, however, include limited access (only those with computers and Internet service may read this type of paper) and portability. There is limited comfort reading it at a terminal versus at the table or in a cozy chair, unless of course the person has a laptop. Advertising with electronic papers is different and organizations often rely on banner advertisements and search engines for consumers to learn about an organization.

Magazines

These glossy publications can be microtargeted to a large variety of consumers. The number of magazines has increased significantly in the past decade, creating the ability to target very specific market segments. High-end bicycle companies who would have relied on *Sports Illustrated* in 1980 can now specifically reach bicyclists who read publications such as *Bike*, *Mountain Biking*, or *Dirt Rag*. Case (2002) found that these new specialized publications, such as *Sports Illustrated for Women*, *Cycleworld*, *Power & Motor-yacht* and *Travel + Leisure Golf* were the only ones who improved in advertising in an oversaturated marketplace. The good news is that they have a long shelf life and are typically high-quality publications. Their cost can be a deterrent for consumers but annual subscription discounts often entice interested consumers.

Phone Book

The telephone book has changed dramatically since deregulation occurred. The greatest challenge for an organization is to identify which telephone books to advertise in and to determine if the target markets use them to access information. Often considered a good referral base for consumers, many view Yellow Page advertising as a "cost of doing business." They provide a 24-hour reference for people and are available in every home and business. An organization's decision to place larger sized advertisements rests in knowing how market segments access organization-related information because the cost for the phone book is surprisingly expensive. A half-page advertisement could cost $300,000 per year in an urban market. Because the amount can be a challenge, national companies offer cooperative advertising in Yellow Pages, which is helpful to organizations. For example, Schwinn may assist a bike shop with advertising dollars to be listed in the ad.

Another challenge for leisure organizations is identifying the Yellow Page categories to be listed under. A health club could be under recreation establishments, fitness centers, exercise and physical fitness, or wellness. Yellow Page companies handle these issues differently and organizations must be aware of all available phone book choices and their requirements.

Understanding target markets' use of the Yellow Pages is important. An organization recently kept track of how consumers heard of them when they called for general information on the telephone. They learned through simple pencil-and-paper analysis that certain types of consumers used certain types of telephone books. Based on their findings, they decided to place more specific versus general organization advertisements (e.g., to the family market) in two of the four area Yellow Page books.

Direct Mail

This has become a very popular targeted approach to reaching consumers that directly fall in an organization's targeted markets. It is one of many forms of direct marketing where, in a personal approach to getting into consumer's homes, customers are more likely to see the advertisement and it will receive more personalized attention than those advertisements targeting larger market segments and areas. Ninety-eight percent of U.S. homes are accessible through direct mail (Peterson, Bryant & Franklin, 2001).

More challenging for those organizations employing this type of communication, however, is the junk mail image. Derryberry (2000) suggested Americans receive more than 350 direct mail pieces each year. International markets do not receive nearly as much—Switzerland ranks second at 120 pieces per person. As more organizations use this type of communication, consumers are less likely to give each personalized attention. Therefore, one key is personalizing the direct mail piece so the generic junk mail objection is overcome. Rohrich (1998) suggested the senior market enjoys this form of advertising because they make more rational than emotional decisions. Organizations such as travel companies have found great benefits in providing well-informed pieces to this market segment.

Arnold and Tapp (2001) conducted a research study to measure 18 types of direct marketing, including direct mail in the nonprofit arts industry. They found that the 200 art organization respondents indicated, "The extent of direct marketing methods employed does not significantly determine performance whether measured as sales revenues or fundraising dollars" (p. 47). Therefore, the data supported the notion that direct marketing activities must be tailored to specific targeted markets. Further, they found that newer forms of direct marketing (e.g., direct response advertising) produced greater sales and fundraising results than traditional methods whereas the opposite held true when organizations looked to use direct marketing as an educational and promotional tool. Friesen (2006) suggests the importance of making the cost of postage count. He further suggests organizations ask for referrals, generate Web traffic, and ask for consumer opinions. Making every piece of mail count is critical. Invoices and account statements should be sent under the same marketing thought process.

Database marketing has enabled organizations to be more responsive to organization issues and demands. For example, when Hyatt Hotel Corporation took over a hotel in Los Angeles, they direct mailed existing Hyatt customers who they knew traveled to the area to announce their newest location instantly because their database of over 2 million frequent card holders and 300,000 leisure travelers provided a easy source to do this (Egol, 1995).

Often organizations send direct mail to large quantities of existing and potential consumers. Direct mail can be very costly, and unless the message is sent first class (which increases the cost) there is little control over the timing of market segments receiving the information. At least once each month something seems to come through the mail that is already outdated.

Organizations must have a database from which to develop a mailing list. This database must be updated and accurate; this alone can be time-consuming. Migala (2002) stated that a study by E-Mail Knowledge showed an e-mail address has an 18- to 24-month shelf life. One organization recently shared they were embarrassed by how many calls they received each month after sending the organization newsletter to people who indicated their names were spelled incorrectly or the person no longer lived there. They sent their publication via bulk mail and, therefore, did not get "incorrect addresses" or "sender unknown" items returned. They just continued to send to everyone on the list—whether they were accurate or not was another question.

Databases can be established internally by using an organization's existing consumer information (e.g., memberships, registrations, loyalty cards). Organizations can also gather consumer information from other sources, including board members, guest books, suggestion boxes, and visitors. Externally, databases can be purchased or shared through membership lists, rosters, subscriptions to publications, and zip code geographic lists. External sources for database access to targeted markets include

- professional association membership lists
- organization partner consumer list (e.g., a community recreation organization partners with a travel organization and share their databases with each other)
- list brokers for mail, e-mail, and fax addresses
- magazine or publication subscribers

The cost for each of these databases varies. Some sample costs for various external databases include

- association list—nominal fee if related to association mission
- partnership—no cost
- list broker—http://www.infousa.com, $950 to $1,250 for a mailing list of 10,000 listings in a predetermined zip code
- magazine—*Ski Magazine* with 296,000 active subscribers cost $85 per 1,000 names

A variety of services provide lists for a price. These list brokers provide a range of services from fax, e-mail, and traditional mail lists to managing organization databases. Table 12.2 (p. 274) provides a list of various list brokers (Twenty Top B-to-B List Brokers/Managers, 2001).

Organizations must be careful to only share their databases with others when consumers are aware of the possibility and approve. Nothing will make a consumer angrier than when they feel they have been "sold off" to another organization and begin receiving information that they do not want. Joint partnerships are appropriate, however, when an organization not originally given the information communicates without the partner, consumers can become angry.

The design of direct mail includes two pieces: the envelope that needs to entice a reader to open it, and the letter that directs a call to action (Peterson, Bryant & Franklin, 2001). Mitchell (2001) suggested self-mailers (the envelope and letter are one connected piece) are a way to avoid having to design two pieces because consumers quickly learn direct mail design techniques to envelopes and begin to throw them away even before being opened. In addition they are much faster and less expensive to produce.

These four print-oriented mediums only represent a small portion of possible advertising vehicles. Four common multimedia sources are identified in Table 12.3. In addi-

Table 12.2
List Broker Organizations and Contact Information

Company	Website	Telephone	Key Lists
24/7 Real Media	http://www.247media.com	877-247-2477	Technology, SoHo
Abacus	http://www.abacusdirect.com	303-410-5100	SoHo, Office Products/Furniture, Computers/Technology, Ad Specialty
Advanstar Lists	http://www.advanstarlists.com	888-736-8547	Advanstar Materfile, Pharmaceuticals, Telecommunications
American List Counsel	http://www.amlist.com	800-252-5478	McGraw-Hill, Dow Jones, National Seminars, G. Neil, IDG
DecisionMaker Media Management	http://www.dm2lists.com	800-323-4958	Martindale Hubbell, Decision Maker IT Marketplace Database, Decision Maker E-mail List Masterfile
Direct Media	http://www.directmedia.com	203-532-1000	Newsweek, American Management Association, Ziff Davis Media
Dun & Bradstreet List Services	http://www.dnb.com	800-234-3867	D&B Hot List, D&B Domain Name, Fax File, Telecommunications File
Edith Roman	http://www.edithroman.com	800-223-2194	Fred Prior Seminars, Career Track, DigiKey Electronics, Edmund Scientific
E-Post Direct	http://www.epostdirect.com	800-409-4443	Bill Communications, Sys-Con Media, Post Newsweek Tech Media
IDG List Services	http://www.idglist.com	888-434-5478	Computer World, InfoWorld, Network World, The Industry Standard
Info USA	http://www.infousa.com	800-321-0869	Auto Dealers, Auto Body Repair, Physicians & Surgeons, Attorneys
Kroll Direct Marketing	http://www.krolldirect.com	609-275-2900	Beyond Computing, Target Marketing, Sterling Publishing Group
Lake Interactive	http://www.lakeinteractive.com	914-925-2400	The Economist, Economist.com, New Media, Edgar Online
List Services Corporation	http://www.listservices.com	203-743-2600	Harris InfoSource, U.S. Manufacturing, American Online Business Direct, Hachette Filipacchi Business DirectBase
Merit Direct	http://www.meritdirect.com	914-368-1000	Advertising Age, HelloDirect, Efax.com, J2 Global Communications, AllBusiness.com
NetCreations	http://ww.netcreations.com http://www.postmasterdirect.com	212-625-1370	IT Professionals, Business Opportunities, Sales Management, SoHo, Webmasters
Penton Lists	http://www.pentonlists.com	216-696-7000	Electronic Design, Internet World, Industry Week, Machine Design
VentureDirect	http://www.venturedirect.com	212-684-4800	Adweek, Brandweek, MediaWeek, DMNews, iMarketing News, American Lawyer Media
Yesmail.com	http://www.yesmail.com	650-620-1200	BizTalk.com, iSubmit.org

tion to highlighted strengths and weaknesses, the costs in a rural, suburban, urban, and national market are shared.

Billboards

Billboards are large, visual displays that are both stationary and mobile. They include everything from large signs along highways to the sides of buses, park benches, barn walls, trucks, kiosks, and even bicycles. Typically they have fairly high reach and frequency but this, of course, varies by location and mobility. Some methods are more measurable than others. Standard roadside billboards are measured by the average amount of traffic or vehicles that drive by each day. Thus, organizations understand that investing in this roadside billboard will produce a certain number of impressions per day.

Table 12.3
Multimedia Advantages, Disadvantages, and Costs

		Billboards	Television	Radio	Internet
Advantages		• Awareness/impact • Readability • Targeted message • Continuity	• Reach • Easy identification • Audio/visual recall	• Targeting • Flexibility • Intrusiveness • Reach • Frequency	• Call to action • Accessibility • Creativity
Disadvantages		• Duration of readability • Graphic research • Visual desensitization	• Expensive • Production time • Audience fragmentation • Zapping • Wasted reach	• Fragmentation • Accessibility • Zapping	• Intimidating • Limited accessibility • Data management • Visual desensitization
Average Cost, Type, Features and Duration	*Rural (pop. 7,900)*	• $300–$470 • 30 sheet 14'x48' $60 for lighting; $110 to create advertisement • 30 days	• $82–$120 • Cost determined by peak hours (5 p.m.–11 p.m.) vs. off-peak • 30 second spot, run once	• Coverage area: 15,100 • $13–$21 • Cost determined by by peak vs. off-peak • 30–60 second spots; runs 7–11 times weekly, 156 annually	
	Suburban (pop. 38,000)	• $450–$1,030 • 8 sheet 6'x12' • $150 space rental; $300 for one-color, $350 for two-color, add $110 per sheet for four-color • 60 days at 6 locations	• Coverage area: 326,000 • $35–$400 • Cost determined by peak hours (7 p.m.–10 p.m.; Sun 6 a.m.–10 am) vs. off-peak • 30-second spot, run once	• Coverage area: three towns • $61–$100 • Cost determined by peak (5 a.m.–10 a.m. 5 p.m.–8 p.m.) vs. off-peak • 60-second spot, run once	
	Urban (pop. 2,896,016)	• $5,515–$8,380 • 30 sheet 14'x48' • Four weeks	• Coverage area: 70,000–575,000 • $50–$15,000 • Cost determined by peak hours vs. off-peak 30 second spot, • run once	• Coverage area: 75 miles • $700–$1,200 • Cost determined by peak (5 a.m–10 a.m.) vs. off-peak (10 a.m.–7 pm) • 30–60 second spot, run close	
	National	• $50,000–$100,000 • To reach 50% of the population $50,000; to do well $100,000 • Four weeks	• $15,000–$200,000 • Cost determined by peak hours (8 p.m.–11 p.m.) vs. early morning and daytime • Run once	• Coverage area: 1,000+ stations • $5,000–$20,000 • Cost determined by peak vs. off-peak • 30–60-second spot, run once	

With mobile types of billboards, however, it is not as easy to measure the number of impressions (Daniels, 2000). Mobile billboards include semi-truck displays that are driven around key distribution areas to gain exposure. Daniels (2000) indicated bike couriers attached a banner to their bike frames and for over two months exposed an organization's brand to consumers in between their 7,000 and 8,000 stops. Regardless of the measurement challenge, this is viewed as the second most popular tool in advertising—second only to the Internet. Overall, billboards remain a popular medium. Not only have the number of drivers increased, the average driver spends more time on the road than eating meals (Edmondson, 1998).

Billboards are a good reminder medium that can target a message very simplistically. Potential challenges include the number of words consumers can read (an average of 7) as the person or advertisement passes by (average read time is 6–10 seconds) and being limited to those who happen to pass by versus finding those to target (http://www.billboards.com). Billboards can be directional or informational. Figure 12.1 highlights a directional billboard.

Three considerations for any billboard advertisement are: (a) directions to help consumers find an organization, (b) effective messages to promote a specific interest to a target market at a certain time of the year (i.e., it should identify the organization's uniqueness and be as simple as possible), and (c) effective design.

One trend in billboard design is developing motion activated billboards, talking billboards, and interactive billboards, where consumers can participate in an engaged activity, such as kicking a virtual soccer ball or painting in a virtual picture (Pierce, 2003). Extended shapes and 3-D features are added to contrast the simple rectangle to draw attention. Further, digital ink technology will allow billboards to be changed instantly based on viewer reactions, time of day, location, sales results, or current events (Powell, 2003).

Television

As the excitement medium, television has enormous reach. It is often (mistakenly) taken as believable and real. *Marketing Week* reported that advertisements with both auditory and visual content were more readily recalled than auditory content alone (Benady, 2003). This suggests the value of a medium that engages multiple senses. The cost of advertisement production and the advertisement itself makes this choice not often available for many leisure and tourism organizations.

The most widely watched U.S. sports event, the Super Bowl, sets television's highest advertising rates (Crawford, 2005). This figure continues to climb—averaging $2 million in 2003 and doubling the cost from ten years ago. Advertisements that aired during the 2004 Super Bowl averaged $2.4 million per 30-second advertisement (Crawford, 2005; O'Connell, 2003). Yet, these organizations are willing to spend this because they believe there is a return for their investment. O'Connell (2003) supported this notion by measuring over 1,500 opinions regarding Super Bowl advertisements. Five days before the Super Bowl and 24 hours following the game, consumers responded to questions regarding their intentions of consuming advertisers' offerings. O'Connell found, on average, 37% of respondents indicated their interest in seeing featured movies whereas only 28% indicated they had interest prior to seeing the advertisements. Organizations with less brand recognition (e.g., Quizno's; myFico.com) found more consumer awareness and purchase intent than brands with greater recognition. This investment, however, is still costly. Of those advertisements receiving a distinction of the ten best Super Bowl ads (as determined by a *USA Today* poll), only two continued to be advertisers in 2003 (Thomaselli, 2003).

A Canadian study of over 1,500 people found that four out of five consumers felt there were too many commercials on TV, with women more often than men stating this was

Figure 12.1
Sample Directional Billboard

the case (Leger & Scholz, 2002). More than half, however, indicated they do watch commercials some of the time, whereas only 9% never watch them. To ignore commercials most read something instead or flip through channels. Few (3%) turn the TV off. However, television remains "the most pervasive leisure-time activity in the United States" (Frank & Greenberg, 2000). Based on these difficulties, advertising prices are lower today than in 1997 according to Lee (2003).

Cable TV and local TV coverage, however, is a more affordable alternative for many organizations and appears more targeted. Advertising revenue has dropped for national network TV but grown in regional and cable TV (Sweet, 2002). Certainly, the advent of the remote control and systems that totally eliminate advertisements has made this choice less popular, but the advent of more targeted programming through digital and cable capabilities has provided more specific options for organizations to consider to reach specific market segments. Timing of the message (when the target market is watching) and during a program the target market would watch are important considerations.

One TV advertising development over the past ten years has been the introduction of direct response television (DRTV) advertisements. These advertisements solicit an immediate response from consumers as they provide an offer during the viewing period. This type of advertising has grown considerably because organizations have not only found results but also are also able to directly measure the impact of this form of advertising (French, 2001, 2000). Danaher and Green (1997) explained there are three basic elements of this type of advertisement: (a) it provides a definite offer, (b) all relevant information is provided in the commercial, and (c) consumers are instructed on how to access or purchase the offering (e.g., through a 1-800 number). DRTV differs from infomercials with the same three characteristics because DRTV only runs a maximum of 60 seconds.

Organizations that employ these strategies are able to immediately measure the impact of the commercial and its timing. Danaher and Green (1997) analyzed 12 advertising campaigns and found DRTV advertisements were least cost-effective for stations during soap operas and dramas and most effective during sports, comedies, and off-peak world news. Afternoons provided the best responses; both morning and afternoons were highly cost-effective. Ads that ran earlier during a show produced higher results as did commercials of longer duration.

Another rising trend in gaining television exposure is sponsorship activities or branded entertainment, also known as *advertainment* (Berger, 2003). This type of effort allows an organization exposure during the television show itself. For example, a Marriott brand logo was prominent in a movie scene where the actors were going into a hotel; soft drinks are readily displayed in actors' hands; and certain food brands are shown in actors' refrigerators. Benady (2003) suggested there has been a significant rise in broadcast sponsorship, yet organizations are hesitant because the measurability of its impact has not been well-studied. Popular television shows, such as *Sex and the City*, highlighted the significance of this type of medium. Berger (2003) suggests this form of advertising will increase significantly, and more brands will be apparent in the entertainment industry as movie and television makers search for revenue streams and organizations search for more brand exposure.

Radio

Radio advertising is effective for calling consumers to action. It easily targets radio listeners because stations reach specific market segments too. Radio is able to reach consumers in automobiles, at their workplaces, outside, or in their homes while they are doing other activities. Therefore, this is a good reminder medium. Digital, satellite, and Internet radio have expanded radio's reach potential. However, channel surfing poses even greater challenges than before as well as advertising-free stations growing in interest. Limited broadcast ranges may not reach some potential markets, but overall radio be a very effective choice. Organizations who use this medium must remember that timing of advertisements and a high frequency to constantly remind consumers is critical. DePelsmaker, Geuens, and Vermier (2004) state that frequency in radio advertisement is important for ad recognition. It was predicted that frequency would increase as the numbers of messages consumers were exposed to increased (Myers, 1993). Today there are more messages hitting consumers than ever before. Therefore, organizations who place one advertisement for 52 weeks will see less return than those who use all 52 advertisements in one month. Should leisure and tourism organizations have limited resources to afford high frequency, Leutz (2004) suggests radio advertising can also be used and have an impact on sales/participation if the "advertising exposure (is) in close proximity to the purchase occasion" (p. 22)

Internet

The opportunity for advertising has expanded largely because of emerging and advancing technologies. The Internet is a cutting-edge medium and the most creative choice. Few limits have been placed on this medium as compared to others. This tool should be used by *all* leisure and tourism organizations. Consumers should have access to an organization 24 hours a day, 7 days a week, year-round even if the organization is closed at times. An organization's brand can be communicated continuously. A website not only allows consumers year-round access but also may indicate to consumers that an organization is up-to-date and less likely to be a fly-by-night organization. A study of the Sporting Goods Manufacturers Association (n.d.) suggests that most all agreed the Internet will have a positive impact on organizations' business in the future, most used e-mail (94%), most accessed industry and competitive data (85%) and over half (52%) felt their organization's website was extremely important to maintaining a competitive edge.

The Internet is a distribution channel in both the marketing mix and communication mix tool. Interactive marketing, including websites, Web advertising, and e-mail marketing, have grown considerably as their role in the marketing, promotions, and communication mix is expanding (White, 2002).

The Internet has several advantages over traditional advertising mediums. First, it can easily solicit consumer feedback. Second, it can track consumer data and provide a database of e-mail addresses from consumers and potential consumers. Third, it can provide a great deal of information in an organized and not overwhelming format. Finally, the Internet is less expensive than many other mediums. Some consumers do not have access to the Internet however; others find the medium intimidating. Consumers also suggest slow and overly complicated sites will receive little attention.

Advertisers use the Internet to reach certain market segments. Migala (2002) found that sports marketing has turned to the Web to attract 12- to 24-year-olds. The Internet, like other media choices understands that they must use this to pursue certain target markets and that the messages must be focused on the needs of these markets. Korgaonkar and Wolin (2002) interviewed over 400 Internet users from a large southeastern metropolitan area to understand behaviors of those with heavy, moderate, and light Internet use. They found that heavier Web users believed that Web advertisements were more entertaining, enjoyable, informative, and helpful (but harder to understand) than lighter users. They also liked advertising better and bought more on the Web. They suggested that developing one type of Web advertisement may not appeal to all types of users and the Internet market could also be segmented according to preferences. There are many sources to gain assistance in the ever-changing world of Web advertising. A list of sources is available at the end of the chapter.

Web advertising is similar to other advertising means. Advertisers provide exposure to a number of consumers, and the advertisements are viewed similarly to traditional methods. Organizations must concern themselves with the timing, production, medium deadline, and process and guidelines for Web advertisements. Every organization will have particular guidelines, requirements, and deadlines it should know in advance. However, Web consumers "surf" and look for information they seek (versus being presented with an advertisement) and may or may not access one organization's information, as they may be overwhelmed with possibilities (Rossiter & Bellman, 1999).

A variety of ways exist for organizations to use the Internet for advertising purposes, including the development of banner advertisements, pop-up screens, rich media formats, and contextual advertising.

Banner advertisements. The first and most popular form of Internet advertising, banner advertisements, are also the most common form of Internet advertising. A "banner" shaped advertisement is displayed on an organization's website, highlighting their brand identity. However, some suggest users ignore banner advertisement and that fewer than one out of every 100 are read and clicked through and those people do see are not recalled (Shaffer, 1999). In an effort to produce advertisements that are read, several technologies have been used to create more effective advertisements such as floating, expandable, and wallpaper advertisements in addition to those identified next.

Pop-up screens. This type of advertising system on the Internet has been described as inviting as fingernails on a blackboard and have often been regarded as digital intruders, though users of this approach have found favorable results. Pop-up screens are advertisements magically presented to Internet users at any time, in any location. They may or may not have any interest to the user, however, they slow access to the intended site and ultimately gain exposure for the pop-up organization as people cannot help but read the screen before clicking it away to return to cyberspace. Pop-up windows appear automatically when a user enters a new page whereas daughter windows appear when a user clicks on a banner advertisement and splash screens appear to reinforce a message or introduce the site. Superstitials even play after a user has left a webpage (Hamm-Greenawalt, 2000).

Rich media formats. This type of advertising includes full-motion video and audio components. It is more advanced and creative than banner or button advertisements. Although historically viewed as negative because they slowed systems down, this is no longer the case (Hyland, 2004). Intermercials use this media to entertain and encourage interaction with consumers. Maddox (2005) states online video advertisements are being embraced as technology continues to improve and formats become standardized. *B-to-B*'s 2006 Marketing Priorities and Plans research found marketing executives estimate 72% of respondents will increase online spending while 33% will increase print spending, and 6% broadcast spending.

Contextual advertising. Hyland (2004) suggested this is the newest form of advertising. Organizations bid at an auction to have their advertisements strategically placed in ways that reach more consumers. Their advertisements run on high-visibility websites and are placed next to valued content. For example, a news story about the benefits of exercise may be followed by an advertisement for exercise equipment, a health club, or an online exercise monitoring system that provides daily fitness support.

Each of these advertising tools via the World Wide Web costs the organization money to produce and deliver. Other Internet communication tools have production costs (e.g., staff time, consulting expertise) but cost little to nothing to deliver (e.g., there may be costs associated with developing an e-mail address list, but no cost to send it to the address list once developed).

Even though there are distinct advantages, most agree that this should not be an organization's only form of communication. A hybrid approach utilizing a mixture of communication tools to achieve an organization's objective has been found to be the most effective choice. As a result, however, more and more traditional communication tools are being simplified with shorter more specific messages that direct consumers to the organization's website for more information.

As discussed in Chapter 10, the Internet is not only viewed as a distribution but also a communication tool. An organization's Internet website links consumers to the organization where they can purchase or consume the organization's offerings/experiences. A technique to enhance this linkage beyond those discussed includes e-mail, search engines and brand spiraling.

E-Mail

E-mail is the 21st century's method for communicating and is an inexpensive and easy communication method. More e-mail messages are sent daily than first class mail delivered by the U.S. Postal Service. As a result, organizations are focused on using this simple tool to communicate with stakeholders. Martin predicted as many as 1,600 messages daily would be sent to consumers in 2005 (Martin, 2001). Consumers also enjoy receiving e-mail in this way. The International Association of Assembly Managers (2003) found their members preferred the e-mail version of their newsletter versus the print version. Seventy-eight percent of respondents indicated they preferred the new method of sharing information over the latter.

Therefore, e-mail has developed (and will possibly continue to develop) into a valued, yet potentially, overused and misused form of marketing communication. Organizations must find ways to break through the myriad messages sent via electronic means. Several ways in which organizations do this include

- Focus on target market needs.

- Consider ways to reach through spam filters, including the following: (a) subject line should be less than 40 characters, should be benefit focused, and should NOT contain the words advertisement, free, or $ characters; (b) body text should NOT contain the words order now, today, or money back; and (c) avoid attachments and use links to the organization's website instead.

- Send messages during business hours versus overnight because organizations may clear junk mail first thing in the morning.

- Ask consumers for their e-mail addresses in all database gathering methods (e.g., registration, website guest book; Go-To-Market Strategies, 2003)

Think about the behaviors of market segments that use e-mail as a form of communication. Which are they more likely to access on a daily basis: their e-mail account, the Internet or their post office mailbox? Frequent e-mail users access their e-mail more often than once each day and learn to expect others to do the same. Eighteen- to twenty-four-year-olds treat their e-mail as *the* form of communication. The first time I had a student e-mail me about an assignment question they had when their paper was due in an hour enlightened me to this issue. This student expected me to be on my e-mail account as they had been— regularly throughout the day. Any e-mail communication will only be as strong as the quality of the database.

Several e-mail messages most any user receives are uninvited messages. These types of e-mail correspondence are called *spam*. Somehow, someone found the e-mail addresses and sent a message to any e-mail address they could access. As a result, consumers are more skeptical about to whom they provide their e-mail address. Although organizations may feel they have "reached" more potential consumers, the reality is very few of these will produce a desirable action. However, e-mail messages designed to create an emotional connection with a user have greater impact, therefore, organizations must find ways to do this. Wright (2001) suggested organizations must engage users quickly. He states that asking questions whether useful (e.g., satisfaction survey) or fun (e.g., trivia) and providing rewards (e.g., free tickets, night stay, membership) for doing so help get people connected. Further, make users feel the letter was specifically for him or her—not a mass e-mail. Do this by customizing the letter. Be careful not to bombard users with e-mail messages once the organization realizes this technique is effective. Remember the target market's needs and share information of meaning to them. Even more ideal is permission-based e-mail. Users on these lists have given permission to organizations to directly communicate with them, therefore, these messages are most likely to be read.

In addition to spam filters there are other ways organizations are blocked from reaching consumers via e-mail. ISP-block of incoming or outgoing mail occurs when an ISP develops a list of denied connections. It is more common to see a blocking of incoming messages; however, some ISP's are known to block outgoing messages as well. Antispam organizations are hired by ISPs or consumers to manage the influx of unwanted e-mail (e.g., Brightmail, Postini) and public lists are maintained by volunteers to eliminate this type of e-mail (e.g., Mail Abuse Prevention System [MAPS], SpamCop). ISP and user content filters keep junk mail to a minimum and can be controlled individually by eother the user or by the organization (Popov & McDonald, 2004).

Listservs

Listservs are groups of targeted consumers with a common interest who are accessible via one e-mail address. Individuals subscribe to the group because they have interest in the topic or information provided. Some listservs are designed to deliver a message to a targeted audience and encourage website traffic. Many groups have developed listservs, including associations, special interest groups, organizations who desire sharing updated offering information, educational institutions, and other groups of people who have a common interest. Because there is only one e-mail address, this type of tool can be used more easily than individual e-mail addresses and subscribers can be added or deleted quickly. Often organizations use a listserv internally to communicate quickly with stakeholders; however, listservs are being used more for target markets and those with common interests.

Search Engines

Entertainment and media projections suggest that from 2003–2007 Internet advertising will increase substantially, and one of the largest growth areas is in keyword search engines (Hyland, 2004). This system is when organizations pay for favorable placements within search engines for their Internet advertising. Those paying money for sponsored links will gain exposure before others.

Free and low cost tools provide an organization the opportunity to be found by consumers who are surfing the Web in search of information. Search engines are, in essence, a computer program designed to identify information on the Internet. They examine webpages automatically and, using algorithms, make decisions on a page's topics and then add selected keywords to their giant databases. When they finish, the search engine retrieves an organization's URL if the noted keywords are used to describe the search. Each search engine operates differently and should be evaluated based on how they operate and how an organization can be accessed successfully (Law, 2000; Raeder, 1997). Search engine management is how organizations strategically approach connecting their organization to the surfers.

E-Professional Commerce Solutions (2003) found search engines were the most important source to find a Web address and that search engines were most valuable for comparison shopping, travel, information/news, and music. They are, however, only as effective as the word(s) used by a consumer to find his or her information. Only if an organization selected the same word(s) will the match be successful. Search engines examine the page title, keyword meta tags (i.e., a preprogrammed list of words or phrases people might use when searching for an organization's offerings) and body text. Therefore, organizations must ensure their HTML tags reflect the site's content. Seventy-three percent of respondents found the design of the search engine is very important because the text of the entry must be clearly arranged, and the title of the website included (E-Professional Commerce Solutions, 2003). For example, if a consumer enters the phrase "recreation center in Baltimore, Maryland," a site will only be found by the search engine if an organization developed its keywords by using the same terms/phrase. The leisure and tourism industry is particularly challenged to find the word(s) to describe their experiences and offerings because there are so many ways to do this. For example, over 28,000 hits were found from the mentioned entry (on MSN's search engine), the first was the Department of Recreation and Parks, the City of Baltimore, Maryland—a success! However, if the consumer was not looking for public facilities and was instead searching for a commercial operation, then they would have to search through 28,000 hits.

This process can be free or can cost an organization if they desire another company to manage this process for them and/or pay the search engine for "pay-per-click" systems. They can be managed internally or for as little as $8/month it can be managed by an outside organization (e.g., Direct Search Engine Registration; http://www.dsr1.com). In this instance, they will submit an organization's information to over 400 search engines and links to gain exposure for an organization.

Links to sites are inexpensive ways to develop a site and to expand the reach to others. Organizations can request links on industry sites, request reciprocal links from partners, and share the organization's site on mailing lists and news groups (Go-To-Market Strategies, 2002).

An Enquiro study prepared by Hotchkiss, Garrison and Jensen (2004) found that even within search engines, user patterns differed related to gender, age, income and education. Google users had higher incomes, loyalty and levels of education,s and were more satisfied than other search engine users.

Brand Spiraling

Harvin (2000) stated brand spiraling is a strategy used for organizations to ensure their Web address is communicated through traditional media sources and designed to attract markets to the online site. Driving traffic to an organization's well-designed and informative website can enhance awareness and participation because more specific details can be provided to address individual market needs. For example, Williams suggested Disney's Wide World of Sports does just this (Janoff, 2003). In each of their communication mix decisions regarding the 30 sports they serve, they drive traffic to their website. This helps keep collateral pieces simpler because the organization can provide the details on the website itself.

Advertising Organizations

For those leisure and tourism organizations that do not have expertise in-house to effectively design and implement a communication mix plan, advertising organizations can provide this assistance for a fee. They "can deliver the expertise and creative spark" to assist organizations in meeting their marketing objectives (Begovich, 2002, p. 35). Even though this expertise costs money, organizations realize that they are actually more affordable, as they can leverage media purchases, provide strategic support for brand development, provide fresh ideas for positioning statements and advertisements, and expand the ability of the internal organization that has limited resources. Cardona (1998) suggested one quarter of all TV advertising is wasted, as it is not well placed. Begovich (2002) identified several steps to identifying the right advertising organization to select:

1. Before selecting a firm organizations should have clearly defined objectives for the advertising agency to accomplish. These objectives can be the same as the organization's marketing objectives.

2. Select an organization that (a) addresses the objectives and (b) complements existing in-house expertise. This way the agency can become more of a partner in achieving your organization's objectives versus being an outsider.

3. Involve all key internal personnel when working with an advertising organization, beginning with the selection process.

4. Solicit several advertising agencies in a request for proposal (RFP) process. The list of potential organizations can be obtained through referral, trade publications, advertisements, and the Yellow Pages. From the completed RFPs, identify a few that you would like to interview and conduct an organization review.

   This review can be as simple as asking the organization to share what they have previously done, or asking them to present mocked-up samples of how they would approach working with a particular leisure organization. Some organizations are understandably hesitant about creating this free coverage because their ideas are how they are employed. Most will produce better work once they understand an organization's culture and delve into the specific issues within the organization.

5. Leisure organizations should review the advertising agency's work and its ability to be creative and compelling. Are they well-managed? Do they have dedicated expertise about an organization's issues? Are the two cultures compatible? Are staff able to work well together? Can the organization afford them? Can the organization afford *not* to have them? Answers to these questions will lead an organization to making the right choice (Begovich, 2002).

A variety of methods can be used to pay an advertising organization. Some rely on commission sfrom running advertisements in various media. They secure a percentage of all costs associated with the media buy (commonly 15%). Others are retained on a monthly basis and paid a set fee for a certain number of hours of work guaranteed. This work includes more than simply media buys and is effective for organizations that rely on advertising firms to do more than manage advertising. Yet another method of payment is when an organization charges a mark-up from suppliers. As such, the advertising organization would charge the leisure organization 18% more for the photographer to take organization photos and would receive payment from this source versus the organization itself. Most organizations, however, use a combination of these payments types and learn what resources they have available internally (Begovich, 2002).

Various staff in an advertising organization have distinct roles to assist leisure and tourism organizations in accomplishing their objectives. Begovich (2002) summarized each main staff members and his or her role:

- The *account executive* acts as the liaison between the leisure organization and the advertising organization.

- The *media buyer* purchases all media and negotiates the best possible prices and placements of advertisements.

- *Copywriters* write all copy from headlines to body; they are the words of all messages.

- The *art director* designs all advertisements visually.

- The *creative director* supervises and coordinates the work of the copywriter and art director.

Organizations need to develop a blend of communication mix items to be effective but they need to ensure they do not spread themselves too thin. For example, if an organization's marketing plan spreads its resources across public relations, direct mail, television commercials, radio advertisements, the Internet, sponsorship, and internal marketing activities, then they may be better off limiting their choices to a few of these if they do not have enough to dominate in any one medium. Buying four radio advertisements, one television commercial, 100-piece direct mail, a new Internet site, a media event, sponsoring a scouting event, and developing an employee referral system may spread an organization too thin. This organization should consider selecting a few that can produce the most effective result because repetition is the key to effective communication. Therefore, limiting choices to 36 radio advertisements, a 500-piece direct mail, and a new Internet site may be in the organization's best interest.

Well-designed commercials include the following four components:

- a specific offer (e.g., 2-for-1 membership at the Wellness Center)

- urgency associated with the message (e.g., call today and tell them Patty sent you to get your discount)

- frequency (e.g., radio advertisement for one week with the commercial airing eight times per day)

- price (e.g., a savings of $200)

Well-designed advertisements have several key components:

- Highlights brand in a distinctive, consistent manner.

- Sets organization apart from competitors by emphasizing a competitive niche or advantage.

- Uses a well-designed layout (as reviewed in Chapter 11) based on a realistic delivery expectations and benefits.

- Offers something people want at a significant enough value/benefit.

- Requests an action by consumers.

Every organization that decides to use any form of advertising should also incorporate public relations (PR) activities into the mix to balance out the paid media coverage. Kathy Backus, Backus Communications

Public Relations

While leisure organizations (as other types of organizations) understand PR activities, they do not fully understand the benefits of integrating it successfully (Brabender, 2003). Public relations is working with the media and others to gain free, positive attention or coverage for an organization. It is about the relationship an organization has with stakeholders. Effective relationships are based on clear communication. The more the public is aware of an organization's offerings, the more likely it will be to achieve its objectives.

Regardless of an organization's profit status (e.g., for-profit, nonprofit), all types of leisure and tourism organizations can benefit from public relations activities. Many believe that simply because they are designed to make a profit, they cannot take advantage of free publicity. However, every organization has newsworthy happenings. A great benefit of the leisure and tourism industry is that it innately has newsworthy events and activities of value to the media if organizations make them available.

"Since the public believes editorial information is more trustworthy than paid advertising, there is incalculable value in publicity if it's positive and it's published," Helitzer wrote in Henninger's (2001, p. 1) article. Consumers are more likely to read or hear a story about an organization and remember them through this free coverage than they will from an advertisement. An organization can use public relation activities in many ways, such as

- press releases
- press/media kits
- public service announcements
- feature or news stories
- newsletters
- bulletin boards
- familiarization tours
- displays
- talk shows
- distribution of collateral materials at no-cost locations (e.g., visitor centers)
- media relations
- news conferences
- interviews
- photographs
- remote broadcasts
- list servs
- websites

Examples of public relations include

- Write a monthly column in the local paper about health issues.
- Pitch a story to the local editor about a "newsworthy" event your staff has volunteered for.
- Distribute collateral at no-cost locations for tourists visiting (e.g., CVB, hotels).
- Conduct familiarization tours of the department for new community members (i.e., Be a welcome wagon!).
- Mail a press kit to related media regarding a new focus of the department.

- Develop a protocol for who speaks to the media and represents the department.
- Gain publicity for any community relations activity you have completed.
- Build a relationship with all local/area media representatives.

Media Relations

In an effort to effectively manage public relations activities, organizations often assign one person as the media liaison and establish an organization-wide media relations policy. The policy is communicated throughout the organization and related staff members are trained on how to successfully implement it.

The leisure and tourism industry is full of interesting, remarkable, and valuable stories that many in the media may consider newsworthy information. Solomon (2002) suggested regardless of organization size, every one can find value in public relations activities. "The key is knowing what is attractive to the media and making sure your program has a realistic built-in news element" (p. 26). The

A dad and daughter at "Date Night."

challenge most leisure and tourism organizations have is to find the story within the leisure experience.

For example, Daddy-Daughter Date Night has been planned by a leisure and tourism organization for the past 15 years. Once again, as part of the program marketing plan, the staff not only produce and distribute a flyer to school-age girls, but also they write a press release and public service announcement with the hopes of gaining exposure in the local paper. This year, as in the past, they do gain exposure on the community relations page and are listed in a one-inch column with 20 other community events for the week. The press release includes information on the event, when it was, who was invited, how much it cost, what time it was being held, and where it was. However, there was nothing interesting about it. Yet, there are many interesting stories, topics, and issues imbedded in this and other leisure and tourism offerings. For example, one story may have been how a dad and daughter had been going to the event for each of the 15 years, first as participants and then as volunteers. Profiling a story about this dad and daughter would have been more newsworthy to a local paper than simply answering who, what, when, where, why, and how. This dad and daughter received so many benefits from the earlier years of attending they wanted to help continue the tradition. This year, the daughter even returned from her college two hours away to participate in this midweek event. Now there is a story!

Leisure and tourism experiences have tremendous benefits for people, communities and society, and the industry needs to do a better job in communicating this through the media. A leisure organization's role is to provide the media with the most newsworthy information in ways that have meaning to the media and their audiences. A leisure services department found a way to develop positive media relations with the student newspaper on one of their volunteer efforts. In 2006, 46 students went to the Mississippi Gulf Coast to assist with restoring nine tourism attractions following the devastation of Hurricane Katrina. The paper found their efforts so compelling they sent a photographer and reporter with the student group to cover their efforts and the aftermath of the hurricane. Upon their return, they dedicated the largest coverage to any story in the paper's history to this student effort. The story covered two pages with accompanying six photographs sharing their experiences. Tying the media to this effort produced positive media coverage of the student's efforts as well as the academic program.

One of the first activities that must be undertaken to develop a comprehensive public relations plan is to develop a list of relevant media in the markets of interest to a leisure and tourism organization. A variety of media sources leisure and tourism organizations may be interested in communicating with exist for any given market. Large daily and small weekly newspapers, all-talk radio stations, weekend television news programs, a.m. radio stations, student newspapers, regionally focused publications, tourism guides, municipal publications, cable television, shopping guides, and community magazines are all possible sources for media exposure. Media lists profile all types of media source information: the contact information, organization liaison, and publication specifications. It is used as a base from which all public relations activities are developed. Organizations develop this type of list for every geographic market with which they wish to communicate. Table 12.4 showcases this type of list.

There are several forms of public relations sources an organization can pursue depending on the type of media coverage desired. It is vital to know your audience and determine which is the best means of reaching them. Many of the examples of how an organization can use public relation activities are explained next.

The newsletter was one of our biggest mistakes. We had been doing it for years and found that people were not reading it. It is never a good idea to rely on what has been done before. You have to be willing to try new things. Rich Fairman, Warwick Hills Country Club

---

Public Relations in Any Type of Medium

Editorials can be developed in two ways. One way to develop an editorial is for the organization to write it themselves; another is to convince an editor to write one. Editorials written by someone recognizable with community influence may have a greater chance of being published and read, thereby gaining support for organization issues. Concerns from key people can assist with this free coverage choice.

Familiarization tours are invitations to key print media reporters, editors, and publishers to visit a leisure organization and ideally gain exposure through positive acknowledgment of the organization. Golf courses conduct these types of tours for golf writers. They invite the writers to an all-expense paid trip to their course where the they are treated like royalty. Writers receive this treatment with hopes the course will be featured in a golf-related article or even recognized as a top course. Resorts do the same with travel writers, and convention and visitor bureaus do the same with nonmedia groups to gain awareness and, ultimately, business from frequent travelers, company decision makers regarding travel, association executives, and travel organizations.

Media kits are a compilation of an organization's information that may be of value to various media outlets. This kit should include the organization's history, a fact sheet, and frequently asked questions in addition to a press release and public service announcement, organization promotional collateral, annual calendar of events, CD with brand-approved logos, photographs to be used in publications, and a cover letter acknowledging the purpose and intent of the kit to the specific media contact. Media kits should be professional, interesting, and unique. Leisure and tourism organizations must find ways to make these kits stand out from other organizations' efforts.

Newsletters are internal and external communications that share important information with stakeholders (e.g.,

employees, members). For example, Disney gets as much good will from making good Ambassadors out of their staff by communicating through the employee newsletter and "Morning News Flash" as they do from direct mail letters to families.

Bulletin boards are eye-catching, often large displays that share an organization's message. They may be internal to or external from the organization itself. A community center has billboards throughout the facility to share information with consumers, regarding anything from basketball league standings to policies, services offered, and special events. A center's offerings could also be promoted on the public library's bulletin board.

Displays come in two forms—tabletop and window—which can be found on-site or at other locations. These are often three-dimensional and provide a unique opportunity

Table 12.4
Sample Media List

Radio

WCFX-95.3 FM
5847 Venture Way
Mt. Pleasant, MI 48858
Phone: 989-772-4173
Fax: 989-772-1236
Contact: Stacey Gibbons
Email: sgibbons@wcfx.com
Website: www.wcfx.com
Deadline: 5:00pm daily

WCEN 94.5 FM
2929 S. Isabella Road
Mt. Pleasant, MI 48858
Phone: 989-773-5961
Fax: 989-772-9420
Contact: Brooke Allen
Email: brookea@wcen.com
Website: www.wcen.com
Deadline: 6:00pm daily

WUPS 98.5 FM
5905 E. Pickard Road
Mt. Pleasant, MI 48858
Phone: 989-773-9899
Fax: 989-773-4545
Contact: Josh Monroe
Email:jmon@wups.com
Website: www.wups.com
Deadline: 5:00pm daily

WXZY 104.3 FM
WMMI 830 AM
4065 E. Wing Road
Mt. Pleasant, MI 48858
Phone: 989-772-9664
Fax: 989-772-5000
Contact: David Curwen
Email: dcurwen1@wxzy.com
Website: www.wxzy.com
Deadline: 5:00pm daily

Television

WWTV/WWUP TV 9&10
(CBS affiliate)
P.O. Box 627
Cadillac, MI 49601
Phone: 1-800-STAR-910
Fax: 231-775-0556
Contact: Randy Miser
Email: news@9and10.com
Website: www.9and10news.com
Deadline: 12:00pm daily

WJRT (ABC-12)
2302 Lapeer Road
Flint, MI 48503
Phone: 810-233-3130
Fax: 810-233-2812
Contact: Mike Steed
Email: wjrt@cris.com
Website: www.wjrt.com
Deadline: 1:00pm daily

WEYI (NBC-25)
2225 West Willard Road
Clio, MI 48420
Phone: 810-867-1000
Fax: 810-867-4925
Contact: Pamela Goddard
Email: weyitv25@aol.com
Website: www.weyi.com
Deadline: 12:00pm daily

WNEM (CBS-5)
P.O. Box 531
Saginaw, MI 48606-0531
Phone: 517-758-2111
Fax: 517-758-2343
Contact: Bob Stacker
Email: wnemtv5@mdp.com
Website: www.wnem.com
Deadline: 11:30am daily

Newspapers

The Morning Sun
711 W. Pickard
Mt. Pleasant, MI 48858
Phone: 989-779-6000
Fax: 989-779-6051
News Department: 989-779-6000
Contact: Lisa Hart
Email: newsone@morningsun.com
Website: www.morningsun.com
Deadline: 10:00am M, W, F

CM Life
8 Anspach Hall, CMI
Mt. Pleasant, MI 48859
Phone: 989-774-3493
Fax: 989-774-7805
Contact: Jim Boone
Email: editor@cm-life.com
Website: www.cm-life.com
Deadline: 11:00am daily

Tribal Observer
7070 E. Broadway
Mt. Pleasant, MI 48858
Phone: 989-775-4011
Fax: 989-772-3508
Contact: Betty Stevens
Email: bstevens@yahoo.com
Deadline: 12:00pm Wednesdays

Other

Mount Pleasant Area Chamber of Commerce
114 E. Broadway
Mt. Pleasant, MI 48858
Phone: 989-772-2396
Fax: 989-772-2909
Contact: Wilson Beck
Email: chmber@mt-pleasant.net
Website: www.mt-pleasant.net
Newsletter: *Business Monthly*

to communicate. For example, a golf course creates a window display in the pro shop featuring merchandise. They may also develop a tabletop display of clubs, equipment, clothes, and photos of golfers to promote golf as a leisure sport at an AARP conference.

Distribution of collateral at no-cost locations includes sites such as visitor centers, hotel lobbies, and convention and visitor bureau offices. There are several sites available for organizations to share calendars of events, brochures, rate cards, and/or maps at no cost. Some organizations have companies distribute these materials at such locations, whereas others manage the process internally. For example, historic attractions hire staff to drive to 25 identified locations throughout a state to restock brochures monthly.

News conferences are planned media events, by invitation, held at a specific time to make a special announcement, such as an amusement park announcing plans for a new roller coaster, new CEO, or a celebrity spokesperson.

Remote broadcasts are when a radio station conducts an on-site broadcast in conjunction with a special event or promotion. These broadcasts can be win-win partnerships: the station provides a high-profile means of sharing an organization's message and develops a new programming twist for its listeners. For example, a climbing wall partners with a local radio station that serves a similar target market of interest. The station broadcasts their morning show from the climbing wall and their contest winners are welcomed for a day of free climbing.

Speaker bureaus are when professionals make themselves available to speak to local groups on various topics related to an organization. A fitness center might offer the following speaker bureau topics: nutrition/fitness, basics of exercise, food for health, benefits of weight training, advantages/disadvantages of home fitness equipment.

Print Publication Public Relations

Organizations can use a variety of ways to get free coverage from print publications, including magazines, newspapers and newsletters, but the organizations must know how each specific medium wants to receive information, then respect that request. Most media prefer the submissions be sent digitally. The following paragraphs highlights several ideas that can be submitted.

Letters to the editor are one place you can offer a personal opinion in a newspaper. This is one of the most influential and widely read sections of a print publication. A well-written, short, and simple letter alerts editors, journalists, and the public about an organization's concern.

Special columns can be suggested to an editor and/or written by an organization for a newspaper, magazine, or newsletter. Oftentimes, publications are seeking high-quality materials that would be beneficial to their readers. Leisure and tourism organizations have built-in expertise on a subject most consumers find of value—leisure and tourism activities. Organizations that make a commitment to a publication to produce a weekly or monthly articles on leisure-related topics benefit from exposure to not only the industry but also the author who represents the specific leisure and tourism organization.

Features or news stories are those a reporter, editor, or publisher find valuable to their readership. They differ in their approach to coverage as a feature story would highlight an issue within an organization versus the hard, specific facts of a story. For example, a news story may include coverage on the development of a new $45 million dollar recreation complex whereas a feature story would discuss the trend in climbing walls, one of which happens to be included in the new recreation complex. Facts, figures, events, and conflicting opinions are traditionally featured in a news story. Leisure and tourism organizations can facilitate this process by tying into current events and "hot" news stories.

Press releases are the most common form of communication between an organization and the print media. It is a concisely written article that summarizes the who, what, when, where, why, and how of a feature or news story that an organization wishes a print medium to publish. Figure 12.2 highlights the proper format and way to write a press release.

Historically, a press release was *the* way to communicate with the print media; however, times are changing. Publishers, editors, and reporters are inundated with press releases from organizations who believe that simply because they are mailing, faxing, or e-mailing these documents they will gain coverage. The truth is 80% of all press releases are never read. Large publishing firms may receive thousands of releases per day where even small town publications receive up to 100 (Edgar, 2002). The likelihood an organization's release will be read without some type of additional efforts is rare, therefore, one rule of thumb is to *never* send a press release without some type of additional effort to improve the possibility of gaining coverage. The following tips and techniques can improve the odds of gaining publicity.

Develop a relationship with key media personnel before requesting coverage. An organization can invite the media to the facility and buy them lunch or personally contact those on the media list to visit with them at their office. Relationships are key. Learn from the media how they prefer to be communicated with (e.g., fax, e-mail, direct mail), how they would like you to approach possible feature or newsworthy articles or pitch stories, what they look for in newsworthy information, and all key information on the media list provided (Table 12.4, p. 285). Editors like information in their format—not necessary the traditional press release format. Therefore it is important to understand the media's needs, including deadlines, policies, and editorial focus. Finally, it is important organizations be accessible to the media.

Think like an editor, reporter, and publisher. Remember a writer's goal is to have someone read his or her piece from beginning to end, and reporters will always be reporters.

LETTERHEAD

FOR IMMEDIATE RELEASE

Date: Month, Day, Year
For Information Contact:
First Name, Last Name, Phone Number(s),
e-mail, fax

<u>HEADLINE, HEADLINE, HEADLINE—BOLD, UNDERLINE, ALL CAPS—CATCHY!</u>

Lead paragraph. Different types of leads include immediate, delayed, summary, and leads with a twist. Press releases should always be double-spaced from the Headline down. Catch the readers' attention and gain interest in this paragraph.

Create a press release by telling a newsworthy story objectively. This is not an editorial letter. It is an event announcment or news item to share for informational purposes; not an opinionated piece. Press releases should be written in the third person.

When you write a release, creativity and accuracy are very important. The five critical elements of a release are: (1) the datelines; (2) the contact's name and phone number; (3) the headline; (4) the body of the release, which includes the who, what, when, where, how, and why of your story; and (5) a "for further information" reference.

Informational releases always close with a reference of whom to call for further information. Feature releases may not. "For further information or to register, call Parks and Recreation at 800-888-8888," "Seating is limited," "Preregistration is required" and other such lines are most common. One-page releases—the most common and probably best utilized in today's news world—end with one of the following messages centered at the bottom of the page: "_end_" "_30_" or "_###_". Two-page releases continue on the second page after you have cued the reader by putting "_more_" at the bottom center of the first page, and end just like a one-page release (with one of the messages from above). Good luck!!

end

Figure 12.2
Proper Format and Content of a Press Release

Reporters are generalists not specialists; it is an organization's job to provide the reporter with any helpful, necessary information. Reporters are human and juggle multiple stories and work under very specific, and often stressful, deadlines (Steinman, personal communication, November 12, 2004).

An editor's goal is to have newsworthy material. A publisher's goal is to sell their publication. Their goal is not to promote an organization unless they are assisting the publication in achieving its goals. Will an organization's idea help sell more newspapers? Be considered newsworthy, interesting, and valuable? Will it be read from beginning to end? Steinman (personal communication, November 12, 2004) stated organizations should be prepared for a fair story, not a favorable one, because the goal of the publication is not necessarily to put an organization in the most positive light possible. If an organization wants a 100% guarantee of positive information, they should purchase advertising.

Think like the media's audience. The media is interested in stories that are interesting to their readers. A story about the new youth playground may have little interest in a senior publication unless the storyline profiles grandparents taking children to the playground's activities and events.

Pitch a story to the media contact prior to developing a press release to learn if it is even of interest to them. This is often done via e-mail or telephone. In either instance, organizations want to be aware of publication deadlines (e.g., ask a reporter if they are on deadline, or if they have a few minutes so you might ask them a few questions). If they are not available, organizations should ask when they may be able to reach them and explain the purpose. If the contact indicates he or she has a few minutes, organizations should be brief and explain their story idea in terms of how it will be useful to readers and what is known about the publication's audience. Organizations who listen to the media contact and modify a release as the contact suggests are more likely to get exposure. Then develop the release in the publication's preferred format to submit it, if necessary. This step will ensure an organization does not waste time, energy, or resources on activities destined to fail. If the organization is turned down, keep trying! Some suggest an organization will get one "yes" for every ten rejections (Edgar, 2002).

Write the release or story following established guidelines. *The Associated Press Stylebook and Libel Manual* (Goldstein, 2002) provides guidelines for writing a story/release and these should be adhered to along with ensuring each release answers who, what, when, where, why, and how. The press release test includes the following:

1. Does this release answer who, what, when, why, where, and how?

2. Is it written in an inverted pyramid format (i.e., does the most important information appear first)? When space is limited and an editor must eliminate some content, he or she will start from the bottom.

3. Does the release have clarity? Is it written in simple language (i.e., free of jargon and complex words)? Is there an active versus passive tone to the story?

4. Is the release written in short sentences that don't make people work to understand it? Try to use no more than 16 words per sentence.

5. Does it describe the story in vivid ways to create an image in people's minds?

6. Is it important, interesting, or unique? People generally like stories about love, death, money, sex, people, conflicts, change, mystery, and surprise.

7. Does it include contact information for a knowledgable or key person?

8. Is it only one page? Two pages are ok *if* a release must be that long. Organizations should have a compelling reason why it *has* to be two pages because length is the enemy of interest.

9. Is the release factual and objective?

10. Is it written in third person?

11. Does the opening headline grab a reader's attention? Is it creative without being cute? Headlines should provide an expressive summary of the entire release.

12. Is the lead sentence compelling? Does it indicate interest, importance, uniqueness, or authority?

13. Is a fact sheet necessary to share specific factual information with the reporter/editor that is not critical to the release?

14. Is the release free of errors? Proofreading is critical.

Send the release. Organizations must follow preferred submission methods; if the seven newspapers in town each use a different format, then send it to them in their preferred format. Be aware of deadlines and honor them. Address the release to a specific individual; do not simply use "To Whom It May Concern" or "Dear Editor." Spell all names, titles, and affiliations correctly—Nothing makes it easier to throw away a release than when an author has not taken the time to address every detail.

Follow up. Organizations need to realize providing newsworthy information to the media makes i easier for them do a better job! Following up with media contacts in a timely manner without hounding or stalking the contact is critical. Follow up two or three days after sending a release. Ask the editor if he or she received the story, if he or she has had a chance to review it, and what his or her thoughts were about it would be some appropriate questions to ask during this conversation.

Remember the publication's priorities. Stories may be bumped routinely by breaking news; others may be held for slow news days. Therefore, there is no guarantee an article about an upcoming event will make the front page of the local paper as the media contact may have indicated.

Continue to build the relationship by thanking the media contact whether or not the organization received any publicity. Even if the organization did not this time, they will another time if the process is handled professionally. Offer and honor "exclusives" to media sources that have been most influential for your organization (Henninger, 2001). Media relationships are critical to successful public relations efforts. This is the heart of gaining exposure through publicity.

Press releases can be sent to the media for various reasons when an organization wishes to share information about organization happenings. Marketingpower.com suggests the following:

- new offering
- modification to offerings
- changes in organization brand image/identity (e.g., new logo, look)
- changes in the organization's structure
- industry trends
- features
- events (e.g., open houses, award ceremonies, speaking engagements)
- new funding/grants received
- personnel changes
- philanthropic activities, such as community relations, cause marketing, volunteer work, or donations
- partnerships/collaborations with other organizations
- ownership/board member changes

- significant new consumer or contract
- media advisories
- milestones (e.g., years in business, number of customers served)
- increase in market share or revenue (*Public Relations Tools*, 2003)

Keep in mind, reporters are always reporters. Be ready for fair, not favorable, coverage when relying on public relations. If you want positive coverage, buy an advertisement. Colleen Steinman, Michigan Department of Natural Resources

Organizations should not feel they are properly implementing a marketing communication mix if they simply send out a bunch of press releases. Was there a return from these efforts? Too often organizations believe they have "done good" by simply completing an activity and do not necessarily ensure a return for the effort. Measuring the impact of public relations activities can be handled in many ways. With press releases, one way is to track effectiveness is to subscribe to a clipping service. A clipping service is an organization that finds any mention of your organization in a variety of publications. Clipping services charge a monthly fee to find, copy, and forward newsclips mentioing an organization so the organization can learn what the media has published about it. Oftentimes smaller leisure and tourism organizations handle this internally. One staff member may be responsible for reading various publications to identify any mention of the organization. Since the advent of the Internet, this search process is simpler because a Google search can identify any organization reference quite effectively (although it is not inclusive of all publications).

Interviews occur when a reporter or editor solicits an organization member's assistance for a story the publication has decided to develop (as opposed to the organization suggesting a story topic for the publication). Organizations need to be prepared for a reporter to contact anyone in their organization about a topic of interest. "Anything goes" and a reporter may ask any type of question, some an organization enjoys answering and others they would rather avoid. Regardless, the organization staff must be prepared for reporters' questions and the organization overall must have a strategy in place about who can speak with the media and what they are able to share.

Ideally, an organization would have established media guidelines. These guidelines outline the process for handling a reporter's telephone call or visit. It would state who in the organization is allowed to speak with the media (about any issue) and the process for directing this person to the media in a positive, cooperative way. Guidelines for managing crisis communication will be presented later in this chapter. However, several guidelines exist regardless of the type of questions a reporter may have:

1. Know the reporter, publication, deadline, audience, type of story, others interviewed, and interview format ahead of time. Be timely in returning telephone calls. Ask if time allows for you to properly prepare for the interview.

2. Identify what you want to say and establish a number of key points you want to emphasize.

3. Practice likely questions and your answers.

4. Include bridging phrases, such as "I think the real issue is," "That brings up an interesting point," "You may be interested to know," "I think the real issue here is," and "What's really important here."

5. Back up main points with facts.

6. Don't overanswer—Short answers are better than long ones.

7. If asked about a problem, discuss the solution.

8. Correct false charges, facts, or figures.

9. Speak clearly and avoid jargon.

10. Be engaging and likeable.

11. Don't be provoked; stay cool.

12. Never say "no comment" or ask to go "off the record." If you cannot yet share specific information, explain why: "We are not ready to release that information until we examine it further. I would be happy to notify you when we are ready to release it."

13. Don't speculate. Tell them what you know and offer to get back with them regarding answers you may not have.

14. Phrase all responses positively.

15. If a reporter fails to ask a question you feel may be important, suggest it at the end and ask if they would like to hear anything about "xyz" subject.

Real Life Story: "Climb for Wishes" Participation Doubles

Tanya Donahue, a commercial recreation undergraduate student, wanted to implement a community event for her honors project required to graduate. She had designed and implemented a student-developed program in her programming class (with a group of five others) the previous year. This year, she wanted not only to improve the event and use what she had learned from last year's program evaluation but also to use the skills she had developed over the past year in her leisure marketing and recreation classes.

The event, entitled "Climb for Wishes," targeted local families with children under age 18. Tanya solicited the assistance of her roommate, Andrea Harris, and began to plan.

The proceeds were to benefit the Make-A-Wish Foundation of Michigan. They set their goal of making a $300 minimum profit, more than what was raised by the previous event for the Foundation. Tanya had no marketing funds and she wanted to donate as much as possible to the Foundation, so she decided to use public relations as a part of her communication mix.

Tanya knew simply sending a press release and PSA would not guarantee any free publicity, therefore, faxing, e-mailing, or mailing these documents were unlikely to produce an effect. Instead, she decided to personally deliver each announcement and she was able to meet with two editors. She followed up with each contact a few days later. As a result of her efforts, two local radio stations made several announcements for the event and one welcomed her to participate in a half-hour talk show to discuss the event and Foundation. Additionally, one newspaper provided 1/4-page of coverage prior to the event; they even sent a photographer to the climbing wall to take Tanya and Andrea's photograph. Another newspaper wrote a story following the event and included a photo from the event itself resulting in another 1/4 page of coverage.

As noted in the postevent story, Tanya and Andrea's event was a great success. Participation doubled from the previous year. They accomplished their goal and donated $342 in proceeds to the Make-A-Wish Foundation. Tanya attributed her public relations as a critical reason for the success because through her evaluation, she learned many participants heard about the event through reading the article.

Tanya applied a strategic approach to public relations, and her efforts paid off. She was diligent in taking the right steps with the media to stand out from other community events that could have received attention or been considered more "newsworthy" than hers. Tanya didn't just send a release and check off "task completed." She took the extra steps while few organizations do this.

16. Don't offer a media person any type of gift that can be perceived as a bribe.

17. Never lie.

18. Do not pester a reporter to find out if you will be in the final copy and when it will be published or ask if you can read the story before it goes to press—This simply isn't done.

19. *Radio interviews* should include effective voice tone and inflection and include short answers (i.e., less than 20 words or 10 seconds). Notes can be used to ensure main points are addressed.

20. *Television interviews* also emphasize appearance and technique. Dark clothing with solid colors are most appealing without large, shiny, or noisy jewelry. Voice and gestures should be natural and short answers are most effective (i.e., less than 20 words or 10 seconds). Use pleasant expressions with appropriate smiles during positive interviews; crisis or concerning topics warrant serious expressions. Finally, maintain interview "on" mode until you are certain the taping is finished.

21. *Print interviews* should pace comments to a reporters note taking. Notes are allowed. Ideally opportunities to correct any mistakes or misinformation will be provided.

Audiovideo Media Public Relations

Public Service Announcements (PSAs) are short 15-, 30- and 60-second messages intended most often for TV, cable, and radio mediums to inform viewers and listeners of the work of charitable and nonprofit organizations and others that serve a public interest (Yes, for-profit organization efforts can also benefit from this type of exposure; for example, a golf course's efforts to protect wetlands should not go unnoticed!). Commercially sponsored PSAs, however, cannot contain any sponsor logos or slogans.

PSAs answer the questions who, what, when, where, why, and how in a concise, acceptable format. They can be in video, written, or verbal forms. Historically the Federal Communication Commission mandated the amount of PSAs to be aired each day; however, broadcasters are no longer obligated to run these announcements. Many still do, though, in a community calendar of events format to provide free local coverage. This is still a good choice to pursue for free coverage for not-for-profit businesses. For example, a for-profit organization can seek free coverage

about information regarding their sponsorship of a blood drive, whereas nonprofits can seek coverage for almost all activities because even though some activities may be profit motivated, the overall organization mission is to break even. The format and content of a properly written PSA is shown in Figure 12.3 (p. 292).

Talk shows are often used in both local radio and television/cable mediums. Organizations that choose to work with this medium need to identify shows whose viewers might be potential customers. For example, one professional recently participated in an "Ask the Travel Professional" segment on the local PBS television station whose coverage reaches half of the state. Another was recently interviewed on a half-hour Sunday morning radio show. Networking with the media to identify their needs and interests and offer your expertise can produce a win-win relationship.

Guest call-in is a technique used to stimulate audience participation. Organizations that have informative and inducing subjects or topics can solicit the media to want to include them.

Crisis Management

As much as every organization would like only positive publicity, it is inevitable all will deal with negative press eventually. It is crucial the leisure and tourism organizations develop a long-term strategy for managing controversial situations resulting from bad publicity because even a positive industry can be faced with crisis situations. In essence, this is what crisis management is all about. *Crisis management* is a strategic, proactive way organizations prepare for and/or reduce the likelihood of crisis situations occurring.

Every leisure and tourism organization is faced with potential crises. Massey (2001) stated a *crisis* is "a major, unpredictable event that threatens to harm the organization and its stakeholders" (p. 157). *Merriam-Webster's Collegiate Dictionary* (2004) defines crisis as "an unstable or crucial time or state of affairs whose outcome will make a significant and decisive difference for better or for worse." Preparing for unforeseen crisis situations cannot be underestimated even though no one plans emergencies. Emergencies are intruders to well-thought-out and prepared plans that an organization has developed. No one wants a crisis to develop, but avoidance is not the answer. How an organization and individual staff manages these situations can be success-defining for the organization and career-defining for the individual.

Crisis management involves every aspect of an organization, including operations, marketing, and legal departments (NyBlom, Reid, Coy & Walter, 2003). A variety of strategies can be used by leisure organizations to reduce the likelihood of crises occurring. Most leisure management textbooks have chapters dedicated to risk management or crisis response topics for establishing strategies to ensure a crisis does not occur and establishing procedures should a crisis occur. This is the first, best preventative measure an organization can take. This is especially true in the leisure and tourism industry, where consumers and employees are engaged in activities and events that are not sedentary in nature. Hopefully, most organizations have developed standard operating procedures for crises such as severe weather, fire evacuation, and bomb threats (Koolbeck, 2003).

It is common for organizations to establish crisis management teams. This crossbreed of staff members (representing all areas) proactively addresses issues related to crisis management. This may include writing, communicating, and training about standard operating procedures related to crises and establishing a communication strategy for managing a situation should it occur. A risk management plan often addresses the specific operational issues related to crises; however, it is often the marketing department that determines, communicates, and trains staff about crisis communication issues.

LETTERHEAD

PUBLIC SERVICE ANNOUNCEMENTS
FOR USE UNTIL THIS DATE

Date: Month, Day, Year
For Information Contact:
First Name, Last Name, Phone Number(s),
e-mail, fax

:15 PSA

P-S-A's ARE WRITTEN EXACTLY AS A PERSON WOULD READ, BECAUSE THEY CAN BE EASILY TAPED

RIGHT OFF YOUR SUBMISSION SHEET. THEY ARE COMMONLY DOUBLEiSPACED AND WRITTEN IN

ALL CAPS, BECAUSE BROADCASTERS ARE USED TO READING FROM A DIGITAL PROMPTER OR

TELEPROMPTER IN ALL CAPITAL LETTERS.

end

:30 PSA

WHY NOT JUST SEND A PRESS RELEASE? WELL, YOU COULD, BUT IF THE RADIO STATION'S NEWS

DIRECTOR RECEIVES SPOTS ALREADY WRITTEN, FORMATTED AND READY-TO-RECORD, IT'S A LOT

EASIER TO GET NEWS ON THE AIR. THIS SPOT, IF YOU WERE TO READ IT ALOUD, SHOULD TIME OUT

AT 30 SECONDS. P-S-A'S LIKE THIS ARE COMMONLY USED AS FILL-IN NEWS OR TO HELP A STATION

MEET THEIR SERVICE QUOTA. CALL 1-888-MORE-FUN FOR FURTHER INFORMATION OR TO REGISTER.

end

Figure 12.3
Proper Format and Content of a Public Service Announcement

Organizations can reduce the likelihood of crises occurring; however, all crises are not directly the result of what an individual or organization has done—some are the result of industry affiliation.

Crisis situations vary greatly and can be caused by the organization directly or not. These range from employment situations where employees have been terminated for unjust or controversial reasons to natural disasters like forest fires that threatened camps in the western United States (Brown & Mickelson, 2002). The media seems to publish issues every day, such as health concerns (e.g., when Toronto's travel industry was plagued by concerns about the SARS outbreak in 2003), confrontations between boards and administrators, consumer accidents, environmentalists protesting an organization's development of wetlands, unethical practices (e.g., tax evasion), and criminal activity (e.g., when a patron was stabbed at a concert at the Fleet Center in Boston; Koolbeck, 2003).

Crises vary in degree and probability but all share the threat of causing damage to organizations, which can be measured in terms of harm to the organization's image and actual financial losses (Williams & Olaniran, 1998, p. 387). The spectrum of potentially difficult situations organizations face is broad and expanding. Evans (2002) suggested this even occurs in the camp industry. Crisis plans have expanded to include issues related to suicides, shootings, hostage taking, pollution and hazardous waste, food poisoning, governmental restriction, and communicable disease outbreaks. He suggests a new level of crisis planning/risk management has emerged. If organizations are unprepared for these situations ,they will be subject to longer-term impacts than those who are well-prepared. The issue has become so prevalent that colleges and universities offer semester-long courses on crisis management and communication (Coombs, 2001).

Most organization crises arise based on operational situations. Lukaszewski (2001) suggested as many as 90% of crises fall into this day-to-day operations category, whereas the remaining occur based on everything from external influences (e.g., crime, environmental threats) to poor employee behavior (e.g., sexual harassment, poor management choices).

Organizations, therefore, must strategically prepare for the reality that a crisis can occur with or without their direct involvement. Crisis management must consider not only how to reduce the likelihood of a crisis situation occurring but also how the organization will react when a situation does occur. Evans (2002) suggested camps consider two simple rules for crisis management: protect the people, and perform actions that demonstrate the camp cares for emotional and physical injuries during and after an occurrence. Further, Bardo (2005) suggests a crisis is an opportunity to demonstrate leadership, and Schoenberg (2005) states leadership skills are critical for all who manage crisis situations.

Organizations that have experienced crises understand crises can attract crowds. Often, the majority of these crowds involve the media because crises sell newspapers, encourage radio listeners, and attract television viewers. Crises are newsworthy events.

The media is one audience that organizations need to be prepared to communicate with; however, there are others as well. Organizations need to address stakeholders in their organization and develop a direct link to consumers, board members, volunteers, and employees to ensure each is kept abreast of the crisis situation and how the organization is prepared to manage it. These audiences should be first priority to the organization's communication effort should an emergency occur. Often organizations use broadcast faxes, e-mail, or phone trees to quickly reach these stakeholder groups.

Therefore, organizations must be prepared to communicate with multiple audiences should a crisis situation develop or occur. Organizations who establish proactive plans to minimize potential confusion, difficulties, or improper messages being shared will be better off than those who have not. Organizations have several choices about how they manage crises communication when a crisis occurs. They may deny the situation, provide an excuse, or justify/ explain why it occurred (Benoit, 1997; Massey, 2001).

Crisis communications are how and what the organization shares with stakeholders they want to reach internally or externally. Crisis communication procedures combined with established operational standards create a solid crisis management infrastructure. Massey (2001) suggests crisis communication, like other communication efforts, must be consistent. He reiterates this is a "key determinant of success or failure" when managing crisis situations (p. 158). He observed this in a quasi-experiment designed to understand messages communicated during airline industry crises. Massey recorded how undergraduate students reacted to written messages developed by an airline facing a situation. Students reacted more favorably to consistent messages provided by the organization regarding the crisis and to those from larger organizations with more complex operations, a broader focus, and established routines. Large organizations were perceived as more legitimate than smaller organizations with simpler organizational charts and focuses. Therefore, everyone needs to hear the same information to reduce potential message error and confusion, which will harm crisis communication efforts.

Authors who manage and deal with crisis situations on a regular basis have suggested steps to sucessfully prepare for crisis situations from a media/communications perspective. King (2002) notes organizations have responsibilities before, during, and after crises. Critical elements of crisis communication include the following (Argenti, 2002; Bardo, 2005; Benoit, 1997; Evans, 2002; Lampton, 1999; Marra, 1998):

1. Identify how an organization's culture and public relations autonomy can support a crisis. Is the organization well-prepared? Do they have the right structure to manage this type of situation?

2. Develop a relationship with the media and emergency personnel (e.g., police, fire) *before* a crisis occurs.

3. Develop a crisis management team. Stanton (2002) stated a "team approach ensures effective communication as well as a collaborative process of crisis management" (p. 22).

4. Prepare and establish effective communication channels with all stakeholders. Organizations can reach employees, board members/investors, and volunteers directly and should do so *immediately* in order to be prepared for media involvement. Zielinski (2001) stated organization employees can be the best supporters or largest critics depending on how an organization chooses to communicate with them during a crisis. Organizations then must quickly communicate with external stakeholders (e.g., consumers) through direct means and/or by relying on the media to assist them.

5. Write and distribute a formal, documented crisis communication plan within an organization. Elements of this document will be explained in the next section.

6. Train staff about how to manage situations and implement the crisis communication plan.

7. Go to the crisis scene. Analyze the crisis, identify the relevant audience(s), and develop the organization's response based on the severity of the situation.

8. View the media as a messenger to communicate through and establish two-way communication with them. Spokespeople must respond to media calls promptly and stick to the facts. Never go "off the record," babble, or volunteer information. Negative relationships with the media during a crisis will adversely impact the communication shared by the organization. Provide the media with information that can be shared as quickly as possible.

9. Work proactively with the media to take control of the communication process (as opposed to allowing the media control the process). For example, an organization should state where, when, and how they will share and distribute information (e.g., press conference, written statement). They should also share who will be involved in the process. Leaders within the organization should be highly visible. The media's audience and organization stakeholders expect an instant response to a crisis situation. Organizations must keep the media abreast of changes and encourage their involvement so the organization's message is the one that reaches the media's audience. Any verbal information shared with the media should be supported by written documentation to ensure an organization's message is clear and not taken out of context.

10. Always tell the truth, never say "no comment," and follow all other public relations principles of working with the media.

11. Document all communication. Written statements should be saved and all interviews videotaped or audiotaped. This could be helpful later if legal issues emerge from the situation.

12. Organizations should try to minimize any interruption to organization operations and conduct "business as usual."

13. Organizations need a plan for repairing its image through restoration and/or renewal. Ulmer and Sellnow (2002) found by using renewal efforts rather than "arguing over guilt and responsibility" (p. 365), organizations reconnect with their core values and communicate their actions based on these issues.

14. Learn from the situation. Organizations that confront these challenges positively and learn from mistakes (or any effort) will be better prepared the next time. Of course, no one would want to see a next time, but organizations will be prepared should another incident occur.

Marketing is about communication—communicating with the public as well as the departments. Lynne Ike, VanAndle Arena

Real Life Story:
National Tour Association Partners Get Message Heard

Freedom—the state of being free; exemption from the power and control of another; liberty; independence

Freedom. This simple, two-syllable word took on a whole new meaning in the months following the events of September 11th. In an effort to help the travel industry rebound and encourage consumers to travel, members of the National Tour Association (NTA) began spreading the word about one of our most important freedoms—the freedom to travel.

NTA launched its grassroots consumer message—"Travel... the perfect freedom"—at its 2001 Annual Convention in Houston. The objective was simple—to join forces in a unified effort to encourage people to travel. Don't stand still—Go, see, do, experience!

The "Travel... the perfect freedom" program was made up of three main components: NTA member grassroots marketing efforts, industry partnerships and a consumer public relations campaign.

One of the primary goals of "Travel... the perfect freedom" was the NTA member grassroots marketing program. NTA provided its members with tools and resources to stimulate consumer interest in their products while stimulating consumer interest in travel.

NTA partnered with nearly 30 other industry organizations and associations throughout North America in an effort to extend the reach of this message to consumers. In order to become a "Travel... the perfect freedom" partner, each organization pledged to help spread the message "Don't stand still—Go, see, do, experience!" Partnering organizations delivered this message in various ways: stories in their member publications, complimentary advertising space, recognition and links on websites and displaying posters in state visitor centers, airports and at governor's conferences.

This message was also distributed to the travel industry and consumers through advertising, supplements and consumer publications. A consumer website (http://www.traveltheperfectfreedom.com) provided information on the message, how to contact NTA tour operators and special travel packages. In the first year, nearly 40,000 consumers visited the site.

Public Service Announcements were distributed to the top 200 television outlets and top 100 radio outlets in the United States. Only three weeks after distribution, the TV PSAs had received 2.7 million viewer impressions, with an estimated value of more than $37,000 in airtime. The TV PSAs

appeared in top markets including New York, Philadelphia and San Francisco.

The travel industry is slowly recovering from the after-effects of September 11th and, in 2004, NTA tour operators reported their best year since the attacks. Most recently, more than 50% of tour operators reported overall sales volume during the first quarter of 2005 was greater than the first quarter of 2004. NTA continues to assist its members through a variety of marketing programs, government relations efforts and product development trips.

Crisis Communication Plan

A *crisis communication plan* is an organization's documented policy on how they will handle any type of crisis situation when communicating with the media or their stakeholders. Stanton (2002) stated a well-developed plan is a method for planning and thinking about crisis situations and preparing people to understand and respond to the demands of these situations. This plan allows employees, volunteers, board members, and other internal stakeholders to understand not only who speaks for the organization but also the steps anyone involved with the organization should take if they are confronted with a crisis situation. The plan provides a process to gather and release information as quickly as possible during a crisis (Marra, 1998). Argenti (2002) stated in his interviews with leaders following September 11th, "Forward thinking leaders realize that managing a crisis-communication program requires the same dedication and resources they give to other dimensions of their business" (p. 109). Yet, not all organizations have them or use them even if they do have them (Samansky, 2002). Specific elements should be included in a crisis communication plan, including the following:

1. Explain what constitutes a crisis situation within the particular organization. The various types of crises are identified as well as scenarios that suggest how the organization should respond to these situations from an operational and communication standpoint.

2. Identify a spokesperson who is responsible for communicating with the media and all stakeholder groups. One organization employee should be assigned this responsibility. He or she needs to be not only an effective communicator (i.e, have exceptional verbal skills and media training) but also needs to be someone who can easily assess and problem solve the situation, anticipate questions, offer answers and solutions, and manage this type of stressful situation. Often this is a senior marketing staff person who reports directly to the top administrator or owner. More than one message creates confusion, and one person representing the organization's opinion and perspective minimizes this. If this person is not the owner or a top administrator, then the owner/top administrator would be expected to inform the media and organization stakeholders that he or she has given this responsibility to the person identified in the plan. The owner/ top administrator

needs to be well-prepared for the media even if he or she is not identified as the spokesperson.

3. Explain the impact for not following the established plan to the organization.

4. Identify contact names, telephone numbers, and other ways to reach key personnel (e.g., administrators, spokesperson, legal counsel).

5. Explain how the organization will handle specific, more common situations since there is no way to prepare for all specific crisis situations.

6. Establish employee, board member, and volunteer roles should a situation occur.

7. State specific protocols to be taken by the organization to communicate with internal and external stakeholders.

8. Communicate with all staff members to ensure clear understanding and acceptance. (Arpan, 2002; Evans, 2002; Lampton, 1999; Marra, 1998; Parsons, 2002)

The crisis communication plan is approved by not only the organization but also the organization's attorney. This ensures any potential legal issues or concerns are minimized. Other legal issues to consider during crisis situations do exist too.

One legal concern is crisis communication plans relate to what an organization is allowed to say should a situation occur. "The corporate apology has become a prime tool in crisis communications handbooks and a means of attempting to restore consumer confidence in battered brands" (Frank, 2000, p. 36). One potentially troublesome issue for many organizations is how they can show empathy and be apologetic without legally harming their organization. Patel and Reinsch (2003) studied this issue and found organizations tend to fail to apologize because legal staff recommend against it due to potential legal liabilities. They suggest, however, this is not necessarily true and several high-profile organization crises have had leaders apologize. It is the way they apologize, however. They suggest "apologies generally do not constitute evidence of guilt and, in fact, they sometimes have positive consequences" for the organization apologizing (p. 9). An apology, they continued, "…has equal or even greater, potential to make a positive contribution" to an organization's legal strategy if it is managed correctly (p. 10). They further suggest apologies should be prepared, communicated, and described at appropriate times.

Organizations should not admit fault but rather express concern. A statement such as "I'm sorry for hurting you" versus "I'm sorry you were hurt" have different legal implications (Patel & Reinsch, 2003). The latter does not admit an organization was at fault. Therefore, organizations must be prepared for both types of apologies and their implications. If an organization was at fault, a complete apology that admits responsibility and an erroneous act may be more appropriate than one that addresses regret and sympathy (without responsibility). An apology that addresses responsibility must also address making amends and taking action to ensure it does not occur again.

The faster an organization is to apologize, the more likely it will be accepted by stakeholders and produce positive consequences. Organizations must determine what type of apology should occur when because a full apology (i.e., showing responsibility) may be better served at a later point due to legal concerns. Organizations could therefore immediately suggest regret and sympathy, then at a later point address their responsibility (Patel & Reinsch, 2003).

There are legal consequences in apologies, therefore organizations must understand the differences and take advantage of apologizing in different ways based on circumstances surrounding the situation and timing. Appropriately worded apologies can have positive impacts for an organization without harm to the legal challenges they may face. Patel and Reinsch (2003) state public relations and legal advice are important for any crisis situation.

Apply What You Know

1. Find several leisure and tourism industry advertisements and critique each.

2. Write a press release and a public service announcement.

3. Interview a staff member responsible for marketing at a leisure and tourism organization and discuss his or her advertising and public relations activities. Are they balanced? Are some ignored? What processes/formats does he or she use?

4. Brainstorm and determine a communication mix using advertising and public relations decisions for the marketing plan you are writing.

5. Develop a crisis communication plan for the organization for which you are developing a marketing plan.

Key Terms

Advertising	Frequency
Audio medium public relations	Listservs
	Media list
Brand spiraling	Media relations
Clipping service	Multimedia
Contextual advertising	Press releases
Crisis communication plan	Print media
Crisis management	Public relations
Direct mail	Reach
Direct marketing	

Review Questions

1. List five suggestions for improving the effectiveness of advertisements.

2. Identify the disadvantages of using electronic newspapers.

3. List the three components every billboard advertisement should have printed on it.

4. What is one of the first activities undertaken to develop a comprehensive public relations plan?

5. Describe the nine factors used for improving media publicity.

6. What are the components of a crisis communication plan?

Internet Resources

Advertising

American Association of Advertising Organizations is the national trade association representing the advertising organization businesses. This association offers its member's expertise, resources, and information about the advertising industry.
http://www.aaaa.org

DoubleClick helps marketers to reach consumers. The company provides tools for online advertising, e-mail delivery, direct marketing, and data management for marketers, advertisers, and Web publishers.
http://www.doubleclick.com/us

WebHitsDirect specializes in online advertising solutions. Their marketing packages include access to live statistics, advertising on other websites, and pop-under advertising.

http://www.webhitsdirect.com

Proceed Interactive helps travel/hospitality and consumer services companies extend brand awareness and drive sales through online marketing strategy, online media, creative design, technology services, and Web consulting.

http://www.proceedinteractive.com

UltimatePromotion.com provides website submission services to help businesses promote their websites to the top search engines and directories.

http://www.ultimatepromotion.com

Public Relations

PR Newswire provides comprehensive communications services for public relations professionals. Their website includes materials about news releases; information distribution to websites, databases, and online services; and additional public relations tools.

http://prntoolkit.prnewswire.com/paloalto

Spread the News helps businesses to create media interest for their products or services. Their services include publicity campaigns and publicity consultations.

http://www.spreadthenewspr.com

The Public Relations Society of America is the world's largest organization for public relations professionals. A great variety of information and public relations materials are available on this website.

http://www.prsa.org

Online Public Relations brings together useful resources for public relations professionals and links to other websites that discuss related topics.

http://www.online-pr.com

The Institute for Public Relations provides research articles, news, lectures, publications, and professional development

forums to improve the knowledge and practice of public relations professionals.

http://www.instituteforpr.com

The International Public Relations Association offers opportunities for its members to network with professionals in the field, and to share knowledge and professional experience with colleagues from the same industry in different parts of the world.

http://www.ipra.org

Crisis Communication

All About Public Relations gathers feature articles on public relations, media relations techniques and tips, careers in public relations, and crisis management challenges.

http://www.aboutpublicrelations.net

The Public Relations Society of America offers professional development seminars for members and nonmembers. The Crisis Communication Strategy seminar provides opportunities for professionals to learn how to deal with difficult situations strategically and immediately.

http://www.prsa.org/_advance/seminars/70024.asp?ident=apr8

Bernstein Crisis Management LLC is a public relations consultancy organization that provides crisis management services including crisis prevention, response, planning, training, and simulations.

http://www.bernsteincrisismanagement.com

Value Based Management.net provides materials and useful links to crisis management resources. Some generic help and tips on crisis management are included.

http://www.valuebasedmanagement.net

Ross Campbell & Associates, a crisis managment consultancy company, provides planning, training, resources, and risk and threat analysis for organizations to control and manage difficult situations.

http://www.crisismanagement.com.au

References

Argenti, P. (2002). Crisis communication: Lessons from 9/11. *Harvard Business Review, 80*(12), 103–109.

Arnold, M. and Tapp, S. R. (2001). The effects of direct marketing techniques on performance: An application to arts organizations. *Journal of Interactive Marketing, 15*(3), 41–52.

Arpan, L. M. (2002). When in Rome? The effects of spokesperson ethnicity on audience evaluation of crisis communication. *The Journal of Business Communication, 39*(3), 314–339.

Bardo, J. (2005). Top management communication during crises: Guidelines and a "perfect example" of a crisis leader. *Public Relations Quarterly, 50*(2), 27–32.

Begovich, R. (2002, February/March). Adding an organization: When it comes to competing for today's consumer, adding an advertising organization to your marketing team can be the right move. *Athletic Management, 14*(2), 35–43.

Benady, D. (2003, April 3). Sharper scrutiny of TV sponsorships. *Marketing Week*, 14–15.

Benoit, W. (1997). Image repair discourse and crisis communications. *Public Relations Review, 23*(2), 177–186.

Berger, W. (2003, March). That's advertainment. *Business 2.0, 4*(2), 90–95.

Brabender, T. (2003, September 23). *The increasing power of publicity*. Retrieved October 9, 2003, from http://www.mplans.com/dpm/article.cfm/155

Brown, D. and Mickelson, R. (2002, March/April). Forest fire: A crisis reality for camp. *Camping Magazine, 75*(2), 22–29.

Cardona, M. (1998, March 30). Study finds half of spot TV buys are wasted money. *Advertising Age, 69*(13), 22.

Case, T. (2002, March 4). Triumph of the niche. *Mediaweek, 12*(9), SR4–SR8.

Cassidy, H. (2002, July). Going to market: In the fight to remain relevant to consumers, some companies are finding that ad spending isn't everything. *Sporting Goods Business, 35*(7), 40–42.

Chaisson, V. (2002). Marketing trends. *Michigan Parks and Recreation*, 14–22.

Clawson, M. and Knetsch, J.L. (1966). *Economics of outdoor recreation*. Baltimore, MD: Johns Hopkins Press.

Coombs, T. (2001). Teaching the crisis management/communication course. *Public Relations Review, 27*(1), 89–101.

Crawford, K. (2005, February 4). *Sanitizing the Super Bowl*. CNN/Money. Retrieved August 21, 2005, from http://money.cnn.com

Danaher, P. and Green, B. (1997). A comparison of media factors that influence the effectiveness of direct response television advertising. *Journal of Interactive Marketing, 11*(2), 46–59.

Daniels, C. (2000, November 27). New ways to put ads in motion. *Marketing Magazine, 105*(47), 20.

DePelsmacker, P., Geuens, M., and Vermeir, I. (2004). The importance of media planning, ad likeability, and brand position for ad and brand recognition in radio spots. *International Journal of Market Research, fourth quarter, 46*(4), 465.

Derryberry, J. (2000). Europe hails snail mail. *Sales and Marketing Management, 152*(9), 118–120.

Edmonson, B. (1998, March). In the driver's seat. *American Demographics, 20*(3), 46–52.

Edgar, S. (2002, October). *Media relations presentation at Publicity Connection Conference*. Mt. Pleasant, MI.

Egol, L. (1995). Why Hyatt prefers the hotel DM. *Direct, 7*(12), 17.

Evans, W. (2002, March/April). Camp crisis management: Responding to new challenges. *Camping Magazine, 75*(2), 16–21.

Fisher, J. (2002, June). Shaving face. *Entrepreneur, 30*(6), 94.

Frank, J. (2000, October 12). Sorry is no longer the hardest word. *Marketing*, 36–37.

Frank, R. and Greenberg, M. (2000). Interest-based segments of TV audiences. *Journal of Advertising Research, 40*(6), 55–64.

French, I. (2000). Brand based DRTV that sells. *Marketing Magazine, 105*(16).

French, I. (2001). Tricks of the trade. *Marketing Magazine, 106*(33), 18.

Friedman, W. and Fine, J. (2003, September 1). Print feels heat as movie dollars shift. *Advertising Age, 74*(35), 17.

Friesen, P. (2006, January). Stretch your postal dollars. *Target Marketing, 29*(1), 21–23.

Goldstein, N. (Ed.). (2002). *The Associated Press stylebook and libel manual*. New York, NY: Addison-Wesley.

Go-To-Market Strategies. (2002, August). *Online marketing techniques every company should use!* Retrieved October 2, 2003, from http://www.gotomarketstrategies.com/tip_08_02.htm

Go-To-Market Strategies. (2003, November). *E-mail marketing success lies in the details*. Retrieved November 11, 2003, from http://www.gotomarketstrategies.com/tip2_11_03.htm

Hamm-Greenawalt, L. (2000, June 15). Those boinging boxes: Interstitials are effective, whether or not they annoy people. *Internet World, 6*(14), 29.

Harvin, R. (2000, January 24). In Internet branding, the off-lines have it. *Brandweek, 41*(4), 30–32.

Henninger, W. (2001) Watch those PR do's and don'ts. *Street and Smith's Sports Business Journal, 4*(16), 1.

Hotchkiss, G., Garrison, M., and Jensen, S. (2004). *Search engine usage in North America: A research initiative by Enquiro*. Kelowna, BC: Enquiro. Retrieved July 17, 2004, from http://www.enquiro.com/research.asp

Hyland, T. (2004). *The global outlook for Internet advertising and access spending, 2003–2007*. Retrieved June 6, 2004, from http://www.pwcglobal.com

International Association of Assembly Managers (IAAM). (2003, May 1). E-mail newsletter a hit with members. *IAAM News*.

Irwin, R., Sutton, W., and McCarthy, L. (2002). *Sport promotion and sales management*. Champaign, IL: Human Kinetics.

Janoff, B. (2003). Disney's quest to brand and market its sports division is a complex matter. *Brandweek, 44*(3), 10.

King, G. (2002). Crisis management & team effectiveness: A closer examination. *Journal of Business Ethics, 41*(3), 235–249.

Koolbeck, T. (2003, January/February). When the cameras start rolling. *Facility Manager, 19*(1), 22–25.

Korgaonkar, P. and Wolin, L. (2002). Web usage, advertising, and shopping: Relationship patterns. *Internet Research, 12*(2), 191–204.

Lampton, W. (1999, January). Critical care in crisis communication. *Perspective, 25*(1), 23–24.

Law, R. (2000). Internet in travel and tourism. *Journal of Travel and Tourism Marketing, 9*(3), 65–71.

Lee, J. (2003, February 14). TV airtime costs falls to lowest rate since 1997. *Campaign*, 2.

Leger, J. and Scholz, D. (2002, February 11). Canadians tuning out on ads. *Marketing Magazine, 107*(6), 25.

Leutz, R. (2004). Sounds advice. *Mediaweek, 14*(19), 22.

Lukaszewski, J. (2001). Managing bad news in the era of instant communication. *Executive Speeches, 16*(1), 11–15.

Maddox, K. (2005, December 12). New media, ROI, deliverability key to success in '06. *B-to-B, 90*(16), 1–4.

Marra, F. J. (1998). Crisis communication plans: Poor predictors of excellent crisis public relations. *Public Relations Review, 24*(4), 461–474.

Martin, C. (2001). The ABC's of e-mail: Think of e-mail as a way to do direct mail marketing without all that messy (and costly) postage. *Bowlers' Journal International, 88*(4), 104–105.

Massey, J. (2001). Managing organizational legitimacy: Communication strategies for organizations in crisis. *Journal of Business Communication, 38*(2), 153–182.

Merriam-Webster's Collegiate Dictionary (11th ed.). (2004). Springfield, MA.

Migala, D. (2002, March). If you want Web advertisers, understand the demographic they chase. *Street and Smith's Sports Business Journal, 4*(48), 18–24.

Mitchell, C. (2001, August 20). The end of the envelope. *Marketing Magazine, 106*(33), 18.

Moses, L. (2003, August 11). Sunday will never be the same. *Editor & Publisher, 136*(29), 10.

Myers, J. (1993). More is indeed better. *Mediaweek, 3*, 14–21.

NyBlom, S. E., Reid, J., Coy, W. J., and Walter, F. (2003). Understanding crisis management. *Professional Safety, 48*(3), 18–25.

O'Connell, V. (2003, January 30). Some Super Bowl ads didn't score—Surveys indicate viewers liked costly commercials but don't intend to buy. *Wall Street Journal*, p. B4.

Parsons, P. (2002). Communicating strategically in a crisis. *Healthcare Executive, 17*(6), 56–57.

Patel, A. and Reinsch, L. (2003). Companies can apologize: Corporate apologies and legal liability. *Business Communication Quarterly, 69*(1), 9–25.

Peterson, J., Bryant, C., and Franklin, B. (2001, March). Making dollars and sense from direct mail marketing: Just because you send it, doesn't mean they'll read it. *Fitness Magazine, 17*(4), 46–50.

Pierce, J. (2003, July 25). From talking tubs to motion-activated billboards. *The Engineer*, 23.

Powell, C. (2003, April 14). Digital ink makes billboards flexible. *Marketing Magazine, 108*(14), 4.

Popov, K. and McDonald, L. (2004, May 12). *E-mail deliverability: The challenges*. Retrieved July 17, 2004, from http://www.clickz.com

Public relations tools. (2003). Retrieved November 25, 2003, from http://www.marketingpower.com

Raeder, A. (1997, July/August). Promoting your website. *Searcher, 5*(7), 63–66.

Raphel, M. (1999, October). How direct marketing increases odds for casinos. *Direct Marketing, 62*(6), 54–55.

Rohrich, K. (1998, October 5). Direct mail can be a truly effective way to sell to the mature market. *Marketing Magazine, 103*(37), 14.

Rossiter, J. and Bellman, S. (1999). A proposed model for explaining and measuring Web ad effectiveness. *Journal of Current Issues and Research in Advertising, 21*(1), 13–31.

Samansky, A. (2002). Run! That's not the crisis communications plan you need. *Public Relations Quarterly, 47*(3), 25–27.

Schoenberg, A. (2005). Do crisis plans matter? A new perspective on leading during a crisis. *Public Relations Quarterly, 50*(1), 2–7.

Shaffer, R. (1999, October 5). Listen up! Pay attention! New Web startups want ads that grab you. *Fortune, 140*(8), 348–349.

Solomon, A. (2002). Good PR doesn't have to break the bank. *Street and Smith's Sports Business Journal, 5*(7), 1.

Sporting Goods Manufacturers Association (SGMA). (n.d.). *Sporting goods manufacturers Internet/website usage survey results*. Retrieved December 11, 2003, from http://www.sgma.com

Stanton, P. (2002). Ten communications mistakes you can avoid when managing a crisis. *Public Relations Quarterly, 47*(2), 19–22.

Sweet, D. (2002). Behind the numbers: How U.S. sports dollars are spent. *Street and Smith's Sports Business Journal, 4*(47), 30.

Tehrani, N. (2002, August). The art of positioning: It all begins with effective advertising. *Customer Interaction Solutions, 21*(2), 2–6.

Thomaselli, R. (2003, January 20). Why some advertisers sit on the sidelines for Super Bowl. *Advertising Age, 74*(3), 4–36.

Twenty top B-to-B list brokers/managers. (2001, July 16). *B-to-B, 86*(14), 23.

Ulmer, R. R. and Sellnow, T. L. (2002). Crisis management and the discourse of renewal: Understanding the potential for positive outcomes of crisis. *Public Relations Review, 28*(4), 361–365.

White, E. (2002, December 18). Web, direct mail get larger share of marketer's pie. *Wall Street Journal*, p. B2.

Williams, D. and Olaniran, B. (1998). Expanding the crisis planning function: Introducing elements of risk communication to crisis communication practice. *Public Relations Review, 24*(3), 387–400.

Wright, S. (2001, January). Avoiding the spam trap: Careful targeting and crafting can produce an electronic newsletter that is valuable and appreciated. *Ski Area Management, 40*(1), 44–46.

Zielinski, D. (2001, February). Crisis presenting: How to deliver bad news. *Presentations, 15*(2), 39–48.

Chapter 13

Relationships: Community, Sponsorships, and Stewardship

Edited by Bill Shepler, Owner
The Crossings and Shepler's Mackinaw Island

Buddy couldn't wait to go to the Click's Pizzeria. It wasn't just a pizza place—It was a child's dream. Click's was a pizzeria with a large variety of child-oriented games and activities including a maze, athletic and skill games, and rides. It was clear the focus of this pizzeria was not the food—It was the fun. Certainly not fun for adults, but fun for kids like Buddy. Based on the amount of money Buddy's mother, Suzanne, spent on games and rides when they last visited, it was undoubtedly a moneymaker for the organization.

Suzanne dreaded the idea of going back there. The first time they went six months ago it was too crowded, the pizza was average, the staff seemed bored (and even rude), and the prices were too high. However, Buddy loved it. He begged his Mom to take him if his report card was all *As*. The good news was that Buddy's did this, so Suzanne knew she had to make this day special.

Suzanne was strategic in finding a day to visit Click's again. She selected a midweek, late lunch hour when she thought the facility would be less crowded. She also clipped a coupon from the local paper for ten free games with the purchase of a pizza. When they arrived Suzanne noticed a sign on the marquis that said "new owners," but she was still not overly optimistic.

Two staff members with smiling, excited faces welcomed them at the door, and Suzanne couldn't help but smile back. When a staff member named Stuart (staff now had nametags) placed a security band on both Buddy and Suzanne, Stuart explained the bands were intended as a safety device to ensure children did not leave without the adult they arrived with. Suzanne smiled even more. Stuart and the staff further highlighted new games, activities, and rides not only for Buddy but also for older children and adults. The new owners had expanded the facility and added more rooms filled with activities. Some of these were designed for specific age groups; others for a variety of ages. Even Suzanne was thinking this could be fun.

As they went from ride to ride, game to game, Suzanne noticed the facility itself looked more professional and well-kept. She noticed other organizations had sponsored rides in the facility. For example, the local bank sponsored a family ride, an amusement park two hours away sponsored a

---

At the end of this chapter, readers will be able to...

- Describe various types of partnerships.

- List examples of community relation activities.

- Identify distinctions of cause-related marketing.

- Depict values associated with community relations, sponsorships, and stewardship activities.

- Define sponsorship and techniques for approaching this type of relationship.

- Distinguish between stewardship and quality service practices.

- Describe various internal and external stewardship activities.

mini rollercoaster, a new travel organization sponsored an Around-the-World game, and a local grocery store sponsored the large fruit-and-vegetable mascots who did a live show and walked to greeting the children playing games throughout the day.

As Suzanne saw these sponsors, she couldn't help but think she was proud her bank was listed as one of the sponsors. She also thought about frequenting that grocery store again. She had used another one for the past two years, but only for convenience. There wasn't a compelling service or offer that kept her going back to the other grocer. Further, she considered buying tickets to the amusement park—If you purchase tickets at Click's, you receive a 20% discount off admission. Although she did not need a travel agent anytime soon, her mother was flying to Europe this fall; she would be sure to tell her about this new travel organization. She found herself thinking positively not only of Click's but also of the organizations that appeared to be involved with the organization's improvements.

Three and a half hours later Suzanne and Buddy left with smiles on their faces a mile wide. The afternoon flew. They had more fun at Click's that day than they had in quite a while, wanted to tell others about Click's and come back again soon.

A week later, Suzanne was even more surprised to receive a thank-you note, discount coupon for a return

visit, and photograph of her and Buddy at Click's. The smile returned to her face again when she saw the photograph and remembered all the fun they had. Buddy grabbed the picture and ran to put it on his bedroom nightstand. Suzanne opened her date book and started to find another day that they could go.

• • • • •

Click's Pizzeria's new ownership realized they would need to do something different to reach their organization goals. They did not have an unlimited budget to make all the changes they wanted, so they found ways to do more with less by developing relationships with other related (and some unrelated) organizations. They found partners who would be interested in targeting the same market segments as they did and developed a sponsorship plan to have each of their activity areas financially sponsored by an organization. The monies received from the sponsoring organizations went into refurbishing and buying new games, activities, and rides. In addition, Click's realized partnering with organizations to offer promotions and discounts would assist in opening the organization up to different target markets who may be unable to afford coming very often or at all.

They also realized hiring, training, and rewarding employees who supported their organization's culture would develop internal and external relationships with consumers because both would be more satisfied. Finally, they knew they needed to focus on relationships they did have with consumers by doing something extra and unanticipated. Sure, it did cost about $1 per group to take, print, and send the photograph with the coupon, but they knew the return was worth much more than that.

An organization's ability to develop relationships with consumers, community organizations, sponsors, and other organization partners (e.g., associations, other related or unrelated organizations) is a powerful tool to reach consumers in today's marketing environment. It is no longer simply good enough to provide a good quality experience for consumers and a good work environment for employees. Organizations must be skilled at forming relationships with all stakeholders and partnering organizations to provide meaning to their experiences and approach marketing throughout an organization holistically. This chapter will review the various types of relationships formed by organizations.

It's all about the people you meet, the people you know, and the relationships you build. Sharon Gaiptman, Alaska Discovery

Relationships, relationships, relationships... If readers take away one main point from this textbook it should be relationships are the fundamental issue that drives successful marketing today. The ability for an organization to form valued relationships with all stakeholders and partners will provide the insight needed to address specific needs; gain buy-in to delivering the expected, deserved quality; and create long-term communication among board members, employees, volunteers, and consumers, which results in achieving organization objectives.

Relationship-oriented marketing has changed the way organizations implement communication mix components. Historically armed with promotion, advertising, public relations and sales, organizations now realize a number of other channels exist to build brand image and awareness. Further, how an organization approaches these relationships has changed. Once thought of as "good thing to do" and based on corporate citizenship and philanthropy, these types of relationships are now strategically formed with organizations that assist in achieving marketing objectives.

In this chapter, the concept of relationships is explained through the belief that partnerships exist when any two organizations or people engage in a way to produce something better. Pung stated a trend in public parks and recreation is greater collaboration and partnerships (Chaisson, 2002). These partnerships are being formed with other recreation providers to manage funding changes and to replace or enhance program and service offerings to the community they serve (Glover, 1999). This phenomenon is occurring in both private and for-profit leisure settings.

Specifically, this chapter discusses partnerships, community relations, sponsorships, and stewardship/quality service. These areas are viewed as increasingly important to organization marketing plans and have grown considerably to represent a growing proportion of a marketing plan's budget. Each of these topics is examined in this chapter and builds on the premise that relationships are fundamental to effective marketing plans.

Partnerships

As stated, a *partnership* is a relationship between at least two organizations (without regard to profit status) that combine efforts or resources for some type of mutual benefit. Acknowledged values of partnering include adding or expanding resources, reducing service duplication, increasing an organization's visibility, enhancing relationships, heightening an organization's credibility, increasing networking opportunities and developing friendships among staff in different organizations (van der Smissen, Moiseichik, Hartenburg & Twardzik, 1999, p. 3). These collaborative

relationships have grown in the past several years. Pybus and Janes (2004) found that 98 of 100 responding public parks and recreation organizations partnered with other recreation providers and 69 projected they will form more partnerships in the next three years. None indicated they will form fewer. Respondents indicated they engaged in partnerships largely based on program offerings, resource issues, and marketing needs. Partnerships helped organizations better deal with funding challenges.

The elements of an effective partnership are well-documented. Often literature states leadership support, target market, workforce, cultural fit, goals and mission, ongoing communication, and the formalization of partnership arrangements are all elements of effective collaborative relationships. Even though these arrangements range from verbal agreements to legal contracts, the trend is to have greater formalization of these relationships to protect all parties and ensure commitment and consistency (Crompton, 1999; Hastad & Tymeson, 1997; Wymer & Samu, 2003).

Barnholt and Jackowski (2002) suggested not all organizations are prepared for developing partnerships and may need to assess their beliefs as to whom may be an effective partner. Public recreation organizations form partnerships with all types of organizations, historically with similar ones. Eighty percent have formed a relationship with other public providers, whereas 42% of respondents have partnered with private/for-profit recreation organizations. This trend is growing, however, with more public providers accepting partnerships with private and for-profit organizations of value to them too (Pybus & Janes, 2004). Partnerships with schools, community education departments, social service organizations, and other human service organizations have existed for decades (Conner & Grady, 1978; Stark & Parker, 1981; van der Smissen, Moiseichik, Hartenburg & Twardzik, 1999, p. 76). Even though this is the oldest form of partnership, over the past 30 years other types have formed as well (van der Smissen, Moiseichik, Hartenburg & Twardzik 1999, p. 76). Increasingly, public recreation organizations are partnering with quasi-public, private, and for-profit leisure and tourism organizations because both sides recognize the benefits of such an arrangement outweigh any perceived disadvantages. These partnerships can be difficult due to conflicting philosophies and operating goals so partners should have similar quality service beliefs and practices because incompatible values can be challenging to overcome.

Partnerships in the leisure industry can change with any change in leadership. A new board president, executive director, or owner may decide an existing partnership is not the direction he or she wishes to pursue. Therefore, organizations must be prepared for a shift in positioning should this occur (Barnholt & Jackowski, 2002; Pybus & Janes, 2004).

Cross promotion partnership or *cobranding* opportunities are a specific type of marketing-related partnership. This type of arrangement allows two or more organizations to leverage their resources ultimately to attract and better serve target markets. Partners in this instance are formed with other strong brands to leverage brand strength and attain a larger share of revenue/participation by linking with another strong brand. Cobranding partnerships can be used (a) to gain access to each others' consumer base, (b) to provide more to existing consumers experiences and keep them loyal, and (c) to expand the consumer base to reach those with additional offerings. The lodging industry has done this with linking their properties with strong restaurant brands. Radisson has joined with T.G.I. Friday's and Marriott with Starbuck's Coffee. Howard Johnson's even cobranded with Crayola to attract young children and families. Organizations engage in these cross-promotion partnerships for many reasons:

1. Use promotional/marketing dollars more efficiently and effectively. Partnerships can expand revenue streams to engage in marketing activities as well as introduce more effective forms to reach and secure targeted markets.

2. Expand reach as more people become aware of an organization's offerings. A partnership may open the organization's doors to markets they have not yet reached or were unable to reach.

3. Expand frequency. People will hear, read, and see the organization's brand more often. This will create greater awareness of the organization's brand.

4. Identify a competitive niche, as aligning with an appropriate partner will reinforce the brand and build credibility.

5. Develop enhanced opportunities to improve the organization's ability to be newsworthy. A partner can create and develop stories.

6. Create enhanced consumer loyalty. Enhanced images reinforce consumer relations.

7. Have more fun. Developing a cobrand partner can be exciting and exhilarating. (Nozar, 2000)

Washburn, Till, and Priluck (2000) found cobranding relationships provide positive results, as perceived by consumers, for both brands with low brand equity and high brand equity. Further, consumers' first experience with a cobrand enhances their evaluations of the cobranded offerings, especially for those with low equity perceptions. Partnerships with low brand/low brand equity were perceived less positively than other combination types (i.e., high brand/low brand, high brand/high brand). However, partnering between low equity brands was perceived more highly than if the two had not cobranded at all. Cobranding relationships between two organizations with high brand equity creates an increased brand perception for both as well. Overall, it appears the selection of a cobranding partner can have a positive impact on both organizations.

Cobranding or crosspromotion partnerships can range from joint collateral and packaging to combined media events, newspaper columns, resource guides, mailings, and coupons to partners consumers. The range of potential crosspromotion opportunities is endless, and organizations can leverage their offerings through this type of partnership approach. The ideal type of partnership, Barnholt and Jackowski (2002) noted, is as varied as the number of leisure industry organizations. Various types of additional partnerships are reviewed throughout this chapter, including community relations, sponsorships, and stewardship/quality service partnerships.

Community Relations and Cause-Related Marketing

Community relations is developing partnerships with local "public service" (i.e., community, service, and social) organizations to communicate with targeted markets. Historically considered an organization's philanthropic focus, today organizations view these activities more strategically because they contribute to a marketing plan and assist in achieving organization objectives. This type of citizenship helps an organization market themselves to stakeholders (Maignan & Ferrell, 2001). It is, in essence, gaining free coverage or exposure from any number of community sources where the organization is viewed as a positive contributor to the local area, industry, and profession. The focus is to positively enhance the organization's image through good news and good efforts. Any public or community relation activities should be focused on mediums or organizations that target similar market segments. Certainly, any positive, free coverage from a media or community source is beneficial, but those geared toward similar market segments will produce the most meaningful returns for an organization.

The "community" in a community relations plan is not limited to the geographic area where an organization is based or the type of organization with which it is involved. Valuable environments to develop this type of relationship are created through involvement and volunteerism in related professional and industry associations. Organizations become involved with their respective industry associations (e.g., National Recreation and Park Association, National Tour Association, International Amusement Parks and Attractions Association, Employee Services Management Association, American Lodging Association, American Camping Association). Additional industry affiliations, (e.g., National Tourism Foundation, State Travel Bureaus, Convention and Visitor Bureaus) and other professional associations (e.g., National Association of Working Women) are all effective relationships supported by a community relations plan.

A variety of strategies can be taken within community relations activities that an organization can undertake in their marketing plan. Mogos stated a trend in marketing

Real Life Story: Courses Partnering in Gaylord's Golf Mecca

A small rural community of 23,000 in Ostego County is host to the Midwest's premier summer golf destination according to *Great Lakes Golf* magazine. Located in northern Michigan, the largely tourism-based economy hoped to expand its presence in the competitive tourism market by partnering lodging and golf operations to market themselves as a golf destination.

Since 1987 Gaylord Area Convention and Tourism Bureau has facilitated a relationship between area golf courses and lodging properties to market Gaylord as a tourism destination. Executive Director Paul Beachnau gained support from seven courses to package lodging and golf tee times in one—an idea new to the Midwest and modeled after Myrtle Beach. Even though it was a new concept, none of the courses hesitated in partnering and developing cooperative promotional material to market the new package. The courses saw immediate results.

The package provided discounted prices to golfers interested in lodging and golf opportunities. It was marketed through a brochure, advertising campaign, and golf show the first year. Courses and lodging properties were jointly displayed on all marketing materials and the community of Gaylord promoted itself as a "Golf Mecca." To facilitate the program, the Convention and Tourism Bureau wanted to empower lodging properties to work with consumers directly. This direct interaction would put visitors at a direct point of contact versus having the Bureau act as an intermediary to consumers and properties/courses. Golf consumers interested in the package simply called the lodging property they wished to stay at and informed them of the courses where they wanted to golf. In turn, lodging properties contacted courses to arrange tee times. Upon arrival to Gaylord, golfers would receive vouchers from the lodging property for the courses they reserved and paid for the entire package there. The vouchers would be redeemed at each course consumers played. Courses then billed the lodging properties for the vouchers they collected.

Since 1987 few changes have been made to the initial system. More courses and lodging properties have joined the cooperative program. To maintain and ensure quality, courses must be approved by the Convention and Tourism Board and meet minimum criteria, such as (a) 18-hole golf course, (b) watered fairways, (c) minimum yardage, and (d) a full-service clubhouse. All courses are within a 40-minute drive of Gaylord.

In 2005, 21 courses participated in the program, generating close to $1 million in golf vouchers. The Bureau spent $198,000 to promote the courses and lodging to the golf market. The plan now includes an aggressive database direct mail with a standard, high-end golf brochure; golf show appearances; and expanded advertising campaigns. The golf industry in Gaylord employs close to 1,400 people and brings in close to $18 million in revenue representing 329,497 golf rounds. This represents an 4% increase in number of rounds from the previous year with an average decrease of 6% in price per round. The net result shows an overall revenue increase of 2.5%.

The Bureau's ability to bring tourism partners together to promote the community has significantly contributed to the economic well-being of the area and developed this small, rural county's image as a "Golf Mecca" destination.

recreation organizations is to get involved in the community because these activities are valued and effective (Robinson, 2002). Again activities should relate to the targeted markets and be a smart use of organization resources (i.e., time, money, expertise). Sample community relations activities an organization can conduct with other organizations include the following:

- *Community service columns* can be prepared by the organization and inserted into community service publications. The content does not directly relate to the organization but the author and his or her organizational affiliation would be identified. Columns may be related or unrelated to what the organization offers to the public, such as a resort that writes columns on travel, a public leisure service organization that writes about community resources, or a health club that writes about wellness.

- *Community service presentations* (e.g., when professional athletes make a presentation to local school children, when organizations are asked to present to a community service group) may or may not relate to the organization directly but somehow contribute to the organization's community service objectives.

- *Organization membership (and participation)* involves joining and participating in an association related to the leisure and tourism industry. The membership benefits vary; however, benefits most often provide resources like education sessions, professional conferences, networking opportunities, industry publications, discounts with other partnered organizations, job searching, and research services.

- *Advisory boards* established by the organization serve two purposes: (a) organization leaders serve the community through leadership on other organization boards and (b) community leaders provide feedback to the organization by serving on the leisure and tourism organization's board.

- *Information booths* are used when an organization is allowed to set up and display organization information to those in attendance at some other organization's event. For example, an annual bridal show allows resorts to display information about their facility at the event.

- *Community events* (e.g., adopt-a-highway programs where an organization would sponsor a mile of highway and bring staff out to clean the roadside twice a year; festival support and donations; donating facility space to host a blood drive) are all examples that build community relationships.

- *Charitable events* promote a charitable cause or function and may involve organization donations, attendance, or in-kind services.

- *Local, professional, and industry organization volunteerism/leadership* involve organization employees providing their services to lead a local (e.g., Kiwanis), professional (e.g., California Professional Women Association), or industry (e.g., state travel bureau) association.

- *Cause-related support* can be in the form of allowing the organization's collateral to be displayed within the organization to financially supporting a cause or to act as a supporter of the cause in presentations or publications (e.g., an organization selects the Nature Conservancy and raises awareness and funds for them).

Another form of community relations is considered *cause-related marketing*, when organizations invest marketing resources in cause-related issues and activities in an effort not only to support a cause but also to create awareness for the organization and show it as a concerned, committed citizen and community member. This type of community relations activity identifies a specific cause (e.g., resource protection) whereby the organization supports the efforts and issues of a cause-related organization. *Direct Marketing* stated over 85% of corporations and 65% of not-for-profit organizations participated in cause-related marketing activities, and it is becoming more important to strategic communications and branding efforts (Direct Intelligence, 2000).

Mohr, Webb, and Harris (2001) found "market segments do consider a company's level of social responsibility in its purchase and investment decisions" (p. 69). They further noted organizations have an opportunity not only to meet their organization objectives but also to contribute to society. Organizations recognize the general image of business held by society today is low. Concerns have emerged regarding the ethical and immoral behaviors exhibited seemingly by so many organizations in the early 21st century that partnerships between cause-related issues are continuing to emerge as a strategy to overcome these attitudes (Lachowetz & Irwin, 2002). A study of the impact of FedEx's sponsorship of the St. Jude Classic charity golf tournament revealed it was a positive component of the company's activities and important to society. An IEG, Inc., study suggests 65% of consumers are likely to switch brands based on cause-related marketing activities (Moler, 2000).

Organizations that participate in cause-related marketing activities seek certain benefits from the relationship, including enhanced brand awareness, enhanced brand loyalty, and consumer brand switching (Lachowetz & Gladden, 2003). They theorize that for this to be successful, organizations must not only completely support the cause throughout their organization but also ensure the consumer recognizes this commitment.

Overall, these types of "community" relationships establish a "giving" strategy for philanthropic activities that involve all types of employees within the organization itself because any employee represents the organization. Being a good community member through involvement in activities and events inside and outside an organization provides many benefits for both the organization and individual, especially when it can positively contribute to an organization's marketing plan. Those who get involved state the value in doing so is the positive impacts provided not only to them personally but also to the organization. Some values of community relations involvement include the following:

- sense of accomplishment and doing something good for the local community, industry, or profession

- expanded network of community, industry, and professional leaders

- positive community perception of an organization's commitment

- expanded opportunities for potential consumers

- improved business relationships and resources

- improved profitability and/or enhanced organization operations

- team building and enhanced internal communication when multiple staff are involved

- potential tax incentives/savings

- enhance business or participation in slow periods by providing organization offerings to specific groups/organizations during slow/down times

Bennett (2002) found UK organizations used mostly commercial motives for choosing community relations/cause-related marketing efforts and these were largely employee determined. They also evaluated the return received from these projects just as they would advertising and sponsorship activities.

Community relations activities are a form of public relations because positive organization representation is the goal; however, it is specialized within community service activities, not the media. To facilitate this in an organization, a *community relations employee volunteer list* highlights all community organizations and assigns staff members' responsibilities to those organizations. This list clarifies information and indicates a commitment to strategically addressing each relationship. Organizations support employee involvement at various levels. Some encourage this type of community involvement through making employees more aware of opportunities in which to be involved; others financially support involvement by paying for annual fees, excusing and paying for meeting attendance, donating organization materials, and sponsoring meetings at the organization itself. Any type of employee can become involved in community relations activities and, the involved staff are often found to be more committed to the organization. Their efforts also produce more returns for the organization as well. The most important issue is for an organization to develop a strategic approach when developing community relationships. Table 13.1 (p. 310) showcases a list from a community leisure and tourism organization for supervisors/administrators to develop local community relations.

In addition to employees volunteering for various local, professional, and industry associations and organizations, an organization should also establish a specific giving strategy to ensure consistency and to eliminate overlapping or excluded efforts. Therefore, organizations should look at their target market segments and identify the type of local, professional, and industry affiliations they should have, participate in, and engage in to improve the likelihood of achieving organization objectives.

Activities do not have to be individually oriented. Community relations efforts can be identified for the entire organization. This joint approach to community relations activities can have additional benefits for the organization. Organizations that collectively focus on a charitable activity state improved internal relations develop through enhanced communication and team building.

Even though community relations activities do not involve the media, all community relations activities should work with the media to spread awareness about the organization's cause, issues, and efforts. Working with the media is a natural extension to these activities. An organization can gain positive media exposure regarding their community relations activities through public relations. For example, an organization that donates to a local charitable cause should also write a press release sharing a newsworthy story about the donation. Leblein (2002) stated water parks could also benefit from community relation activities because they could use off-peak hours to assist community organizations to not only use the park to introduce it to new market segments but also to foster good will and provide resources at slower time periods. She further noted it could be as simple as discounting tickets for those in their scout uniforms or providing the venue to a charitable organization for free. Organization can provide endless activities to use community relations as a tool to reach consumers and ultimately achieve organization objectives. Examples include

- Establish a philanthropy for the organization's employees to donate (e.g., American Heart Association).

- Host an event for a local charity (e.g., Boys and Girls Clubs) at no cost. Get the press to cover it and it becomes public relations.

- Act as a blood donation center for a community blood drive.

- Buy tickets for and attend other charity events.

Table 13.1
Sample Community Relations List

Canton Leisure Services
Staff Liaison to Community, Service, and Social Organizations

Keith Alexander
Recreation Supervisor
Exchange Club of Canton, Public Safety Education Committee
Partners with: Canton Historical Society

Debra Bilbrey-Honsowetz
Manager of Recreation and Facilities
Canton Chamber of Commerce, Canton's 100 Days to Health Committee

Ann-Marie Carravallah
Recreation Coordinator (Sports)
Canton Community Junior Baseball Softball Association, Canton Lions Football Club, Canton Soccer Club, Canton Community Basketball Association, Canton Amateur Hockey Association

Ann Conklin
Leisure Services Director
Canton Chamber of Commerce, Public Safety Education Committee, Plymouth/Canton Community Schools

Robert Dates
Recreation Coordinator (Programming)
Partners with: Canton Lions, Canton Historical Society, Plymouth/Canton Morning Optimists

Susan Doughty
Marketing Specialist
Canton Chamber of Commerce

Jennifer Eubanks
Recreation Specialist (Special Events)
Partners with: Canton Lions, Canton Historical Society, Plymouth/Canton Morning Optimists

Rosemary Globke
Banquet and Conference Center Coordinator
Partners with: Canton Chamber of Commerce

Dave Horstman
Manager of Golf Operations
Canton Chamber of Commerce, St. Joseph Mercy Hospital Pro-Am Steering Committee

Jon LaFever
Recreation Specialist (Youth)
Exchange Club of Canton, Michigan Special Olympics
Partners with: Growth Works

Amy Lockmondy
Recreation Specialist (Health & Wellness)
Canton's 100 Days to Health Committee

Dianne Neihengen
Recreation Coordinator (Seniors)
National Council on the Aging, National Institute of Senior Centers, Michigan Association of Senior Centers, Vice Chair of The Senior Alliance
Partners with: Canton Civitan Club, Canton Goodfellows, Canton Lions Club

Dan Plamondon
Recreation Specialist (Sports)
Canton Community Junior Baseball Softball Association, Canton Lions Football Club, Canton Soccer Club, Canton Community Basketball Association, Canton Amateur Hockey Association

Brad Sharp
Manager of Parks
Partners with: Canton Rotary Club

Jennifer Tobin
Performing Arts
Wayne County Council for the Arts, History and Humanities, Michigan Association of Community Arts Agencies, ArtServe Michigan, Cultural Initiatives Alliance of Northville, Plymouth, Canton, and Belleville, Project Arts

Abraham Vinitski
Parks Supervisor
Council for Community Excellence, American Cancer Society Relay for Life
Partners with: Canton Historical Society

- Serve in an executive board member capacity for an industry association.

- Serve on a committee for a professional association to raise money for student scholarships.

- Donate free materials/services for other charities' fundraisers.

- Develop a community relation employee volunteer list to encourage and support employee participation in community relations activities.

- Sponsor local community campaigns (e.g., Adopt-a-Mile, Be a Good Neighbor).

- Provide a leisure service facility, program or service to consumer groups in need (e.g., health club facilities during slow or closed periods to rehabilitation patients from a local hospital).

The lines between corporate philanthropy, community relations, cause-related marketing and sponsorship have blurred in the last ten years because organizations have approached these functions with similar intent. They have thought, "If I do good things for my local, professional, and industry community through employees volunteering, giving donations, sponsoring activities, and supporting specific causes I not only feel good about what I am doing and assist others in their organization's missions but also achieve my organization objectives." However, a distinction of sponsorship allows sponsorship to be separated from other community relations functions.

Sponsorships

A *sponsorship* is a cash or in-kind fee paid to an organization in return for access to the exploitable commercial potential associated with the organization (McKnight, personal communication, December 8, 2004). With in-kind sponsorship, no money is exchanged but a dollar amount is determined by each partner to identify whether the services are equal. An example would be a sports venue offering $450 worth of tickets to a newspaper for $450 worth of ad space for the week leading up to the event.

Sponsors affiliate with events, experiences, or organizations in an effort to expose their organization to the market(s) served by the sponsoring organization. It is also a partnership relationship where one organization agrees to provide support for another organization in return for enhanced awareness of their organization brand.

The sponsorship field has changed dramatically in the past decade. Once viewed as a way to be a good commu-

Real Life Story: Tourism Caring for America

Tourism Caring for America is a volunteer program providing the tourism industry the opportunity to "give back" by cleaning up and/or restoring tourism-related sites in need of care or rejuvenation. Past projects have included Ellis Island, New York, the first point of entry for many immigrants to the United States during the late 19th and early 20th century. St. Louis Cemetery #1, commissioned in 1789, marking the beginning of aboveground burial in New Orleans, a most popular destination for tourists visiting the city. Mount Vernon, Virginia, George Washington's estate and grounds was the site for the 2005 gathering.

Tourism Caring for America volunteers provide sweat equity to their projects. While many philanthropic organizations provide monetary assistance, the participants involved with the Tourism Caring projects provide true physical labor. At Mount Vernon, the mission was to clear the forest floor of debris accumulated over the years and exacerbated by Hurricane Isabel in 2003. The removal of the debris and deadwood allows the forest to regenerate at a faster pace and lessen the risk of a catastrophic forest fire, which would threaten the historic mansion and out buildings visited by 1,000,000+ annually. The close to 400 volunteers provided a combined 2,250 hours of physical labor and completed in one day what would have taken more than ten years by the grounds crew of Mount Vernon, assuming the time and funding were available.

Generosity is a character trait of all those who choose a profession within travel, tourism and hospitality. From frontline sales to chief executives, the desire to provide assistance is the backbone of our profession. By offering sweat equity, participants are able to see the results of their labor by the end of the day. Participants have commented, after their first participation, they look forward to the following year's project. The ability to work as a team towards the betterment of a tourism-related site and to "give back" to the local community is the motivation of many to offer their personal time and financial contribution to these projects.

nity member, it is now also viewed as a strategic marketing decision because more and more organizations are engaging in this type of marketing communication. Sponsorship has also changed as the number of media choices have expanded, resulting in greater interest in other forms of communication (Fitzgerald, 2002). In addition, sponsorships are viewed as relatively inexpensive compared to other communication choices. As a result, different and additional types of organizations are pursuing leisure-oriented sponsorships (e.g., car companies, credit card corporations). Recreation facility organizations that have not capitalized on sponsorship opportunities are missing a tremendous opportunity (Moler, 2000). Sponsorship is a way to more effectively reach target markets with less clutter than other communication choices because the organization's brand can directly touch valued target markets (Mack, 1999).

Sponsorships have always been of value to the organizations soliciting the sponsor, but historically they have not been used by public leisure and tourism organizations. Today, even public parks and recreation organizations have turned to sponsorship techniques as a means to expand funding sources and growth because the value of using this form of communication has become evident (Mowen & Graefe, 2002; Mowen & Havitz, 2002). Although researchers disagree about how much sponsorship spending has increased, they all agree it has grown in the past decade. Some estimate these expenditures have as much as quadrupled. In relation, marketing budgets have increased proportionately toward these activities (McKnight, personal communication, December 8, 2004; Sponsorships Expected to Grow This Year, 2002; Verity, 2002).

Sponsorship comes in many forms. These forms include money, goods or services, or in-kind support (e.g., use of an organization's facilities or staff time). Bednall, Walker, Curl, and LeRoy (2001) found during organization interviews that most organizations showed support for some type of sponsorship, donation, or partnership with nonprofit organizations. Donations of cash and in-kind support were the most often used types of support provided. More firms, however, predicted they would see a decrease in support offered because more a return for their contributions was needed versus simply being a good thing to do.

Engaging in a sponsorship occurs in two different ways for organizations: (a) by determining appropriate and effective sponsors for an organization's activities and events, and (b) by establishing a strategy for events and activities an organization will sponsor. Regardless of the type of sponsorship engagement, organizations do so for four main objectives:

1. to achieve broad organization objectives, such as enhanced image

2. to achieve specific target market objectives

3. to leverage media and marketing communication exposure with target markets

4. to align with a partner and be perceived as one, versus two, separate organizations

Types of Sponsorships

Large corporations like Nike are not the only ones that can participate in securing sponsors for their activities. Although these organizations secure more corporate-oriented funding opportunities, smaller organizations depend on local and regional support, and likewise support these smaller type organizations with their own sponsoring efforts (Hirschkorn, 2002; Mack, 1999). A variety of ways an organization can be involved in sponsorship activities are highlighted in Table 13.2.

Over 100 small organizations responded to a questionnaire designed to understand sponsorship practices. Little support was found for sponsorship activities beyond the local area; most often cited forms of sponsorship included local events and charities. Small organizations indicated modest growth of this as a communication mix item for the future. Smaller organizations relied on other forms of relationship communication including word-of-mouth, quality service to consumers by managers and employees, and direct personal selling. Small organizations were also more spontaneous about these decisions and did less strategic planning (Webb & Carter, 2001).

These findings would suggest smaller organizations may not be as strategic in their approach to sponsorship and other marketing initiatives. Even though the mediums best suited for large and small organizations varies, a more

Sponsors allow programs to happen.

strategic approach for any size organization can provide significant results regardless of the availability of marketing resources. Smaller organizations can also appeal to larger sponsors by *sponsor sharing*. This process is when two or more smaller organizations partner to appeal to a sponsor (Cruice, 2002). Smaller organizations that did partake in more advanced forms of sponsorship found similar benefits as larger organizations would (Webb & Carter, 2001).

Value of Sponsorships

A tremendous body of literature suggests why organizations would want to engage in some type of sponsorship relationship. However, evidence suggests some sponsorship arrangements are more effective and valued than others. Organizations value sponsorships and have interest in forming these types of partnerships for several reasons:

1. expanded marketing efforts when associated with a positively viewed brand

2. enhanced image and reputation with targeted markets

3. altered or enhanced public perception

4. build business trade relations and good will

5. greater organization awareness, revenue, market share and participation

6. improved employee morale and relations

7. organization differentiation from competitors

8. improved stakeholder support (Bennett, 2002; Clark, Cornwell & Pruitt, 2002; Verity, 2002)

Simply because value exists in establishing sponsorship relationships does not mean all are successful. Several studies evaluated these relationships and found various influences.

Copeland, Frisby, and McCarville (1996) studied Canadian organizations who supported sports sponsorships. They discovered the most often cited reasons for discontinuing a sponsor relationship was organizations viewed little return or value for the investment made or their objectives were not being achieved. Less often cited were changing priorities, budget reductions, poor execution by sponsoring organizations, increased sponsorship costs, and conflict between organizations.

Berrett (2001) found in his study of 34 Canadian national sport organizations that two environmental factors contributed to their ability to raise sponsorship funds: media exposure and participation rates. These were the prime considerations in sponsorship decisions/selections.

Sponsorship support of a women's golf event with the LPGA was based on the organizations' interest in using sponsorship as a growing trend, value of the association of a strong brand in women's sport, and the unique opportunity for participants (Williams, 1998)

Sparks and Westgate (2002) found the Canadian Hockey Association's sponsors had different reasons for being involved with women's ice hockey sponsorship versus other sport industry sponsorship:

1. The growing participation and attendance in the sport.

2. Female players are viewed as more courteous, approachable, and easier to work with than their male counterparts.

Table 13.2
Examples of Sponsorship Partnerships

Type of Sponsorship	Example
On-site sampling	A portable climbing wall where a for-profit organization sponsors free climbs at a community recreation department event
On-site signage	A camp sponsors signage at an ice arena for exposure to the same market that may attend camp. One trend in signage is virtual advertising, where multiple sponsors share the same space as images are virtually displayed and rotated.
Event partnership	A fitness center partners with a senior center to offer a Healthy Seniors Day event
On-site usage partnership	A for-profit tennis club provides tennis lessons for community recreation participants at a significantly reduced cost
Brand awareness in promotional literature	A soft drink company pays for all brochures to be printed if their logo is prominently displayed on the promotional piece
Organization privatization partnership	A hotel company is hired to manage the lodging operation in a National Park

3. Women's hockey is growing in Canada and is receiving a great deal of media attention.

4. It is a low-cost/high-value relationship.

5. Women influence a family's buying decisions.

Therefore, it is important for organizations to identify the reasons their offerings should be selected over other potential choices a sponsor may have.

A study of Australia's 20 largest sports sponsors suggested the greater market orientation (i.e., integration of market-oriented practices in an organization), the greater the benefits associated with the sponsorship relationship. Farrelly, Quester, and Mavondo (2003) found that a positive relationship exists with commitment to the sponsorship relationship and market orientation. More specifically, an organization's market orientation is positively associated with relationship variables including communication, trust, and commitment. Those organizations with higher market orientation also had greater commitment to the relationship.

Traditional means for securing sponsors and maintaining long-term relationships are no longer working as they once did. The popularity of on-site signage, logos on or in programs, and on-site sampling are changing. Simply showcasing the sponsors brand is no longer enough. Sponsors now want to create experiences and communicate their brands' values by engaging in more emotionally charged sponsorship means. This starts with how a sponsor relationship is approached, developed, and maintained.

Approaching Sponsorship Relationships

Bunting (personal communication, 2004) stated sponsorships are like dating relationships—To obtain a new sponsor an organization must

1. **Grab the sponsor's attention.** The organization must be prepared and attractive to a potential buyer.

2. **Court the potential sponsor.** It must research the sponsor and understand the sponsor's likes, wants and needs. One must also understand others influence the decision to sponsor or not to sponsor.

3. **Ask the potential sponsor for a date.** A face-to-face meeting with a potential sponsor is always the ideal—either invites them to lunch or to the organization itself so the sponsor can see leisure and tourism experiences occurring

and better understand the type of exposure they may receive.

4. **Get to know the sponsor.** On the first date, it is important to get to know the sponsor before trying to sell them on your organization. Any direct sales activity should be based on the sponsor's individual needs. Do not push the sponsor either—No one likes a pushy date.

5. **Follow up after the date.** Thank the potential sponsor for the date and continue to court them eventually asking for a commitment.

6. **Commit.** The potential sponsor becomes an actual sponsor, and they must feel engaged and important to the organization. The agreement is a win-win arrangement to benefits both organizations when each is completely satisfied with the contract.

7. **Do what you say.** Organizations must fulfill their end of the commitment agreement and uphold their end of the arrangement.

8. **Establish a long-term relationship.** As long as commitments are fulfilled and the needs of the sponsor or the organization do not change (or they change together), then the likelihood of a long-term relationship is possible. If either party is dissatisfied, then the relationship will breakdown and there may be hurt feelings toward one another. The potential sponsor may look for other organizations that want to form a relationship with them instead. Therefore, staying in tune with the needs of the sponsor and addressing how well the organizations is meeting the sponsor's needs is of particular importance in this relationship (as all others!).

Successful sponsors are found by

1. Identifying a target list of potential sponsors. Which potential sponsors fit the organization's target markets, objectives, needs and mission?

2. Learning *everything* about a potential sponsor. What do they do? Who do they serve? Who do they compete with? Who do they sponsor? What are their marketing objectives? What is their organization's history? Resources to assist with this process include trade and general publications, websites, business or research publications, networking with other professionals, and conferences. Bednall, Walker, Curl, and LeRoy (2001) found Australian organizations were

more likely to donate, sponsor, and partner with nonprofit organizations if their competitors were known to do so.

3. Understanding how the sponsors and your organization are similar.

4. Identifying potential mutually beneficial opportunities where each can have a win-win situation.

5. Following the "dating process" as outlined previously.

What Organizations Consider Before Agreeing to Sponsor

Organizations are concerned with the following:

- their objective
- target market solicited by the sponsor organization
- amount of exposure they will receive for their sponsor contribution
- type of direct exposure they can be provided (e.g., distributing the organization brochure to all in attendance)
- use of logos on promotional materials
- type of advertising/promotion that will be done
- what specific pieces will include the organization's brand
- return on investment (Gabriel, 1999)

Further, organizations now realize that additional public relations exposure can also occur because of the sponsorship arrangement. Therefore, understanding an organization's plan for creating positive media attention is also a consideration when valuing sponsorship arrangements. *Sport Business* suggested "increasingly sophisticated public relations programs are key to establishing, building and nurturing the relationship between sponsor and the all-important media" (Sponsor Services, 1999, p. 15). Organizations recognize they must develop a sponsorship package that includes media and public relations exposure, as well as more completely integrate the sponsor with the organization itself. Organizations ask themselves several questions to be sure sponsorship is the right choice:

- Is there a connection with the target market that the organization is interested in serving?

- What type of recognition is the organization giving or getting from this sponsorship?
- What is the return the organization will get for sponsoring?
- What are the benefits of this sponsorship for the organization or the sponsoring organization?
- How is the sponsorship package more competitive and valued than other choices a potential sponsor may have?

Positive answers to these questions will surface when sponsorship choices are best suited for an organization.

Sponsorship Packages

One way of meeting the needs of sponsors is by providing a menu of sponsorship choices. Historically completed in nonprofit organizations, these types of sponsorship packages are designed to offer a variety of sponsorship opportunities. In an attempt to appeal to each individual organization's needs and resources, this type of approach allows leisure and tourism organizations to solicit various sizes and types of establishments.

Measuring Sponsorship Investments

Even though sponsorships as a marketing communication mix item are growing in the myriad communication possibilities, there is concern that this area of the mix is difficult to measure its return. Some suggest evaluating sponsorships is subjective at best and there are few ways to identify concrete findings regarding the return of the sponsorship investment. Yet, others don't seem to care, as some believe that any controlled, positive exposure cannot hurt revenue or participation (Copeland, Frisby & McCarville, 1996; Maloney, 2002; Verity, 2002). Still other suggested sponsorships need to be evaluated to determine how it engages consumers.

Yet, the sponsorship environment is continuing to change. Organizations are more demanding that sponsoring organizations are able to formally evaluate the worth of their sponsorship investment. Williams (1998) found only three out of seven LPGA sponsors formally evaluated the impact of their sponsorship of the women's golf event. The formal methods employed included surveys, focus groups, media audits, and other commercially available research. The other four sponsors relied on verbal feedback and other informal methods to measure their return. They indicated time, cost, and a lack of measurable means to do so were

Real Life Story: Sponsorship and Bowling

The Professional Women's Bowling Association (PWBA) was the first to find a way to be proactive concerning individual tour player sponsorships. Kim Adler, PWBA star, "established a new entrepreneurial standard when she auctioned off logo space on her bowling apparel" on eBay (p. 102).

Instead of approaching organizations one-by-one to see which one might be interested in sponsorship, Adler decided to take responsibility for managing the process and promote herself to various organizations in a competitive format. She put her auction item on eBay and allowed organizations to bid on the sponsorship package. Pacific Pools won the sponsorship auction with a $14,389.88 bid. Their Director of Marketing stated their market was middle America and bowling attracted the same type of market segments.

Adler then contacted organizations that had bid but did not receive the sponsorship package. She individually negotiated with them to see if they had interest in increasing their bids to sponsor her and receive awareness through their organization logo on her bowling shirt too. Overall, this new approach to sponsorship created a great deal of publicity and awareness not only for the PWBA tour but Pacific Pools. Before the tour season began, Pacific Pools stated they had recouped their investment with this coverage already (Dressel, 2002).

reasons few sponsors actually formally evaluated the impact. Those using formal evaluation tended to view their sponsorship as a means to achieve their marketing objectives, whereas those that did not evaluate viewed their sponsorship as a means of pubic relations and awareness. Those who did conduct formal evaluation did so for the following reasons:

1. to justify sponsorship
2. to identify support for future involvement
3. to measure sponsorship objectives
4. to secure lower level sponsors
5. to understand audience demographics

Some organizations have found ways to measure the sponsors' return and to prove sponsorship is a positive investment for organizations through asking consumers. *Olympic Review* (Salt Lake City, 2002) stated their study of Olympic spectators found overwhelming support existed for sponsors, and spectators expected and understood the importance of sponsorship to the Olympic's success. Further, 45% of spectators stated they would buy more from an Olympic sponsor because of the affiliation. Seventy-five percent of spectators felt sponsorship builds organization awareness, 39% believed it increased organization sales, and 30% felt it boosted the organization's image. IEG, Inc., supported this, suggesting in their study that 83% of consumers have a more positive image of sponsoring organizations (Moler, 2000).

Yet, others measure sponsorship success based on participation/revenue. Mackin (personal communication, 2004) suggested a radio partnership with the city's annual haunted forest event increased awareness and attendance by 300% the year they were added as a sponsor. He noted this was the only tactical change the recreation department employed in the program marketing plan that year.

Strategies for Determining Which Organizations to Sponsor

A variety of sponsorship choices are available for an organization to select from. Data gathered on corporations' sponsorship activities suggest they invest mostly with sports sponsorship activities. Data from 1998 suggested 67% of sponsorship dollars went to sports sponsorship activity, 10% funded entertainment tours and attractions, 9% festivals and fairs, 8% causes, and 6% the arts. Leisure and tourism organizations must determine if they will sponsor other organization's activities and who will receive their marketing resources (The Parade of Corporate Sponsors, 1999).

Lardinoit and Derbaix (2001) studied the ability of television viewers to recall two different types of sponsorship: *field sponsorship*, where an organization sponsors a sport team and receives some type of exposure at the event itself, and *television sponsorship*, where an organization sponsors the show itself. Field sponsors would receive exposure during an event, such as when the television shows a football play occurring in the end zone and a view of the billboard at that end of the stadium is seen on the television. Television sponsors would receive exposure at the beginning or end of a televised sporting event allowing uninterrupted view of their few seconds of exposure. They found that both are more effective in viewer recall than no exposure, however, television sponsorship is more effective than field exposure with both unaided and aided recall.

A study by MediaLab, polling 12,000 consumers in 18 countries, found different market segments have appeal to different types of sponsorship relationships (Kaplan, 2002). More specifically, men remember sports sponsors, women tend to buy products from good-cause sponsors, younger viewers more often cite sports sponsors influence buying decisions, affluent consumers notice sponsors more, "but mid-market viewers are more likely to buy products from a sponsor" (p. 1).

Burnside (2002) interviewed author and former leader of the International Festival and Event Association, Bruce Skinner, who stated event sponsorship is still a relatively new form of sponsorship because it was not until the 1984 Olympics that this concept emerged. Further, he noted organizations get involved with events for several reasons, including exposure as a communications method, community visibility, support for a cause, directly serving consumers, and various other organization objectives.

In determining the reason for the sponsorship, it is vital to look at another important dynamic of the relationship. The organization, with the potential partner, should decide whether to instate a sole or exclusive partnership versus the organization looking to multiple partnerships to reach its objectives. When food and beverage companies sponsor events, they want to ensure their offerings are the only ones being used. Heinz did this in their stadium sponsorship, as did Maxwell House with the Taste of Chicago. Burnside (2002) suggested their market share improved dramatically after this relationship was formed. They moved from number three to number one in the marketplace.

Sponsorship can also assist with exposing an organization to market segments it wants to reach, as Intel did in Oregon. They supported a festival when first moving to town to expose their organization to potential employees. It appears that organizations cannot simply rely on historic methods for sponsorship and must look at new ways to reach consumers through these relationships. Sponsors must become actively involved in the organization's operations to maximize sponsorship impact (e.g., booth at a festival, promotional items distributed at events, developing activities for consumers, ensuring offerings are available to consumers).

Fans with strong team support had more favorable attitudes about purchasing from team sponsors and having more sponsor recognition, patronage, and satisfaction than those less loyal to a team (Dalakas & Kropp, 2002; Gwinner & Swanson, 2003). Gwinner and Swanson (2003) suggested organizations may want to segment consumers in this instance to those with high fan support and low fan support. Either market segment may be worthy of sponsor focus but more loyal fans may naturally support sponsor efforts, therefore specific tactics should be focused on communicating more aggressively with less loyal fans. Conversely, enhanced communication activities through loyalty programs may further engage loyal fans to a sponsor's offerings.

The popularity of venues acquiring sponsors for the naming rights to their buildings suggests organizations must find value in this type of exposure. Although this concept started in 1966 with Anheuser-Busch naming Busch Memorial Stadium (the venue of the St. Louis Cardinals), it really wasn't until 1973 that a true sponsorship emerged because Anheuser-Busch owned both the team and the stadium in St. Louis. The first sponsorship occurred when Rich Products, a dairy food company, sponsored the Buffalo Bill's stadium renamed the Rich Stadium. This practice did not significantly expand, however, until 20 years later (Clark, Cornwell & Pruit, 2002). Clark, Cornwell, and Pruitt (2002) believe it took so long for this phenomenon to expand due to the ignorance about the impact of such a relationship.

Organizations have since viewed investing $1 million per year to create tens of thousands of exposures daily as a "relatively low-cost communications medium" (Clark, Cornwell & Pruit, 2002, p. 18), and they have overcome their concern of the effectiveness of simply sharing a name brand (vs. an entire message with traditional sport advertising). With the more recent addition of new, refurbished, and expanding venues, there also have been more opportunities for organizations to be involved. They studied 49 stadiums and venues to understand a measurable impact of the association since some suggested these types of sponsorships were only to enhance egos within organization leadership. They found stock prices increased by 1.65% at the time of the sponsorship announcement for the stadium. Further they found "variables positively and significantly correlated with perceived sponsorship success include the team's winning percentage (i.e., greater awareness for stadiums hosting winning teams), contract length, and high-technology and locally based companies."

Although naming rights are viewed as acceptable in the commercial-oriented leisure industry, some suggest public parks and recreation organizations do not view this in the same manner. Mowen and Havitz (2002) suggested naming rights should be used sparingly. They should be used when a substantial percentage of the facility investment is from the sponsoring organization. Temporary associations (e.g., an event) are more readily accepted than permanent associations (e.g., a park). Size and content restrictions should exist, and public organizations should establish acceptable standards the public agrees to and supports. They further noted appropriate locations for sponsor recognition should be considered at indoor rather than outdoor locations, and off-site (e.g., publications) versus on-site means are preferred. Public settings have issues to consider that commercial leisure and tourism organizations do not. Understanding the interests, needs, and desires of the target market segments is once again a critical concern.

Even in public parks and recreation organizations, research suggests public parks and recreation organization's corporate sponsorship is supported by more than half of respondents; only 15% opposed corporate sponsorship. The types of sponsorships perceived most favorably included those with local companies, those for money, and those supporting free programs provided by the parks and recreation organization. Further, the public supported sponsorship activities with nationally recognized organizations, and preference would be to develop relationships with those "that are subdued, nonpermanent and consistent with the natural character of park settings" (Mowen & Graefe, 2002, p. 46).

Sponsorship decisions are emerging as viable options for communicating with target markets and achieving organization objectives in all types of leisure and tourism organizations. Some sponsorship examples include

- Sponsor food and beverages at a youth community event.

- Financially sponsor an adult hockey tournament at the local arena.

- Financially sponsor datebook calendars at local elementary schools with your calendar of events and organization information listed.

- Solicit sponsors who seek to reach the same target market as you (e.g., schools and youth, commission on aging and seniors, daycare centers for infants, toddlers, preschoolers), and develop a sponsorship package from which the sponsors can select.

- Host a chamber after-hours event at the leisure facility.

In any sponsorship relationship it is important to draw guidelines and have a clear understanding of how the sponsor will be acknowledged. Naming rights can pose challenges for organizations if a shift in brand identity occurs and the brand needs to become reestablished. For example, an arena had a sponsor who wanted to spend $20,000 on "something." The arena allowed this company to sponsor a circus coming to town and receive naming rights for their investment. They renamed the circus with the company's name in the title, which no one recognized, so the circus had poor attendance as a result.

Quality is never an accident. It is always the result of high intention, sincere effort, intelligent direction and skillful execution. It represents the wise choice of many alternatives. Author Unknown

Stewardship: Providing Quality Service Internally and Externally

Because Chapter 3 has already been dedicated to the quality movement, there may be some confusion about how this is perceived as a communication mix variable and an overall organization concern. As suggested earlier, quality service deals with exceeding expectations. Quality service practices must permeate all aspects of an organization. A quality service system is an integrated approach that occurs throughout an organization. It is not a pieced-together effort that allows one department to "train staff on service practices" and another to "address guest dissatisfaction through empowerment." It must be accepted, created, acknowledged and delivered by *everyone* in an organization. Quality is a group effort built on individual responsibility.

Once this approach is accepted and integrated by an organization, it is more likely to apply more effective marketing practices because it has successfully managed the five critical phases of the leisure service experience—anticipation, travel to, destination, travel from, and reflection (see Clawson and Knetsch's model, Figure 2.2, p. 36). It is assumed, therefore, that organizations which have accepted and embodied the quality movement are better prepared to achieve marketing and organization objectives. The acceptance of quality as a part of an organization's culture, however, does not specifically address target market objectives and additional quality efforts may need to be employed to assist an organization in reaching these specific focus areas. Quality is a journey and not a destination.

There are additional considerations an organization can take to apply the same quality service practices as a strategic means to achieve a marketing objective. Hence, quality service actions are considered a communication mix decision *and* an overall organization philosophy. In this chapter, specific quality service actions designed to assist in achieving an organization's marketing objective will be referred to as stewardship.

The word *stewardship* is a term that began in the Middle Ages in Europe when those who had a great deal of property hired a "steward" to protect the estate and those within it. In the philanthropic environment today, this same term is used to describe how organization stewards protect donors, how relationships are developed to preserve the "property" (e.g., donor) and the public relations or positive attention given to an organization. Environmental stewardship practices protect and care for natural resources (Charbonneau, 1997; Dustin & Wolffe, 1998; Worley & Little, 2002). The same concepts apply here, except the "protection" is not geared toward an environmental resource, donor, or property. In this instance, it is applied to human capital resources (e.g., consumers, employees). Stewardship represents the organization's specific decisions designed to protect and preserve long-term relationships with targeted markets and achieve marketing objectives.

The employees' or guests' experience in a leisure and tourism organization should be the best it can be. When guest expectations are exceeded, they will tell others to go to the organization, whereas poor service experiences result in guests and employees telling others not to come or not to work there. Quality is an overall organization issue, and several things can be reinforced within each particular target market.

External Stewardship

Specific stewardship actions or initiatives are another choice leisure and tourism organizations should make for each marketing objective. Building stewardship relationships with consumers contributes to an organization's success as it helps to attract and to retain consumers (Priluck, 2003).

Consider the following marketing objective: A live theater wants to increase the number of senior citizen motor coach tour groups interested in Missouri as a destination from 500 seats in 2004 to 5,000 seats by December 31, 2005. Even though the organization may indeed employ quality service practices, they may not have considered the unique needs of this senior market in their specific quality actions. Therefore, the organization may choose to identify additional quality-oriented/stewardship actions that can be taken to assist in achieving this specific objective. In this

example, the organization may decide there are specific stewardship actions they could take to improve their ability to achieve their objective. The actions they consider relate to how they will communicate with and reach this market. For instance, they could:

- Train staff about serving senior citizens because they have served so few before that their staff is not prepared to deal with the unique needs of this market segment.

- Provide the tour operator and motorcoach driver(s) with a welcome basket complete with regional specialties and a handwritten welcome note.

- Meet the tour group on arrival, and have at least two actors perform a song aboard the motor coach as a welcome to the group.

- Provide a welcome bag to all senior citizens with promotional items from the theater (e.g., playing cards) and additional information on the entertainers and the particular performance beyond what is already provided in the program.

- Following their visit, mail handwritten thank-you notes to each senior citizen and include a photograph of their tour group with the cast.

Each of these ideas would more directly meet the needs of the senior citizen motorcoach group and would assist in ensuring their expectations were exceeded as well as acheiving marketing objectives. If this set of decisions was not considered, the organization would not necessarily have addressed the individual target market needs. This list does not suggest an organization would do each of these to better reach and communicate with the intended audience. However, this short list of items are intended to be considered, along with the other communication mix variables (e.g., public relations, sponsorship, community relations, direct sales, internal marketing, advertising) and from that complete list, the most effective choices selected (as discussed in Chapter 10).

Stewardship communication mix decisions should also reconsider each of the five phases of a leisure experience to identify the specific ways the organization could ensure this market segment had an experience that exceeded their expectations. The theater should consider how they can ensure each consumer leaves with this occurring. Going the extra mile to develop loyal relationships with consumers is viewed as how organizations not only weather potential negative influences (e.g., price wars) but also achieve marketing objectives.

Internal Stewardship

Staff is a vital factor in the ability of an organization to establish consumer relationships. A marketing plan that does not address staff specifically is lacking a critical element. Staff are the delivery system that supports critical service moments in a consumer's experience. Verstraete (2002) stated, "If staff performance is not up to [an organization's] expectations, the marketing campaign will fail" (p. 4). Therefore, issues related to stewardship focus not only on specific target market objectives but also on how an organization can assist staff in ensuring those relationships exist. From top management to the front lines, staff are charged with bringing an organization's culture to life. Staff are less likely to build relationships with consumers if the organization has failed to build a relationship with them.

Capes (2002) shared her experience about selecting a new health clubbecause the one she had gone to for years was no longer meeting her needs. She thought she found the perfect new facility that met all her initial needs relating to price, amenities, and location. On a referral and free trial for two weeks at another club, however, she found that this may not have had all the other services but it had much

more—a higher level of personalization and quality service delivery by employees and other consumers alike. She found and supported that organizations that create something special for consumers are the ones that will ultimately win.

An organization should employ several quality service oriented practices to develop relationships with its workforce, including applying quality practices to every part of the human capital relationship. Some of these concepts were highlighted in Chapter 3. Others, however, were not and include issues ranging from hiring, training, and evaluating staff performance to understanding if employees are satisfied, providing opportunities to grow, and ensuring leaders utilize quality-oriented practices (e.g., coaching, motivating, communicating with, caring for, rewarding employees). One noted study by Enz and Siguaw (2000) focused on understanding quality-oriented human resource practices in the lodging industry and profiled several organizations' best practices. Table 13.3 summarizes several of these.

This list, however, indicates organizations which have applied progressive, quality-oriented human resource practices have proven results that contribute to organization objectives. The same stewardship consider-

Table 13.3
Lodging Industry Human Resource Best-Practice Champions

Human Resource Champion	Practice Initiated	Measure of Success
The Boulders Resort	Created three-person housekeeping teams responsible for determining their own work patterns	Retention and morale of room attendants improved; rooms are readied faster; guests have fewer intrusions on their privacy
Day Hospitality Group	Mandates a sabbatical leave for GMs with five years' tenure	Used as a recruiting tool; anticipates reduced management turnover and enhanced morale
Marriott International	Develops future leaders through a management development program	Established consistent framework for developing leaders; increased rigor of filling senior positions; customer should experience improved service
Hilton Airport, Minneapolis/St. Paul	Line-level employees are empowered to make guest-satisfaction decisions	Dramatic improvement in guest comment cards; increased occupancy and Average Daily Rate on the executive level; cost savings in training, advertising and other expenses; boosted morale; guest expect immediate solutions to problems
Motel Properties, Inc.	Employee recognition program	Increased employee retention; boosted revenues and improved profits; improved customer satisfaction
Ritz-Carlton, Tyson's Corner	Self-directed work teams	Cut employee turnover in half; reduced payroll costs; reduced manager-to-staff ratio; greatly improved employee satisfaction ratings
Rodeway Inn, Orlando International	Developed employee satisfaction and rewards programs	Improved job performance and morale; became first hotel to receive Choice Hotels President's Award for guest service
Towneplace Suites by Marriott	Cross-trained employees	Employees have high job satisfaction; guest service improved

ations should, therefore, be made for staff, as well as consumers in the marketing plan process. Organizations should ask themselves the following questions regarding internal stewardship:

1. What can the organization do for the staff to facilitate buy-in to the organization's culture to ensure consistency?

2. What has the organization done to create a quality-oriented experience for their workforce?

3. What can the organization do to build better relationships with staff?

4. What actions can the organization implement to go out of their way to care for employees?

5. What resources can the organization provide for staff to help them do their job successfully (e.g., training, time off, equipment)?

6. What does the organization need to provide for staff so they can serve the targeted markets better and ensure marketing objectives are met?

7. What steps does the organization need to take to have the opportunity to take time to be critical when hiring staff? What is the best way to relay expectations of the staff?

8. What is the best way to include staff as part of the process (e.g., consider their ideas, communicate with them, discuss organization ideas with them)?

An organization can integrate stewardship type activities into organization day-to-day activities on behalf of employees and consumers in a variety of ways. Table 13.4 shows how this tool could be used for internal or external communication approaches beyond the quality human resources practices already identified:

As a result of successful stewardship, the development team is able to secure additional gifts—sometimes in higher amounts. The donor feels appreciated knowing the donation was a sound investment. In Easter Seals' plan, various market segments (based on the level of giving) have different stewardship plans, such as when the gift is for a certain program or how it was received (e.g., at a special event, during a face-to-face visit, through a specific campaign). Donors of more than $25,000 have a different plan than those who give from $1,000 to $24,999, or those who give under $1,000 (see *Real Life Story*, p. 322).

Priluck (2003) found in his research on service failures that consumers who had established relationships with organizations were more likely to overlook instances of poor performance. They feel more trust and commitment for the organization, are more satisfied and are less likely to leave an organization. Therefore, relationships can make up for times when an organization falters. Even though some believe those with stronger organization relationships would have higher expectations when confronted with dissatisfaction, Priluck suggested otherwise. Expectations play a lesser role when a strong relationship is formed between organization and consumer. Finding ways to enrich a relationship between an organization and consumer, therefore, is of particular importance. Stewardship allows an organization to continue to build and reinforce critical relationship issues. Examples of stewardship include

Target Market

- Ask a community member to conduct a mystery shopping experience to better learn of what a particular market segment experiences.

- Develop comment cards and make them available for visitors.

Table 13.4
Internal and External Stewardship Activities

Internal Employees

1. Tie employee incentives to performance.
2. Give employee gifts on special occasions (e.g., anniversary, birthday) or for exceptional performance.
3. Send notes to employees (e.g., thank you).
4. Use verbal compliments.
5. *Wow* them—Do something unexpected!
6. Host an employee appreciation event.
7. Host annual employee get-togethers.

External Consumers

1. Offer loyalty programs.
2. Send consumer gifts (e.g., anniversary, birthday).
3. Send notes to consumers (e.g., thank you).
4. Use verbal compliments.
5. *Wow* them—Do something unexpected!
6. Host consumer appreciation events.

- Call a patron after he or she has visited to see how he or she enjoyed the experience.

- Mail random surveys community members to identify the quality of the department.

- Do something special for people—wow them.

Employees

- Provide incentives for good performance.

- Send a thank you for providing great guest service.

- Give an extra paid day off for superior performance.

Real Life Story: Easter Seals Tennessee

Easter Seals Tennessee prides itself in developing quality service-oriented marketing plans. However, they struggled to identify concrete ways to apply specific actions to ensure they exceeded the expectations of targeted markets. That was until they developed a stewardship plan for their financial donors.

The purpose of a stewardship plan is to communicate with donors about how their donation made an impact and how their donation was used as the donor requested. Donors seek accountability from this organization.

Different stewardship tools can be used to fulfill this goal—a personal thank-you note from a parent whose child receives services; touring a program site or facility to meet the clients they are assisting; or receiving special gifts made by clients, scrapbooks with photos, and newsletters that focus on giving impacts.

Three of the main areas where development staff seek relationships with donors and sponsors in an effort to achieve their organization's mission are Easter Seals Turner Family Center, Easter Seals Camp, and Easter Seals McWhorter Family Children's Center. Since 2000, their marketing plan included a targeted stewardship plan to develop a more specific relationship with donors and begin to exceed the donors' expectations because other nonprofit organizations that rely on donors and sponsors were not employing the same type of practices.

Easter Seals Tennessee Communication with Donors FY 04/05

Acknowledgment	Time
All Gifts—Donation, In-Kind and Event	
1 Standard thank-you letter with impact statement and story (change quarterly)	24 hrs
OR	
1 New donor—Welcome kit with gift receipt	24 hrs
$100 to $999	
1 Standard thank-you letter with impact statement and story (change quarterly)	24 hrs
OR	
1 New donor—Welcome kit with gift receipt	24 hrs
1 Thank-you call from Staff (AF or MG)	2–4 wks
$1,000 to $4,999	
1 Standard thank-you letter with impact statement and story (change quarterly)	24 hrs
OR	
1 New donor—Welcome kit with gift receipt	24 hrs
1 Handwritten note from Staff	12 hrs
1 Thank-you call from CEO	2–4 wks
$5,000 to $9,999	
Same as $1,000 level PLUS	
1 Letter from ES Board member	1–3 mos
$10,000 to $24,999	
Same as $5,000 level PLUS	
1 Naming opportunity based on size of gift	
$25,000 to $99,999	
Same as $1,000 level PLUS	
1 Naming opportunity based on size of gift	
1 Letter from ES National president	4 wks
More than $100,000	
1 Plaque from ES National president	Aug or Feb

Additional Areas	Time
Event Volunteers	
1 Client call to thank for participation	4 wks
Board members	
1 Client call for being a board member	Jun

Fiona (left), who has brittle bone disease, and Rose Mary, who has a spinal cord injury, receive physical and occupational therapy at the Easter Seals McWhorter Family Children's Center in Nashville, Tennessee. As part of Tennessee's stewardship plan, Fiona and Rose Mary's parents have spoken with and written letters to the facility's financial donors about the girls' successes.

- Mail birthday/work anniversary cards.

- Conduct an exit evaluation for employees leaving your employment.

- Empower staff to handle guest situations.

- Provide staff the training necessary to be experts at their jobs.

- Ensure employees are easily identifiable (e.G., Nametags, uniforms, standards for appearance).

- Develop a script for handling all telephone calls efficiently and effectively.

Real Life Story: Easter Seals Tennessee (continued)

Easter Seals Tennessee Communication with Donors FY 04/05

Stewardship	Time
Gifts below $100	
1 Postcard with Impact Statement/Photo	June
$100 to $999	
4 Quarterly newsletter (Oct, Dec, Mar, Jul)	Quarterly
6 Stew e-mail (if have e-mail)	Bimonthly
1 Holiday card	Dec
1 United Way postcard	Jun
$1,000 to $4,999	
Same as $100 level PLUS	
Add quarterly PC letter to NewsL Mailing	
1 Annual report	Mar
1 Mail item made by child (6 mos later)	All
1 Invite to annual PC reception (give PC pin if didn't in previous visit)	
$5,000 to $9,999	
Same as $100 level PLUS	
Add quarterly PC letter to NewsL Mailing	
1 Invite to annual PC reception	
1 Annual report	Mar
1 Stewardship visit (3–9 mos later; take item made by child)	All
1 Parent impact letter (Jan, Apr, Jul, Oct)	3–6 mos
More than $10,000	
Same as $5,000 level PLUS	
1 Lunch with CEO and Volunteer	

Additional Baseline Stewardship	Time
1 SESAC Golf Donors	Jan
1 CDC Donors	Feb
1 TFC Donors	Mar
1 10K Run Sponsors	Mar
1 Building Dreams Donors	Apr
1 NOY Event Donors	May
1 Camp Donors	Jul
1 Century 21 Donors	Aug
1 McWhorter Event donors	Oct
1 BDGG Event Donors	Nov

Other Mailings	Time
More than $1,000	
1 Invite to golf events	May
1 Invite to NOY Event	Dec
1 Invite to McWhorter Event	Apr

Apply What You Know

1. Brainstorm to determine a communication mix using relationship-oriented tools (e.g., sponsorships, community relations, stewardship) for the marketing plan you are writing.

2. Interview leisure and tourism organizations to identify stewardship actions taken to build employee relationships.

Key Terms

Cause-related marketing
Cobranding
Community relations
Community relations employee volunteer list
Crosspromotion partnership
External stewardship
Industry associations
In-kind sponsorship
Internal stewardship

Organization privitization partnerships
Partnerships
Relationship-oriented marketing
Sole sponsorship
Sponsorship
Sponsorship packages
Stewardship

Review Questions

1. Identify why cobranding partnerships are used.

2. What were the criteria established by the Gaylord Area Convention and Tourism Bureau to ensure quality for golf courses?

3. Name and describe the nine community relation activities.

4. Determine why organizations solicit sponsors or become sponsors.

5. Out of the sponsorship types listed, which offers logos being prominently displayed on promotional pieces in exchange for paying for the cost of printing?

6. What actions need to be performed to find successful sponsors?

7. Identify the quality-oriented practices leaders should utilize with employees.

Internet Resources

IEG develops surveys on sponsorship and the results are available to media industries. Information on industry size and scope, spending trends and opportunities are available.

http://www.sponsorship.com

The *National Council for Public-Private Partnerships* facilitates the formation of public-private partnerships at the federal, state, and local levels. Their website includes materials that discuss how partnerships work, issue papers, and case studies.

http://www.ncppp.org

Partnerships for Parks promotes community support for parks. Their mission is to join community efforts to restore and to preserve natural areas.

http://www.partnershipsforparks.org

The *Sponsorship Report* is a newsletter that aims to develop successful partnerships between Canadian corporations and art groups, sports organizations, charities, government initiatives, events, and festivals.

http://www.sponsorship.ca

References

Barnholt, J. and Jackowski, M. (2002, June). First place: Before pursuing a partnership, analyze your ability to reposition your organization. *Athletic Business*, 56–60.

Bednall, D., Walker, I., Curl, D., and LeRoy, H. (2001). Business support approaches for charities and other nonprofits. *International Journal of Nonprofit and Voluntary Sector Marketing*, 6(2), 172–187.

Bennett, R. (2002). Corporate perspectives and cause-related marketing. *Journal of Nonprofit & Public Sector Marketing*, 10(1), 41–59.

Berrett, T. (2001, May). A framework for the analysis of strategic approaches employed by non-profit sport organisations in seeking corporate sponsorship. *Sport Management Review*, 4(1), 21–45.

Burnside, M. W. (2002). Book it: Skinner gives tips on event sponsorships. *Amusement Business, 114*(49), 12.

Capes, L. (2002). Could your club earn my business? *Club Industry Magazine, 18*(9), 14.

Chaisson, V. (2002). Marketing trends. *Michigan Parks and Recreation*, 14–22.

Charbonneau, P. (1997, February/March). Environmental stewardship: A golf course perspective. *Greenmaster, 31*(6), 13–14.

Clark, J., Cornwell, T. B., and Pruitt, S. W. (2002). Corporate stadium sponsorship, signaling theory, organization conflicts, and shareholder wealth. *Journal of Advertising Research, 42*(6), 16–32.

Conner, J. A. and Grady, K. (1978). Getting the pieces to fall into place. *Parks and Recreation, 13*(4), 37–39.

Copeland, R., Frisby, W., and McCarville, R. (1996). Understanding the sport sponsorship process from a corporate perspective. *Journal of Sport Management, 10*(1), 32–48.

Crompton, J. L. (1999). *Financing and acquiring parks and recreation resources.* Champaign, IL: Human Kinetics.

Cruice, M. (2002). A sporting chance: How community sports clubs should approach their marketing. *Australian Leisure Management, 31*, 58–59.

Dalakas, V. and Kropp, F. (2002). Attitudes of youth toward purchasing from sponsors: A crosscultural perspective. *Journal of Euromarketing, 12*(1), 19–39.

Direct Intelligence. (2000, September). 85 percent of corporations use cause marketing tactics. *Direct Marketing, 63*(5), 10.

Dressel, J. (2002). The best of publicity stunts are those that aren't. *Bowlers Journal International, 89*(10), 102.

Dustin, D. and Wolff, R. (1998, February). 50 years of stewardship: The ongoing struggle to preserve Everglades National Park. *Parks and Recreation, 33*(2), 80–84.

Enz, C. and Siguaw, J. (2000, February). Best practices in human resources. *Cornell Hotel and Restaurant Administration Quarterly*, 48–61.

Farrelly, F., Quester, P., and Mavondo, F. (2003). Collaborative communication in sponsor relations. *Corporate Communications: An International Journal*, 8(2), 128–138

Fitzgerald, K. (2002, March). Sports sponsorships get a workout. *Credit Card Management, 14*(12), 44.

Gabriel, A. (1999, November/December). Marketing. Corporate giving: More than just a tax advantage. *Commercial Law Bulletin, 14*(6), 36–37.

Glover, T. D. (1999). Propositions addressing the privatization of public leisure services: Implications for efficiency, effectiveness, and equity. *Journal of Park and Recreation Administration, 17*(2), 1–27

Gwinner, K. and Swanson, S. R. (2003). A model of fan identi-fication: Antecedents and sponsorship outcomes. *The Journal of Services Marketing, 17*(3), 275–294.

Hastad, D. N. and Tymeson, G. (1997). Demonstrating visionary leadership through community partnership. *JOPERD, 68*(5), 47–50.

Hirschkorn, J. (2002, March). The perfect match. *Director, 55(8)*, 19.

Kaplan, D. (2002, September). How to play the naming game. Mediaedge: Cia surveys consumer attitudes on sponsorships. *AdWeek Southeast, 24*(36), 2(1).

Lachowetz, T. and Gladden, J. (2003). A framework for under-standing cause-related sport marketing programs. *International Journal of Sports Marketing and Sponsorship, 4*(4), 313–333.

Lachowetz, T. and Irwin, R. (2002). FedEx and the St. Jude Clas-sic: An application of a cause-related marketing program. *Sport Marketing Quarterly, 11*(2), 114–116.

Lardinoit, R. and Derbaix, C. (2001, February). Sponsorship and recall of sponsors. *Psychology & Marketing, 18*(2), 167–190.

Leblein, J. (2002, June). A novel approach: Let "Tom Sawyer" help you increase revenue and attendance and community relations. *Aquatics International, 14*(5), 14–15.

Mack, R. (1999). Event sponsorship: An exploratory study of small business objectives, practices, and perceptions. *Journal of Small Business Management, 37*(3), 25–30.

Maignan, I. and Ferrell, O. (2001). Corporate citizenship as a mar-keting instrument—Concepts, evidence and research direc-tions. *European Journal of Marketing, 35*(3/4), 457–484.

Maloney, P. (2002, July 8). Do sponsorships measure up? Lacking concrete numbers, marketers look elsewhere to prove pro-motion success. *Marketing Magazine, 107*(27), 13.

Mohr, L, Webb, D., and Harris, K. (2001). Do consumers expect companies to be socially responsible? The impact of cor-porate social responsibility on buying behavior. *The Jour-nal of Consumer Affairs, 35*(1), 45–72.

Moler, C. (2000, September). Wanted: Not-for-profit to take money. *Parks and Recreation, 35*(9), 164–172.

Mowen, A. and Graefe, A. (2002). Public attitudes toward the corporate sponsorship of park organizations: The role of promotional activities and contractual conditions. *Journal of Parks and Recreation Administration, 20*(2), 31–48.

Mowen, A. and Havitz, M. (2002, September). Citizen-driven guidelines for sponsor recognition in parks and recreation settings. *Parks and Recreation, 37*(9), 83–90.

Nozar, R. (2000, June 5). Cobranding can build guest loyalty, boost occupancy. *Hotel and Motel Management, 215*(10), 13.

Priluck, R. (2003). Relationship marketing can mitigate product and service failures. *The Journal of Service Marketing, 17*(1), 37–52.

Pybus, D. and Janes, P. (2004). Expanding public recreation programs through partnership arrangements. *Current Mu-nicipal Problems, 30*(4), 408–422.

Robinson, R. A. (Spring 2002). Moving the message: Parks and recreation marketing. *Michigan Parks and Recreation*, 13–23.

Salt Lake City 2002: Unprecedented marketing success. (2002, August/September). *Olympic Review, 27*(46), 47–48.

Sparks, R. and Westgate, M. (2002). Broad-based and targeted sponsorship strategies in Canadian women's ice hockey. *International Journal of Sports Marketing and Sponsorship, 4*(1), 59–84.

Special Report—Sponsorship: Be a Sponsor (2005, March 24), *Marketing Week,* 37.

Sponsor services. (1999, November). *Sport Business, 39*, 15–18.

Sponsorships expected to grow this year. (2002, May 13). *Mar-keting Magazine, 107*(19), 19.

Stark, S. L. and Parker, P. E. (1981). A viable partnership: Com-munity education and parks and recreation. *Journal of Physical Education and Recreation, 52*(3), 17–18.

The parade of corporate sponsors. (1999, July 16). *New York Times,* p. C1.

van der Smissen, B., Moiseichik, M., Hartenburg, V. J., and Twardzik, L. F. (Eds.). (1999). *Management of park and recreation organizations.* Ashburn, VA: National Recre-ation and Park Association.

Verity, J. (2002). Maximising the marketing potential of sponsor-ship for global brands. *European Business Journal, 14*(4), 161–173.

Verstraete, P. (2002, January). Bolster the success of your mar-keting campaigns by implementing concrete performance standards. *Club Success, 8*(1), 4–5.

Washburn, J., Till, B., and Priluck, R. (2000). Cobranding: brand equity and trial effects. *The Journal of Consumer Marketing, 17*(7), 591–604.

Webb, J. and Carter, S. (2001, July). Sponsorship activities and the small firms sector. *Managing Leisure, 6*(3), 168–179.

Williams, J. (1998). *Sponsorship evaluation practices of Ladies Professional Golf Association title sponsors.* Doctoral dis-sertation, University of Oregon.

Worley, D. and Little, J. (2002, February). The critical role of stewardship in fund raising: The Coaches vs. Cancer Cam-paign. *Public Relations Review, 28*(1), 99–112.

Wymer, W. and Samu, S. (2003). Dimensions of business and nonprofit collaborative relationships. *Journal of Nonprofit & Public Sector Marketing, 11*(1), 3–22.

Chapter 14

Direct Marketing:
Internal and External Sales

Edited by Bill Underdown
Director of Alliance Account Sales, Marriott International

Spending two days at the Adventure Amusement Park was a family tradition. For the past 20 years the Conlin family set aside the last weekend in July to get together and to enjoy the park and family fun in the heat of summer.

At 20 and 22, respectively, Lori and Jennifer were cousins who looked forward to the annual get together. It seemed finding a time they were both free was more difficult than ever. This year the family booked rooms at the park's adjacent resort, Timber Creek. They were excited to stay at the brand new facility because the families liked to hang around the pool early morning and late evening to share the events of the day.

Jennifer's mom made all the reservations with the sales department staff and explained all the particulars for the ten rooms needed. She was assured those with nonsmoking, adjoining, and two double bed requests would not be a problem.

Upon check-in, however, Jennifer and Lori were disappointed right off—the adjoining rooms were not available at all. The desk clerk, seeing their disappointment, tried to find other solutions to correct situation. However, because they were sold out, the best he could do was put their rooms away from each other. Adding to the frustration, the desk clerk, although nice, could not answer any questions regarding the park hours and any specials resort guests would receive there. Jennifer's mom thought she read somewhere that there would be some special offers.

Trying not to focus on this small but important issue, the girls decided to quickly go to their rooms and change

---

At the end of this chapter, readers will be able to...

- Define direct marketing and provide examples of this communication mix element.

- Describe the eight components of the strategic sales cycle.

- Identify the distinctions of internal marketing definitions.

- Understand how direct marketing, personal selling, and internal marketing benefit an organization and its communication mix.

- Describe an employee's involvement in and the values for an organization with these types of communication mix decisions.

to meet at the pool and relax in the hot tub. Jennifer and Lori were again disappointed to arrive and find the hot tub out-of-order and empty. A housekeeper by the pool was unable to offer insight about when it might be repaired.

So girls went to swim. Afterward, they thought the resort recreation department might be planning some events they would be interested in. So, they contacted the recreation desk. Unfortunately, no one answered. The recorded message stated to contact the front desk or leave a message with any questions. Lori called the front desk to inquire only to learn they did not know of any planned events. She was advised to try to contact the recreation desk again. It was common, according to the clerk, for "that department to forget about us up here."

The girls started to feel like they were spinning their wheels. They just wanted someone to answer their questions so they could have some idea of what there was to do around the resort. This was the only full day they had planned there and their next two days would be in the park.

When they arrived, however, they did notice a Family Fun Center with a rock climbing wall, go-carts and other activities about a mile away. So they decided to go there instead. There, they had a great time.

The next morning all 26 family members went to the park. The complimentary transportation to and from the park was a great resort service; it worked like a charm. On the shuttle, a park employee named Kathy welcomed them and acted as host. She answered everyone's questions about the park, resort, and surrounding area. The family learned they could show their resort key and receive a 20% discount on admission tickets and a complimentary bottle of sunscreen. The family further learned about specific attractions in the park, strategies for minimizing wait time in lines, other things to do in the park Kathy called "the hidden wonders," and the shuttle's hours of operation.

Kathy was exactly what the family had needed a day earlier. They were disappointed in the resort staff who seemed unaware and unknowledgable about basic resort questions, but Kathy made up for it. The family searched her down all weekend long. She helped not only by answering their questions but also by providing information they didn't even realize they needed to know.

• • • • •

Sales skills are valuable in *all* staff—not just the sales staff—and effective communication is vital. The resort staff had multiple opportunities to "sell" their offerings to these customers, yet, they were not prepared to do so. From the sales staff promise of adjoining rooms to ignorance over resort amenities, the staff seemed unprepared and unknowledgable. Conversely, Kathy exhibited a great deal of sales skills: she listened to what they family needed, anticipated their needs, and provided what they needed. Had the resort

staff had the same skills, the family experience would have been far better. Thank goodness Kathy helped; however, one person cannot do it alone.

This example highlightes an employee-consumer relationship, however, this same premise holds true with an employee-to-employee and a consumer-to-consumer relationship. People sell to people everyday. Building an organization that has consumers and employees alike selling the organization's "experiences" are those that have integrated marketing practices successfully. These concepts will be explored throughout this chapter.

Pushy, aggressive, in-your-face salespeople are often those people think of when they think "salesperson." Certainly, until the 1990s this was often the case. Sales people, often commissioned off the revenue they could sell, would do anything to make a sale—even if a consumer was dissatisfied. This type of behavior seemed acceptable in the retail, automotive and manufacturing industries, and it was even considered acceptable in the leisure setting.

Thank goodness the sales culture of the past has changed. Organizations no longer find a win-lose relationships acceptable with consumers and other stakeholders. A short-term sale with no concern of consumer satisfaction is not where quality-oriented organizations focus. Therefore, the skills of the sales force have changed as well.

Everyone in an organization has marketing responsibilities. This is most true when considering a direct, personal selling relationship. Every day, every staff member sells to someone. They may be selling an idea to the board or the staff, they may be selling while on their day off to a peer, or actually dealing with a consumer who has interest in a service. Any staff member who has contact with a consumer or other stakeholder has sales responsibilities.

The first challenge organizations have, therefore, is to help all staff see how they have a role direct sales efforts. Staff are selling every day, whether they realize it or not. As was shown, some people are better salespeople than others. Not because they are more pushy, but because they have a genuine interest in exceeding the expectations of individuals they interact with whether external consumer, internal staff member or other stakeholder. This chapter explores the direct marketing and sales efforts taken by organizations to achieve marketing objectives.

Direct Marketing

Direct marketing is a form of personal selling that creates and establishes an intimate relationship between a seller and an individual consumer. *Personal selling* is a one-on-one (or small group) personal presentation designed to gain commitment from individuals/organizations to be consumers.

Direct marketing activities have been a concept for over 25 years (Suman, Yorgey & Paul Loyle, 2002); however, personal selling has been in existence since the beginning of time. Joan of Arc succeeded in convincing France she had a divine mission to save the country from England and end the Hundred Years' War, Christopher Columbus convinced Spain the world wasn't flat, and the list goes back through history even further.

This more personalized approach to marketing communication is often associated with offerings that have moved from the introduction stage into the growth and maturity stages of the product life cycle. Even though these activities may be employed throughout an offering's life, personal selling is a critical communication element when an organization's strategy is to develop loyalty and secure one consumer, or small groups of consumers, at a time.

Like other quality-oriented practices, this too must be supported throughout an organization. The belief that all staff is indeed part of the organization's sales force must be an established part of an organization's culture—one that accepts, encourages, and rewards these behaviors in all staff. Organizations develop a workforce of salespeople by taking the following steps:

1. Establish a culture that supports positive sales skills from all staff members.

2. Train employees about positive, effective sales techniques from developing rapport with consumers, staff and stakeholders to how to identify and respond to theei needs and overcome objections and misconceptions.

3. Establish organization expectations through stated sales functions in all employee job descriptions.

4. Reward employees who exhibit effective sales skills.

5. Provide tools for staff to develop internal and external relationships.

Leisure and tourism organizations realize the more skilled staff is in being prepared to exceed consumer and stakeholder expectations, the more successful they will be. In turn, staff are not only better prepared to provide onsite sales assistance but also they can consider other direct marketing strategies geared toward selling to consumers before the experience begins. Direct marketing has several advantages including

- more personalization—direct, personal contact to establish a one-on-one relationship

- better understanding of individual consumer needs and reactions (i.e., acceptance, misconception, objection) to an organization's offerings

- ability to respond faster to consumer inquiries, questions, and concerns

- allows for two-way personal communication to occur

- greater personalization develops staff-consumer relationships

- ability to use this communication as reinforcement for other forms of communication or as a stand-alone activity

- as a workforce becomes engaged as sales staff, the marketing communication mix becomes less reliant on other forms of reaching target markets

- when successful, this approach expands marketing efforts through consumer endorsements

Direct marketing, as established, is the responsibility of all staff. However, many leisure and tourism organizations have specifically assigned staff members to implement their direct marketing activities as established by the organization's marketing plan. As with other communication choices, organizations may also choose to more aggressively conduct direct sales activities to assist in achieving specific target market objectives. Many forms of direct marketing organization can consider, and ultimately select from, exist. Direct marketing options for organizations include

- presentations, tours, and meetings

- seminars, workshops, or training programs

- door-to-door distribution

- telemarketing

- direct sales letters

- network or multilevel marketing consumer support centers

- lead referral programs

- sales blitzes

- trade shows

Sales presentations, tours, and meetings are provided as one-on-one or to small groups and use the formal direct sales approach. These direct marketing activities are designed to sell the benefits of participation to potential consumers and stakeholders. These interactions can occur face-to-face or through multimedia. Infomercials are this form of sales presentation using the television as the medium to reach consumers and sell them on the benefits of consumption or participation. The direct personal sales methods utilized are discussed throughout this section.

Seminars, workshops, or training programs can be provided by an organization to a target market group to sell them an organization's offerings. For example, a golf course may provide a free golf workshop for junior high students or women to introduce the game to them and encourage their participation as consumers. A health club may conduct a seminar on the benefits of an active, aerobic lifestyle to a senior center group who may be more passive than active. This direct marketing tool builds relationships without selling directly. As consumers get to know the organization and value their expertise, they develop comfort, trust, and confidence. Go-To-Market Strategies (2002) stated consumers can "try before they buy" with this type of sales activity. It further provides a base of potential leads/ prospects who can become future consumers.

Door-to-door distribution includes the personal delivery of marketing materials to consumer homes or businesses. This "pound the pavement" technique provides one-on-one personalization and interaction.

A form of direct marketing that establishes a one-on-one relationship via telephone with a consumer and a seller is called *telemarketing*. Popular since the early 1990s, this form of personal selling has grown to be considered one of the most successful, as well as one of the most annoying, forms of marketing communication. A 2003 Congressional ruling was established that limits telemarketers' access to people. The legislation allows consumers to place themselves on a "do not call" list which prohibits telemarketers from contacting them to solicit their offerings. This was a disappointment for this form of direct marketing.

Direct sales letters are considered a one-on-one relationship tool even though they oftentimes are delivered in impersonal ways through the postal service, fax, e-mail, or other forms of distribution. This type of correspondence is sent to a specific individual (vs. a generic "to whom it may concern"). Ideally letters relate specifically to a topic the recipient has inquired about or can easily relate to. It is presumed that, unlike many direct mail pieces, this letter will be read by an individual because it is of interest to them.

The words used in a sales letter are of utmost importance because they may be the only communication a target market reads. The words chosen by the author—in this case the organization—are critical to convey a message that will cause the market to respond favorably. Westphal (1998) suggested the use of several terms (e.g., pledge, testimonial, strong, promise, secure, stable, protects, performs, gets results, time-tested, world-renowned, rigorous standards) effectively communicates a strong brand. She states the

way an organization develops and communicates sales letters will have an impact on the organization's outcome. A letter stating "We hope you always feel that you make a difference to us" versus "We appreciate our customers" conveys two different impression of the organization. Letters are important communication pieces that should be written, edited, and reflected on prior to sending.

The professionalism of the letter is another important issue worthy of consideration and reflection. Not too long ago, a sales letter marketing a communication consulting firm came across the fax machine. It had ten typographical and grammatical errors in it. This organization received their letter back with concerns about their consulting ability if they couldn't even send a professional, error-free letter! All too often, organizations and individuals send letters that have not been formatted using acceptable business letter standards. In addition, they fail to be evaluated properly for potential errors. Although one would think this is common sense, there probably isn't one leisure industry professional who has not made a mistake in his or her past. The key is the attention to detail, learning from mistakes, and developing systems to minimize the possibility of errors.

E-mail correspondence should follow the same business guidelines as any written business communication. However, this form of communication has resulted in some organizations and individuals approaching it with less professionalism than many consumers desire. There is a distinction between personal, casual letterwriting and professional business writing that is even more critical in an e-mail setting because casual communication is very different with this tool.

Network or multilevel marketing is the process of securing a small group of consumers who, in turn, sell to another small group of consumers. The multilevel marketing process is used to develop a sales force who is then, in turn, financially rewarded for continuing to expand the sales force which results in increased sales.

Consumer support centers can be referred to as everything from a concierge desk, reservation center, box office, consumer help desk, or customer service centers. Organizations that develop systems to directly engage consumers and assist with facilitating an organization's experience fall under this type of direct marketing activity.

Lead referral programs are direct marketing activities designed to provide incentives to people/organizations involved in making consumption decisions. For example, a hotel may provide financial incentives for business meeting planners (or their organizations) who book sleeping/meeting rooms. Staff could also be provided this type of incentive when they are rewarded for bringing in new business.

Sales blitzes are concentrated bursts of one-on-one direct sales activities designed to spread awareness and generate sales leads to prospects interested in an organization's offerings. These are typically limited to a specific geographical area and occur over a one-day to two-week time frame. The greatest benefit of this type of direct marketing is the immediacy of the results. A number of staff are trained and placed on sales teams to canvas a geographical area and ultimately identify potential consumers in the assigned area. The amount of time it takes to complete a blitz is contingent on the number of staff involved, the size of the geographical area, and the blitz goals. A sales blitz with few staff, a larger area, and/or higher goals will take more time.

Each trained sales team of two to four people is created with skill levels in mind; staff can be trained before the blitz and do not have to be experienced salespeople. They introduce themselves and the organization to individuals or businesses, share organization collateral and contact information and, oftentimes, offer a "premium" item to people in exchange for organization information regarding potential interest in their organization's offerings. In addition, contact information about who is responsible for making organization decisions is also collected. For example, in a health club sales blitz, the sales team stops at every business within a large office complex, the team introduces themselves, indicates they are there only to share information about their organization and to learn if the organization might have interest in corporate health club memberships for staff. If they may have interest, the sales team asks who the contact person would be. They write down the information, including the organization name and contact information, so a staff member will contact this person at a later time. Upon leaving the office building the team may have identified four leads from a building of 30 businesses. There is no set formula for the number of leads generated by a blitz, but an organization can feel comfortable they have personally reached many organizations and developed a list of initial leads to pursue.

In today's world of heightened security, it is more difficult to enter some office buildings without permission. Therefore, leisure and tourism organizations have employed new means to access secured buildings, discover prospective information, and expose the organization to potential consumers. For example, another way to blitz a building could include offering refreshments to associates entering the building on their way to work or offering complimentary items in the common cafeteria/break area.

By the end of a sales blitz, the organization will have generated a number of leads to follow, have an established list of potential consumers, have a better understanding of market demand, and feel more confident in their ability to reach a target market. Keys to effective sales blitzes include the following:

- a well-organized approach to the overall effort
- clearly established objectives (e.g., number of leads expected)
- outlined geographical areas for teams
- coordinated resources for distribution and data collection
- trained sales teams (e.g., knowledge about the organization's offerings, how to complete a call, overcoming objections, key phrases to use, how to write a lead)
- a motivating, orchestrated theme to encourage sales team efforts

One known theme is the creation of lead contests among teams (e.g., most leads collected, most calls made, largest potential lead). This helps to keep teams motivated and excited about making calls and generating leads. The sales blitz process is a demanding, challenging experience as teams "pound the pavement" and generate leads. Teams can become frustrated because few leads may be generated and no one enjoys rejection. However, a carefully planned and executed event can not only generate needed information but also it can develop staff morale and a team focus.

Leisure and tourism organizations often benefit from attending or exhibiting in a trade show. This is yet another type of communication that many organizations utilize.

Trade shows are a place where consumers meet suppliers in one large setting and organizations have the opportunity to showcase their experiences in exhibits. For example, in the slow season, golf courses regularly attend trade shows to meet with golf consumers and prepare for the upcoming season; fitness equipment companies share their offerings at industry trade shows where health and

St. Ives golf course attends a trade show.

wellness organizations attend to see what the latest trends are in fitness and purchase equipment for their organization. Some trade shows are designed solely to bring these audiences together; professional associations also host trade shows as part of their conferences. The National Recreation and Park Association (NRPA) hosts its annual congress where hundreds of organizations sponsor trade show booths to highlight their offerings to the thousands of NRPA Congress attendees.

"Getting the most out of a trade show takes careful planning and preparation" though and many organizations are not well prepared for the experience either as attendee or exhibitor (Thill, 2002, p. 27). Strategies for effective trade show participation include

1. Organizations identify specific objective(s) for attending or exhibiting at a trade show. Are they there to identify 100 new prospects or to make $50,000 in sales? Are they there to purchase equipment, or to simply meet with each supplier and learn what is available?

2. Attendees and suppliers develop a strategy for whom to meet with and how to attract consumers to the organization's booth. Time is minimal at a trade show; therefore, making the most of each and every encounter is critical.

3. Organizations prepare for the hard work and long hours required in trade shows. They wear comfortable shoes and comfortable, but professional, clothing.

4. Organizations do not mix business and pleasure. Even though trade shows include a great deal of social opportunities, these are designed to provide networking—not social parties.

5. Organization booths should be set up in a professional, high-quality manner to encourage consumers to stop. In addition to an easy entrance and exit, there must be a compelling reason for them to stop. Certainly, consumer need is one factor; however, freebies, attractive displays, and contests can help to draw in customers. There must be enough samples, brochures, and gifts for everyone who is interested. Running out of matierial can be disastrous when communicating an organization's message.

6. Staff attending a trade show must be educated about the organization's offerings and be able to answer all anticipated questions in a positive way. They must employ aggressive hospitality skills to encourage people to visit the booth, and they must enjoy meeting with and talking to a wide variety of people. They must have fine-tuned sales skills that focus on the consumers' needs and match those needs to the organization's benefits and its features.

7. Contacts made during a trade show must be followed up with immediately. Sending simple thank-you cards to all those met and indicating a time to follow up with those who are prospects sets one organization apart from others (Thill, 2002).

8. Remember, everyone is a potential customer!

Organizations have many choices with regard to direct and personal marketing that selecting the best ones to achieve an organization's objectives can be problematic. Organizations, must therefore, consider each option carefully with regard to the following tips to select the most effective direct marketing activities:

1. Understand the target market and how an organization can reach them most effectively. For example, if few of the organization's target market are known to use e-mail, then pursuing this type of communication means would not be an effective choice.

2. Learn which methods produce the best results. A 2003 study by Go-to-Market Strategies stated the following response rates for various direct marketing methods:

Direct Marketing Method	Average Response Rate
Permission e-mail	4 – 12%
Bulk e-mail	0.05 – 0.2%
Bulk direct mail	0.2 – 2%
Targeted direct mail	1 – 4%
Banner Ads	0.5 – 1%

3. Utilize effective design formats and messages.

4. Consider resource limitations including budget, time frame, and expertise.

Other forms of direct marketing reviewed in previous chapters include direct mail and direct response advertising.

Direct Sales Process

Just because someone is outgoing and pleasant does not mean they will be a good salesperson. Salespeople learn to be great salespeople. Some qualities evident in effective salespeople may be natural, however, all can be learned skills. Even great salespeople build, develop, and refine their sales skills. Those salespeople who develop these skills often do so following a formal process or system for "selling" an organization and its experiences. It is not only a salesperson's skills that impact selling effectiveness, however, because the entire organization is involved.

Sales efforts lack when the following conditions occur:

1. ineffective listening—often stated as the number one problem with sales staff—they do not listen

2. a lack of understanding regarding the consumer and his or her buying process

3. a lack of an integrated support process for the sales staff and operational organization (i.e., conflict between the organization and the sales staff)

4. failure to establish an accepted process for developing, implementing, and evaluating the sales effort

5. failure to provide staff the tools needed to successfully develop relationships

Effective salespeople are win-win focused. The bottom line is people buy from people they like. Hence the relationship is the focus of effective sales experiences.

The leisure and tourism industry has not explored direct sales because many public leisure and tourism organizations are just beginning to view these activities are valuable. Yet, research in other industries suggests the relationship sales staff form with consumers is vital in developing long-term loyal relationships. Beverland (1999) studied New Zealand's wine industry and found a trend of sales staff forming closer relationships with retailers and distributors. Staff were becoming more interactive, direct, and long-term focused. In this industry, salespeople needed to focus more on making their consumers more successful. This is true in the leisure industry as well. Organizations that focus on the success of their consumers develop a more loyal following. For example, health clubs that take a personal interest in helping consumers achieve fitness goals build a more loyal consumer base that those who do not. Lodging salespeople who focus on ensuring the meeting planner is not disappointed help make the meeting planner look good to his or her own organization, which results in a more loyal consumer.

The Strategic Sales Process

Regardless of an organization or individual's interest in "selling" as a career, every leisure and tourism organization uses personal selling in their activities whether they have a staff member with that title or not. Personal selling may include selling memberships at a health club, selling a bride and groom on having their wedding reception at a convention facility, or contacting a list of attendees at a trade show who indicated they were interested in visiting a golf facility.

How many times have you wandered into a store, intending to just look, and leave spending hundreds of dollars? Most people will have this type of experience at one time in their life (others more often!). Often it was the result of a sales incentive (e.g. 50% off) or a direct sales person. Great sales people recognize their sales increase when they develop and use effective sales skills.

Effective salespeople have developed their sales skills. Just because a person has a good personality does not mean they are a good salesperson. Certainly, it will help, but a lot of unsuccessful salespeople have good personalities. Direct sales are critical in so many organizations, so understanding the professional steps necessary to become a highly skilled salesperson are important. The remaining portions of this section highlight a seven-step process to strategic selling. Each of the steps is a vital component to the process and should be understood by all because everyone is a salesperson.

Step 1: Prospecting

The fundamental issue surrounding all direct marketing applications is one's ability to develop effective leads/

Alta Ski Resort salespeople find that effective sales skills pay off.

prospects. Organizations should develop a lead management system to identify potential leads as well as prioritize and manage these through the process.

Prospecting is the art of determining with whom you will try to interact. Some leisure and tourism organizations are fortunate to have so many incoming calls that prospecting is not an issue; the potential sales come to the organization. This is considered reactive versus proactive sales. However, all organizations are not so fortunate and just because interested consumers contact an organization does not mean they are the type of calls they would want. Potentially there are other businesses a leisure and tourism organization would be more interested in. The success of the organization may rely on an organization's ability to find qualified leads to pursue. Places where an organization may find leads, depending on organization type, include

- feasibility study
- guest history report (e.g., database of past guests)
- sales prospector
- business section of local newspaper
- travel organization commission list
- sales blitz reports
- past sales call reports and files
- referrals from existing customers
- business journals
- National Tour Association membership directory
- American Society of Travel Agents membership roster
- trade show attendee list or people dropping off business cards for an organization's raffle

Some organization resources for prospecting are industry specific. The following examples are for the lodging industry:

- Who's Who in Association Management
- Reader Boards from competing lodging properties
- Turn Down Report
- The Nationwide Directory of Association Meeting Planners
- The Directory of Corporate Meeting Planners
- Meeting Planners International Membership Directory.

Step 2: Planning and Preparing

Planning and preparing are critical steps in the sales call process. In today's information society, knowledge is a powerful resource. Organizations can increase their chances of gaining commitment from a prospect by knowing their prospects and knowing their needs. This knowledge will provide organizations the foundation upon which they can establish goals. It is imperative to have a clear objective before you enter into a sales call and have a strong action plan to achieve that objective. Before any call organizations should (a) research the company, (b) establish sales call objectives, and (c) develop an action plan.

Precall planning is important to both organizations and their prospects. Organizations will be better organized and more prepared to make an effective sales call. Prepared, organized organizations show prospects they are concerned about the prospect and care about the prospects' needs.

Researching prospects. The first step in planning is to research the company the organization will be contacting. In this step, organizations must find out general information about companies:

- What does the company do?
- Where are they located?
- Is this the main branch or a satellite office?
- How many people does this company employ?
- How is the company organized?
- What is the economic environment of the company?

Seven-Step Process to Strategic Selling

The first two steps occur before a salesperson interacts with a potential user. The remaining steps outline the process taken during an actual sales call.

1. **Prospecting:** Figure out who to contact
2. **Planning and Preparing:** Find out all an organization can about a prospect, and clearly identify a sales objective
3. **Establishing Rapport:** Establish a relationship, and state the purpose for meeting
4. **Questioning:** Ask questions to understand needs
5. **Supporting:** Support needs with benefits and features
6. **Summarizing:** Summarize benefits accepted
7. **Closing:** Identify a customer's buying signal and ask for the sale.

Consumers appreciate organizations taking the time to research. It will demonstrate they not only have an interest in the prospect but also have respect for the customer's time. When a customer says, "You've certainly done your homework" to a salesperson, the salesperson knows he or she has started to build credibility in the customer's mind. Credibility and confidence in the customers' mind is essential to the success of the sales call.

Sales call objectives. Organizations key objective for every sales call is to secure business. The salespersons' dream is to achieve this on the first call. And, sometimes that dream comes true. However, salespeople won't always be able to achieve this on each and every sales call. It can take many calls with several intermediate goals before a salesperson can reach the final objective of having the prospect become a consumer. Regardless of the number of calls however, a salesperson should always have a sales call objective in mind. Remember, the sales process is much like a long-distance trip—organizations map the journey with intermediate objectives to reach the final objective—the destination. A salesperson's single sales call objective should advance them to the next milestone, and ultimately, the final objective. It is imperative organizations chart their direction if they hope to achieve their ultimate objective.

The sales call goal must be something observable, must objectively happen, and must require customer commitment. Understanding needs is not a useful sales call objective. It is an essential portion of the process, yet it does not require customer commitment. Organizations must assess the needs of their consumers via fact-finding questions but they must also formulate an action plan requiring consumer commitment if they want to advance the sale. Salespeople also should formulate back-up objectives before going into a call if you sense there may be an objection to the primary objective. Try to role-play the call with a sales associate or colleagues. Was the "customer" interested and would they buy

Now that the salesperson/organization is knowledgable about the prospect and has set realistic sales call objectives, he or she is ready to actually make contact with them. The remaining steps relate to communicating directly with a prospect—someone who may need your organization's offerings.

Step 3: Establishing Rapport

The first step in the sales cycle once contact has been made with a prospect is to quickly develop rapport with him or her. Generally, this step in the sales cycle takes only minutes yet is critical to establishing a relationship. Taking time to develop rapport with a prospect develops trust, comfort, connectedness, and relationships.

Rapport development should only take several seconds to a few minutes during the sales call. Generally, the salesperson takes the lead on rapport-developing questions with the prospect. First, a salesperson introduces themselves and then asks the prospect a few questions. The questions do not directly relate to the sales call at hand; they are more general about the person. The type of questions a salesperson asks to develop rapport differ depending on the scene in which the sales call takes place. For example, if the call occurs at a leisure and tourism organization, a question like "Welcome, did you have any trouble finding your way here?" would be effective. If the call is at the prospect's office, with an opportunity to observe his or her personal and professional interests, it would help to develop questions, such as "I see you must be an avid golfer. What are your favorite local courses?" Yet, a telephone sales call can have rapport developing questions also, such as "I wanted to tell you that Sue Smith says 'Hello.' It seems we have a mutual friend."

In addition to building an initial relationship, it is important for everyone involved to quickly understand the purpose of the meeting. Spending a minute clarifying the intent of the meeting is an important step that is often overlooked by salespeople. Skilled salespeople set the stage for the meeting with the prospect to gain agreement with each party's expectations about the call's intent or purpose. Sentences to state the purpose of a sales call may include

Today I thought we could spend some time discussing more of your needs from a hotel for this convention and then take a tour of the hotel. How does that sound?

I recently learned you may have interest in a corporate fitness membership for employees, and I wanted to speak with you more about this possibility.

Thank you for meeting with me at your office. I would like to better understand your interest in hosting a golf outing next year.

By gaining commitment from the prospect about the meeting agenda, the prospect feels the time was spent appropriately, and the prospect then is more likely to buy-in to the call and commit to the forthcoming action. Sharing expectations clarifies any communications issues so prospects and salespeople are on focused on the same item. If a prospect does not agree then he or she is able to share their expectations, such as, "I really wanted to take a tour first because I am limited on time. Could we talk while we tour?

Step 4: Questioning

Questioning is the skill of gathering information and uncovering customer needs for an organization's offerings. There are two types of questions: open and closed. Both are used to gather general and specific information from a prospect.

Open questions. To encourage a customer to respond freely, you should use an open question. Open questions elicit broad answers and are often used early in early stages of a sales call to uncover customer needs. Key words to help identify an open question include who, when, where, why, tell me, what, and how.

Closed questions. Conversely, closed questions limit the range of a customer's response to a "yes" or "no" answer or to a choice among supplied alternatives. Key words to help identify a closed question include do, does, are, have, which, is, and has.

Generally, its a good idea to keep questions as open as possible. By doing so, salespeople provide prospects with more chances to freely reveal their problems, needs, and attitudes. Otherwise, the type of question salespersons use largely depends on what a prospect says or doesn't say. For example, if a prospect is responsive (i.e., talkative) and providing useful information, salespeople should use as many open questions as possible. If a prospect is unresponsive, or although talkative, is not providing you with useful information, questions will have to be more closed. You can effectively qualify a customer's needs through tactical questioning strategy.

Clarifying questions. Salespeople clarify information through a strategy of restating the prospect's remarks or referring directly to the prospect. Clarifying questions are used to verify an understanding of the prospect's needs.

If I understand you correctly...

If I hear you right...

These questions may be used successfully to check understanding of what the prospect has said. They can also be used to clarify ambiguities and broad generalizations. Finally, they can uncover what is on the prospect's mind.

Developmental questions. Asking for further information on a subject already introduced is a developmental question. These are designed to draw out a wide range of responses on an identified general need:

You mentioned security is important to you. Can you elaborate a little on that for me?

Of course a variety of services are important. Could you help me to understand what type of services are important to you?

These questions ask for more detailed additional information. They also encourage the prospect to expand and elaborate on the topic being pursued.

Some strategies for questioning include

- Start with questions on general needs then narrow the focus with subsequent questions.

- Keep questions free of buzz words, jargon, and technical terms that may confuse a prospect.

- Keep questions simple—One idea at a time is most effective.

- Keep questions focused.

- Keep questions nonthreatening.

- Explain why a question is being asked.

- Maintain a consultive atmosphere.

- Phrase questions so they are easy to answer.

- Phrase questions according to the perceived behavior of the prospect. Matching the style of the prospect will help him or her feel more comfortable with the salesperson and the sales process.

Questioning to understand potential. Throughout the questioning process, salespeople gather data on the potential of the prospect to the organization. Questions should help clarify if an opportunity exists, and if it does, whether the sale is in the organization's best interest. Just because a leisure and tourism organization can secure consumers/business does not mean it is in their best interest to do so.

This step may have occurred during your qualification process. However, during some sales call an assessment must take place regarding the organization's interest in securing the business. Tactical questioning should provide a salesperson with the necessary information to allow him or her to formulate a strategy about whether this business is a good fit, and if this prospect can make a commitment to the organization. Salespeople must consider three situational factors throughout a sales call: potential, authority, and resoures

Salespeople consider potential. What is the potential business opportunity? Is there a general need for your product or service? Does the prospect see the need (if are you dealing with unrealized needs)? How easy will it be to get the prospect to see the need? If the need does in fact exist, how great a need and how urgent is it? Are you likely to face tough competition?

Salespeople consider authority. Who can authorize the purchase of your product or service? Is this the person you should be talking to at this time? Is this person a decision maker or influencer? Who else might play a decision-making or influencing role to purchase your product or service? Where should you be focusing your selling efforts, and how can you get there?

Salespeople consider resources. Does the company have the appropriate resources to justify your selling efforts? Does it have the dollars required to purchase your product or service? Does it have the internal resources to justify and implement the purchase of your product or service?

Step 5: Supporting

To be successful in sales, a salesperson must be able to enter a sales call with an open mind and with few preconceived notions—Never assume what the prospect will need. When the salesperson is ready to discuss business with a prospect, it is important he or she fully understand the prospect's needs. Only then can he or she link benefits and features of the organization's offerings/experiences to the prospect's specific needs. Features and benefits must be structured to meet the customer's objectives.

A *benefit* is something of value to the prospect that results from one or more features at the leisure and tourism organization. It will only be of value to the prospect if it meets one of the prospect's needs. Generally speaking, benefits are intangible, yet people buy benefits. Prospects buy how an organization's features directly benefit them.

A *feature* is a characteristic of the organization's experiences. A feature is important to a prospect if it meets a prospect's need and produces a valuable benefit. For example, during a sales call for a health club membership, the prospect identifies the need for a variety of cardiovascular activities. Based on this, the following benefits and features were identified having considered this need:

Benefits	Features
Get into shape	Aerobic classes
Lose weight	Life cycles, Stairmasters and a running track
Reduce cholesterol	Nutrition counseling services

Needs-benefit feature (NBF) relationships. The logical connections a salesperson makes between what the prospect wants and the offerings an organization can provide are an essential part of the sales process. To make logical connections between prospects' needs (i.e., what the prospect wants) and features (i.e., the characteristics of the organization and its offerings), salespeople identify and share the benefits produced by the features of an organization that help prospects achieve their needs. By relating prospects' specific needs to the benefits and features of a

leisure and tourism organization, salespeople show them how they will achieve their needs at their organization.

Each prospect's needs vary and prospects often have a variety of needs in multiple areas. Organizations have a unique set of features as well. Depending on the prospect's priorities, the organization's features may or may not produce benefits that interest them. Features can be described without any references to the customer's needs and objectives. Benefits, on the other hand, must deal with a prospect's needs and objectives. An accurate description of features would apply to any potential purchaser; a description of benefits might apply to one prospect, but not another, based on the needs each prospect has. A description of features focuses on the organization's offerings, whereas a description of benefits focuses on the prospect.

Because a potential consumer may or may not be interested in the benefits of a particular feature, receiving the feature may or may not move him or her closer to a decision to purchase. People do not purchase a product or service because it has features—they do so because they see benefits in the product or service that match their needs and objectives.

Step 6: Summarizing

Summarizing accepted benefits is valuable. It takes into account the listening ability of both the salesperson and the prospect. Most people are not very effective listeners yet this is the most important skill found in salespeople today. By summarizing what was learned frmo the call, a salesperson helps the prospect remember what he or she agreed was important. This shows the prospect that a salesperson is focused in on their specific needs. Salespeople must sharpen their own listening ability to remember the accepted benefits. If at the end of a call, he or she can't remember the benefits the customer accepted, it will show the prospect he or she has not listened and may not care.

Summarizing accepted benefits increases the probability that the prospect will agree to the action plan a salesperson suggests because the benefits supply reasons to the prospect for making a commitment. Phrases to begin a benefit summary include

Let's review what we've agreed on...

We've agreed that...

Let's summarize...

Let's go over what we've talked about so far...

You've agreed that...

Step 7: Closing

The last phase of a sales call is getting commitment from a prospect. This phase begins when the prospect agrees that the benefits accepted will meet his or her needs. A salesperson can now ask the prospect to do what he or she came to achieve in their sales call objective. This is a commitment to take action or to close the sale.

A salesperson closes when the prospect gives a buying signal. Buying signals can be subtle or overt. A gesture, facial expression, word, phrase, or question can be cues the prospect is ready to closed. A salesperson does two things when he or she closes:

1. Summarize the benefits the prospect accepted during the call.

2. Formulate an action plan requiring commitment.

Of course all sales calls aren't that easy. Prospects have objections, hesitations, or skepticisms about buying an organization's experience. Therefore, salespeople should develop skills to overcome these potential obstacles in the sales process. These advanced sales skills are taught in the many sales specific books.

Many choices are available to organizations within the direct marketing and personal selling communication mix. Activities an organization could conduct to achieve its marketing objectives include the following:

- Conduct a sales blitz of the local area to obtain prospect leads, then follow up on those leads.

- Attend a trade show to meet with individuals/ groups to inform then about the organization.

- Obtain written testimonials of satisfied community members that can be shared with other potential patrons.

- Present to the local Boy Scouts or other youth group about the benefits of healthy living.

- Offer tours around the facility to potential group contacts which highlights the features that match the benefits he or she is seeking.

- Develop an incentive for staff who refer groups.

- Write personal letters/make personal contact with individuals who have referred groups (and follow up!).

Most leisure service organizations think marketing is just promotion. Everybody in the organization does marketing but half are unaware of what or how they are contributing to the whole package. It is important for the organization to understand and then educate employees on just how much they make a difference.
Maureen McGonagle, DePaul University

Internal Marketing

A form of direct marketing already discussed stated how valuable employees are to the direct sales effort because all staff members are indeed a part of the sales force regardless of their job titles. The final communication mix variable outlined in this textbook relates to this concept. The practice of internal marketing has grown over time, yet is still approached differently. Confusion exists in the marketing literature as to what internal marketing really means (Rafiq & Ahmed, 2000). Two basic definitions, however, seem to have emerged.

The first is a concept mentioned by John McKitterick as early as 1957 and by many other authors since. Internal marketing, in this instance, is described as the concept in which organizations apply employee service management issues, select employees, and treat them as consumers where they are treated to the same type of marketing focus (e.g., develop jobs to meet employee needs, utilize marketing communications to reach them). Internal marketing efforts are designed to create an organization in which employees treat each other as guests and provide the same high-quality services to each other that they do consumers. As a result, employees who are better treated will in turn treat consumers better (Cahill, 1996; Czaplewski, Ferguson & Milliman, 2001; Ewing & Caruana, 1999).

The second definition portrays internal marketing as a communication vehicle for reaching target markets. Internal marketing is a strategic approach for communicating through employees or other stakeholders to reach targeted markets. It is where an organization insures every employee/ target market is aware of the various offerings/promotions the entire organization is providing. It is the process by which employees become an organization's best brand advocate. Practical applications of internal marketing have also been referred to as crossmarketing and four-walls marketing where employees share information with consumers regarding other aspects of the organization's offerings. For example, an employee in a resort's dining room may share information regarding the resort's recreation services.

Gronroos (1981) was the first to establish this distinction of internal marketing—employees should not only be quality-oriented but also involved with marketing. Specifically, employees should be consumer-oriented and sales-oriented (Rafiq & Ahmed, 2000). Further definitions of internal marketing continued to expand on this belief. Rafiq and Ahmed (2000) summarized the variations of the definitions by highlighting the common characteristics of each:

- employee motivation and satisfaction oriented

- customer orientation and satisfaction oriented

- integration focused

- marketing approached

- implementation of specific strategies

These approaches combine the elements of human capital or human resource practices with marketing practices to best meet consumer and organization needs. These definitions approach integrated internal marketing as a specific communication mix activity and are viewed as a part of an organization's strategic approach to achieving target market objectives. This is one more instance where marketing and management practices continue to blend as each is involved with the other. Schultz (2002) stated, "Marketing can help by working with human resources departments to identify the key elements in employee motivation including the effect of incentives and the development of training and improvement programs" (p. 8).

There are a variety of ways an organization can identify specific actions to take toward reaching an organization's objectives through internal marketing. Examples of internal marketing efforts that can be applied in leisure and tourism organizations include

- Train employees on new programs (e.g., inside signage, promotions).

- Create table tents for the employee break area to highlight the organization's programs/offerings and new ideas.

- Write and distribute an employee newsletter to highlight marketing programs.

- Present to various departments (e.g., golf,) about new offerings (e.g., preschool fitness class).

- Feature a "fun fact" about a department with a stuffer in employee paychecks (e.g., new equipment in the sports programming department and how it is helpful to this area).

As noted, it is a misunderstood, underutilized tool for reaching consumers through employees and other stakeholders. More methods to utilize internal marketing activity follow.

Interdepartmental and cross-training opportunities to provide staff with the knowledge, skills, and abilities to work in several areas/positions successfully. This not only provides the organization with greater flexibility but also develops a staff that understands multiple areas and becomes more competent in representing the entire organization to consumers.

Employee newsletters are often designed to share both organization and personal information within the workforce. Produced anywhere from weekly to monthly, this communication piece highlights organization accomplishments, future plans, and staff promotion or changes. It also shares information to assist staff. It could provide a list of organization resources available for staff and even unrelated organization resources like a newspaper's classified section would do.

Bulletin boards to display collateral for employees should be placed in a common area away from consumers, and be used to maintain an indirect dialog with staff. It is important to keep the information on it current so employees maintain interest. Bulletin boards provide a consistent location where employees are informed about events and changes. Postings can also be utilized to boost morale with written public praise and novelty concepts like "thoughts for the week."

Table tents, paycheck stuffers, and other collateral specifically designed to communicate with staff can be visually displayed in employee areas (e.g., break rooms, by time clocks, in paychecks, rest rooms). These pieces should be developed with the same professional care as other stakeholders' pieces and clearly communicate organization offerings, staff incentives and current/future happenings.

Employee business cards that highlight promotions can be produced to allow staff to further connect with stakeholders and indicate their empowerment in the organization. In the Warwick Hills Country Club Real Life Story (p. 340), staff business cards included a promotional coupon from another facet of the organization, so staff could provide consumers with discount opportunities for benefits from the organization's other services.

Employee sales incentives are financial rewards given to staff for securing business for the organization. For example, community center staff are given a $25 bonus for each service group referred to the organization to conduct a team-building activity.

Organizations have only recently begun to integrate employees in their marketing communication mix, yet gaining support from other stakeholders is also a strategy that can be taken. Clark (personal communication, April 2000) shared that a large percentage of their YMCA membership is acquired through word-of-mouth. One strategic way in which they involved existing consumers was through an internal "member get a member" promotion. In this promotion, members received a free month's membership for recruiting a new member.

Sometimes employees are the last to know—as it frequently happens. Upon a visiting an establishment and inquiring about an organization's offerings or marketing communication piece, employees stare blankly back at the consumer because this was the first time he or she heard about it. Somehow, consumers were better informed than employees.

Internal marketing formalizes this approach for organizations, ensuring everyone is well-informed of the organization offerings, marketing, and overall objectives. It ensures the organization will not fail at reaching employees because they establish a routine for communicating with all employees regarding these issues. Eventually, it becomes a part of an organization's culture. Fram and McCarthy (2003) stated "…by weaving brand messages into employees' everyday experiences, managers can ensure that on-brand

behavior becomes instinctive" (p. 101). Yet, organizations have not yet adopted these practices. *Marketing Week* cited a study by Intercommunic 8 who found that 1,000 respondents from both the public and private sector indicated organizations did not have sufficient internal marketing strategies and actions (Survey Reveals, 2003). Further, Booker (2003) stated organizations that have made small investments in this communication approach and have made poor choices as a result because employees are the catalyst to external consumers.

Marketing has a role for every function in an organization, and everyone has a role in marketing. Todd Leinberger, Spring Hill Camp

Every employee should be knowledgable about an organization's marketing program. Certain employees should be responsible for implementing the organization's

---

Real Life Story: Warwick Hills Country Club

As general manager of Warwick Hills Country Club, Rich Fairman was making his rounds about the facility one morning. He stopped as he approached the first tee at the golf course where he overheard a starter enjoying a conversation with a foursome.

The foursome questioned the ranger about a good place to eat dinner that evening. "There are several nice restaurants in the area," he replied, "I recommend the Silver Lake Inn. It's about seven miles from here, and it specializes in steaks." Pleased with the insight, the foursome thanked the starter and hit their first tee shot.

Rich, on the other hand, was mortified. Their club had two restaurants these visitors could have enjoyed—one casual dining and other fine-dining that specializes in steaks.

Once the visitors had left, Rich approached the ranger. "I enjoy hearing how helpful you are with the guests," he said, "but why didn't you recommend one of the club's own restaurants? They serve steaks."

The starter replied, "We have a fine-dining restaurant that serves steaks?"

Rich was shocked, amazed, and saddened. The starter had volunteered there for several years. How was it that the organization had never focused their marketing efforts at educating golf volunteers about the various offerings at the resort? The organization had missed years of opportunities.

Now that a problem was identified, the club could do something about it. Because of this incident, the club implemented internal marketing in several ways. They now have weekly staff meetings, 5- to 10-minute "mini meetings" before and after shifts, and the Club

has implemented staff incentives to sell and cross-sell the organization.

One example of this that the club provides business cards to all employees with the latest club promotion printed on the back of each card. The staff member whose name is on the most promotional cards redeemed by consumers wins an incentive. In addition, the club now places table tents promoting other offerings, conducts a familiarization tour for employees/volunteers, and develops promotions to get the staff to use the facilities themselves to become more familiar with and knowledgable about the club. During off-peak times, the club often allows employees to stay for free, play golf for free, and it holds employee events in the bar/lounge. By involving staff (and volunteers) in the solution, they develop ownership in decisions.

marketing plan. Yet, there can be a strategic approach to maximizing how employees will be involved with the sales and marketing process. Internal marketing is deciding how employees can be a part of this communication process with consumers and stakeholders—It is establishing a strategic approach to employee involvement in the marketing process. Again, focusing on target market objectives, organizations ask themselves how employees can be involved in directly helping the organization achieve its marketing objectives. What type of communication channels must be used to reach employees who in turn will reach consumer and stakeholder groups?

There are many benefits for organizations that use internal marketing as a communication strategy. Fram and McCarthy (2003) found that employees who participated in their employer's offerings were prouder, enjoyed working for the employer more, and felt the organization was more customer focused and better managed than those who had lower brand loyalty to their employer. Further, they stated that internal marketing increases employee brand loyalty, which in turn develops higher consumer loyalty, sales, profits, and participation. Developing internal marketing practices has many benefits, including the following:

Expanded market awareness. Unrelated to their work itself, employees naturally communicate with and reach family, friends, and neighbors who serve as potential consumers for leisure and tourism organizations. In addition, employees themselves can be a market segment an organization wishes to attract. For example, a city parks and recreation department is employed by a municipality who also employs others not in this department. Access to additional, unrelated but affiliated employees provides an opportunity to expand a market quite easily. Existing parks and recreation employees are also an accessible market to attract.

Expanded sales force. Employees based on their affiliation represent the organization to anyone who asks "Where do you work? What is an experience like there?" Employees who positively respond to questions regarding the affiliation provide additional opportunities to have one-on-one, personal contact with existing or potential consumers or stakeholders (e.g., How do you like working there?).

More knowledgable staff and satisfied consumers. This results in more satisfied consumers as questions they may have are answered, their needs better anticipated and fulfilled, and expectations exceeded. Employees understand and can deliver on an organization's brand promise (Jacobs, 2003).

More satisfied staff. Staff included in organization decisions and empowered and trusted to represent the organization are more committed and loyal than staff who are not. Mitchell (2002) suggests that internal marketing efforts help employees become emotionally connected to an orga-

nization and its offerings. "Employees' attitudes and opinions about their colleagues and the work environment may make all the difference between workers' merely doing a good job and delivering exceptional guest service" (Arnett, Laverie & McLane, 2002, p. 87).

More loyal staff. Staff who are more involved with the organization are more likely to take ownership and have pride in their workplace and efforts of themselves and those around them. Staffs that are committed are motivated to work harder and as a result become more loyal. Internal marketing efforts have been shown to reduce employee turnover as well (Taylor & Cosenza, 1997).

Competitive advantage. Most organizations fail to recognize this form of marketing communication and have not yet developed a strategic approach to internal marketing. Therefore, investing in an organization's human capital is reinforcing a competitive advantage for the organization.

More business. Whether an organization's objective is profit or participation, internal marketing not only expands market awareness but ultimately achieves organization objectives.

Apply What You Know

1. Brainstorm a communication mix using the internal marketing, direct marketing, and personal sales decisions for the marketing plan you are writing.

2. Create a leisure and tourism organization sales situation (e.g., a potential consumer walks up to the front desk of a community center and inquires about gymnastic lessons for her children). Role play the consumer, salesperson, and observer using the direct sales cycle.

3. For your organization, identify a typical customer need. List at least five benefits that satisfy this need, then list at least two features that support each of the benefits.

Key Terms

Cross-marketing
Direct marketing
Direct sales
Four walls marketing
Internal marketing
Multilevel marketing
Needs-benefit-feature relationships

Personal selling
Prospecting
Questioning
Sales blitz
Strategic sales cycle
Telemarketing
Trade shows

Review Questions

1. Identify how organizations develop a workforce of salespeople.

2. Describe the direct marketing options for organizations.

3. List the five ways organization sales efforts can lack.

4. Explain the eight-step process of strategic selling.

5. What are the three situational factors salespeople must consider throughout a sales call?

6. Identify and describe the benefits of internal marketing.

Internet Resources

MarketingTeacher.com provides materials on key marketing topics for marketing learners, teachers, and professionals. The implementation process of internal marketing and its practicalities are described.

http://www.marketingteacher.com

The *Information Technology Services Marketing Association* (ISTMA), consulting organization for businesses, markets and sells technology services. The organization helps companies improve their profitability, growth, and costumer loyalty. Materials and information on internal marketing are available at their website.

http://www.itsma.com/europe/notes/040803.htm

BrandBuilding.com is the online site of Upshaw Consulting, a business that provides marketing consulting services for businesses. An article on the organization page describes the components of an internal marketing plan.

http://www.brandbuilding.com/best/buildinginternal.html

Senior Internet specializes in providing Internet needs, from website design and promotion to e-business process development. The company provides intranet and extranet services and methods to help organizations improve their internal and external communications.

http://www.senior.proweb.co.uk/marketing/internal.htm

CIO.com provides information, news, reports, and other resources for IT and business executives. An article by Alice Dragoon talks about internal marketing as a secret strategy for businesses to become successful internally.

http://www.cio.com/archive/050104/marketing.html

The *Direct Marketing Association* is the largest trade association for businesses interested in direct, database, and interactive global marketing. The association's mission is to encourage the education, growth, and profitability of their members.

http://www.the-dma.org

References

Arnett, D., Laverie, D., and McLane, C. (2002, April). Using job satisfaction and pride as internal marketing tools. *Cornell Hotel and Restaurant Administration Quarterly, 43*(2), 87–96.

Beverland, M. (1999). Are salespeople relationship oriented? (And do they need to be?) A study based on the New Zealand wine industry. *International Journal of Wine Marketing, 11*(1), 47–64.

Booker, E. (2003, February 10). Spend some serious time, money on internal marketing. *B to B, 88*(2), 8.

Cahill, D. (1996). *Internal marketing: Your company's next stage of growth.* New York, NY: Haworth Press.

Czaplewski, A., Ferguson, J., and Milliman, J. (2001, September/October). Southwest Airlines: How internal marketing pilots success. *Marketing Management, 10*(3), 14–17.

Ewing, M. and Caruana, A. (1999). An internal marketing approach to public sector management: The marketing and human resources interface. *The International Journal of Public Sector Management, 12*(1), 17–26.

Fram, E. H. and McCarthy, M. S. (2003). From employee to brand champion. *Marketing Management, 12*(1), 24–29.

Go-To-Market Strategies. (2002, December). *Seminars as sales tools: Increasing revenues and sales leads.* Retrieved October 2, 2003, from http://www.gotomarketstrategies.com

Go-To-Market Strategies. (2003, April). *Your guide to effective lead generation planning.* Retrieved October 2, 2003, from http://www.gotomarketstrategies.com/tip_04_04.htm

Gronroos, C. (1981). Designing a long-range marketing strategy for services. *Long Range Planning, 13*, 36–42.

Jacobs, R. (2003, April). Turn employees into brand ambassadors. *ABA Bank Marketing, 35*(3), 22–26.

Mitchell, C. (2002, January). Selling the brand inside. *Harvard Business Review, 80*(1), 99–105.

Rafiq, M. and Ahmed, P. (2000). Advances in the internal marketing concept: Definition, synthesis and extension. *The Journal of Services Marketing, 14*(6), 449–462.

Schultz, D. (2002, October 14). Study internal marketing for better impact: New forum researches what motivates workers. *Marketing News, 36*(21), 8–9.

Suman, A. O., Yorgey, L. A. B., and Paul Loyle, D. (2002). Celebrating 25 years of change in direct marketing. *Target Marketing, 25*(5), 36–46.

Survey reveals 'inadequate' state of internal marketing. (2003, July 3). *Marketing Week*, 8.

Taylor, S. and Cosenza, R. (1997, December). Internal marketing can reduce employee turnover. *Supervision, 58*(12), 3–5.

Thill, G. (2002, September). Floor exercises: Whether you're an exhibitor or attendee, getting the most out of a trade show takes careful planning and preparation. *Aquatics International, 14*(7), 26–29.

Westphal, L. (1998, November). How to create believability when you write. *Direct Marketing, 61*(7), 24.

Appendix A: Market Research Resources

Industry Associations with Research Information

The amount of research conducted varies by association, however, a wealth of information in specific related industries can be obtained ranging from human resource, trend, legislative, and consumer data. Although this list is not inclusive of all leisure related associations, those listed indicate research availability through their association.

American Hotel & Lodging Association
The trade association representing the lodging industry in the United States. It is a federation of state lodging associations.
www.ahma.com

Hospitality Sales & Marketing Association International
Site promotes the Association's events and publications and includes links to some additional sources of information
www.hsmai.org

Hospitality Net
Provides links to news, books, events, vendors, and a discussion forum related to hospitality. Resources are listed by topic through the Hospitality Index.
www.hospitalitynet.org/index.html

National Tourism Database
A joint project of Michigan State University and the National Tourism Education Design Team. The purpose of the database is to provide a comprehensive inventory of extension resource materials related to tourism education.
www.msue.msu.edu/msue/imp/modtd/mastertd.html

Academy of Leisure Sciences
Includes information on the Academy and its members along with texts of Academy white papers on leisure, recreation aad tourism.
www.academyofleisuresciences.org/index.html

American Academy for Park and Recreation Administration
AAPRA site provides information about the Academy and about its publication, the Journal of Park and Recreation Administration. Includes an abstract search database for the journal
rptsweb.tamu.edu/AAPRA/index.html

American Association for Physical Activity and Recreation
AAPAR includes information on membership, publications and communications, programs and professional services
http://www.aahperd.org/aapar/

American Camping Association
ACA includes information about the organization, a camp directory, listings of conferences and professional development opportunities and more. Also has links to job placement web sites.
www.aca-camps.org

American Therapeutic Recreation Association
ATRA includes information about the organization, standards of practice, a newsletter, job listings and more.
www.atra-tr.org/atra.htm

National Recreation and Park Association
NRPA focuses on the organization and its activities, provides online access to *Parks & Recreation magazine*, and lots of link to related websites.
www.nrpa.org

National Park Service: ParkNet
Information about the National Park Service and its programs including park history, job listings, and links to individual park's web pages.
www.nps.gov

American Academy of Advertising
Organization of scholars and professionals with the purpose to foster research and exchange ideas among its members
advertising.utexas.edu/AAA/index.html

American Advertising Federation
Functions as advocates for the rights of advertisers and combine mutual interests of corporate advertisers, agencies, media companies, suppliers and academia
www.aaf.org

American Marketing Association
Purpose is to promote education; assist in career development among marketing professionals; and advance the science and ethical practice of marketing disciplines
www.marketingpower.com

American Alliance for Health, Physical Education, Recreation and Dance
www.aahperd.org

Association for Environmental and Outdoor Recreation
www.aeoe.org

Club Managers Association of America
http://www.cmaa.org/

Employee Services Management Association
www.esmassn.org

International Association for Amusement Parks and Attractions
www.iaapa.org

International Association of Assembly Managers, Inc.
www.iaam.org

Destination Marketing Association International
www.iacvb.org

International Facility Management Association
www.ifma.org

International Festivals and Events Association
www.ifea.com/

Meeting Professionals International
www.mpiweb.org

National Sporting Goods Association
www.nsga.org

The Park and Recreation Trades
http://www.parktrades.com

State Travel Bureaus and related links (e.g., Michigan Tourism Business)
http://www.eletra.com/tourism

International and National Data

The Statistical Abstract of the United States
Provides data on particular leisure industries and participation rates.
http://www.census.gov/statab/www/

The Public Register's Annual Report Service
www.prars.com

Wall Street Journal Annual Reports Service
wsj.ar.wilink.com/asp/WSJ1_search_eng.asp

Canadian Market Research
Canadian Market Research provides links to Canadian news, market statistics and trends, and Canadian government sites.
www.bplans.com/sbs

Market Research.com
A directory of market research to be purchased.
www.marketresearch.com/default.asp?SID=56421931-215316718-260675269&PartnerID=811788012

American Demographics Magazine
http://adage.com/americandemographics/

National Bureau of Economic Research
www.nber.org

Stat USA/Internet
www.stat-usa.gov

USA Data
www.usadata.com

World Factbook
Political, economic, social facts, and statistics about countries.
www.odci.gov/cia/publications/factbook/index.html

Corporate Internet Strategy
Describes a methodology for Internet strategic planning, highlights possible application, and supplies illustrative Internet example and case studies.
www.mbendi.co.za/strategy/

U.S. Census Bureau: Foreign Trade Statistics
Statistics covering a number of different topics
www.census.gov/foreign-trade/www

Organization of American States Quantitative Trade Data
Access links to tariffs, trade data, and statistical agencies
www.sice.oas.org/datae.asp

Statistics Canada
Daily news, census data, and articles
www.statcan.ca/start.html

UK Office for National Statistics Databank Service
Click on "United Kingdom in Figures" for links to the economy, people, state, and land.
www.statistics.gov.uk

Aneki.com
Contains country information, regional, and world rankings in a variety of socioeconomic conditions
www.aneki.com

Latin America & the Caribbean (World Bank)
General marketing information, sectoral and product specific information, general economic information, and business travel and etiquette
wbln0018.worldbank.org/external/lac/lac.nsf

Mexican Consulate General (New York)
Locate speeches, press releases, and documents from various federal government departments
www.consulmexny.org

Middle East & North Africa
General marketing information, sectoral and product specific data, general economic information, business travel and etiquette
www.menareport.com

Australia Guide
Link to general fact and figures, geography, culture, tourism, travel, and government history
www.csu.edu.au/australia

Canadiana: The Canadian Resources Page
References to Canadian news, media, facts and figures, travel and tourism, government servers, politics and history, and heritage, culture, and entertainment
www-2.cs.cmu.edu/Unofficial/Canadiana

Canadian Government Primary Internet Page

Information about Canada (e.g., fact sheets, map, information by subject), government overview, and federal institutions canada.gc.ca/main_e.html

Simmons Study of Media and Markets

(Sports and Leisure Volume)

Provides participant demographics, competing sports and leisure activities, and consumer media habits.

The Gallop Poll: Public Opinion

Provides data on public views on social issues and popular topics of the day.

Dun & Bradstreet's Industry Norms and Key Business Ratios

Allows the comparison between organization and industry financial performance measures.

Also check with the U.S. Small Business Administration, Small Business Development Corporation, and U.S. General Accounting Office

Local Data

Lifestyle Market Analyst

Provides a compiled list of millions of respondents demographic and lifestyle data in over 200 major U.S. metropolitan areas. Data is provided by area and activity.

The Sourcebook for ZIP Code Demographics

Provides U.S. data on dozens of demographic variables by five-digit zip code.

County and city data resources

http://fisher.lib.virginia.edu/collections

See also area Chambers of Commerce, and consult market research firms

Databases for Secondary Market Research

ABI/Inform

Index to periodical articles on all areas of business from U.S. and international publications. Covers 1971 to present and is updated weekly. Many articles are in full text libnet.ac.il/~libnet/abi.htm

Business Dateline

Citations on regional business activities and trends as well as major stories on local firms, their products and executives. Covers 1985 to present and is updated weekly. Articles are full text.
library.dialog.com/bluesheets/html/bl0635.html
www.proquest.co.uk/products/business_dateline.html

FactSearch

Facts and statistics on topics of current interest.
www.oclc.org/support/documentation/firstsearch/databases/dbdetails/details/FactSearch/htm

Interuniversity Consortium for Political and Social Research (ICPSR)

www.icpsr.umich.edu

LexisNexis

Statistics produced by the U.S. government, major international intergovernmental organizations, professional and trade organizations, commercial publishers, independent research organizations, state government agencies, and universities.
global.lexisnexis.com/us

General Secondary Sources

Web Digest for Marketers

wdfm.com

Business eJournals

A listing of hundreds of electronic journals
www.libraries.rutgers.edu/rul/rr_gateway/research_guides/busi/busejour.shtml

Entrepreneurmag.com

The online version of *Entrepreneur Magazine*
www.entrepreneur.com

Fast Company

Magazine that aims to be the "handbook of the business revolution."
www.fastcompany.com

Forbes

www.forbes.com

Fortune

www.fortune.com/fortune

Harvard Business School Publishing

www.hbsp.harvard.edu/home.html

Internet Statistics Refdesk.com—Internet Usage Snapshot

Links to sites providing data on Internet usage
www.refdesk.com/netsnap.html

Pew Internet & American Life

Aims to create and fund original, academic-quality research that explores the impact of the Internet on children, families, communities, the workplace, schools, health care and civic/political life.
www.pewinternet.org/index.asp

Appendix B: Brainstorming Cards and Charts

The Stage 1 worksheet concisely highlights each step an organization should take to develop a marketing strategy. Ideally, each box of the sheet would be completed thoroughly to best prepare an organization for identifying and writing target market objectives. Each box represents valuable information that ensures an organization targets the most appropriate markets, which will result in a more effective outcome. Chapter 6 explains each component (or box) further.

The Stage 2 worksheet and corresponding cards helps an organization identify all the marketing, promotional, and communication decisions that are directly tied to each target market objective (completed in Stage 1). These are designed to give anyone in an organization the opportunity to contribute to brainstorming and decision making. As illustrated in Chapter 4 (p. 76), utilizing others results in more effective outcomes. Each card front defines what each box means while the back shares real examples of how these concepts can be applied.

Ideally, the following steps would be taken to ensure an organization capitalizes on identifying as many ideas as possible when selecting the most effective way to achieve the target market objective. One worksheet should be completed for each of the organization's target market (objectives). Chapter 9 explains the process and each box further while Chapters 10–14 provide detailed insight into each concept.

Stage 2 Worksheet/Card Steps

1. Each participant has a set of cards and a worksheet.

2. Write the target market objective in the box provided. Chapter 8 (p. 197) discusses writing proper objectives.

3. Discuss quality issues and organization philosophies because these are the foundation of effective marketing (Chapter 3, p. 50).

4. Discuss the target market's needs (e.g., What do they look for/expect in the organization's offerings?) and behaviors (e.g., Where do they shop? eat? visit? What do they watch? listen to? read? What are they doing when not with your organization?); What is the competitive environment like? What are the organization's conclusions from the SWOT analysis (Chapter 6, p. 153)? What is the target market objective?

5. Brainstorm how the organization can specifically address the needs of the target market and achieve the target market objective through the utilization of the five phases of a leisure and tourism experience (Step 1; Chapter 2, p. 36).

6. Starting with the Marketing Mix (Step 2) section from left to right, use one card at a time to discuss each topic jointly. Brainstorm all the possible offerings the organization can provide to meet the market's needs and be *the* organization that provides for them. After completing the offerings box, move to the next box (i.e., distribution, then pricing).

7. Once Step 2 is complete, review the marketing mix list. Select only the most effective ideas that will allow the organization to reach the target market objective. Chapter 9 (p. 212) highlights considerations that should be made *prior to* identifying what the organization will be able to provide.

8. Reflect on the decisions just made as well as the needs/behaviors of the target market and the objective. Brainstorm promotional mix items including brand message, collateral, and event ideas.

9. After brainstorming for Step 3, review the promotional mix list. Select only the most effective ideas that will allow the organization to reach the target market objective. Chapter 9 (p. 212) highlights considerations that should be made *prior to* identifying what the organization will be able to provide.

10. Reflect on both the marketing and promotional mix choices just made as well as the needs and behaviors of the target market and objective. Brainstorm communication mix items (Step 4). These are all the ways an organization will reach the target market and communicate directly with them about the organization and changes identified in the marketing and promotional mix. Without this section, no one would know about the organization's ability to serve the market. This critical step will communicate what the organization offers and promises to the market.

11. After brainstorming for Step 4, review the communication mix list. Select only the most effective ideas that will allow the organization to

reach the target market objective. Chapter 9 (p. 212) highlights considerations that should be made *prior to* identifying what the organization will be able to provide.

12. Organizations should reflect on the five phases list (Step 1). Select the most effective ones that will assist in achieving the target market objective for each phase of the experience.

13. Each final decision should be evaluated upon completion to measure its worth and determine future value (Chapter 4, p. 88; Chapter 9, p. 220). For example: Was using a coupon an effective decision? Was direct mail effective?

14. Organizations should consider gathering additional information/data that would be helpful to future marketing decision making. This may include anything from understanding who the organization serves currently and how satisfied the customers/consumers are to gaining a better understanding of the needs of the target market (Chapter 5, p. 98).

As a result of completing these worksheets, an organization has drafted a marketing plan and can now apply the final steps to ensure the plan's acceptance and implementation as discussed in Chapter 9 (i.e., identify costs and projected revenue as a result of the plan and achieving the target market objective).

stage one
Marketing, Promotional, and Communication (MPC)
Strategy Development

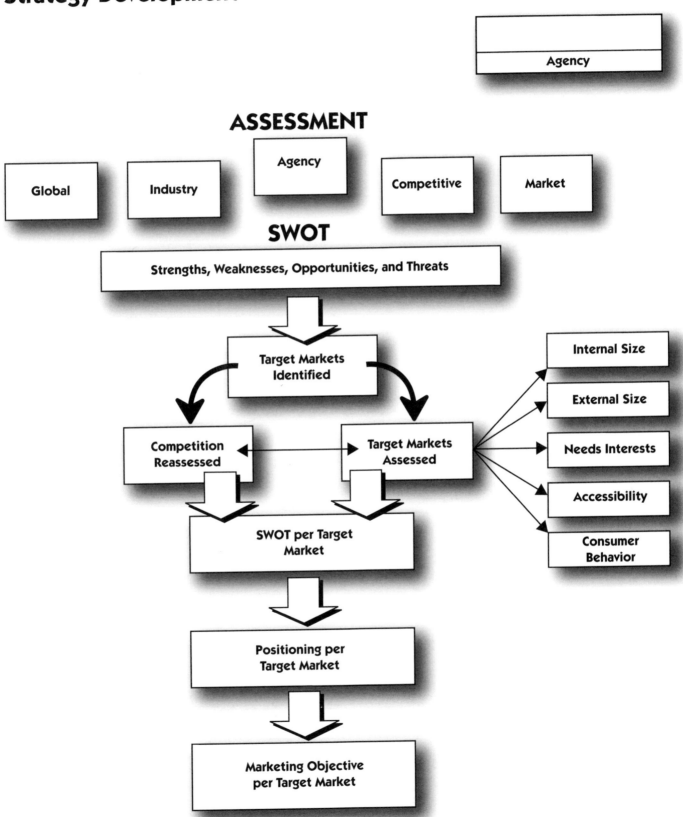

stage two
Marketing, Promotional, and Communication (MPC) Mix
Achieving Objectives by Creating High Quality Experiences

Organization Name

1: Five Phases of an Experience

Marketing Objective Per Target Market

Anticipation

Travel to

Destination

Travel From

Reflection

2: Marketing Mix

Offerings

Distribution Place

Pricing

3: Promotional Mix

Brand Message

Collateral

Promotional Events

4: Communication Mix

Public Relations

Community Relations

Advertising

Direct Sales

Sponsorship

Internal Marketing

Quality Service & Stewardship

5: Evaluation & Market Research

Promotional Events

Promotional Mix

Promotional events are temporary "shot in the arm" incentives or special events designed to stimulate interest in an organization's offerings.

Notes

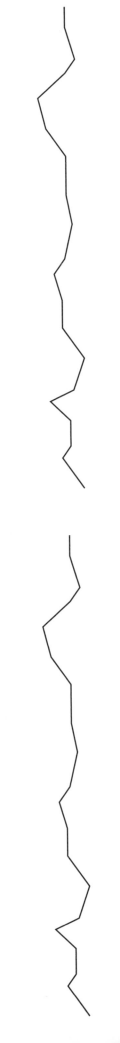

Collateral

Promotional Mix

Collateral is a visual aid that supports an organization's communication activities and is used to create awareness and offer incentives for participation.

Notes

Promotional Events

Examples

- Host an open house and invite the target market to tour the facility.
- Work with a radio station on a joint promotion—Educate people about the benefits of recreation.
- Create a float to use in all local parades.
- Create a point-of-sale display with a contest for school offices/ hallways to promote your offerings and engage people.

BRAINSTORMING HELP: **Events:** open houses, charity events, demonstrations, celebrity events, point-of-sale displays/exhibits, combined with free samples, coupons, sales incentives, contests, sweepstakes, giveaways

Collateral

Examples

- Create coupons for the target market to provide an incentive.
- Create brochures about each department as well as the agency overall.
- Have a mascot distribute stuffed animals of itself for the department that visits children in hospitals, schools, etc.
- Buy a large number of trinkets to distribute with your logo, name, and slogan.
- Create a point-of-sale display with tear-off information for school offices to promote your offerings.

BRAINSTORMING HELP: **Collateral:** postcards, brochures, letterhead, business cards, newsletters, flyers, posters, websites, annual reports, catalogs, and CD/DVDs; point-of-sale displays/exhibits, novelty items, free samples, sandwich board, mascot, videos, and photographs, trading stamps, coupons, sales incentives, contests, sweepstakes, giveaways

Community Relations

Communication Mix

Establish a "giving" strategy for philanthropic activities that involves employees and the agency. Be a good community member through involvement in other charitable events both within and outside your agency.

Internal Marketing

Communication Mix

Referred to as "four-walls" marketing, an agency insures every employee and target market is aware of the various offerings/promotions the entire agency provides. Educate employees and consumers on the overall agency focus.

Brand Message

Promotional Mix

A brand message identity establishes the image organizations wish to create in consumer minds through visuals and written words. These should be reviewed regularly by an agency.

Quality Service/Stewardship

Communication Mix

The employees' or guests' "experience" at your department should be the best it can be. When guest expectations are exceeded, guests will tell others to come to the organization as well. Poor service results in guests telling others not to come. Quality is an overall agency issue; however, several things can be reinforced within a particular target market.

Community Relations

- Establish a philanthropy to which the agency's employees can donate (e.g., Make-A-Wish Foundation, Red Cross, a local shelter).
- Host an event for a local charity (e.g., Boys and Girls Clubs) at no cost. Get the press to cover it and it becomes public relations.
- Act as a blood donor center for a community blood drive.
- Buy tickets for and attend other charity events.
- Donate free materials/services for other charity events.
- Establish a "giving" strategy to ensure consistency and better manage charitable requests.

BRAINSTORMING HELP: Establish one or more charities to which the agency and employees contribute, financially support other charity fundraising events (e.g., United Way dinner), volunteer staff for other charities' events, host charity events at your agency, sponsor local community campaigns (e.g., Adopt a Mile, Be a Good Neighbor)

Brand Message

- Create a website design.
- Design a logo.
- Establish a slogan for the department.
- Write a positioning statement for each target market.

Internal Marketing

- Train employees about the new sponsorship program the agency has for inside signage.
- Create table tents for the employee break area that highlights the department's programs/offerings and new ideas.
- Create a biweekly employee newsletter to highlights marketing programs.
- Inform all departments (e.g., golf) about the new preschool fitness classes.
- Feature one "fun fact" within a department to stuff in employee paychecks (e.g., new equipment that the sports programming department has and how it is helpful to this area).

BRAINSTORMING HELP: Interdepartmental training, interdepartmental presentations, table tents, bulletin boards, employee newsletter, other

Quality Service/Stewardship

Employees: Feedback, Rewards, Training, and Care

- Provide employees meaningful incentives for good performance.
- Send a thank you to an employee for providing great guest service.
- Give an employee an extra paid day off for superior performance.
- Mail employee birthday/work anniversary cards.
- Conduct an exit evaluation for employees leaving your employment.
- Empower staff to handle guest situations.
- Provide staff the training necessary to be experts at their jobs.
- Ensure employees are easily identifiable (e.g., nametags, uniforms, standards for appearance).
- Develop a consistent script for handling all telephone calls efficiently/effectively.

Target Market: Feedback, Rewards, Effective Systems, and Care

- Ask a community member to conduct a mystery shopping experience.
- Create a feedback system for guest dissatisfaction.
- Develop systems to evaluate service (e.g., comment cards, questionnaires, focus groups).
- Call a patron after he/she has visited to see how they enjoyed the experience.
- Do something special and unexpected for people...Wow them!

Sponsorship

Communication Mix

Sponsorship occurs in two different ways for agencies:

1) By determining appropriate, effective sponsors for your activities and events.

2) By establishing a strategy for events and activities that you will sponsor.

Direct Sales

Communication Mix

One-on-one or one-on-small-group presentations with an interest in achieving agency objectives.

Advertising

Communication Mix

Paying for positive media-related attention.

Consideration should be given to the strengths and weaknesses of each medium as well as issues related to frequency and reach.

Public Relations

Communication Mix

Most often, working with the media to obtain "free" coverage of your agency's offerings and events to enhance a positive image for the agency.

Direct Sales

Examples

- Conduct a sales blitz of the local area to obtain prospecting leads, then follow up on those leads.
- Attend a trade show and meet with individuals/groups about the agency.
- Obtain written testimonials of satisfied consumers that could be shared with other potential patrons.
- Present to the local Boy Scouts about the benefits of healthy living and your offerings.
- Give a potential group contact a tour around the facility, highlighting the features that match the benefits he or she is seeking.
- Develop an incentive for staff who refer groups.
- Write thank-you letters, and make personal contact with individuals who have referred groups.

BRAINSTORMING HELP: Sales blitzes, trade shows, testimonials (written or verbal), public speaking engagements, telemarketing, sales presentations/tours (in-house), personal sales meetings (another location), lead referral programs, one-on-one correspondence, other

Public Relations

Examples

- Write a monthly column in the local paper about health issues.
- Pitch a story to the local editor about a "newsworthy" event for which your staff has volunteered.
- Distribute collateral at no-cost locations for tourists (e.g., CVB, hotels).
- Conduct familiarization tours of the department for new community members...
- Be a welcome wagon!
- Mail a press kit to related media regarding a new focus of the department.
- Develop a protocol for whomever speaks to the media and represents the department.
- Gain publicity for any community relations activity you have completed.
- Build a relationship with the media... Start by introducing yourself/the agency to all key media representatives.

BRAINSTORMING HELP: Press releases, public service announcements, press kits, community service column/presentations, feature stories, familiarization tours, displays, talk shows, collateral at no cost, organization membership, media relations, advisory boards, news conferences, interviews, remote broadcasts, information booths, other

Sponsorship

Examples

- Sponsor the food and beverages at a youth community event.
- Sponsor an adult hockey tournament at the local arena.
- Sponsor annual planners for students at local elementary schools.
- Solicit sponsors that are looking to reach and serve the same target market as you (e.g., schools=youth; commission on aging=seniors; daycare centers=infant, toddler, preschooler) for various marketing and communication mix ideas.

SPONSORSHIP CONSIDERATIONS: Is there a connection with the target market either of you is interested in serving? What type of recognition am I giving or getting from this sponsorship (e.g., logo on flyers, announcement at event, signage)? What are the benefits of this sponsorship for our agency or the other agency?

Advertising

Examples

- Buy a full-page advertisement in a magazine that targets the same market.
- Add a listing in the Yellow Pages under "recreation," "athletics," and/or "health."
- Create a video of your department to broadcast on a local cable channel.
- Lease a billboard for six months to promote a department.
- Develop a Website and e-mail distribution letters.
- Send direct mail to past patrons.
- Send a paycheck stuffer to large area employers so their employees can consider your offerings.
- Create a bulletin board focusing on leisure/recreation opportunities at a complementary agency (e.g., health club).

BRAINSTORMING HELP: Airplane, Yellow Pages, church bulletins, Chamber/CVB programs, school programs, newspapers, television (e.g., cable, local, national), radio, Internet site and e-mail, billboards, signage, magazines/journals, electronic displays, cooperative advertising, other

Distribution Place

Marketing Mix

Identify ways to reach the intended target market through:

1) Offering your products, programs, and services at other locations; and/or

2) Linking what you provide through another agency, person, and/or source

Pricing

Marketing Mix

Permanent pricing decisions are determined by first establishing a pricing objective (e.g., profit, break-even, disincentive, usage), then a strategy (e.g., skimming, penetration, variable).

Use these cards with the Stage 1 and 2 worksheets for brainstorming exercises
(see p. 349 for instructions)

Offerings:
Products, Programs, Facilities, Services & Experiences

Marketing Mix

Regular/permanent changes in your agency's offerings focused on the needs and wants of the target market.

Distribution Place

- Offer mobile recreation services (i.e., take recreation offerings to the people).
- Provide a golf clinic at a local employer's worksite.
- Have the local school sell open-skate discount tickets for the recreation department.
- Provide a $1 commission for each ticket the local senior citizen complex sells for your upcoming special event.
- Develop an Internet site where consumers can register, purchase products/services, and communicate with the agency.

Pricing

- Provide a discounted price for senior citizens.
- Offer different prices depending on the day/time the facility is desired.
- Establish different rates for residents versus non-residents.

Offerings:
Products, Programs, Facilities, Services & Experiences

- Develop a new "eating right" class.
- Provide transportation to/from the facility and parking lot.
- Have a greeter at each entrance (yes, just like Wal-Mart!).
- Provide a snack/waiting area for parents of children involved in programs.
- Provide new, state-of-the-art equipment.
- Offer daycare/babysitting for employees and visitors.